DATE DUE

JE 2 6 '14			

DEMCO 38-296

The World Since 1945

FOURTH EDITION

The World
Since 1945

A History of
International Relations

Wayne C. McWilliams & Harry Piotrowski

LYNNE
RIENNER
PUBLISHERS

BOULDER
LONDON

Published in the United States of America in 1997 by
Lynne Rienner Publishers, Inc.
1800 30th Street, Boulder, Colorado 80301

and in the United Kingdom by
Lynne Rienner Publishers, Inc.
3 Henrietta Street, Covent Garden, London WC2E 8LU

Library of Congress Cataloging-in-Publication Data
McWilliams, Wayne C.
    The world since 1945 : a history of international relations /
Wayne C. McWilliams & Harry Piotrowski. — 4th ed.
    Includes bibliographical references and index.
    ISBN 1-55587-788-5 (hc : alk. paper).
    ISBN 1-55587-621-8 (pbk. alk. paper)
    1. World politics—1945– 2. Military history, Modern—20th
century. 3. Developing countries—Economic conditions.
I. Piotrowski, Harry. II. Title.
D843.M34   1997
327'.09'045—dc21   97-17880
                                                        CIP

British Cataloguing in Publication Data
A Cataloguing in Publication record for this book
is available from the British Library.

Printed and bound in the United States of America

        The paper used in this publication meets the requirements
  ∞ of the American National Standard for Permanence of
        Paper for Printed Library Materials Z39.48-1984.

    5 4 3 2 1

In Memoriam

Bill Sladek
1938–1993

friend and colleague

■ Contents

■ Maps

■ Preface to the Fourth Edition

The events of the late 1980s and early 1990s not only brought the postwar era to a close, but continued to transform the world in a manner that was nothing short of revolutionary. What will emerge is impossible to predict, but it is certain that the new era will have a different look from the one that came out of World War II. The factors that brought about the onset of the new era demand an updated and revised history.

We can no longer, for example, continue to speak of the Cold War in the present tense. We ended a previous edition of this book with the event that marked the end of the Communist Party's monopoly in the Soviet Union. Less than two years later, however, the Soviet Union itself ceased to exist. The age of the post–World War II superpower rivalry had ended. With it came the dissolution of the Soviet Union's military alliance in Eastern Europe and agreements to cut drastically the strategic nuclear arsenals of the United States and the successor states to the Soviet Union.

There were other significant developments. For more than forty years, international competition was largely military and ideological in character; in the early 1990s it became primarily economic in nature, and once again blocs began to take shape. The 1990s saw attempts to resolve a number of lingering problems, such as the civil strife in Nicaragua and El Salvador, contention between North and South Korea, and the quest for nonracial democracy in South Africa. Efforts were again made to establish the foundations of representative societies in parts of Africa, Asia, and Latin America. With the end of the Cold War, the main focus in nuclear weapons discussions shifted from disarmament to nonproliferation. In all these endeavors, the United Nations began to play the role for which it was initially created. All the while, however, civil strife, brought about by a reassertion of ethnic differences, emerged with a force not seen since the days before World War II.

If history is a combination of continuity and change, it was change that was the dominant factor during the recent past. With the end of one era, the world now faces an uncertain future.

Wayne C. McWilliams
Harry Piotrowski

■ Introduction

A survey of current world conditions and a reading of the recent past reveal that the world is neither a fair nor a friendly place. Insurrections and wars abound, and more than half the world's inhabitants live in misery and hunger while others live in comfort and luxury. In this age of modern science and technology, of space exploration and heart transplants, how does one account for the absence of peace and the prevalence of poverty in a world of plenty? What are the roots of the perilous condition of human affairs? Today's students, young and old, must ask and seek to answer these questions. This book, a history of the world since 1945, was undertaken in order to assist them in that endeavor.

Tribal hostility and war between nations have been common throughout history, but in modern times, and especially in the twentieth century with the development of modern military technology, war has become increasingly deadly. World War II brought death and destruction on an unprecedented scale, and it ended with the use of a powerful new weapon of mass destruction, the atomic bomb. From the ruins of that war came a cry, expressed even by military leaders, that there must never be another such war. Yet, even as the ashes of World War II were still smoldering, friction developed among its victors, and they—the United States and Britain on one side and the Soviet Union on the other—became locked in a new power struggle that threatened the very peace they had sacrificed so much to attain. The postwar friction between them rapidly hardened into a political Cold War that soon turned into a military confrontation between East and West marked by mutual mistrust, suspicion, and hostility. After World War II the Cold War continued for more than forty-five years as the major determinant of international affairs. The two superpowers, the United States and the Soviet Union, aggressively sought to establish and maintain blocs of allies, thus dividing the world into two hostile camps. And since each claimed to be the champion of a superior system, one capitalist and the other Communist, the world became the arena of an enduring ideological conflict.

1

Meanwhile both superpowers began rearming, and a relentless arms race was soon under way. Each claimed that security—both national and global—lay in military strength, but that the other's armaments threatened world peace. Thus they justified the building of massive arsenals containing thousands of nuclear weapons far more powerful than the ones used against Japan in 1945. Their arsenals have long since been large enough to destroy each other many times over and possibly extinguish human life on this planet, and yet year after year they continued piling up more weapons, spending at a rate of millions of dollars per hour. The military standoff between the nuclear powers brought about a precarious peace between them, but the world has not been free of war. On the contrary, there have been more than one hundred wars since World War II, and many of these lesser brushfire wars, though contained geographically and limited to conventional weapons, carried the potential of igniting a larger conflagration. Indeed, the combatants were all too often clients of the major powers and were armed by them.

Equally dangerous to the safety and well-being of humanity was the growing gulf between the world's rich and poor, between the industrially advanced nations of the North and the underdeveloped nations of the South. In the South, often referred to as the Third World, one finds the world's lowest standards of living, lowest economic growth rates, lowest levels of education, lowest rates of life expectancy, and the highest population growth rates and infant mortality rates. Thus, millions of the inhabitants of the Third World are dreadfully impoverished, malnourished, disease-ridden, and unable to live productively and in dignity. Governments of Third World nations have struggled, usually ineptly, to lift their countries from such impoverishment, and while some have made marginal progress, many others are merely marking time or slipping even further behind. Many of these countries have contracted enormous foreign debts, which they are unable to pay, and their indebtedness threatens the financial stability of the wealthier nations of the North. Economic failure made the Third World more volatile politically and more vulnerable to intervention and militarization by the superpowers. Nearly every war fought since World War II has been fought in Third World countries, and they all have been fought with weapons supplied by industrialized nations.

This is the world into which the youth of today were born. Their chances of resolving the immense problems they have inherited, of reducing the nuclear threat and of alleviating the misery of the majority of mankind, thus making this world a safer and more civilized place, depend to a great extent on what they know of the causes of these problems. The clear-eyed vision needed to come to terms with these difficult problems and to progress toward a resolution of them must be based on an understanding of the past. To remain ignorant of that past is to compound the chances of either perpetuating the current problems or committing grievous and possibly irretrievable errors.

It was for the purpose of combating such ignorance and supplanting it with a knowledge of world affairs that we undertook the writing of this text. Our aim is to provide our readers with an evenhanded, yet critical explanation of the political history of this troubled world and to expose them to more than one viewpoint. We seek to advance our readers' knowledge of the recent past and to develop a better understanding of the difficult issues and dangerous conditions in the world today. Above all, we hope to instill an appreciation of the need for greater objectivity and for careful, critical thinking about political issues. It is, therefore, our hope that this text will serve as a primer for responsible global citizenship.

It should be emphasized that we are primarily dealing with political history in this text, except in certain chapters where economic themes are particularly relevant. We do not address social or cultural dimensions of recent world history, as interesting or important as they may be. We also wish to point out that a text with a scope as broad as the world cannot help but be selective. Obviously, not every political development around the globe is discussed within these pages. We have attempted to provide a balanced coverage of global history, rather than a Western world or U.S.-centered approach. Thus, a substantial portion of the text is devoted to Asia, Africa, and Latin America.

The study of the recent past is no substitute for studying the longer haul of human history. Obviously, World War II had antecedents, the knowledge of which deepens our understanding of that momentous event, its consequences, and the course of events in the postwar period. Nonetheless, because World War II represents a historic watershed, one of the landmarks in history, it is not inappropriate that it be taken as a starting point for the study of recent world history. And because the postwar period is distinctly a new era with many new features—the advent of nuclear warfare, the development of high-speed aviation, the emergence of two superpowers, and the end of European colonialism, to name just a few—it makes sense to treat it as a distinct historical period. (To be sure, for certain topics treated in this text, such as the Arab-Israeli conflict or the revolution in China, it will be necessary to trace historical roots further back in time, but our focus remains on the postwar period.)

■ SEVEN MAJOR CONSEQUENCES OF WORLD WAR II

The enormous consequences of World War II gave shape to the postwar world, and they are treated as major themes in this text. We have identified the following as the most important of those consequences:

1. *The end of the European age.* Europe ceased to be the center of international power. At war's end, Europe was in shambles; its nations

were prostrate, its cities in ruins, its people exhausted, and its economies shattered. The total defeat and destruction of Germany created a power vacuum in central Europe, and since nature and politics both abhor a vacuum, the victors inevitably filled it.

2. *The rise of the United States to superpower status.* Having played a decisive role in the global war and emerging from it militarily and economically supreme among the nations of the world, the United States shed for good its earlier isolationism and assumed a leadership role in the international arena.

3. *The expansion of the Soviet Union and its rise to superpower status.* Despite its severe war damage and its dire economic condition, the Soviet Union was determined to extend its power, especially in Eastern Europe, and play a major role in world affairs.

4. *The emergence of the Cold War.* Contention, mistrust, and hostility between the two emerging superpowers, the United States and the Soviet Union, developed quickly and produced an ongoing, global, bipolar power struggle.

5. *The beginning of the nuclear age.* The use of the atomic bomb by the United States and the world's failure to achieve international control of atomic energy resulted inevitably in the ever-growing nuclear arms race.

6. *The rise of nationalism and independence movements in Asia and Africa.* Although the roots of nationalism may be traced back to prewar times, it was not until the postwar period that nationalist movements became strong enough to challenge the colonial order in Asia and Africa. The struggle for independence was stimulated by the defeat of Japan and the weakening of the European colonial powers, and, in a remarkably short span of time, many Asian and African states won their independence.

7. *A renewed effort to secure lasting peace through international organization.* The United Nations was created in the hope that it might achieve the global peace and security that the old League of Nations had failed to maintain.

Most of these interrelated themes are discussed in Part 1, "The Origins of the Cold War." In it we examine the global state of affairs at the end of World War II, and analyze the origins of the Cold War and its development in both Europe and Asia. In Part 2, "Nationalism and the End of Colonialism," the sixth theme is taken up. In this part, we also trace the development of Arab and Israeli nationalism and the course of the Middle East conflict. Part 3, "The Shifting Sands of Global Power," focuses mainly on the 1960s. In it we examine the changing configuration of the Cold War, the strains within the Eastern and Western blocs, the Sino-Soviet split, and the resulting emergence of multipolarity, which replaced the bipolar confrontation of the earlier Cold War period. This section also includes coverage of the Vietnam War and its consequences. Part 4, "The Third World," takes us back to Asia and Africa to trace their postindependence progress—or lack thereof—and to Latin America as well to examine its similar problems.

In addition to investigating the political and economic patterns on the three Third World continents, we also devote sections to such topics as the problem of the Third World debt, the issue of apartheid in South Africa, the economic progress of certain Asian nations, and the revolution in the Philippines. Part 5, "The End of the Postwar Era," treats the major global developments and issues in the 1980s and 1990s. We have selected for special attention the rise of militant Islam, especially as manifested in the Iranian revolution, the rise of Japan and the European Community as new economic superpowers, and such Cold War issues as the rise of Solidarity in Poland, the Soviet invasion of Afghanistan, and the nuclear arms race, potentially the most dangerous challenge to modern man. Finally, in Part 5, we analyze the momentous changes in the Soviet Union and Eastern Europe since the end of the 1980s, changes that signal the end of the postwar era.

We urge our readers to join with us in a quest for a fuller, more objective understanding of the world of turmoil in which we live. And we would remind them that history, especially recent political history, is not merely the compilation of dead facts; it is alive with controversy and conflicting ideas. We challenge our readers to confront these controversies, to weigh the conflicting ideas and viewpoints, and to formulate their own opinions.

PART 1

THE ORIGINS
OF THE COLD WAR

In light of the enormous impact of the Cold War on human life since World War II—the immeasurable human energies it has exhausted, the gargantuan amounts of wealth it consumed, the shifting of national priorities it demanded, the attention it diverted from other global concerns, the civil liberties it has impinged on and the intellectual freedom it strained, the anguish and fears it caused so many people, and the threat it posed to the earth's inhabitants—it becomes necessary to inquire into its origins and to question whether it was avoidable.

By its very nature, the Cold War was for many years so divisive a subject that it was all but impossible to study it with detachment and objectivity. So strong were the feelings and so total the commitment of each side to its cause, and so contemptuous and mistrusting was each of the other side, that each had its own self-serving version of the history of the Cold War and of each and every confrontation between East and West.

The United States and the Soviet Union each perpetuated a series of Cold War myths that sustained them over the years. On the one hand, the people of the United States generally felt or still feel (1) that the Soviet Union broke its postwar promises regarding Eastern Europe and was therefore responsible for starting the Cold War; (2) that its aggressive action in Eastern Europe was a manifestation of the determination of the Soviet Union to capture the entire world for Communism; (3) that so-called international Communism was a monolithic (that is, singular) movement centered in and controlled by the Soviet Union; (4) that Communism was enslavement, and was never accepted by any people without coercion; and (5) that the great victory of the United States in World War II, as well as its immense prosperity and strength, attested to the superiority of its values and its system—that, in short, the United States represented humanity's best hope.

On the other hand, the Soviets seem to have felt (1) that the United States and the Western allies purposely let the Soviet Union bleed in World War II, and furthermore lacked gratitude for the role that it played in the defeat of Hitler, as well as for the losses it suffered in that cause; (2) that the United States was committed to the annihilation of Communism in general and to the overthrow of the Communist government of the Soviet Union in particular; (3) that the laws of history were on its side, meaning that capitalism was in decline and Communism was the wave of the future; (4) that the U.S. political system was not really democratic but was completely controlled by Wall Street, or at any rate by a small clique of leading corporate interests; and (5) that capitalist nations were necessarily imperialistic and thus responsible for the colonization of the Third World, and that the leading capitalist nation, the United States, was the most imperialistic of them all.[1]

As unquestioned assumptions these myths became a mental straitjacket. They provided only a narrow channel for foreign policy initiatives by either country. When notions such as these were imbedded in the thinking of the two adversaries, it was almost impossible for the two countries to break out of the Cold War and equally impossible to analyze objectively the history of the conflict.

The myths came into play throughout the Cold War, and especially in its earliest phase even before the defeat of Nazi Germany—when the Allied leaders met at Yalta in February 1945. For this reason, in the opening chapter of this book, we examine the wartime relationship between the United States and the Soviet Union, and their respective strengths at the end of the war. We also analyze the U.S. decision to use the atomic bomb against Japan and the impact it had on U.S.-Soviet relations. In Chapter 2, we turn to the Yalta Conference and examine its bearing on the beginning of the Cold War. We then trace the hardening of Cold War positions over critical issues in Europe in the four years following the end of World War II. By 1947, when the U.S. policy of "containment" of Communism was in place, the Cold War myths were firmly entrenched on both sides.

The Cold War quickly became global, and in fact it was in Asia that it became most inflamed in the first decade after the war. In Chapter 3, we pursue the Cold War in Asia by treating the Allied Occupation of defeated Japan, the civil war in China, and the Korean War—all Cold War issues. The Allied Occupation of defeated Japan was thoroughly dominated by the United States over the feeble objections of the Soviets, and eventually the United States succeeded in converting Japan into a major ally in the global Cold War. The Chinese revolution, which brought the Communists to power in 1949, was fought entirely by indigenous forces, but the stakes were great for the two superpowers. The United States responded to the Communist victory in China with still firmer resolve to stem the advance of Communism in Asia. Less than a year later, that resolve was tested in Korea where Cold War tensions grew most intense and finally ignited in the Korean War. The armed conflict between East and West was contained within one Asian country, but it threatened to explode into the dreaded World War III.

After the standoff in Korea, Cold War tensions oscillated during the remainder of the 1950s. During this period, covered in Chapter 4, new leaders—Dwight Eisenhower in the United States and Nikita Khrushchev in the Soviet Union—exhibited a new flexibility, which made possible some reduction in tensions and the solution of a few of the issues that divided the two nations. But the Cold War mentality, the embrace of the Cold War myths, remained undiminished during this period as manifested by sporadic crises and the substantial growth in the nuclear arsenals of both countries. The two superpowers came to the brink of nuclear war in the early 1960s over the deployment of Soviet nuclear missiles in Cuba. The Cuban missile crisis was the most dangerous of the many confrontations between East and West.

NOTE

1. These myths are an adaptation of a similar set of Cold War myths presented in Ralph B. Levering, *The Cold War, 1945–1972* (Arlington Heights, Ill.: Harlan Davidson, 1982), pp. 8–9.

1

The End of World War II and the Dawn of the Nuclear Age

World War II was a cataclysmic event. It was by far the most deadly and destructive war in human history. The war raged on for almost six years in Europe, beginning with Nazi Germany's attack on Poland in September 1939, and ending with the surrender of Germany to the Allied Powers led by the United States, the Soviet Union, and Great Britain on May 9, 1945. The war lasted even longer in Asia, where it began with the Japanese invasion of China in July 1937 and ended with Japan's capitulation to the Allies on August 14, 1945. World War II represented a new dimension in warfare: total war. It was total in the sense that all of the great powers and most of the nations of the world were engaged in it, and in that it involved or affected the entire population of nations, not just the men and women in uniform. Because a nation's military might rested ultimately on its industrial capacity, the civilian work force had to contribute to the war effort; moreover, entire populations, especially urban dwellers, became targets and victims of new and more deadly modern weapons.

Another major dimension of World War II that was of immense importance in ending the war and shaping the postwar world was the introduction of atomic weapons. There are many difficult questions to ponder concerning the U.S. use of the atomic bomb against Japan at the end of World War II, one of the most important and most controversial issues in modern history. But the fundamental question remains: Was it necessary or justifiable to use the bomb? It is also important to consider what bearing the emerging Cold War had on the U.S. decision to drop the bomb on Japan, and what bearing its use had on subsequent U.S.-Soviet relations.

After the war, it was the victorious nations—mainly the United States and the Soviet Union—that took the lead in shaping the postwar world. In order to better understand their respective postwar policies, one must consider the impact World War II had on these two nations, which emerged as "superpowers" and as major adversaries in the ensuing Cold War.

The "Grand Alliance" fashioned by the United States, the Soviet Union, and Great Britain during the war hardly lasted beyond it. But before the alliance began to crumble and give way to Cold War hostility, leading political representatives of these and other nations endeavored to create a new international structure for the maintenance of global peace through collective security—the United Nations. Although the founding of the United Nations was attended by great hope, it was from the beginning very severely limited in its capacity to attain its objective of world peace.

■ HISTORY'S MOST DESTRUCTIVE WAR

The carnage of World War II was so great as to be beyond comprehension. Most of Europe and East Asia were in ruins. Vast stretches of both continents were destroyed twice, first when they were conquered and again when they were liberated. Germany and Japan stood in ruins. It is impossible to know the complete toll in human lives lost in this war, but some estimates run higher than 70 million people. The nation that suffered the greatest loss of life was the Soviet Union. It lost an incredible 27 million people in the war, a figure that represents at least half of the total European war fatalities. Poland lost 5.8 million people, about 15 percent of its population. Germany lost 4.5 million people, and Yugoslavia, 1.5 million. Six other European nations—France, Italy, Romania, Hungary, Czechoslovakia, and Britain—each lost more than a half million people. In Asia, perhaps as many as 20 million Chinese and 2.3 million Japanese died in the war, and there were large numbers of casualties in various Asian countries from India in the south to Korea in the northeast. In some European countries and in Japan, there was hardly a family that had not lost at least one member in the war.[1]

Over one-half of those who died in World War II were civilians. Never before had warfare taken such a heavy toll of noncombatants. (In World War I only about one-twentieth of the dead were civilians.) An estimated 12 million civilians were killed as a direct result of military action, mainly bombing, and millions more died of starvation or epidemics in Europe and Asia, although we have no way of knowing exactly how many. An estimated 12 million people—Jews, Slavs, gypsies, the disabled, conscientious objectors, and political opponents (notably Communists)—were systematically exterminated as a result of the policy of Adolf Hitler, the dictator of Nazi Germany. This unspeakable act of barbarism, known as the Holocaust, was aimed primarily at exterminating the Jewish people; it resulted in the reduction of the Jewish population in Europe from 9.2 million to 3.8 million. All mankind was indelibly scarred by this most heinous of crimes committed by the Nazi rulership against the Jewish people.

The main cause for this huge toll of civilian lives was no doubt the development of air power—bigger and faster airplanes with longer range and greater carrying capacity. Indiscriminate bombing of the enemy's cities, populated by noncombatants, became common practice during the war. It began with Hitler's effort to bomb Britain into submission early in the war with a relentless bombing of British cities.[2] Later in the war, British and U.S. bombers retaliated with a massive bombardment of Germany. One Anglo-U.S. bombing raid on the German city of Dresden, in February 1945 (when Germany was all but defeated), killed some 135,000 people, mainly civilians. The Japanese, who also used air power, suffered the destruction of virtually all of their cities by the saturation bombing carried out by U.S. bombers. And the war ended with the use by the United States of a dreadful new weapon of mass destruction, the atomic bomb, which wrought the horrible devastation of Hiroshima and Nagasaki in August 1945. In total war fought with these methods and weapons, there was no place to hide. In the end, the nations that fought in the name of democracy in order to put an end to militarism resorted to the barbaric methods of their enemies. If unrestrained warfare had come to mean sustained, indiscriminate bombing of noncombatants with weapons of mass destruction, what hope was there for mankind should total war ever again occur?

The suffering and sorrow, the anguish and desperation of the survivors of the war lingered long after the last bombs had fallen and the victory celebrations had ended. Never in history had so much of the human race been so uprooted. In Europe alone there were between 20 and 30 million homeless refugees. Many of these displaced persons were people who fled their homelands to escape political persecution and to seek a greater measure of security and freedom elsewhere. Some were fleeing bombed-out cities and others were fleeing the advancing Soviet Red Army. Still others included those who had been forcibly moved to Germany during the war to work in its fields and factories. And then there were those, such as the several million ethnic Germans who had lived in Eastern Europe, whose homelands were transferred to the victors. (Former German territories, which became parts of Poland, Czechoslovakia, and the Soviet Union, remained among the unresolved issues of the Cold War.) For these millions of homeless people the struggle for survival was especially difficult, and we have no way of knowing how many of them did not survive.

There was also a large refugee problem in Asia, where the Japanese had forced population transfers during the war and where some 6 million Japanese—half of them military personnel—were scattered all over Asia at war's end. After the war, the United States transported most of these Japanese back to safety in Japan and returned Koreans, Chinese, and others to their homelands. However, in Manchuria, which was temporarily occupied by the Soviet Union after the war, several hundred thousand Japanese were never repatriated. They succumbed either to the severity of the Manchurian winter without adequate food, shelter, or clothing or to the brutality of Soviet labor camps in Siberia. Elsewhere in Asia, particularly in China, there were large population movements as millions of people, who had earlier fled from the Japanese invaders, returned to reclaim their lands and homes. In China, cities such as Beijing (Peking) and Shanghai were swollen with weary, desperate people for whom there was no livelihood and insufficient food and other staples. In these places people were plagued by disease, poverty, the black market, inflation, and corruption, all of which ran rampant in China during and well after the war.

The inferno of World War II left many cities gutted and vacant. Dresden, Hamburg, and Berlin in Germany and Tokyo, Yokohama, Hiroshima, and Nagasaki in Japan were virtually flattened, and many other cities in these and other countries were in large part turned to rubble. Some were entirely vacated and devoid of life for a while after the war, and most lost a substantial portion of their people. For example, the huge and once crowded city of Tokyo, which lay mostly in ruins, saw its population dwindle to only a third of its prewar size. In these once bustling cities, survivors scrounged in the debris in hopes of salvaging anything that might help them in their struggle for survival. At war's end homeless people moved into those few buildings that still stood—an office building, a railroad station, a school—and lived sometimes three or four families to a room, while others threw up shanties and shacks made of scraps of wood. Decades later one could still find here and there in many of these cities rubble left over from the war.

The physical destruction wrought by the war estimated at over $2 trillion continued to cause economic and social disruption in the lives of survivors long afterwards. Not only were cities and towns destroyed but so too were industrial plants and transportation facilities. The destruction of factories, farmlands, and livestock and of railroads, bridges, and port facilities made it extremely difficult to feed and supply the needy populations in the war-torn nations of Europe and Asia. Thus, acute shortages of food and scarcity of other life essentials continued well after the fighting was over. In these dire circumstances, many became desperate and demoralized, and some sought to insure their survival or to profit from others' misfortune by resorting to hoarding goods and selling them on the black market. These were grim times in which greed, vengeance, and other base instincts of humanity found expression.

The widespread desolation and despair in Europe bred cynicism and disillusionment, which in turn gave rise to a political shift to the left. Shaken and bewildered by the nightmarish devastation all about them, many Europeans lost confidence in the old political order and turned to other more radical political doctrines and movements. Many embraced Marxism as a natural alternative to the discredited fascism and as an ideology that offered hope for the future. The renewed popularity of the left was reflected primarily in postwar electoral victories of the moderate left, such as the Labour Party in Great Britain and the Socialist Party in Austria.

But the Communists, too, were able to make strong showings, particularly in France and Italy. In Asia the political swing to the left could be seen in China, Indochina, and to a lesser extent in Japan. Alarmed by this resurgence of the left, U.S. leaders soon came to the view that massive aid was necessary to bring about a speedy economic recovery and thereby eliminate the poverty that was seen as the breeding ground for the spread of Communism.

During the war the United Nations Relief and Rehabilitation Administration (UNRRA) was created to rehabilitate war-torn areas after liberation. Economic aid from this agency as well as from the United States directly not only provided relief for the destitute peoples of Europe and Asia, but also provided much needed credit that made possible the beginnings of economic recovery. By the fall of 1946, many of the transportation facilities and factories in Western Europe had been rapidly repaired, and industrial production began to climb slowly toward prewar levels. But the harsh winter of 1946–1947 brought new economic setbacks with a depletion of food supplies, raw materials, and financial reserves. Economic stagnation and attendant deprivation therefore continued for masses of people throughout Europe, especially in Germany, which had suffered the greatest physical destruction in the war, and in Great Britain, one of the victors. A similar situation prevailed in the war-ravaged nations of Asia, especially China and Japan.

When we consider all the death, destruction, suffering, and social dislocation that it caused for so many people, we realize that World War II was much more than a series of heroic military campaigns, and more than a set of war games to be played and replayed by nostalgic war buffs. It was human anguish and agony on a scale unprecedented in the history of mankind. And nowhere were the scars any deeper than on the two Japanese cities, Hiroshima and Nagasaki.

■ THE ATOMIC BOMBING OF JAPAN

On August 6, 1945, the United States dropped an atomic bomb on Hiroshima, and three days later it used another one on Nagasaki. In each instance a large city was obliterated and tens of thousands of its inhabitants were either instantly incinerated, or left to succumb to radiation sickness weeks, months, or even years later. According to Japanese estimates, about 140,000 people were killed in Hiroshima by the atomic bomb strike, and about 70,000 in Nagasaki.[3] Thus, World War II ended and the nuclear age began with the use of this new weapon of unprecedented destructive power, a weapon that one scientist later called "a magnificent product of pure physics."[4]

The people of the United States and their wartime president, Franklin Roosevelt, were determined to bring about the earliest possible defeat of

Japan. The costly war in the Pacific had been raging for almost three and a half years by the time Germany surrendered in May 1945. President Roosevelt, who had commissioned the building of the atomic bomb, was prepared to use it against Japan once it was ready, but he died in April 1945. The decision to employ the revolutionary new weapon fell to the new president, Harry S. Truman, who had not even been informed of its existence before he took office. In consultation with the secretary of war, Henry Stimson, Truman set up an advisory group known as the Interim Committee, which was to deliberate on the matter of introducing the new weapon into warfare. Ultimately, the Interim Committee recommended that the atomic bomb be used against Japan as soon as possible, and without prior warning, on a dual target (meaning a military or war plant site surrounded by workers' homes, that is, a Japanese city).[5] The rationale for this strategy for the use of the bomb was to enhance its shock value. The atomic bomb was successfully tested in a remote New Mexico desert on July 16, just as Truman was meeting British Prime Minister Winston Churchill and Soviet leader Joseph Stalin at Potsdam, Germany. Nine days later, on July 25, Truman, elated by the news of the test, approved the military orders for its use. The following day he issued the Potsdam Proclamation, which contained the final surrender terms for Japan and warned of

Hiroshima, Japan, Aug. 1945. Located near ground zero, this building with its "A-Bomb Dome" has been preserved as a peace monument. *(National Archives)*

"prompt and utter destruction" for noncompliance, but which made no specific reference to the new weapon. The proclamation was rejected by the Japanese government, and thus the orders for the first atomic bomb strike were carried out as planned.

On the official level, the Japanese government dismissed the proclamation, for it was silent on the most important question, a guarantee that the victors would retain the most sacred of Japanese institutions, the emperor. The U.S. intelligence community, which from the very beginning of the war had been able to decode Japanese diplomatic cables, had become well aware that the Potsdam Proclamation had a "magnetic effect" on the emperor, Prime Minister Suzuki, and the army. Some Japanese officials thought that Article 10 of the Potsdam Proclamation implied the retention of the emperor and thus could be used as the basis of a Japanese surrender; others wanted a clarification. The Potsdam Proclamation, far from triggering an expression of Japanese intransigence, had the earmarks of the terms of surrender of the armed forces of the empire of Japan. Only one question remained: Would the U.S. government clarify Article 10 and accept a Japanese surrender before or after atomic weapons were used?[6]

Many people have since questioned the use of the atomic bomb, and opinions differ sharply. The orthodox view, presented by U.S. officials after the event and generally shared by the U.S. public, is that, by cutting short the war and sparing the casualties that would have occurred in the planned invasion of Japan, the atomic bomb actually saved many lives, Japanese as well as U.S. This explanation concludes that, although use of the bomb was regrettable, it was nonetheless necessary. Japan's diehard military leaders were determined to fight to the bitter end, as they had in the Pacific islands, and they were prepared to fight even more fanatically on their own soil to prevent defeat. Thus, in order to bring about the earliest possible surrender of Japan and an end to the long and costly war,[7] the United States was compelled to use the revolutionary, powerful new weapon its scientists and engineers had secretly produced.

However, this interpretation, basically a justification of the atomic bombing of Japan, neglects many important historical facts. First, Japan was all but defeated. Its home islands were defenseless against the sustained naval and air bombardment they were undergoing, its navy and merchant marine were sunk, its armies were weakened and undersupplied, and it was already being strangled by a U.S. naval blockade. U.S. leaders, who had underestimated the Japanese at the beginning of the war, were now overestimating Japan's remaining strength. Although the diehard determination of its military leaders kept Japan from surrendering, the nation's capacity to wage war had been virtually eliminated.

Second, before the United States had tested the atomic bomb in midJuly, the Japanese were already attempting to begin negotiations to end the war through Soviet mediation. (Direct communication between Tokyo and

Washington was not possible because of the state of war between the two countries, but Japan was not at war with the Soviet Union.) The U.S. government was fully aware of these efforts and of the sense of urgency voiced by the Japanese in their communications to Moscow. U.S. decision makers chose to ignore these diplomatic overtures, which they dismissed as unreliable and possibly a trick. The major obstacle to Japan's effort to achieve a diplomatic settlement to the war was the U.S. insistence upon unconditional surrender. (Unconditional surrender calls for the enemy's acceptance of complete submission to the will of the victor, as opposed to a negotiated settlement to end the war.) This was entirely unacceptable to the Japanese, who wanted at least a guarantee of the safety of their sacred imperial institution—which is to say, they insisted on the retention of their emperor, Hirohito, in whose name the imperial forces had fought the war. The U.S. government steadfastly refused to offer any such exception to the unconditional surrender policy. The Potsdam Proclamation, the final Allied ultimatum, issued on July 26, 1945, did not offer Japan any guarantees regarding the emperor, and thus the Japanese could not accept it as a basis for surrender. This condition was the only one the Japanese insisted upon, and eventually it was granted by the United States, *after* the nuclear destruction of Hiroshima and Nagasaki. On August 11, the Japanese government agreed to surrender provided that it "does not comprise any demand which prejudices the prerogatives of His Majesty as a sovereign ruler."[8] This was a condition the United States accepted in its reply when it demanded the unconditional surrender of the Japanese forces. If this condition had been granted beforehand, the Japanese may well have surrendered and the atomic bombs been unnecessary to attain that objective.

Third, the Japanese might have been spared the horrendous fate of Hiroshima and Nagasaki had the U.S. government provided them with an explicit warning about the nature of the new weapon and possibly an actual demonstration of an atomic blast as well. If they had still refused to accept the surrender terms after such a warning or demonstration, the use of the atomic weapons might have been morally justifiable. The Japanese were given no warning of the atomic bombing outside of the vague threat in the Potsdam Proclamation of "prompt and utter destruction." The Interim Committee ruled out the idea of providing Japan with either a warning or a demonstration of the bomb in favor of its direct use on a Japanese city in order to shock the Japanese into surrender. It was also argued that a demonstration would be risky because of the possibility of the bomb's failing to work, thus causing the United States to lose credibility and the Japanese military leaders to gain confidence.

Fourth, an unquestioned assumption of most of those who defend the use of the two atomic bombs is that it produced the desired results: Japan quickly surrendered. But questions do arise. Did the atomic bombings actually cause the Japanese to surrender? And was the second bomb necessary to bring it about? (It should be pointed out that there was no separate set of orders to drop a second atomic bomb on Japan. Instead, the plan was to use a "one-two punch" using both bombs in rapid succession, and, if necessary, a third, which was to be ready within ten days, so as to maximize the new weapon's shock value and force Japan to capitulate as rapidly as possible.)

Those who specifically protest the bombing of Nagasaki as unnecessary, and therefore immoral, assume that the bombing of Hiroshima was sufficient to cause Japan's surrender, or that Japan should have been given more time to assess what had hit Hiroshima. One may indeed question whether the interval of three days was long enough for the Japanese military leaders to assess the significance of the new force that had destroyed one of their cities. But a more fundamental question is whether the atomic bombings—the first or both—actually caused Japan's surrender. Japanese newspapers, the testimony of Japanese leaders, and U.S. intercepts of Japanese diplomatic cables provide reason to believe that the Soviet entry into the war against Japan on August 8 was as much a cause for Japan's surrender as the dropping of the two atomic bombs. The Soviet Union was the only major nation in the world not at war with Japan, and the Japanese leaders were still desperately hoping for Soviet neutrality or possible Soviet mediation to bail them out of the war. They took heart in the fact that the Soviet Union had not signed the Potsdam Proclamation or signified support for it, even though Stalin was meeting with Truman and Churchill when it was issued. But with the Soviet attack the last shred of hope was gone, and Japan could no longer avoid admitting defeat. As for the effect of the atomic bombings on Japanese leaders, Japan's inner cabinet was divided three-to-three for and against accepting the Potsdam Proclamation before the bombing of Hiroshima, and it remained so afterward. And it remained equally divided after the Soviet entry into the war and the bombing of Nagasaki, until finally the emperor himself broke the deadlock in favor of ending the war.

What were the thoughts of the U.S. leaders about the role of the Soviet Union in bringing about Japan's defeat? Clearly, at the Yalta Conference in February 1945, President Roosevelt and his military advisers strongly desired the early entry of the Soviet Union into the war against Japan and he was willing to concede much to Stalin to attain this. But five months later, after the atomic bomb was successfully tested, leading figures in the Truman administration were not so sure they wanted the Soviet Union to enter the war against Japan. Nor did they want the Soviets to know anything about the atomic bomb. In fact, both Roosevelt and Truman pointedly refused to inform Moscow about the development of the new weapon and the plans to use it against Japan, despite the advice of some of the leading atomic scientists to do so in order to prevent a nuclear arms race after the war.

Nagasaki before.

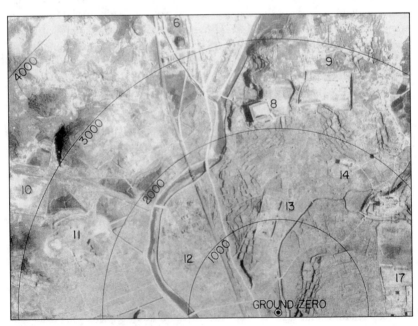

Nagasaki after. (*National Archives*)

This last point raises intriguing and important questions about the connection between the U.S. use of the bomb and its policies toward the Soviet Union at the end of the war. One historical interpretation asserts that the United States used the atomic bomb on defeated Japan not so much as the last attack of World War II, but as the first attack in the Cold War. In other words, the bomb was used in order to coerce the Soviet Union into behaving itself in Europe, Asia, and elsewhere. This interpretation would explain the hurried use of the bomb before the Soviet Union had entered the war against Japan and nearly three months prior to the planned invasion of Japan by U.S. forces. And it would explain Truman's refusal to inform Stalin officially about the new weapon before (or even after) its use against Japan. In this way it is argued that the United States sought to maintain its nuclear monopoly (shared with Britain) and to use it as a means to curb Soviet expansion. This has been referred to as nuclear diplomacy.

Although this interpretation by revisionist historians is based on rather substantial evidence and logic, it remains speculative, and those who hold the orthodox view, of course, reject it and offer counterarguments. They emphasize the fanaticism and intransigence of the Japanese military leaders, who even resorted to suicidal kamikaze airplane attacks on U.S. ships. And they argue that the atomic bomb was needed to subdue an irrational enemy who seemed determined to fight suicidally to the bitter end. Therefore, they conclude, it was solely for military purposes that President Truman decided to use the atomic bomb. They also argue that President Truman, as commander in chief, had the responsibility to use the military power at his command to produce the earliest possible defeat of Japan, and that, if he had not used the atomic bomb and more U.S. military personnel had died in the continuing war, he would surely have been condemned as being politically and morally liable for their deaths.

Those who hold this view also point out that Truman could hardly have decided against use of the atomic bomb. As a new occupant of the White House following the popular Roosevelt, Truman inherited Roosevelt's cabinet, his policies, and specifically his resolve to treat the new weapon as a legitimate one of war. Gen. Leslie Groves, head of the Manhattan Project (the code name of the secret program to build the atomic bomb), certainly assumed and fully expected that it would be used as soon as it became operational. The military planning for its use was well under way. There was, among the scientists and military personnel involved in the project, a rising anticipation of the successful deployment of the weapon they had brought into being after four years of herculean effort. It is argued that Truman, who had only learned about the new weapon when he took office in April, could hardly have stemmed the momentum. The military leaders, and General Groves in particular, seemed especially determined to deploy the new weapon in order to know its destructive force.

They had decided upon a set of Japanese cities as targets and had ordered that these cities be spared from conventional bombing so that they would remain unspoiled targets for the new weapon.

■ THE POLITICAL FALLOUT

Historians are also in disagreement over the impact of the atomic bomb on the Cold War. Did the Truman administration actually attempt to employ nuclear diplomacy after the war? If it did, it is safe to say that it did not work. The nuclear threat, implicit in the exclusive Anglo-U.S. possession of the atomic bomb, did not seem to produce any significant change in Soviet behavior and policies anywhere. But it did, no doubt, affect attitudes on both sides that contributed to Cold War mistrust. U.S. possession of the bomb caused its leaders to be more demanding and less flexible in dealing with the Soviet Union, and the U.S. possession and use of the bomb surely caused the Soviet leaders, in turn, to increase their suspicions of the West.

It is fairly certain that the secretive manner of the United States in building and then using the atomic bomb made a postwar nuclear arms race likely, if not inevitable. Truman's secretary of state, James Byrnes, who also served on the Interim Committee, contended that it would take the Soviet Union at least ten years to develop an atomic bomb and that in the interval the United States could take advantage of its "master card" in dealing with the Soviet Union. However, leading U.S. nuclear scientists, including Robert Oppenheimer, predicted that the Soviet Union could build the bomb within four years.[9] Several of the Manhattan Project scientists attempted to warn the Truman administration that the atomic monopoly could not be maintained for long and that a nuclear arms race would surely follow and threaten the peace of the world if the U.S. government did not share information about this revolutionary new weapon of mass destruction with its ally, the Soviet Union, and did not attempt to bring it under international control. This advice, given both before and after the Hiroshima and Nagasaki bombings, went unheeded, and the result was exactly what the scientists had predicted. Indeed, Oppenheimer's prediction that the Soviets would have their own atomic weapons in four years was right on target.

The U.S. government did, however, after months of careful study of the complicated issues involved, offer a proposal for international control of atomic power. This proposal, the Baruch Plan, presented to a committee within the United Nations in June 1946, was unacceptable to the Soviet Union because, among other reasons, it permitted the United States to retain its nuclear arsenal indefinitely, while restricting Soviet efforts to develop one. The Soviets countered by proposing the immediate destruction of all existing nuclear weapons and the signing of a treaty outlawing any future production or use of them. The United States, understandably unwilling to scuttle its atomic monopoly, flatly rejected this. Talks continued for the next three years at the United Nations, but they proved fruitless. In the meantime, the Soviet Union's frantic effort to build an atomic bomb did bear fruit as early as the U.S. atomic scientists had predicted—July 1949. The nuclear arms race was joined.

■ THE UNITED STATES AND THE SOVIET UNION AT WAR'S END

The two nations that emerged from the war as the most powerful shapers of the postwar world, the two new superpowers, the United States and the Soviet Union, had very different wartime experiences. No nation suffered as many casualties as the Soviet Union, and no major nation in the war suffered as few as the United States.

In June 1941, the German army of more than 2 million soldiers invaded the Soviet Union. Immense areas of the Soviet Union were devastated by the ensuing war, leaving some 1,700 cities and 70,000 villages in ruins and some 70 percent of its industries and 60 percent of its transportation facilities destroyed. During the war, the Germans took several million Soviet prisoners, many of whom did not survive their ordeal, and several million others were forcibly conscripted to labor on German factories and farms during the war. The horrors of the German invasion and occupation policies and the siege of Soviet cities aroused the patriotism of both the Russian and non-Russian peoples of the Soviet Union who fought heroically to defend the nation in what is still called the Great Patriotic War. Ultimately, these people endured, and the Soviet Red Army drove the shattered German armies off their land and across Eastern Europe back to Germany where they were finally defeated. But the cost in lives was enormous: an estimated 7.5 million military deaths and twice—possibly three times—as many civilian lives. Any discussion of postwar policies of the Soviet Union and its relations with the United States must begin with a recognition of the incredible losses it suffered in its war against Nazi Germany and its insistence that there be no repetition of this history.[10]

In contrast, the United States emerged from the war virtually unscathed. Except for the Japanese attack on Pearl Harbor at the outset of the war, it had not been invaded or bombed and there had been no bloody battle lines across its terrain. In comparison with the huge Soviet death toll, the number of U.S. soldiers killed in the war—approximately 330,000—was small. For every U.S. death resulting from the war there were 85 to 90 Soviet deaths. The Soviet Union lost more people in the siege of Leningrad or in the battle of Stalingrad than the United States did in the entire war.

In comparison to the immense physical destruction sustained by the Soviet Union, the United States suffered very little damage. On the contrary, the U.S. economy experienced a great wartime boom, which brought it out of the Great Depression. While the Soviet Union's industrial output fell by 40 percent during the war years, that of the United States more than doubled. And while the Soviet Union sorely needed economic rehabilitation to recover from the ravages of war, the United States possessed unparalleled economic power. Indeed, no nation has ever achieved such economic supremacy as that achieved by the United States at the end of World War II. In a war-ravaged world where every other industrial nation had suffered extensive damage and declining production, the U.S. economy, with its wartime growth, towered over all others like a colossus. What is more, the United States had the capacity to greatly extend its huge lead. It possessed in great abundance every resource necessary for sustained industrial growth in the postwar era: large, undamaged industrial plants, skilled labor, technology, raw materials, a sophisticated transport system, and, last but not least, a huge supply of capital for investment.

The United States emerged from the war with another important although intangible asset: a greatly inflated national ego. The nation was brimming with renewed confidence and optimism. The pessimism spawned by the Great Depression was a thing of the past. The U.S. people saw their victory in war as proof of the superiority of their way of life. With their nation standing tall at the pinnacle of power in the war-torn world, the people exhibited what has been called an "illusion of American omnipotence."[11] Bolstered by this new confidence and sense of supremacy, the United States now displayed a new determination to play the role of a great power and to exercise its leadership in shaping the postwar world.

■ THE QUEST FOR COLLECTIVE SECURITY

The task of establishing a new world order after the defeat of Germany and Japan fell, of course, to the victors, especially the most powerful among them, the United States, the Soviet Union, and to a lesser degree Great Britain. During the war, the leaders of these countries—the "Big Three," Franklin Roosevelt, Joseph Stalin, and Winston Churchill—met not only to coordinate war plans but also to lay plans for the postwar settlement. These men, especially Roosevelt, were confident that the harmony and trust developed during the war would endure and that through personal diplomacy they could settle the enormous problems of the postwar world, such as the future of Germany, Eastern Europe, Japan, and the rest of Asia. However, before the war ended, two of the three were no longer in power: Roosevelt died in April 1945, and Churchill was defeated in the British election of July of that year. But it was already apparent before Roosevelt's death that the wartime alliance would not outlast the war. In retrospect, it is clear that the Big Three had little more in common than a common enemy, and once Nazi Germany was defeated their conflicting interests came to the fore.

The wartime solidarity attained by the personal diplomacy of the Big Three could not be counted on to guide the postwar world to safety and security, and would not in any case endure beyond the war; however, they did endeavor, albeit cautiously, to erect a new international structure of peace. While sharp differences arose among the Big Three over a number of issues as the war was coming to an end, they were in general agreement on the concept of maintaining peace through collective security. President Roosevelt was most ardent in advocating the creation of a new international peacekeeping organization to replace the defunct League of Nations. Early during the war years, Roosevelt began sounding out Churchill on this idea and then found occasion to discuss it with Stalin as well. All three were concerned about maintaining a postwar working relationship among the "united nations," as the Allied powers were sometimes called. Roosevelt wished to avoid a return of his country to isolationism, and Stalin seems to have had a similar concern; he did not want the Soviet Union to be isolated as it had been prior to World War II.

Within each of the three governments there was much discussion about the shape the new collective security organization should take, its structure, functions, and authority. The most difficult issue was that of internationalism versus nationalism, or more concretely, whether member nations were to surrender part or all of their own sovereignty to the new supranational body in the interest of maintaining world peace. How would it be possible to provide the international organization with enough authority to enforce its decisions on member nations and yet permit each nation the right to pursue and protect its national interests? Another key question was the relationship of the major powers to the many smaller nations in the international body. From the outset the Big Three were in agreement that they would not sacrifice their power to majority rule. They insisted that their own nations, which had played the major role in defeating the aggressor nations in World War II, should be entrusted with the responsibility to maintain the postwar peace, and that the new international organization should invest authority in them to exercise leadership unobstructed by the collective will of the more numerous, smaller member states.

These issues were resolved among the Big Three at a series of wartime conferences. At a meeting in Moscow in October 1943, the Allied foreign ministers agreed in principle to the creation of the organization that would come to be known as the United Nations (or simply the UN). In August 1944, as victory in the war approached, representatives of the Big Three, now joined by China, met at Dumbarton Oaks (in Washington) to hammer out the shape of the new international body. At the Yalta Conference in February 1945 (see Chapter 2), the Big Three came to terms on the matter of securing for each of the major powers the right to veto decisions of the new international body. This cleared the way for convening a conference at San Francisco in April 1945, where the United Nations Charter, which spelled out the principles and the powers of the new organization as well as its organizational structure, was signed by representatives of the fifty-one founding nations. In September 1945, the United Nations officially opened at its headquarters in New York City.

The principal organs of the United Nations were the Security Council, the General Assembly, the Economic and Social Council, the International Court of Justice, and the Secretariat. The most powerful and important of these was the Security Council, which was given the responsibility to keep the peace. It was empowered to determine whether an action such as armed aggression by a member nation constituted a breach of the United Nations Charter and to recommend corrective measures or sanctions, including the use of force under the principle of collective security. The Council was composed of five permanent members (the five great powers: the United States, the Soviet Union, Great Britain, China, and France) and six other nations elected for two-year terms. The permanent members were given veto power, which is to say the Council could not act (pass a binding resolution) unless there was unanimity among the five. It was in this manner that they intended to protect themselves against actions by the world body against their individual interests. It must be noted that both the United States and the Soviet Union insisted on this veto power, and without it they would not have joined the United Nations. And it should also be noted that it was this same provision that soon rendered the United Nations Security Council ineffective, because in the ensuing Cold War unanimity among the major powers was all but impossible to attain. In the early years of the United Nations, the Soviet Union, which often stood alone against the other four major powers, resorted again and again to the veto.

The UN General Assembly was composed of all of the member nations, each of which had an equal voice and a single vote. It acted as an open forum in which international problems and proposed solutions were discussed. The Assembly passed resolutions by majority vote, but these were treated merely as recommendations and were not binding on the member nations. This body was important mainly for giving the smaller nations a greater voice in world affairs. The UN Secretariat was the permanent administrative office concerned primarily with the internal operations of the organization. It was headed by a secretary general, who was the highest and most visible officer of the United Nations.[12] Although actual authority was limited, the secretary general was able to exert considerable diplomatic influence owing to the prestige of the office. The other bodies of the United Nations, especially the specialized agencies under the Economic and Social Council (e.g., the World Health Organization), functioned more effectively than the Security Council precisely because they were more operational than political in nature, and the problems they addressed could be separated from Cold War polemics. This also was essentially true for such UN bodies as the International Court of Justice, UNESCO (United Nations Educational, Scientific, and Cultural Organization), and UNRRA.

The founding of the United Nations was an expression of hope by the survivors of catastrophic World War II, and it was greeted by them as the fulfillment of dreams for an organization that would ensure international peace and order. The political leaders who actually took part in its creation also had high hopes for it. It was not long, however, before the United Nations proved unable to fulfill those dreams and even became an object of derision for many. The United Nations did on several occasions intervene to settle or moderate international disputes in such places as Iran, India, Malaya, and the Middle East, when and where the interests of both the United States and the Soviet Union were either minimal or not in conflict. However, the veto power that both superpowers had insisted on and the Cold War contention between them rendered the Security Council all but powerless to keep the peace in the postwar era.

RECOMMENDED READINGS

World War II

Calvocoressi, Peter, and Guy Wint. *Total War Causes and Courses of the Second World War*. New York: Pantheon Books, 1972.
 A comprehensive account of the war both in Europe and Asia.
Dower, John W. *War Without Mercy: Race and Power in the Pacific War*. New York: Pantheon, 1986.
 A frank analysis of the racial nature of the war.
Hart, B. H. Liddell. *History of the Second World War*. New York: Putnam, 1971.
 One of the most highly regarded single-volume studies of World War II.
Saburo, Ienaga. *The Pacific War: World War Two and the Japanese, 1931–1945*. New York: Pantheon Books, 1978.
 A strong indictment of Japanese militarism.
Toland, John. *The Rising Sun*. New York: Random House, 1971.
 One of the best books on Japan's war.
Werth, Alexander. *Russia at War, 1941–1945*. New York: Dutton, 1964.
 Excellent on the Soviet Union's wartime experience, by a British war correspondent, a native of Leningrad.
Wright, Gordon. *The Ordeal of Total War*. New York: Harper and Row, 1968.
 A classic study of the war.

The Atomic Bomb

Alperovitz, Gar. *Atomic Diplomacy: Hiroshima and Potsdam*. New York: Simon and Schuster, 1965.
 The foremost revisionist interpretation of the atomic bomb decision.

Bernstein, Barton J., ed. *The Atomic Bomb: The Critical Issues.* Boston: Little, Brown, 1976.
An excellent anthology, which provides excerpts from the writings of some of those involved in the atomic bomb project and by various other writers.
Committee for the Compilation of Materials on Damage Caused by the Atomic Bombs in Hiroshima and Nagasaki. *Hiroshima and Nagasaki: The Physical, Medical and Social Effects of the Atomic Bombs.* New York: Basic Books, 1981.
The definitive study on these subjects.
Feis, Herbert. *The Atomic Bomb and the End of World War II.* Princeton: Princeton University Press, 1966; originally published as *Japan Subdued,* 1961.
A standard work that focuses on both the military and diplomatic aspects of the atomic bomb decision.
Herken, Gregg F. *The Winning Weapon: The Atomic Bomb in the Cold War, 1945– 1950.* New York: Knopf, 1981.
A discussion of the role of the atomic bomb in immediate postwar diplomacy.
Hersey, John. *Hiroshima.* New York: Bantam Books, 1959.
A classic on the death and destruction caused by the first atomic bomb attack.
Rhodes, Richard. *The Making of the Atomic Bomb.* New York: Simon and Schuster, 1986.
Sherwin, Martin J. *A World Destroyed: The Atomic Bomb and the Grand Alliance.* New York: Knopf, 1975.
Among the best studies of the politics and diplomacy involved in the decision to drop the atomic bomb on Japan.

NOTES

1. The magnitude of the slaughter was such that no exact figures are possible. For a breakdown of the figures, particularly in Asia, see John W. Dower, *War Without Mercy: Race and Power in the Pacific War* (New York: Pantheon, 1986), pp. 295–301.
2. Aerial bombardment actually began before World War II. Its effectiveness was demonstrated by the German bombing of Spanish cities in the Spanish civil war and the Japanese bombing of Chinese cities in Manchuria. In World War II, Britain carried out bombing raids on Berlin before Germany began its bombardment of Britain, but the latter represents the first sustained, large-scale bombing attack on the cities of another country.
3. U.S. estimates of the death toll from the atomic bombings are 70,000 in Hiroshima and 40,000 in Nagasaki. The discrepancy in the fatality figures apparently results partly from different methods of calculation and partly from differing intentions of those doing the counting.
4. Dr. Yoshio Nishina, "The Atomic Bomb" Report for the United States Strategic Bombing Servey (Washington, D.C.: National Archives), p. 1, Record Group 243, Box 56.
5. "Notes of the Interim Committee," Record Group 77, Manhattan Engineering District Papers, Modern Military Branch, National Archives (Washington, D.C.: National Archives, May 31, 1945), pp. 9–10.
6. Pacific Strategic Intelligence Section, intelligence summary of August 7, 1945, "Russo Japanese Relations (28 July 6 August 1945)," National Archives, Record Group 457, SRH-088, pp. 3, 7–8, 16. For the Japanese attempts to surrender, beginning on July 13, 1945, see "Magic Diplomatic Extracts, July 1945," MIS,

War Department, prepared for the attention of General George C. Marshall; National Archives, Record Group 457, SRH-040, pp. 1–78.

7. One commonly finds the figure of 1 million as the estimate of Allied (mainly U.S.) soldiers who would have been killed in the invasion of Japan if the atomic bomb had not been used, but this figure seems grossly exaggerated. It is more than three times the total number of U.S. military deaths resulting from World War II—both in Europe and in the Pacific in four years of warfare. The 1 million figure was used by Secretary of War Stimson after the war in an article intended to justify the use of the atomic bomb on Japan. In point of fact, at a meeting of top U.S. military officials to discuss the planned invasion of Japan on June 18, 1945, General George C. Marshall, the army chief of staff, expressed the view that it was impossible to give an estimate of the casualties in such an invasion, but he said that in the first month they would probably not exceed those suffered in the invasion of Luzon—31,000. See Herbert Feis, *The Atomic Bomb and the End of World War II* (Princeton: Princeton University Press, 1966), pp. 8–9.

8. Harry S. Truman, *Memoirs, I, 1945: Year of Decisions* (New York: Signet, [orig. 1955] 1965), p. 471.

9. "Notes of the Interim Committee," May 31, 1945, pp. 10–12; Gregg Herken, *The Winning Weapon: The Atomic Bomb in the Cold War, 1945–1950* (New York: Random House, 1981), pp. 109–113. Byrnes was apparently less influenced by the views of the scientists than he was by General Groves, who speculated that it would take the Soviet Union from ten to twenty years to produce an atomic bomb.

10. It is estimated that there were about as many Soviet deaths in the Battle of Stalingrad alone as the United States suffered in the entire war (330,000), and it is estimated that over 1 million died in the siege of Leningrad.

11. Sir Denis Brogan cited in Louis Halle, *The Cold War as History* (New York: Harper and Row, 1967), p. 25.

12. The secretary general was appointed by the General Assembly on the recommendation of the Security Council. In effect, this meant finding a neutral candidate from a neutral country acceptable to the two sides in the Cold War. The first secretary general was Trygve Lie of Norway (1946–1953), who was followed by Dag Hammarskjöld of Sweden (1953–1961), U Thant of Burma (1961–1971), Kurt Waldheim of Austria (1972–1981), Javier Pérez de Cuéllar of Peru (1982–1991), Boutros Boutros-Ghali of Egypt (1992–1996), and Kofi Annan of Ghanha (1997–   ).

2

The Cold War Institutionalized

At the end of 1944, it became clear that it was only a matter of time until the Allies would defeat Nazi Germany. It also became evident that the reason for the wartime alliance—always a marriage of convenience—was coming to an end. Postwar considerations were beginning to play an ever increasing role in the relations between the Allies. Throughout the war, the Allies had made it clear repeatedly that they fought for specific aims and not merely for the high-sounding principles of liberty and democracy. In 1945, the moment thus came to consider the postwar world, to present one's claims. For these reasons the Allied heads of state—Franklin Roosevelt of the United States, Joseph Stalin of the Soviet Union, and Winston Churchill of Great Britain—met in February 1945 in the Soviet resort of Yalta on the Crimean Peninsula in the Black Sea. It was here that the Big Three attempted to sort out four central issues.

■ THE YALTA CONFERENCE

The main topic at Yalta was the status of postwar Eastern Europe, and mainly that of Poland, which had been—and still was at the time of the conference—an ally in the war against Germany. It had been on behalf of the government of Poland that Great Britain and France had declared war on Germany in 1939. This action by the Western powers had transformed the German-Polish war into a European conflict, which then spilled over into the Atlantic, the Mediterranean, and North Africa, and with the Japanese attack on Pearl Harbor in December 1941, into Asia and the Pacific. In short, the governments of France and Great Britain had taken the momentous decision to go to war—and thus risk the welfare and the independence of their own nations, not to mention their people's lives and fortunes—to prevent the German conquest of a nation in Eastern Europe.

As the war drew to a conclusion and the Germans were expelled from Poland, the fate of that nation became the overriding political concern of

The Big Three. Soviet Marshal Joseph Stalin, U.S. President Franklin D. Roosevelt, and British Prime Minister Winston Churchill at the Tehran conference in Nov. 1943. (*National Archives*)

the Allies. To complicate matters for the West, the government of Poland, virulently anti-Russian and anti-Communist, had fled Warsaw in the wake of the German invasion and had taken up residence in London, waiting to return to power at the end of the war. The Poles in London now insisted that the West had an obligation to facilitate their return to Warsaw as the legitimate government of Poland. The Western leaders, Churchill and Roosevelt, wanted to oblige, but it was the Red Army of the Soviet Union that was in the process of occupying Poland. It became increasingly clear that Stalin, not Roosevelt or Churchill, held the trump cards.

The second issue at Yalta was one of prime importance for the U.S. armed forces, which at that time were still engaged in a bitter war with Japan that promised to continue perhaps into 1946. Japanese resistance was as fierce as ever. The sustained bombing of Japanese cities was under way, but the Battle of Okinawa (where the United States first set foot on Japanese soil) had not yet taken place. For the U.S. Joint Chiefs of Staff, therefore, Yalta was primarily a war conference with the aim of bringing the seasoned Red Army into the war against Japan in the Pacific.

The third question was the formation of the United Nations to replace the old League of Nations, a casualty of World War II. Roosevelt sought an organizational structure for the United Nations acceptable to Churchill and

Stalin, as well as to the U.S. people back home. Roosevelt firmly believed that there could be no effective international organization without U.S. and Soviet participation.

Finally, there was the question of what to do with the German state, whose defeat was imminent. The Allies, after all, would soon be in control of the devastated land of the once-powerful German, whose uncertain future was in their hands.

☐ The Polish Question

The first question, the status of Poland, proved to be the thorniest. It came up in seven of the eight plenary (full, formal) sessions. Roosevelt and Churchill argued that Poland, an ally, must be free to choose its own government. Specifically, they sought the return of the prewar government of Poland, which had gone into exile in London during the war and was anxious to return to power in Poland.

But there was a problem. This "London government" consisted of Poles who did not hide their strong anti-Russian and anti-Communist sentiments, the result of age-old struggles between the Russians and Poles. Their animosity toward the Communist government in Moscow was so great that on the eve of the war with Germany they had refused even to consider an alliance with the Soviet Union. Stalin then made his famous deal in 1939 with Hitler whereby the two agreed to a Non-Aggression Pact,[1] by which Stalin hoped to sit out the war. As part of the bargain, Hitler offered Stalin the eastern portion of Poland, a large piece of territory that the victorious Poles had seized from a devastated Soviet state in 1921. The Polish conquest of what the Soviets considered part of their empire and the Soviets' reconquest of these lands with Hitler's complicity were but two events in the long and bloody relationship between these two peoples. In 1941, Hitler used Poland as a springboard to invade the Soviet Union and at the end of the war the Soviets returned to Poland with a powerful army once more.

Stalin understood only too well the nationalistic and bitterly anti-Russian attitudes of the Poles, particularly that of the prewar government, which had sworn eternal hostility to his government. As the Soviet soldiers moved into Poland they became targets of the Polish resistance, which took time out from fighting the Germans to deal with the invader from the east. Stalin had no difficulty understanding the nationalistic and religious divisions in Eastern Europe. He himself, an ethnic Georgian, was after all a product of the volatile ethnic mix of the old tsarist empire. He knew, as he told his Western allies at Yalta, that the Poles would be "quarrelsome."[2]

Hitler's invasion of the Soviet Union cost the Soviet Union an estimated 27 million lives. At Yalta, Stalin was determined to prevent the reestablishment of a hostile Poland along his western border. Stalin had no intentions, therefore, of permitting the London Poles to take power in Warsaw. This was a major concern Stalin repeatedly conveyed to his allies who grudgingly accepted in principle the reality that Eastern Europe in general, and Poland in particular, had already become part and parcel of the Soviet Union's sphere of influence. To this end, even before Yalta, Stalin had created his own Polish government, with its seat in the eastern Polish city of Lublin, which consisted primarily of Communists and socialists.

Roosevelt and Churchill faced a dilemma. World War II had been fought for the noble ideals of democracy and self-determination. But in postwar Poland there would be neither. Britain, moreover, still had a treaty obligation with the London Poles.[3] Yet, Stalin held the trump card; the Red Army controlled Poland.

The long disputation on the Polish question pitted the demands of Roosevelt and Churchill for self-determination against Stalin's insistence on a government answerable to Moscow. Specifically, it came down to an argument over the composition of a provisional (interim) government, with Stalin arguing for recognition of the Lublin regime as the provisional government and Roosevelt and Churchill insisting that Poland's provisional government include as many "democratic" politicians as Communist. Finally, the two sides arrived at an ambiguous agreement that papered over their broad differences. The agreement stated that the Polish government was to be "reorganized on a broader democratic basis with the inclusion of democratic leaders from Poland itself and Poles abroad."[4] It went on to say that this reorganized government was to be provisional and was to hold elections on the basis of which a permanent government would be established later. The ambiguity of the agreement allowed both sides to interpret it as they saw fit.

After the conference, Roosevelt and Churchill chose to accentuate Stalin's concession to allow "free elections" so as to claim that they had won a victory for the London Poles and for democracy at Yalta. Stalin, however, had no intention of allowing "democratic" politicians—that is, the Western-oriented and anti-Soviet London Poles—into the provisional government or of permitting them to run for office later. In any case, his definition of free elections was so narrow that the supposed promise of free elections became meaningless. When elections were finally held, the slate of candidates was restricted to "safe" political figures who posed no threat to the Soviet domination of Poland.

Stalin apparently was under the impression that the Western powers had essentially yielded at Yalta to the Soviet Union's presence in Poland and that their complaints were largely cosmetic and for domestic consumption. He thus considered the question resolved. But in Britain, and in particular the United States, the Soviet Union's control of Poland never sat easily. After all, Stalin had, in effect, violated his promise of free elections, his control of Poland was in direct conflict with the Western war aims, such as freedom and democracy, and the Red Army in Poland had pushed Stalin's political and military influence toward the center of Europe.

From these events came the following arguments, which Roosevelt's Republican critics often made: (1) Roosevelt had yielded Poland (as well as the rest of Eastern Europe) to Stalin; and (2) Stalin had broken his promise at Yalta to hold free elections, and this act of infidelity precipitated the Cold War. The Democrats, stung by these charges, replied that Roosevelt had not ceded Eastern Europe to the Soviets. Geography and the fortunes of war, they contended, had been responsible for putting the Red Army into Eastern Europe, not appeasement on the part of Roosevelt or of his successor, Harry Truman, who became president upon Roosevelt's death on April 12, 1945.

The ghost of Munich. At this juncture the two major allies in World War II became locked into positions that were the result of their peculiar readings of the lessons of history—particularly, the "lessons of Munich." This refers to the event that many politicians and historians have considered the single most important step leading to World War II.

In the autumn of 1938, Adolf Hitler insisted that a part of western Czechoslovakia—the Sudetenland with a population of 3 million ethnic Germans—must be transferred to Germany on the basis of the principle of national self-determination, a principle ostensibly dear to the victors of World War I, who had created the sovereign state of Czechoslovakia. Germans must live in Germany, Hitler threatened, otherwise there will be war. France had a treaty of alliance with Czechoslovakia that committed France to war in case Germany attacked that country. But the French government was psychologically and militarily incapable of honoring its treaty and sought a way out to resolve the crisis Hitler's threats had created. At this point England's prime minister, Neville Chamberlain, stepped in. The result was the Munich Conference, by which the Western powers avoided war, if only for the time being, and Hitler obtained the Sudetenland. Hitler promised that this was his last demand in Eastern Europe. Chamberlain returned to London proclaiming that he had "brought peace in our time."

Events quickly showed that Hitler had lied. In March 1939, he annexed the rest of Czechoslovakia and then pressured the Poles to yield on territorial concessions. When the Poles refused to budge, the British, and later the French, determined that the time had come to take a stand and offered the Poles a treaty of alliance. Hitler then invaded Poland, and a European war was in the making.

The lessons of Munich for the West were clear. A dictator can never be satisfied. Appeasement only whets his appetite. In the words of the U.S. secretary of the navy, James Forrestal, there were "no returns on appeasement."[5] When Stalin demanded his own sphere of influence in Eastern Europe, the

West quickly brought up the lessons of Munich and concluded that Western acceptance of the Soviet Union's position would inevitably bring further Soviet expansion and war. Western leaders, therefore, proved to be psychologically incapable of accepting the Soviet Union's presence in Eastern Europe: there could be no business-as-usual division of the spoils of victory.

The Soviets had their own reading of these same events. To them, Munich meant the first decisive move by the capitalist West against the Soviet Union. The leaders in the Kremlin always believed that they, and not the West or Poland, were Hitler's main target. Throughout the latter half of the 1930s, the Soviet Union had repeatedly called for an alliance with the West against Germany, but the pleas had always fallen on suspicious ears. Instead, the West's deal with Hitler at Munich appeared to have deflected Hitler toward the East. In rapid order Hitler then swallowed up Czechoslovakia and a host of other East European nations, confirming the Soviet leaders' deep suspicions. By June of 1941, when Hitler launched his invasion of the Soviet Union, he was in control of all of Eastern Europe—not to mention most of the rest of Europe as well—and proceeded to turn it against the Soviet Union.

For the Soviets the lessons of Munich were obvious. Eastern Europe must not fall into the hands of hostile forces. Stalin would not tolerate the return to power of the hostile Poles in London, nor of the old regimes in Hungary, Romania, and Bulgaria, which had cooperated with the Nazis. No foreign power would have the opportunity to do again what Hitler had done and turn Eastern Europe against the Soviet Union. The old order of hostile states aligned with the Soviet Union's enemies must give way to a new reality that served Moscow's interests.

From the same events the two antagonists in the Cold War thus drew diametrically opposed conclusions. The Western position held that its containment of the Soviet Union and its unwillingness to legitimize the Kremlin's position in Eastern Europe kept the peace. A lack of resolve would surely have brought war. The Soviets in their turn were just as adamant in insisting that the buffer they had created in Eastern Europe kept the capitalist West at bay and preserved the security of their nation. These opposing visions of the lessons of history were at the core of the conflict between the West and the Soviet Union.

Polish borders. At Yalta, Stalin also insisted on moving Poland's borders. He demanded a return to the Soviet Union of what it had lost to the Poles in the Treaty of Riga in 1921 (after the Poles had defeated the Red Army). At that time Lord Curzon, the British foreign secretary, had urged the stubborn Poles to accept an eastern border 125 miles to the west since that line separated more equitably the Poles from the Belorussian and Ukrainian populations of the Soviet empire. But in 1921, the victorious

PRE-WORLD WAR II BOUNDARIES
POST-WORLD WAR II BOUNDARIES
TERRITORIAL CHANGES RESULTING
FROM WORLD WAR II

CENTRAL AND EASTERN EUROPE:
TERRITORIAL CHANGES AFTER WORLD WAR II

Poles rejected the Curzon Line and, instead, imposed their own line upon the defeated Soviets. In 1945, it became Stalin's turn to redraw the border.

To compensate the Poles for land lost to the Soviet Union, Stalin moved Poland's western border about 75 miles farther west into what had been Germany, along the Oder and Western Neisse rivers. At Yalta, Stalin sought his allies' stamp of approval for the Oder-Neisse Line but without success.

A third readjustment of Poland's border called for the division between the Soviets and the Poles of East Prussia, Germany's easternmost province. Stalin intended that East Prussia become part of the spoils of war. His reasoning was simple. The Soviet Union and Poland had suffered grief at the hands of the Germans and the peoples of both nations felt that they deserved compensation. The West reluctantly acceded to Stalin's demands.

Since 1945, the Soviets and Poles have considered the border changes at the expense of Germany as a fait accompli. Germans, however, were reluctant to accept these consequences of the war. When, after World War II, the Western powers and the Soviet Union failed to reach an agreement on the political fate of Germany, the result was the division of that nation into the U.S.-sponsored Federal Republic of Germany (commonly known as West Germany) and the Soviet creation, the Democratic Republic of Germany (or East Germany). The East German government had little choice but to accept the new German-Polish border. The West German government always insisted that it was the sole legitimate German government and that it spoke for all Germans, East and West. The original West German government of Chancellor Konrad Adenauer—the champion of German territorial integrity—bitterly opposed Soviet expansion westward and refused to accept the new, Soviet-imposed boundaries. In the late 1960s, the West German government, under the leadership of Willy Brandt, began to acknowledge that new borders existed in fact; but for more than forty years after the conclusion of the war, no West German government formally accepted the legality of the transfer of German territory. Until the reunification of Germany in 1990, it remained one of the unresolved consequences of the war.

☐ The Japanese Issue

The second issue at Yalta was more straightforward. The U.S. Joint Chiefs of Staff wanted the Soviet Red Army to enter the war against Japan. The Soviets, as it turned out, needed little prodding. Stalin promised to enter the Japanese war ninety days after the end of the war in Europe. The Japanese had handed Russia a humiliating defeat in the Russo-Japanese War of 1904–1905. In the wake of the Bolshevik Revolution of 1917 and the civil war that followed, the Japanese had invaded eastern Siberia and remained there until 1922.[6] In the 1930s, it seemed for a while as if the Soviet Union might become Japan's next target after the Japanese annexation of the northern Chinese region of Manchuria. In fact, in late summer 1939, the Red Army and the Japanese clashed along the border at Khalkin Gol. Only Japan's thrust southward—which ultimately brought it into conflict with the United States—and the Soviet Union's preoccupation with Nazi Germany kept the two from resuming their old rivalry. When the Soviets attacked the Japanese army in Manchuria at the very end of World War II, it marked the fourth Russo-Japanese conflict of the twentieth century. From the Soviet point of view, here was a golden opportunity to settle past scores and to regain lost territories.

☐ The UN Question

The third major topic at Yalta dealt with the organization of the United Nations. Roosevelt proposed, and Churchill and Stalin quickly accepted, the power of an absolute veto for the world's great powers, of any United Nations action they opposed. In 1919, when President Woodrow Wilson unsuccessfully proposed the U.S. entry into the League of Nations, his opponents argued that in doing so, the foreign policy of the United States would be dictated by the League. A U.S. veto would prevent such an eventuality in the new United Nations. Naturally, however, the United States could not expect to be the only nation with a veto. Roosevelt proposed that each of the "Big Five"—the United States, the Soviet Union, Great Britain, France, and China—be given the power to veto a UN action. It also meant that the United Nations could not be used against the interests of any of the big powers. The United Nations, therefore, could act only when the Big Five were in concert—and that proved to be a rare occasion. The weakness of the United Nations was thus built into its charter.

An example of what this sort of arrangement meant in practice may be seen in this exchange between Stalin and Churchill at Yalta (concerning the issue of Hong Kong, a colony Great Britain had taken from China in the 1840s):

Stalin: Suppose China . . . demands Hong Kong to be returned to her?
Churchill: I could say "no." I would have a right to say that the power of [the United Nations] could not be used against us.[7]

☐ The German Question

The fourth question, the immediate fate of Germany, was resolved when the Big Three decided that as a temporary expedient the territory of the Third Reich—including Austria, which Hitler had annexed in 1938—was to be divided into zones of occupation among the three participants at the

Yalta Conference. Shortly, the French insisted that as an ally and a major power they, too, were entitled to an occupation zone. Stalin did not object to the inclusion of another Western, capitalist power but he demanded that if France were to obtain a zone it must come from the holdings of the United States and Great Britain. The result was the Four-Power occupation of Germany and Austria, as well as of their respective capitals, Berlin and Vienna.

As the Big Three returned home from Yalta, they were fairly satisfied that they had gotten what they had sought. But, as events would show, Yalta had settled little. Instead, it quickly became the focal point of the Cold War. The issues under discussion at Yalta—Poland and its postwar borders, the United Nations, the Red Army's entrance into the war against Japan, and the German and Austrian questions—all became bones of contention between East and West in the months ahead.

■ THE POTSDAM CONFERENCE

By mid-summer 1945, with Berlin in ruins and the defeat of Japan all but a certainty, the Grand Alliance of World War II fell apart with remarkable speed. The first signs of tension had appeared upon the conclusion of the war in Europe when both the Western powers and the Soviet Union sought to carve out spheres of influence in Eastern Europe. Whatever cooperation had existed during the war had turned into mutual suspicion. Still, the two sides were consulting with each other and they were slated to meet again in July 1945, this time for a conference in Germany at Potsdam (not far from Berlin, the bombed-out capital of Hitler's Third Reich).

The Big Three at Potsdam were Joseph Stalin, Harry Truman (who had succeeded Roosevelt in April 1945), and Winston Churchill (who later in the conference would be replaced by Britain's new premier, Clement Attlee). This meeting accomplished little. The Polish question came up at once, particularly the new border drawn at the expense of Germany, which the Western leaders reluctantly accepted. The Western leaders also grudgingly recognized the new socialist government in Poland, but they repeatedly voiced their objections to other client governments Stalin had propped up in Eastern Europe, particularly those of Romania and Bulgaria. The Soviets considered the transformation of the political picture in Eastern Europe a closed issue, comparing it to the creation of the new government in Italy under Western supervision, replacing the previous fascist government that had been an ally of Nazi Germany. The sharp exchanges at Potsdam only heightened suspicions and resolved virtually nothing.

Another source of disagreement was the issue of reparations from Germany. The Soviets insisted on $20 billion from a nation that was utterly destroyed and could not possibly pay such a huge amount. This demand would therefore mean the transfer of whatever industrial equipment Germany still possessed to the Soviet Union. Such measures would leave Germany impoverished, weak, and dependent on outside help. This scenario presented several disadvantages to the West: a helpless Germany was no physical deterrent against potential Soviet expansion westward; it might succumb to Communism; and it could become neither an exporter of the goods it produced, nor an importer of U.S. goods. Moreover, the United States was already contemplating economic aid to Germany, and thus the Soviet demand meant that U.S. money and equipment would simply pass through Germany to the Soviet Union as reparations.

The Soviets insisted that at the Yalta Conference in February 1945 their allies had promised them the large sum of $20 billion. U.S. representatives replied that this figure was intended to be the basis of discussion depending upon conditions in Germany after the war. The devastation of Germany at the very end of the war, therefore, meant that the Soviets would have to settle for far less.

To Truman the solution was simple. He would exclude the Soviets from the Western zones of occupation, leaving the Soviets to find whatever reparations they could come up with in their Eastern zone. They did so by plundering the eastern part of Germany. The reparations question marked the first instance of the inability of the wartime allies to come to an agreement on how to govern Germany. It established the principle that in each zone of occupation the military commander would have free reign. As such, the occupation powers never came up with a unified policy for Germany. The main consequence of this was the long-enduring division of Germany. Within three years there was no point in pretending that a single German state existed.

The only thing on which Truman and Stalin seemed to agree at Potsdam was their position on Japan. Neither, it seems, was willing to let the Japanese off the hook. Surrender could only be unconditional. While at Potsdam, Truman was notified that the first atomic bomb had been successfully tested at Alamogordo, New Mexico. Truman knew of Japanese efforts to end the war, but with the atomic bomb he could now end the conflict on his own terms and keep the Soviet Union out of postwar Japan. Stalin, for his part, did not want a quick Japanese surrender. At Yalta he had pledged to come into the war with Japan ninety days after the war against Germany had ended, and he had every intention of doing so. It would give him the chance to settle old scores with the Japanese and to extend his influence in the Far East. Truman did not tell Stalin about the atomic bomb and his plans to use it against Japan. He was led to believe that Truman still wanted the Soviet Union to attack Japan. With the United States secretly planning to drop atomic bombs on Japan and Stalin secretly planning to attack its forces in Manchuria, there was apparently no way out for the Japanese.

The defeat of Japan, however, brought no improvement in East-West relations. Both sides constantly voiced their grievances and suspicions of

President Harry S. Truman and Gen. Dwight Eisenhower, Jan. 1951.
Two years later, the general would succeed Truman as president.
(*National Archives*)

each other. The U.S. bombing of Hiroshima and Nagasaki gave the Soviets still more reason to distrust and suspect the intentions of the United States. Each point of disagreement was magnified, each misunderstanding became a weapon; each hostile act was positive proof of the other side's evil intentions. But one could not yet speak of a full-blown, irreversible Cold War. This came in 1947, when the conflict reached a new plateau. In fact, many historians, in the Soviet Union as well as in the West, see that year as the true beginning of the Cold War. It was then that the United States declared its commitment to contain—by economic as well as military means—all manifestations of Communist expansion wherever it occurred. In the same year a Soviet delegation walked out of an economic conference that concerned itself with the rebuilding of Europe. With this act all East-West cooperation came to an end and the battle lines were clearly drawn.

■ THE TRUMAN DOCTRINE

"The turning point in American foreign policy," in the words of President Truman, came early in 1947 when the United States was faced with the prospect of a Communist victory in a civil war in Greece.[8] The end of World War II had not brought peace to Greece. Instead, it saw the continuation of a bitter conflict between the right and the left, one which in early 1947 promised a Communist victory. The British, who for a long time had played a significant role in Greek affairs, had supported the right (the Greek monarchy), but they were determined to end their involvement in Greece. The British were exhausted; they could not go on. Unceremoniously, they dumped the problem into Truman's lap: If the United States wanted a non-Communist government in Greece it would have to see to it, and it would have to go it alone. Truman, a man seldom plagued by self-doubt, quickly jumped into the breach. But he also understood that the U.S. public would be slow to back such an undertaking. At the end of World War II, the U.S. public had expected that within two years the U.S. military presence in Europe would end. Truman's involvement in Greece would extend it and postpone the U.S. disengagement from Europe indefinitely. In fact, it meant an increased, continued U.S. presence in Europe. To achieve his aim, Truman knew he would have to "scare the hell out of the American people."[9] And he succeeded admirably.

In March 1947, Truman addressed a joint session of Congress to present his case. In his oration, one of the most stirring Cold War speeches by a U.S. political leader, Truman expounded his views: the war in Greece was not a matter between Greeks; rather, it was caused by outside aggression. International Communism was on the march and the orders came from its center, Moscow. It was the duty of the United States "to support free peoples who are resisting attempted subjugation by armed minorities or by outside pressures." The United States must play the role of the champion of democracy and "orderly political processes."[10] Truman argued that there was even more at stake here than the upholding of political and moral principles. A Communist victory in Greece threatened to set off similar events in other countries, like a long chain of dominoes. "If Greece should fall under the control of an armed minority, the effect upon its neighbor, Turkey, would be immediate and serious. Confusion and disorder might well spread throughout the entire Middle East."[11] This speech, which became known as the Truman Doctrine, firmly set U.S. foreign policy on a path committed to suppressing radicalism and revolution throughout the world.

But there was no clear evidence that the guiding hand of Stalin was behind the Greek revolution. Stalin, it seems, kept his part of the bargain made with Churchill in October 1944, by which the two agreed that after the war Greece would fall into Britain's sphere of influence. Churchill later wrote that Stalin adhered to this understanding.[12] If anything, Stalin wanted the Greek revolt to "fold up . . . as quickly as possible" because he feared precisely what ultimately happened.[13] He told the Yugoslav vice president, Milovan Djilas: "What do you think? That . . . the United States, the most powerful state in the world will permit you to break their line of communications in the Mediterranean Sea? Nonsense, and we have no navy."[14] But to Truman and most of the U.S. public it was a simple matter: all revolutions in the name of Karl Marx must necessarily come out of Moscow.[15] The Republican Party, not to be left behind in the holy struggle against "godless Communism," quickly backed Truman. Thus, a national consensus was forged, one which remained intact until the divisive years of the Vietnam War.

The first application of the Truman Doctrine worked remarkably well. U.S. military and economic aid rapidly turned the tide in Greece; the Communists were defeated and the monarchy was spared. And this was achieved without sending U.S. troops into combat. There appeared to be no limits to U.S. power. This truly appeared to be, as Henry Luce, the influential publisher of *Time* and *Life* had said earlier, the "American Century."[16] Yet, at about the same time, events in China showed that there were in fact limits on the ability of the United States to affect the course of history, when the position of the U.S.-supported government there began to unravel.

■ THE MARSHALL PLAN

Three months after the pronouncement of the Truman Doctrine, the United States took another step to protect its interests in Europe when the Truman administration unveiled the Marshall Plan, named after Gen. George Marshall, Truman's secretary of state, who first proposed the program. The program was intended to provide funds for the rebuilding of the heavily damaged economies of Europe. The Marshall Plan was in large part a humanitarian gesture for which many Europeans expressed their gratitude. Because of it, the United States was able to draw on a residue of goodwill for decades after the war. The Marshall Plan was also intended as a means to preserve the prosperity the war had brought to U.S. society. At the very end of the war, the United States had taken the lead in establishing an international system of "free trade" or at least relatively unrestricted trade. But international commerce demanded a strong and prosperous Europe. The United States proved to be extremely successful in shoring up the financial system of the Western, capitalist world. In this sense, the Marshall Plan became a potent political weapon in the containment of Soviet influence.[17] It well complemented the Truman Doctrine. The Marshall Plan, Truman explained, was but "the other half of the same walnut."[18]

The United States was willing to extend Marshall Plan aid to Eastern Europe, including the Soviet Union, but not without a condition. The money would have to be administered there, as in Western Europe, by the United States, not by its recipients. Several Eastern European states were receptive to the plan, particularly Czechoslovakia, which was governed by a coalition of Communist and non-Communist parties. The Soviet Union, too, at first appeared to be ready to participate in the rebuilding of Europe under the auspices of the Marshall Plan.[19] Its foreign minister, Viacheslav Molotov, came to Paris with a large entourage of economic experts to discuss the implementation of the plan. But shortly afterward, he left the conference declaring that the Marshall Plan was unacceptable to the Soviet Union since its implementation would entail the presence of U.S. officials on East European and Soviet soil and would, therefore, infringe upon his country's national sovereignty. Molotov did not say publicly that the presence of U.S. representatives in Eastern Europe would reveal the glaring weaknesses of the Soviet Union and its satellites. The Marshall Plan was a gamble Stalin apparently felt he could not afford. Stalin then pressured the governments of Poland and Czechoslovakia to reject the Marshall Plan.

In February 1948, Stalin went beyond merely applying pressure on Czechoslovakia. A Communist coup in that country ended the coalition government and brought Czechoslovakia firmly into the Soviet orbit. This act regenerated in the West the image of an aggressive, brutal, and calculating leadership in Moscow. The Communist coup in Czechoslovakia, only ten years after Hitler had taken the first steps to bring that nation under his heel, did much to underscore in the West the lessons of Munich.[20] The coup had a deep impact on public opinion in the West and it became prima facie evidence that one could not do business with the Soviets.

Stalin's rejection of Marshall Plan aid also meant that the East European countries would have to rebuild their war-torn economies with their own limited resources and without U.S. aid and Western technology. In fact, Stalin's economic recovery program for Eastern Europe was exploitative since it favored the Soviet Union. As Churchill had remarked in his speech in Fulton, Missouri, in 1946, an "Iron Curtain" had descended across Europe from Stettin on the Baltic Sea to Trieste on the Adriatic Sea.

■ LIMITS OF SOVIET POWER

Yet, immediately after Stalin appeared to have consolidated his position in Eastern Europe, the first crack appeared in what had been a monolithic facade. The Yugoslav Communist leadership, under the direction of Joseph Tito, broke with the Kremlin over the fundamental question of national sovereignty. Moscow insisted that the interests of a foreign Communist party must be subordinate to those of the Soviet Union, officially the center of an international movement. The Yugoslavs insisted, however, on running their own affairs as they saw fit. In the summer of 1948, the bitter quarrel became public. Tito refused to subordinate the interests of his state to those of Stalin and the result was the first Communist nation in Eastern Europe to assert its independence from the Soviet Union.

Stalin understood only too well that "Titoism" (that is, a nationalist deviation from the international Communist community) was no isolated phenomenon. Other East European nations could readily fall to the same temptation. In order to forestall such an eventuality, Stalin launched a bloody purge of East European "National Communists." The purge was so thorough that until Stalin's death in March 1953, Eastern Europe remained quiet. The prevailing—and, as events later showed, incorrect—view in the West was that Titoism had proven to be an isolated incident.

In 1948, it also became evident that the division of Germany and Berlin would become permanent. All talks on German reunification had broken down and the West began to take steps to create a separate West German state, with Berlin, a city 110 miles inside the Soviet sector, becoming a part of West Germany. When the Soviets had agreed on the division of Berlin among the allies, Stalin had not bargained on such an eventuality. The last thing he wanted was a Western outpost inside his zone. Berlin had little military value for the West since it was trapped and outgunned by the Soviet Red Army which occupied East Germany. But it served as a valuable political, capitalist spearhead pointing into Eastern Europe. Most important, West Berlin was invaluable as a center of espionage operations. In June 1948, Stalin took a dangerous, calculated risk to eliminate the Western presence in that city. He closed the land routes into West Berlin in the hope of convincing the West to abandon Berlin. The West had few options. It wanted neither World War III nor the abandonment of West Berlin and its 2 million people to the Communists. The result was the "Berlin Airlift," by which the West resupplied West Berlin by transport planes flying over East Germany. During the next ten months over 270,000 flights were made carrying an average of 4,000 tons a day to the beleaguered city. Stalin dared not attack the planes for he would not risk World War III either. Finally, in May 1949, Stalin yielded by reopening the highways linking the city once again with West Germany. Stalin had lost his gamble and there was no point in perpetuating the showdown. This crisis, which had brought both sides to the edge of war, was over if only for the time being.

Throughout the late 1940s, the U.S. assumption was that the Soviet Union was preparing for an attack on Western Europe, an assumption based largely on fear rather than on fact. The image of an expansionist, aggressive Soviet Union was the result of three conditions. First, the Red Army had pushed into the center of Europe during the war. Second, in the West, this act was regarded not so much as the logical consequence of the war but as the fulfillment of Soviet propaganda stressing the triumph of socialism throughout the world. Third, the differences of opinion between the Soviet Union and the West quickly took on the character of a military confrontation, and people began to fear the worst.

Once the specter of an inevitably expansionist Soviet state gripped the Western imagination, it became almost impossible to shake this image.

This view of Soviet intentions buttressed the U.S. arguments that the Soviet Union must be contained at all cost. The "containment theory," first spelled out in 1947 in a lengthy essay by George Kennan, a State Department expert on the Soviet Union, seemed to be working reasonably well with the application of the Truman Doctrine and the Marshall Plan. But Kennan never made clear the nature of the containment of the Soviet Union he had in mind. Later, he insisted that he had meant the political, and not the military, containment of the Soviet Union. Yet, the central feature of Truman's containment policy was its military nature. In 1949, the United States created NATO, the North Atlantic Treaty Organization, an alliance that boxed in the Soviet Union along its western flank. One person's containment theory is another person's capitalist encirclement. Stalin responded by digging in.

RECOMMENDED READINGS

Andrzejewski, Jerzy. *Ashes and Diamonds*. London: Weidenfeld and Nicholson, 1962; orig. 1948.
    The classic novel on life in Poland at the very end of World War II.
Clemens, Diane Shaver. *Yalta*. New York: Oxford University Press, 1970.
    The best monograph on the Yalta Conference, which sees Yalta not as an ideological confrontation but an exercise in horse-trading.
de Zayas, Alfred M. *Nemesis at Potsdam: The Anglo-Americans and the Expulsion of the Germans: Background, Execution, Consequences*. 2d rev. ed. London: Routledge and Kegan Paul, 1979.
    Focuses on the refugee problem after the war, a topic generally ignored in Cold War histories.
Fleming, D. F. *The Cold War and Its Origins, 1917–1960*. 2 vols. Garden City: Doubleday, 1961.
    By one of the first practitioners of the revisionist school of history of the Cold War.
Halle, Louis J. *The Cold War as History*. New York: Harper & Row, 1967.
    One of the few books on the Cold War that puts it into a historical perspective.
Ulam, Adam B. *The Rivals: America and Russia Since World War II*. New York: Viking, 1971.
    Discusses the first phase of the East-West confrontation.
Ulam, Adam B. *Expansion and Coexistence: Soviet Foreign Policy, 1917–1973*. 2d ed. New York: Frederick A. Praeger, 1974.
    A useful treatment of Soviet foreign policy.

NOTES

1. Often called the Molotov-Ribbentrop Pact, after the foreign minister of Nazi Germany, Joachim Ribbentrop, and the Soviet Union's commissar for foreign affairs, Viacheslav Molotov, who worked out the details of the arrangement.

2. Winston S. Churchill, *The Second World War, VI, Triumph and Tragedy* (New York: Bantam, [orig. 1953] 1962), p. 329.

3. The treaty with the Polish government in London consisted of an obligation on the part of Britain to defend its ally only against Germany, not the Soviet Union, a point the British government stressed in April 1945 when it released a secret protocol of the 1939 treaty. With this release, Britain's legal obligation to the Polish government came to an end. But there was still the moral duty to defend a former ally against the aspirations of a totalitarian ally of convenience.

4. Quoted from "The Yalta Declaration on Poland," as found in U.S. Department of State, *Foreign Relations of the United States: The Conferences at Malta and Yalta, 1945* (Washington, D.C.: U.S. Government Printing Office, 1955), p. 938.

5. A cabinet meeting of September 21, 1945, in Walter Millis, ed., *The Forrestal Diaries* (New York: Viking, 1951), p. 96.

6. The U.S. president, Woodrow Wilson, too, sent troops into eastern Siberia at that time, ostensibly to keep an eye on the Japanese. Earlier, at the end of World War I, Wilson also sent troops into European Russia, ostensibly to protect supplies that had been sent to the Russian ally—led at the time by Tsar Nicholas II—to keep them from falling into German hands. The Soviets have always rejected this explanation and have argued that U.S. intentions were to overthrow the fledgling Communist government.

7. James F. Byrnes, *Frankly Speaking* (New York: Harper and Brothers, 1947), p. 37.

8. Harry S. Truman, *Memoirs, II, Years of Trial and Hope* (Garden City: Doubleday, 1956), p. 106.

9. The words are Senator Arthur Vandenberg's, cited in William A. Williams, *The Tragedy of American Diplomacy*, rev. ed. (New York: Delta, 1962), pp. 269–270.

10. "Text of President Truman's Speech on New Foreign Policy," *New York Times*, March 13, 1947, p. 2.

11. Ibid.

12. Churchill's report to the House of Commons, February 27, 1945, in which he stated that he "was encouraged by Stalin's behavior about Greece." *The Second World War, VI*, p. 334. In his "Iron Curtain" telegram to Truman, May 12, 1945, Churchill expressed concern about Soviet influence throughout Eastern Europe, "except Greece"; Lord Moran, *Churchill: Taken from the Diaries of Lord Moran, The Struggle for Survival, 1940–1965* (Boston: Houghton Mifflin, 1966), p. 847. Churchill to the House of Commons, January 23, 1948, on Greece: "Agreements were kept [by Stalin] when they were made." Robert Rhodes James, *Winston S. Churchill: His Complete Speeches, 1897–1963, VII, 1943–1949* (New York: Chelsea House, 1974), p. 7583.

13. Milovan Djilas, *Conversations with Stalin* (New York: Harcourt, Brace and World, 1962), pp. 181–182.

14. Ibid., p. 182.

15. After World War II, the most militant Communist head of state was Joseph Tito of Yugoslavia. It was Tito, rather than Stalin, who openly supported the Greek Communist insurgency by providing them weapons and refuge in Yugoslavia. Tito's actions were seen in the West as evidence of Stalin's involvement via a proxy; yet, even Tito, once he broke with Stalin in 1948, shut his border to the Greek Communists and abandoned them.

16. Henry Luce, "American Century," W. A. Swanberg, *Luce and His Empire* (New York: Dell, 1972), pp. 257–261.

17. The political move to the left in Western Europe after World War II had in fact largely burned itself out by 1947, at the time the Truman administration proposed the Marshall Plan. The Soviet Union's influence in Western Europe was

dependent on the strength of the Communist parties. After initial strong showings, particularly in France and Italy, the Communist parties' fortunes declined. The Marshall Plan then helped to accelerate the swing to the right.

18. Quoted in Walter LaFeber, *America, Russia, and the Cold War, 1945–1984*, 5th ed. (New York: Knopf, 1985), pp. 62–63.

19. At the end of World War II, after the U.S. wartime Lend-Lease Program to the Soviet Union had come to an end, Moscow had applied for economic assistance from the United States, but nothing came of it. Lend-Lease, a massive wartime assistance program to U.S. allies, provided the Soviet Union with $11 billion in aid. Subsequent U.S. aid to the Soviet Union, however, was dependent upon proper Soviet behavior in Eastern Europe.

20. During the coup, Czechoslovakia's foreign minister, Thomas Masaryk, was murdered under mysterious circumstances, an act generally attributed in the West to Stalin.

3

The Cold War in Asia: A Change of Venue

The Cold War, which had its origins in Europe where tensions mounted between East and West over the status of Germany, Poland, and other Eastern European countries, became even more inflamed in Asia. In 1945, U.S. policy in East Asia was focused primarily on the elimination of the menace of Japanese militarism and on support of the Nationalist government of China under Jiang Jieshi (Chiang Kai-shek)[1] as the main pillar of stability in Asia. But within five short years the United States was confronted with a set of affairs very different from what Washington had envisioned just after the war.

The Nationalist regime in China was defeated by the Chinese Communists who, under the leadership of Chairman Mao Zedong (Mao Tsetung), proclaimed the founding of the People's Republic of China on October 1, 1949. The largest nation on earth was now under Communist rule. Only nine months later the Communist forces of North Korea invaded the U.S.-supported, anti-Communist regime in South Korea, and in the Korean War, for the first time, the rivals of the Cold War, East and West, clashed in the field of battle. These two major events had a profound effect on the military occupation of defeated Japan, which had begun immediately after Japan's surrender. All three of these interrelated events developed in the context of the Cold War and contributed toward making Cold War tensions ever more dangerous in this area of the world. The contention between East and West, evident from the very outset of the military occupation of defeated Japan in 1945, hardened by the early 1950s.

■ THE ALLIED OCCUPATION OF JAPAN

The Allied Occupation of Japan, which lasted almost seven years (from September 1945 to May 1952), is unique in the annals of history, for, as the historian Edwin Reischauer says, "Never before had one advanced

49

nation attempted to reform the supposed faults of another advanced nation from within. And never did the military occupation of one world power by another prove so satisfactory to the victors and tolerable to the vanquished."[2] From the outset, the U.S. policy in Japan was benevolent and constructive, although it would also have its punitive aspects as well. The Japanese, who had never in their long history been defeated and garrisoned by foreign troops, expected the worst. Not only did their fears of U.S. brutality prove unfounded, but so also did U.S. fears of continued hostility by Japanese diehards. The two nations, which had fought each other so bitterly for almost four years, made amends, and in a remarkably short time they established enduring bonds of friendship and cooperation. This was partly the result of the generous treatment by the U.S. occupation forces, and partly the result of the receptivity and goodwill of the Japanese themselves. They welcomed the opportunity to rid themselves of the scourge of militarism that had led their nation into the blind alley of defeat and destruction. And they appreciated the sight of U.S. GIs brandishing, not rifles, but chocolate bars and chewing gum. Even more important for securing the active support of the Japanese was the decision by U.S. authorities to retain the emperor on the throne rather than try him as a war criminal, as many in the United States had demanded. Indeed, one important reason why the Japanese were so docile and cooperative with the U.S. occupation forces was that their emperor, whom they were in the habit of dutifully obeying, had implored them to be cooperative.

Prior to the defeat of Japan, officials in Washington were already planning a reform program to be implemented under a military occupation. The Allied Occupation of Japan was, as the name implies, supposedly an Allied affair, but it was in fact dominated by the United States, despite the desire of the Soviet Union and other nations to play a larger role in it. Gen. Douglas MacArthur was appointed Supreme Commander of Allied Powers (SCAP), and under his authority a broad-ranging reform program was imposed on Japan. The government of Japan was not abolished and replaced by a military administration as was the case in defeated Germany; rather, the Japanese cabinet was maintained as the instrument by which the reform directives of SCAP were administered. Also, unlike the case of Germany, Japan was not divided into separate occupation zones, largely because of the insistence of the United States on denying the Soviet Union its own occupation zone in Japan.

The principal objectives of the U.S.-controlled occupation program were demilitarization and democratization. Demilitarization was attended to first and was attained promptly. Japan's army and navy were abolished, its military personnel brought home from overseas and dismissed, its war plants dismantled, and its weapons destroyed. Some 3 million Japanese soldiers were repatriated to Japan from all over Asia and the Pacific

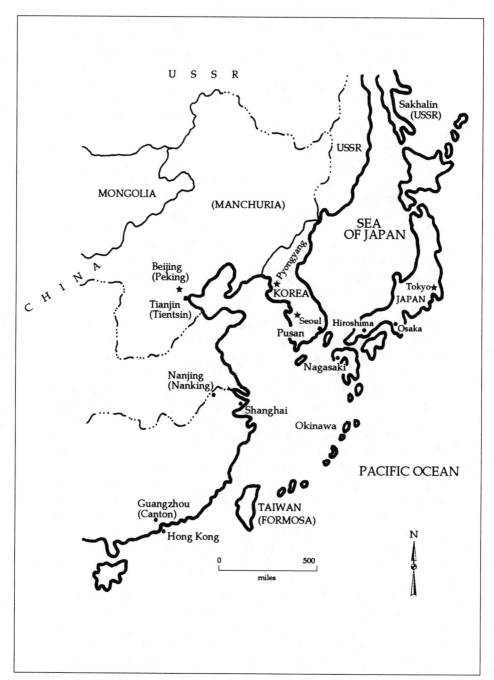

EAST ASIA (1945)

mainly by U.S. ships, as were almost as many Japanese civilians. Also, as a measure to rid Japan of militarism, Japanese wartime leaders were put on trial at an international military tribunal in Tokyo. In court proceedings similar to the Nuremberg trials of Nazi war criminals, twenty-eight leading figures were accused of "planning a war of aggression" and "crimes against humanity," found guilty, and given severe sentences. Seven were sentenced to death and seventeen were sentenced to prison for life. Additionally, several thousand other Japanese military officers were tried and found guilty of a variety of wartime atrocities.

The occupation reformers also sought to rid Japan of its ultranationalist ideology, often referred to as emperor worship. On New Year's Day 1946, the emperor was called upon to make a radio speech to the nation renouncing imperial divinity. Steps were also taken to abolish "State Shinto," the aspect of the religion native to Japan that promoted the belief in the divine descent of Japan's imperial ruler. Textbooks were censored to rid them of such ideas and other content considered militaristic.

Democratization of Japan was a more complex matter and would take longer to achieve, but the first major step in that direction was taken with the writing of a new constitution for Japan in 1947. The new constitution, which was actually drafted by MacArthur's staff, provided for a fundamental political reform. It provided Japan with a parliamentary system similar to that of Britain, and consistent with Japan's own prewar political experience. The people of Japan were made sovereign (meaning, in effect, that government power ultimately rested on the consent of the governed, the people). The emperor, who had been sovereign in the old constitution, became no more than a symbol of the state, which is to say, he would no longer have any political authority. All laws were to be passed by a majority in the popularly elected House of Representatives in the Diet (Japan's parliament). The 1947 constitution also included extensive Bill of Rights provisions spelling out the civil rights of Japanese citizens in great detail. The most striking feature of the new constitution—one in keeping with the demilitarization objective—was Article Nine, which outlawed war and forbade Japan to maintain land, sea, or air forces. MacArthur himself ordered that this provision be put into the constitution, but the idea was enthusiastically endorsed by the political leaders and the common people of war-weary Japan.

As the occupation continued under the watchful eye of MacArthur, a host of other reforms were imposed upon the Japanese. The economic reforms included the dismantling of the old *zaibatsu* (the huge financial cartels that dominated Japan's prewar economy), a land reform that redistributed farmland for the benefit of poor farmers and at the expense of wealthy landowners, and a labor reform creating Japan's first genuine trade union movement. There were also far-reaching social and educational reforms, all of which were intended to make Japan a more democratic society. Generally, these various reform programs were remarkably successful, largely because they addressed real needs in Japan and because the Japanese themselves desired the reforms. Indeed, the Japanese genuinely rejected past militarism and wholeheartedly embraced the new democracy.

One of the anomalies of the occupation is that democracy was being implanted in Japan by a military command, that is by General MacArthur and his staff. SCAP's mode of operation was military. It censored the Japanese press, disallowing free speech, and it ruled by fiat, its directives to the Japanese government not being arrived at by democratic means. Also anomalous was the character of General MacArthur as a reformer. In Japan he was aloof, arrogant, and almighty. The defeated Japanese seemed to need an august authority figure, and the imperious MacArthur seemed destined to play just such a role. Although he claimed to like the Japanese people, his manner toward them was condescending, and he often expressed contempt for their culture. In his view, the Japanese were but twelve-year-old children who must be shown the way from "feudalism" to democracy.[3] But despite MacArthur's arrogance and the military cast of the occupation, he and his staff possessed a genuine reformist zeal, and their sense of mission contributed greatly toward the successful rooting of democratic ideas and institutions in Japan.

The menace of Japanese militarism was thus eliminated and supplanted by democracy, but U.S. minds soon perceived a larger menace looming on the Eastern horizon: the spread of Communism in Asia. The Communist victory in the civil war in China in 1949, and Communist aggression in Korea in the following year, caused the U.S. government to recast its policy in Japan reflecting Cold War exigencies. Safely under U.S. control, Japan was to be prepared to play a key role in the U.S. policy of containment of Communism.

It is difficult to arrive at a final assessment of the occupation of Japan, for opinions differ greatly according to one's ideology and nationality. That the occupation program, with its various reforms, was in every instance a grand success is certainly debatable. Many Japanese historians as well as revisionist historians in the United States argue that the U.S. exercise of power in postwar Japan was excessive, that the "reverse course" policies (see p. 42) negated the democratic reforms, and that Japan was victimized by zealous U.S. anti-Communist policies. But there is little question that Japan emerged from the experience with a working democratic system of government and a more democratic society, a passionate pacifism, the beginnings of an economic recovery, and a large measure of military security. And the United States emerged with a new, potentially strong, ally strategically located in a part of the world confronted with the spread of Communist revolution.

■ THE CIVIL WAR IN CHINA

The victory of the Chinese Communists over the Nationalist government of China in 1949 was the culmination of a long struggle between two revolutionary parties—the Communists and the Nationalists—that began back in the 1920s. After winning the first round of that struggle and coming to power in 1928, the Nationalist Party, under its domineering leader Jiang Jieshi, sought to exterminate the rural-based Communist Party led by Mao Zedong. In 1935, the Communists barely escaped annihilation by embarking on the epic "Long March," a trek of over 6,000 miles, after which they secured themselves in a remote area in northwest China. When the war with Japan began in mid-1937, Mao persuaded Jiang to set aside their differences and form a united front for the purpose of defending China from the Japanese invaders. During the war against Japan (1937–1945), the Chinese Communist Party (CCP) and its army grew enormously while the Nationalist regime deteriorated badly. The Communists' success was the product of inspired leadership, effective mobilization of the peasantry for the war effort, and skillful use of guerrilla warfare tactics against the Japanese. By the end of the war the Communists controlled nineteen "liberated areas," rural regions mainly in northern China, with a combined population of about 100 million, and the size of their army had increased tenfold from about 50,000 to over half a million. In contrast, the Nationalist government and army retreated deep into the interior to Chungking during the war and failed to launch a successful counteroffensive against the Japanese. Meanwhile, wartime inflation became rampant, as did corruption within Jiang's Nationalist government and army. Growing political oppression was met by growing public discontent and declining morale. The Nationalist Army, supplied and trained by the United States, was hardly used against the Japanese, but rather was deployed to guard against the spread of Communist forces or languished in garrison duty. Thus, military morale sank as well.

When World War II ended with the U.S. defeat of Japan, civil war within China was all but a certainty as the two rivals, Nationalists and Communists, rushed to fill the vacuum created by the defeated Japanese. Both sought to expand their areas of control, and particularly went after the major cities in northern China. Jiang issued orders sanctioned by the United States that Japanese commanders were to surrender only to Nationalist military officers rather than turn over areas under their control to the Communists. Moreover, the United States landed some 53,000 marines to take and hold several key cities in northern China until the Nationalist forces arrived.

While the United States continued to support Jiang's government as it had during the war, it wished to avert the impending civil war and thus urged Jiang Jieshi to find a peaceful solution to his conflict with the Communists.

Before World War II had ended Washington had sent a special envoy, Patrick Hurley, to China to serve as a mediator between the two sides. He was successful only in bringing the rivals Mao and Jiang to the negotiating table in August 1945, but not in finding a solution to their feud. After his efforts ended in failure, President Truman sent Gen. George C. Marshall to China in December 1945 to mediate the dispute. Despite Marshall's initial success in getting the two sides to agree—on paper at least—to an immediate cease-fire and to a formula for mutual military demobilization and political cooperation, he too ultimately failed as the conflict escalated into a full-fledged civil war in the spring of 1946. The U.S. efforts to mediate between the CCP and Jiang's regime were destined to failure largely because Jiang refused to share power with the Communists. Essentially, Mao demanded the formation of a coalition government, followed by the mutual reduction and integration of Communist and Nationalist military forces, whereas Jiang insisted on the reduction of Communist forces and their integration into the Nationalist Army as the precondition for sharing power with the Communists. The U.S. position as mediator was weakened by its lack of neutrality, for continued U.S. military and economic aid to the Nationalists served to alienate the Communists. However, the civil war that the United States had tried so hard to prevent was not initiated by Mao, but rather by Jiang, who was convinced that the only solution to the problem was a military one and that it was obtainable.

Mao Zedong (Mao Tse-tung), chairman of the Chinese Communist Party, Oct. 1, 1950, the first anniversary of the founding of the People's Republic of China. (*National Archives*)

At the outset of the Chinese civil war, the Nationalists had good reason to be confident of victory. Despite Communist gains, the Nationalist Army still had a numerical superiority of three to one over the Communist forces. The Nationalist Army was much better equipped, having received huge amounts of U.S. military aid, including artillery pieces, tanks, and trucks, as well as light arms and ammunition. Moreover, the Nationalists benefited by having the use of U.S. airplanes and troop ships for the movement of their forces. In contrast, the Communist army, reorganized as the People's Liberation Army (PLA), was relatively poorly equipped and had practically no outside support. Given the Nationalist edge, it is not surprising that Jiang's armies were victorious in the early months of the war, defeating the PLA in almost every battle in northern China. But within a year of fighting the tide began to shift.

The battle for China took place mainly in Manchuria, the northeastern area of China, which had been under Japanese control since the early 1930s. It was prized by both sides for its rich resources and as the most industrialized area of China (thanks to the Japanese and to the earlier imperialist presence of Russia). Immediately after World War II, Manchuria was temporarily under the control of the Soviet Union, whose Red Army had attacked the Japanese forces there in the closing days of the war and "liberated" the area. On August 14, 1945, the Soviet Union concluded with the Nationalist government of China a treaty of friendship, which included provisions for the withdrawal of Soviet forces from Manchuria to be completed within three months of the surrender of Japan. Before the Nationalists could occupy the area with their forces, the Soviet Red Army hastily stripped Manchuria of all the Japanese military and industrial equipment it could find and shipped it—together with Japanese prisoners of war—into the Soviet Union, thus depriving the Chinese of a valuable industrial base. Meanwhile, Chinese Communist forces had begun entering Manchuria immediately after the surrender of Japan. A poorly equipped PLA force of about 100,000 troops was rapidly deployed in rural areas surrounding the major cities of Manchuria. Jiang was determined to maintain Nationalist military control of Manchuria, and he decided—against the advice of his U.S. military advisers—to position his best armies in that remote area, where they could be supported or reinforced only with great difficulty. Thus, when the battle for Manchuria began, Jiang's Nationalist forces held the major cities, railways, and other strategic points, while the PLA held the surrounding countryside. The Chinese Communists were not assisted by the Soviet Red Army in Manchuria (or elsewhere), but before the Soviets left Manchuria they did provide the PLA with a much-needed cache of captured Japanese weapons (mainly light arms—machine guns, light artillery, rifles, and ammunition).

In the major battles in Manchuria in late 1947 and 1948, the Chinese Communists were big winners. Not only did the Nationalist Army suffer great combat casualties, running into the hundreds of thousands, but it lost almost as many soldiers to the other side either as captives or defectors. Moreover, the PLA captured large amounts of U.S. weapons from the retreating Nationalist Army. The Communist forces, which were better disciplined and had stronger morale, used their mobility to advantage, since they were not merely trying to hold territory as were the Nationalists. In the end, it was they, not the Nationalists, who took the offensive. With their greater maneuverability they were able to control the time and place of battle and to inflict great losses on their less mobile enemy. The Nationalists, on the other hand, had spread their forces too thin to maintain defensive positions and were unable to hold open the transportation lines needed to bring up reinforcements and supplies.

After the last battle in Manchuria in 1948, the momentum in the civil war shifted to the Communists. The last major engagement of the war was fought in the fall of 1948 at Xuzhou (Hsuchow), about a hundred miles north of the Nationalist capital of Nanjing (Nanking). In this decisive battle Jiang deployed 400,000 of his best troops, equipped with tanks and heavy artillery. But after two months of fighting, in which the Nationalists lost 200,000 men, the larger and more mobile Communist army won a decisive victory. From that point it was only a matter of time before the Nationalist collapse. During the spring and summer of 1949, Jiang's forces were rapidly retreating south in disarray, and in October Jiang fled with the remainder of his army to the Chinese island of Taiwan. There the embattled Nationalist leader continued to claim that his Nationalist regime (formally titled the Republic of China) was the only legitimate government of China, and he promised to return to the mainland with his forces to drive off the "Communist bandits." In the meantime, on October 1, 1949, Mao Zedong and his victorious Communist Party proclaimed the founding of the People's Republic of China (PRC) with Beijing (Peking) as its capital.

The Chinese civil war, however, was not entirely over, but instead became a part of the global Cold War. The new Communist government in Beijing insisted it would never rest until its rival on Taiwan was completely defeated; conversely, the Nationalist government was determined never to submit to the Communists. The continued existence of "two Chinas," each intent on destroying the other and each allied to one of the superpowers, would remain the major Cold War issue and source of tension in East Asia for the next three decades.

The outcome of the Chinese civil war was the product of many factors, but direct outside intervention was not one of them. Neither of the superpowers, nor any other nation, became engaged militarily in the conflict once it began in 1946. By that time the United States had pulled its troops out of China. Nor was indirect foreign assistance a major factor in determining the outcome of the conflict. If military aid had been a major factor, the Nationalists surely should have won, for the United States provided them far more assistance, military and otherwise, during and after World War II than the Soviet Union provided the Chinese Communists. The United States had provided Nationalist China with a massive amount of military and economic aid since 1941, amounting to more than $2 billion.[4]

The postwar policy of the Soviet Union toward China was ambivalent, as was its attitude toward the Chinese Communists. It is noteworthy that at the end of World War II Stalin signed a treaty with the Nationalist government of China and publicly recognized Jiang's rulership of China. The Soviet Red Army did little to deter the takeover of Manchuria by Jiang's Nationalist Army, and it withdrew from Manchuria not long after the date to which the two sides had agreed.[5] The Soviet Union's looting of Manchuria for "war booty" was of benefit to neither of the combatants in China and was objectionable to both. Moreover, Stalin made no real effort to support or encourage the Chinese Communists in their bid for power in China, except for turning over the cache of Japanese arms in Manchuria. On the contrary, Stalin is known to have stated in 1948, when the victory of the Chinese Communists was all but certain, that from the outset he had counseled the Chinese Communist leaders not to fight the Nationalists because their prospect for victory seemed remote. Indeed, when we take all this into account and take note of how guarded Moscow was in its dealings with the Chinese Communists after their victory, we can speculate that Stalin might have been happier with a weak Nationalist government in China rather than a new and vigorous Communist government. Jiang's regime could more readily be exploited than could a strong fraternal Communist regime.

More important as a determinant of the civil war's outcome than outside support (or the lack of it) were domestic factors: the popular support of the peasantry for the Communists, the high morale and effective military strategy of the Communist forces, the corruption of the Nationalist regime, the low morale and ineffective strategy of its army, and the inept political and military leadership of Generalissimo Jiang Jieshi. Still another factor was the deteriorating situation on the Nationalist home front, where runaway inflation, corruption, and coercive government measures combined to demoralize the Chinese population. The Communists, by contrast, enjoyed much greater popular support, especially from the peasantry (which made up about 85 percent of the population), because of its successful land redistribution programs. The Nationalists had alienated the peasantry for lack of a meaningful agrarian reform, having provided neither a program of land redistribution nor protection for tenant farmers against greedy and overbearing landowners.

The turn of events in China had immediate political repercussions in the United States. Shortly before the civil war ended, the U.S. Senate Foreign Relations Committee heard the testimony of U.S. teachers, businesspeople, journalists, and missionaries who had lived in China for years. They were unanimous in their criticism of Jiang's regime and warned that any additional aid would only fall into the hands of the Communists. The Truman administration understood this, but it nevertheless continued to provide aid. It knew that to cut off aid to its client promised to invite the inevitable political charges that Truman had abandoned a worthy ally, albeit a hopelessly corrupt one, in the struggle against international Communism. The Republicans, of course, who had been sharpening their knives for several years, did not disappoint him. No sooner had the civil war ended in China than they were blaming the Democratic administration of President Truman for "losing China." Republican Senator Joseph McCarthy went so far as to blame the "loss of China" on Communists and Communist sympathizers within the State Department. Although McCarthy's charges proved unfounded, the Democrats were nonetheless saddled with the reputation of having lost China to Communism.

The loss of China to Communism, as perceived by the U.S. public, and the intensified Cold War mentality it engendered within the United States, served to drive the Truman administration still further to the right in its foreign policy. Consequently, Truman became ever more vigilant to check the spread of Communism to other parts of Asia, and when, soon afterward, he was faced with Communist aggression in Korea and the prospect of losing Korea, it is little wonder that he responded immediately and forcefully.

■ THE KOREAN WAR

On June 25, 1950, only nine months after the Communist victory in China, the armed forces of Communist North Korea launched a full-scale attack on South Korea. The United States and its major allies responded swiftly and decisively to halt what they perceived to be the forceful expansion of international Communism and a blatant violation of the United Nations Charter. Korea thus became the first real battleground of the Cold War and the first major threat of an all-out war between the East and West. Even though it remained a limited war, it proved to be a bitter and bloody conflict that lasted over three years, produced over 1 million fatalities, and left Korea devastated and hopelessly divided. The Korean War was a product of the Cold War and had profound effects on its continuation.

The roots of the Korean conflict go back to the last days of World War II when the United States and the Soviet Union divided the Korean peninsula at the 38th parallel. The division, which was agreed to by U.S. and Soviet diplomats at Potsdam in July 1945, was meant to be a temporary arrangement for receiving the surrender of Japanese military forces in Korea after the war. The Soviet military occupation of northern Korea after Japan's defeat and the U.S. occupation of the southern half of Korea were to last only until a unified Korean government could be established—an objective agreed to by both parties. However, before any steps were taken to achieve that objective, Korean Communists, who had been in exile in either the Soviet Union or in northern China during the war, established in the north a Soviet-styled government and speedily carried out an extensive land reform program. Meanwhile, in the south, U.S. occupation authorities attempted to bring order to a chaotic situation. Korean nationalists opposed continued military occupation of their country and agitated for immediate independence. Rival nationalist parties, some of which were virulently anti-Communist, contended with each other in a political free-for-all. Political disorder, which was exacerbated by economic problems—namely, runaway inflation and the demand for land redistribution—continued in the south, even after an authoritarian and staunchly anti-Communist regime was established in 1948 by the Korean nationalist Syngman Rhee.

Under these circumstances, unification of the north and the south proved impossible. U.S. and Soviet diplomats had agreed in late 1945 to set up a provisional Korean government, which for five years would be under a joint U.S.-Soviet trusteeship, and a joint commission was set up in Seoul to implement this plan. However, the first session of this commission in March 1946 produced a typical Cold War scene with the U.S. and Soviet delegates hurling accusations at one another. The Soviet side accused the U.S. military command in South Korea of fostering the development of an undemocratic anti-Communist regime in the south, and the U.S. side similarly accused the Soviets of implanting an undemocratic Communist regime in the north. The Soviets insisted that no "antidemocratic" (meaning anti-Communist) Korean political party be allowed to participate in the political process, while U.S. representatives insisted on the right of all parties to participate. The Soviets also proposed the immediate withdrawal of both Soviet and U.S. occupation forces from Korea; but the United States, concerned about the Soviet advantage of having a better organized client state in the north, insisted on a supervised free election to be carried out in both the north and the south prior to troop withdrawal.

Failing to solve the impasse in bilateral talks, the United States took the issue of a divided Korea to the United Nations in September 1947. As a result, the UN General Assembly passed a resolution calling for free elections throughout Korea and a UN commission to oversee these elections. In May 1948, the National Assembly elections were held under UN supervision, but in the south only, since the Communist regime in North Korea refused to permit the UN commission into the north. On the basis of his party's victory in the UN-sanctioned election, Syngman Rhee proclaimed the founding of the Republic of Korea, which purported to be the only legitimate government of all of Korea. Less than a month later, in

September 1948, the Communist regime in the north, led by Kim Il Sung, formally proclaimed the founding of the Democratic People's Republic of Korea, and it too claimed to be the rightful government of all of Korea. With the peninsula now divided between two rival regimes there seemed little prospect of unification. Despite this and despite the steadily mounting tensions between the two opposing regimes, both the Soviet Union and the United States began withdrawing their forces from the peninsula, and by mid-1949 the withdrawal was completed. (There remained in North Korea a 3,500-troop Soviet military mission and in South Korea a 500-troop U.S. Military Advisory Group.)

Not only were tensions mounting in Korea, but elsewhere in the global Cold War struggle. By the end of the 1940s, the U.S. policy of containment of the Soviet Union began to show signs of weakness, especially when, in August 1949, the U.S. public was hit with twin shocks. First, the Soviet Union successfully tested an atomic bomb, thus breaking the U.S. monopoly in four short years. Second, the civil war in China came to an end with a Communist victory and with it the world's most populous nation had fallen to what the West perceived to be militant, expansionist Communism. Predictably, the people of the United States believed that the Communist triumph in China somehow had been engineered by Moscow.

As noted previously, the loss of China to Communism had immediate political repercussions in the United States. The Republican charge that Truman had lost China to the Communists just as Roosevelt had lost Eastern Europe to the Soviets served to create a perception of dominoes falling one after another. The relentless Republican criticism of the Democrats for being "soft on Communism" caused the Truman administration (and especially Secretary of State Dean Acheson, a favorite target of McCarthy) to strengthen even more its resolve to stand up to the Communists.

In April 1950, President Truman received and accepted a set of recommendations from his National Security Council, the president's own advisory committee.[6] These recommendations, known as NSC-68, were based on the premise that there could be no meaningful negotiations with the Kremlin until it "changed its policies drastically." According to NSC-68, Stalin understood only force. It recommended, therefore, that the United States develop the hydrogen bomb to offset the Soviet Union's atomic bomb, and that it rapidly increase its conventional forces. The cost of such a program would have to be borne by a large increase in taxes. The U.S. people would have to be mobilized; the emphasis must be on "consensus," "sacrifice," and "unity." NSC-68 urged the creation of regional alliances, similar to NATO, to create global positions of strength. NSC-68 also expressed the hope of making "the Russian people our allies in this enterprise" of ridding the world of "Communist tyranny." This hope, however, was based on the questionable assumptions that people never willingly accept Communism, that it is always forced on them, and that they will always welcome U.S. forces as liberators. This set of assumptions later produced fatal consequences for U.S. foreign policy in Cuba and in Vietnam where the local populations refused to rally to the U.S. cause.

The first test of the mobilization of the U.S. people came two months after the president approved NSC-68, when the Korean War broke out and, as a consequence, the remilitarization of the United States began in earnest. It should be noted, however, that earlier in the year top U.S. military leaders (including the Joint Chiefs of Staff and Gens. Dwight Eisenhower and Douglas MacArthur) had concluded that Korea was not of sufficient importance to U.S. national interests to be included within its defensive perimeter. This assessment was based mainly on the higher priority given to defending Europe and Japan and on the insufficiency of U.S. ground forces at the time. Secretary of State Acheson stated publicly in January 1950 (as MacArthur had done earlier) that the U.S. defense perimeter stretched from Alaska through Japan to the Philippines, and that Korea was outside that perimeter. In making this statement Acheson can hardly be faulted for inviting the North Korean attack on the south as his critics would later charge, because he was merely stating what was already quite clear to the Soviet Union. Moscow was well aware of U.S. strategic priorities and troop limitations. U.S. military doctrine at the time emphasized preparation for "total war" and focused primarily on resisting the Soviet threat in Europe, not in Asia.

When the invasion came on June 25, 1950, Washington acted as if it had been caught off guard and denounced it as an unwarranted surprise attack. In fact, however, both MacArthur's military intelligence and that of Syngman Rhee had monitored North Korean troop movements and preparations and had abundant evidence of the impending attack. It appeared that both Rhee and MacArthur withheld this information to maximize the psychological impact of what they called a "surprise attack."[7]

It is not altogether clear what roles the Soviet Union and Communist China played in the decision of North Korea to attack the south, but neither Soviet nor Chinese troops were involved initially. Nor were they deployed near Korea prior to the war. North Korea, however, was a Communist state that received substantial Soviet political, economic, and military support and was considered in the West to be under Soviet control. The United States and its allies concluded, therefore, that this was another case of Soviet aggression, and they were quick to lay the blame at Joseph Stalin's feet. Recent testimony by men who were close to Stalin, which has come to light only since the collapse of the Soviet Union, makes it clear that Kim Il Sung did visit with Stalin in Moscow in March 1949 and again in March 1950 and in the latter meeting sought Stalin's support for an invasion of South Korea aimed at unifying Korea by force. But the Soviet dictator's response is less clear. By some accounts Stalin acknowledged Kim's plans for war and wished him success but did not offer specific instructions, much less orders for carrying out such plans. Stalin neither blocked Kim's proposed war nor gave it enthusiastic support. Stalin did advise Kim to consult first with Mao Zedong, which Kim did in Beijing in May 1950. It seems that he was there merely to inform the Chinese leader of his plans and that Mao, although skeptical, raised no objections and speculated that the United States was not likely to intervene in such a distant and small country.[8] Thus, on the evidence available, it is reasonable to conclude that the decision for war—specifically the strategy and timing of the attack—was made by Kim himself in Pyongyang, the North Korean capital, after he had secured at least acquiescence from both Stalin and Mao.[9] Kim, whose nationalist convictions were as strong as his Communist ones, was convinced that his North Korean army was strong enough to gain a swift victory by waging a full-scale offensive. He also assumed that the United States lacked either the will or the means to come to the rescue of South Korea, but this would prove to be a serious miscalculation.

Far from ignoring or standing by idly while its former client was being overrun by a superior Communist force, the U.S. government rapidly swung into action. First, President Truman immediately ordered U.S. naval and air support from bases in nearby Japan to bolster the retreating South

United Nations Security Council session, New York, June 27, 1950, at which the resolution condemning North Korean aggression was approved in the absence of the Soviet representative who was then boycotting the UN. (*National Archives*)

Korean army, and, second, he immediately took the issue of North Korean aggression to an emergency session of the United Nations Security Council. In the absence of the Soviet delegate, who was boycotting the United Nations in protest against its refusal to seat the People's Republic of China in the world body, the Security Council passed a resolution on June 25 condemning the invasion by North Korea and calling for the withdrawal of its forces from South Korea. Two days later the Security Council passed a second resolution calling for member nations of the United Nations to contribute forces for a UN "police action" to repel the aggression. (It seems unlikely that the Soviet delegate to the United Nations would not have been at his seat in the Security Council—or even in New York—if Moscow had known in advance of, much less planned, the North Korean attack on the south.)

By virtue of the second resolution, U.S. military involvement in Korea was authorized by the United Nations. Actually, Truman had already, the previous day, ordered U.S. ground troops (in addition to air and naval support) into action in Korea. The Soviet Union made use of this point to argue that U.S. military action in Korea was an act of aggression. Moreover, Moscow contended that the war in Korea was started by South Korea and that the deployment of UN forces in Korea was in violation of the UN Charter because neither the Soviet Union nor the People's Republic of China was present at the Security Council session to cast a vote. The Soviets protested that the UN operation in Korea was actually a mask for U.S. aggression. In point of fact, some planners within the U.S. National Security Council welcomed the outbreak of war in Korea as an opportunity for the United States to roll back Communism on the Korean peninsula.[10] Clearly, the UN engagement in Korea was largely a U.S. operation. Although some sixteen nations ultimately contributed to the UN forces in Korea, the bulk of UN troops, weapons, and matériel were from the United States; UN operations in Korea were largely financed by the U.S. government; the UN forces were placed under the command of U.S. Army Gen. Douglas MacArthur; and the military and diplomatic planning for the war was done mainly in Washington.

The swift and resolute U.S. response to halt Communist aggression in Korea belied the Acheson statement of January 1950. It instead reflected the thinking of NSC-68. The Truman administration, which had been ready to write off Korea earlier in the year, decided that the United States must meet the Communist challenge to the containment policy. On second look, it determined that South Korea's defense was vital to the defense of U.S. interests in Asia, especially since the prospect of a Soviet-controlled Korea would threaten the security of Japan, which had suddenly become the major U.S. ally in Asia. Moreover, President Truman saw the defense of Korea as important to the maintenance of U.S. credibility and defense commitments elsewhere in the world, and thus to the maintenance of the

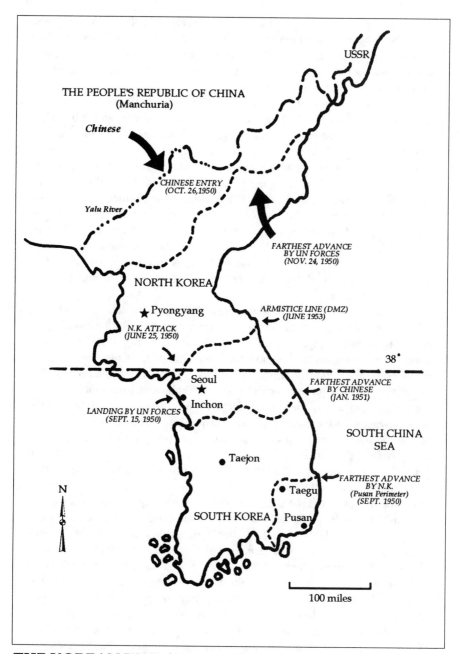

THE KOREAN WAR (1950–1953)

Western alliance. Indeed, he likened the situation in Korea in June 1950 to the Nazi aggression in the late 1930s and invoked the lesson of Munich: appeasement of an aggressor does not bring peace but only more serious aggression. Korea represented a test of U.S. will. Thus, the United States must not fail to stand up to that test.

The South Korean army, which lacked tanks, artillery, and aircraft, was no match for the heavily armed North Korean forces, and it therefore took a beating in the early weeks of the war. It was barely able to hang on to keep from being driven off the peninsula. The first units of U.S. ground troops to come to its rescue were also undermanned and ill-equipped, but still they succeeded in holding the Pusan perimeter in the southeastern corner of Korea. Then, in September 1950, MacArthur engineered a dramatic reversal of the war with his successful landing of a large U.S./UN force at Inchon several hundred miles behind the Communist lines. Taken by surprise by this daring move, the North Korean forces then beat a hasty retreat back up the peninsula. By early October the North Koreans were driven across the 38th parallel; the U.S./UN forces had gained their objective in a spectacular fashion.

At this juncture the U.S. government had a critical decision to make: whether or not to pursue the retreating enemy across the 38th parallel. General MacArthur, riding the wings of victory, was raring to go, and so, of course, was Syngman Rhee, who hoped to eliminate the Communist regime in the north and bring the whole of the country under his government. But the use of military force to achieve the unification of Korea had not been the original purpose of the UN engagement; the June 27th resolution called only for repelling the North Korean invasion. Moreover, U.S./UN military action in North Korea ran the risk of intervention by Communist China and possibly the Soviet Union as well in an expanded conflict. At the United Nations, the United States rejected proposals by the Soviet Union and by India aimed at achieving an overall peace in Asia including both an armistice in Korea and the seating of the People's Republic of China in the United Nations. Instead, the United States succeeded in getting a resolution passed in the UN General Assembly that called for nationwide elections in Korea after "all appropriate steps [are] taken to ensure conditions of stability throughout Korea." The United States had opted for a UN General Assembly resolution because the Soviet Union would surely have vetoed any Security Council resolution sanctioning the use of UN forces to unify Korea. (No nation has veto power in the General Assembly.)

Tentatively, Washington then decided first to authorize the entry of the South Korean army into the north and then to give the go-ahead to MacArthur's UN forces on the condition that they would halt their advance northward if either Chinese or Soviet forces entered the war. Nonetheless, the U.S. war objective was now significantly altered; the goal was no longer limited to repelling an attack but was extended to eliminating the Communist regime in the north and militarily unifying the whole of Korea. Despite the caution manifested in Washington, General MacArthur, sensing the imminent collapse of the North Korean army, pressed on, rapidly advancing his forces toward the Yalu River, the boundary between Korea and China. In doing so he ignored the repeated warnings from Washington and those from Beijing, which threatened intervention by Chinese forces if its territory were threatened. To Beijing, the prospect of a hostile "imperialist" military presence across the border from the most industrialized area of China was intolerable.

MacArthur's aggressive pursuit of the enemy caused Washington and its allies qualms. In mid-October President Truman met with his field commander on Wake Island in the Pacific in order to urge caution against provoking the Chinese or Soviet entry into the war, but at that meeting MacArthur confidently predicted an imminent victory and assured Truman that if the Chinese dared to intervene they could get no more than 50,000 troops across the Yalu and the result would be "the greatest slaughter."[11] Back in Korea, MacArthur launched a major offensive, which, he predicted, would have the U.S. soldiers back home in time for Christmas.

With U.S. forces rapidly advancing toward the Chinese border, the Chinese did exactly as they had warned they would; they sent their armed forces into battle in Korea. Beijing insisted that these troops were "volunteers" thereby disclaiming official involvement in the war in order to ward off a possible retaliatory attack by UN forces on China itself. After an initial surprise attack on October 25, the Chinese made a strategic retreat for about a month only to come back in much greater numbers. MacArthur's intelligence reports badly underestimated the number of Chinese troops involved and China's capacity to increase the size of its forces. Suddenly, on November 26, a vast Chinese army of over 300,000 soldiers opened a massive counteroffensive. Overwhelmed by this superior force, MacArthur's UN forces soon beat a hasty retreat southward over 250 miles to below the 38th parallel.

The Chinese intervention with a force much larger than MacArthur thought possible made it, in his words, "an entirely new war," and it also provoked a sharp dispute with President Truman over political and military policy. MacArthur, frustrated by having an imminent victory denied him and by the limitations placed on him by his superiors in Washington, favored widening the war, including using Chinese Nationalist forces from Taiwan, bombing Chinese Communist bases in Manchuria, and blockading the coast of China. The president, his military advisers, and his European allies feared that such steps might touch off World War III—a nuclear war with the Soviet Union—or that the overcommitment of U.S. forces in an expanded Korean War would leave Europe defenseless against a possible Soviet attack. MacArthur publicly criticized the policy of limited warfare that he was ordered to follow. In March 1951, he clearly exceeded his authority by issuing a public statement threatening China with destruction if it refused to heed his demand for an immediate disengagement from Korea. It was this unauthorized ultimatum that caused President Truman to dismiss the general from his command. Truman, who later stated that this was the most difficult decision he had ever made, felt it necessary to reassert presidential authority over the military and make it clear to both enemies and allies that the United States spoke with a single voice. Moreover, there was good reason to fear that continued insubordination by MacArthur, in his quest for total victory, might indeed instigate an all-out war between East and West. For his part, MacArthur minimized such prospects and argued that the West was missing an opportunity to eliminate Communism not only from Korea but from China as well.

It has been frequently alleged that it was General MacArthur's advocacy of use of the atomic bomb against the Chinese that resulted in his dismissal. Although there may be some truth to the allegation, it must be pointed out that on at least three separate occasions U.S. presidents considered the use of the bomb in the Korean War. Truman threatened use of the bomb in a press conference in November 1950 just after Chinese soldiers entered the war in large numbers, and he suggested that the decision rested with the field commander in Korea. The latter point caused so much consternation among his allies and advisers that Truman quickly modified his statement, saying that the final decision on the use of the bomb rested with the president. Several months later, when a new UN offensive was stymied by Chinese forces near the 38th parallel, Truman conferred with his advisers on the possibility of using the bomb. And near the end of the war, in June 1953, when armistice talks were deadlocked, the new U.S. president, Dwight Eisenhower, seriously considered using the atomic bomb to break the stalemate.

The dismissal of MacArthur on April 11, 1951, brought no change in the war. His replacement, Gen. Matthew Ridgeway, held against a new Chinese offensive in late April, and several weeks later he was able to force the Chinese to retreat to near the 38th parallel. Soon thereafter the war stalemated with the battle line remaining in that general vicinity. The war dragged on for two more years without a major new offensive by either side. Still, the toll of casualties mounted as patrol action on the ground continued, as did dogfights in the air between U.S. jet pilots and Chinese and North Korean pilots flying Soviet jet fighters. All the while, the United States conducted devastating bombing attacks on North Korea, destroying virtually every city as well as hydroelectric plants and irrigation dams.

The military deadlock of the spring of 1951 brought about the beginning of peace talks. In June of that year, Moscow and Washington agreed to begin negotiations for a cease-fire in Korea, and both Beijing and Pyongyang concurred. Talks began in July and continued on-again-off-again for the next two years at Panmunjom, a town situated along the battle line. Two main questions divided the negotiators: the location of the cease-fire line and the exchange of prisoners. The Communist side insisted on returning to the 38th parallel, but finally agreed to the current battle line, which gave the South Koreans a slight territorial advantage. On the second issue, the Communists insisted on a complete exchange of all prisoners, but the U.S. negotiators called for allowing the prisoners to decide for themselves whether they wished to be returned to their homelands. The truce talks remained deadlocked on this issue, which carried great propaganda value for the United States. In point of fact, many North Korean captives—perhaps as many as 40,000—did not wish to be repatriated, and the United States wanted to exploit this matter as much as the Communists wanted to prevent this mass defection, and thereby deny the United States a major propaganda victory.

After the emergence in 1953 of new leadership in Moscow with the death of Stalin and in Washington with the inauguration of Eisenhower, the two sides finally exhibited the flexibility necessary to break the impasse in Korea and to end the costly stalemated war. On June 8, 1953, the negotiators at Panmunjom signed an agreement that made repatriation of prisoners voluntary, but allowed each side the opportunity (under the supervision of a UN commission) to attempt to persuade their defectors to return home. However, a truce settlement was delayed because of a drastic attempt by South Korean President Syngman Rhee to sabotage it. Rhee, who desired to continue the fight to unify the country under his regime, released some 25,000 North Korean prisoners, who allegedly rejected repatriation to the north. The Chinese responded with a new offensive against South Korean units. Finally, after U.S. negotiators offered assurances to pacify and restrain Rhee, the two sides signed a truce on July 23, 1953. The fighting ended with the final battle line as the truce line, which was widened to become a two-and-a-half-mile-wide demilitarized zone (DMZ). The truce, however, did not mean the end of the war; it merely meant a halt in the fighting by exhausted adversaries. Officially, a state of war has continued ever since, and the truce line between North and South Korea has remained the most militarized border anywhere in the world. For over forty years it remained a potential flash point in the Cold War.

Even though the Korean War ended at about the same place it began, both its costs and its consequences were enormous. The United States lost over 33,000 men in the conflict; South Korea, an estimated 300,000; North Korea, 52,000; and China, 900,000 (Washington estimates).[12] While its outcome represented something short of victory for either side, both could claim important achievements. The United States succeeded, with the help of its allies, in standing firm against Communist aggression. This brought greater security to Japan and it contributed to the strengthening of NATO as well. The Chinese emerged from the Korean conflict with greatly enhanced prestige, especially insofar as its now battle-hardened army had stood up to technically superior Western armies in a manner that no Chinese army ever had.

For the Koreans in both the north and the south, the war was disastrous. The war had been fought with great ferocity by Korean partisans who did not hesitate to inflict vicious punishment on their enemies—not only enemy soldiers but civilians thought to be informers or collaborators. Consequently, many atrocities were committed by both sides, and caustic bitterness would persist for years to come. In addition to the great death and destruction suffered by the Koreans, the division of their country was made permanent, and there would be no reduction of tensions and animosity between the Communist regime in the north and the anti-Communists in the south. The war produced millions of refugees, and when the fighting ended several hundred thousand Korean families remained separated. The Cold War thus remained deeply entrenched in Korea.

■ THE UNITED STATES AND THE COLD WAR IN ASIA

The Communist victory in China represented a major setback for U.S. foreign policy. The threat to U.S. power in East Asia was made all the greater when the new Communist government of China promptly cemented its relations with the Soviet Union with a thirty-year military alliance aimed at the United States, and vehemently denounced U.S. "imperialism." The United States was then confronted by what seemed to be a global Communist movement that had suddenly doubled in size and now included the world's most populous nation. The turn of events in China meant that the United States's immediate postwar Asian policy, which had envisioned the emergence of a strong, united, democratic China to serve as the main pillar of stability in Asia, was completely shattered. Now the U.S. government fashioned a new Asian policy that called for the containment of Communism and featured Japan, the United States's former enemy, in the role of its strategic partner and base of operations.

In 1948, when it became apparent that the Chinese Communists would defeat the Nationalists in the civil war raging in China, the U.S. occupation policy in Japan took a strong turn to the right. The new policy, often called the "reverse course," called for rebuilding the former enemy, Japan, so that it would play the role of the United States's major ally in Asia, acting as a bulwark against the spread of Communism in that part of the world. Beginning in 1948, Washington, which heretofore had made no effort to assist Japan economically, now began pumping economic aid into Japan and assisting Japan's economic recovery in other ways. The reverse course was evidenced by a relaxation of the restrictions against the *zaibatsu*, a new ban on general labor strikes, and the purge of leftist leaders. And with the outbreak of war in nearby Korea in 1950, the security of Japan became an urgent concern to the United States. In order to maintain domestic security within Japan, General MacArthur authorized the formation of a 75,000-person Japanese National Police Reserve, thus reversing his earlier policy for an unarmed Japan. This step was the beginning of the rearmament of Japan, and it was bitterly disappointing to many Japanese who were sincere in their conversion to pacifism.

In the midst of the intensified Cold War, the United States not only groomed Japan to become its ally, but also took the lead in framing a peace treaty with Japan in 1951 that would secure the new relationship. The treaty, which formally ended the Allied Occupation and restored full sovereignty to Japan, was crafted by the U.S. diplomat John Foster Dulles in consultation with major U.S. allies. The Communist bloc nations, which were not consulted, objected to the final terms of the treaty and they chose not to sign it. Tied to the treaty, which went into effect in May 1952, was a U.S.-Japan Mutual Security Pact, which provided that the United States would guarantee Japan's security. It also allowed U.S. military bases to remain in Japan to provide not only for Japan's security but also for the defense of U.S. interests in Asia, or, more specifically, for the containment of Communism. Moreover, the United States retained control of the Japanese island of Okinawa, on which it had built a huge military installation. The reborn nation of Japan thus became a child of the Cold War, tied militarily and politically as well as economically to the apron strings of the United States.

Within Japan the Cold War was mirrored by political polarization between the right and the left. The right (the conservative political parties, which governed Japan for the next four decades) accepted the Mutual Security Pact and favored the maintenance of strong political and military ties with the United States. It recognized the threat that the war in nearby Korea represented and the advantages provided by the security arrangement with the United States. Moreover, it was fully aware of Japan's economic dependence on the United States and did not wish to jeopardize these vital economic ties. The left (comprised of the opposition parties, affiliated labor unions, and many—probably most—of Japan's intellectuals and university students) was bitterly opposed to the Security Pact, to U.S. military forces remaining on Japanese soil, and to the rearmament of Japan. It favored instead unarmed neutrality for Japan, rather than its becoming a party to the Cold War. But since the conservative party remained in power, Japan continued to be a close partner of the United States in the international arena, and over 40,000 U.S. forces remained on U.S. military bases in Japan.

The Korean War had a great and lasting impact on the global Cold War. Beyond the fact that the two sides fought to a standstill in Korea, the war occasioned a large general military buildup by both East and West, and this meant the militarization of the Cold War. "Defense" budgets of both the United States and the Soviet Union skyrocketed during the Korean War to record peacetime levels, and they continued to grow thereafter. The military budget of the People's Republic of China also grew commensurately, and that nation remained on a war footing in the years that followed.

A less tangible, but no less important, consequence of the Korean War was the great intensification of hostility between the United States and the People's Republic of China. The possibility for accommodation between them, which still existed before they crossed swords in Korea, vanished. Both continued to accuse each other of aggression, and both increased their vigil against each other. For the PRC, the increased U.S. military presence in Asia meant a rising threat of U.S. "imperialism," and for decades to come this perceived threat remained the central point of Chinese diplomacy and security policy. For the United States, the continuing threat of "Chinese Communist aggression" required a greatly strengthened commitment to the containment of Communist China, and this became the central feature of the U.S. Asian policy for the next twenty-five years. This was reflected in the policy of making Japan the United States's major ally and base of operations in Asia, a decision to guarantee the security of South Korea and maintain U.S. forces there, a commitment to defend the Nationalist Chinese government on the island of Taiwan against an attack from the mainland, and a growing U.S. involvement in Vietnam in support of the French in their efforts to defeat a Communist-led revolutionary movement. The United States thus locked itself into a Cold War position in Asia in its endeavor to stem the spread of Communism, and its Communist adversaries in Asia strengthened their own resolve to resist U.S. intervention and "imperialism." The Cold War battle lines were thus drawn by the early 1950s, and for the next two decades, the two sides maintained their respective positions in mutual hostility.

RECOMMENDED READINGS

Japan

Dower, John W. *Empire and Aftermath, Yoshida Shigeru and the Japanese Experience, 1878–1954*. Cambridge, Mass.: Harvard University Press, 1979.
   An in-depth analysis of the policies of and politics between U.S. occupation authorities and the government of occupied Japan.
Kawai, Kazuo. *Japan's American Interlude*. Chicago: Chicago University Press, 1960.
   A critical "inside view" of the occupation by a Japanese-American scholar who edited an English-language newspaper in Japan during the period.
Minear, Richard. *Victor's Justice: The Tokyo War Crimes Trials*. Princeton: Princeton University Press, 1971.

Argues that the war crimes trials were unjust.

Perry, John C. *Beneath the Eagle's Wings: Americans in Occupied Japan.* New York: Dodd, Mead, 1980.

Reischauer, Edwin O. *Japan: The Story of a Nation.* 4th ed. New York: Knopf, 1988.

China

Bianco, Lucien. *The Origins of the Chinese Revolution, 1915–1949.* Stanford: Stanford University Press, 1971.

    A lucid analysis of the Communist revolution in China stressing the strengths of the Communists and the failures of the Nationalists.

Fairbank, John K. *The United States and China.* 4th ed. Cambridge, Mass.: Harvard University Press, 1979.

Pepper, Suzanne. *Civil War in China: The Political Struggle, 1945–1949.* Berkeley: University of California Press, 1979.

Purifoy, Lewis M. *Harry Truman's China Policy: McCarthyism and the Diplomacy of Hysteria, 1947–1951.* New York: New Viewpoints, 1976.

    Strongly critical of the U.S. policy of supporting Jiang Jieshi.

Tsou, Tang. *America's Failure in China, 1941–1950.* Chicago: Chicago University Press, 1963.

    Argues that the United States had neither the means nor the will to achieve its goals in China.

Tuchman, Barbara. *Stilwell and the American Experience in China, 1911–1945.* New York: Macmillan, 1970.

    A blistering attack on Jiang Jieshi and critical of U.S. support for him.

Korea

Cumings, Bruce. *The Origins of the Korean War: Liberation and the Emergence of Separate Regimes, 1945–1947.* Princeton: Princeton University Press, 1981.

Cumings, Bruce, ed. *Child of Conflict: The Korean American Relationship, 1943–1953.* Seattle: University of Washington Press, 1983.

    Essays by revisionist historians that refute orthodox (Western) interpretations of the origins of the Korean War.

Cumings, Bruce. *The Origins of the Korean War: II, The Roaring of the Cataract, 1947–1950.* Princeton: Princeton University Press, 1990.

    The best scholarly analysis of the background and the early stages of the Korean conflict.

Rees, David. *Korea: The Limited War.* Baltimore: Penguin, 1964.

    A military history focusing on the uniqueness of this conflict as the first U.S. limited war.

Spanier, John W. *The Truman-MacArthur Controversy and the Korean War.* New York: W. W. Norton, 1965.

Stone, I. F. *The Hidden History of the Korean War.* New York: Monthly Review Press, 1952.

    A provocative early revisionist version of the Korean War.

Whiting, Alan S. *China Crosses the Yalu: The Decision to Enter the Korean War.* New York: Macmillan, 1960.

NOTES

1. One finds in English-language materials on China two quite different spellings of Chinese names depending on when they were published. The pinyin system of romanization of Chinese names and words, the method used in the People's Republic of China, was adopted by U.S. publishers in 1979 in place of the Wade-Giles system that had been standard previously. Prior to 1979, Jiang Jieshi's name was rendered Chiang Kai-shek, and Mao Zedong's name was rendered Mao Tse-tung. In this text the pinyin system is adopted, but in most instances, the old spelling of a Chinese name will also be provided in parentheses. Also note that personal names for Chinese, Japanese, and Koreans are given in the manner native to their countries, that is, the surname or family name precedes the given name.

2. Edwin O. Reischauer, *Japan: The Story of a Nation* (New York: Knopf, 3d ed., 1981), p. 221.

3. MacArthur referred to the Japanese as twelve-year-olds in his testimony to the joint committee of the U.S. Senate on the military situation in the Far East in April 1951. Cited in Rinjiro Sodei, "Eulogy to My Dear General," in L. H. Redford, ed., *The Occupation of Japan: Impact of Legal Reform* (Norfolk, Va.: The MacArthur Memorial, 1977), p. 82.

4. After Jiang launched a full-scale civil war in mid-1946, General Marshall made it clear to him that the United States would not underwrite his war. Thereafter, Washington turned down Jiang's urgent requests for additional military aid and provided only a reduced amount of economic aid after the end of 1946.

5. Soviet withdrawal from Manchuria was completed in May 1946, four months later than called for in the initial agreement with Nationalist China, but this was partly because Jiang Jieshi actually requested the Soviets to postpone their withdrawal until the Nationalist forces were prepared to take control.

6. The National Security Council duplicates much of the work of the State Department and during the days of the Kennedy administration (1961–1963) a tendency emerged whereby presidents began to consult the NSC rather than the professionals in the State Department. The discussion in 1950 on the nature of the Soviet threat proved to be one of the first instances where the professionals in the State Department played second fiddle to the National Security Council. The State Department's experts on the Soviet Union, Charles Bohlen and George Kennan, both of whom later served as ambassadors to Moscow, challenged the argument that Stalin had a master plan of conquest. They saw the Soviet threat largely as a potential political problem in Western Europe. But they were overruled by Dean Acheson, who sided with the hard-liners on the National Security Council who argued that the United States must create order throughout the world.

7. The first to make this case was I. F. Stone, *The Hidden History of the Korean War* (New York: Monthly Review Press, 1952), pp. 1–14. Also see Bruce Cumings, "Introduction: The Course of Korean-American Relations, 1943–1953," in Bruce Cumings, ed., *Child of Conflict: The Korean American Relationship, 1943–1953* (Seattle: University of Washington Press, 1983), pp. 41–42.

8. See Sergei N. Goncharov, John W. Lewis, and Xue Litai, *Uncertain Partners: Stalin, Mao, and the Korean War* (Stanford: Stanford University Press, 1993), pp. 136–146.

9. Soviet sources show that throughout 1949, Stalin opposed a North Korean attack on the south, repeatedly telling Kim that "the 38th parallel must remain peaceful." Stalin feared that a war would give the United States a pretext for getting involved in Korean affairs. Kim, however, continued to lobby for a green light from Stalin. It was not until April 1950 that Stalin accepted Kim's view that the

war could be contained to the Korean peninsula and would not draw foreign intervention. See Natal'ia Bazhanova, "Samaia zagadochnaia voina XX stoletniia," *Novoe vremia* 6 (1996), pp. 29–31.

10. Cumings, "Introduction: The Course of Korean-American Relations, 1943–1953," pp. 29–38.

11. Quoted in Richard Rovere and Arthur Schlesinger, Jr., *The General and the President* (New York: Farrar, Straus, 1951), pp. 253–262.

12. Bruce Cumings estimates that the total number of fatalities was as high as 2 million; *The Origins of the Korean War: II, The Roaring of the Cataract, 1947–1950* (Princeton: Princeton University Press, 1990).

4

Confrontation and Coexistence

For centuries the nations of Europe have struggled against one another. France and Britain were often enemies in past centuries, and in modern times the strife between France and Germany has been even bloodier. They have fought each other in three major wars within the span of seventy-five years. Twice in the first half of the twentieth century, the nations of Europe divided into warring camps and fought each other furiously with ever more destructive consequences. During and immediately after World War II, leading political representatives of war-ravaged Europe spoke fervently of the necessity of burying the violent past and embarking on a new future of peace, friendship, and unity among Europeans.

The onset of the Cold War and the closing of the Iron Curtain by Stalin over Eastern Europe meant that Western designs for European unity would be limited to Western Europe. Indeed, the East-West division of Europe and the perceived threat posed by the Soviet Union to the security of Western European nations served to reinforce the need for greater unity among them. In order to counter the Soviet Union's hegemony in Eastern Europe, the United States and its allies began to take steps in the late 1940s to secure the integration of Western Europe. In its turn, Moscow set out to create its own unified empire in Eastern Europe. The result was a rigid political division of Europe.

■ WEST EUROPEAN ECONOMIC INTEGRATION

The division of Europe into hostile East-West camps and the subsequent development of unity within each was the product of the Cold War, and from the outset the United States, no less than the Soviet Union, was involved in a major way. From the beginning of the postwar era, the focal point in the East-West power struggle in Europe was Germany, which had been divided into four occupation zones. Disagreements over reparations to be extracted from Germany and other issues led to a closing off of the Russian zone in East Germany from the U.S., British, and French zones in West Germany. By early 1947, less than two years after the conclusion of the war, it became clear to Washington that the chances for a settlement of the German question had vanished in the Cold War climate of acrimony, suspicion, and fear. The time had come to consolidate the U.S. position in Western Europe, a position centered around a North Atlantic community of nations with common economic and political systems and security interests. In essence, it meant an attempt to integrate the parliamentary, capitalist nations of Western Europe, such as Great Britain, France, Italy, Belgium, the Netherlands, Luxembourg, Denmark, and Norway (but excluding the dictatorial states of Spain and Portugal). Shortly, West Germany, by virtue of its location, size, and economic potential, was also to be integrated into this community and it was destined to play a major role in it. Thus, in the late 1940s, West Germany became, like Japan in East Asia, the first line of defense for the United States against Soviet expansion.

The creation of a separate West German state and its economic recovery were matters of high priority in U.S. foreign policy in the late 1940s. The United States, with the concurrence of Britain and France, took the lead in creating a West German parliamentary government, officially known as the Federal Republic of Germany. From the very moment of its formation in May 1949, the West German government insisted that it spoke for all of Germany, including what at the time was still the Soviet zone of occupation.[1] In rapid order, the United States integrated West Germany into a system of international trade, supplied it with generous amounts of economic aid (through the Marshall Plan), introduced a new currency, and eventually brought West Germany into the U.S.-led military alliance, NATO. Under such circumstances, West German democracy flourished, as did the economy of the rebuilt nation. Indeed, West Germany was the first of the world's war-torn industrial nations to attain a complete economic recovery, and by the late 1950s its postwar growth was considered an economic miracle, or *Wirtschaftswunder.*

When the United States and West Germany introduced the new German mark into West Berlin, the Soviets realized that not only had the United States created a new German state, but that this state now had an outpost 110 miles inside the Soviet zone. When, during the war, the Soviets had agreed to the Allied occupation of Berlin, they did not expect a permanent Western outpost in their zone. This U.S. and West German action triggered a Soviet response. In June 1948, the Soviets attempted to force the West to abandon Berlin by closing the overland routes into West Berlin from West Germany. The Allies responded with the Berlin Airlift, an operation involving daily flights of U.S., British, and French transport planes over East Germany delivering food and other goods to the West

Berliners. For political, psychological, and practical reasons, the West was in no mood to yield.[2] When Stalin finally relented by lifting the overland blockade in May 1949, it was a tacit recognition that West Berlin would remain part of West Germany.

Once West Germany officially came into existence in 1949, its chancellor, Konrad Adenauer, doggedly pursued a policy of integrating the state into the community of West European nations. He insisted that the postwar German state develop democratic, liberal institutions under the aegis of the West. In fact, there is ample evidence to suggest that Adenauer, who came from the westernmost part of Germany—the Rhineland—and whose credentials as an opponent of the Nazi regime were impeccable, did not trust the German people. He feared that left alone, they would succumb once more to the lure of political, economic, and, in particular, military power. Germans needed to be under the lengthy tutelage of the Western democracies. A West Germany under Western control suited him and many of his compatriots just fine. In fact, in March 1952, when Stalin sought talks with the West about the possibility of establishing a neutral, unified Germany, it was Adenauer who lobbied strenuously—and successfully—with his Western allies to reject Stalin's diplomatic note without even bothering to discuss it.[3] For Adenauer, the inclusion into the company of Western nations was more important than German unification. The unification of Germany had to wait, and it had to be accomplished on Western terms.

What endeared the Roman Catholic Adenauer to the Western powers was his conservatism and staunch opposition to Communism. The West German voters, not inclined to another round of social experimentation, gave their votes to Adenauer's conservative Christian Democratic Union. *Der Alte* ("the old man") Adenauer, already seventy-three years of age at the time of his first election as chancellor, held that post until 1963 and put West Germany firmly onto its postwar path.

During Adenauer's tenure, West Germany experienced rapid economic recovery, established viable democratic institutions, and tried to come to grips with its recent past. It acknowledged Germany's responsibility for World War II and the Jewish holocaust and paid large sums in reparations to the Jewish victims. It took steps to purge the nation of its Nazi past; the Nazi Party and its symbols were outlawed, and students were taught the causes and consequences of the rise of Nazism.

When dealing with the West, Adenauer always said the right things, but he and many Germans had a more difficult time acknowledging the consequences of German actions in the East. Not only did Adenauer insist that Poland and the Soviet Union return German lands they had seized at the end of the war, but his government refused to pay reparations to the millions of Poles, Russians, and others in Eastern Europe who had worked in Nazi slave labor camps or had family members murdered. There was no opening to the East under Adenauer. Stalin had created the Iron Curtain, but politicians such as Adenauer also played a role in maintaining the partition of Europe. (For details on Adenauer's foreign policy and that of his successors with regard to Eastern Europe, see Chapter 10.)

The notion of creating a fully integrated, supranational union of Europe—a "United States of Europe"—faded as the emotional idealism generated by the war gradually gave way in the postwar period to a more realistic and pragmatic approach toward integration. In May 1948, some 750 political leaders met at The Hague to create the Council of Europe, designed to be a permanent European assembly. However, this organization floundered from the beginning largely because Britain objected to joining a supranational integration of Europe. At Britain's insistence, the Council's Assembly was not given legislative authority, and its only decisionmaking body, the Council of Ministers, was comprised of the foreign ministers of the member states. As such it was merely the sounding board for each nation's interests. The failure of this attempt at European political integration was signaled by the resignation of its first president, the Belgian foreign minister, Paul-Henri Spaak, in 1951. When he resigned, Spaak, one of the Council's founders and ardent supporters, strongly denounced the nationalism of those who obstructed its efforts to achieve a meaningful integration of Europe. Although the idea of European political integration was revived from time to time thereafter, the only significant progress toward European unity in the early postwar era was the creation of a set of economic and military organizations, which addressed more pragmatic concerns.

Western European economic integration had its beginnings in the Marshall Plan, the U.S. economic aid program announced in June 1947, which was intended primarily to rescue Europe from the economic devastation of the war. However, insofar as the Marshall Plan was rejected by Moscow for all of Eastern Europe, the aid and the integrative impact of the program was limited to Western Europe.

After the initial impulse from the Marshall Plan, the countries of Western Europe took bold steps toward greater economic integration. In May 1950, France proposed the creation of a European Coal and Steel Community, and in April 1951 six nations—France, West Germany, Italy, and the Benelux countries (Belgium, the Netherlands, and Luxembourg)—signed a treaty establishing this joint venture. This program, designed primarily by the French economist Jean Monnet and French Foreign Minister Robert Schuman, called for the pooling of the coal and steel resources of the member nations. It created a High Authority, which on the basis of majority vote was empowered to make decisions regulating production and development of coal and steel in the six countries. In effect, it internationalized the highly industrialized Saar and Ruhr regions of West Germany. Not only did this program eliminate a source of national contention and greatly raise production, but it was considered at the time as the platform on which to build both the economic and political integration of Europe.

So well did the integrated coal and steel program work that in 1955 the same six nations decided to form a European Economic Community (EEC), and in March 1957 they signed the Treaty of Rome, which brought this more comprehensive organization formally into existence on January 1, 1958. In addition to coordinating economic production, the EEC (commonly referred to as the Common Market) established a customs union, which involved the lowering of tariffs among the member states and the erecting of one common tariff rate on imports from outside countries. This easing of trade restrictions greatly increased the flow of goods, which in turn stimulated production, provided jobs, and increased personal income and consumption. Thus, the Common Market contributed significantly to the economic growth and higher standards of living of its member states, and it allowed Europe to reemerge as one of the thriving economic regions of the world. In fact, the economic growth rate of the Common Market countries surpassed that of the United States by the end of the 1940s and remained significantly higher for many years thereafter.

Great Britain did not share in the benefits of the Common Market because it initially chose not to join. Britain already enjoyed the benefits of a preferential tariff system within its own community of nations—the Commonwealth—and it could not reconcile its Commonwealth trade interests with those of its European neighbors in the Common Market. Other reasons for Britain's rejection of the Common Market included its conservative inclination to retain the old order rather than join in the creation of a new one, its reliance on its strong ties with the United States and Commonwealth friends, and its reluctance to give up a measure of its national sovereignty to a supranational body whose decisions were binding on member nations. However, after both its economy and its international status faltered in the 1950s, Britain saw fit in 1961 to apply for membership in the Common Market, only to find that admission now was not for the mere asking. The issue of Britain's entry was hotly debated both within Britain, where the Labour Party opposed it, and in France, where President Charles de Gaulle had his own terms for British admission. After over a year of deliberation, de Gaulle, who had attempted in vain to draw Britain into a European military pact, suddenly announced in January 1963 his firm opposition to British membership in the Common Market. Since voting within the Common Market structure was not by majority but required unanimity—a point de Gaulle insisted upon—the French president's veto unilaterally kept Britain out. When Britain renewed its application to join the Common Market in 1966, de Gaulle—who was critical of Britain's close political and economic ties with the United States and with the Commonwealth nations in other parts of the world—still objected, and it was only after de Gaulle's resignation as president of France in 1969 that Britain gained entry. Although the heads of the six Common Market states declared their approval of Britain's entry in December 1969, negotiations among them and the British government were protracted by technical complications, and it was not until January 1973 that Britain (together with Denmark and Ireland) finally entered the Common Market.[4]

The success of the Common Market revived the hopes of some of its members for achieving political as well as economic integration, and efforts were made to make use of its organizational machinery for that purpose. From its inception there existed a division between the "supranationalists," who desired total integration, and the "federalists," who wished to retain for each nation essential decisionmaking power. Within the Common Market structure the primary decisionmaking body was its Council of Ministers, comprised of the foreign ministers of member states. It voted on proposals brought to it by the Commission, an elected body made up of delegations from each of the member nations according to their size. Since decisions on key issues were binding for all member states, certain members (most notably France and later Britain) insisted on consensus rather than majority voting on such issues. Also, within the EEC structure was the European Parliament (located in Strasbourg, France), a deliberative body that best represented the supranationalist interests, but this body was given only a consultative role. Because it had no power over decisions made by the executive branch of the EEC, it remained toothless and thus was not an effective vehicle for political integration.

■ NATO: THE MILITARY INTEGRATION OF WESTERN EUROPE

While the efforts to achieve meaningful political integration did not achieve results commensurate with the progress toward the economic integration of Western Europe, more was accomplished in the realm of military affairs. But here, too, efforts to bring about an integrated military establishment ran up against formidable obstacles. Nonetheless, a significant degree of military coordination, if not unity, was achieved. Once again the main obstacle to military integration was the force of nationalism, especially as personified by France's Charles de Gaulle.

In April 1949, the United States took the lead in the formation of the North Atlantic Treaty Organization (NATO) as a collective security system for Western Europe and North America. It was the military equivalent of the Marshall Plan, designed to extend U.S. protection to its allies in Western Europe. The ten European countries that originally joined NATO (Britain, France, Iceland, Norway, Denmark, Belgium, the Netherlands, Luxembourg, Portugal, and Italy), with the United States and Canada, attained a twenty-year guarantee of their security against attack by the Soviet Union. Ultimately, it brought U.S. air power and nuclear weapons to bear as the primary means to prevent the Soviet Union from using its large land forces against West Germany or any of the member states. Each of the NATO nations was to contribute ground forces to a collective army under a unified command.

The first serious question facing NATO was whether to include West Germany. Its territory was covered by the initial NATO security guarantee, but it was not a treaty member; in fact, it was still under Allied military occupation until 1952 and had no armed forces of its own. As early as 1950, after the outbreak of the Korean War, U.S. officials began to encourage the rearmament of Germany and integration of its forces into NATO. But the French and other Europeans, fearing the return of German militarism, were reluctant to see the rearmament of Germany. As an alternative, France proposed in 1952 the creation of the European Defense Community (EDC), a genuinely integrated military force in which German soldiers could serve together with those from other European countries in multinational units placed under a multinational European command center. For four years the EDC was under debate among the NATO members, but ultimately it failed mainly because of Britain's refusal to join it and France's own opposition to an EDC without Britain.

The fear of a reappearance of German militarism was, however, overshadowed by the fear of Soviet aggression. Moreover, German troops were badly needed to beef up the under-strength NATO ground forces. Therefore, at the urging of the United States, Britain, and West Germany itself, the NATO members agreed by the end of 1954 on West Germany's entry into NATO—on the conditions that it supply twelve divisions of ground forces and that it be prohibited from the development of nuclear, bacteriological, and chemical weapons; warships; or long-range missiles and bombers.

The Soviet Union, too, opposed the rearmament of Germany and it made an eleventh-hour attempt to block West Germany's entry into NATO. In March 1952, Stalin proposed the immediate and total evacuation of all occupation forces from Germany—East and West—the reunification of Germany, and the creation of a security pact to defend it as a neutral nation. It is idle to speculate whether such a generous proposal would have received a better reception in Western capitals had it been made earlier, but the plan was rejected out of hand as a Soviet propaganda ploy aimed merely at disrupting the strengthening of the Western military alliance.

In its first decade, the weak link in the NATO collective security system was France, which lacked political stability until the emergence of Gen. Charles de Gaulle as president of the newly established Fifth French Republic in 1958. France was unable to supply its share of ground troops to NATO because they were needed first in Indochina and later in Algeria where France was engaged in struggles to retain its colonial empire. The new French president was intent on cutting France's losses abroad and regaining for France a dominant position in Europe. De Gaulle, France's great World War II hero and always the supreme nationalist, wished to re-make Europe in his own way. His vision of a powerful Europe was not one of political integration as suggested by the Common Market, but rather an association of strong nations. He was staunchly opposed to any notion of supranationalism, for his real objective was to elevate the role of France in a reinvigorated Europe. His determined pursuit of French domination of the new Europe was the cardinal point of what came to be called Gaullism.[5]

De Gaulle's boldly assertive nationalism was also reflected in his view of the security needs of France (and Europe). Because he sought the strengthening of the posture of France within Europe and the reassertion of European power in global affairs, de Gaulle wished to put the United States at a greater distance from Europe. He felt that Europe, especially NATO, had been dominated in the postwar period by the United States and, secondarily, by its closest ally, Great Britain. Specifically, de Gaulle questioned the commitment of the United States to the defense of Europe and, therefore, he considered NATO to be flawed. He thought that, while the United States might enter a nuclear war in defense of its West Euro-pean allies if they came under a nuclear attack from the Soviet Union, it

French President Charles de Gaulle and visiting U.S. President John F. Kennedy, Paris, June 2, 1961. (*National Archives*)

could not be counted on to risk its own destruction in nuclear warfare in order to defend Western Europe from an invasion by conventional ground forces. After rejecting a U.S. offer to place nuclear weapons in France, de Gaulle went ahead with the development of France's own nuclear arsenal, its *force de frappe*, or "strike force." Not only did he wish to enhance France's international prestige by joining the exclusive club of nuclear powers, but his idea was that, even if France's nuclear force were far smaller than that of the superpowers, it still might serve as a deterrent. In the 1960s, de Gaulle turned a deaf ear to foreign critics who castigated France for its refusal to join other major powers in signing a series of nuclear arms control agreements and for its refusal to halt its atomic bomb testing program in the Pacific Ocean.

Charles de Gaulle persistently challenged U.S. leadership of the Western alliance as he sought to assert France's independence. In 1964, he broke ranks with the United States by extending diplomatic recognition to the People's Republic of China. Later, in 1966, de Gaulle again challenged U.S. dominance of the Western alliance when he decided to withdraw all French troops from NATO (although he did not formally withdraw France from the NATO alliance) and when he called for the withdrawal of all U.S. forces from French soil. French security, the general insisted, must remain in French hands.

De Gaulle disliked the confrontational approach taken by the United States in the Cold War, especially in the 1962 Cuban missile crisis (to be discussed later), and he did not want to be left out of diplomatic meetings between the superpowers where decisions might be made affecting the security and interests of France. He sought to counter U.S. Cold War diplomacy and its domination of the Western allies by conducting his own diplomacy with the Soviet Union and Communist China, and by strengthening France's ties with the most powerful continental West European state, West Germany.

The *entente* (understanding) between France and West Germany was achieved by the political skill of de Gaulle and West Germany's aged chancellor, Konrad Adenauer. After Adenauer accepted an invitation to meet with de Gaulle in Paris in July 1962, de Gaulle made a triumphant tour of West Germany two months later. This exchange of visits was followed by the signing of a Franco-German treaty aimed at strengthening their relations and thereby making it the cornerstone of Western European solidarity. This act served to check the Anglo-U.S. domination of the Western alliance, but it did not result in putting greater distance between West Germany and the United States, as de Gaulle had wished. It did, however, symbolize the marked improvement in the postwar era of the relations between these two major European nations, which had been hostile for so long.

■ EAST EUROPEAN INTEGRATION

In Eastern Europe, Moscow had its own program of political and economic integration. What had begun in 1944–1945 as a military occupation by the Red Army shortly became a social, political, and economic revolution with Stalin's Soviet Union serving as the model. In 1949, in response to the Marshall Plan, Stalin's foreign minister, Viacheslav Molotov, introduced the Council of Mutual Economic Aid, commonly known as COMECON. Its purpose was to integrate the economies of the East European nations of Poland, Hungary, Romania, Czechoslovakia, and Bulgaria (and later Albania) with that of the Soviet Union. It was designed to aid in the postwar reconstruction of the Soviet Union and in the industrial development of Eastern Europe, which was still largely an agricultural region. It also supplemented the Kremlin's political control of Eastern Europe by giving it an economic lever.

The transformation of the East European economies took place along Soviet lines. The emphasis was on heavy and war industries, with consumer goods taking a back seat. Expropriation decrees, issued as early as September 1944 in Poland, led to the confiscation of the estates of nobles and the churches. These measures eliminated the "landlord" classes and paved the way for collectivization of agriculture.

The economic transformation of Eastern Europe was accompanied by sweeping political changes. In Bulgaria, Albania, Yugoslavia, and Romania the monarchies were officially abolished. Moscow's East European satellites followed the Soviet example by adopting constitutions similar to Stalin's Constitution of 1936. Everywhere, parties in opposition to the new political order were declared illegal.

The dominant force in Eastern Europe since the end of World War II was the Soviet Army, augmented by the forces of the new socialist regimes. In 1955, the Soviet Union, ostensibly in response to the inclusion of West Germany into NATO, created its own military alliance, the Warsaw Treaty Organization, commonly known as the Warsaw Pact. Its membership included Albania, Bulgaria, Czechoslovakia, East Germany, Hungary, Poland, Romania, and the Soviet Union. Unlike NATO, its members did not have the right to withdraw from the organization, an act the Kremlin considered the supreme political sin its satellites could commit. Albania, by virtue of its geographic position and relative lack of importance, did manage to leave the Warsaw Pact in 1968, but Hungary's flirtation with neutrality in 1956 met with an attack by the Soviet Army. When Czechoslovakia in 1968 and Poland in the early 1980s moved dangerously close to a position similar to that of Hungary in 1956, the Soviet leadership made it clear that it would not tolerate the disintegration of its military alliance.

The most interesting manifestation of the force of nationalism in Eastern Europe was that of Romania, which since the mid-1960s sought to carve out a measure of independence from Moscow. Under the leadership of Nicolai Ceausescu, the Romanian Communist Party successfully maneuvered to secure a limited economic and political independence, particularly in its dealings with Western Europe. Over the years, Ceausescu rejected his nation's role in agricultural and petrochemical production as allocated by COMECON, retained diplomatic ties with Israel after all other East European nations had broken relations with Israel in the wake of the 1967 "Six Day" war (see Chapter 7), refused to participate in Warsaw Pact maneuvers, maintained correct relations with the People's Republic of China at a time of ever-increasing hostility between Moscow and Beijing, gave warm receptions to visiting U.S. presidents, and sent his athletes to the 1984 Olympic Games in Los Angeles in defiance of the Soviet boycott of the games. Throughout, the Kremlin cast a wary eye on the Romanian maverick but refrained from taking drastic action. After all, there was no pressing need to discipline Ceausescu since he remained a loyal member of the Soviet Union's military alliance and, perhaps even more important, he showed absolutely no tendency toward any sort of political reform. Moscow always considered political reform in Prague and Warsaw as a greater threat to its hegemony in Eastern Europe than Ceausescu's actions, which, although an irritant, did not pose a major problem. As long as Ceausescu retained the most harshly repressive political system in Eastern Europe, the Kremlin was willing to tolerate his unorthodox behavior in certain matters.

Despite the Kremlin's insistence on maintaining its hegemony over Eastern Europe, the forces of nationalism repeatedly made it clear that Eastern Europe contained restless populations with whom the Kremlin's control did not sit easily. In the face of repeated Soviet pronouncements that considered Eastern Europe a closed issue (notably General Secretary Leonid Brezhnev's statement in 1968 that the Soviet Union's defensive borders were at the Elbe River separating East and West Germany), the region remained a potentially volatile problem.

■ THE FIRST ATTEMPTS AT DÉTENTE

The Korean War, one of the most dangerous moments in the Cold War, brought about the remilitarization of both the United States and the Soviet Union. Immediately upon the conclusion of World War II, the two nations had reduced their armed forces despite the shrill accusations in Washington and Moscow focusing on the evil intentions of the other. U.S. intelligence records show that a Soviet attack was not in the cards—unless an uncontrolled chain of events led to miscalculations on the part of the leaders

EUROPE (1990)

in the Kremlin. By early 1947, U.S. forces had dwindled from a wartime strength of 12 million to fewer than 1 million soldiers under arms. Because of this reduction, Western Europe was exposed to a possible assault by the Soviet Army. If that occurred, U.S. troops in Western Europe were under orders not to fight but to find the quickest way across the English Channel.

But the Soviets showed no inclination to initiate World War III on the heels of the just-concluded, bloody conflict. Stalin reduced the Soviet Army to its prewar level of about 3.5 million soldiers, much of the Soviet Union was in ruins and in need of rehabilitation, and there was always the U.S. trump card, the atomic bomb. If the leaders in Washington did not consider it likely that Stalin would direct his armed forces across the Iron Curtain, similarly, those in the Kremlin did not contemplate a U.S. attack. For the next five years the protagonists maintained their forces at a level just sufficient to repel a potential attack. But by 1950 the arguments were in place to transform the political Cold War into a military confrontation. The Korean War proved to be the catalyst for this transformation.

In the United States in April 1950, nine weeks prior to the outbreak of the war in Korea, National Security Council directive NSC-68 recommended to President Truman a drastic increase in the military budget. The prospects of attaining this were slim, for popular sentiment was against it. Yet, the opportunity to implement NSC-68 came in June 1950 when, according to Secretary of State Dean Acheson, "Korea came along and saved us."[6]

In the Soviet Union a similar process was taking place. Stalin long ago had demanded unity and sacrifice from his people. In the late 1940s, he renewed his insistence that the socialist, Soviet fatherland must be defended at all cost. There could be no deviation from this principle. A renewed emphasis on ideological rigidity and conformity became the order of the day, and with it purges of individuals suspected of ideological nonconformity. When the war in Korea broke out, Stalin rapidly increased the size of the Red Army from 3.5 million to about 5 million troops, the approximate level the Soviet armed forces retained until the late 1980s. The five-year period during which both sides had reduced their armed forces and curtailed their military expenditures was at an end. Both sides began to think that, if diplomacy and compromise could not resolve the issues, perhaps elemental force could.

Truman's retirement from political life took place in January 1953, and Stalin's death came six weeks later. The exit of the two chief combatants in the Cold War made it possible for the new leaders to try a different tack, for they were not locked into the old positions to the same degree their predecessors had been. (In late 1952, there had been a brief flurry of speculation that Stalin and Truman might meet for the first time since 1945. Nothing came of it for apparently they had nothing to talk about.)

President Dwight Eisenhower and the new Soviet Premier Nikita Khrushchev, who had emerged as one of the Soviet Union's leading figures by September 1953, began a dialogue that resulted in the lessening of tensions. It was in this context that the word "détente" (relaxing the strain) first entered the vocabulary of the Cold War.[7] Eisenhower, the hero of World War II, had no need to establish his anti-Communist credentials. He had, therefore, greater latitude in dealing with the Soviets than did Harry Truman or his secretary of state, Dean Acheson, whom the Republicans (notably Joseph McCarthy and Richard Nixon) had berated time and again for being "soft on Communism." There was nothing they could do to shake off the Republican charges and, in fact, McCarthy had gone far beyond charging Truman with a lack of vigilance. He went so far as to allege that Truman's State Department was filled with Communist subversives.

Khrushchev and his colleagues began to move away from the Stalinist pattern of conduct at home and abroad shortly after they buried Stalin. Khrushchev was determined to avoid a military showdown with the West and declared, by dusting off an old Leninist phrase, that "peaceful coexistence" with the West was possible. With it he rejected the thesis of the inevitability of war between the socialist and capitalist camps.

At Geneva in 1954, the great powers convened to deal with the central problems of the day. The more relaxed climate, the "Spirit of Geneva," made possible the disengagement of the occupying powers from Austria. It proved to be the first political settlement of any significance by the belligerents of the Cold War.[8] In May 1955, Austria, under four-power occupation since the end of the war, gained its independence as a neutral state. Austria became a nonaligned buffer in the heart of Europe, separating the armies of the two superpowers. The Iron Curtain shifted eastward, to the borders of Czechoslovakia and Hungary. Western and Soviet troops thus disengaged along a line of about 200 miles. In return, Austria pledged its neutrality in the Cold War, a condition that suited the Austrian temperament perfectly. In particular, Austria was not to join in any alliance—particularly military or economic—with West Germany. Austria quickly became a meeting ground between East and West. Its capital city, Vienna, became a neutral site for great-power meetings—a city with one of the largest concentrations of foreign spies in the world.

A solution similar to the Austrian settlement had earlier been envisioned for Germany. But in contrast to Austria, by 1955 two Germanies already existed. Austria's good fate was that at the end of the war it was treated not as a conquered, but a liberated nation. Also, it had a relatively small population of just over 7 million and was insignificant as an economic and military power. Yet, the latter may be said of Korea and Vietnam, while no political solution was ever found for these nations. One of the main reasons why a solution for Austria ultimately proved to be feasible was Stalin's unilateral action in April 1945. He appointed the moderate socialist Karl Renner as the new head of Austria and in this fashion Austria, unlike Germany, Korea, and Vietnam, was from the very beginning under one government, which all of the occupying powers eventually recognized. Churchill and Truman were unhappy with Stalin's action, not because they objected to Renner, but because it was unilateral, high-handed, and accomplished without their consultation. Nevertheless, they grudgingly accepted Stalin's choice. Renner then proceeded to guide his nation carefully on a middle course between the superpowers. When the time came to disengage in 1955, Austria already had a neutral government ten years in existence. The German experience had been quite different. At the end of the war the Allies had spoken of creating a German government that all sides could accept but it never happened.

The partial rapprochement between the United States and the Soviet Union made possible Nikita Khrushchev's visit to the United States in 1959. Khrushchev's itinerary took him to New York City, a farm in Iowa, Los Angeles, and the presidential retreat of Camp David in the hills of western Maryland, where he and Eisenhower conferred in private. The "Spirit of Camp David" produced recommendations for disarmament and a decision for the two men to meet again at a summit meeting in Paris in May 1960, to be followed by an Eisenhower visit to the Soviet Union.

The Austrian settlement and talks between the heads of state did not mean that the Cold War was over. Nor did it mean that a process of disengagement had begun. Détente was always tempered by a heavy residue of mistrust and a continued reliance on military might. (The leadership in Washington and Moscow was always divided on which approach to take— diplomacy or force.) At the high-point of détente in the 1950s, the Cassandras were always in the wings warning of dire consequences.

The Soviets spoke of peaceful coexistence—as they called détente— but the ideological struggle and the preservation of the empire continued. Nikita Khrushchev always had his critics at home, particularly the old Stalinist, Viacheslav Molotov, who remained foreign minister until Khrushchev replaced him in 1956.[9] Détente did not mean, therefore, the abandonment of influence and power. The Soviets were unwilling to abandon an inch of territory within what they considered their sphere of influence vital to their security. When they were challenged in Eastern Europe they did not hesitate to act. They quickly suppressed rebellions in East Germany in 1953 and in Hungary in 1956. The empire, the Soviet bloc, remained one and indivisible.

A similar conflict between détente and Cold War aspirations was also evident in the United States. The Republican president, Eisenhower, pursued the high road of compromise and negotiations; his secretary of state, John Foster Dulles, was an uncompromising anti-Communist. Dulles went beyond the stands his Democratic predecessors (Dean Acheson and George Marshall) had taken. Containment of the Soviet Union was not enough, for it suggested tolerance of an evil, godless system. To Dulles, the Cold War was not merely a struggle between two contending economic and political orders; it was also a clash between religion and atheism. Dulles, therefore, proposed the "rollback" of the Soviet Union's forward position and the "liberation" of lands under Communist rule. Officially, U.S. foreign policy abandoned what had been a defensive position, and took on a "new look," an offensive character.[10] But as events showed, particularly in Hungary in 1956, it is the president who ultimately determines foreign policy, and Eisenhower had no desire to start World War III by challenging the Soviets in their sphere. Despite Dulles's rhetoric, U.S. foreign policy had to settle for containment.

Dulles acted vigorously to preserve and protect the U.S. presence throughout the world. When in 1954 the Communist Viet Minh of Vietnam triumphed over the French, he moved to preserve the southern half of that country for the Western camp. When the United States felt its interests threatened in Iran in 1953 and in Guatemala in 1954, the CIA, under the guidance of Allen Dulles, John Foster's brother, quickly moved into covert action and accomplished some of its most successful coups. In Iran, the CIA returned the shah to power when it engineered the overthrow of Premier Mohammed Mossadegh, who had sought to nationalize the nation's oil industry in order to take it out of the hands of British and U.S. companies. In Guatemala, the CIA replaced the socialist Jacobo Arbenz, who had proposed the nationalization of lands held by U.S. corporations, with a military junta.[11]

■ MOSCOW'S RESPONSE
TO CONTAINMENT

In the mid-1950s, the Kremlin's foreign policy underwent a significant transformation when Khrushchev took the first steps to negate the U.S.-led system of alliances designed to contain the Soviet Union. Until that time the country had resembled a beleaguered fortress, defying what it perceived to be an aggressive West, a view not without foundation. The United States was in the process of implementing one of the provisions of NSC-68, the creation of regional alliances directed against the Soviet Union. In 1954, the United States created the Southeast Asia Treaty Organization (SEATO) and in 1955, the Baghdad Pact. In conjunction with NATO and its military ties in the Far East (South Korea, Japan, and Taiwan), the United States was about to close a ring around the Soviet Union.

The Baghdad Pact was intended to be a Middle Eastern alliance, consisting largely of Arab states, led by the United States and Great Britain. Yet, the only Arab state to join was Iraq; the other members were Turkey, Pakistan, and Iran. In March 1955, Egypt's Gamal Abdel Nasser created an Arab alliance, which included Syria and Saudi Arabia, to counter the West's influence in the Middle East. In this fashion, Nasser sought to establish his independence from the West. Nasser's act of defiance and his anti-Western rhetoric contributed to the rapid deterioration of relations. The United States sought to bring Nasser to heel by withdrawing its funding for the Aswan High Dam on the upper Nile. Nasser then turned to the Soviet Union to complete the dam. By that time he had already concluded an arms agreement with the Soviet Union (its first with a non-Communist state). When, in the summer of 1956, Nasser nationalized the Suez Canal, which had been in British hands since 1887,[12] the stage was set for a re-taliatory strike by the West. In October 1956, France and Britain joined Israel in an attack on Egypt (see Chapter 7). The Cold War once again had spilled over into the Third World.

In 1954, when Kremlin leaders began to take the first steps in arming a client beyond the Communist world,[13] this change in Soviet foreign policy did not come without intense debate in the high echelons of the Soviet Union's ruling circle. From the end of World War II until Stalin's death, the Soviet Union had conducted a relatively conservative foreign policy. To be sure, Stalin had refused to yield to the West on a number of central issues, notably Eastern Europe, but he had not challenged the West outside the confines of his own empire. The successful Communist insurgencies in Vietnam and China, for instance, had not been of his making. Stalin had dug into his fortress behind his massive land army. Shortly after Stalin's death, the CIA, in a special report to President Eisenhower and the National Security Council, described Stalin as a man "ruthless and determined to spread Soviet power," who nevertheless "did not allow his ambitions to lead him to reckless courses of action in his foreign policy." The CIA warned, however, that Stalin's successors might not be as cautious.[14]

Events quickly bore out the CIA's prediction. In 1954, a bitter debate took place in the Kremlin over the nation's foreign policy. One faction, led by Prime Minister Georgi Malenkov and Foreign Minister Viacheslav Molotov, urged caution, favoring a continuation of the Stalinist pattern of defiance and rearmament. The majority in the Presidium of the Central Committee of the party, led by Nikita Khrushchev, who was the first secretary of the party and thus its leader, argued for a more active foreign policy, calling for a breakout from what they called capitalist encirclement.[15] This argument stressed that those who accept the status quo and merely stand still will suffer defeat at the hands of the capitalists. (Interestingly, this position echoed that of John Foster Dulles, who could not tolerate the mere containment of the foe. The conflict, both sides argued, must be taken to the enemy.)

Molotov and his allies warned that involvement in the Middle East was bound to fail. After all, British and U.S. navies controlled the Mediterranean Sea and were bound to stop all shipments, as the United States had intercepted a Czechoslovak arms shipment to Guatemala earlier in 1954. But Khrushchev and his faction prevailed and the Soviet Union began early in 1955 to arm Nasser in secret, a *fait accompli* revealed to the world later that year.

In return for its support of Nasser, the Soviet Union obtained a client in the Middle East, and it was thus able partially to offset the effects of the Baghdad Pact.[16] For the first time the Soviet Union was able to establish a foothold in a region beyond the Communist world. The person largely responsible for this significant departure in Soviet foreign policy and who reaped handsome political dividends at home was Nikita Khrushchev. He had begun to challenge the West in what had formerly been a Western preserve. The monopoly of Western influence in the Third World was no more. It marked the beginning of a contest for the hearts and minds of the nonaligned world. With this in mind, Khrushchev undertook in 1955 a much-publicized journey to South Asia. He visited India and on his way home stopped in Kabul, the capital city of Afghanistan, to forestall apparent U.S. designs on that country. "It was . . . clear that America was courting Afghanistan," Khrushchev charged in his memoirs. The U.S. penetration of that country had "the obvious purpose of setting up a military base."[17] In 1960, Khrushchev paid a second visit to Asia. Eisenhower, concerned with the growing Soviet influence in southern Asia, followed in 1960 in Khrushchev's footsteps when he visited India and several other nonaligned nations.

In May 1960, relations between the Soviet Union and the United States took a sudden turn for the worse when a U.S. spy plane, a U-2, was shot down deep inside the Soviet Union. The Soviet Rocket Force Command had finally been able to bring down one of the high-flying U.S. spy planes, which had periodically violated Soviet air space since 1956. This event wrecked the summit between Khrushchev and Eisenhower later that month, and it canceled Eisenhower's scheduled goodwill visit to the Soviet Union. Khrushchev's vehement denunciation of Eisenhower overstepped the boundaries of both common sense and good manners.[18] Western historians have often speculated that Khrushchev had to placate the hard-liners at home who had never been happy with his rapprochement with the West.

The year 1960 was also a presidential election year in the United States. Presidential election campaigns have never been known for elevated discussions of the issues, and this was no exception. The "outs," in this case John Kennedy and his Democratic Party, accused the "ins," Richard Nixon (Eisenhower's vice-president) and the Republicans, of having fallen asleep on their watch. The Soviets had (supposedly) opened up a "missile gap" that endangered the security of the United States. The Cold War was back in full bloom.

■ **THE CUBAN MISSILE CRISIS**

The division of Europe and its integration into two distinct blocs was both the result of the Cold War and a source of the continuation of the conflict. The belligerents continued to arm for a military showdown that neither wanted. The main feature of the Cold War during the 1950s was the arms race, both conventional and nuclear. In conventional forces, the Soviet bloc always held the lead, while the West relied primarily upon the U.S. nuclear umbrella. The U.S. nuclear monopoly, however, was short-lived. In 1949 the Soviet Union tested its first atomic weapon; in the early 1950s it exploded its first thermonuclear bomb; and in 1955 it obtained the capability of delivering these weapons by means of intercontinental bombers. By the end of the 1950s, both Washington and Moscow had successfully tested intercontinental missiles. The stage was set for the escalation of the arms race and the dangers inherent in it.

The Cold War reached its most dangerous stage in a most unlikely place. It was over Cuba in 1962 that the first and only direct nuclear confrontation between the United States and the Soviet Union took place. The showdown came in the wake of the Cuban revolution of the late 1950s, a revolution by which Fidel Castro took Cuba out of the U.S. orbit and gave it a new political and economic direction. Castro's revolution made Cuba another arena for the superpowers.

Castro's direct challenge to the existing Cuban order and its president, Fulgencio Batista, began on July 26, 1953, when he led an unsuccessful attack on the Moncada army barracks. He spent eighteen months in prison and then went to Mexico, only to return to Cuba for a second attempt in December 1956. On May 28, 1957, Castro and his band of eighty guerrillas scored a significant psychological victory with an attack on the garrison at Uvero. For the next year and a half, Castro's forces, which never numbered more than 300 guerrillas under arms, remained in the field as a

Soviet leader Nikita Khrushchev and Cuban President Fidel Castro, at the United Nations, New York, Nov. 1960. (*National Archives*)

visible challenge to the bankrupt Batista government, which at the end could count on no one to come to its defense. Because of Castro's small force and the fact that Batista's support rapidly began to crumble, the revolution never did reach the magnitude of a civil war in the proper sense of the word. Castro himself admitted that had Batista enjoyed a measure of popular support, his (Castro's) revolution would have been easily crushed. Instead, whatever support Batista had melted away and on January 1, 1959, Castro and his small band triumphantly entered Havana. Batista then fled the country. It was not that Castro had won political power, but that Batista had lost it.

Castro was by no means the first Cuban to seize power by force, but he certainly was the first to take steps to challenge the unequal relationship between the United States and his country, one which had been in existence since the days of the Spanish-American War of 1898 when the United States gained a foothold in Cuba. Castro demanded the nationalization of U.S. property in Cuba and its transfer into Cuban hands. At first Castro appeared to be willing to offer compensation to U.S. companies, but not at the high level that the U.S. businesses demanded. The result was a deadlock with severe repercussions. It was not so much the differences in opinion over the value of U.S. property as it was ideological principles that led to the impasse. The United States became the champion of the right to private property of U.S. citizens in Cuba; Castro became the defender of Cuban national sovereignty.

Shortly, high-ranking U.S. officials in the Eisenhower administration became convinced that Castro was a Communist. At what point he did in fact become a Communist is difficult to say. His brother Raul had long been a Communist. Castro's conversion apparently came sometime after the revolution. The United States had dealt successfully (that is, forcefully) with radical Latin American leaders before, most recently in Guatemala in 1954; it now took steps to put pressure on Castro.

Thus far, events in Cuba had paralleled those in Guatemala in 1954, after Jacobo Arbenz had won an electoral victory. President Arbenz had proceeded to take steps to limit the power of foreign corporations, notably that of the United Fruit Company, a U.S. concern, which owned 10 percent of the nation's land. Arbenz nationalized uncultivated land and supported strikes against foreign businesses. The U.S. secretary of state, John Foster Dulles, raised the specter of Communism, but he obtained no support of his interpretation of events from other Latin American nations. The actions of Arbenz did not sit well with Dulles or his brother Allen, the director of the CIA. They decided to act for reasons of national security, ideology, and the fact that both owned stock in the United Fruit Company and had previously provided legal services for the company. The Dulles brothers went into action. The CIA organized and outfitted disaffected elements of the Guatemalan army. The successful coup took place in June 1954.[19] For

Washington, the crisis was over. For Guatemala, a succession of military regimes—some of them of extraordinary brutality—became the order of the day until the mid-1990s.

There was little reason to believe that the United States could not repeat the Guatemalan scenario and reestablish its economic and political position in Cuba. The first weapon Washington employed was economic; if needed, other weapons would be employed later. The United States closed its market to Cuba's main source of income, the export of sugar cane. The U.S. market previously had taken half of Cuba's exports and provided nearly three-quarters of its imports. Predictably, the U.S. trade embargo had severe repercussions on the Cuban economy.

At this point events began to move rapidly. Castro refused to yield to U.S. pressure. Instead, he turned to the Soviet Union for economic, political, and military support. Also, he saw his revolution as a model for other revolutionaries throughout Latin America and as such he posed a direct challenge to U.S. hegemony in Latin America. His reform program at home acquired a Marxist flavor and it resulted in the exodus of thousands of Cubans who opposed the accompanying political and economic restrictions and sweeping changes. They settled mainly in Florida, waiting to return to their native land. In March 1960, a frustrated Eisenhower administration turned the Cuban problem over to the CIA and subsequently to the new president, John Kennedy.

Cuba became Kennedy's first foreign policy adventure. In the spring of 1961, Allen Dulles assured Kennedy that Castro could be removed with little difficulty. After all, the CIA had dealt with similar problems before and had handled them successfully. Dulles then put together a plan for Cuba. It called for Cuban exiles, trained and supplied by the CIA, to land on the beaches of Cuba and call upon the Cuban population to rise up against Castro. The plan was based on the assumption that the Marxist regime of Cuba had no popular support and would collapse. All that was needed was a push and the corrupt house of cards would come down.

President Kennedy decided to put the CIA plan into operation in April 1961. But something went wrong. The population did not rise against Castro and his armed forces destroyed the force of 1,500 Cuban exiles who had landed on the beaches of the Bay of Pigs. It was all over in forty-eight hours. A vague understanding between the CIA and the Cuban exiles had led the exiles to believe that the United States would not abandon them on the beaches. They expected direct U.S. military intervention in case they ran into difficulty. When Kennedy did not respond militarily to the fiasco at the Bay of Pigs, many Cubans in the United States felt betrayed. But Kennedy never had contemplated the need for such a contingency. Moreover, such an action would have been in violation of international law and promised international and domestic repercussions. Kennedy had planned only for a covert operation.

Kennedy, stung by this defeat, blamed Allen Dulles for the fiasco. Castro's Cuba then became an obsession with him. Three days after the Bay of Pigs, Kennedy offered Castro a warning: "Let the record show that our restraint is not inexhaustible. . . . I want it clearly understood that this Government will not hesitate in meeting its primary obligations which are to the security of our Nation."[20] Kennedy's obsession, coupled with domestic politics and questions of national security, made it difficult for him to accept the presence of Castro in nearby Cuba.

The Soviet Union could do little to aid Castro. It could not readily challenge the United States in the Caribbean in an attempt to protect a client. The United States enjoyed a vast naval superiority, particularly in the Gulf of Mexico, not to mention a large advantage in delivery systems of nuclear weapons. When John Kennedy entered the White House, the United States possessed over 100 intercontinental and intermediate-range ballistic missiles, 80 submarine-launched missiles, 1,700 intercontinental bombers, 300 nuclear-armed airplanes on aircraft carriers, and 1,000 land-based fighters with nuclear weapons. In contrast, the Soviets possessed 50 intercontinental ballistic missiles, 150 intercontinental bombers, and an additional 400 intermediate-range missiles capable of reaching U.S. overseas bases.[21]

In the presidential election of 1960, Kennedy had charged that the Eisenhower administration had been responsible for a "missile gap" to the detriment of the United States. But that political myth was laid to rest shortly after Kennedy became president. In October 1961, Deputy Secretary of Defense Roswell Gilpatric announced that there was no missile gap; on the contrary, there was a gap favoring the United States. "We have a second-strike capability," Gilpatric stated, "which is at least as extensive as what the Soviets can deliver by striking first."[22]

The Soviet premier, Nikita Khrushchev, understood this all too well. His boasts of Soviet military might had only masked the reality. There seemed to be little he could do about this state of affairs. But one day in 1962, a solution came to him in a flash. He reasoned that if he could establish a Soviet nuclear presence in Cuba he could solve several problems in one bold stroke.[23] The implementation of such a plan promised three dividends. First, Khrushchev would be able to present himself as the defender of a small and vulnerable state. Second, and more important, medium-range missiles in Cuba would essentially give the Soviet Union nuclear parity—if only symbolically—with the United States. The missile gap, which favored the United States, would be no more. Third, nuclear parity with the United States would greatly enhance the international prestige of the Soviet Union.

Khrushchev quickly decided to act. His memoirs suggest that neither he nor his advisors spent much time considering the consequences of this rash act. (He was, after all, always a man of action, not of reflection.) In the past, Khrushchev had several times taken decisive, yet potentially dangerous steps that, however, had brought him political rewards. Now the stakes were higher than ever before. Success promised to bring great gains, but failure promised to contribute to the early end of his political career. And in fact, two years after the Cuban missile crisis, when his party turned him out, he was accused of "hare-brained" and "wild schemes, half-baked conclusions and hasty decisions," none too subtle reminders of what had gone wrong in the Caribbean.[24]

When the CIA became aware of the construction of Soviet missile sites in Cuba, Kennedy had to act. Military and domestic political considerations demanded it. The Joint Chiefs of Staff understood that the presence of ninety Soviet intermediate-range missiles in Cuba, while posing a formidable threat to much of the eastern part of the United States, did not change the balance of terror whereby both sides were capable of annihilating the other. But when Kennedy and his advisers met, they knew that theirs was first and foremost a domestic political problem. At the height of the crisis, Secretary of Defense Robert McNamara told National Security Advisor McGeorge Bundy: "I'll be quite frank, I don't think there is a military problem here. . . . This is a domestic, political problem. . . . We said we'd *act*. Well, how will we act?"[25]

One option was to launch preemptive air strikes against the missile sites, which could bring about the deaths of Soviet military personnel and would mean the humiliation of a great power. Such an action could touch off a nuclear war. Two of Kennedy's advisers, Air Force chief of staff, Gen. Curtis LeMay, and the commander of the Strategic Air Command, Thomas Power—both of whom for over a decade had advocated a preventive nuclear war against the Kremlin—now took the opportunity to urge a nuclear resolution of the confrontation over Cuba, even to the point of launching a nuclear attack on the Soviet Union, which, they argued, would be able to inflict only minimal damage on the United States.[26] The Joint Chiefs of Staff and the CIA, however, pointed out that in an all-out war the Soviet nuclear arsenal was capable of destroying the United States without the Cuban missiles. This bleak assessment had a sobering impact on Kennedy and his advisers, who met around the clock in an effort to find a solution to the crisis.

A second possibility was an invasion of Cuba, but such action was as dangerous as the first option. The destruction of Soviet forces in Cuba would leave Khrushchev with few options. He could accept a defeat, contemplate a nuclear exchange, or attack the West's isolated and vulnerable outpost in Berlin where the Soviet Army had a marked advantage.

Kennedy decided on a third option, a blockade of Cuba (which he called a "quarantine" since a blockade is an act of war) that would give both sides additional time to resolve the issue. The blockade was a limited one since its purpose was only to intercept ships carrying missile components. Khrushchev, in the face of U.S. action, was prepared to back down.

But he, not unlike Kennedy, had his own political problems at home. Since he could not afford to come away from the confrontation empty-handed, Khrushchev demanded concessions from Kennedy. First, he insisted on the Soviet Union's right to place defensive missiles in Cuba. After all, the United States had done the same when it had placed missiles in Turkey, along the Soviet Union's southern border. At the least, therefore, the U.S. missiles should be removed from Turkey. But Kennedy refused publicly to discuss this demand. He, too, could not afford to appear to back down, despite the fact that the U.S. missiles in Turkey were obsolete and already had been scheduled for removal. Second, Khrushchev wanted a pledge from the United States not to invade Cuba and to respect the sovereignty of that nation.[27] For several days the standoff continued. A false move could mean disaster for everyone involved.

Eventually, Kennedy saw the absurdity of his position. He was at the verge of bombing a small nation, an act that could touch off a nuclear war, over the issue of obsolete missiles in Turkey—missiles that he had already ordered to be removed. Kennedy ignored Khrushchev's belligerent statements and instead decided to reply to a conciliatory letter from the Soviet prime minister in which Khrushchev expressed his desire to resolve the dilemma:

> We and you ought not to pull on the ends of the rope in which you have tied the knot of war, because the more the two of us pull, the tighter that knot will be tied. And a moment may come when that knot will be tied too tight that even he who tied it will not have the strength to untie it. . . . Let us not only relax the forces pulling on the ends of the rope, let us take measures to untie that knot. We are ready for this.[28]

Robert Kennedy, the president's brother and closest adviser, met with Soviet Ambassador Anatoly Dobrynin to tell him that the United States was prepared to pledge not to invade Cuba in the future and that after a sufficient interval it would remove the missiles from Turkey. But there would be no official U.S. acknowledgment of this second concession. On the next day, Dobrynin told Robert Kennedy that the Soviet missiles would be withdrawn. The crisis was over.

After the first Soviet ships were turned back by the U.S. blockade, Secretary of State Dean Rusk said: "We looked into the mouth of the cannon; the Russians flinched."[29] But it was not merely the Soviets who had flinched. The United States had reacted in a similar fashion. The Cuban missile crisis had a profound, sobering effect on the nuclear powers. Both the United States and the Soviet Union realized that the constant state of confrontation had been in part responsible for the nuclear showdown. The time had come for a constructive dialogue. And, in fact, relations between the United States and the Soviet Union improved markedly shortly thereafter. The most notable, immediate achievement was the partial Nuclear

Test Ban Treaty of 1963, which forbade nuclear testing in the atmosphere. It set the stage for further East-West discussions and the beginning of the détente of the late 1960s.

In the aftermath of the crisis, historians, politicians, and soldiers have sought to determine the lessons of this confrontation. A view commonly held in the United States emphasized that the crisis showed that the Soviets yielded only in the face of determination and will. Force was the only thing they understood. On the surface, Khrushchev had surrendered to Kennedy's demands by removing the Soviet missiles from Cuba. But this explanation has several serious flaws. On balance, the victory did go to Kennedy. But it came at a price. Until the very end, Khrushchev always insisted on a *quid pro quo* (something in return) and he continued to hold out for concessions until he received them. In the meantime, his government granted Kennedy nothing. As long as the deadlock persisted, the Soviets continued to work on the Cuban missile sites and they challenged the U.S. U-2 spy planes that continued their surveillance flights. A Soviet missile— fired by Cubans at the express order of Fidel Castro—shot down and killed Maj. Rudolph Anderson, the pilot who had initially brought back the information on the missile sites. And when, during the crisis, a U.S. intelligence plane took off on a routine flight over the Soviet Union, the Soviet air force met it and chased it back.

The Cuban missile crisis was first and foremost a political test of wills. Nothing that either side did or contemplated doing would have changed the military balance of power. The crisis was political in nature, one that called for a political solution, namely, a *quid pro quo*. And that is how, in fact, it was resolved, not by one side dictating a settlement to the other. It ended only after Kennedy gave assurances on the missiles in Turkey and a pledge of noninterference in Cuban affairs. As Khrushchev emphasized in his memoirs, the crisis had been settled by political compromise, and he spared no words in thanking John Kennedy for settling it in that fashion rather than going to war.[30]

The Cuban missile crisis sobered up the belligerents and ushered in a climate of cooperation and the reduction of tension. The crisis revealed the Soviet Union's relative weakness in the face of U.S. military might. This imbalance in favor of the United States was in part the result of a modest build-down on the part of the Soviets, which had begun in the late 1950s. But after Kennedy's demand for an increase in the U.S. nuclear arsenal, Kremlin leaders committed themselves to the quest for genuine—and not just symbolic—nuclear parity with the United States. The Soviet Union's rearmament program, however, had done nothing to change the balance of power by the time of the Cuban crisis of October 1962. The Soviets then vowed that the United States would never again humiliate them. The result was a renewed Soviet effort to close the gap or, at the least, to create parity between the two nuclear powers.

RECOMMENDED READINGS

Western Europe

Calmann, John. *The Common Market: The Treaty of Rome Explained.* London: Blond, 1967.
An analysis of the origins of the Common Market.

Hiscocks, Richard. *The Adenauer Era.* Philadelphia: Lippincott, 1966.
A study of the accomplishments of the architect of West Germany.

Sampson, Anthony. *Anatomy of Europe: A Guide to the Workings, Institutions, and Character of Contemporary Western Europe.* New York: Harper and Row, 1968.
A readable analysis of postwar Europe.

Williams, Philip, and Martin Harrison. *Politics and Society in de Gaulle's Republic.* New York: Doubleday, 1971.
A book that focuses on the politician most responsible for the political orientation of postwar France.

The Cold War, 1953–1962

Beschloss, Michael R. *Mayday: Eisenhower, Krushchev and the U-2 Affair.* New York: Harper and Row, 1986.
A detailed analysis of the U-2 incident and its impact on U.S.-Soviet relations.

Dallin, David. *Soviet Foreign Policy After Stalin.* Philadelphia: Lippincott, 1961.
A scholarly treatment of Soviet foreign affairs during the 1950s.

Lebow, Richard Ned, and Janice Gross Stein. *We All Lost the Cold War.* Princeton: Princeton University Press, 1994.
Analyses of how three confrontations were resolved: the Cuban missile crisis, crisis management during the Yom Kippur War of 1973, and management of the nuclear deterrent.

Ra'anan, Uri. *The USSR Arms the Third World: Case Studies in Soviet Foreign Policy.* Cambridge, Mass.: M.I.T. Press, 1969.
A most valuable account of the debates in the Kremlin over foreign policy.

Cuba

Abel, Elie. *The Missile Crisis.* Philadelphia: Lippincott, 1966.
A journalist's scholarly account of the nuclear confrontation.

Kennedy, Robert F. *Thirteen Days: A Memoir of the Cuban Missile Crisis.* New York: W. W. Norton, 1969.
By the president's brother and close adviser, who presents what may be called the official U.S. view.

Schlesinger, Stephen, and Stephen Kinzer. *Bitter Fruit: The Untold Story of the American Coup in Guatemala.* New York: Anchor Books, 1990.
The definitive account of the CIA's coup of 1954.

Szulc, Tad. *Fidel: A Critical Portrait.* New York: Morrow, 1986.
A detailed biography that offers the thesis that Castro was already a Communist before seizing political power.

Walton, Richard J. *Cold War and Counterrevolution: The Foreign Policy of John F. Kennedy.* New York: Viking, 1972.
Contains two chapters highly critical of Kennedy's handling of the Bay of Pigs and the missile crisis.

Weyden, Peter. *Bay of Pigs: The Untold Story.* New York: Simon and Schuster, 1979.
A detailed account of the CIA's ill-fated attempt to overthrow Fidel Castro.

NOTES

1. West Germany's choice of a capital, the small provincial city of Bonn, signified the capital's provisional and temporary status. The traditional German capital, Berlin (which was divided into East and West German sectors), was within East German territory. Over the years, Bonn was transformed and acquired large complexes of government office buildings and foreign embassies befitting a capital city.

2. West Berlin's main practical strategic value to the West was that it was a most important center of intelligence operations. One psychological benefit was that the steadily improving standard of living in West Berlin stood in sharp contrast to that of East Germany, by which it was surrounded.

3. For details, see Rolf Steininger, *Eine Chance zur Wiedervereinigung? Die Stalin-Note vom 10. März 1952: Darstellung und Dokumentation auf der Grundlage unveröffentlichter britischer und amerikanischer Akten* (Bonn: Verlag Neue Gesellschaft, 1985).

4. The Common Market later expanded to include Greece in 1981, Spain and Portugal in 1986, and Austria, Finland, and Sweden in 1995, bringing the membership to fifteen nations.

5. Gaullism also entailed the vigorous ascension of executive power within France and the build-up of France's military forces, specifically its nuclear arsenal.

6. Quoted in Walter LaFeber, *America, Russia, and the Cold War: 1945–1990* (New York: McGraw-Hill, 6th ed., 1991), p. 98.

7. "Détente" is a French word meaning an unbending or relaxing; specifically, in the case of the Cold War, the relaxation of strained international relations.

8. A bold and sweeping statement, to be sure. Other agreements on trade, arms limitations, travel, and the like, must not be lightly dismissed. Yet, none of them settled a major political problem. The stubborn fact that it took the two sides ten years and new leaders to agree on the Austrian solution—and on little else in the succeeding thirty years—is testimony to the intensity of the Cold War.

9. The man who replaced Molotov was Dimitri Shepilov, who was replaced in 1957 by Andrei Gromyko, who retained his post until July 1985, when he was kicked upstairs to take the ceremonial post of president of the Soviet Union.

10. Dulles's "rollback" and "liberation" and Eisenhower's "New Look" are discussed in Stephen E. Ambrose, *Rise to Globalism: American Foreign Policy, 1938–1970* (Baltimore: Penguin, 1971), pp. 221–225.

11. Peter Wyden, *Bay of Pigs: The Untold Story* (New York: Simon and Schuster, 1979), pp. 94–99.

12. The Suez Canal was owned by a joint-stock company in which British and (to a lesser extent) French money had been invested.

13. Charges in the West that Nasser was a Communist were incorrect. In fact, Nasser had outlawed the Egyptian Communist Party. The Soviet Union turned a blind eye to Nasser's actions in order not to jeopardize its new relationship with the Arab world. Similarly, when the Soviets began to sell arms to the Sukarno government of Indonesia, the powerful Indonesian Communist Party complained bitterly. The party's fears were well founded; in October 1965, the Indonesian army launched a bloodbath that destroyed the Communist Party.

14. CIA special estimate, advance copy for National Security Council, March 10, 1953, "Probable Consequences of the Death of Stalin and of the Elevation of Malenkov to Leadership in the USSR," p. 4, in Paul Kesaris, ed., *CIA Research Reports: The Soviet Union, 1946–1976* (Frederick, Md.: University Publications of America, 1982), Reel II, frames 637–648.

15. The Presidium (known as the Politburo during, 1966–1991) of the Central Committee of the Communist Party was the decisionmaking body, which consisted of approximately a dozen individuals. The number was not fixed; it varied frequently.

16. The Baghdad Pact, at any rate, did not last long; nor did it accomplish much. Similarly, the Soviet Union's national interests were hardly served by supplying arms to Nasser. These actions of the superpowers had little more than symbolic value.

17. N. S. Khrushchev, *Khrushchev Remembers: The Last Testament* (Boston: Little, Brown, 1974), pp. 299–300.

18. The event had embarrassed Eisenhower, who had first lied about it and then had to acknowledge that he had approved the spying mission. It had also proven to be an embarrassment for Khrushchev, whose military and scientific establishment had launched the first earth satellite and the first intercontinental missile and yet had been unable to bring down a U.S. plane at 75,000 feet until engine trouble apparently forced it to a lower altitude.

19. For details of the operation, see Stephen Schlesinger and Stephen Kinzer, *Bitter Fruit: The Untold Story of the American Coup in Guatemala* (New York: Anchor Books, 1990).

20. Quoted in Richard J. Walton, *Cold War and Counter-Revolution: The Foreign Policy of John F. Kennedy* (Baltimore: Viking, 1972), p. 50.

21. David Horowitz, *The Free World Colossus: A Critique of American Foreign Policy in the Cold War* (New York: Hill and Wang, rev. ed., 1971), pp. 342–345. Also, Edgar M. Bottome, *The Balance of Terror: A Guide to the Arms Race* (Boston: Beacon Press, 1971), pp. 120–121, 158–160.

22. "Gilpatric Warns U.S. Can Destroy Atom Aggressor," *New York Times,* October 22, 1961, pp. 1, 6.

23. In 1955, Khrushchev had argued for a secret arms shipment to Nasser's Egypt, and it had proven to be a bold and successful plan of action. In Cuba, he could perhaps do the same.

24. "Nezyblemaia leninskaia general'naia linia KPSS," *Pravda,* October 17, 1964, p. 1.

25. Kai Bird and Max Holland, "Dispatches," *The Nation,* April 28, 1984, p. 504.

26. LeMay thought the Soviets would not retaliate with nuclear weapons because the United States held the trump cards. During the crisis he stated that "the Russian bear has always been eager to stick his paw in Latin American waters. Now we've got him in a trap, let's take his leg off right up to his testicles. On second thought, let's take off his testicles too." After the political resolution of the crisis, LeMay publicly berated Kennedy for having "lost" the showdown. See Richard Rhodes, *Dark Sun: The Making of the Hydrogen Bomb* (New York: Simon and Schuster, 1995), pp. 571, 574–575. LeMay thought the bear would accept his castration without somehow trying to reclaim his manhood.

27. The standoff was resolved with the help of two unlikely intermediaries. Soviet journalist Alexander Feklisov (who was also a KGB agent) and U.S. journalist John Scali (who had contacts in the White House) met in a restaurant in Washington on October 26 to discuss the crisis. Feklisov pointed out that "mutual

fear" drove the two superpowers: Cuba feared a U.S. invasion, and the United States feared the rockets in Cuba. A U.S. pledge not to invade Cuba would resolve the matter. Feklisov got in contact with his embassy, Scali with the White House. They met again for dinner that same day, and Scali informed Feklisov that "the highest power"—namely, John Kennedy—had accepted the deal to trade the Soviet rockets in exchange for a public pledge that the United States would not invade Cuba. See A. S. Feklisov, "Neizvestnoe o razviazke karibskogo krizisa," in M. V. Filimoshin, ed., *KGB otkryvaet tainy* (Moscow: Patriot, 1992), pp. 118–132.

28. Robert F. Kennedy, *Thirteen Days: A Memoir of the Cuban Missile Crisis* (New York: Norton, 1969), pp. 89–90.

29. Ibid., p. 18.

30. *Khrushchev Remembers: The Last Testament,* pp. 513–514.

PART 2

NATIONALISM AND THE END OF COLONIALISM

After World War II a wave of nationalism swept across Asia and Africa, and in its wake a host of new nations proclaimed independence from their European colonial masters. Within two decades about one-third of the world's population was freed from colonial rule. The scope and the speed of the dismantling of the colonial empires were unforeseen. But by 1960, it had become clear to even the more conservative rulers of the colonial powers that they could no longer resist the demands rising from the colonized peoples of Asia and Africa for independence and nationhood. None stated it better than British Prime Minister Harold Macmillan in his famous "Wind of Change" speech delivered at the end of a tour of Africa in January 1960:

> We have seen the awakening of national consciousness in peoples who have for centuries lived in dependence upon some other power. Fifteen years ago this movement spread through Asia. Many countries there of different races and civilisations pressed their claim to an independent life. Today the same thing is happening in Africa and the most striking of all the impressions I have formed since I left London a month ago is the strength of this African national consciousness. The wind of change is blowing through the continent, and whether we like it or not this growth of national consciousness is a political fact, and our national policies must take account of it.[1]

Several historical developments merged to bring about this rise of nationalism and rapid decolonization in the postwar period. First, the war itself caused strains on the European colonial powers, which caused them to lose grip on their overseas colonies. Some of them had lost their colonies during the war and found it difficult to restore control of them afterward, while others were so exhausted by the war that they came to view the maintenance of a colonial empire as a burden greater than it was worth. Another factor was the emergence of a Western-educated elite among the natives of the colonies who took seriously the lessons they had learned in the Western universities they attended and demanded democracy, self-government, and nationalism. In some cases the colonial peoples took part as allies in the war and, having contributed to the victory of freedom, they now demanded a measure of that freedom for themselves.

Still another factor with relevance to Asia, as we shall see in Chapter 5, was the role of Japan in bringing an early end to European colonialism. On the one hand, Japan lost its own colonies, and on the other hand, it had promoted and provoked in various Asian countries nationalist movements, which opposed the return of the colonial powers after the war. Britain responded with greater alacrity than did France and the Netherlands to the strength of the independence movement in Asia and took the lead in decolonization. Once it granted independence to India, long the most important of its colonies, the grounds for maintaining its rule over lesser colonies vanished. France, however, resisted granting independence to its colonies, for it seemed to find in the restoration of the French empire a means of compensating for its humiliating defeats in World War II. In Chapter 5, we relate the frustrations of France in Indochina, where it was met and ultimately defeated by a determined Vietnamese nationalist movement led by Ho Chi Minh.

In Africa, decolonization came later than in Asia largely because national consciousness and strong nationalist movements were slower to develop. There are several historical reasons for this, but as we explain in Chapter 6, the persistence of ethnic divisions in Africa was a major obstacle to the development of nationalism. As in Asia, the pattern of decolonization in Africa was determined, to a great extent, by the policy of the European colonial nations. In general, Britain did more to prepare its African colonies for self-rule and independence than did France or the other European powers. In fact, the abrupt departure of France and Belgium from Africa left their former colonies particularly ill-prepared for either political or economic independence. France, in addition, refused to abandon Algeria, which many French citizens called home and which their government considered a province of France and not a colony. But the Muslim majority among native Algerians was determined to win independence from France, and the result was that France had on its hands another long and bitter revolutionary struggle.

Nationalism was a key ingredient in the postwar struggles in the Middle East as well. Here, two peoples, Jews and Arabs, clashed over claims to the same land on which to establish their nations. The Jews, fortified by their particular brand of nationalism—Zionism—returned to settle a land they had parted from centuries before, while the Palestinians, who had occupied this same land for centuries, were determined not to make room for the Jews who came in greater and greater numbers after the war. Chapter 7 provides a review of the long historical background to their conflicting claims, without which their postwar feud cannot be understood. The state of Israel came into being in 1948, at the expense of the Palestinians, and ever since it has been embattled by its Arab neighbors.

The continuing struggle for national self-determination in Vietnam is treated in Chapter 9 in the following section, and the postindependence drive of the new nations of Asia and Africa for political and economic modernization is taken up in Part 4, "The Third World."

NOTE

1. James H. McBath, ed., *British Public Addresses, 1828–1960* (Boston: Houghton Mifflin Co., 1971), pp. 75–83.

5

Decolonization in Asia

Independence movements in Asian nations had been brewing since about the beginning of the twentieth century, and by the end of World War II they had become boiling cauldrons, the contents of which the lid of colonialism could no longer contain. The demand for self-determination and national independence was sounded by ardent nationalists throughout Asia, in India and Burma, in Vietnam and Malaya, in Indonesia and the Philippines. In some cases, independence was achieved peacefully, because the imperial nation became resigned to the termination of its colonial rule, as was the case of the United States in the Philippines and Great Britain in India and Burma. In other cases, imperial powers were determined to resist the national independence movements in their colonies and ultimately granted independence only after engaging in a long and bloody struggle, as was the case of the French in Indochina and the Dutch in the East Indies.

The primary ingredient in all independence movements was nationalism. The beginnings of nationalist resistance to European colonial rule in Asia may be traced to the turn of the century. Gradually, the colonized peoples awakened to their precolonial traditions and developed a sense of national consciousness. Their quests for national independence were mixed with strong anti-imperialist and anti-white racial sentiments. They were outraged by imperialist domination, by being treated as inferior citizens in their own native lands. They could point out to the Europeans the blatant contradiction between their own professed ideals of democracy and self-government and their denial of the same to their Asian colonies. After witnessing the destruction European nations had wrought upon one another in World War I, the Asian colonial peoples began to doubt the superiority of their colonial masters. By the end of World War II, Asian nationalist movements had become quite strong, and they were determined to fight for an end to colonial rule and for full national independence.

■ THE IMPACT OF WORLD WAR II

World War II, and especially the role played by Japan in the war, greatly stimulated the national independence movements in Asia. During the war, several of the imperial powers of Europe were either defeated by Nazi Germany, as were France and the Netherlands, or were fighting desperately for survival, as was Great Britain. These nations were unable to maintain their colonial regimes in Asia, or did so only with difficulty. Moreover, Japan quickly took advantage of this situation and filled the power vacuum by its own conquest of most of Southeast Asia at the outset of the war. The Japanese claimed that they came not as enemies of the Asian peoples but as their liberators, fighting to free Asia from the chains of Western imperialism and to make Asia safe for Asians. While it is true that the Japanese merely replaced the former colonial regime with one of their own, they nonetheless did much to generate nationalism and independence movements in the various countries they occupied in Southeast Asia—the Philippines, Indochina, the Dutch East Indies, Malaya, and Burma. The swiftness and apparent ease with which the Japanese defeated the European forces in Asia signaled to the Vietnamese, Indonesians, Burmese, and others that their former European masters were not as powerful as they had thought.

In Indonesia the Japanese released native political prisoners from the jails and threw the Dutch colonial officials into the same cells. They banned the use of the Dutch language and promoted the use of native languages. They granted nominal independence to the Philippines and to Burma in 1943, and promised it to others. In some cases, such as in India and Burma, Japan helped arm and train national armies to fight the British. By the end of the war, when Japan was forced out, the nationalist organizations Japan had assisted stood ready to oppose the efforts by the European powers to reimpose their colonial rule. This was especially the case in Indonesia, where nationalist leaders immediately issued a declaration of independence at the time of Japan's surrender.

The United States, too, played a role in hastening the end of colonialism in Asia. During the war, U.S. leaders, especially President Roosevelt, had been outspoken in their opposition to the continuation of European colonialism in postwar Asia. The United States became the first Western nation to relinquish its colonial power there after the war. The U.S. government had long before promised independence to the Philippines, a U.S. colony since 1898, and no sooner was the war over than plans for the transfer of power were made. In 1946, with great fanfare, the Republic of the Philippines was proclaimed on an appropriate date, July 4th.

■ INDEPENDENCE AND THE PARTITION OF INDIA

The decolonization of British India has deeper historic roots. The nationalist resistance to British rule began back in the nineteenth century with

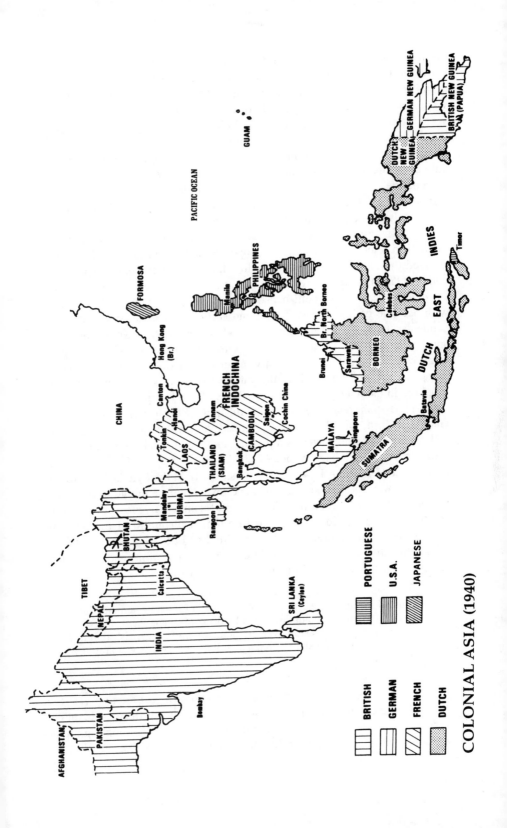

COLONIAL ASIA (1940)

the founding of the Indian National Congress (a political party usually known as Congress). Prior to World War II, the British were already committed to eventual self-government and independence for India, but the war speeded up the timetable. In May 1942, the British government sent a special envoy, Sir Stafford Cripps, to India on a mission aimed at placating the Indian nationalists (and world opinion). In what became known as the Cripps proposal, he promised India dominion status (self-government but continuing membership in the British Commonwealth) and an election for a native constituent assembly to draft an Indian constitution—*after* the war. This provoked a negative reaction from Indian nationalist leaders, notably Mahatma Gandhi and Jawaharlal Nehru, who were determined to turn Britain's disadvantage—the war emergency—into India's advantage. Their firm rejection of the Cripps proposal and their inspirational rhetoric aroused the nationalism of their fellow Indians, which found expression both in Gandhi's passive resistance movement as well as in violent political demonstrations. Gandhi had become a unique force to be reckoned with because of his long-suffering and selfless pursuit of national independence using such nonviolent methods as organizing work stoppages and fasting until near death.[1] Flushed with the heady wine of nationalism, Congress, in August 1942, not only rejected the British offer for eventual independence but passed the Quit India Resolution, which demanded instead the immediate departure of the British from India.

The British response to the Quit India Resolution was to arrest Gandhi, Nehru, and the entire Congress Working Committee. Congress followers rebelled but were suppressed in several weeks. One expatriate Indian nationalist leader, Subhas Chandra Bose, went so far as to put an army in the field (with Japanese assistance) to fight the British. Toward the end of the war, the British viceroy, the crown's representative in India, repeatedly advised London that the demand for independence in India was so strong that it could be postponed no longer. Prime Minister Winston Churchill, the guardian of Britain's empire, had little tolerance for the Indian nationalist movement and had no intention of granting independence. His public reaction to the Quit India Resolution was:

> We intend to remain the effective rulers of India for a long and indefinite period. . . . We mean to hold our own. I have not become the King's First Minister in order to preside over the liquidation of the British Empire. . . . Here we are, and here we stand, a veritable rock of salvation in this drifting world.[2]

Churchill reduced the issue in India to two clear-cut alternatives: the British could either stand and rule or they could cut and run, and he never seriously considered the latter. He did, however, consider adopting a policy aimed at undermining the Indian National Congress by enlisting the support of the impoverished rural masses of India with a land reform program that would benefit them at the expense of wealthy landowners, who were identified with Congress.[3]

In June 1945, in anticipation of the end of the war, British authorities in India convened a conference of Indian leaders (several of whom were released from prison so that they could take part) aimed at creating an interim coalition government pending the granting of independence after the war. These talks, however, were complicated by the presence of a third party, the Muslim League. The Muslims made up a large religious minority in India, and they feared being swallowed up by the far more powerful Hindu majority. They did not wish to become a helpless minority in an Indian nation in which the Hindu-Muslim population ratio was about five to one. Therefore, the Muslim League, led by Mohammed Ali Jinnah, insisted on nothing less than a separate state for the Muslims. Gandhi and the Congress leaders were staunchly opposed to such a division, and they tried to reassure Jinnah and the British that Muslim autonomy and safety would be guaranteed within the new Union of India. The British, too, wished to preserve the unity of India, but Jinnah remained adamant in his demands for a separate Muslim nation.

In London, the new prime minister, Clement Attlee, whose Labour Party had unseated Churchill's government in July 1945, declared that the goal of his government was to transfer power to the Indian people as soon as possible, and at the same time to preserve the unity of India. However, these two goals were in conflict because of the Muslim insistence on a partition of India. In an effort to resolve the partition/unity issue, Attlee dispatched, in March 1946, a cabinet mission to India, where tensions were rapidly mounting. Indian nationalist aspirations for independence clashed with Muslim aspirations for nationhood. Indian nationalism was made manifest in a mutiny by Indian sailors against their British naval officers, by expressions of popular support for Indians who were put on trial for having taken up arms against the British during the war, and by the outpouring of the inspired nationalist rhetoric of Gandhi and Nehru. The Muslim leader, Jinnah, was equally articulate and passionate in his demand for the creation of a separate nation for the Muslims. After conducting a two-month-long investigation in India, the cabinet mission released its report, rejecting partition as impractical but favoring instead a formula for assuring the autonomy of Muslim provinces within a greater Indian unity. But efforts to implement this plan were forestalled by mutual mistrust and quarreling. With the outbreak of communal violence between Hindus and Muslims (and among other minorities), there was too little time to work out a peaceful solution.

The tense situation developing in India caused the British to advance the timetable for independence. A new initiative was made with the appointment of Lord Louis Mountbatten, the popular wartime hero, to the

Indian Prime Minister Jawaharlal Nehru, addressing an audience in the United States, Oct. 11, 1947, two months after independence was granted to India. (*National Archives*)

Mohammed Ali Jinnah, president of the Muslim League and later the first president of Pakistan, Aug. 9, 1945. (*National Archives*)

post of viceroy of India. On his arrival there in March 1947, Mountbatten announced July 1948 as the new deadline for the transfer of power from the British to the Indians. Instead of pacifying the Indians—both Hindus and Muslims—as he had intended, his announcement excited them all the more. As violence mounted and thousands of people were being killed in the strife, negotiations among the three parties intensified. Although Mountbatten at first reaffirmed the British desire to preserve the unity of India, he could not satisfy the Muslim League with anything less than partition, and he therefore decided to settle the matter speedily on the basis of establishing two successor states. The result was a hasty agreement in June 1947 on the division of India to go into effect on the new, earlier date set for independence: August 15, 1947.

On that day, not one but two nations came into being: India and Pakistan, the new Muslim state. This event, known as the partition, was followed by the movement of some 15 million people from one area to another, mainly the flight of Muslims from various regions of India to their new nation. A commission was set up to define the boundaries of the new state of Pakistan, one part of which was to be in the northwest and another part in the northeast (the Bengal region). The agreement on the partition of India did not specify the future status of the Sikhs, another religious minority, and the 560 small, independent princely states scattered throughout the Indian subcontinent. It was presumed, however, that they would look to one or the other of the two new governments for protection and thus be integrated into either India or Pakistan.

While the partition met the nationalist aspirations of the Muslims, who were jubilant over the birth of Pakistan, it was a disappointment to both the Indian nationalists and the British, who would have preferred the preservation of a united India. But none of the three could be pleased by the terrible brutality that attended the partition. Under the best of circumstances, hardship always accompanies the dislocation of peoples. Instead of putting an end to the civil strife between Hindus and Muslims, partition led to much greater bloodletting. Hysterical mobs of Hindus, Muslims, Sikhs, and others savagely attacked one another in acts of reprisal, bitterness, and desperation. In many cities terrorism raged out of control for many days when arson, looting, beatings, murder, and rape became common occurrences. Numerous villages became battlegrounds of warring groups and massacres were frequent along the highways clogged with poor and usually unprotected migrants. Before it was over, almost 1 million people lost their lives. The British, in fact, had warned the two impatient and obstinate sides of this possible result of moving too hastily on partition, but it had been to no avail. Indeed, the British laid themselves open to charges of moving with excessive haste and without adequate planning for an orderly population transfer.

■ THE BRITISH AND DUTCH IN SOUTHEAST ASIA

The process of decolonization in Southeast Asia varied from country to country but, in general, it was more orderly in the U.S. and British colonies (excepting, of course, the violence involved in the partition of India) than it was in the French and Dutch colonies.[4] The British granted independence to Ceylon (now known as Sri Lanka) in 1947 and to Burma in 1948. They were prepared to transfer power to a Malayan union in 1948, but this was delayed for a decade by internal strife between the Malays, the Muslim majority, and the Chinese, who were in the minority except in the city of Singapore.[5] An unsuccessful ten-year-long Communist insurgency complicated matters further. Finally, in August 1957, after the Communist movement was suppressed and a greater degree of ethnic harmony between the Malays and the Chinese was attained, the British granted full independence to the Federation of Malaya.

Britain also relinquished control of its other colonies on the periphery of Malaya. Singapore remained a British crown colony until it became an independent nation in 1959. Sarawak and North Borneo, British colonies located on the northern side of the island of Borneo (the southern part of which belonged to the Dutch East Indies), were granted independence in 1963 and, together with Singapore, joined Malaya to form the new state of Malaysia.[6]

In contrast to the British, the Dutch had no intention of granting independence to the Dutch East Indies, a colony made up of many Southeast Asian islands, which the Dutch had exploited for three centuries. But Dutch intransigence was met by equally strong resistance on the part of the Indonesian nationalists. During World War II, the Japanese military rulers who controlled the Dutch colony gave their active support to an anti-Dutch, nationalist organization known as Putera. By the end of the war, this organization, under the leadership of Achem Sukarno, had developed a 120,000-troop army. When news of Japan's surrender reached Jakarta, the capital, Sukarno, who had been under intensive pressure from the more radical student element in Putera, quickly drafted a declaration of Indonesian independence. He read it on August 17, 1945, to a huge crowd that had gathered to celebrate the event. At about the same time the British landed an occupying force to receive the Japanese surrender and to maintain order until Dutch forces could arrive.

The Dutch returned with a design to restore colonial rule, only to be confronted by a strong nationalist movement with a large, well-equipped army and by an even more hostile Communist movement. Negotiations produced a compromise plan in late 1946 whereby the Dutch would recognize Indonesian independence only on the islands of Java and Sumatra, on the condition that this new Indonesian republic remain within the Dutch colonial empire in a "Union of Netherlands and Indonesia." Indonesian leaders, however, rejected this plan, and when the Dutch resorted to police action to quell demonstrations in July 1947, they were met by armed resistance. Despite United Nations efforts to arrange a cease-fire and diplomatic pressures by the United States and Britain on the Dutch, the Indonesian war of independence continued for another two years, with thousands of casualties on both sides. Finally, in 1949, the Dutch conceded, and a fully independent Federation of Indonesia came into being with Sukarno as its president.

■ THE FRENCH IN INDOCHINA

The French, not unlike the Dutch, were also opposed to granting independence to their Asian colony in Indochina, and their efforts to reimpose colonial power there would also meet with failure.

France's colonial presence in Vietnam dates back to 1858, when its troops occupied the Mekong River delta in the south. By 1883, when the native ruling dynasty submitted to French rule, the French extended their rule to the Red River delta in the north. The conquest of Vietnam was then complete. But, according to the Museum of the Revolution in Hanoi, the struggle against this latest manifestation of foreign domination of Vietnam began on the very day the French had extended their dominion over all of

Vietnam.[7] At first, defiance consisted of unorganized peasant uprisings, which the French quickly suppressed. At the turn of the century, French rule, not unlike that of other colonial powers elsewhere, appeared to be secure. Vietnamese nationalists, humiliated by the French presence, found themselves incapable of challenging the colonial power. Imprisonment and the public use of the guillotine had their intended impact.

The early career of Ho Chi Minh is a case in point. Later in life he fought and defeated the French, but as a young man he could do no more than humbly request justice for his native land. In 1919, he happened to be living in Paris, where the victors of World War I were meeting to decide the fate of the losers. U.S. President Woodrow Wilson had come to the conference as the champion of national self-determination, the one who spoke for the rights of all subjugated peoples. Ho Chi Minh submitted a petition to the U.S. delegation in the hope that Wilson would intervene on Vietnam's behalf. But the delegates had more pressing issues to consider, and the French, whose overriding concern was the punishment of Germany, were in no mood to discuss with a U.S. president (with whom relations were strained as it were) their colonial rule in a faraway land. Ho's calls for amnesty for all political prisoners, equal justice, freedom of the press, and "the sacred right of all peoples to decide their own destiny" fell on deaf ears.[8]

In the following year, Ho became one of the founders of the French Communist Party. His attraction to Communism, he wrote later, was because he saw it as the only political movement in France that concerned itself "a great deal with the colonial question." Communism, for Ho Chi Minh, thus became a vehicle for national liberation of his native land from a succession of French governments that professed the sacred principles of liberalism and democracy. Ho's identity as a Marxist and anticolonialist made it impossible for him to return to Vietnam and took him to Moscow in 1924, at a time when the Kremlin began to officially focus on domestic problems and all but abandoned its ideological commitment to international revolution. By the late 1920s, he made his way to China, where revolutionary ferment promised to spread to the rest of Asia. For nearly twenty years, he remained a man without a country, living in exile and waiting for a chance to return to Vietnam to challenge the French.

The opportunity came in 1941, during the early years of World War II. The French army, the world's best on paper, had collapsed in the face of the German attack in the spring of 1940. In the following year, when the Japanese swept over Southeast Asia, the French again offered little resistance. Japan had humbled one of Europe's great powers, but this proved to be little solace for the Vietnamese since they merely exchanged one master for another. The Japanese conquest of Southeast Asia, however, put into sharp focus the vulnerability of the European colonial presence in Asia, a lesson that was not lost on the Vietnamese, who at the end of the war demanded the end of French colonial rule.

In the meantime, Ho Chi Minh returned to Vietnam in 1940 to create a native resistance movement, the Viet Minh (the League for the Independence of Vietnam), and turned against the Japanese, who now controlled Vietnam. Thus, by a strange twist of fate, Ho and the United States became allies during World War II in their common struggle against the Japanese empire. The United States recognized the usefulness of the Viet Minh, and in fact the OSS (the U.S. Office of Strategic Services, the forerunner of the CIA) provided Ho with weapons and supplies.

When the war ended in 1945, it was Ho and his men who controlled much of Vietnam. France's colonial ambitions in Southeast Asia seemed to be at an end. Toward the end of the war, President Roosevelt had urged the French to follow the U.S. example in the Philippines and grant Vietnam its independence. But the French, humiliated in World War II and insisting on the restoration of France as one of the world's great powers, refused to accept the loss of a prized colony. They sought refuge in a page out of the nineteenth century, which equated colonialism with national pride and prestige. They insisted on reasserting their authority as they had done in the past.

In the meantime, Ho Chi Minh declared the independence of Vietnam in Hanoi on September 2, 1945. He drew on hallowed French and U.S. political documents to justify a Vietnam free from colonial rule. Ho made use of The Declaration of the Rights of Man and Citizen from the French Revolution of 1789 and the U.S. Declaration of Independence, a copy of which was given to him by an OSS official. Talks between Ho and the French came to nothing. At a minimum, the Vietnamese insisted on a genuine measure of autonomy within the context of the French empire. The French, however, were not interested in coming to the conference table to oversee the dissolution of their empire. The French navy eventually replied with a classic example of gunboat diplomacy. In November 1946, the French fleet bombarded the Vietnamese sector of the port of Haiphong. According to French estimates, 6,000 civilians died in the shelling of the city. The French then marched into Hanoi, and the first Indochina War began.

■ THE FIRST INDOCHINA WAR

Initially, the Viet Minh proved to be no match for the French army, which possessed superior weaponry as well as more troops. The French were able to put airplanes, tanks, trucks, and heavy artillery into battle. In a conventional head-to-head clash the French were destined to win. The Viet Minh, therefore, had no choice except to pursue the tactics of the weak against the strong: guerrilla warfare.

Guerrillas (from the Spanish meaning "little war") have no chance of defeating their more powerful enemy in a decisive battle, because they simply do not have the means to do so. They rely instead on a series of small campaigns designed to tie down the enemy army without engaging it directly. Once the enemy forces bring their superior power into play, the guerrillas break off the fight and withdraw, leaving the battlefield to the conventional forces who then plant their banners and proclaim victory. Armies fighting guerrillas can often point to an uninterrupted string of "victories," in the traditional sense of the word. The guerrillas are almost always "defeated."

But such a scenario is frequently misleading. Ché Guevara, who was one of the better known practitioners of guerrilla warfare and who had fought alongside Fidel Castro in Cuba in the 1950s, compared a guerrilla campaign to the minuet, the eighteenth century dance. In the minuet, the dancers take several steps forward and then back.[9] The "steps back" are of central importance to the guerrillas. They cannot afford to hold their ground since they know they will be decimated; therefore, they must always retreat after going forward. They must gather their dead and wounded and their supplies, and then reorganize to fight another day. Little wonder that the conventional forces are always able to claim that they are winning the war and that it will only be a matter of time until the guerrillas suffer their "final" defeat.

The guerrillas' victory comes only after a prolonged struggle that wears down the enemy physically and psychologically. Of utmost importance for the guerrillas is the conduct of political action necessary to gain recruits for their cause. For conventional forces, the conflict is frequently of a purely military nature; in contrast, successful guerrilla movements always focus on the psychological and political nature of the conflict. The French Colonel Gabriel Bonnet reduced this to a quasi-mathematical formula: "$RW = G + P$ (revolutionary warfare is guerrilla action plus psychological-political operations)."[10]

In Vietnam, the French forces generally held the upper hand, and with it came repeated predictions of victory. But they were unable to suppress the insurrection. The Viet Minh always managed to reappear and fight again. And, thus, what was intended as a short punitive action by the French turned into a long and costly war of attrition. And because all wars have political and economic repercussions, successive French governments were beginning to feel the heat. At the outset of the war, the French public had supported the efforts to suppress an anticolonial rebellion, but as the years went by and the financial burden became increasingly heavy, public dissatisfaction grew.

In 1950, the United States became involved in the Korean War, which it considered part of a general Communist offensive in Asia across a wide front. Its view of the Viet Minh insurgency was no different. President Harry Truman became concerned with the French position in Vietnam, and he thus became the first U.S. president to involve the United States in that region when he offered the French financial aid. (When the war ended in 1954, most of the French expenditures in Vietnam were being underwritten by the U.S. taxpayer.)

But the U.S. line of reasoning that revolutions have no indigenous causes but are fomented instead from the outside (a view that lies at the core of Washington's view of the Cold War) proved to be a questionable one in this case. The Soviet Union offered the Viet Minh no aid, and when the Chinese Communists came to power in 1949, Ho Chi Minh emphatically rejected the idea of using Chinese troops against the French although he did accept Chinese supplies, particularly artillery. Chinese-Vietnamese enmity is age-old, and Ho feared the Chinese, their Communism notwithstanding, as much as he did the French. But once the Truman administration took the position that the struggle in Indochina was part of a global Communist movement, the anticolonial rebellion in Southeast Asia was destined to become a focal point of the Cold War.

After years of fighting, the French public grew tired of the war. Predictions of victory by French generals and politicians had proven to be hollow promises. In desperation, the French military command hoped to find a solution to the elusiveness of the Viet Minh guerrillas, to entice the Vietnamese to stand up and wage a conventional battle. The bait was the enticement to attack the remote outpost of Dien Bien Phu, near the border of Laos. If the Viet Minh took the bait, it would result in a conventional showdown and they would be crushed. The French, after all, possessed superior firepower and they controlled the air and the roads leading to Dien Bien Phu.

General Vo Nguyen Giap, the military genius of the Viet Minh, decided to oblige the French, but only after he had made adequate preparations for the battle. With great difficulty he brought into combat heavy artillery, which the Viet Minh had not used previously to any great extent. To the surprise of the French, Giap managed to place the artillery on the hilltops overlooking the valley of Dien Bien Phu, and the decisive battle of the war began. The French soon realized their position was doomed and they appealed for U.S. intervention. Some of President Eisenhower's advisers urged a nuclear strike, but Eisenhower rejected this option because he understood that nuclear weapons are tools of destruction, not war. It made no sense to incinerate Dien Bien Phu—French and Vietnamese alike—to "save" it. Eisenhower refused to become involved in Vietnam, particularly after the Senate majority leader, Lyndon Baines Johnson, told him that the U.S. people would not support another war in Asia, particularly in light of the fact that the cease-fire in Korea had been signed only the previous year.[11]

The battle of Dien Bien Phu ("hell in a very small place," in the words of the French historian Bernard Fall) took place in the spring of 1954. In early May, the French garrison finally fell and with it some of France's finest soldiers. Two thousand of the French forces died; 10,000 were taken prisoner, and only 73 managed to escape.[12] The French defeat was total and the French role in Indochina was over. The French government and the public both welcomed the end.

By coincidence, the world's leading powers—both Communist and capitalist—were engaged at that time in discussing several issues in Geneva. The French and Vietnamese agreed, after the battle of Dien Bien Phu, to take their dispute to this forum. At the conference, however, the Vietnamese Communists received precious little support from the other Communist powers, the Soviet Union and China, both of whom were more interested in other issues. As a consequence, the talks produced a strange agreement. The Geneva Agreement called for a Vietnam temporarily divided along the 17th parallel with a Communist government in the north and a non-Communist government in the south. This division was to last only until a nationwide election, scheduled for July of 1956, could be held. The election was intended to give the country a single government and president and to bring about the "unity and territorial integrity" of Vietnam. In the meantime, the agreement demanded the neutrality of both regions of Vietnam, north and south.[13]

The U.S. delegates at Geneva were hypnotized by a specter of a monolithic Communism. But they need not have worried. Both the Communist Chinese and the Soviets were more interested in cutting a deal with the French than in coming to the aid of their Vietnamese comrades. It appears that it was the Chinese foreign minister, Zhou Enlai (Chou En-lai), much to the surprise of the French, who first proposed a division of Vietnam. The Vietnamese, under Chinese and Soviet pressure, finally yielded, but they insisted on a dividing line along the 13th parallel, which would leave the Viet Minh two-thirds of the country. The French insisted on the 18th parallel; under Chinese and Soviet pressure, the Vietnamese backed down and accepted the 17th parallel, which cut the country roughly in half. At the farewell banquet, Zhou hinted to the South Vietnamese delegation that he favored a permanent partition of Vietnam. This suggestion reflects China's centuries-old animosity toward Vietnam rather than solidarity among Communist nations.

The Viet Minh also yielded on the question of the timetable for the scheduled election. They wanted an election as soon as possible to cash in on their stunning defeat of the French. It was the Soviet foreign minister, Viacheslav Molotov, who asked rhetorically: "Shall we say two years?"[14] The French and the U.S. delegates quickly endorsed Molotov's proposal. It was the best deal the U.S. delegation could hope to obtain. Secretary of State John Foster Dulles was not happy with the prospect of pitting a candidate hand-picked by the United States against the popular Ho Chi Minh. He knew full well that a free election throughout all of Vietnam would bring Ho to power. Earlier in the conference, Dulles had cabled the U.S. ambassador in Paris:

Thus since undoubtedly true that elections might eventually mean unification Vietnam under Ho Chi Minh this makes it all more important that they should be held only as long after cease-fire agreement as possible and in conditions free from intimidation to give democratic elements best chance. We believe important that no date should be set now.[15]

As it was, losing even half of the nation to Communism did not sit well with Dulles. It was for this reason that the United States refused to sign the Geneva Agreement. In a separate statement, however, the U.S. negotiator, Gen. W. Bedell Smith, on behalf of President Dwight Eisenhower, pledged U.S. adherence to the agreement.

The postponement for two years of the creation of a single government for Vietnam had predictable consequences. In a development reminiscent of Korea and Germany, two separate governments came into being: a pro-Western regime in the south (with its capital city of Saigon) and a Communist dictatorship in the north (with the capital in Hanoi). The United States soon began to prop up the anti-Communist government in the south, which it dubbed as "democratic," and which refused to abide by the Geneva Agreement calling for free elections. The elections were never held. Instead, the United States became increasingly tied to the unpopular and repressive regime of Ngo Dinh Diem in South Vietnam. From the very beginning, the United States provided military assistance, as well as economic aid, thus sowing the seeds for direct U.S. intervention once the very existence of the Diem regime was threatened.

For U.S. government leaders, South Vietnam became the gate guarding the "free world," and the United States became "the guardian at the gate." Once that metaphor took root in popular thought, the anti-Communist regime in South Vietnam became identified with the very survival of the United States. For psychological, geopolitical, and domestic political reasons, therefore, U.S.–South Vietnamese relations became a Gordian knot that a succession of U.S. presidents did not dare to cut. When Diem was challenged by an insurgency in the late 1950s, the second Indochina War began.

RECOMMENDED READINGS

India and Pakistan

Brown, W. Norman. *The United States and India, Pakistan, Bangladesh.* 3d ed. Cambridge, Mass.: Harvard University Press, 1972.
   A lucid treatment of Indian independence and partition and the subsequent division of Pakistan.
Hutchins, Francis G. *India's Revolution: Gandhi and the Quit India Movement.* Cambridge, Mass.: University Press, 1973.
   An excellent analysis of Gandhi's role in the Indian nationalist movement.

Merriam, Allen H. *Gandhi vs Jinnah: The Debate Over the Partition of India*. Calcutta: Minerva, 1980.
   Recreates the debate between Gandhi and Jinnah over partition, with many quotations from the speeches and writings of each man.
Thorne, Christopher. *Allies of a Kind: The United States, Britain, and the War with Japan*. Oxford: Oxford University Press, 1978.
   An authoritative study of Britain's wartime and immediate postwar policies regarding its colonies in Asia.

Vietnam

Giap, Vo Nguyen. *People's War, People's Army*. New York: Frederick A. Praeger, 1962.
   Giap's assessment of the nature of wars for national liberation and the reasons for his victory at Dien Bien Phu. Introductory biographical sketch by Bernard B. Fall.
Fall, Bernard B. *Hell in a Very Small Place: The Siege of Dien Bien Phu*. Philadelphia: Lippincott, 1966.
   The definitive history of the battle by a recognized French expert.
Fall, Bernard B., ed. *Ho Chi Minh on Revolution: Selected Writings, 1920–66*. New York: Praeger, 1967.
   A valuable collection of primary sources.
The Joint Chiefs of Staff and the War in Vietnam: History of the Indochina Incident, 1940–1954. Washington, D.C.: Joint Chiefs of Staff, 1955; declassified 1981.
   The Pentagon's critical assessment of why the French lost.
Lacouture, Jean. *Ho Chi Minh: A Political Biography*. New York: Random House, 1968.
   A standard biography of the Vietnamese revolutionary.
Patti, Archimedes. *Why Vietnam? Prelude to America's Albatross*. Berkeley: University of California Press, 1980.
   An account of immediate postwar Vietnam by a U.S. OSS officer who established a working relationship with Ho Chi Minh in 1945.

NOTES

1. Gandhi's career of passive resistance to the laws of Britain that he considered immoral drew upon the writings of the nineteenth-century U.S. writer Henry David Thoreau, and in turn Gandhi's philosophy influenced the U.S. civil rights leader, Martin Luther King, Jr.
   2. As quoted in Francis G. Hutchins, *India's Revolution: Gandhi and the Quit India Movement* (Cambridge, Mass.: Harvard University Press, 1973), p. 143.
   3. Churchill once expressed the view that the Indian National Congress represented hardly anybody except lawyers, moneylenders, and the "Hindu priesthood." Ibid., p. 284.
   4. Southeast Asia refers to the area of Asia stretching from Burma to the Philippine Islands, and includes such countries as Thailand, Vietnam, Indonesia, and Malaysia.
   5. Given the large Chinese population in Singapore, the Chinese would have been the majority population in the new Malaysian union that Britain proposed, and it was for this reason that Muslim leaders opposed its creation.

6. Brunei, another British protectorate in northern Borneo, was scheduled to join its neighbors, Sarawak and North Borneo, in becoming members of the new union of Malaysia, but, prompted by Indonesia, it refused to do so at the last minute. It remained a source of contention among Britain, Malaysia, and Indonesia until it attained self-government under British tutelage in 1971. Singapore separated from Malaysia in 1965 and became a sovereign state.

7. Harrison E. Salisbury, *Behind the Lines—Hanoi: December 23, 1966– January 7, 1967* (New York: Harper and Row, 1967), pp. 52–53.

8. Jean Lacouture, *Ho Chi Minh: A Political Biography* (New York: Random House, 1968), pp. 24–25; Chalmer M. Roberts, "Archives Show Ho's Letter," *Washington Post,* September 14, 1969, p. A 25.

9. Ché Guevara, *Guerrilla Warfare* (New York: Vintage Books, 1969), p. 13.

10. Bernard B. Fall, *The Two Vietnams: A Political and Military Analysis,* 2d rev. ed. (New York: Frederick A. Praeger, 1967), pp. 349–350. For an analysis of Bonnet's formula, see Bernard B. Fall, *Last Reflections on a War* (Garden City: Doubleday, 1967), pp. 209–223.

11. David Halberstam, *The Best and the Brightest* (New York: Random House, 1969), p. 141; also Stanley Karnow, *Vietnam: A History* (New York: Viking, 1983), p. 197.

12. Bernard B. Fall, "Dienbienphu: A Battle to Remember," in Marvin E. Gettleman, ed., *Vietnam: History, Documents, and Opinions* (Greenwich, Conn.: Fawcett, 1965), p. 107.

13. The text of the Geneva Agreement may be found in several anthologies, as well as in Appendix 2, in George McTurnan Kahin and John W. Lewis, *The United States in Vietnam,* rev. ed. (New York: Delta, 1969), pp. 422–443, particularly the Final Declaration, pp. 441–443.

14. Karnow, *Vietnam,* pp. 198–204.

15. Neil Sheehan, et al., *The Pentagon Papers* (New York: Bantam, 1971), p. 46. Dulles also sent a copy of the cable to the U.S. delegate at Geneva, Bedell Smith. Eisenhower wrote in his memoirs that Ho Chi Minh would have won an election with 80 percent of the vote.

6

Decolonization in Africa

Africa was the last frontier of white colonialism. At the close of World War II, the European powers—Britain, France, Belgium, Portugal, and Spain—still held firmly to their African colonies, which collectively encompassed virtually the entire continent. But this was soon to change with the awakening of African nationalism. In 1945, there were only three independent nations on the African continent (Ethiopia, Liberia, and South Africa), but by 1970 there were no less than fifty-two independent African nations.

By the mid-1950s the British government recognized the inevitability of decolonization and began preparing for it rather than resisting it. By the end of that decade the French, too, had resigned themselves to the new reality, and they, too, willingly handed over political power to the nationalist leaders in all of their African colonies, except Algeria. The 1960s in Africa were full of excitement and expectation as power changed hands from the white colonial rulers to new black African rulers who were flushed with nationalistic pride and eager to face the new challenges of nationhood. The transition was remarkably smooth and was achieved faster and with far less bloodshed than an earlier generation—black or white—dreamed possible.

The decolonization process in Africa differed from region to region and colony to colony, and it is therefore difficult, if not impossible, to generalize about it. Africa has two distinct regions: North Africa, bordering the Mediterranean Sea, and sub-Saharan Africa, consisting of the remainder of the continent south of the Sahara Desert. And there are distinct areas within the sub-Saharan region, namely, West Africa, East Africa, Central Africa, and Southern Africa. The colonial system and the pattern of decolonization varied not only according to region but also according to the European nation involved. British colonial rule differed substantially from the French or Belgian colonial systems. There were also great differences in native populations from colony to colony, and from tribe to tribe within a colony.

The bloodiest struggle for national independence in Africa took place in Algeria, where the French made their last stand for colonial empire. The revolution in Algeria, which lasted for eight years, was an especially violent one, and it may be considered an archetype of an armed struggle for national liberation that features terrorism as a means toward a political end.

■ THE RISE OF NATIONALISM

The ethnic makeup of the African population had an important bearing on the decolonization process. The various colonies that sought nationhood had boundaries that had been artificially created by the Europeans in the past century. The black African inhabitants of any given colony were not usually all of the same tribe or ethnic group, and in some cases one ethnic area was in more than one colony. The growth of nationalism required that loyalty to tribe be shifted to loyalty to nation. The timing of decolonization in the various colonies therefore depended, to a great extent, on the growth of national consciousness and the development of a sense of political unity in the native population. This was a slow process and was still far from complete in the 1950s. The persistence of tribal loyalties retarded the growth of nationalism and the birth of independent nations in Africa, and it continued to plague the new African nations once independence was granted.

Prior to World War II, European colonial rule was hardly challenged by the subject peoples of Africa. The colonial administrations seemed so secure that they needed little military force to protect them. In some cases, especially in British colonies, this was achieved by use of the protectorate system, whereby local African rulers were allowed to retain considerable autonomy and were protected by the colonial "overlords." Local rulers were made more secure by the military, political, and financial support supplied by their colonial masters. Also, the European rulers used the divide-and-rule method, whereby they retarded or blocked the development of African unity, or even tribal unity, that might threaten their colonial rule. In general, the Africans, the majority of whom were illiterate, viewed the Europeans with mixed awe and fear, and they were hesitant to attempt armed insurrection. And since political consciousness remained relatively low, there seemed little prospect of an effective, organized anticolonialist action by the African blacks.

Gradually this situation changed as more Africans received an education—ironically, at the hands of the Europeans—and gained more experience in and exposure to the world of the Europeans. The very presence of Europeans in Africa fundamentally altered African society, particularly in the cities. On the one hand, the Europeans created a labor class among the

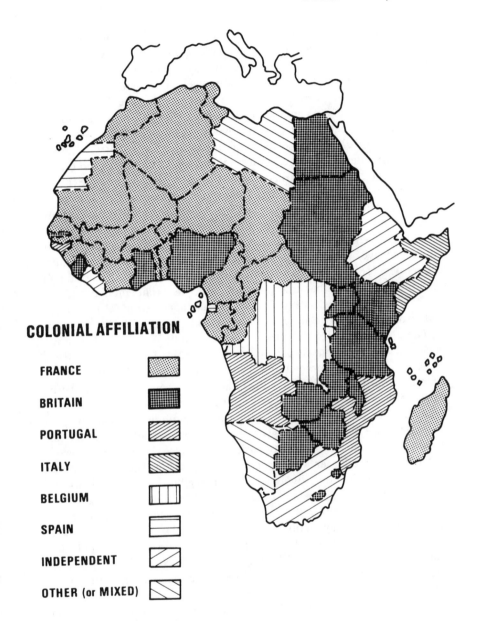

COLONIAL AFFILIATION

FRANCE

BRITAIN

PORTUGAL

ITALY

BELGIUM

SPAIN

INDEPENDENT

OTHER (or MIXED)

COLONIAL AFRICA (1945)

blacks, whose cheap labor was exploited; and on the other hand, the Europeans created new educational and economic opportunities as well as new models for the Africans. One might say that colonialism carried within it the seeds of its own destruction, especially when the colonial powers were nations that espoused democracy and civil liberties. Some Africans, the more privileged and able among them, became well educated, urbanized, and Westernized. Thus, after several generations under colonial rule, a native elite emerged, marked by its Western education and values. It is this class that first developed a sense of grievance and frustration, and then a political consciousness marked by a strong desire to liberate black Africans from colonial rule. It was from this class that the new leaders of the independence movements emerged: leaders who educated their fellow Africans and aroused in them a political consciousness and who established bonds with nationalist leaders of other colonies to strengthen their mutual endeavor for independence. The bond among these new nationalist leaders developed into a pan-Africanist movement in which they found unity in the cause of liberating the whole of Africa from colonial rule.

Although some signs of African restiveness appeared in the prewar period, especially as African businesspeople and workers felt the effects of the Great Depression of the 1930s, it was not until World War II that nationalism and the demand for independence gained strength in Africa. Some African leaders pointed out that their people, who had been called upon to participate in that war to help defeat tyranny and defend liberty, deserved their just reward, a greater measure of that liberty. Their military experience in the war suggested a means of gaining national independence—the use of armed force. They were also stimulated by the example of colonies in other areas of the world, mainly in Asia, winning their independence from the same Europeans who ruled them. These new nations, especially Nehru's India, vigorously championed the cause of decolonization in the United Nations and other forums. The founding of the United Nations also gave heart to the African nationalists, who looked forward to the day when their new nations would join its ranks as full-fledged member nations. It may be added that initially the two superpowers, the United States and the Soviet Union, both urged early decolonization. All these factors contributed to the growing force of nationalism in Africa in the postwar period.

As important as the growth of nationalism in Africa was in preparing the way for independence, that objective would not have been achieved so swiftly or smoothly had Britain, France, and the other colonial nations not come to the realization that it was not in their interest to perpetuate their colonial empires on that continent. Economically underdeveloped colonies were increasingly viewed as both an economic and political liability. The British were the first to come to that realization, but within the decade of the 1950s the French and Belgians also came to the same view.

■ THE BRITISH DEPARTURE

The British colonial system after the war envisioned eventual independence for its colonies. In a gradual, step-by-step manner, the British permitted greater participation by the native peoples in the governing of their colonies. They established executive and legislative councils to advise the governors of the colonies, and began to appoint a few well-educated, black Africans to these councils. Next, black political leaders were permitted to seek election to the legislative council. Once this was granted, the nationalist leaders began convening national congresses and organizing political parties, which became organs of nationalistic, anti-imperialist propaganda. They also began agitating for expanding the right to vote in the legislative council elections. The granting of universal suffrage (extending the right to vote to native populations) was the turning point, for it paved the way for the nationalist, pro-independence parties to gain power. According to the parliamentary system that operated in British colonies, the party that won the election and gained the majority in the legislative council earned a majority of seats in the executive council. The leader of the majority party was then chosen to fill the post of chief minister. The first native Africans to achieve this position were usually charismatic figures who had long been recognized as leaders of the national independence movement. Typically, the one chosen was an able and articulate leader, who had a Western education, had spent many years as a political organizer and agitator, and had spent not a few years in the jails of the British colonial administration before gaining the opportunity to lead the independence party to power. Finally, when the British authorities judged that the new ruler could maintain order and govern responsibly, they prepared for a transfer of power to this responsible leader and his party and granted the colony self-rule and ultimately full independence.

This procedure took place first in the Gold Coast, which became the first of Britain's African sub-Saharan colonies to gain independence. In this West African colony, the able nationalist leader, Kwame Nkrumah, organized an effective political organization and aggressively fought for independence. He took advantage not only of the legal political process, but also of various forms of illegal political pressure, including "positive action"—namely, strikes and boycotts. In 1951, in the first election under universal suffrage, Nkrumah managed his party's campaign while sitting in a British prison. His party won a large majority, and on the basis of this electoral victory, the British governor released Nkrumah, now a national hero, and granted him a seat on the executive council. Three years later the colony, now renamed Ghana, was made self-governing under Nkrumah's leadership, and in March 1957 Nkrumah, now prime minister, was able to announce that Ghana had won its full independence.

Ghana immediately became the model for other African independence movements, and Nkrumah became the continent's most outspoken champion

Kwame Nkrumah, on a visit to the United States, addresses a New York audience. (*National Archives*)

Kenyan Prime Minister Jomo Kenyatta, Nov. 1964, ruler of Kenya from independence in 1963 until his death in 1980. (*National Archives*)

of liberation. In 1958 Nkrumah invited leading African politicians, representing African peoples from the entire continent, to two conferences at Accra, the capital of Ghana. These conferences (the first in April and the second in December 1958) greatly promoted the cause of pan-African unity. It was at these conferences that the Organization of African Unity was created. The delegates at the December 1958 conference unanimously endorsed Nkrumah's pronouncement that all Africans must work together for the complete liberation of all of Africa.

The demand for independence thus spread rapidly across Africa. In general, the British were more responsive to these demands than were the other Europeans. The British attempted to institute a decolonization process similar to that employed in Ghana in its other colonies in Africa, but the timing differed according to the particular circumstances involved. For example, in Nigeria, the most heavily populated British colony whose nationalist leaders were among the earliest and most vocal in demanding liberation, the process was delayed by serious ethnic conflicts. And in East Africa, Kenya's independence was forestalled by other, very different problems.

Kenya, like some other British colonies in Eastern and Southern Africa (but unlike those in Western Africa), was a settlers' colony, meaning that there were European settlers on the land. These white settlers, numbering about 50,000, lived in the Kenyan highlands, possessed the best lands, and discriminated against the black population in numerous ways. They were, of course, opposed to any independence movement based on majority rule. Instead, they insisted upon the creation of a multiracial state that would permit them to maintain their land, wealth, power, and privilege. The largest tribe in Kenya, the Kikuyu, reacted against the domination of the white settlers, and in 1952 it launched a movement known as the Mau Mau. The primary aim of the Mau Mau was to return the land to the black population, which had become overcrowded on reservations. The Mau Mau uprising terrorized the British settlers, but it in fact directed most of its violence toward other blacks who collaborated with the British. The Mau Mau were forcibly suppressed by 1955, but the threat of continued violence remained long afterward to hamper the decolonization process.

The Kikuyu and other tribes eventually formed a national party under the able leadership of Jomo Kenyatta. Kenyatta, a Western-educated member of the Kikuyu tribe, had languished in a British jail for over seven years as a political prisoner. After he was released in 1959, he led his party to electoral victories and eventually to independence in December 1963. Kenyatta's party and the outgoing British colonial authorities worked out a political formula, embodied in a new constitution, designed to provide for majority rule and yet protect the white minority. Still, fear caused most of the settlers to leave. But those who remained in the country were neither victimized by Kenya's black majority nor by the new government. Under Kenyatta's enlightened rule, Kenya became one of the most politically stable of Africa's new nations—at least until the mid-1970s.

In South-Central Africa there remained three British settler colonies: Nyasaland, Northern Rhodesia, and Southern Rhodesia. These three joined together to form a federation in 1953, partly for economic reasons and partly as a means of retaining rule by the white minorities. However, in response to increasing pressure by the majority black populations, the British dissolved the federation and imposed on Nyasaland and Northern Rhodesia constitutions guaranteeing majority rule, thus ending white minority rule. In 1961, Nyasaland under black rule became independent Malawi, and in 1963 Northern Rhodesia became the African-ruled state of Zambia. In Southern Rhodesia, however, a white minority regime, led by Ian Smith, defied the British government and its own black majority by rejecting its British-made, majority-rule constitution and by unilaterally declaring its independence in 1965. Only after prolonged guerrilla attacks by African nationalist parties from bases in neighboring countries and sustained international pressure did Smith finally relent, accepting a plan in 1976 to allow majority rule two years afterward. Continued fighting among rival nationalist parties delayed until 1979 the creation of a black majority government in the country, now known as Zimbabwe.

■ THE FRENCH DEPARTURE

The French colonial system was different from the British, and this meant that the decolonization process was also different, even though the timetable was similar. The aim of French colonial policy had been the assimilation of its African colonies into the French empire and the transformation of the African natives into French citizens. The blacks were enjoined to abandon their own culture in favor of the "superior" French civilization. They were taught the French language and culture, and the elite among them received their higher education at French universities. No attempt was ever made to prepare the native Africans for independence; however, because the colonies were part of the French empire, they were permitted to send elected representatives to Paris where they held seats in the French National Assembly.

There always was a problem with the French program of assimilation in that it assumed that the population of the French African colonies wanted to become and in fact were somehow capable of becoming "French." In the case of Algeria, the assimilation of Muslim Arabs proved to be impossible, as the French settlers and the Arabs both rejected it. The Arabs always understood that they were, first and foremost, conquered subjects. The lot of the Africans south of the Sahara was little different. There was no point for black schoolchildren to recite the lessons written for their counterparts in Paris: "Our ancestors the Gauls had blue eyes and blond hair." At its worst, assimilation as Paris envisioned it was racist; at its best, it was unabashedly ethnocentric. A greater French union of France and the former colonies could only have succeeded on the basis of equality and on the recognition of cultural and racial diversity.

Until the mid-1950s none of the short-lived cabinets in postwar France responded to the African demands for self-rule. However, at this juncture, shortly after abandoning its colonial empire in Asia, France was faced with a revolutionary movement in Algeria and a growing demand for independence in its other African colonies. With the exception of Algeria, where the French refused to budge, the African colonies of France were surprised to find a new French receptiveness to change. The French no longer insisted upon assimilation; instead, they began to search for a workable alternative.

African nationalists who desired the liberation of their people still found it necessary to work within the French system. The most politically successful of the black African leaders from the French colonies was Félix Houphouët-Boigny, a medical doctor from the Ivory Coast. Shortly after World War II, he had taken the lead in forming an African political party, which championed the cause of the blacks. As a member of the French National Assembly, Houphouët-Boigny played a leading role in drawing up a new colonial policy that set in motion the movement for colonial self-government. The effect of this bill, which was passed by the assembly in 1956, was to permit greater autonomy for the separate French colonies, which heretofore were under one centralized colonial administration. Each colony was now to have a French prime minister and African vice-ministers, and elections for legislative assemblies under universal suffrage. Meanwhile, in the various French colonies, Houphouët-Boigny's party established branches, which began organizing for elections under the banner of nationalism.

Still, it remained the intention of France to maintain some form of indirect control over its African colonies. A plan for continued association was endorsed by President Charles de Gaulle, after he came to power in Paris in May 1958. Later that year he offered the twelve separate sub-Saharan colonies the option of membership in the French Community or immediate and full independence. The former meant autonomy, but continued association with France; more important, it meant continued French economic and military aid. This was the preference of all of the colonies except Guinea, which courageously opted instead for independence. In response to Guinea's decision, France immediately pulled out all of its personnel and equipment and terminated all economic aid in hopes of forcing the maverick back into the fold. Guinea, however, stuck with its decision.

The example of Guinea, and nearby Ghana as well, inspired the nationalist leaders in the neighboring French colonies in West Africa. In 1960, after two years of agitation and negotiations, President de Gaulle abruptly granted independence to all of the remaining French colonies in sub-Saharan Africa. These new nations were relatively unprepared either politically or economically for independence, and consequently they tended to remain politically unstable and economically dependent on France for years to come.

■ **THE FRENCH STRUGGLE IN ALGERIA**

France's determination to retain control over Algeria must be viewed in the historical context of its war in Vietnam, a conflict that had drained the French people emotionally, physically, and economically. When defeat came in 1954, the French accepted the loss of Vietnam without bitter recrimination. Vietnam had become a burden to be lifted from their shoulders. There were few dissenting voices in the spring of 1954 when Prime Minister Pierre Mendès-France promised to end the war by granting the Vietnamese their independence. With the Geneva Conference of July 1954, the French colonial presence on the Asian mainland came to an inglorious end.

Yet, within five months of the Geneva settlement, the French faced once more the prospect of losing a colony. This time it was Algeria. The French, however, having lost one colony, were in no mood to accept again a humiliation at the hands of a colonized people of a different color and religion. At stake were France's honor, its role as a great power, and its position in Africa.

The French insisted that Algeria was not a colony but an integral part of France, a province across the Mediterranean, in the same manner that Brittany, Alsace, or Lorraine were provinces of France. More important, Algeria was the home of 1 million French citizens who considered themselves to be living in France. Algeria is "part of the republic," Mendès-France insisted; it has "been French for a long time. Between it and the mainland, no secession is conceivable. . . . Never will France . . . yield on this fundamental principle." The minister of the interior, François Mitterand, added: "Algeria is France."[1]

France's presence in Algeria dated back to 1830 when its troops first landed there. It took the French seventeen years to complete the conquest of a people who spoke Arabic and professed the faith of Islam, a religion remarkably impervious to Christian missionaries. (For a summary of Islam, see Chapter 18.) In 1848, the first French, Roman Catholic settlers arrived. The French quest for empire here became a bitter struggle between two cultures and two religions. In 1870–1871, in the wake of France's defeat in its war with Prussia, the Arab population rose in rebellion. The uprising was put down in blood and was followed by the widespread confiscation of Muslim lands. Algeria became a land divided between the immigrant French, who had seized the best lands along the coast and who enjoyed the rights and protection of French citizenship, and the native Algerians for whom the law offered little protection. The French always justified their colonial conquest as part of their civilizing mission, yet the blessings of French democracy were meant only for Europeans in Algeria, not for the indigenous Arab and Muslim population.

In the years between the two world wars (1918–1939), the French government grappled repeatedly with the question of the status of native Algerians. Liberals, both French and Algerians, urged the integration of the Muslim Algerians into French society by granting them citizenship without first having to convert to Catholicism. To that effect, in 1936 France's premier, Leon Blum, proposed a bill granting a number of select Arabs—soldiers with distinguished records in World War I, teachers, graduates from French institutes—the privilege of French citizenship even though they continued to profess the faith of their ancestors.[2] Unrelenting opposition killed the bill—and with it the opportunity of integrating Algeria with France.

A synthesis of Algerian and French societies was a pipe dream pursued by a liberal minority. The French settlers in Algeria refused to consider it; the same may be said of most Muslims. They, too, could not envision themselves as French. As one Muslim scholar put it: "The Algerian people are not French, do not wish to be and could not be even if they did wish."[3] Children in Muslim schools were taught to recite: "Islam is my religion. Arabic is my language. Algeria is my country."[4]

World War II was fought for the noblest of reasons: against fascism, racism, and colonialism, and for democracy and human rights. It was little wonder that at the end of the war the colonial peoples in Asia and Africa demanded the implementation of these ideals for which, moreover, many of their compatriots had died fighting in the armies of the colonial powers. Inevitably, after the war the Algerians presented the bill for their services to the French.

The first manifestation of the new Algerian attitude became apparent even before the guns fell silent in Europe. On May 1, 1945, during the May Day celebrations in Algiers, Algerian demonstrators staged an unauthorized march carrying banners denouncing French rule and demanding Algerian independence. The French attempt to halt the demonstration led to the deaths of ten Algerians and one Frenchman. The French then boasted that they had ended all disorder. But several days later, on May 8, 1945, the V-E (Victory-in-Europe) Day parade in the Algerian city of Setif turned into a riot. The French had hoisted their victorious *tricolor*. Algerian participants, however, had their own agenda. Again they came with banners calling for the independence of Algeria—and one young man defiantly carried Algeria's forbidden green-and-white flag with the red crescent. A police officer shot him to death.

This act touched off an anticolonial rebellion. The heavy-handed French response brought into combat police and troops as well as airplanes and warships to bomb and strafe villages. The British, as they did later that year in Vietnam when they secured that colony for the French upon the defeat of the Japanese, came to the assistance of the French colonial administration when they provided airplanes to carry French troops from France, Morocco, and Tunisia. When the fighting was over, the French conducted wholesale arrests—the traditional French policy after colonial outbreaks. The French killed between 1,165 (according to their official count) and 45,000 Arabs (according to Algerian estimates).[5] The OSS (the Office for Strategic Services), the U.S. wartime intelligence-gathering organization, put the number of casualties between 16,000 and 20,000, including 6,000 dead.[6] The rebellion claimed the lives of 103 Europeans. On May 13, the French staged a military parade in Constantine to impress upon the Algerians the decisive nature of their victory. The Algerians quickly found out that World War II had been a war for the liberation of the French from German occupation, not for the liberation of the French colonies from French domination.

French society was nearly unanimous in its response to Algerian defiance. Politicians of all stripes, including the Communist Party—whose official position was one of anticolonialism and which later opposed the war in Indochina—strongly supported the suppression of the uprising. The

French colonial authorities admitted that the violence had been in part the result of food shortages. They refused to acknowledge, however, that the rebellion had been fueled primarily by a deep-seated opposition to French colonialism.

For nine years relative stability prevailed in Algeria. When the next rebellion broke out it was not a spontaneous uprising as had been the case in 1945. This time the revolution was organized by the FLN (Front de libération nationale), which turned to the traditional weapon of the weak—terror.[7] Terrorists have little hope to defeat an adversary whose military strength is formidable. They seek, instead, to intimidate and to keep the struggle alive in the hope of breaking the other side's will. The conflict became one of extraordinary brutality. The FLN resorted to bombing attacks against European targets; the Europeans then, logically and predictably, bombed Muslim establishments. Moreover, the French army responded with its own version of terror by torturing and executing prisoners in order to uncover the FLN's organizational structure. In 1956, Parliament—with the express support of the Communist Party—granted Gen. Jacques Massu of the Tenth Parachute Division absolute authority to do whatever was necessary. The subsequent "Battle of Algiers" ended with the destruction of the FLN's leadership. Brute force had triumphed over brute force and within a year the uprising appeared to be over.

But the rebellion continued, nevertheless, as new leaders emerged. Algerians, such as Ferhat Abbas, who had devoted their lives to cooperation with the French, joined the rebellion. The million French settlers in Algeria demanded an increase in military protection. French military strength, initially at 50,000, rose to 400,000. In the end, between 2 and 3 million Arabs (out of a population of 9 million) were driven from their villages to become refugees, and perhaps 1 million had died.

Gradually, many in France began to comprehend the unpalatable truth that Algeria would never be French. By the late 1950s, the French, who had been unified on the Algerian question in 1954, began an intense debate of the subject. The war now divided French society to the point that it threatened to touch off a civil war. One of the telling arguments against the continued French presence in Algeria was that it corrupted the soldiers who were serving in an army guilty of repeated atrocities. Many French (not unlike many of their U.S. counterparts during the war in Vietnam) became more concerned about the effect the killing, the brutality, and the torture had on their own society than their impact on the Arab victims. The costs of the continuing struggle were outweighing the benefits. The time had come to quit Algeria.

It took an exceptional political leader to take a deeply divided France out of Algeria. The colonials in Algeria continued to insist that as French citizens they had the right of military protection; the army, too, was determined to stay. By 1957, the gravest issue before France was no longer the

Algerian uprising, but a sequence of "white rebellions," which threatened to topple the constitutional government of France itself. Only a politician of the stature of Gen. Charles de Gaulle was able to accomplish the difficult task of resolving the Algerian dilemma without plunging France into civil war. De Gaulle had emerged from World War II as the sacred symbol of French resistance to Nazi Germany and had thus salvaged France's honor. In May 1958, he announced that he was ready to serve his nation once again. After he became president in June 1958, he sought at first to resolve the conflict by offering the Algerians what all previous French governments had refused. He announced the rectification of inequalities between Arabs and Europeans, which included the Algerians' right to vote. In this way, Algeria was to remain a part of France. Arab nationalists, however, rejected this solution, which may have worked before hostilities had commenced in 1954. Now nothing short of independence would do. De Gaulle's choices were now narrowed down to two. He could either crush the rebellion—or withdraw. He chose the latter. In the summer of 1960, he began talking publicly of an *"Algérie algeriénne,"* which, he declared, would have "its own government, its institutions and its laws."[8] When he took an inspection trip to Algeria in December 1960, the European residents organized a general strike to protest his policies. They demanded an *"Algérie française!"* But it was to no avail. The time had come to put to rest the myth that native Algerians could be French and that Algeria was part and parcel of France.

In July 1962, de Gaulle quit Algeria in the face of intense opposition within his own army and from the settlers in Algeria, nearly all of whom left for France and never forgave de Gaulle for his act of betrayal. Only 170,000 French residents remained when Algeria formally declared its independence in July 1962. This event essentially marked the end of France as a colonial power.

■ THE BELGIAN AND PORTUGUESE DEPARTURES

The Belgian government paid even less attention than France to preparing its colonial possession, the Congo, for self-government, and yet it quite abruptly granted independence to that huge colony in June 1960. The Belgian Congo, which had once been the private domain of King Leopold, was one of the largest and richest of the African colonies. The Belgian colonial policy of enlightened paternalism was designed to allow the African workers a modicum of material advancement while denying them political rights. In response to the wave of nationalism that had spread over the continent, and especially to the outbreak of insurrection in the city of Leopoldville in early January 1959, the Belgian government hastily issued plans for the creation of what was meant to be a new democratic order for the Congo. The new government in Leopoldville was to be based on universal suffrage and was to guarantee the liberties of all of its people and eliminate any further racial discrimination. In January 1960, the Belgian government made the stunning announcement that in only six months it would formally transfer power to the new sovereign state of the Republic of the Congo.

However, the turbulent events that followed independence suggest that the Congo was ill-prepared for self-rule and that it had been too hastily abandoned by Belgium. The explosion of ethnic rivalry and separatist wars was, in part, the consequence of the lack of development of a nationalism sufficient to pull its approximately 200 tribes into a national union. Even before the Belgians exited, a rift had developed between the two most noted nationalist leaders: Patrice Lumumba, who favored a unitary state with a strong central government, and Joseph Kasavubu, a long-time nationalist leader who insisted upon a loose federation of autonomous regions based on tribal affiliation. No sooner had these two leaders established rival regimes than Moise Tshombe, the separatist leader of the rich copper-mining province of Katanga, announced the secession of that province from the new republic. The result was not only a complicated three-sided political struggle, but a tragic war that soon involved outside forces, including UN forces, the CIA, and Soviet troops. It was an extraordinarily violent war that lasted over two years and left tens of thousands dead.

The Congolese army, weakened by the mutiny of black soldiers against their white officers and divided in loyalty between the contending leaders, Lumumba and Kasavubu, was unable to maintain order or prevent savage attacks by blacks against the white settlers. Nor could either leader match the Katangan forces of Tshombe, whose army remained under the command of Belgian officers. Tshombe, who had the support of the Union Minière, the huge corporation that controlled the copper mines, and of the white settlers, invited Belgian reinforcements into Katanga to defend its independence. Desperate to maintain Congolese national unity, Lumumba requested military assistance from the United Nations. The UN Security Council called upon Belgium to withdraw its forces from the Congo and dispatched a peacekeeping force with instructions to prevent a civil war. The UN intervention, however, proved unsuccessful, as its member states were in disagreement about its role in the Congo.[9] Frustrated by the UN's failure to act decisively against Katanga, and still unable to defeat Katanga's Belgian-led forces, Lumumba then turned to the Soviet Union for support. This complicated the situation all the more as the Western powers sought to make use of the UN presence in the Congo as a means to check Soviet influence. Lumumba was then overthrown by a military coup (supported by the CIA) and delivered to his Katangan enemies, who murdered him.

After a long and costly struggle, the Republic of the Congo, later re-named Zaire, managed to survive with the province of Katanga included, but only after Kasavubu brought Tshombe and his followers into the government on their own terms. About a year later, in November 1965, both Kasavubu and Tshombe were overthrown in a military coup by General Joseph Mobutu, who then established a lasting, brutal, and dreadfully corrupt regime. In addition to having a ruinous effect on the political and economic development of Zaire, the Katangan war and its aftermath severely damaged the credibility of African nationalists who had insisted on the readiness of Africans for self-government. It also had the effect of tarnishing the reputation of the United Nations as a neutral, peacekeeping body, and of draining its resources as well. Moreover, the conflict in the Congo proved to be a forerunner of recurrent East-West power struggles now shifting into the arena of the Third World.

Not all of Africa was liberated from colonial rule by the end of the 1960s. In Southern Africa, Portugal still stubbornly held onto its colonies, Angola and Mozambique. Portugal, a very small country that had remained under the dictatorship of Dr. Oliveira Salazar from 1929 to 1969, regarded its African possessions—which together amounted to twenty times the size of Portugal itself—as "overseas provinces." Thus, they were considered an integral part of the nation and not colonies at all. Portugal savagely suppressed a nationalist insurrection in Angola in 1961, killing about 50,000 people, and quashed a similar uprising in Mozambique in 1964. The Salazar regime ignored the UN condemnation of its colonial policies and continued its use of military force to subdue guerrilla resistance in the colonies. Not until the autocratic regime was overthrown in Portugal in April 1974 did that country take steps to grant independence to its African colonies. The transfer of power to an independent Angola in 1975 was accompanied by the eruption of warfare between rival nationalist parties, each of which had international supporters, and the country remained a scene of domestic turmoil and East-West contention for many years. The Portuguese, exhausted by the conflict in Angola, decided in June 1975 to grant independence to Mozambique as well.

After most of Africa was liberated by the early 1960s, the remnants of colonialism and white minority rule in Southern Africa served as an impetus for pan-Africanism. African leaders sought an early end not only to colonialism but to the white supremacist rule in the independent nation of South Africa (see Chapter 12). Although they persisted in their quest for black African solidarity, the goal remained elusive, partly because the concept itself remained vague and ill-defined. While all the black African leaders affirmed that the liberation of the entire African continent was their first order of business, they in fact lacked the military power and the economic leverage, either singularly or in unison, to achieve that objective. In reality the various leaders were forced to direct their immediate attention to the very difficult tasks of nation building awaiting them in their own countries. They were confronted with a host of political, economic, and military problems, which came with independence. The greatest political challenge was that of creating and maintaining an effective central government whose authority was accepted and whose power was sufficient to enforce its laws throughout the entire nation.

The African nationalist leaders who had led in the struggle for independence also championed the cause of democracy, but it soon became clear that the attainment of the former did not guarantee the success of the latter. Even where genuine efforts were made to establish democratic institutions and to operate according to declared democratic principles, those who gained power by the democratic electoral process were, all too often, loath to risk their positions in another election. The principle of a loyal opposition (that is, tolerance of opposing political parties) was never firmly established. Eventually, most elected African governments gave way to dictatorships, the notable exceptions being Senegal, the Ivory Coast, Tanzania, and Botswana.

The rulers of the newly independent African nations, especially the former French colonies, also found it extremely difficult to maintain a sound economy and raise their people's standard of living—as they had earlier promised. They were soon to find that independence itself brought no magic solution to the struggle against poverty, and that they would remain far more dependent economically on their former colonial rulers than they had hoped. One unanticipated financial burden on the new governments of Africa was the ever-increasing cost of building armed forces that were deemed necessary to guard the borders and maintain internal security. Eventually, such armies everywhere became the major threat to the security of African rulers and their governments.

Yet, despite the numerous problems that lay ahead (see Chapter 11), the liberation of Africa stands as a momentous historical event. The peoples of the new nations of Africa and their proud leaders were swept up in the wave of nationalism and were understandably euphoric about the future of nationhood. In retrospect, however, the tasks of nation building, economic growth, and the maintenance of democratic institutions proved to be more difficult than anyone had anticipated.

RECOMMENDED READINGS

Black Africa

Cameron, James. *The African Revolution.* New York: Random House, 1961.
    A stirring contemporary account of the independence movement in Africa by
    a British journalist.
Cartey, Wilfred, and Martin Kilson, eds. *The African Reader: Independent Africa.*
    New York: Random House, 1970.

A useful anthology of writings by participants in the African independence movement.

Mazrui, Ali A. *The Africans: A Triple Heritage*. Boston: Little, Brown, 1986.
An introduction to the culture and politics of Africa by a native of Kenya whose emphasis is on the European colonial heritage; a companion volume of the BBC/WETA television series.

Mazrui, Ali A., and Michael Tidy. *Nationalism and New States in Africa*. London: Heineman Educational Books, 1984.
A survey of the decolonization process in Africa, focusing on Ghana.

Oliver, Roland, and Anthony Atmore. *Africa Since 1800*. 3d ed. New York: Cambridge University Press, 1981.
A survey focusing mainly on former British colonial regions.

Algeria

Fanon, Frantz. *A Dying Colonialism*. New York: Monthly Review Press, orig. 1959; English edition, 1965.
By a native of the West Indies, a psychiatrist, whose focus is the psychological oppression and disorientation French colonialism created in Algeria.

Fanon, Frantz. *The Wretched of the Earth*. New York: Grove Press, 1963.
Fanon's most influential book on the impact of colonialism.

Horne, Alistair. *A Savage War of Peace: Algeria, 1954–1962*. New York: Viking Press, 1977.
Another fine explanation of a brutal anticolonial conflict.

Talbott, John. *The War Without a Name: France in Algeria, 1954–1962*. New York: Random House, 1980.
A fine history of the Algerian war.

NOTES

1. Pierre Mendès-France and François Mitterand cited in John Talbott, *The War Without a Name: France in Algeria, 1954–1962* (New York: Random House, 1980), p. 39.

2. During the first year, 21,000 Muslims were to be admitted to French citizenship. In later years the list was to increase.

3. Abdelhamid Ben Badis, one of the founders in 1931 of the Society of Reformist Ulema, in Tanya Matthews, *War in Algeria: Background for Crisis* (New York: Fordham University Press, 1961), p. 20.

4. Ibid., p. 20.

5. Frantz Fanon, *A Dying Colonialism* (New York: Monthly Review Press, 1965), p. 74.

6. "Moslem Uprisings in Algeria, May 1945," Record Group 226, OSS Research & Analysis Report 3135, May 30, 1945, pp. 1–6, National Archives, Washington, D.C.

7. The distinction between terrorism and guerrilla tactics has always been blurred, particularly when the charge of terrorism became a political buzzword. Guerrilla action is a type of warfare (which frequently uses terror); terror is a form of political propaganda. The FLN in Algeria was primarily a terrorist organization. The guerrillas of the NLF in Vietnam, no stranger to the uses of terror, went into combat. (All guerrilla movements have been labeled by their opponents as terrorists,

bandits, and the like.) None of the studies on contemporary terror have yet come up with a generally accepted definition of the term. Richard E. Rubenstein, *Alchemists of Revolution: Terrorism in the Modern World* (New York: Basic Books, 1987) defines it as "politically motivated violence engaged in by small groups claiming to represent the masses." That would include the FLN and the French government. To complicate matters further, no one ever admits to being a terrorist.

8. The political discussions revolved around the fate of Algeria: *Algérie française* or *Algérie algérienne*. In 1947, de Gaulle had tied the fate of Algeria to the sovereignty of France. "This means that we must never allow the fact that Algeria is our domain to be called into question in any way whatever from within or from without." For de Gaulle's position in 1960, see Samuel B. Blumenfeld's epilogue in Michael Clark, *Algeria in Turmoil: The Rebellion, Its Causes, Its Effects, Its Future* (New York: Grosset and Dunlap, 1960), pp. 443–454.

9. Secretary General of the United Nations Dag Hammarskjöld made great efforts to resolve conflicts among the disputants in the Congo and among member states of the United Nations disputing the Congo issue. In this effort, he made frequent trips between the UN headquarters in New York and the Congo, and on a trip to Katanga in September 1960 he was killed in an airplane crash.

.

7

The Middle East:
The Arab-Israeli Conflict

The Middle East did not escape the anticolonial revolts of the twentieth century. There, however, the resistance to foreign domination was first directed not against a European power but against the Ottoman Turkish Empire, which had been in control of the region for several centuries. But with the defeat of Turkey in World War I, the Middle East fell under the dominion of other outside forces, namely, Britain and France. Thus, the Arab states merely exchanged one master for another and, predictably, the anticolonial movement continued. The result was the gradual weakening of the hand of the European colonial overlords who slowly began to understand that ultimately they would have to leave. The Arab world had long been impervious to European cultural penetration, a lesson hammered home to the French during their bloody attempt to suppress the Algerian revolution. Arab nationalism and culture steeped in the Islamic tradition undermined, gradually yet irrevocably, the French and British positions in the Middle East.

Yet, by a twist of fate, at the same time Arab cultural and political nationalism began to assert itself, the Middle East saw the introduction in the 1880s of another cultural and political element: the first attempts to re-create a home for the Jews, to reestablish the biblical Zion in Jerusalem, in a region populated largely by Arabs. The Zionists, primarily of European background, thus launched their experiment at a time when the European presence in the world beyond Europe was under direct challenge and retreat. The subsequent political, religious, and cultural conflict between Arabs and Jews remains a volatile and unresolved issue more than a century later.

■ THE REBIRTH OF ZIONISM

Contemporary Zionism has its origins in the rebirth of European nationalism, which soon became transformed—in Germany and elsewhere—into a virulent manifestation of racism. The late eighteenth and early nineteenth centuries witnessed the revival of romantic national consciousness among Europeans who sought to define their histories, origins, and unique contributions to civilization. The result was an increased fragmentation of what is commonly called European civilization. The Germans, Italians, Russians, and Irish, to mention just a few, discovered their uniqueness in their ancient histories and professed cultural superiority over their neighbors. They all had this in common: they sought to find their proper places in the context of European civilization.

The Jews of Europe were another case in point. Their religion set them apart from the rest of Christian Europe and generally made it impossible for them to achieve cultural and political assimilation. Moreover, the nineteenth century was an extraordinarily race-conscious age. The relative toleration of Jews during the previous century, the Age of Reason, was no more. The legal status of Jews was beginning to deteriorate, particularly in Eastern Europe. As a consequence, a number of European Jews began to contemplate the re-creation of the ancient Jewish state in the biblical land of Zion. The result was the rebirth of the concept of Jewish nationalism.[1] It was intended to become an escape from the destructive fury of a rejuvenated anti-Semitism during the last decades of the nineteenth century.

Appropriately, the father of the concept of a Jewish state was Leon Pinsker, a Jew from Russia, a nation where anti-Semitism had become a state policy. The *pogroms* (massacres) of 1881, in the wake of the assassination of Tsar Alexander II, convinced Pinsker that self-preservation demanded the creation of a Jewish state. Jews made up a large percentage of the revolutionary movement, and although ethnic Russians had carried out the murder of the tsar, the assassination let loose anti-Semitic passions of unprecedented scope and intensity. This produced an exodus of Jews; some went to Palestine, although a much larger number went to the United States and other nations overseas. In 1882, Pinsker published his pamphlet, *Auto Emancipation: An Appeal to His People by a Russian Jew.* The book was instrumental in the creation of a Zionist organization (the "Lovers of Zion") that launched the first wave of emigrants to Palestine. By the end of the 1880s, the Jewish population of Palestine was between 30,000 and 40,000, about 5 percent of the total population.

In 1897, an Austrian Jew, Theodor Herzl, became the best-known publicist of the Zionist cause when he organized the First World Zionist Congress and published his pamphlet, *The Jewish State.* The creation of such a Jewish state, however, faced numerous obstacles. Palestine, as well as nearly the entire Middle East, was in the hands of the Ottoman Empire, a power that sought to suppress manifestations of Jewish nationalism, as well as resurgent Arab nationalism. It was little wonder that Herzl called the first Zionists "beggars . . . with dreams."[2] The nationalist movements of modern times (that is, since the end of the Middle Ages) have grown up in the main as reactions to foreign imperialism. The Napoleonic Wars gave birth to German nationalism; the Mongol invasion of Russia gave rise to Russian nationalism; American nationalism came with the struggle against the British. Modern Jewish nationalism was the product of an assault on the culture and, ultimately, the very existence of the Jews. Similarly, the resurgence of Arab nationalism came with the struggle against the Turkish Ottoman Empire. Jewish and Arab nationalism thus reappeared at about the same time. Arabs sought to reclaim their lands; desperate Jews sought a safe haven from the gathering fury of anti-Semitism. In the process, both sought the same piece of land.

The early Zionists were slow to grasp the fact that their struggle would ultimately be against the Arabs. Eventually, it became clear to them that the defeat of Turkey would be but the first step of a long journey. David Ben-Gurion, one of the early Zionist settlers and later Israel's first prime minister, had overlooked the Arabs until 1916. It was a friend, a Palestinian Arab, who awakened him to the prospect of an Arab-Jewish conflict. The Arab expressed his concern over Ben-Gurion's incarceration when he visited the Zionist in a Turkish military prison. "As your friend, I am deeply sorry," he told Ben-Gurion, "but as an Arab I am pleased." "It came down on me like a blow," Ben-Gurion later wrote, "so there is an Arab national movement *here*."[3]

The possibility of a Jewish state came during World War I when Great Britain launched a drive against Turkey, an ally of imperial Germany. In December 1916, the British advanced from Egypt, and in the following month they entered Jerusalem. By this time, the British and their French allies had already decided to carve up the Middle East after Turkey's defeat. By this arrangement, the secret Sykes-Picot Agreement of May 1916, Britain was to extend its influence into Palestine, Iraq, and what shortly became Trans-Jordan while France claimed Lebanon and Syria.

The British did not foresee the troubles ahead. While fighting the Turks, they had enlisted Arab support and had promised the Arabs nationhood after the war. These pledges had contributed to anti-Turkish rebellions in Jerusalem, Damascus, and other cities long controlled by the Turks. At the same time, however, the British government also enlisted Jewish aid and in return "viewed with favour" the creation of a "national home for the Jewish people" in Palestine. This pledge came in 1917 in the Balfour Declaration (named after the British foreign secretary) in a one-page letter to Lord Rothschild, a representative of the Jewish community in England. The declaration also insisted, however, that "nothing shall be done which may prejudice the civil and religious rights of the existing non-Jewish communities in Palestine."[4] The declaration and its later endorsement by the League of Nations gave international sanction to what since 1881 had been a haphazard experiment to create a homeland for Jews.

The Arabs rejected the Balfour Declaration. The promises made by the British, they argued, were at best limited and conditional. A Jewish "national home" in Palestine, they insisted, did not constitute a Jewish state. Moreover, Great Britain had no right to give away Palestine over the heads of its inhabitants, particularly at a time when Britain had not yet gained possession of Palestine. If anything, Britain earlier had promised Palestine to the Arabs in the Hussein-McMahon Letters of 1915–1916. This exchange of letters had led to the Hussein-McMahon Agreement of 1916 (between Sherif Hussein, emir of Mecca, and Sir Henry McMahon, Britain's high commissioner in Egypt) whereby the Arabs, in exchange for Britain's recognition of a united Arab state between the Mediterranean and Red Seas, joined Britain in the war against Turkey.

The best that can be said about the British policy is that the authorities in London did their best to satisfy all claimants to the lands of the Middle East that were a part of the British postwar mandate. First, to satisfy the Arabs, they granted Abdullah, the second son of Sherif Hussein, a stretch of territory east of the Jordan River. With this action, the British transferred the easternmost portion of Palestine to what became the Emirate of Trans-Jordan, today's Kingdom of Jordan. The creation of this artificial realm constituted the first partition of Palestine. The remainder of Palestine west of the Jordan River, with its restless Arab and Jewish populations, remained under British rule.

The British soon found out, however, that one cannot serve two clients with conflicting claims. Arabs and Jews both suspected that the British were backing away from the commitments they had made. Arabs feared the British were in the process of creating a Zionist state; Jews feared the British favored the numerically superior Arabs and thus had no intention of honoring the Balfour Declaration. The British had no clear policy except to try and keep the antagonists apart. The consequence of British fence straddling was that the British were destined to come under a cross fire when they incurred the enmity of both Jews and Arabs.

After World War I, both Jews and Arabs were determined to create their own national states in Palestine. In this age of rejuvenated nationalism, the clash between Zionists and Palestinians became a conflict fueled by passion, anger, and hatred between two nationalist movements insisting on their historic and religious rights to the same land. The Balfour Declaration had asserted the rights of two peoples whose claims and aspirations clashed. The result was that Jews and Arabs acted out a tragedy of classic proportions in which the protagonists became victims of inexorable forces over which they had but little control.

During the 1920s, Jews and Arabs were engaged in mortal combat. Each side engaged in acts of violence, which in turn led to additional violence. Particularly bloody were the riots of 1929, the first instance of large-scale bloodshed between Jews and Arabs. In Jerusalem, in a dispute over the Wailing Wall, 133 Jews and 116 Arabs lost their lives. In Hebron, the Jewish inhabitants, a people with an ancient linear connection to biblical times, were driven out of the city in a riot that claimed 87 Jewish lives. The British authorities sought to keep the peace but with limited success. Both sides felt the British had betrayed them for not fulfilling the promises made during the war. In 1939, Britain, to placate the Arabs who had risen in bloody rebellion (1936–1939), issued its controversial White Paper, or position paper. With it the British authorities sought to limit the Jewish population of Palestine to one-third and to severely curtail the transfer of land to Jews. (The Jewish population at that time was already at 30 percent, up from 10 percent in 1918.)

The new British directive came at a time when life in Nazi Germany had become unbearable for the Jews. Yet, no country would take them in, and Hitler later initiated his program for the extermination of the Jews. Militant Zionists began to suspect collusion between the British and the Nazis. The British decision, which had the effect of closing the door of a safe haven for Jews seeking to escape the inferno of Nazism in Europe, created a legacy of bitterness. After the war this bitterness led to violence between the British army and militant Jewish organizations, such as the Irgun (Irgun Zvai Leumi, or National Military Organization) headed by Menachem Begin.

The destruction of the European Jews at the hands of Nazi Germany during World War II, all too frequently with the collusion of peoples—Poles, Ukrainians, French, and others—who themselves had been conquered by the Germans, seared the consciousness of Jews everywhere. The re-creation of the state of Israel now became more than a spiritual quest to return to one's ancient home; it became a matter of self-preservation. Such a state seemed to be the only place where a Jew could be assured a safe haven against the fury of anti-Semitism. Israel would be created by the survivors of the holocaust, whose actions were constantly marked by the remembrance of that cataclysmic event. Several years later, when Egyptian President Gamal Abdel Nasser spoke of the destruction of Israel, its citizens could not help but invoke the memory of Hitler's attempt to annihilate the Jews.

After World War II, the British decided to wash their hands of Palestine. At this point the United Nations agreed to take its turn in trying to solve this problem. It was clear by then that a single Palestinian state consisting of Arabs and Jews, as the Balfour Declaration had suggested, was an impossibility. Few Zionists and Arabs were interested in such a solution. Both saw themselves as the legitimate heirs to the land of Palestine. Moreover, too much blood had already been shed between them. In November 1947, the United Nations, therefore, called for the creation of separate Israeli and Arab states. Jerusalem, a holy city for both Jews and Muslims, was to have international status with free access for all worshipers. The UN decision marked the second partition of Palestine. It divided what was left after the British had initially granted the east bank of the Jordan River to the emir of Trans-Jordan.

Nearly all Arabs rejected the UN resolution. They were in no mood for such a compromise with what they considered to be a foreign presence in their land. The Arabs also harbored the suspicion that Zionism in control of only half of Zion—not to mention the fact that the very heart of Zion itself, Jerusalem, was slated to remain a separate entity, apart from the state of Israel—would ultimately satisfy few Israelis and inevitably lead to a renewal of Zionist expansion. In 1947, however, most Jews were generally willing to accept the borders the United Nations had drawn, despite the fact that they fell far short of what the Zionist movement had originally envisioned. David Ben-Gurion, Israel's first prime minister, who once had argued that Israel's eastern border must reach the Jordan River, rejected all pressure for expansion in the hope of gaining Arab recognition of what in his youth had been but a dream—the state of Israel. The early Zionists, particularly people such as Begin whose Irgun had as its logo a map of Israel with borders beyond the Jordan River, had a much different map of Israel in mind than the one that came into existence in 1948. The territorial confines of Israel in the wake of the 1948 war were at the heart of the conflict between Ben-Gurion and Begin.

The Arabs remained adamant in their refusal to recognize Israel's existence. At best, some were willing to accept the presence of a Jewish minority in an Arab state. More significant, many Arabs were convinced that they could prevent the establishment of the Israeli state by military means and could drive the Zionists into the sea. The UN resolution and the Arab rejection of the partition of Palestine were but the last of a series of events that made the first Arab-Israeli war inevitable.

In 1947, the Zionist dream had finally borne fruit. The state of Israel (no longer merely a homeland for Jews) had obtained international sanction. The first state to extend diplomatic recognition to Israel was the United States; the Soviet Union and several Western nations quickly followed suit. No Arab state, however, recognized Israel.[5] Arab intransigence—coupled with the threat of another holocaust a scant three years after Hitler's defeat—made it clear that Israel's right to exist would have to be defended by the sword.

■ THE ARAB-ISRAELI WARS

Inevitably, an escalation of violence took place. The British were slated to withdraw from Palestine in May 1948, and both sides prepared for that day. Violence between Arabs and Jews, already endemic, escalated. On April 9, 1948, Begin's Irgun killed between 116 and 254 Palestinians (depending upon whose account one credits) in the village of Deir Yassin, and three days later an Arab reprisal caused the deaths of 77 Jews. These and other acts of violence became etched into the collective memory of both peoples.

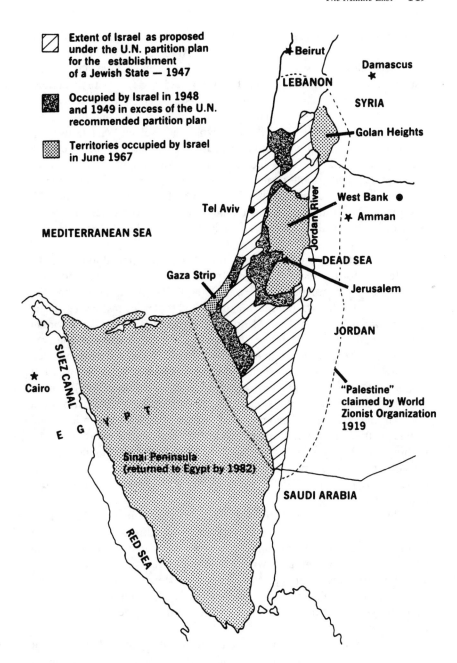

THE EXPANSION OF ISRAEL

Each massacre had its apologists who defended the bloodletting as a just action in a just war. In this fashion the first Arab-Israeli war began.

The 1948 war was over in four weeks. A number of Arab states—Jordan, Syria, Egypt, Lebanon, and Iraq—invaded Israel, but their actions were uncoordinated and ineffectual. The Israeli victory resulted in the third partition of Palestine. The Israelis wound up with one-third more land than under the UN partition plan when they seized West Jerusalem, the Negev Desert, and parts of Galilee. Jordan, in its turn, carried out the fourth partition of Palestine when its King Abdullah made the best of his defeat at the hands of the Israelis by annexing the West Bank and the rest of Jerusalem. As a result of this joint action by Israel and Jordan, the UN-designated Palestinian state never came into being. The Palestinians had been defeated by the state of Israel and betrayed by the Kingdom of Jordan.

The war also produced a refugee problem that continued to plague the Middle East for decades afterward. By the end of April 1948, before the outbreak of the first Arab-Israeli war, 290,000 Palestinian Arabs had become refugees. The war produced another 300,000 refugees. By 1973, the number was over 1.5 million. Most of the refugees fled across the Jordan River into Jordan.[6] The flight of the Arabs settled the nature of the new state of Israel. It guaranteed that Israel would be a Zionist state dominated by a Jewish majority at the expense of what was now an Arab minority left behind. Whatever land the Arabs had abandoned, if only to seek shelter elsewhere during the war, was confiscated. Neighboring Arab nations did not want the refugees; moreover, most refugees did not want to leave the refugee settlements, which in any event they considered temporary. Migration to other Arab lands, the Palestinians reasoned, was tantamount to the acceptance of the permanent loss of Palestine and the recognition of the triumph of Zionism. Half a century later, the Palestinian refugee problem remained.

When the war ended, the Israelis considered the armistice lines, which gave them the additional lands, to be permanent and refused to permit the return of the refugees whose lands were now confiscated. To the Arabs, the new borders and the refugees were a humiliating reminder of their defeat, and they remained incapable of accepting the consequences of the war. These factors, coupled with Arab intransigence on the question of Israel's right to exist, remained at the core of the continuing deadlock in Arab-Israeli relations.

The partitions of Palestine were the result of actions taken by Great Britain, the United Nations, Israel, and Jordan with the complicity of the nations of Europe, both capitalist and Communist. From the beginning, the United States and other major Western powers had offered the Israelis diplomatic support, whereas the Soviet Union had provided most of the weapons for the Jewish victory in the first Arab-Israeli war.

It was only a matter of time until the second war broke out between Jews and Arabs. The 1948 war between Israel and the Arabs had been a bitter blow to the pride and national consciousness of the Arabs. The war had exposed their weaknesses and their inability to unite. Throughout the war, Israeli forces outnumbered those of the Arabs by a ratio of roughly two to one. Arabs spoke fervently of Arab unity and of fighting another war against Israel to drive the Israelis into the sea, but their rhetoric only masked their impotence and frustration.

A palace revolution in Egypt in 1952 swept aside the ineffectual King Farouk and in 1954 brought to power one of the conspirators, Gamal Abdel Nasser, who promised the regeneration of both Egypt and the rest of the Arab world. He envisioned a pan-Arab movement uniting all Arabs, and for a short time Egypt and Syria were in fact merged into one nation, the United Arab Republic. This show of unity, however, did not last long. Nasser's rejuvenation of Arab pride and ethnic consciousness also called for the ouster of the Western presence—notably that of the British, French, and Israelis—which in the past had been responsible for the humiliation of the Muslim world. Another war between Israel and the Arabs seemed inevitable. Nasser, instead of coming to grips with the reality of Israel, was busy putting another Arab-Israeli war on the agenda. All that was needed was a spark to touch it off.

As tensions in the Middle East increased, so did the arms race. Nasser turned to the Soviet Union and in September 1955 announced a historic weapons deal by which he became the recipient of Soviet MIG-15 fighter planes, bombers, and tanks. The Soviet Union, in turn, gained for the first time a client outside its Communist sphere of influence. Israel immediately renegotiated an arms agreement with France. The Middle East was now on a hair-trigger alert waiting for a crisis to unfold. The wait was not long. In July 1956, Nasser boldly seized the Suez Canal, thus eliminating British and French control and operation of that important waterway.

The British and French prepared a counterattack to retake the Suez Canal. They were joined by the Israelis, who had their own reasons to enter the fray. For a number of years, Israelis had listened to Nasser's bloodcurdling rhetoric promising the destruction of their state. They now saw their chance to deal with Nasser and to halt the border raids by the Arab *fedayeen* (literally "those who sacrifice themselves"). These raids had produced an unbroken circle of violence, a series of "little wars" consisting of incursions and reprisals, which in turn led to other raids and reprisals. These actions produced a small but deadly momentum with a life of its own.

In October 1956, Britain, France, and Israel signed the secret treaty of Sèvres in preparation for the second Arab-Israeli war. Israel attacked in Egypt's Sinai Desert and, with the support of French planes, swept all the way to the Suez Canal and the southern tip of the Sinai at Sharm-el-Sheikh. British and French naval, air, and land forces joined the battle against the outgunned Egyptians. The war lasted only a few days, from October 29 until November 2, 1956. Egypt's defeat on the battlefield—not to mention its humiliation—was complete.

When the Anglo-French forces launched an assault aimed at retaking the Suez Canal, President Eisenhower's stated opposition to more war, Soviet threats of intervention, and UN condemnations persuaded Britain, France, and Israel to halt the attack. Israel eventually agreed to withdraw from the Sinai, whereas Egypt pledged not to interfere with Israeli shipping through the Straits of Tiran, which gave Israel an outlet to the Red Sea. The United Nations negotiated the evacuation of the British and French from the canal zone, leaving Nasser in control of the canal, which remained bottled up with war-damaged ships for several years. The United Nations also agreed to patrol the border between Egypt and Israel and in this fashion helped to preserve an uneasy truce for more than ten years.

The 1956 war resolved none of the grievances the belligerents in the Middle East had accumulated over the years. Officially, the state of war between the Arabs and the Jews continued. Israel was still unable to obtain recognition from any Arab government, and the Arabs continued to seek the destruction of the Israeli state. Both sides had no illusions that another war was in the offing, and they took steps to prepare for it.

In spring 1967, Nasser, in an attempt to negate the consequences of the 1956 war, closed the Straits of Tiran to Israeli shipping in the face of Israeli warnings that such an action constituted a *casus belli,* a cause for war. Inevitably, tensions rose rapidly. Nasser then demanded that the UN forces leave Egyptian territory along the Israeli border and concluded a military pact with King Hussein of Jordan. When Iraq also joined the pact, the Israelis struck. Their pre-emptive attack initiated the inevitable third war, the Six Day War of June 1967—a classic case of a preventive war. The Israelis claimed that theirs had been an attack to counter an intended Arab offensive.

As its name suggests, the war was over in less than a week, by which time Israel had decimated the forces of Egypt and Jordan. Once again—as it had done in the 1956 war—Israel conquered the Sinai all the way to the Suez Canal. It then turned against Syria and took from that country the Golan Heights, a 20-mile-wide strategic plateau rising 600 feet above Galilee from which the Syrian army had fired repeatedly on Israeli settlements below. But more important, Israel also took what had been Jordanian territory west of the Jordan River and the Dead Sea—a region generally known as the West Bank (west of the Jordan River). With it, Israel came into possession of the entire city of Jerusalem, which immediately became the nation's new capital. The Six Day War rearranged the map of the Middle East, and its political repercussions still haunt the region. All the conquered territories—the Sinai peninsula, the Golan Heights, the West Bank, and Jerusalem—became Israeli-occupied lands, and as such they became the source of still further contention between Arabs and Israelis.

In November 1967, the great powers once again sought to use the United Nations to resolve the conflict. The United States and the Soviet Union were fearful of being increasingly drawn into the Arab-Israeli wars, each backing one of the belligerents. In a rare display of U.S.-Soviet cooperation, the UN Security Council sought to resolve the crisis by passing Resolution 242, which called for an Israeli withdrawal from territories conquered in the Six Day War, accompanied by a political settlement that would include Arab recognition of Israel and a fair deal for the Palestinian refugees. After some hesitation, Egypt and Jordan accepted Resolution 242, but Syria and the militant Palestinians rejected it. The Israelis were not inclined to give up all the spoils of victory, and they, too, rejected it. For over twenty-five years, leaders of various political and national persuasions repeatedly reached for Resolution 242 as a potential answer to this deadly dispute. But the overwhelming strength of Israel's military in effect negated the resolution. The Israeli government had no pressing need to return to its pre-1967 borders; moreover, it never contemplated the return of Jerusalem. And the Arabs have always insisted that in Resolution 242, "the territories occupied [by Israel] in the hostilities" meant "all territories."[7] Gen. Moshe Dayan, the architect of Israel's victory in the Six Day War, expressed the extremist conviction when he said, "I would rather have land than peace," to which King Hussein of Jordan replied, "Israel can have land or peace, but not both."[8] The resultant deadlock became but another manifestation of how in the Middle East the militants have nearly always carried the day.

With the acquisition of the West Bank, Israel now came into possession of a territory containing 750,000 hostile Arab inhabitants. For years the Israeli government remained largely undecided over what to do with this territory. And when no solution acceptable to both Arabs and Jews was found, the status quo prevailed. In 1977, a general election in Israel brought to power Menachem Begin, who had always insisted that the West Bank was not merely conquered Arab territory or a bargaining card to be played eventually in exchange for Arab recognition of Israel's right to exist. Instead, he argued, it consisted of the biblical lands of Judea and Samaria, an integral part of Israel's religious heritage. For Begin, there was no question that these lands should ever be returned to the Arabs. He proceeded to treat them as a natural part of Zion, and for that reason he urged that Israelis settle in the region. Despite the objections of Arab states, the United Nations, the United States, and other nations, Begin considered the annexation of the West Bank a closed matter. His government also annexed the Golan Heights and considered that matter closed as well.

The problem of the West Bank is complicated by the fact that its largest city, Hebron, contains the tomb of Abraham, who is revered by both Jews and Muslims. Both groups consider Abraham God's messenger and their spiritual and physical patriarch. The Jews consider themselves the direct descendants of one of Abraham's sons, Isaac; the Arabs see themselves as children of his other son, Ishmael.

The 1967 Arab defeat had another, unexpected result. It strengthened the hand of Palestinian liberation/terrorist organizations, which now operated under the aegis of a newly established umbrella organization, the Palestine Liberation Organization (PLO), led by Yassir Arafat. It has been guerrilla fighters of this organization, rather than the armies of the Arab nations generally, that since 1967 have kept the Middle East in turmoil by conducting private wars against the Israelis. During the 1972 summer Olympic Games in Munich, for instance, Palestinian terrorists dramatized their cause before a worldwide audience by kidnapping and killing fifteen Israeli athletes. This act propelled the Palestinian question into the consciousness of the Western world. But this example of "propaganda by the deed" (to use a phrase from the Russian revolutionary movement of the nineteenth century) only strengthened the hands of the extremists on both sides and continued to impede any and all efforts to resolve the questions. It should not have been surprising, therefore, that the consequence of the inability to resolve Arab-Israeli differences was another war.

The fourth Arab-Israeli conflict, the Yom Kippur War, took place in October 1973, when Egyptian President Anwar Sadat, who had succeeded Nasser in 1970, initiated an offensive against the seemingly impregnable Israeli position across the Suez Canal. Owing to its surprise attack, Egypt enjoyed some initial successes, but Israeli forces successfully counterattacked and threatened to destroy the Egyptian army. The United Nations and the two superpowers, the United States and the Soviet Union, hastily intervened to stop the war. Neither Israel nor Egypt was to be permitted to destroy the other. Egypt was permitted to retain a foothold on the east side of the Suez Canal, and the United Nations then created a buffer zone to keep the two sides apart.

This Egyptian offensive proved to be the first time an Arab state had been able to wrest any territory from the Israelis. After suffering one humiliation after another for a quarter of a century, an Arab army had finally proven its battleworthiness. Sadat felt he could now negotiate with Israel as an equal. With encouragement from Washington, he began to take steps to recognize the existence of the state of Israel and in this fashion became the first Arab head of state to do so. In an act of supreme courage, Sadat responded to an invitation from the Israeli government and flew to Jerusalem in 1977 to address the Knesset, Israel's parliament. Israeli Prime Minister Begin reciprocated with his own visit to Cairo.

These remarkable diplomatic actions set the stage for a summit meeting of the two leaders together with U.S. President Jimmy Carter in September 1978 and for the Camp David Agreement signed by all three, which

Egyptian President Anwar Sadat, U.S. President Jimmy Carter, and Israeli Prime Minister Menachem Begin after signing the Middle East peace treaty at Camp David, Maryland, Mar. 27, 1979. (*AP/Wide World Photos*)

led directly to the Egyptian-Israeli peace treaty. The treaty ended a state of war of thirty years' duration between Egypt and Israel and brought about the diplomatic recognition of Israel by Egypt. In turn, Israel pledged to return the Sinai to Egypt and did so by April 1982. This marked the first and only instance whereby an Arab state managed on its own to regain territory lost to Israel. Sadat had achieved through negotiation what no Arab nations had achieved by war. For their efforts, the three leaders were nominated for the Nobel Peace Prize. In the end, Begin and Sadat—former terrorists turned diplomats—shared the prize; inexplicably, Jimmy Carter was excluded.

But the Camp David agreement of 1979 did not adequately address the thorny questions of Jerusalem, the West Bank, and the Palestinian refugees. Sadat wanted Palestinian independence from Israel; Begin spoke vaguely of Palestinian "autonomy" within the state of Israel. Begin was more interested in peace with Egypt and diplomatic recognition than in discussing the fate of the inhabitants of what he considered to be an integral part of Israel and thus an internal matter. Nor did the Camp David agreement settle the issue of Jerusalem, Israel's capital city, on which virtually no Israelis were willing to compromise. They insisted on their claim to Jerusalem and that it remain one and indivisible. But the Palestinians, too, envisioned Jerusalem as the capital of their future state.

The PLO was not consulted in these negotiations. Begin refused to talk to the PLO, which he considered only a terrorist organization. Nor was the PLO's leadership interested in joining the talks. Participation in the negotiations, after all, would have meant the de facto recognition of Israel. The PLO instead continued its attacks against the Israelis.

Inevitably, many Arabs saw Sadat as a man who had betrayed the Palestinian and Arab cause. His dealings with Israel contributed to his domestic problems. As his critics became more vocal, his regime became increasingly dictatorial and his opponents, in turn, became increasingly embittered. He was assassinated by Muslim extremists in Egypt in 1981.

The festering Palestinian problem continued to rile the region. In 1970, King Hussein of Jordan had driven the PLO leadership from his country after it had become clear that its presence in Jordan posed a threat to his regime.[9] Searching for a home, the PLO found a new base of operation in southern Lebanon, a nation already divided between a politically dominant Christian minority and the majority Muslim population. In the early 1970s, Lebanon was on the edge of civil war with a government incapable of maintaining order. Lebanon's political factions operated private armies in an unrestricted manner. It was into this volatile environment that the Palestinians introduced their own private armies. And it was from Lebanon that the PLO launched its raids into Israel.

The Israelis, predictably, responded in kind. Raids and reprisals were the order of the day along the Lebanese-Israeli border. In July 1981, however, the PLO and Israel agreed on a "cessation of all armed attacks." The cease-fire over the next ten months was in part the work of the special U.S. envoy to the Middle East, Philip Habib. Both sides abided by the terms of the agreement until June 1982, when the government of Menachem Begin attempted to eliminate the Palestinian threat in Lebanon once and for all by launching an invasion into southern Lebanon.

The Israeli government's official explanation for the resumption of war against the Palestinians was to secure "Peace for Galilee" and to root out the Palestinians across the border. This rationale for the invasion had a hollow ring to it since there had been no Palestinian attacks across that border for nearly a year. The scope of the operation, the Begin government announced, would be limited. The Israeli army would go no farther than forty kilometers (twenty-five miles) into Lebanon. Events proved, however, that Begin, and his defense minister, Ariel Sharon, had more ambitious plans.

In December 1981, Sharon outlined the following scenario to Philip Habib. Sharon contemplated a strike into Lebanon in the hope of quickly resolving several problems at once. He sought to dislodge the Syrians, who had been invited several years earlier by the Lebanese government to restore order at a time when the country was beginning to disintegrate into civil war. Once invited, however, the Syrians stayed. Sharon considered the Syrians, with whom the Israelis had been on a war footing since 1948, to be the real masters of Lebanon. Second, Sharon intended to destroy the Palestinian base in southern Lebanon and with it to subdue the restless Palestinian population of about half a million. "What can be done," Sharon told Habib, "and this is not actually a plan, but it is practicable, is a swift and vigorous strike of 24 to 48 hours, which will force the Syrians to retreat and inflict such heavy losses on the PLO that they will leave Lebanon." Sharon also expected the Lebanese government to regain control of the Beirut-Damascus highway, thus driving the Syrians further north.[10] In this fashion the PLO, a "time bomb" in Sharon's words, would be destroyed. When Habib asked of the fate of the 100,000 Palestinians directly across the border in Lebanon, Sharon told him that "we shall hand them over to the Lebanese. . . . Fifty-thousand armed terrorists won't remain there, and the rest will be taken care of by the Lebanese." Habib protested the impending violation of a cease-fire he had worked out. Shortly afterward, President Reagan warned Prime Minister Begin against any moves into Lebanon, but to no avail.

The invasion of Lebanon did bring about the military (although not the political) defeat of the PLO and the Israeli bombardment and destruction of parts of Beirut containing Palestinian populations. The invasion also provoked the massacre of Palestinian civilians by Lebanese Maronite Christian Phalangist (right-wing) militia forces that had long been engaged in bitter conflict with the Palestinians. Israeli forces also crippled Syrian forces in Lebanon and destroyed much of the military hardware the Soviets had provided them, but the Syrians quickly recovered their losses and remained as deeply entrenched in Lebanon as ever. Israel did not withdraw completely but left some of its forces in a self-imposed buffer region in southern Lebanon. Egypt recalled its ambassador from Jerusalem in protest over Israeli action in Lebanon.

The cost of the invasion is incalculable. The greatest losers were the Palestinians, who suffered at the hands of first the Israelis, then the Christian Phalangists, and finally the Shiite Muslims in Lebanon. The war also pitted the Israelis against the Shiites; the Shiites against the Maronite Christians and their army, the Phalangists; and a faction of the PLO (the rebels supported by the Syrians) against Arafat's faction. It produced the evacuation of the PLO guerrillas, the deaths of over 600 Israeli soldiers, the de facto partition of Lebanon between Syria and Israel, and a deep emotional split within the population in Israel. The volatile political debates in Israel centered on whether the invasion had been necessary, for this was the first war initiated by Israel in which the survival of the state had not been an immediate issue.

The invasion of Lebanon did not resolve the central issues of the region. Instead, it added fuel to the fire of the multisided civil war in that country. Under UN auspices, a peacekeeping force made up of U.S., French, and Italian troops was deployed to oversee the evacuation of PLO fighters. Soon afterward, the U.S. peacekeeping force ran head-on into an opposition of fury and anger few U.S. citizens were able to understand when a truck filled with explosives blew up a U.S. military encampment, killing 240 marines. More than a decade and a half later the bloodletting continued. Israeli forces were still in southern Lebanon engaged in sporadic combat with Lebanese Shiites.

■ THE ISRAELI-PALESTINIAN IMPASSE

In the mid-1980s, the PLO was no closer than before to achieving its stated goal—the creation of a Palestinian state and the destruction of Israel. After the 1982 expulsion from Lebanon, the PLO was in disarray, as PLO fighters were now openly split with various Arab countries supporting contending factions. For the next several years the nominal leader of the PLO, Yassir Arafat, now based in Tunisia, struggled to maintain the unity of the organization. His main conflict was with Syrian President Hafez Assad, with whom some of the more radical elements of the PLO became linked. Arafat gravitated toward more moderate Arab leaders— Hussein of Jordan and Hosni Mubarak, Sadat's successor in Egypt—and began to explore the possibility of a negotiated settlement with Israel, as opposed to a military one.

As the PLO floundered for lack of unity and Arab nations remained divided over policy toward Israel, Israel itself was immobilized by its own political disunity. The leading parties, the right-wing Likud and the left-of-center Labor Party, which shared power in an awkward coalition after an inconclusive parliamentary election in 1984, were unable to find a consensus on how to deal with the PLO.

Nothing changed until December 1987, when the Palestinian population in Gaza and the West Bank took matters into its own hands and by doing so stirred the other parties to move off dead center. The Palestinian uprising, the intifada (literally, "shaking off" the Zionist yoke), began in Gaza when an Israeli truck collided with two cars, killing four Palestinian refugees. The protests escalated and spread to the West Bank. Israel put itself into the uncomfortable position of using armed soldiers against stone-throwing Palestinians. By early 1990, more than 600 Palestinians had been killed by Israeli soldiers. Israeli hard-liners tried to deflect criticism by blaming the violence on the PLO.

The intifada spurred debate within Israel over the future of Gaza and the West Bank and within the PLO over strategy and tactics. Israel's problem was compounded by the fact that it had built settlements on the West Bank for some 70,000 of its citizens. Moreover, for Israel the fate of Jerusalem was not negotiable. In Israel, the Likud and the Labor Party squared off in another parliamentary election in November 1988, the central issue being the future of the occupied territories. Yitzhak Shamir, incumbent prime minister and head of the Likud, took a hard line, insisting on no mercy for the intifada, no talks with the PLO, no Israeli participation in an international conference on the Middle East, and no trading land for peace (the last two ideas were supported by Washington by this time). His opponent, Shimon Peres, took a more flexible approach, favoring an international conference to resolve the conflict. In short, Shamir held that to survive, Israel must keep the West Bank and Gaza, whereas Peres held that Israel must trade land for peace. The election produced another deadlock, with neither party winning a majority in the Knesset. Once more, no consensus was possible.

Meanwhile, the PLO decided to take advantage of the opportunity presented by the intifada. It convened a meeting of the Palestinian National Council in Algiers in November 1988, at which it passed a resolution proclaiming its willingness to recognize the state of Israel on the condition that Israel officially endorse UN Resolutions 242 and 338, which called for Israeli withdrawal from the occupied territories and for the right of all parties in the Middle East to live in peace and security. For the PLO, this was a remarkably conciliatory position. Arafat also declared and repeated that "we [the PLO] totally and absolutely renounce all forms of terrorism."[11] Washington then announced that for the first time it would enter discussions with the PLO to prepare for an international conference on the Middle East.

Israel was now virtually isolated. The major Western powers, the dominant element in the PLO, key Arab countries, and the Soviet Union were all in essential agreement on the need for an international peace conference that would lead to the creation of an autonomous Palestinian state on at least part of the occupied territories. But Shamir stood firm. He did not believe the peaceful protestations of his mortal enemies; there would be no international conference, no talks with the PLO, and no Palestinian state. He could not forget that the PLO had vowed in the past to destroy the state of Israel and that, in fact, several of its factions still held this position.[12] Shamir offered instead a proposal to conduct an election in the occupied territories to produce a Palestinian leadership with which he could negotiate the future of the West Bank and Gaza. Neither the PLO nor other Arab nations found this plan acceptable; nor did Washington. The political deadlock remained.

The end of the Cold War in 1990 led to significantly improved relations between Israel and the Soviet Union. The two nations reestablished diplomatic relations (which the Soviet Union had broken off after the Six Day War of 1967), and when Moscow opened its doors for the emigration of Jews, Israel welcomed them. The mass immigration of Jews to Israel (200,000 in 1990 alone) had consequences beyond the domestic issues of providing housing and jobs. The Soviet Jews were settled in large numbers in the West Bank and Eastern Jerusalem, areas the Palestinians claimed. Although intifada violence had subsided, the influx of the Soviet Jews into the occupied lands inflamed Arab passions. Shamir, however, reiterated his pledge that he would keep intact for future generations the "Greater Israel," by which he meant all areas currently under Israeli control.

■ THE SEARCH FOR A POLITICAL SOLUTION

The Arab-Israeli dispute became more acute during the Gulf crisis occasioned by the invasion of Kuwait by Iraqi forces in August 1990 (see Chapter 18). Israel's most urgent concern was for its own security since earlier in the year Iraqi ruler Saddam Hussein had threatened to "scorch half of Israel" in reprisal of any Israeli action against Iraq. In his efforts to secure Arab support, Hussein proclaimed his willingness to withdraw from Kuwait if Israel were to withdraw from all the occupied territories. Although most Arab leaders shunned this pretension, the PLO announced its support for Hussein, and Palestinians stepped up the intifada against Israel.

The defeat of Iraq by the U.S.-led coalition in the Gulf War in early 1991, however, as well as the demise of the Soviet Union, greatly improved conditions for achieving a breakthrough in the Middle East. After the Gulf War, it was clearer than ever that Israel was a permanent fact of life in the Middle East. The PLO had publicly contemplated recognition of Israel in exchange for some of the land taken by the latter in 1967. Afez Assad of Syria, too, took a new tack in his quest to regain the Golan Heights. Deprived of Soviet backing, there was little point in Assad continuing to pretend he could force a military solution on Israel. Many Israelis, too, sought an end to the costly confrontation. The time had come to sit down and talk.

Washington called for a comprehensive peace conference, and U.S. Secretary of State James Baker played the role of the honest broker, bringing the warring sides to the negotiating table. Shamir proved the most reluctant to participate in such a conference because he knew discussions would focus on the return of Israeli occupied territory. When Shamir continued to balk, the Bush administration announced that it was withholding $10 billion in loan guarantees Israel had requested to finance the settlement of Soviet immigrants. The defiant Shamir finally agreed to participate in the talks but only on the condition that the Palestinian negotiating team include no members of the PLO or residents of East Jerusalem.

When the long-awaited international Middle East peace conference opened with considerable fanfare in Madrid, Spain, in October 1991, Shamir was determined to make no territorial concessions, and the Arabs came insisting on nothing less. The four-day meeting was marked by bitter exchanges, especially between Israel and Syria, and ended inconclusively. As soon as the conference ended, Shamir promptly founded new settlements for Soviet Jews in both the West Bank and the Golan Heights. A second round of negotiations began in Washington in December 1991, but before any headway could be made, Shamir's cabinet lost its parliamentary majority in February 1992 because of the defection of two minor right-wing parties, and he was forced to call for parliamentary elections. Peace talks were suspended until elections were held in June 1992.

In a tight race, Labor Party leader Yitzhak Rabin defeated Shamir. Rabin had promised greater flexibility in the search for peace and was willing to trade some land for peace. Rabin was a military man who in January 1964 became the chief of staff of the Israeli army. His hawkish position contributed to rising tensions in the years leading up to the Six Day War of 1967; during that war, he was as responsible as anyone for the Israeli conquest of Arab lands. Yet, it was this man who now had to deal with the consequences of that war.

Rabin declared that the most urgent task was to negotiate self-rule for Palestinians in the West Bank and Gaza, and toward that end he announced a curb on building new settlements in the occupied lands. Still, progress toward a negotiated solution was slow. Although Rabin was willing to trade land for peace, he was not willing to return to the 1967 borders. The moderate Palestinians with whom Israel was negotiating knew many Palestinians saw them as traitors negotiating away their patrimony. Hamas ("zeal" in Arabic), a militant Islamic organization based in Gaza, gained considerable support with its call for the destruction of Israel. Syria, in turn, demanded all, not merely a part of, the Golan Heights.

☐ The Oslo Agreements

At the end of summer 1993, secret negotiations in Oslo, Norway, between PLO functionaries and members of Israel's Peace Now movement (acting at first independent of the Rabin government) came to a successful conclusion. The negotiations produced a remarkable breakthrough when Arafat and Rabin accepted the broad outlines of the agreement. The signing ceremony for the agreement took place at a historic meeting at the White House in Washington, D.C., on September 13, 1993, where a reluctant Rabin shook Arafat's hand. The highlights of the agreement were as follows:

- A five-year period of limited autonomy for Palestinians in the occupied territories
- A withdrawal of Israeli forces from Gaza and the Jericho section of the West Bank and the establishment of Palestinian control of internal affairs in these areas within four months (with Jewish settlements there remaining under Israeli control)

- Palestinian elections in the occupied territories to create a governing body to be known as the Palestinian Authority (the embryo of a future Palestinian state)
- The creation of a Palestinian police force to include former PLO guerrillas
- Promise of Israeli financial support for economic development in Gaza and the West Bank

Although the agreement broke the long-standing Arab-Israeli logjam, it still left much unclear and unresolved, most significantly the future of East Jerusalem and its Palestinian population. Arafat expressed optimism that the talks would lead to the creation of a sovereign state of Palestine to be composed of Gaza and most of the West Bank, including East Jerusalem. Not surprisingly, there was strong opposition to the agreement from radical elements in both Israel and the Palestinian community. As Rabin's foreign minister, Shimon Peres, later put it, "A peace negotiation is with your own people as well as with the other one."[13] Jewish militants, particularly those who had set up residence in the West Bank city of Hebron (which contained the tomb of Abraham, the revered patriarch of both Jews and Muslims), cried that Arafat was still a terrorist and that allowing him control of the West Bank would lead to the extermination of Jewish settlers and threaten the survival of Israel. Hamas charged that Arafat had obtained too little and had betrayed the Palestinian cause, and the group began terrorist actions aimed at radicalizing public opinion in Israel, as well as among Palestinians. Israel and the PLO now became allies, each pinning its hopes on the other as they faced the same enemies—extremists who sought to derail the peace process.

The Oslo agreement prompted Jordan's King Hussein to get on board the peace process. Secret talks between representatives of Jordan and Israel soon produced a peace treaty, signed in Washington in July 1994, officially ending forty-six years of undeclared war. The treaty also opened border crossings between the two countries. The contagion of peace talks next spread toward Syria where the stalwart President Assad, no longer fortified by Soviet backing, began to respond to prodding by Washington and overtures from Rabin's government. The issue was the Golan Heights, the strategically located plateau about twenty miles wide and forty miles long, which had been under Israeli occupation since 1967. As early as 1993, Rabin spoke of the possibility of withdrawing Israeli forces from that region in exchange for peace with Syria, and he later spoke of a partial return of the territory. But Assad insisted on full Israeli withdrawal, including the evacuation of Israeli settlers.

All the while, the PLO-Israeli peace process continued according to the timetable laid out in the Oslo agreement, despite attempts by extremists to subvert it. In February 1994, a U.S.-born Zionist, Baruch Goldstein, carried out a mass murder of twenty-nine Muslim worshipers at the Tomb of the Patriarch (the resting place of Abraham) in Hebron. The killer was a member of an extremist organization whose attitudes were capsulized by a statement a rabbi made in a eulogy to the killer: "One million Arabs are not worth a Jewish fingernail."[14] The PLO condemned the massacre but did not abandon the pursuit of peace, as the perpetrators had hoped. Instead, Arafat and Rabin resolved to go forward. A supplementary agreement in May 1994 prepared the way for the withdrawal of Israeli military forces from Gaza and Jericho and for the establishment of internal control in these areas by the Palestinian Authority and its police force. In July 1994, Arafat made his triumphant return to Gaza as the president of the Palestinian Authority.

Arafat found Rabin and Peres, two former arch enemies, to be partners with whom he was able to negotiate various issues. The peace process itself, as Peres later explained, was more important than a plan because "plans don't create partners, but if you have a partner then you can negotiate a plan."[15] As long as the process remained in force, the possibility continued that even the most intractable issues, such as the final status of Jerusalem, could be resolved. It was for this reason that the Nobel Peace Prize committee, as it had done several times in the past, offered its award to former enemies—Rabin, Arafat, and Peres—who attempted to resolve their differences at the conference table rather than on the battlefield.

Arafat now had to shoulder the work of governing the Palestinians and improving their livelihood. Poverty was especially severe in Gaza, where the unemployment rate was almost 50 percent. The World Bank and several nations collectively contributed $180 million in developmental aid to Arafat by the end of 1994, but the amount was far less than was needed or than had been pledged. In addition to having to fend off complaints about the economy, Arafat faced critics of his autocratic rule. Most serious was the challenge posed by Hamas. In October 1994, a Hamas suicide bomber blew up a crowded bus in Tel Aviv, killing twenty-one people. A rally in Gaza drew over 20,000 Hamas supporters who praised the bomber as a martyr and denounced the PLO's agreement with Israel.

Another issue that blocked the road to peace was the unresolved status of Jerusalem. Palestinians had never accepted the 1967 Israeli annexation of the eastern half of Jerusalem and the city's designation by Israel as its capital. The population of East Jerusalem was almost exclusively Palestinian, and the PLO regarded it as an integral part of the West Bank and thus part of the envisioned state of Palestine. The issue came to the fore again in 1995 when Israel announced plans to expand Jewish settlements in and around Jerusalem and to seize 130 acres of Palestinian-owned property to build housing for Jewish residents. Arafat protested vehemently and even took the issue to the UN Security Council, where only a veto by the United States prevented passage of a resolution condemning the Israeli property seizure. Three months later, however, the Rabin government canceled the land confiscation plan, and the issue of Jerusalem remained in abeyance.

The struggle between the PLO and Hamas for the allegiance of the Palestinians continued unabated. In August 1995, Hamas carried out two more bus bombings, claiming twelve lives. Terrorism now made Israel and the PLO de facto allies, as they cooperated in efforts to apprehend and punish the terrorists and tighten security. With PLO cooperation, Israeli police hunted down those responsible and in a shoot-out killed two Hamas leaders and captured thirty others.

In September 1995, Arafat and Rabin affixed their signatures to a detailed plan that established a timetable for the withdrawal of Israeli forces from about 30 percent of the West Bank (including its major cities and about 400 towns) and put the Palestinian Authority immediately in charge of public services for most of the residents of the West Bank. The new agreement also called for the election of a Palestinian president and legislature and for the release of 5,000 Palestinian prisoners. The implementation of this agreement meant the end of the fifteen-year effort of previous right-wing governments of Israel to create a Greater Israel that would include the West Bank.

Hamas bombings produced in Israel ever-increasing hostility toward the peace process. Benjamin Netanyahu, the leader of the opposition Likud Party, went so far as to accuse Rabin of treason. One of Netanyahu's campaign posters showed Rabin wearing the *kaffiyeh,* Arafat's trademark Arab headdress. And in November 1995, a twenty-one-year-old Israeli extremist, Yigal Amir, assassinated Rabin. He justified his act on religious grounds: a Jew who harmed Jewish society must be killed.

Rabin's successor was his foreign minister, Shimon Peres, who had been a major architect of the peace process and was committed to it. Before the end of the year, Peres announced that the scheduled withdrawal of Israeli troops from seven West Bank cities had been completed, leaving 90 percent of the West Bank's 1 million Palestinians under PLO control.

☐ Return to Impasse

The first direct election of an Israeli prime minister took place in May 1995 under the shadow of escalating violence. Both Peres and his Likud Party opponent, Netanyahu, viewed the election as a referendum on the nearly three-year-long peace process. Peres hoped to improve his election prospects by making progress in the stalled negotiations with Syria, but these talks were abruptly derailed by a renewed flare-up between Hezbollah guerrillas in Lebanon and Israeli forces. Hezbollah opened fire on Israeli towns with rockets, and Israel retaliated with much greater force—as it had done so many times in the past—causing half a million civilians to take flight and bombing Beirut for the first time since 1982. With his eye on the election, Peres no doubt felt it necessary to convince Israeli voters of his resolve to defend the nation. At the same time, he hastened to assure Arafat that he had no intention of abandoning negotiations with him. In fact, even before a cease-fire was arranged in Lebanon, Peres promised Arafat that he would withdraw Israeli forces from Hebron in exchange for an official revocation by the PLO of clauses in its original charter calling for the destruction of Israel.

But neither his assault on Hezbollah nor this coveted concession from Arafat won Peres the election. By a razor-thin margin, the victory went to Netanyahu, a hard-liner who had opposed the Oslo peace process agreements every step of the way. Netanyahu rejected Rabin's "land for peace" formula, instead promised "peace with security," and would trade only "peace for peace." He also had the reputation of knowing how to deal with terrorists; he had even published a recent handbook on the topic, *Fighting Terrorism*. Peres had his own book, *Battling for Peace*.[16] The majority of voters decided that the battle for peace contained too many dangers, and they were willing to hand over power to someone who just might defeat the terrorists.

After the election, prospects for a continuation of the peace initiatives looked dim. Netanyahu refused to make any commitments and for almost four months refused to meet with Arafat, whom he still considered a terrorist and not a worthy negotiating partner. Peres saw the snub of Arafat as a needless "humiliation for the sake of humiliation." With Rabin dead and Peres defeated at the polls, the peace process was derailed. Netanyahu, instead of resuming negotiations with the PLO, took actions that made it clear that Israel—including the West Bank and all of Jerusalem—contained but one sovereign ruler. He demolished Palestinian homes, authorized the building of additional Jewish settlements and Jewish-only access roads in the West Bank, and delayed the previously agreed upon withdrawal of Israeli troops from Hebron.

In September 1996, Netanyahu sent a message that Israel alone was sovereign in Jerusalem and that the Palestinians had no choice but to accept what the Israeli government was meting out. In the dark of night, he opened a tunnel that ran into the heart of East Jerusalem along the Temple Mount, on which rested two of the most sacred shrines of Islam—the Dome of the Rock and the Al-Aksa Mosque. This unilateral act symbolized that the Oslo agreements were all but over. Arafat called for an angry protest by Palestinian residents of Jerusalem, which quickly escalated into widespread riots and shoot-outs. The intifada had consisted mainly of an uprising by young Palestinians armed with rocks and Molotov cocktails, but this time it was different. The clashes produced shoot-outs between Israeli forces and some of the 30,000 Palestinian police officers. Israeli and Palestinian police had established a remarkable degree of cooperation since 1993, but now they were shown on television killing each other. In three days of fighting, over sixty Palestinians and fourteen Israelis were killed, and many more were wounded. To cut short the violence before it completely destroyed the peace process, U.S. President Bill Clinton invited Netanyahu, Arafat, and other Arab leaders to Washington for talks. But he was able to secure only an agreement on the need to continue negotiations indefinitely. In follow-up talks, Netanyahu steadfastly refused to yield on any issue. Finally, in January 1997, Netanyahu allowed a partial withdrawal of Israeli forces from Hebron, but the concession fell short of what Peres had earlier promised Arafat. One month later, in yet another affront to the PLO, Netanyahu authorized the construction of a large apartment complex for Jews at a site on the periphery of East Jerusalem. It was an act aimed at rejecting Palestinian claims to that part of the city and destroying the PLO's dream of making it the capital of the future state of Palestine. Under Netanyahu's best-case scenario, the Palestinians would have to accept meekly the end of the Oslo process. Such was his vision of "peace for peace." The Arab-Israeli impasse continued.

RECOMMENDED READINGS

Avineri, Shlomo. *The Making of Modern Zionism: The Intellectual Origins of the Jewish State*. New York: Basic Books, 1981.
    An explanation of the intellectual climate of the nineteenth century that produced the Zionist movement.
Elon, Amos. *The Israelis: Founders and Sons*. New York: Holt, Rinehart and Winston, 1971.
    A classic treatment of the roots of Zionism and the first two decades of the existence of Israel.
Kimmerling, Baruch, and Joel S. Migdal. *Palestinians: The Making of a People*. New York: Free Press, 1993.
    How a clan-centered Arab population acquired a national collective character.
Lilienthal, Alfred M. *The Zionist Connection: What Price Peace?* Rev. ed. New Brunswick, N.J.: North American, 1982.
    A critical explanation of the Zionist movement.
Oz, Amos. *In the Land of Israel*. New York: Random House, 1983.
    By an Israeli novelist who dwells on Israel's dilemma.
Peters, Joan. *From Time Immemorial: The Origins of the Arab-Jewish Conflict over Palestine*. New York: Harper and Row, 1984.
    An ambitious and controversial attempt to prove that the Jews did not displace the Arabs in Palestine but instead that Arabs had displaced Jews.
Reich, Walter. *A Stranger in My House: Jews and Arabs in the West Bank*. New York: Henry Holt, 1984.
    An evenhanded and judicious attempt by a U.S. psychiatrist to understand the historical, sociological, and theological arguments of the inhabitants of the West Bank.
Said, Edward W. *The Question of Palestine*. New York: Random House, 1980.
    By a U.S. scholar of Palestinian descent, this is the classic study championing the Palestinian cause.
Segev, Tom. *1949: The First Israelis*. New York: Free Press, 1985.

A controversial best seller in Israel; a reinterpretation by an Israeli journalist of the early history of the state.

Shehadeh, Raja. *Samed: Journal of a West Bank Palestinian*. New York: Adama Publishers, 1984.

Life on the West Bank from a Palestinian's perspective.

Shipler, David K. *Arab and Jew: Wounded Spirits in a Promised Land*. New York: Times Books, 1986.

By a *New York Times* correspondent.

NOTES

1. Jewish nationalism has existed ever since the diaspora, the dispersion of the Jews that began in the sixth century B.C. with the destruction of Solomon's temple and culminated with the destruction of the second temple in Jerusalem in A.D. 70 and the defeat of Bar Kochba in A.D. 135. British philosopher Bertrand Russell, in reminding his readers that modern nationalism is a relatively new concept, pointed out that at the end of the Middle Ages "there was hardly any nationalism except that of the Jews."

2. Quoted in Amos Elon, *The Israelis: Founders and Sons* (New York: Holt, Rinehart and Winston, 1971), p. 106.

3. Palestinian Arab and Ben-Gurion cited in ibid., p. 155 (emphasis in the original).

4. "Balfour Declaration," in London *Times,* November 9, 1917, p. 7.

5. In fact, when King Abdullah of Jordan, the grandfather of King Hussein, sought to come to terms with the state of Israel (he met in secret with several Zionists in 1949), it cost him his life at the hand of an assassin. The first Arab nation to exchange ambassadors with Israel was Egypt in 1979. For this, as well as for domestic reasons, Egyptian President Anwar Sadat suffered the fate of Abdullah when he, too, was assassinated.

6. As a result, 70 percent of the population of the Kingdom of Jordan consisted of Palestinians, from which came the argument in some quarters in Israel that a Palestinian state already existed.

7. "UN Resolution 242," *Yearbook of the United Nations: 1967* (New York: United Nations, 1969), pp. 257–258.

8. Moshe Dayan and King Hussein quoted in Dana Adams Schmidt, *Armageddon in the Middle East* (New York: John Day, 1974), p. 249. For a discussion of the positions of Dayan and Hussein, see Bernard Avishai, *The Tragedy of Zionism: Revolution and Democracy in the Land of Israel* (New York: Farrar, Straus, Giroux, 1985), pp. 275–278.

9. Despite King Hussein's suppression of the PLO in 1970, the king and the PLO made common cause in 1985 in an uneasy alliance that proposed a Jordanian-Palestinian federation that would include the West Bank. President Hosni Mubarak of Egypt sought to peddle the plan to Washington but with no success. Israel rejected the proposal outright.

10. From a report of a U.S. diplomatic summary of the conversation between Sharon and Habib, published by the Israeli Labor Party newspaper, *Davar.* The U.S. ambassador to Israel, Samuel W. Lewis, and the State Department confirmed the basic outlines of the conversation. Thomas L. Friedman, "Paper Says Israeli Outlined Invasion," *New York Times,* May 26, 1985, p. 15.

11. Text of Arafat statement, *Baltimore Sun,* December 15, 1988.

12. Yitzhak Shamir, "Israel at 40: Looking Back, Looking Ahead," *Foreign Affairs,* 66, 3 (1988), pp. 585–586.

13. Peres cited in Connie Bruck, "The Wounds of Peace," *The New Yorker,* October 14, 1996, p. 64.

14. Cited in William Pfaff, "Victory to Extremists," *Baltimore Sun,* March 7, 1994, p. 14A.

15. Peres cited in Bruck, "The Wounds of Peace," p. 66.

16. *Fighting Terrorism: How Democracies Defeat Domestic and International Terrorism* and *Battling for Peace: A Memoir,* reviewed by Avishai Margalit in "The Terror Master" and "The Chances of Simon Peres," *New York Review,* October 5, 1995, pp. 17–22, and May 9, 1996, pp. 18–23.

PART 3

THE SHIFTING SANDS OF GLOBAL POWER

From the outset the Cold War created a bipolar world in which the two contending superpowers pulled other nations toward one pole or the other. But gradually this bipolar East-West confrontation underwent a transformation marked by divisions within each camp and the emergence of other centers of power. In the first eight years of the Cold War there existed a straightforward adversary relationship featuring the hard-nosed diplomatic combat of Joseph Stalin and Harry Truman. It also featured the Soviet Iron Curtain, the U.S. containment policy, a tense standoff in Europe, the creation of two military alliances (NATO and the Warsaw Pact), a war in Korea, persistent ideological attacks and counterattacks, and the massive rearmament of both sides. Despite the conciliatory gestures by the successors of Stalin and Truman and talk of peaceful coexistence, the bipolar struggle carried over into the 1960s and grew even more intense as the two superpowers squared off in the Cuban missile crisis.

However, by that time, it was becoming clear to both superpowers that they had lost the capacity to make military use of their huge nuclear arsenals and that the day of direct confrontation had ended. Also by the early 1960s, the two superpowers could no longer take for granted the solidarity of their respective alliances. The bipolar world of the 1950s began to give way to multipolarity in the 1960s.

In order to understand this process, the political legacy of Joseph Stalin in the Soviet Union is our point of departure in Chapter 8. Here we trace the efforts of his successor, Nikita Khrushchev, to put to an end the excesses of Stalinism, the terror and the arbitrary and abusive use of state power, and to institute reforms aimed at restoring orderly and legal procedures to Soviet rulership and revitalizing the economy. The consequences of this reform effort and the pattern of Soviet politics under Khrushchev's successors are also discussed. Additionally, we examine the stresses and strains within the Communist bloc and particularly the impact of Khrushchev's reforms in Eastern Europe. The impact of de-Stalinization was controlled within the

Soviet Union, but that was not the case in the satellite countries, especially in Poland and Hungary, where it rekindled nationalist sentiments and unleashed pent-up desires for political liberalization and liberation from Moscow's control.

But if the resulting revolts in Poland and Hungary and later in Czechoslovakia could be snuffed out by the Soviet Union, a recalcitrant Communist China could not so easily be dealt with. In Chapter 8, we analyze the causes and the course of the Sino-Soviet split, which divided the Communist world. Their bitter and long-lasting feud signified that ideological bonds are not stronger than national interests and that international Communism was not the monolithic movement it was generally thought to be.

Meanwhile, in the 1960s, the U.S. government, still convinced that Communism was monolithic, went off to war in distant Asia to stop its spread. In Chapter 9, we explain how and why the United States took up the fight in Vietnam. We argue that the staunch anti-Communist logic of U.S. leaders caused them to misread the revolution in that country, its causes and strengths, and come up with the erroneous conclusion that its source was Beijing-based Communist aggression rather than Vietnamese nationalism. We next offer an explanation of the prolongation and expansion of the war in Indochina and the difficulty the United States had in extracting itself from that war. We also examine the tragic consequences of U.S. involvement in Vietnam, the trauma of its defeat, the impact of its departure on the remainder of Indochina, especially Cambodia, and the tragedy of the refugees, the "boat people."

In the late 1960s, when the United States was still mired in Vietnam, progress was made in lowering East-West tension on other fronts. New leadership in West Germany, specifically that of Chancellor Willy Brandt, took bold steps seeking to break up the twenty-year-old Cold War logjam in Central Europe. In Chapter 10, we examine Brandt's conciliatory policy toward the Communist nations of Eastern Europe and the role it played in bringing détente—the relaxation of tension—to East-West relations. By the early 1970s détente became the basis of Soviet-U.S. diplomacy.

The new relations between Washington and Moscow left Beijing isolated as an enemy of both. In fact, the U.S.-Soviet détente at first brought jeers from China, which suspected an anti-Chinese conspiracy. But as we show in Chapter 10, Chinese leaders came to realize the dangers of China's continued isolation and judged that it had more to gain in terms of economic development and national security by normalizing its relations with the United States. In a dramatic diplomatic turnabout the United States and Communist China, two nations that had been the most intransigent of ideological foes for two decades, suddenly in 1972 buried the hatchet.

With U.S.-Soviet détente and the normalization of U.S.-Chinese relations, a new era of delicate tripolar power relations had arrived.

Moreover, with the resurgence of Western Europe and the emergence of an economically powerful Japan, the international arena was now multipolar with at least five centers of power. The simpler world of East versus West, of the struggle between the "free world" and the "Communist world," gave way to a more complex world of power-balancing diplomacy, one calling for greater political flexibility.

8

The Communist World
After Stalin

When Stalin died in March 1953, he had ruled the Soviet Union for nearly thirty years and in the process left his imprint on the Communist Party and the nation. In the late 1920s, Stalin and his party had set out to initiate a program of rapid industrialization with a series of Five-Year Plans. In order to feed the growing proletariat (the industrial work force), he introduced a program of rapid collectivization whereby the small and inefficient individual farms were consolidated into larger collectives. In effect, it made the Soviet peasant an employee of the state. The state set the price the collective farms received for their agricultural commodities, a price kept low so that the countryside wound up subsidizing the cities where an industrial revolution was taking place. In this fashion, agriculture became one of the "stepchildren" of the Communist revolution in the Soviet Union.

At the time of the Communist revolution of 1917, the peasants had realized an age-old dream, the private and unrestricted ownership of their land. Predictably, they resisted the Stalinist drive toward collectivization. Stalin, faced with intense opposition, had two choices: curtail the program of collectivization and industrialization or pursue it with force. He chose the latter. Collectivization became a bloody civil war during the late 1920s and early 1930s in which several million peasants perished and which witnessed widespread destruction of equipment and livestock. In such wasteful and brutal manner, the countryside subsidized the industrial revolution and the growth of the city.

Stalin subordinated Soviet society to one overriding quest, to create an industrial state for the purpose of bringing to an end Russia's traditional economic backwardness, the root cause of its military weakness. In 1931, Stalin spoke to a conference of factory managers on the question of whether the mad dash toward industrialization could be slowed. He offered his audience a capsule history of Russia:

> To slacken the tempo would mean falling behind. And all those who fall behind get beaten. . . . One feature of the history of old Russia was the

continual beatings she suffered because of her backwardness. She was beaten by the Mongol khans. She was beaten by the Turkish beys. She was beaten by the Swedish feudal lords. She was beaten by the Polish and Lithuanian gentry. She was beaten by the British and French capitalists. She was beaten by the Japanese barons. All beat her—because of her backwardness, military backwardness, cultural backwardness, political backwardness, industrial backwardness. . . . Such is the law of the exploiters, to beat the backward and the weak. . . . Either we do it [catch up with the capitalist West], or we shall be crushed. . . . In ten years we must make good the distance which separates us from the advanced capitalist countries. . . . And that depends on us. Only on us![1]

Stalin's Five-Year Plans gave the Soviet Union a heavily centralized economy capable of withstanding the supreme test of fire, the German attack on the Soviet Union in 1941. In fact, during World War II the Soviet war economy, despite massive destruction at the hands of the Germans, outproduced that of Germany. Studies conducted after the war for the U.S. Joint Chiefs of Staff repeatedly paid tribute to Stalin's industrial revolution, which had transformed the Soviet Union from a weak, backward country into a formidable opponent that all too soon broke the U.S. nuclear monopoly (1949) and later was the first to venture into the frontiers of space (1957).

All of this did not come without a heavy price. Stalin contributed to the transformation of what initially had been meant to be a "dictatorship of the proletariat"[2] into a dictatorship of the party over the proletariat and the peasantry, and eventually into a dictatorship of the secret police over the proletariat, the peasantry, and the party itself. In 1937, Stalin initiated the bloodiest of a series of purges of the party by which he eliminated all opposition within the Communist Party to his regime. The Bolshevik Revolution of 1917, which had begun as an uprising by the proletariat, rank-and-file soldiers, and peasants, had become a monument to the triumph of the secret police.

■ KHRUSHCHEV AND STALIN'S GHOST

When Stalin died in 1953, the party immediately took steps to reassert the position of preeminence it had enjoyed in the days of Vladimir Lenin, the architect of the Bolshevik Revolution, who had led the Soviet Union until his death in 1924. Within a week after Stalin's death, the party forced Stalin's designated successor, Georgi Malenkov, to give up one of the two posts he held. The party told him to choose between the post of first secretary of the party (that is, the head of the party) or that of prime minister. Malenkov, inexplicably, decided to hold on to the position of prime minister. As a result a lesser member of the Politburo, Nikita Khrushchev, took charge of the daily operations of the party. The party then took another step to prevent the consolidation of power in the hands of one person. It officially established a collective leadership, a *troika* (Russian for a sled pulled by three horses) consisting of Malenkov as prime minister, Viacheslav Molotov as foreign minister, and Lavrentii Beria as the head of the secret police. Beria, who had been an agent of Stalin's terror, remained a threat to the party. In the summer of 1953, the party, with the help of the leadership of the Soviet Army (which also had suffered greatly during the secret police's unchecked reign of terror), arrested Beria. It charged him with the abuse of power and then shot him.

The party then continued to attempt to come to terms with the Stalinist legacy. The reformers repeatedly clashed with those who sought to prevent meaningful changes. Gradually, in the mid-1950s the reformers gained the upper hand and some of the shackles of the Stalinist past were cast off. A general amnesty freed political prisoners. Writers, many of whom had been "writing for the desk drawer," succeeded in seeing their works in print. The first version of détente with the West now became a possibility. Western visitors began to arrive in Moscow.

The most dramatic assault on the status of Stalin came in February 1956, at the Communist Party's Twentieth Congress, when Nikita Khrushchev

Soviet leader Nikita Khrushchev, flanked by Foreign Minister Andrei Gromyko and Marshal Rodion Malinovski, at a press conference in Paris, May 16, 1960. (*National Archives*)

delivered a scathing attack on Stalin's crimes. It became known as the "Secret Speech," but it did not remain secret for long—since an address before an assembly of several hundred delegates, many of whom had much to gain by making it public, would certainly reach the light of day. The speech was the result of a commission the party had set up to report on Beria's and Stalin's crimes, mostly those committed against the party itself. The Communist Party announced through Khrushchev that Stalin's terror, including the destruction of its role in the affairs of the state, had been an act of lawlessness, one which the party now sought to prevent in the future. "Socialist legality" was to take the place of one-person rule.

The speech was essentially an attempt by the party at self-preservation. And it was limited to just that. It did not address the larger question of Stalin's terror directed against the peasants, religious organizations, writers and composers—in short, the public at large. One of Khrushchev's Western biographers wrote that the Secret Speech was a smokescreen as well as an exposure.[3] It did not tackle the question of one-party rule by the "vanguard of the proletariat," namely the Communist Party. Neither did it challenge the Stalinist system of agriculture, which the party admitted at the time was in ruin, nor the system of industrial production, which still worked reasonably well. Instead, Khrushchev's speech focused on the dictatorship of the police over the party.

The Secret Speech signaled the end of the arbitrary terror of Stalin's time. The secret police was brought under the party's control and its wings were clipped, particularly in dealing with party members. Arbitrary arrests were largely ended. Censorship restrictions were partially lifted, breathing new life into the Soviet Union's intellectual community. Throughout his tenure Khrushchev repeatedly waged war against the memory of Stalin, particularly in 1957 and then in 1961 when he went so far as to remove Stalin's body from the mausoleum it shared with Lenin's body and to rename cities and institutions that had been named in Stalin's honor. The city of Stalingrad, for example, the supreme symbol of the Soviet Union's resistance to Hitler, where an entire German army found defeat, became merely the "city on the Volga," or Volgograd.

After Khrushchev's ouster in October 1964, the party made no concerted effort to rehabilitate Stalin's image, although overt criticism of Stalin was brought to an end. It was clear, however, that one day Soviet society had to come to grips with Stalin's legacy. The transformation of Stalin's image from a hero and generalissimo, to a murderous tyrant in violation of "Leninist legality," and finally to a shadowy figure who appeared scarcely to have existed, simply would not do. In 1961, the party published the long-awaited second edition of its *History of the Communist Party of the Soviet Union*. The first edition had been published in 1938 under Stalin's direct editorship and as such had heaped voluminous praise on Stalin. The second edition, in contrast, was an example of revisionist history with a vengeance. It never mentioned Stalin's name. It was Mikhail Gorbachev who in 1987 forced Soviet society once again to deal with its past and reopened the discussion of Stalin's role.

To many observers in the West, these changes were of little consequence. The Communist Party still retained its control and the economy remained unchanged. But in the context of Russian and Soviet history, these liberalizing changes were nothing short of revolutionary. This is something on which both the Soviet opponents and defenders of Khrushchev agreed. What Khrushchev needed to do was continue to introduce innovations without major repercussions, for, as Alexis de Tocqueville (the French political writer of the nineteenth century) wrote, the most difficult time in the life of a bad government comes when it tries to reform itself.[4] Khrushchev soon found that out.

Philosophically, Khrushchev expressed the view that art must not be censored. But the flood of writings that sought to portray Soviet reality as it in fact existed, warts and all, soon overwhelmed the party, and Khrushchev himself became a censor. In 1962, Khrushchev permitted the publication of Alexander Solzhenitsyn's exposé of Stalin's labor camps, *One Day in the Life of Ivan Denisovich,* the literary sensation of the post-Stalin age; yet, several years earlier, Khrushchev had supported "administrative measures" to prevent the publication of Boris Pasternak's *Doctor Zhivago,* admittedly without having read it. Late in life, a repentant Khrushchev wrote that "readers should be given a chance to make their own judgments" and that "police measures shouldn't be used."[5] As the first secretary of the party, however, Khrushchev never did manage to come to grips with his contradictions. The result was that he was unable to bring the restless writers under control. This task fell to his successor, Leonid Brezhnev.

By the early 1960s, Khrushchev had worn out his welcome. The majority of the party was increasingly beginning to view his erratic moves and innovations as hare-brained schemes. The classic case in point was the attempt to place nuclear missiles in Cuba in 1962, a rash impulsive act. Poorly thought out and hasty reforms in the areas of agriculture and industry also came back to haunt Khrushchev. In October 1964, Khrushchev contemplated a shake-up in the party. It proved to be the last straw, for it threatened the exalted positions of many. By then Khrushchev had lost the support of the majority in the Central Committee, officially the major decisionmaking body of the Communist Party. The party, in a vote of no confidence, sent him out to pasture with the stipulation that he stay out of politics. Leonid Brezhnev succeeded him as the head of the party.

Khrushchev's demise proved to be his finest hour. He had dealt with his opponents within the bounds of "socialist legality," that is by using the rules and procedures written into the party's statutes and by using the support many in the party at one time gave him enthusiastically. But when his behavior became increasingly irrational, embarrassing, and reckless, the party then turned against him. Once he faced the cold, hard fact that he had lost the support of the majority, he stepped down. There was never a question of using the military or the secret police.

Khrushchev's successors gave the Soviet Union twenty years of stability, a significant increase in the standard of living, and rough military parity with the West. At the same time, this was an era when the status quo was maintained. A free-wheeling discussion of Stalin's role in Soviet history, therefore, had no place in the scheme of the Brezhnev vision of Soviet society. The intellectuals were eventually brought under control by intimidation, jailing, and, in several cases, notably that of Solzhenitsyn, expulsion from the country. Brezhnev, the first secretary of the party, and particularly his prime minister, Alexei Kosygin, contemplated economic reforms but they were soon shelved when it became apparent that all too many factory managers had their fill of reforms under Khrushchev and fought for the retention of the status quo.

By the time Brezhnev died in 1982, the party was beginning to accept the need for another round of reform, this time primarily in the field of industry and agriculture. Yuri Andropov and Konstantin Chernenko initiated the first modest steps, but both were hampered by what turned out to be incurable illnesses. In 1985, Mikhail Gorbachev, the new first secretary of the party, took on the nation's problems.

The Communist Party stood to come full circle. Nikita Khrushchev began the attack on Stalin's political legacy, the terror against the party and people. Mikhail Gorbachev inherited the unenviable task of tackling Stalin's economic legacy, top-heavy industrialization and collectivized agriculture. For more than three centuries, successive rulers of Russia have repeatedly introduced significant departures from the policies of their predecessors. Gorbachev, in a direct challenge to Brezhnev's political, economic, and intellectual inertia, committed his nation to a free-wheeling discussion of its shortcomings, to the restructuring of the economy, and to the acceleration of the process of transformation (see Chapter 21).

■ EASTERN EUROPE: THE SATELLITES

As the Communist Party in the Soviet Union wrestled with Stalin's ghost, a similar drama began to unfold in Moscow's East European satellites. There, the conflict was fought with much more intensity and conviction. The reformers were willing to go much further than their counterparts behind the Kremlin walls. Although much of Eastern Europe subsequently moved further from the Stalinist model than the Soviet Union, Moscow always made it clear that the reforms must remain within certain perimeters, which, although not rigidly defined and constantly shifting, must nevertheless not be transgressed. Moscow's position vis-à-vis Eastern Europe followed along the classic lines of the carrot, in the shape of a tolerance of reforms, and the stick, wielded by the Soviet Army to maintain control.

The West considered the expansion of Soviet political and military power after World War II as a threat to its security and saw it as a source of Soviet strength. But Stalin saw it in a different light. He knew that the East European buffer offered his state security, but that it was also a potential source of headaches. At the Yalta Conference he had described the Poles as "quarrelsome." He well understood the volatile mix of nationalism, religion, and anti-Russian sentiments in Eastern Europe. Soviet occupation of Eastern Europe had given him a measure of military strength in any future confrontation with the capitalist West, but it also promised to bring problems.

By 1948, Stalin appeared to have consolidated his position in Eastern Europe. The Communist parties of that region were for the most part the creation of the Soviet Union and on the surface loyal members of the socialist camp lined up in solidarity against the capitalist threat. But the Communists of Eastern Europe were soon showing nationalist tendencies whereby they were more interested in championing the causes of their own nations instead of serving the interests of the Soviet Union.

☐ Yugoslavia

The classic example of such "nationalist deviation" was the case of Joseph Tito, the Communist ruler of Yugoslavia. In the 1930s Tito had spent time in Moscow under Stalin's tutelage, and during World War II he had fought with the Allies against Nazi Germany. His loyalty to Stalin and the cause of international Marxist solidarity appeared beyond reproach. Soon after the war, however, at the very moment the West and the Soviet Union were taking steps to consolidate their respective positions, the Yugoslav and Soviet Communists had a falling out over the question of who was to play the dominant role in running Yugoslavia. The upshot of this quarrel was that Tito established his independence from Moscow. He did not, however, move into the capitalist camp. He accepted aid from the West, but always maintained a position of neutrality between East and West.[6] The Tito-Stalin split pointed to a central problem the Soviets faced in Eastern Europe, the volatile force of nationalism.

The immediate consequence of Tito's defection was Stalin's reorganization of the Communist governments of Eastern Europe. He executed and jailed Communists (such as Poland's Wladyslaw Gomulka, of whom more later) whom he suspected of nationalist (or Titoist) tendencies. Foreign Communists were to have one loyalty and that was to be to the Soviet Union, not their native lands. Stalin's definition of a loyal Communist was one who faithfully served the interests of the Kremlin. An international *"revolutionary,"* Stalin wrote in 1927, is one "who is ready to protect, to defend the U.S.S.R. without reservation, without qualification."[7] In short, the interests of the Soviet Union outweighed the considerations of all other socialist governments. Stalin never budged on this definition of an international revolutionary. Only one Marxist was permitted to be a nationalist, namely, Stalin himself.

The damage Stalin did to Communist movements beyond the Soviet Union was seldom adequately appreciated in the West. Not only did he subordinate the Communist parties to the interests of his state, but in doing so he tainted them with a brush wielded by a foreign power. As such, these movements found themselves struggling for support. That was particularly true in Europe after both world wars. Within two to three years after the wars, the radical shifts for which the wars and subsequent disillusionment had been largely responsible had burned themselves out. All that remained were Communist parties struggling to survive, their association with Moscow having become a millstone dragging them down, and their thunder stolen by reformist socialists. In short, the shifts to the left were not the creation of Stalin; the left's demise, however, was in part Stalin's responsibility.

Stalin's brutal cleansing ("purging") of the East European Communist parties did have its desired effect. Until Stalin's death in March 1953, these parties were outwardly loyal to the Soviet Union, and Eastern Europe remained calm.

☐ Poland

But soon after Stalin's death the East European Communist parties began to work toward partial independence from Moscow. This did not mean that they sought to leave the socialist camp or legalize capitalist political parties, but they did insist on dealing with their own internal problems without direct intervention by Moscow. An element of self-preservation played a large part in the restructuring of the relationship between the East European Communist parties and Moscow. The East Europeans sought to do away with Moscow's repeated and arbitrary purges of their ranks and interference in their internal affairs. The Polish party took the lead when it quietly released (December 1954) and later readmitted (August 1956) into the party the nationalist Wladyslaw Gomulka whom Stalin had jailed in 1948.

Stalin had good reason to mistrust Gomulka. As early as 1945, Stalin's agents in Poland had warned him that the deviationist Gomulka had repeatedly and publicly advocated a "Polish road" to socialism, a "Polish Marxism." Gomulka's variation of Communism, unlike the Soviet version, sought a peaceful rather than a bloody transformation of society. It rejected the collectivization of agriculture, spoke of a "parliamentary democracy" for Poland, and even suggested that the Polish Communist Party had seized political power in 1945 in its own right—as it was "laying in the street" ready to be picked up—thus failing to show proper gratitude for the role of the Red Army. What we are dealing with here, the agents pointed out, is more a case of "Polish nationalism" than of Communism based on the Soviet model.[8]

The return to power of East European Communists who had been driven from power by Stalin was greatly speeded up when the new Soviet leader, Nikita Khrushchev, denounced Stalin's "mistakes" and "excesses," namely his crimes against members of the Communist Party in the Soviet Union itself. Khrushchev sought to discredit his Stalinist political opponents at home, but his action had unforeseen and important repercussions in Eastern Europe.

When Khrushchev's first attack on the dead Stalin took place in his Secret Speech at the Twentieth Congress of the Communist Party of the Soviet Union in February 1956, the Polish Communist Party, which had sent delegates to the congress, leaked a copy of the speech to the West. Khrushchev later wrote in his memoirs: "I was told that it was being sold for very little. So Khrushchev's speech . . . wasn't appraised as being worth much! Intelligence agents from every country in the world could buy it cheap on the open market."[9] If Khrushchev could denounce Stalinism at home, the Poles reasoned, then they ought to be able to do the same. The Poles then used the speech to justify their attempt to travel their own road toward socialism without, however, leaving the Soviet camp.

At home the Polish Communist Party had its work cut out. The summer of 1956 saw rioting by workers, particularly in Poznan where seventy-five workers lost their lives in confrontations with police, and the country became unmanageable. To deal with this crisis, the party convened in October 1956 to initiate a program of reform and to elect Gomulka as its first secretary. Upon his election, Gomulka delivered a speech in which he affirmed Poland's right to follow a socialist model other than the one the Soviet Union offered. He also insisted on his country's "full independence and sovereignty," as part of every nation's right to self-government. Polish-Soviet relations, he said, must be based on equality and independence.

What particularly had galled the Poles was that their defense minister, Konstantin Rokossovsky, was a Soviet citizen. Rokossovsky, a native of Poland, had left his country for the Soviet Union and had risen to the highest rank, that of marshal of the Red Army. As Poland's minister of defense he thus served a foreign master. Understandably, Rokossovsky became one of the first casualties of Poland's peaceful "October Revolution."

The behavior by the Polish Communists alarmed their Soviet comrades. A high-level Soviet delegation, led by Khrushchev, arrived uninvited at the October 1956 party meeting in Warsaw. In the resulting confrontation the Poles refused to back down. They made it clear that they would travel the socialist road, yet at the same time they insisted on the right to take care of their own internal problems. In addition, they pledged their loyalty to the Warsaw Pact, the Soviet-led military alliance. They eventually convinced Khrushchev to return to Moscow.

The Soviet Union, here, gave tacit assent to the principle that there exist several different roads to socialism, that the Soviet model was not the only one and thus not necessarily the correct one. In effect, the Kremlin yielded and accepted the legitimacy of what once was a heresy, the right to nationalist deviation. If the Soviets had the right to find their own path to socialism, so did the other socialist countries. In fact the Soviets had already buried the hatchet in their ideological dispute with Tito. In May 1955, Khrushchev had gone to Belgrade on a state visit and when he and Tito embraced it signaled an end to the intra-Marxist feud. The Soviet Union's monopoly on interpreting the writings of Marx and Engels was no more. The Italian Communist Palmiro Togliatti coined a word to describe the new reality, "polycentrism."[10] This term made it clear that the world now had not one but many centers of Marxist orthodoxy.

The Poles, although still in the shadow of the Soviet Union, embarked on their own road to socialism, and the Communist Party took steps to placate the restless population. Workers gained concessions, and the gradual process of collectivizing farmland was halted and then reversed. (Unlike the Soviet Union where the state owned all land, most farmland in Communist Poland was in the hands of private farmers.) Political parties other than the Communist Party were permitted to exist and they received subordinate representation in the government. Gomulka released from jail the prelate of the Roman Catholic Church in Poland, Stefan Cardinal Wyszynski, and the church regained the traditional right to administer its own affairs. In turn, Gomulka received the church's endorsement.

☐ Hungary

Across the border, the Hungarians watched the developments in Poland with increasing intensity. If the Poles could eliminate some of the baleful effects of Stalinism, why could not they? Heated discussions took place in intellectual circles and within the Hungarian Communist Party. The upshot was that the Stalinists were forced to resign and Imre Nagy, Hungary's "Gomulka," took over.

Initially, events in Hungary paralleled those in Poland. But Nagy could not control the rebellious mood that was building up in his country. It was not enough to rid the nation of the Stalinists; nothing short of independence from Moscow would do. A reformed Communist Party was not enough; the Communist Party was, after all, a creation of the Russians. Deep-seated Hungarian animosity toward the Russians had its historic roots in the intervention by the Russian army during the revolution of 1848 when Hungarians had sought to free themselves of Austrian domination.

Resistance fighters in the Hungarian revolt, Budapest, Oct. 11, 1956. (*National Archives*)

Also, the Stalinist secret police had bred deep resentment. These factors, as well as economic grievances, led to massive street demonstrations and the lynching of secret police agents. Budapest had become unmanageable and on November 1, 1956, Nagy suddenly announced that Hungary was now an independent nation. With this declaration came the pledge to hold free elections—elections that promised to end Communist Party rule in Hungary.

The events in Hungary left Nikita Khrushchev few choices, particularly when Radio Free Europe, a station operating out of Munich under the aegis of the CIA, encouraged the Hungarians by offering vague promises of U.S. aid. In this highly charged moment in the Cold War, a neutral Hungary was out of the question. John Foster Dulles, the U.S. secretary of state, had said earlier that neutrality in this holy war against the forces of absolute evil was the height of immorality.[11] The leaders in the Kremlin held a similar view. Hungary was thus destined to be but a pawn in an ideological and military tug-of-war. Its fate was to serve either the interests of Washington or those of Moscow. With the Soviet position in Eastern Europe beginning to disintegrate, Khrushchev acted.

For several days, the Soviets did not know what to do. At first, they saw the disturbances in Budapest as anti-Soviet (as had been the case in Poland) but not anti-Communist. They expected to work with Nagy and even discussed the possibility of withdrawing their troops from Hungary. But then came the news that Communists were being lynched in the streets of Budapest. Any withdrawal, Khrushchev now argued, would "cheer up the imperialists." "We had to act," he declared in his memoirs, "and we had to act swiftly."[12]

The Soviet Army attacked Budapest three days after Nagy's proclamation. After a week of savage fighting during which an estimated 25,000 people died, the Soviets reestablished their control over Hungary. The Kremlin installed János Kádár as the Hungarian party's new first secretary, and he had Imre Nagy executed in 1958. Kádár, who came to power with blood on his hands, proved in time to be a cautious reformer.[13] Gradually over the next three decades he introduced the most sweeping economic reforms anywhere in the Soviet bloc, culminating in the legalization of private enterprises in the early 1980s. This combination of the carrot (tolerance of reforms) and the stick (the Soviet Army) lifted many restrictions, raised the standard of living, and kept Hungary quiet.

The United States could do little but watch with indignation the Soviet suppression of the Hungarian uprising and offer political asylum to many of the nearly 200,000 Hungarians who fled their country. John Foster Dulles, who in the past had repeatedly stated that the aim of the United States was the liberation of Eastern Europe and the roll-back of the Soviet presence there, could do no more than watch in frustration. The events in Hungary offered him the opportunity to put his policy into operation, but President Eisenhower's cautious response revealed that Dulles's rhetoric was just that. The Hungarian rebellion also revealed that the United States would not challenge the Soviet Union in Eastern Europe; it would not start World War III over Poland or Hungary. The lesson was not lost on the Soviets when they had to deal with Czechoslovakia in 1968.

☐ Czechoslovakia

Events in Poland and Hungary did not affect Czechoslovakia during the 1950s. The country continued to be ruled by Antonin Novotny, whom Stalin had placed in power in 1952. In the late 1960s, Czechoslovakia, therefore, appeared to be the least likely candidate for social and political reform. Yet, the unreconstructed Stalinist Novotny was bitterly resented by many in Czechoslovakia, particularly the writers but also members of his own party. When a writers' rebellion began late in 1967, Novotny found himself unable to deal with it because his own party did not support him. In short order the party asked him to resign, and he did so in January 1968. After the party dutifully checked with the Kremlin, Leonid Brezhnev responded that "this is your matter." The party then elected Alexander Dubček as its first secretary.

The writers, many of whom were Communists, had raised a number of basic questions—those of civil rights, censorship, and the monopoly of the Communist Party in the political, economic, and social affairs of the nation. Under Dubček's stewardship, the Communist Party introduced numerous reforms at breakneck speed. It attempted to create a "socialism with a human face," one that sought to combine Eastern-style socialism with Western-style democracy. One restriction after another was lifted. The results were freedom of the press, freedom to travel, freedom from fear of the police. An intense and open debate of the nature of the reforms took place in the uncensored pages of the press. In the spring and summer of 1968, euphoria swept a nation that became oblivious to the inherent dangers of such radical reforms. Soon there was the inevitable talk of neutrality and the possibility of leaving the Soviet bloc.

Both the United States and the Soviet Union watched these developments intensely. Several high-ranking delegations arrived from Moscow and other East European capitals. The Communist parties of Eastern Europe urged Dubček and his party to bring the movement under control before it completely got out of hand. Several of the East European governments (particularly those of Yugoslavia and Hungary) did not want to give the Soviet Union an excuse for intervention. But it was to no avail. Dubček neither wanted to nor was he able to put an end to the discussions and experiments. The hopeful "Prague Spring" continued unabated. The border between Czechoslovakia and Austria became but a line on a map that Czechs—and visitors from the West—crossed without restriction. The Iron Curtain had ceased to exist in this part of Europe.

Until August 1968, the Soviet leadership appeared to be divided on what course to take. But by that time the hard-liners in Moscow became convinced that Dubček and his party were no longer in control. What was happening in Czechoslovakia was no longer a local matter. To the Soviets, a counterrevolution was in the making, one Dubček was unable to bring to an end. Dubček was well aware of the inherent danger of this situation, that the Soviets had a contingency plan to use force. In a telephone conversation with Brezhnev on August 13, a week before the invasion, Dubček said, "If you consider us traitors, then take the measures which your Politburo considers necessary."[14]

Events in Czechoslovakia also threatened to create repercussions in the Soviet Union. The non-Russian population of the Soviet empire—approximately half of the population—watched the events in Czechoslovakia with growing interest. The party chiefs in the non-Russian republics, particularly those of the Ukraine and Lithuania, took the lead in urging strong action. Brezhnev convened a plenary session of the party's Central Committee to inform the party that the Warsaw Pact was about to put an end to the "Prague Spring." On August 20, 1968, Brezhnev ordered the Soviet

Army to put its contingency plans into operation. When the Soviet tanks and troops rolled into Prague, the Czechs, as expected, did not resist to any appreciable degree. The Soviets then proceeded to replace Dubček with Gustav Husak.

The Soviets justified their invasion of Czechoslovakia by claiming that they had to protect that nation against a counterrevolution. Moreover, they declared they had an inherent right to intervene in all socialist countries similarly threatened. This Soviet right of intervention in Eastern Europe became known in the West as the Brezhnev Doctrine. In 1979, Brezhnev used it anew to justify intervention in Afghanistan when he sent the Soviet Army to bail out a bankrupt socialist government. And in 1980, Brezhnev resurrected it to warn Poland's Solidarity movement against going too far.

Ironically, the Soviet Union had been able to count on a certain measure of goodwill among the population of Czechoslovakia until the invasion of 1968. After all, it had been the Red Army in 1945 that had liberated Prague from the Germans, and only the Soviets had appeared to be willing to come to the aid of Czechoslovakia when Hitler had carved it up in 1938. But whatever goodwill had existed before 1968 became a thing of the past.

☐   **East Germany**

East Germany was unique among the Communist states in Eastern Europe. For one, it was the last of the Communist states Stalin established. It is not clear what Stalin had in mind for Germany after World War II, but after the West had formally created West Germany in May 1949, Stalin had little choice but to create his own state in October of that year. As late as March 1952, Stalin still proposed to the West a unified—but demilitarized and neutral—Germany. A West German historian concluded that East Germany was "Stalin's unloved child,"[15] a burden he wanted to be rid of. Stalin's proposal to unload East Germany came too late, however, as the Cold War by 1952 was in full bloom and attitudes had hardened. By then, West Germany was well on its way to rearmament as a member of NATO.

Second, East Germany was the Communist state with the least popular support. Its leaders understood only too well that without Soviet backing their state had no chance of existing. The politicians in Bonn considered it part of West Germany and bided their time until reunification. As a result, East German leaders, such as Walter Ulbricht and Erich Honecker, were the most hawkish of all the East European Communist rulers. They wanted the Soviets to dig in as deeply as possible in defiance of all Western aspirations. Shortly after Stalin died in March 1953, politicians in Moscow once again contemplated the abandonment of East Germany. But when widespread uprisings took place on June 17, 1953,[16] Moscow, after initial hesitation, came to the "fraternal" assistance of a Communist client in deep political trouble. It was Soviet Army tanks that put an end to the disturbances in East Berlin and other cities.

Third, the Western challenge East Germany faced was not only political but also economic. As East Germany gradually rebuilt its economy under Soviet auspices, West Germany experienced a sustained economic boom. By the late 1950s, West Germany had reached its prewar standard of living, and it continued to improve. As a booming West German economy suffered from a shortage of skilled workers, many East Germans left their country to participate in the political and economic benefits in the West. East Berliners were able to travel by public transport to West Berlin, where they automatically received West German citizenship. Berlin had become the biggest hole in the Iron Curtain. By the early 1960s, the hemorrhage had become so serious for East Germany that Khrushchev repeatedly threatened war to drive the West out of Berlin.

The Berlin Blockade (1948–1949) and Khrushchev's saber rattling had proven to be ineffective in dislodging the Western powers; another solution had to be found. The erection of a ten-foot wall around West Berlin was Khrushchev's new solution. The Berlin Wall, built in August 1961, solved East Germany's most pressing problem when it sealed off the last remaining gap in the Iron Curtain. The East Germans left behind were shut off from the rest of the German-speaking world. The Berlin Wall thus became the supreme symbol of the division of Europe and the most visible manifestation of the Iron Curtain.

* * *

On paper the forces of the Warsaw Pact always looked formidable. But the Soviets could never actually rely on most of the East European armies. Yugoslavia and Albania left the Soviet camp during the late 1940s and early 1960s respectively. Romania conducted its own foreign policy since the mid-1960s. The East Germans, Poles, Czechs and Slovaks, and Hungarians were never as reliable as the Kremlin wanted them to be. Only Bulgaria appeared to be a loyal ally. In the West, Communist Eastern Europe was generally viewed as a potential forward base for the Soviets. At the same time it served as a defensive barrier protecting the Soviet Union's borders. But increasingly, as the events of 1989 would later show, it also became a glacier protecting Western Europe through which the Soviet Army could cross only at its peril.

■ THE SINO-SOVIET SPLIT

The Soviet leadership faced another crisis within the Communist world. By the mid-1950s, the Communist rulers of the People's Republic of China

(PRC) began to strike out on their own. Before long, it became apparent that the two Communist giants were at loggerheads. The rift between them became more serious with each passing year, and by the early 1960s, relations were openly hostile. The feud between the two Communist giants had a great impact on international relations. As the Sino-Soviet split emerged, the Cold War, initially a bipolar struggle between East and West, gave way to a triangular pattern of relations among the Soviet Union, China, and the United States.

From the time of its formation in October 1949 the People's Republic of China sought to establish and maintain close relations with the Soviet Union. At the time Moscow and Washington were engaged in a potentially dangerous rivalry, which already had turned into a nuclear confrontation. As early as 1950, Beijing sent its troops against the U.S.-led forces of the United Nations in Korea. Moscow and Beijing thus faced a common foe and professed a common ideology. There was little reason to believe that their alliance would be short-lived. Yet, only six years later the two began to pull apart. Chairman Mao Zedong's mission to Moscow in early 1950 seemed to confirm the suspicion that Mao and Stalin were comrades united in the cause of international Communism and mutually dedicated to the defeat of the capitalist world. In Moscow, in February 1950, they signed a thirty-year military alliance aimed at the United States, and the Soviet Union took up the cause of seating the PRC in the United Nations to replace the Republic of China (Nationalist China). The Soviet Union also provided much needed economic assistance to China in the form of loans, technicians, and advisers. The two nations also rallied in support of Communist North Korea during the Korean War. And of course they spoke the same Marxian language, which denounced U.S. imperialism.

It was little wonder then that the United States was skeptical about the early reports of difficulties between the two Communist states. The U.S. assumption, fostered by the Cold War, was that Communism was a monolith, a single, unitary movement directed by Moscow. This assumption was much slower to die than the reality of Communist unity.

In retrospect, we can recognize signs of friction between Beijing and Moscow from the very outset. The Chinese could hardly be pleased by the rather cavalier manner in which Stalin treated them. The terms of the Moscow agreement were not at all generous. Stalin offered Mao a development loan of no more than $300 million to be spread over five years and to be repaid by China in agricultural produce and with interest. As a price for that loan China agreed to continued Soviet use and control of the principal railroads and ports in Manchuria and to the creation of joint Sino-Soviet stock companies to conduct mineral surveys in Xinjiang (Sinkiang), the innermost province of China. The paucity of Soviet aid and the concessions Stalin demanded from China suggest that Stalin's purpose was to accentuate Soviet supremacy and Chinese dependency. Indeed, it would seem that Stalin was wary of this new Communist friend and that he would have preferred dealing with a weaker, more vulnerable Nationalist China than with a vigorous new Communist regime in China. If the Chinese harbored ill feelings toward Stalin or resented the continued Soviet presence in Manchuria and Xinjiang, they prudently remained silent, publicly accepting Stalin's leadership and extolling the fraternal relationship with the Soviet Union. The backwardness of China's economy was such that Chinese leaders considered Soviet economic assistance and diplomatic support too important to sacrifice on the altar of national pride.

The unspoken misgivings between Moscow and Beijing of the early 1950s did not lead directly to the Sino-Soviet split of the late 1950s. Nor is that feud to be explained as a direct consequence of earlier Sino-Russian troubles. One can surely trace the historical roots of animosity between the two countries back in time, to tsarist imperialism in the nineteenth century, or even to the Mongol invasions of Russia in the thirteenth century. But it would be too simple to argue that the conflict in the late 1950s was, therefore, the inevitable result of that history. The two sides dredged up the conflicts of the past, such as territorial claims, only after the dispute began to develop over other contemporary issues in the mid-1950s.

The first strains of conflict between Moscow and Beijing came in consequence of Soviet leader Nikita Khrushchev's famous Secret Speech in February 1956. The Chinese leaders were caught by surprise by this sudden, scathing attack on Stalin and by Khrushchev's call for peaceful coexistence with the capitalist world. Chinese Communists had no particular reason to defend the departed Stalin, but they feared that the attack on Stalin's "cult of personality" might, by implication, undermine Mao's dictatorship in China. Moreover, they questioned the wisdom of peaceful coexistence, and more important, they disputed the right of Moscow to unilaterally make such a major ideological shift with significant global implications. The Chinese leaders chafed at Khrushchev's bold reinterpretation of Marxist-Leninist doctrine, without so much as consulting with Mao Zedong in advance. Mao, who had led the Chinese Communist Party (CCP) since 1935, was the world's senior ranking Communist leader, and he had reason to object to being ignored by the brash new leader of the Soviet Union. The Chinese were, in effect, questioning Khrushchev's authority to dictate policy to the Communist world.

The new Soviet line of peaceful coexistence was soon to become the major bone of contention between Moscow and Beijing. The Soviet leadership had become alarmed about the nuclear arms race and came to the conviction that the Soviet Union must avert a devastating nuclear war with the United States, whose burgeoning nuclear arsenal posed a serious threat to the survival of their country. Khrushchev, therefore, concluded that it would be necessary to coexist peacefully with the capitalist superpower. However, at the same time that they were offering the olive branch to the other side, the Soviets worked feverishly to close the gap in the arms race, and in 1957 they made two remarkable technological breakthroughs. They launched their first ICBM (inter-continental ballistic missile) in August, and in October they stunned the world with Sputnik, the first satellite sent into orbit around the earth. The enormous strategic significance of this Soviet advance in military technology was not lost on the Chinese. Mao Zedong, attending a meeting of world Communist leaders in Moscow in November 1957, contended that the international situation had reached a new turning point and that the Communist world had stolen the march on the capitalist world in the contest for global power. Mao asserted that "at present, it is not the west wind which is prevailing over the east wind, but the east wind prevailing over the west wind."[17] He argued that the Communist camp should put its newfound military superiority to work to attain the final victory over capitalism. Khrushchev strongly rejected these ideas and concluded the meeting with a reaffirmation of peaceful coexistence.

This was the origin of a dispute over global strategy that ultimately split the two Communist giants. The Chinese argued that, by making peace with the capitalists, the Soviet Union was departing from essential Marxist-Leninist doctrine. Peaceful coexistence might suit the Soviet Union because it was already an industrialized nation with secure borders and nuclear weapons, but it was unsuited to China, which had none of these. Mao argued that Communist nations should continue the international struggle, for example, by assisting Communist forces engaged in wars of national liberation. Moreover, the PRC sought assurances of Soviet support in its own unfinished war of national liberation: the civil war against Jiang Jieshi's Nationalist regime, which controlled the island of Taiwan. In 1958, Beijing intensified the pressure on Taiwan by launching a sustained artillery barrage against two off-shore islands, Quemoy and Matsu, which were occupied by the Nationalist forces. It seems that Mao's purpose was to test the resolve of the United States to defend Nationalist China and to test Soviet willingness to provide active military support to the PRC. The United States made clear its commitment to the defense of Taiwan, but the Soviets, instead of pledging support, denounced China's actions as reckless. The Soviet Union would not allow itself to be drawn into a nuclear war with the United States over Taiwan.

In addition to disputing global strategy, the two Communist powers also disagreed on the means to attaining Communism. The Chinese had adopted the Soviet model for economic development when, in 1953, they put into operation a Soviet-style Five-Year Plan. But by 1957, the leaders in Beijing were beginning to question the appropriateness of the Soviet model for China, and Mao in particular became very critical of its top-heavy, bureaucratic nature. In early 1958, Mao called for scrapping the Second Five-Year Plan and replacing it with a new program known as the Great Leap Forward. Mao thus abandoned the Soviet model in favor of his own program designed to achieve industrial development and the collectivization of agriculture simultaneously. Boldly, Mao proclaimed that China had overtaken the Soviet Union in the quest to build a Communist society. But Mao was too quick to trumpet success, for within a year the Great Leap Forward, with its hastily created communes, produced an economic disaster (see Chapter 15). The Soviet leadership, concerned about the implications for the Eastern European satellites of China's departing from the Soviet model, was from the beginning critical of the new experiment in China. Indeed, Khrushchev heaped scorn on Mao's heralded Great Leap all the more when it failed.

The growing feud with Moscow was reflected in a political crisis that occurred in Beijing in the summer of 1959. The Chinese defense minister, Peng Dehuai, who had just returned from a visit to the Soviet Union, dared to condemn Mao for the disastrous failure of the Great Leap Forward and spoke out in favor of retention of the Soviet model, which he regarded as necessary for China's military modernization. Mao led a blistering counterattack against Peng, charging him with conspiring with Moscow against the Chinese revolution and denouncing him as a traitor. At a meeting of the Central Executive Committee of the CCP in August 1959, Mao accepted criticism of the Great Leap Forward failures, but he secured the party's support for the expulsion of Peng from the government and the party. Peng was replaced as defense minister by Lin Biao, a supporter of Mao, who immediately declared that China was in no need of Soviet technical or military assistance for its national defense.

Only a month later, Khrushchev gave Mao added reason to suspect that the Soviet Union was plotting against China. At the invitation of President Eisenhower, Khrushchev made a two-week visit to the United States. Mao, who remained adamantly opposed to peaceful coexistence, obviously took a dim view of this diplomatic venture, and he was left to speculate on what had transpired at Camp David in the private talks between Khrushchev and Eisenhower. He suspected that Khrushchev was making concessions at China's expense, specifically, striking a bargain that would trade Western concessions on the Berlin question for a Soviet commitment to oppose the PRC's use of force to settle the Taiwan question.

In 1960, the polemical feud between Moscow and Beijing became an open confrontation as each side, for the first time, made public their attacks on the other. The Chinese struck first, in April 1960, with an article titled "Long Live Leninism" in *Red Flag*, an official organ of the Chinese Communist Party. It argued that peaceful coexistence was contrary to the precepts of Leninism:

> We believe in the absolute correctness of Lenin's thinking: war is an inevitable outcome of systems of exploitation and the source of modern wars is the imperialist system. Until the imperialist system and the

exploiting classes come to an end, wars of one kind or another will always occur.[18]

The Soviet government responded quickly. In July 1960, it abruptly pulled out of China its 1,300 economic advisers and military technicians, who took their blueprints with them and left behind many unfinished projects. This was a serious blow to China's industrialization efforts. At about this time, Moscow rescinded an earlier agreement to provide China nuclear technology to build the atomic bomb.

Khrushchev's purpose was not to terminate the alliance but to force Beijing back into line and to coerce its acceptance of Moscow's policies and position of leadership. In the year that followed, Beijing seemed to acquiesce to an extent while a more conciliatory Moscow seemed to be backing away from détente with the United States. But this proved to be but a brief respite, for in October 1961, at the Twenty-second Party Congress of the Communist Party of the Soviet Union, Khrushchev again lashed out at the Chinese. He attacked China's economic policies and ideology and argued that modern industrial development must precede experiments with creating communes. Communism was to be achieved by following the Soviet lead. In response, Chinese Foreign Minister Zhou Enlai led the entire Chinese delegation out of the congress and back to Beijing.

In 1962, new diplomatic issues divided Moscow and Beijing and exacerbated their conflict. China and India engaged in a brief war in October over a border dispute, and Moscow, instead of supporting China (with which it had a military alliance), offered diplomatic support to India while joining the United States in condemning China for its reckless aggression. And shortly afterward, in the wake of the Cuban missile crisis, in which the United States and the Soviet Union came perilously close to a nuclear war, the Chinese scorned Khrushchev as weak-kneed for caving in to U.S. demands to pull out the Soviet missiles from Cuba. Moreover, the year that followed the Cuban missile crisis brought a new thaw in Soviet-U.S. relations with ominous consequences for China. In August 1963, the two superpowers signed a treaty banning atmospheric testing of nuclear weapons. For Beijing this was devastating, for it signified that China was being abandoned by its Communist comrades in favor of the capitalist world. It meant more than diplomatic isolation; it implied strategic isolation.

The Chinese originally had hoped to draw from the strength of the Soviet-led Communist movement and specifically to attain from Moscow a firm commitment to provide military support for the "liberation" of Taiwan. Having failed in this, Beijing then sought to strengthen its position by cultivating its relations with other Communist and national liberation movements in Asia, Africa, and Latin America—that is, the Third World. China had already made a major step in identifying itself with the nonaligned nations of these parts of the world by its participation in the Bandung Conference in Indonesia in 1955.[19] Increasingly in the 1960s, the PRC sought to befriend leaders of revolutionary movements and those of newly independent nations in the Third World even to the point of providing economic aid that China, with its own economic problems, could ill afford. Additionally, Beijing engaged in a propaganda program aimed at convincing Third World nations that the Maoist revolution was the correct path to Communism.

In the early 1960s, when the breach with China became wide open, Khrushchev seemed to have become as obsessed with the recalcitrant China as Mao had become obsessed with what he regarded as Soviet treachery. After publishing an open letter demanding Beijing's submission to Soviet leadership, Khrushchev began formulating plans for a meeting of world Communist leaders at which he would either force China back into the fold or force it out. Several Communist parties, however, declined invitations because they opposed Khrushchev's confrontational approach. Before this meeting could be arranged, Khrushchev himself was suddenly ousted from power in Moscow. And on the very day that this was reported in the world press, October 16, 1964, the PRC announced it had successfully tested an atomic bomb. Proudly, the Chinese proclaimed that the PRC too was now a superpower. They had successfully defied Khrushchev's efforts to dictate policy and his efforts to deny them nuclear weapons.

No significant change occurred in Sino-Soviet relations in consequence of the fall of Khrushchev and his replacement by Leonid Brezhnev. Nor did the escalation of the U.S. involvement in the Vietnam War in 1965 bring the two Communist powers together; instead, they rivaled one another for influence over the Communist regime in North Vietnam. In April 1965, Moscow proposed to Beijing that the two nations cooperate in support of North Vietnam. It asked the Chinese to allow Soviet aircraft use of Chinese airports and airspace. After lengthy debate within ruling circles in Beijing, Chairman Mao, who opposed any cooperation with the Soviets, rejected the proposal. Mao and his comrades in Beijing feared not only a Soviet military presence in China but also the possibility of a full-scale war with the Soviet Union. The specter of a preemptive nuclear strike against the PRC and its fledgling nuclear arsenal caused great alarm in China.

Mao Zedong's bombastic attack on the Soviet Union reached new heights in the summer of 1966, when he launched the Great Cultural Revolution, a campaign designed to revitalize the Chinese revolution by mass mobilization (see Chapter 15). This political program contained a strong anti-Soviet aspect, for Mao called upon the Chinese people to purge the party of leaders whom he condemned for trying to establish a Soviet-type Communism in China. He pronounced them guilty of the same crimes that he pinned on Soviet leaders: bureaucratic elitism, revisionism, sabotage of the Communist movement, and taking it down the capitalist road. The political and economic chaos caused by his Cultural Revolution gave the Soviet Union still more reason to ridicule Mao and Maoism. Nevertheless, despite the upheaval it caused, Mao proclaimed that he had set the revolution back on the track to true Communism, and he called upon all Communists and would-be Communists throughout the world to abandon the revisionist Soviets and turn instead to China for their model.

Tensions between the two Communist giants mounted even higher on yet another front: the Sino-Soviet border. From time to time during their feud, Mao had called into question the Soviet claim to territory north of the Amur River boundary between the two countries in Eastern Asia.[20] During the 1960s, as their feud heated up, both the Soviets and the Chinese fortified their common border with larger and larger forces. Within the Ussuri River, which separates China and the Soviet Maritime Province, were several disputed islands, and in March 1969 a skirmish between Chinese and Soviet armed forces suddenly broke out on the island of Damanskii. After the Chinese launched an assault, the Soviets struck with artillery, tanks, and aircraft and drove the Chinese back. The warfare left about 800 Chinese troops dead as compared with about 60 Soviet dead.

Although a cease-fire was arranged, a war of nerves continued throughout the year. A full-scale war between China and the Soviet Union seemed imminent. It was in this context that leaders in Beijing began to consider ending their diplomatic isolation and improving their relations with the United States. Tension along the border continued into the 1980s as both sides reinforced their border security with greater military force. Ultimately, the Soviet Union deployed an estimated 2 million troops along its long China borders and armed them with the most modern of weapons, including tactical nuclear weapons. China's border forces were thought to be as large as the Soviets, but not as well equipped.

One of the major consequences of the Sino-Soviet split, and specifically of the near war between the two Communist nations, was the normalization of relations between the PRC and the United States in the early 1970s. This had a profound effect on global power relations, supplanting the bipolar Cold War with what was called a strategic triangle. Throughout the 1970s and 1980s, the PRC moved closer to the United States and still further away from the Soviet Union. It charged the latter with "socialist imperialism" and "hegemonism." In fact, "anti-hegemonism" became the main pillar of China's foreign policy in the 1970s, when it endeavored to attain the active support of the United States, Japan, and other nations in its struggle against Soviet global expansion. Its fears of Soviet aggression largely accounted for its great efforts since the late 1970s to speed up its retarded industrialization and to close the technology gap.

■ THE THIRTY-YEAR FEUD IS ENDED

The open estrangement between the two Communist giants continued into the late 1980s. Although Moscow showed signs of desiring a thaw, Deng

Xiaoping, the new Chinese Communist ruler who came to power after Mao's death in 1976, hunkered down with an inflexible policy. Deng identified three specific paramount issues on which he insisted on a change in Soviet policy before relations could be normalized. He demanded a withdrawal (or at least a substantial reduction) of Soviet forces from the Chinese border, an end to the Soviet invasion of Afghanistan, and an end to Soviet support for the Vietnamese army in Cambodia. Although bilateral trade and diplomatic exchanges were gradually restored, further progress was blocked by Chinese intransigence on the "three obstacles."

As both Beijing and Moscow focused their attention on economic reform in the 1980s, the prospects for Sino-Soviet rapprochement improved. Mikhail Gorbachev, who came to power in the Kremlin in 1985, brought a dynamic new pragmatism to Soviet diplomacy. Determined to regenerate the faltering Soviet economy, Gorbachev saw it necessary to reduce the size of its military establishment, including the large deployment of Soviet forces in Asia, and toward that end to take steps to reduce tensions in Asia. With these ideas in mind, in July 1986 Gorbachev went to Vladivostok, the largest Soviet city in East Asia, to deliver a speech that boldly proclaimed a new Soviet initiative to establish peaceful relations with China and other Asian nations. In this conciliatory speech, Gorbachev addressed Beijing's three burning issues, declaring Soviet readiness to seek accommodation on all three. He indicated that steps were already being taken toward the evacuation of Soviet forces from Afghanistan, that Soviet troops would be withdrawn from Mongolia on the Sino-Mongolian border, and that Moscow was prepared to discuss the issue of mutual reduction of military forces on the Sino-Soviet border and the Vietnam-Cambodia issue.

Deng Xiaoping reacted positively. In April 1987 Chinese and Soviet negotiators began addressing "regional issues" (that is, border disputes) and the Cambodian question. Negotiations continued on various levels through the following year as both parties reciprocated with confidence-building gestures and agreements. They entered into an agreement, for example, on barter trade across the border, which resulted in a vast increase in mutually beneficial contacts between the two peoples along their 4,000-mile-long boundary. A new bridge built across the Amur River not only served the practical needs of the Chinese and Soviets on each side, but also served as a symbol of their renewed ties. By 1989, substantial improvement had been made toward the restoration of peaceful relations. The Soviet Union withdrew from Afghanistan, reduced its troops along the Chinese border,[21] and pressured Vietnam to begin evacuation of its troops from Cambodia. Placated by these conciliatory measures, Deng accepted Gorbachev's proposal for a summit meeting, and extended an invitation to him to visit Beijing in May 1989.

Gorbachev's visit to China signaled the end of the thirty-year-long rift. He arrived in Beijing, however, in the midst of the mammoth student demonstrations in the Chinese capital, and his historic visit was upstaged by this tumultuous event (see Chapter 15). The summit meeting was, nonetheless, a success. Gorbachev, who acknowledged that the Soviet Union was partly to blame for the deep split between the two countries, proclaimed the summit a "watershed event." The two sides pledged to continue talks aimed at mutually reducing military troop strength along their long shared border "to a minimum level commensurate with normal, good-neighborly relations," to seek expanded trade and cultural relations, and to restore relations between the Communist parties of the two countries.[22] On Cambodia, they acknowledged a lack of agreement but pledged to continue efforts to avert a civil war in that country and to help it become independent and nonaligned. On the whole, the summit meeting advanced the new rapprochement between China and the Soviet Union and reflected their mutual objectives of lessening tensions and improving economic relations.

In 1992, the Russian parliament ratified Gorbachev's agreement with China. It recognized that Damanskii Island on the Ussuri River, where the fighting had broken out in 1969, was indeed Chinese territory. Russian historians estimated that Soviet troop deployment along the Amur and Ussuri rivers from the onset of hostilities in 1969 to Gorbachev's visit to Beijing cost the state the massive sum of between 200 and 300 billion rubles (in 1960s rubles), roughly the equivalent of $200–$300 billion.[23]

RECOMMENDED READINGS.

Bethell, Nicholas. *Gomulka: His Poland, His Communism.* New York: Holt, Rinehart and Winston, 1969.
An explanation of the Polish road to socialism.
Clubb, O. Edmund. *China and Russia: The "Great Game."* New York: Columbia University Press, 1971.
A comprehensive, detailed, and evenhanded analysis of the Sino-Soviet split by a U.S. diplomat-turned-scholar.
Crankshaw, Edward. *Khrushchev: A Career.* New York: Viking Press, 1966.
The standard Western biography of Khrushchev.
Deutscher, Isaac. *Stalin: A Political Biography.* Rev. ed. New York: Oxford University Press, 1966.
The classic biography by a Trotskyite.
Hinton, Harold C. *China's Turbulent Quest.* 2d ed. New York: Macmillan, 1973.
An analysis of the Sino-Soviet rift.
Kecskemeti, Paul. *The Unexpected Revolution: Social Forces in the Hungarian Uprising.* Stanford, Calif.: Stanford University Press, 1961.
London, Kurt, ed. *Eastern Europe in Transition.* Baltimore: Johns Hopkins University Press, 1966.
A study of the forces of nationalism in Eastern Europe.
Medvedev, Roy A. *Let History Judge: The Origins and Consequences of Stalinism.* New York: Knopf, 1971.
An indictment of Stalin by a Soviet "Leninist" historian.
Shipler, David K. *Russia: Broken Idols, Solemn Dreams.* New York: Times Books, 1983.

An explanation of Soviet society by a correspondent of the *New York Times*.

Solzhenitsyn, Alexander. *One Day in the Life of Ivan Denisovich.* New York: Praeger, 1962.

An exposé of Stalin's forced labor camps, the novel that brought Solzhenitsyn international acclaim.

Tatu, Michel. *Power in the Kremlin: From Khrushchev to Kosygin.* London: William Collins Sons, 1968.

A well-received study of Soviet politics by a French expert.

Ulam, Adam. *Stalin: The Man and His Era.* New York: Viking Press, 1973.

A highly readable, detailed biography written from a Western perspective.

Valenta, Jiri. *Soviet Intervention in Czechoslovakia in 1968.* Baltimore: Johns Hopkins University Press, 1979.

A detailed explanation of the Kremlin's reasons for ending the Czechoslovak experiment in liberalization.

NOTES

1. J. V. Stalin, "The Tasks of Business Executives," February 4, 1931; J. V. Stalin, *Works* (Moscow: Foreign Languages Publishing House, 1955), XIII, pp. 40–41.

2. A proletarian—a member of the proletariat—is a wage earner or, more commonly, a factory worker. In Marxist jargon, the words "proletarian" and "worker" are used interchangeably.

3. Edward Crankshaw, *Khrushchev: A Career* (New York: Viking, 1966), p. 228.

4. De Tocqueville quoted in Bernard B. Fall, *The Two Vietnams: A Political and Military Analysis* (New York: Praeger, 1963), p. 253.

5. N. S. Khrushchev, *Khrushchev Remembers: The Last Testament* (Boston: Little, Brown, 1974), p. 77.

6. Tito's independence of both the Soviet Union and the West led him to take a "third" road. Tito, Nehru of India, and Nasser of Egypt became the early leaders of the Third World, that is, nations that refused to align themselves with either the Western or socialist blocs. The term later lost its original meaning, for it came to designate the world's underdeveloped nations.

7. J. V. Stalin, "The International Situation and the Defense of the U.S.S.R.," speech delivered on August 1, 1927, to the Joint Plenum of the Central Committee and Central Control Commission of the C.P.S.U. (b); J. V. Stalin, *Works* (Moscow: Foreign Languages Publishing House, 1954), X, pp. 53–54.

8. G. M. Adibekov, *Kominform i poslevoinnaia Evropa* (Moscow: Rossia molodaia, 1994), pp. 90–95.

9. Khrushchev, *Khrushchev Remembers,* p. 351; for the full text, pp. 559–618.

10. Adam B. Ulam, *Expansion and Coexistence: The History of Soviet Foreign Policy, 1917–67* (New York: Praeger, 1968), pp. 578–579.

11. For a summary of Dulles's views on Communism, see his testimony before Congress, January 15, 1953; Walter LaFeber, ed., *The Dynamics of World Power: A Documentary History of United States Foreign Policy, 1945–1973, II, Eastern Europe and the Soviet Union* (New York: Chelsea House, 1973), pp. 465–468.

12. Khrushchev, *Khrushchev Remembers,* pp. 416–420. See also the documents made public at a conference in Budapest commemorating the fortieth anniversary of the uprising: Timothy Garton Ash, "Hungary's Revolution: Forty

Years On," *New York Review*, November 16, 1996, pp. 18–22; Reuters, "Soviets Almost Recognized Hungary Revolt, Data Show," *Baltimore Sun*, September 28, 1996, p. 7A; and Jane Perlez, "Thawing Out Cold War History," *New York Times*, October 6, 1996, p. 4E.

13. "Blood on his hands" is a reference to Kádár granting safe conduct to Nagy (whom he nevertheless executed in 1958) and the bloody suppression of the rebellion. Kádár then became known as the "butcher of Budapest."

14. R. G. Pikhoia, "Chekhoslovakiia, 1968 god. Vzgliad iz Moskvy: Po dokumentam TsK KPSS," *Novaia i noveishaia istoriia*, 1 (January–February 1995), p. 42.

15. Wilfried Loth, *Stalins ungeliebtes Kind: Warum Moskau die DDR nicht wollte* (Berlin: Rohwolt-Berlin, 1994).

16. That day became an official holiday in West Germany, the Day of Unity, commemorating the victims of the uprising and underscoring the committment to unification. After Germany was unified in 1990, October 3 became the new official Day of Unity.

17. Mao: "At present it is not the west wind," *Survey of the China Mainland Press*, U.S. Consulate General, Hong Kong, no. 1662, December 2, 1957, p. 2.

18. Mao on Lenin, *Current Background*, U.S. Consulate General, Hong Kong, no. 617, April 26, 1960.

19. At this conference of twenty-nine African and Asian nations, China's representative, Zhou Enlai, shared the spotlight with India's neutralist prime minister, Nehru. China joined with these Third World nations in pledging peace and mutual noninterference.

20. In two separate treaties in 1858 and 1860, China relinquished to tsarist Russia territory north of the Amur River and east of the Ussuri River (the latter territory known as the Maritime Province). But Mao now (the 1950s) contended that these were ill-gotten gains and that, since the treaties were forced on China by an imperialist government, they should not be honored or considered binding.

21. Gorbachev pledged in December 1988 at the United Nations to cut Soviet military forces by half a million, 200,000 of which would be from military units in Asia. He also announced plans to withdraw three-quarters of the Soviet troops in Mongolia and indicated that the first contingent of 12,000 soldiers was already being taken out.

22. Scott Shane, "Gorbachev Returns Home from 'Watershed' Summit," *Baltimore Sun*, May 19, 1989.

23. Viktor Usov, "'Goriachaia vesna' na Damanskom," *Novoe vremia*, 9 (1994), pp. 36–39.

9

The War in Indochina

The Vietnam War, the United States's longest war, was one of the most tragic experiences in the history of the United States. It was even more tragic for Vietnam, the country in which it was fought. The United States became engaged in a conflict in a distant Asian nation, confident that its great military capability could produce a victory and stop the spread of Communism in that part of the world. By getting involved in a war against an Asian people fighting in defense of their homeland, the United States ignored the lessons of the past—the Chinese resistance against an over-powering Japan in the 1930s and 1940s, and the success of the Viet Minh guerrillas in their eight-year-long battle against the French in Vietnam.

The massive U.S. intervention began in 1965, but continued to esca-late until U.S. troops numbered well over half a million by 1968. This huge armed force with its modern weaponry was, however, denied victory by a resilient, determined Vietnamese enemy. In time, Washington learned that piling up the dead higher and higher would not necessarily bring vic-tory. However, for political reasons, it would prove much more difficult to get out of Vietnam than it was to get in. In this chapter, our first concern is how and why the United States became involved in this war. Secondly, we will examine U.S. difficulties in getting out of the war and the war's costs and consequences.

■ THE ESCALATION OF U.S. INVOLVEMENT

The Geneva Conference of 1954 called for the withdrawal of France from Indochina after the French defeat at Dien Bien Phu. The agreement estab-lished the independent states of Laos and Cambodia, and made a tempo-rary separation of Vietnam into two zones divided at the 17th parallel. In the north a Communist government, the Democratic Republic of Vietnam, was already established with Hanoi its capital and Ho Chi Minh its president.

In the south, the French transferred power to the native monarch, Bao Dai, in Saigon. The Geneva Accords called for the unification of Vietnam on the basis of an internationally supervised election to be held two years later, in July 1956. It also provided that, until unification, the people in Vietnam would be free to relocate across the dividing line, and that neither part of Vietnam would introduce foreign troops or make any military alliances. French troops were to remain in the south until the unification process was completed.

The United States sought from the start to strengthen the Saigon regime and weaken the Hanoi regime. The United States, which had already assumed the greater part of the financial burden of France's war in Vietnam, now took up the task of supporting a client state in South Vietnam, financially, politically, and militarily. Even before the Geneva Accords had been signed (the United States never signed them, but did pledge to abide by them), U.S. Army officers arrived in Saigon to establish a military mission and prepare for "paramilitary operations."

In Saigon, the most effective political leader was not the playboy king, Bao Dai, known as the "emperor of Cannes," but his prime minister, Ngo Dinh Diem. Diem, a Roman Catholic from North Vietnam, was not in his homeland during its struggle for independence against the French but was instead in the United States where he cultivated some important friendships, particularly with influential clergy. In October 1955, Diem deposed Bao Dai in a referendum and with it he became the president of the newly created Republic of Vietnam. It was a smashing electoral victory for he won an incredible 98 percent of the votes cast, and in the city of Saigon he received 130 percent of the registered vote.[1] The French had little faith in Diem's ability to unify the country, but U.S. leaders saw in him the strongman needed to govern and defend South Vietnam. He was the "Churchill of Southeast Asia," a decisive, staunchly anti-Communist leader who was determined to prevent the unification of Vietnam under Ho Chi Minh's Communist government and to smash any resistance to his own government in the south.[2] So determined was he that he willfully ignored the terms of the Geneva Agreement regarding the nationwide elections. With the silent support of Washington, Diem defied the Geneva Accords on the matters of the elections and military alliances, and went on to entrench himself in the south with ever more U.S. aid.

Ngo Dinh Diem soon encountered an opposition movement in the villages of South Vietnam, and his own policies and authoritarian style gave it cause. First, his rejection of the elections in 1956 stirred protests, especially by former Viet Minh soldiers who had remained in the south in expectation of the reunification of the country. Diem sought to silence this protest by conducting a campaign of terror against the Viet Minh involving arrests, beatings, torture, and execution of suspected Viet Minh members. A second cause of the growing unrest in rural areas was the peasants'

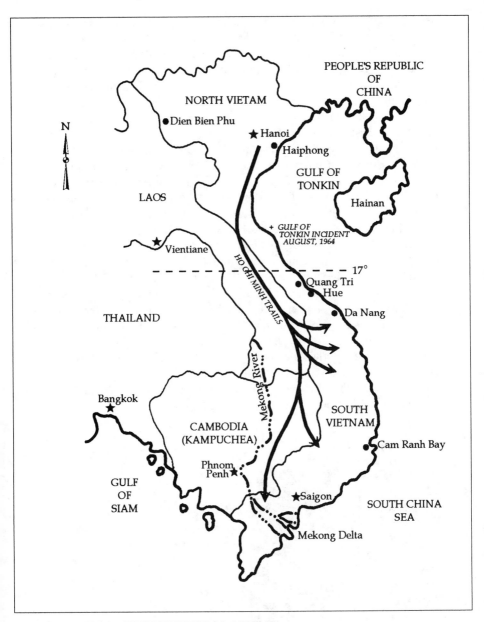

INDOCHINA: THE VIETNAM WAR

demand for land reform. A radical redistribution of farm land was being instituted in North Vietnam, and Diem's government had promised one in the South. The peasantry, which made up 85 percent of the population, felt betrayed by Diem's refusal to carry out a genuine land reform program. This discontent was exploited by the Communist Party, which was formed mainly by Viet Minh veterans. It took the lead in organizing the anti-government elements in the countryside and preparing them for a program of forceful resistance, which is to say, insurrection. Diem's increasingly repressive policies played into its hands. When Diem began rounding up suspected dissidents—Communist and non-Communist alike—and placing them into detention camps, the new Communist-led revolutionary movement began to wage guerrilla warfare against his regime. Government terror was met with guerrilla terror, and the level of violence steadily increased in the late 1950s and early 1960s.

In December 1960 various opposition groups and parties, including the Communist Party, formed the National Liberation Front (NLF), and this organization directed the revolutionary movement in South Vietnam thereafter. The guerrilla forces of the NLF were commonly known as the Viet Cong, short for Vietnamese Communists. It was a derisive term Diem used to label his enemies. The more brutal Diem's regime became in its efforts to root out and destroy the insurrection, the more popular and active the NLF revolutionaries became and the larger their forces grew. When Diem replaced local village headmen with his own bureaucrats in an attempt to control the countryside, these new leaders became targets for assassination by the Viet Cong. After trying several schemes to reorganize

Ngo Dinh Diem,
president of the Republic of
Vietnam from 1955 to Nov. 1963,
when he was killed in a coup.
(*National Archives*)

and secure the villages of South Vietnam, Diem finally resorted to the drastic measure of resettling the villagers in compounds called strategic hamlets. Although these met with the approval of U.S. advisers who financed them, the peasants were strongly opposed to them and the NLF condemned them as concentration camps.

Diem's government was no more popular in the cities. He adopted the style of a benevolent dictator, which he rationalized by his own doctrine, called "personalism." According to his Confucian-like doctrine, individual freedom must take second place to the collective betterment of society, which is achieved by dutiful loyalty to the morally superior ruler. In practice this meant absolute obedience to Diem, even to the point of requiring all citizens to hang official photographs of him in their homes. Meanwhile, he gathered around himself a tightly knit clique of loyal supporters, several of whom were his own brothers. The most notable among these was Ngo Dinh Nhu, who matched his brother in arrogance and who gained notoriety as the ruthless head of Diem's secret police.

The Diem regime resorted to forceful measures to demand the active support of the various Buddhist organizations in the country, and when they resisted, Nhu used brute force against them. In protest, several Buddhist priests resorted to self-immolation. In a public square they doused themselves with gasoline, and while seated in the posture for meditation they ignited themselves. This spectacle, seen around the world on television, signaled the degree to which Diem's government had alienated South Vietnamese society. Even the South Vietnamese army turned against him and made an unsuccessful attempt to topple him. Despite—and because of—the brutal methods used by Diem and his brother Nhu, the opposition grew stronger. And the stronger the insurrectionist movement grew the more repressive Diem's regime became. It became a vicious circle.

Finally, U.S. observers in Saigon came to the conclusion that, because Diem had become so ruthless, especially in his attacks on the Buddhists, and because his regime was so weak both in the countryside and in Saigon itself, he should be replaced by a new regime more capable of defeating the Communist-led insurrection. A group of South Vietnamese army officers, encouraged by the U.S. embassy, staged a coup d'état in November 1963, murdering Diem and his brother Nhu in the process. They then formed a junta (a military ruling group) to govern in Saigon and to direct the military effort to crush the NLF.

The new government had the blessing of the United States from the outset, but it proved to be no more effective than the previous one. When it became apparent in the following year that the NLF was winning the struggle for control of South Vietnam, the Pentagon and State Department planners began laying plans for a greatly increased U.S. role in the conflict. During the Kennedy administration, the U.S. presence grew from several hundred advisers to 18,000 "special forces" troops. Lyndon Johnson, who succeeded the slain Kennedy as president in November 1963, confronted the prospect that the South Vietnamese government, one which the United States had propped up for ten years, would soon be overthrown by a Communist-led insurrection. President Johnson inherited the commitment to defend Vietnam against that fate, and he committed himself fully to that cause.

The thinking in Washington at this time was that the NLF was completely controlled by the Communist regime in Hanoi, which in turn was under the control of Communist China. If South Vietnam were to fall to Communism, then other neighboring states would also fall one by one to this Beijing-directed Communist aggression. (This scenario was referred to as the domino theory, a term that had been widely used in Washington since the Eisenhower administration.) Therefore, the U.S. commitment in South Vietnam was to defend this "free" (non-Communist) nation against "Communist aggression from outside." Officially, the Johnson administration saw the war in Vietnam as an international conflict, never a civil war among the Vietnamese. President Johnson told the nation in October 1964 that "We are not going to send American boys nine or ten thousand miles away from home to do what Asian boys ought to be doing for themselves," but at the same time he declared that the United States would "defend freedom" in South Vietnam and stop the "Communist aggression" from the north.[3] He was determined to prevent his administration from being charged with losing the battle against Communism in yet another Asian country. Moreover, he feared that such a major foreign policy setback would do political damage to his presidency and thus endanger the Great Society program that he had launched at home.

The United States's Communist opponents in Vietnam, whose voice was generally not heard in Washington, had a very different view of the realities in that country. The NLF disputed the legitimacy of the Saigon government, protesting that the Diem regime and its successors in Saigon were merely puppets of U.S. forces in Vietnam. It called for the implementation of the 1954 Geneva Accords, the withdrawal of U.S. military forces from the country, and the creation of a coalition government in South Vietnam. Ho Chi Minh's government in Hanoi took the same position. In April 1965, it set forth a four-point proposal, which called for (1) withdrawal of U.S. forces, (2) an end of hostilities against North Vietnam, (3) honoring the Geneva Accords, and (4) allowing the Vietnamese to solve their own problems. Hanoi did not sway from this position throughout the war.

Critics of President Johnson's policy—and they were still rather few at this stage—disputed the claim that the Saigon government was the victim of foreign aggression and raised the key question of the relationship between the NLF and the Communist government in Hanoi. The official U.S. position was that the NLF was a puppet of Hanoi, and thus Johnson consistently refused to recognize it in any formal capacity. His critics argued that the NLF was neither created nor controlled by Hanoi, but was the organized center of the revolution within South Vietnam and was essentially independent of Hanoi. The relationship between the two is still debated by historians. As noted above, they had similar objectives and had the same enemies, and the NLF no doubt looked for and received guidance and supplies from Hanoi. However, it is fairly clear that the NLF fought its own battle against the Saigon regime and its U.S. supporters, at least until the massive intervention by U.S. troops in 1965. In June 1966, Senator Mike Mansfield (D-Montana) revealed that when sharp U.S. escalation began in early 1965, only 400 of the 140,000 enemy forces in South Vietnam were North Vietnamese soldiers. The Defense Department confirmed these figures.[4] *The Pentagon Papers* point to similar such low estimates of North Vietnamese forces during the years 1963–1964. Washington's panicky reaction to developments in South Vietnam was not a response to North Vietnamese strength in that country, but to the weakness of South Vietnam and the fear of a Viet Cong victory.[5] It was not until 1965, after the sustained U.S. bombing of North Vietnam began in February of that year, that North Vietnam regulars entered the war in the south with military units.

In its effort to prepare the U.S. public for the escalation of the war, the U.S. State Department, headed by Dean Rusk, sought to prove that the war in South Vietnam was the result of Communist aggression from the north. In early 1965 it published, with great fanfare, its famous White Paper (or position paper) in which it sought to prove its case. For that purpose it produced evidence that, among weapons captured from the NLF, a number were of Communist origin. But the number—179 out of 15,100—only proved that the NLF was depending more on weapons captured from the inept and demoralized South Vietnamese army than on outside Communist sources.[6]

■ THE AMERICANIZATION OF THE WAR

In early August 1964, during the U.S. presidential election campaign, President Johnson found the pretext he needed for the United States to intervene directly in the war in a major way and to do so with congressional support. This was the Gulf of Tonkin incident. The U.S. government reported that one of its naval ships, the destroyer *Maddox,* had been attacked by North Vietnamese torpedo boats. Although Johnson claimed that the attack took place on the high seas (that is, in international waters) and that it was unprovoked, the destroyer was in fact within the twelve-mile limit of North Vietnam gathering intelligence electronically and providing support for covert military operations against North Vietnam by South Vietnamese commandos (which had been going on since January 1964.) After an alleged second North Vietnamese "attack" two days later—one that was never confirmed by an investigation—President Johnson ordered retaliatory air strikes against selected targets in North Vietnam.[7] But more importantly, he also went to Congress for authorization to use military force in Vietnam. The result was the Gulf of Tonkin Resolution, which authorized the president to take "all necessary measures to repel any armed attacks against the forces of the United States and to prevent further aggression." This resolution was passed unanimously by the House of Representatives and by a ninety-eight to two vote in the Senate. Supporters of the war called it a "functional equivalent of a declaration of war."[8] Both President Johnson and his successor, Richard Nixon, used it as the legal basis for massive military operations in Vietnam and in neighboring countries.

Not until he was elected and inaugurated for a new term of office did President Johnson actually use these new powers. During the election campaign he had wanted to appear as a "dove" compared to his "hawkish" Republican opponent, Barry Goldwater. Thus, he repeatedly vowed that he was against committing American boys to fighting a war in Vietnam. But, after the election, on the advice of his political and military advisers, a group of men who had served under Kennedy, Johnson decided to step up the U.S. involvement in the war. It became evident that in order to save the South Vietnamese government, the United States had to take an active combat role. Johnson then ordered sustained bombing raids on North Vietnam in February 1965, and in the weeks that followed U.S. combat troops landed in large numbers on the shores of South Vietnam to take up the battle.

Meanwhile, in June 1965, another military coup in Saigon brought to power a new set of officers who were more strongly committed to the anti-Communist cause in which the United States was so heavily engaged. The leaders of the new ruling group were Air Marshal Nguyen Cao Ky and Army Gen. Nguyen Van Thieu. Their regime was quite willing to use force against any and all political opposition, and did so against the Buddhists in Hue in May 1966. They resolutely refused any negotiations or compromise with the NLF. In September 1967, a controlled election was held and Thieu was elected president and Ky vice-president. The election served to provide the semblance of democracy that Washington needed to support its case that the United States was fighting in defense of a government that represented the will of the people of South Vietnam.

The continued bombing of North Vietnam and its supply routes into the south (nicknamed the Ho Chi Minh Trail) and the heavy commitment of U.S. forces in search-and-destroy missions seemed to promise certain victory. In late 1967, Gen. William Westmoreland, the commanding officer of U.S. forces in Vietnam, felt confident enough to state "we have reached an important point, when the end begins to come into view."[9] The United States introduced an incredible amount of firepower into the war, and inflicted an ever-increasing number of casualties on its enemy. Every week U.S. television viewers were treated to higher and higher body counts of dead Communist soldiers. However, despite their increasing losses, the Communist forces seemed to grow ever stronger. Hanoi continued to infiltrate more supplies to arm the Viet Cong, who were able to recruit more soldiers to fight and die for their cause against the foreign army. Nationalism was surely on the side of the NLF, as its appeals to avenge the dreadful toll of Vietnamese deaths and the devastation of their country were answered by hundreds of thousands of their own people. The more that the United States bombed and strafed and napalmed, the more that it killed and captured, the stronger its Vietnamese enemy grew.

And so the weary war went on through 1966 and 1967. No longer did South Vietnam carry the chief burden of the war; it had become the United States's war. And with North Vietnam now engaged in the fight in South Vietnam it became an entirely different conflict, one which belied President Johnson's 1964 campaign promise that he sought no wider war. By the beginning of 1968, the optimism in Saigon and in Washington began to give way to pessimism. The war was proving to be "an escalated military stalemate." By this time, after three full years of large-scale warfare and increasingly volatile political protests at home, Lyndon Johnson could hear voices within his own administration and his own party urging him to consider getting out of Vietnam.

The Vietnam War had become a dreadful nightmare that went on and on. It grew more and more costly to both sides. For the Vietnamese the cost was death and destruction on an unprecedented scale. For the United States the cost was, in addition to the increasing number of war dead, a huge drain on the U.S. economy, strained relations with U.S. allies many of which opposed the U.S. position, and loss of influence in the Third World. The war also caused serious political and social upheaval in the United States itself. In fact, it became one of the most divisive issues in U.S. history. It ruined the political career of President Lyndon Johnson, and contributed to the downfall of the next president, Richard Nixon. In 1968, both men—Johnson as he was leaving the presidency and Nixon as he campaigned for and prepared to assume the office—came to the realization that the United States must pull out of this costly war.

That realization came to President Johnson in the wake of the February 1968 Tet Offensive. After a lull in the fighting, which the United States interpreted as a sign that the enemy had finally been worn down, the Viet Cong and the army of North Vietnam launched a surprise offensive throughout South Vietnam during Tet, the lunar New Year holiday. At the outset, they were able to take thirty-six of the forty-four provincial capitals in the country, and most surprising of all, they staged a major attack on Saigon, where suicide commandos even penetrated the grounds of the U.S. embassy. The impact of the Tet Offensive, as Communist forces had calculated, shattered the popular illusion the U.S. leaders had created, that the United States was on the verge of victory. However, the U.S. military command in Vietnam, in an effort to demonstrate its supremacy, launched a furious counterattack making full use of its massive firepower.

The Communist losses were staggering as they were driven out of Saigon and the other cities and towns they had taken. Within a month General

Vietnamese President Nguyen Van Thieu and Vice-President Nguyen Cao Ky meet with U.S. President Lyndon Johnson, Honolulu, Hawaii, Feb. 7, 1966. (*National Archives*)

Viet Cong prisoners under U.S. military guard. (*National Archives*)

Westmoreland could claim that the Tet Offensive was a disaster for the enemy, that it had wasted its remaining strength. This was not an empty claim, for subsequent evidence has made it clear that the U.S. counterattack all but eliminated the Viet Cong as a fighting force, leaving only North Vietnamese forces to fight the war from this point on.

Particularly harsh were the fates of the old imperial city of Hue and of Ben Tre, a provincial capital in the Mekong Delta. After the North Vietnamese conquered Hue, they immediately rounded up and executed an estimated 3,000 residents of the city suspected of collaboration with Saigon and U.S. forces. The U.S. military command, in an effort to drive the North Vietnamese out of Hue, subjected the city, particularly its huge citadel, to sustained bombardment. In all, 10,000 soldiers and civilians died in the battle for Hue. In late February 1968, U.S. marines reoccupied a city largely in ruins.

Ben Tre suffered a similar fate. U.S. artillery destroyed it completely. When asked why the city had been leveled, a U.S. major offered what became his country's epitaph in Vietnam: "We had to destroy it in order to save it."[10] It was the only answer he could give. The U.S. military involvement in Vietnam no longer made sense.

The Tet Offensive was a military setback for the Communists. It was, however, a psychological and political victory for them, because of its impact on the people of the United States and on the Johnson administration. Hanoi was well aware that 1968 was an election year in the United States. In addition to seeking a sudden military victory, Hanoi's purpose seems also to have been to give notice that the war was far from over, despite the optimistic pronouncements by U.S. generals and politicians alike. In this the Communists were quite successful. President Johnson, faced with mounting opposition to his Vietnam policy even in his own party, was forced to reassess the entire war effort. At about this time, he received from General Westmoreland in Vietnam a request for 206,000 more soldiers. This request would have surprised the U.S. public if it had known of it, for General Westmoreland had consistently maintained that his troops were winning the war. President Johnson, who had also promised victory, could not in this election year meet this request. Instead, after making a reappraisal of the situation in Vietnam, he made a televised address to the people of the United States, announcing that he would call a halt to the bombing of North Vietnam as an inducement to Hanoi to seek a negotiated settlement and—the real surprise—that he would not seek reelection. Lyndon Johnson wanted to wash his hands of Vietnam.

The winner of the 1968 presidential election, Richard Nixon, proclaimed during the campaign that he had a secret plan to end the war. Several years later he admitted that he had no specific plan, but once in office he devised a war strategy that was designed to gradually end the U.S. involvement in Vietnam, but which in fact kept U.S. soldiers in the war for four more years. Nixon's strategy called for the "Vietnamization" of the war, a plan whereby the United States would gradually disengage itself from the war while strengthening the ARVN (the Army of South Vietnam). This would allow him to placate his domestic opponents of the war by announcing periodic withdrawals of U.S. troops, and yet was intended to produce a victory against the Communists. But this plan took time to implement, and in the meantime the war raged on, as did opposition to it at home. Subsequently, thousands more U.S. and Vietnamese soldiers died in battle during the years of Vietnamization, from 1969 to 1973. Ultimately, the Vietnamization scheme failed, despite the enormous amount of military provisions supplied by the United States, mainly because, no matter how well equipped, the corrupt and undisciplined ARVN was no match for its more determined Communist foes.

■ THE U.S. EXIT

President Johnson had tried persistently to persuade Hanoi to come to the bargaining table, but Hanoi just as persistently refused his terms. North Vietnam had presented its peace plan in April 1965, a four-point proposal calling for the withdrawal of U.S. forces from Vietnam, the end of hostilities against North Vietnam, adherence to the Geneva Accords, and allowing the Vietnamese alone to settle their problems. It also insisted, as a condition for negotiations, that the NLF be recognized and be allowed to take part in the negotiations. But the Johnson administration and the Thieu-Ky government in Saigon steadfastly refused to have any dealings with the NLF. This remained the main obstacle to starting negotiations until the very end of the Johnson administration. Finally, in October 1968, the two sides agreed to begin peace talks in Paris with the NLF and Saigon represented as well as Hanoi and Washington.

The four-party peace talks began in January 1969, just as the Nixon administration took office in Washington, but they were immediately deadlocked. The Communist side demanded a commitment by the United States on a timetable for the complete withdrawal of U.S. forces from Vietnam and the replacement of the Saigon regime by a coalition government made up of all parties, including the NLF. The Nixon administration rejected these demands, and further talks were postponed indefinitely. However, in 1971 the U.S. negotiator, Henry Kissinger, and the North Vietnamese representative, Le Duc Tho, met in Paris to conduct secret negotiations. Still, the two sides refused to make the kind of concessions or compromises that were necessary to end the war. Neither wished to give up at the bargaining table that for which they had been fighting so long. Neither side wished to dishonor its war dead by compromising the cause for which they had died in battle.

And so the war dragged on. Even though U.S. troop levels were reduced from 542,000 soldiers in February 1969 to 139,000 in December 1971, the warfare did not diminish; in fact, it was expanded into Laos and Cambodia. Richard Nixon, as Lyndon Johnson before him, was determined not to be the first president to lose a war. He counted on the destruction of North Vietnam's sanctuaries and supply routes in the neighboring countries to bring victory in Vietnam.

The prelude to the entry of ARVN and U.S. forces into Cambodia[11] was the overthrow of the ruler of that country, Prince Norodom Sihanouk, in March 1970. Prince Sihanouk had managed to keep his country out of the Vietnam conflict by professing a policy of neutrality while in fact allowing Vietnamese Communist forces to make use of Cambodian jungle areas along the eastern border and accepting U.S. retaliatory air strikes against them. He was overthrown by his own prime minister, General Lon Nol, who then turned to the United States for military aid. In response to reports of the spreading military operations of Vietnamese Communists in Cambodia, President Nixon, in April 1970, authorized joint U.S.-ARVN attacks into that country to clean out the Communist bases. For over a month U.S. and ARVN troops, numbering over 50,000, searched the jungles of eastern Cambodia in a futile effort to find the headquarters for the Communist Operations in South Vietnam (COSVN).[12] This widening of the war caused an uproar of protest from anti-war activists in the United States. It was at this juncture that anti-war students at Columbia University and other colleges in the United States sought to forcibly shut down their schools in protest. They were intent on "bringing the war home," and in a sense that is what happened on the campus of Kent State University, where four anti-war student protesters were shot to death by the National Guard on May 4, 1970.

An incursion into Laos in early 1971 demonstrated the failure of the Vietnamization plan, because the ARVN forces who had entered Laos with U.S. air support were badly routed. Television crews sent back images of panic-stricken ARVN troops hanging on the skids of evacuation helicopters in a desperate effort to escape the North Vietnamese counterattack.

As the 1972 election rolled around, the Vietnam War was still raging; 15,000 additional U.S. soldiers had died since Nixon had come to office. Nixon intensified his effort to achieve a negotiated settlement. Secret talks between Kissinger and Le Duc Tho resumed in Paris in April 1972. Meanwhile, both sides sought to strengthen their bargaining positions, as Hanoi launched an offensive on the ground and U.S. B-52 bombers pounded North Vietnam with the heaviest bombing yet, and U.S. ships blockaded and mined the Haiphong harbor. On the eve of the U.S. election, Kissinger was able to announce that "peace is at hand."[13] He and Le Duc Tho had secretly hammered out a preliminary agreement for ending the war. Its main terms were that within sixty days after the cease-fire the United States

Refugees on Route 1 near Quang Tri, South Vietnam, 1972. (*National Archives*)

President Lyndon Johnson meets with Gen. Creighton Abrams and key cabinet members at the White House for a discussion of the war, Oct. 29, 1968. (*National Archives*)

would complete the withdrawal of all of its troops from Vietnam, Hanoi would release all U.S. prisoners, and the political settlement in South Vietnam would be left for the Vietnamese to work out. The contending Vietnamese factions were to form a "National Council of Reconciliation and Concord" with equal representation for the Thieu regime, the NLF, and neutral parties. But one major problem remained, namely South Vietnamese President Thieu, who refused to accept these terms. To win him over Kissinger traveled to Saigon carrying with him President Nixon's pledge of continued U.S. protection for his government and a billion dollars worth of additional armaments for his armed forces. Thieu, however, remained opposed to the peace terms.

Before the peace agreement was reached, the United States delivered one final, savage punishment to North Vietnam. In an effort to break a new deadlock in the Paris peace talks and to demonstrate his continuing commitment to defend Thieu's government, President Nixon, who had recently been reelected in a landslide victory, ordered another bombing of Hanoi and Haiphong. The around-the-clock bombing raids (called the "Christmas bombings"), which began on December 18 and continued until the end of the month, turned large parts of these two cities into rubble. This final act of war gave a hollow ring to Nixon's insistence on "peace with honor." Curiously, the bombings did not bring any significant change in the terms of the peace agreement finally signed in January 1973; its terms were essentially those agreed to by Kissinger and Le Duc Tho in October.

With the signing of the peace agreement on January 27, 1973, the United States finally exited from the Vietnam War. This long-awaited event brought great relief to the United States, but it did not bring an end to the war in Vietnam. Saigon staged a new offensive of its own, seemingly in order to sabotage the peace agreement and keep the United States in the war. But as the battle raged on, the ARVN forces with all of their U.S. arms proved to be no match for the North Vietnamese army. Re-intervention by the United States was impossible, for once the troops had been withdrawn surely the U.S. public would not have allowed their return. Moreover, the Nixon administration was by this time in shambles over the Watergate affair,[14] and Congress, reflecting the will of the nation, cut off further aid to South Vietnam. Finally, in January 1975, ARVN collapsed when a North Vietnamese attack in the northern highlands produced a panic that spread throughout the country. The expected battle for Saigon never took place. In April 1975, North Vietnamese forces entered the city unopposed and in triumph, and South Vietnam fell to the Communists. The U.S. embassy in Saigon was the scene of a frantic airlift of the remaining U.S. citizens in the country and as many of their Vietnamese cohorts and friends as they could crowd onto the last helicopters.[15]

The full dimensions of the U.S. defeat in Vietnam are still to be learned. The final cost of the war for the United States includes nearly

58,000 soldiers killed and more than 300,000 wounded. Economically, the war cost an estimated $165 billion. The indirect economic cost is beyond estimation, but the huge expenditures for the prolonged war surely contributed to the inflation, the deficit, and the balance of payments problems that plagued the United States during the 1970s. The social, political, and psychological damage of the Vietnam tragedy is also incalculable. U.S. society was divided as it had not been since the Civil War a century earlier. Vietnam aroused intense feelings and bitter struggles among the people and brought them the frustration of defeat. It also brought on strong-arm police action against anti-war protesters and the use of armed force against student demonstrators. The war generated a political awakening for the country's young people—a new activism and a heightened political consciousness. But later, as it dragged on and on, the war, together with the Watergate scandal, caused deep feelings of mistrust, apathy, and skepticism toward government. Thus, sadly, another of the casualties of the war was the credibility of the U.S. government.

In 1995, over three decades after the Americanization of the war, Robert McNamara, who had been the U.S. secretary of defense and one of the principal architects of the U.S. military enterprise in Vietnam, published his memoir in which he confessed in retrospect that the United States "could and should have withdrawn from South Vietnam" in late 1963. At that point, only 78 U.S. soldiers had been killed in the conflict there; by the time the war was over it had claimed over 58,000 U.S. lives and between 1 and 2 million Vietnamese lives. McNamara, looking back, saw things much clearer than he had when he played a leading role in committing U.S. forces in a mistaken war. In 1995, he listed eleven major errors, or causes for, the Vietnam disaster, including misjudging the strength of North Vietnam, underrating nationalism as a force in Vietnam, failing to understand the history and culture of Vietnam, and failing to recognize the limitations of modern technological warfare.[16]

The cost of the war to the peoples of Indochina was also enormous and incalculable. The U.S. estimate of the military deaths of the South Vietnamese army was over 200,000, and for the Communist Vietnamese almost 500,000 (including both NLF and North Vietnamese forces). We will never know how many civilian casualties there were or how many refugees, but in both cases the numbers were in the millions. The physical mutilation of the country was staggering. The United States dropped three times more bombs on Indochina than it dropped on its enemies in World War II. In addition, it defoliated over five million acres with chemicals such as Agent Orange. Yet, as great as the physical destruction was, it could eventually be repaired. Less visible and less readily repaired was the serious damage done to the social order, to the Vietnamese way of life.

■ THE CONTINUING TRAGEDY OF INDOCHINA

In the short term, the outcome of the "fall of Vietnam" to Communism was not as grim as the U.S. government had predicted, but in the long term it was even worse. Vietnam was, of course, unified under the Communist rule of Hanoi, but the idea that a Communist victory in Vietnam would be a victory for Communist China proved entirely wrong. After the war, Chinese-Vietnamese relations deteriorated, becoming so hostile that the two nations became engaged in war four years after the fall of Saigon. Predictions of a dismal future for the people of Vietnam proved correct; however, not all the blame is to be placed on the Communist rulers of the country. The causes for the ensuing tragedy in Vietnam and in neighboring Laos and Cambodia are more complex.

In the wake of the Communist military victory, the South Vietnamese braced themselves for the terrible, vengeful "bloodbath" that President Nixon had predicted, but it did not come. Hanoi initially allowed South Vietnam to retain its separate identity under a Provisional Revolutionary Government. The government in Hanoi adopted a policy of gradualism in imposing its system on the people of the south and was much less forceful and heavy-handed than expected. To be sure, those identified as high-ranking former government or military officers of the overthrown Saigon regime were singled out for severe punishments, usually involving confiscation of property, arrest, and long sentences to hard labor in remote rural "reeducation" camps.

The new order in the south meant, of course, a transformation of the city of Saigon, renamed Ho Chi Minh City. Quickly, the bars and dance halls were closed and the prostitutes disappeared, as did other traces of the twenty-year-long U.S. presence in that city. But beyond this and the introduction of revolutionary broadcasts and music over street loudspeakers, change in the city was rather minimal. The city was grossly overpopulated as a result of the influx of refugees during the war years, and its economy had been almost entirely dependent on the U.S. presence. The U.S. departure left almost two-thirds of the 3 million people in the city unemployed. The dire lack of goods and housing to provide for this huge unproductive population gave rise to rampant inflation and black marketeering.

Within a year, severe economic problems gripped Vietnam, and conditions steadily worsened year after year. The government's plan to quickly restore the agricultural productivity of the south to complement the industrial development of the north proved too optimistic. In part, the failure at economic recovery was the result of legacies of the war. Not only were the cities blighted, but vast areas of the countryside were no longer under cultivation due to the flight of the peasants and the defoliated and bomb-cratered land. And there were many other problems. The government lacked trained administrators to carry out policies; machinery, draft animals, fertilizer, and irrigation systems were are all lacking; and the transport system was in shambles. The army, instead of being demobilized, was put to work reclaiming wastelands and developing irrigation. Hundreds of thousands of unemployed city dwellers were lured to rural New Economic Zones with promises of houses, land, and food. Many of these people would soon flee from the harsh, almost primitive conditions of these rural developments back to the cities, causing the government to resort to forced relocation and detention in the New Economic Zones. To compound matters, southern Vietnam experienced three successive years of natural disasters, including both droughts and devastating floods, causing crop failures. As a result, the country was left desperately short of rice by early 1978. The agricultural failure was ruinous for the nation, as it now required large imports of food, lacked capital for industrial development, and was forced to resort to still more austere measures, which caused still greater despair for the people.

Nor was there international deliverance. Vietnam was unable to attract foreign investment, without which its hopes of economic recovery were dim. It had hoped for reparation payments from the United States, such as President Nixon had once promised, but Washington was not so forgiving or generous. Instead, it refused to provide either economic aid or investment, and it pressured international lending agencies to reject Vietnam's pleas. Other Western nations were also unsympathetic. Hanoi's efforts to court favor with members of ASEAN (Association of Southeast Asian Nations—Malaysia, Thailand, Brunei, Indonesia, Singapore, and the Philippines) were also unsuccessful. Increasingly, Hanoi was forced to turn to the Soviet Union for economic assistance, and as it did so, aid from other sources diminished. Moreover, reliance on the Soviet Union contributed to a worsening of relations with China, which until 1978 had provided a modicum of aid to Hanoi. Vietnam's economic and diplomatic difficulties worsened in 1979, when it sent its military forces into Cambodia.

☐ The Plight of Cambodia

In the aftermath of the Vietnam War, the anticipated bloodbath occurred not in Vietnam but in neighboring Cambodia, and it is to the historical background of that part of the Indochina tragedy that we must now turn. When the United States disengaged from Vietnam in early 1973, it also terminated its military support for the Lon Nol government in Cambodia, which was embattled by the Khmer Rouge, a native Communist force. But in a final effort to deny the Cambodian Communists a victory, the United States unleashed its heaviest yet B-52 bombing raids on Communist-held areas of Cambodia, disregarding its neutrality. The Khmer Rouge, which had the support of North Vietnam at this time, battled with renewed intensity and seized much of the countryside. In April 1975, at the same time that Saigon fell to the North Vietnamese, the Khmer Rouge defeated Lon Nol's forces and swept into Phnom Penh, the Cambodian capital.

Cambodia braced itself for a new order under the Communist government led by Pol Pot, who immediately began a horrendous reign of revolutionary terror. Pol Pot, unlike most other revolutionaries, did not merely advocate a revolutionary transformation; he was willing to eradicate completely the old order, root and branch, and to reorganize society to a degree no revolutionary regime had ever attempted. The entire urban population was evacuated to the countryside, where it was placed in armed work camps. Pol Pot's ideal was to create a nation of workers and peasants who would modernize industry and agriculture. All other classes were to be transformed, and if they resisted they would be exterminated. In the space of three years, at least 1.5 million Cambodians—almost one-fifth of the population—were murdered. Pol Pot and the Khmer Rouge directed their fury against the old order, the Western-educated elite, city dwellers, and all real or suspected "enemies" of the revolution.

Not only did Pol Pot employ brutal force against his own people, but he initiated attacks against neighboring countries: Thailand on the western border and Vietnam, his former ally, on the east. Pol Pot, who was vehemently anti-Vietnamese, regarded Vietnam as the greatest threat to the independence of the Cambodian revolution. He perceived a rebellion against his regime developing in the eastern part of the country, which had a substantial ethnic Vietnamese population. In 1978, he unleashed a furious attack against the suspected rebels in the east, slaughtering thousands of people, Cambodians and Vietnamese alike, and driving many of the latter across the border into Vietnam. In pursuit of rebel forces, the Khmer Rouge army attacked Vietnamese forces in the Parrot's Beak border area. The purpose of these attacks was not only to eliminate native resistance, but also to settle old scores with Vietnam and assert Cambodia's claim to certain disputed borderlands.

In retaliation, Vietnam, with its superior, battle-tested army, drove into Cambodia in January 1979, scattered the forces of the Khmer Rouge, took control of Phnom Penh, and installed a former Khmer Rouge officer, Heng Samrin, as head of a new pro-Vietnamese government of Cambodia. The Vietnamese conquest of Phnom Penh, however, did not bring peace to Cambodia. A Vietnamese army of about 170,000 occupied the country and continued to battle remnants of Pol Pot's forces as well as other resistance forces. The war threatened to spill over into Thailand as thousands of the fleeing rival Cambodian forces and civilians took refuge in camps across the border.

The military occupation of Cambodia and the continuing struggle against its opponents in remote jungle encampments near the Thai border put an enormous strain on an already exhausted Vietnamese nation. It meant withdrawing its army from food production and reconstruction and diverting dwindling treasury funds to the military. It also meant still greater reliance on Soviet economic assistance to prop up its stagnant economy.

The international consequences of Vietnam's military occupation of Cambodia and the increased dependence of Vietnam on the Soviet Union were profound. Even though Hanoi ended the genocide of the Pol Pot regime in Cambodia and used this to legitimize its military intervention, it was roundly rebuked by the United States, by other Western countries, by the ASEAN countries, and most strongly by China. In response to Vietnam's "invasion" of Cambodia, China invaded Vietnam in February 1979 in order to "teach it a lesson." This warfare was costly for both sides, but proved inconclusive, because the Chinese withdrew within a month, leaving Vietnam in control of Cambodia and Laos. The Chinese continued to support the deposed Pol Pot regime as a means to force Vietnam to withdraw its army from Cambodia. The United States, too, condemned Vietnam for its invasion of Cambodia. Mainly because of this issue, Washington strengthened its resolve not to extend official recognition to the government of Vietnam or to provide it desperately needed economic assistance. Meanwhile, Hanoi turned to the Soviet Union not only for continuing economic assistance but for military support as well. The Soviet Union signed a twenty-year defense agreement with Vietnam, and thereby gained unlimited access to Cam Ranh Bay, the naval base that had been built up by the United States during the Vietnam War as one of the largest naval supply depots in the world. Both China and the United States were, of course, disturbed by the increased Soviet presence in Indochina. Ironically, the United States, which had entered Vietnam initially to stem Chinese Communist aggression in Indochina, found itself several years after that war on the side of China in the ongoing struggle in that region. And China, which had earlier feared the U.S. military presence in Indochina, now had to contend with the extension of Soviet power in that very same region on its southern border.

The tragedy of Cambodia continued through the 1980s as it remained a cockpit of international struggles. Determined to dislodge both the Vietnamese from Cambodia and the Soviets from the region, China persisted in its aid to the Khmer Rouge, which remained under the command of the mass murderer Pol Pot. In 1982, the Khmer Rouge formed a coalition with two other resistance forces in order to keep up the fight against the Vietnamese-backed regime in Phnom Penh. The two groups (supporters of the deposed Lon Nol and Sihanouk governments, respectively) were aided by neighboring ASEAN countries and by the United States. (Critics of U.S. policy in Cambodia pointed out that this U.S. military aid was, in effect, support for the Khmer Rouge, the dominant member of the coalition.) Even with foreign support, the coalition of resistance forces was not able to mount a serious threat to the Vietnamese forces in Cambodia in the fighting that continued through the 1980s.

Conditions that had sustained the civil war in Cambodia since its beginning in 1979 began to change about a decade later. The impasse in Cambodia had been prolonged by foreign power involvement. The Soviets supported the Vietnamese-imposed Heng Samrin regime in Phnom Penh, the Chinese supplied arms to the Khmer Rouge, and the United States pursued an anomalous policy of opposition to both the Phnom Penh regime and the Khmer Rouge but allowed its aid to the two other rebel groups to pass into the hands of the Khmer Rouge.

In the summer of 1991, as the Soviet Union was disintegrating, a major shift occurred in the policies of the foreign powers involved in Cambodia as well as in the position of the combatants within the war-torn country. With the Soviet Union removed as a threat, China ceased supplying arms to the Khmer Rouge and lent support to a UN-sponsored peace process. At the same time Vietnam, in desperate need of international aid, took steps to improve its relations with China as well as with the United States. Thus, with the Soviets out of the picture and the Chinese, the United States, and the Vietnamese all pressuring the contending Cambodian factions to adopt the UN peace plan, things began to happen quickly. In June 1991, Prince Sihanouk took the lead in calling a meeting of the leaders of the four factions (the three rebel groups and the Phnom Penh regime) at which they agreed to the main elements of the UN plan: formation of a twelve-member Supreme National Council (SNC) with equal representation for each of the four factions, a cease-fire, a ban on foreign military aid to all combatants, and a demilitarization plan requiring each group to cut its troop strength by 70 percent.

Finally, in October 1991, leaders of the four factions and representatives of eighteen nations met in Paris to sign the UN peace agreement formally ending the thirteen-year-long civil war in Cambodia. The comprehensive peace agreement authorized the Sihanouk-led SNC to establish a transitional administration in Phnom Penh and called for the formation of the UN Transitional Authority in Cambodia (UNTAC) to oversee the implementation of the peace accords. This UN peacekeeping operation, its largest and most expensive to date, was to consist of some 22,000 soldiers, police, and civilian officials from twenty countries. UNTAC's mission also included monitoring the cease-fire, administering several government ministries, repatriating some 360,000 refugees from camps in Thailand, and finally, preparing for free, UN-supervised elections scheduled for May 1993.

But not all went according to plan. The Khmer Rouge remained the chief obstacle. In the countryside Khmer Rouge guerrillas continued to conduct raids against villages and government installations. In addition, they refused to commit themselves to demobilization of their forces or even allow UNTAC officers into their zone. They argued that Vietnamese forces still remained in the country and insisted on the immediate dismantling of the interim government in Phnom Penh, which they claimed was still Vietnamese-dominated.[17] In reality, they were holding out for a dominant position in the new political order. Prince Sihanouk and UNTAC officials and peacekeeping forces, through firmness and persistence, managed to overcome Khmer Rouge resistance and finally, in 1993, establish a government based on UN-supervised elections and headed by Sihanouk, who handily won the elections.

☐ The Refugees of Indochina

Another dimension of the continuing tragedy of Indochina was the desperate flight of hundreds of thousands of people from Vietnam, Cambodia, and Laos. Driven to escape by the hardships and dangers that confronted them, desperate people attempted to flee from their homelands, even at great risk to their lives. From Cambodia and Laos they trekked overland to Thailand, and in Vietnam, many thousands of people managed to escape the country by boarding vessels and taking to the sea. The risk was great, for many of those attempting to flee were arrested and punished, and many of those who did escape on overcrowded makeshift boats perished before finding safe harbor. Even if these "boat people" did succeed in reaching the shores of neighboring countries, there were no guarantees that they would be sheltered or would find their way to other nations where they could settle and begin new lives.

Since the fall of Saigon in April 1975 over 1.5 million refugees fled Vietnam by boat, and of this number some 200,000 died on the South China Sea from exposure, drowning, and attacks by pirates while attempting their perilous voyage. The first wave of boat people came at the time of the fall of Saigon, when about 100,000 people fled the country. The exodus diminished during the next three years, but in 1978 and 1979, when the war between Cambodia and Vietnam occurred, a second and much larger wave of refugees fled Vietnam. The new flood of boat people, arriving in neighboring countries at the rate of over 12,500 a month, quickly caused an international crisis as such nations as Malaysia (where most of them landed), Thailand, and Singapore refused to accept them and began driving them away forcibly. In July 1979, a UN Conference on Refugees was called at Geneva. It secured an agreement from Vietnam to limit the refugee outflow, provided relief to the nations of "first asylum" such as Malaysia, and received promises from other nations to open their doors to the refugees.

The majority of those who left Vietnam were ethnic Chinese, who had long dominated private business in southern Vietnam and fell victim to government policies in early 1979 that abolished "bourgeois trade" and introduced a currency reform that rendered their accumulated savings almost worthless. Deprived of much of their wealth and livelihood, they saw no better choice than to flee the country. Curiously, many were assisted in their flight by the Communist authorities, who collected exit fees of $2,000 in gold from each departing refugee. In northern Vietnam the exodus of the Chinese amounted to expulsion. In the wake of the Chinese invasion of Vietnam in February 1979, ethnic Chinese were dismissed from Vietnamese military and government posts and were deprived of work and business opportunities. About 250,000 of the approximately 300,000 ethnic Chinese in northern Vietnam fled northward to find sanctuary in the People's Republic of China.

Still another sad refugee drama unfolded in Laos, Cambodia, and Thailand. After the Communist takeover in Laos in 1975, some 250,000 Hmong tribesmen, who had earlier fought on the U.S. side, fled overland into Thailand. And from Cambodia came at least 150,000 survivors from the scourge of Pol Pot and the Vietnamese invasion in 1979. The entry of these thousands of pathetic refugees presented the Thai government an enormous problem. Not all those who crossed over into Thailand were refugees; at times Pol Pot's guerrilla troops also found it expedient to take refuge there. In any case, there was a limit to Thailand's ability to accommodate this influx of people in its already swollen refugee camps, and it resorted to driving newcomers away. For the vast majority of the Laotian and Cambodian refugees, the temporary asylum in Thailand would last many years while the war in Cambodia went on interminably.

RECOMMENDED READINGS

Arnett, Peter. *Live from the Battlefield: From Vietnam to Baghdad: 35 Years in the World's War Zones.* New York: Touchstone, 1994.
  By a reporter from New Zealand who first made his mark as a correspondent for AP in Southeast Asia and more recently as the CNN correspondent in Baghdad during the Gulf War.
Caputo, Philip. *A Rumor of War.* New York: Holt, Rinehart and Winston, 1977.
  The reminiscences of a loyal marine who, by the end of his tour of duty, questioned the purpose of the U.S. involvement.
Fall, Bernard B. *Vietnam Witness, 1953–1966.* New York: Praeger, 1966.
  By the French historian who was widely considered the West's leading authority on Vietnam.
FitzGerald, Frances. *Fire in the Lake: The Vietnamese and the Americans in Vietnam.* New York: Random House, 1972.
  An award-winning study that places the U.S. intervention in a context of Vietnamese history.
Halberstam, David. *The Best and the Brightest.* New York: Random House, 1972.
  A critical account of how the leaders in Washington drifted into a war on the other side of the globe.
Herring, George C. *America's Longest War: The United States and Vietnam, 1950–1975.* New York: John Wiley and Sons, 1979.

Herrington, Stuart A. *Peace with Honor: An American Report on Vietnam, 1973–75.* Novato, Calif.: Presidio Press, 1983.
A critical view of U.S. responsibility for the fall of Saigon to North Vietnamese forces.

Hersh, Seymour. *My Lai Four: A Report on the Massacre and Its Aftermath.* New York: Random House, 1970.

Isaacs, Arnold R. *Without Honor: Defeat in Vietnam and Cambodia.* Baltimore: Johns Hopkins University Press, 1983.

Karnow, Stanley. *Vietnam: A History.* New York: Viking, 1983.
A major work by a noted journalist who served as the consultant for a thirteen-part television documentary on the Vietnam War.

McNamara, Robert S. *In Retrospect: The Tragedy and Lessons of Vietnam.* New York: Times Books/Random House, 1995.
The mea culpa of the secretary of defense for presidents Kennedy and Johnson.

Shawcross, William. *Sideshow: Kissinger, Nixon and the Destruction of Cambodia.* New York: Simon and Schuster, 1979.
An analysis of the widening of the war into Cambodia, faulting the policy of President Nixon and Henry Kissinger for causing the bloodbath that occurred subsequent to the U.S. withdrawal from that country.

Sheehan, Neil. *A Bright Shining Lie: John Paul Vann and America in Vietnam.* New York: Random House, 1988.
A critical account of the U.S. conduct of the war in Vietnam.

Sheehan, Neil, et al. *The Pentagon Papers.* New York: Bantam, 1971.
A most useful collection of primary sources on the U.S. involvement in the Vietnam War, revealing the plotting and planning of Washington decision-makers.

Summers, Harry G. *On Strategy: A Critical Analysis of the Vietnam War.* Novato, Calif.: Presidio Press, 1982.

NOTES

1. Bernard B. Fall, *Last Reflections on a War* (Garden City, N.Y.: Doubleday, 1967), p. 167. In Saigon, Diem received 605,025 votes from 450,000 registered voters.

2. Vice-President Lyndon Johnson's characterization of Diem, cited in Frances FitzGerald, *Fire in the Lake: The Vietnamese and the Americans in Vietnam* (Boston: Random House, 1972), p. 72; also John Osborne, "The Tough Miracle Man of Vietnam: Diem, America's Newly Arrived Visitor, Has Roused His Country and Routed the Reds," *Life,* May 13, 1957, pp. 156–176.

3. Quoted in Richard J. Barnet, *Intervention and Revolution: The United States in the Third World* (New York: New American Library, 1968), p. 216.

4. Theodore Draper, "The American Crisis: Vietnam, Cuba and the Dominican Republic," *Commentary,* January 1967, p. 36.

5. Neil Sheehan et al., *The Pentagon Papers* (New York: Bantam, 1971), documents 61–64, pp. 271–285.

6. For the White Paper, "Aggression from the North," and I. F. Stone's reply, see Marcus G. Raskin and Bernard B. Fall, eds., *The Viet-Nam Reader: Articles and Documents on American Foreign Policy and the Viet-Nam Crisis,* rev. ed. (New York: Vintage, 1967), pp. 143–162.

7. More than thirty years later, even then Secretary of Defense Robert McNamara did not know precisely what had taken place at the Gulf of Tonkin. In his

memoirs he concluded, however, that it appeared no second attack had taken place. See Robert S. McNamara, *In Retrospect: The Tragedy and Lessons of Vietnam* (New York: Times Books/Random House, 1995), pp. 128–142.

8. First used by President Johnson's acting attorney general, Nicholas Katzenbach; Stanley Karnow, *Vietnam: A History* (New York: Viking, 1983), p. 362.

9. General Westmoreland, ibid., p. 479.

10. FitzGerald, *Fire in the Lake*, p. 393.

11. In 1975, the government of Cambodia adopted an alternate spelling of the nation's name, Kampuchea, but for consistency we have retained the spelling that continues to be most commonly used in the West.

12. President Nixon was already conducting a secret war in both Laos and Cambodia prior to the entry of U.S. ground forces into Cambodia in April 1970—secret only in the sense that the Nixon administration did not make public U.S. military operations (mainly heavy bombing by B-52s) in these two countries and, in fact, repeatedly denied reports of these military operations.

13. Transcript of Kissinger's news conference, *New York Times,* October 27, 1972, p. 18.

14. Watergate was a direct outgrowth of the war in Vietnam. In June 1971, Daniel Ellsberg, who had once served as a zealous administrator of official U.S. policy in Vietnam and who had since become an equally zealous opponent of the war, leaked to the *New York Times,* the *Washington Post,* and other newspapers copies of a study of the war, the "Pentagon Papers" as they became popularly known, that had been commissioned by President Johnson's secretary of defense, Robert McNamara. President Nixon, furious at this and other leaks of classified information, created a group, the White House "plumbers," whose task it was to plug intelligence leaks and to investigate Ellsberg and other "subversives" undermining his presidency and conduct of the war. For reasons still not clear, in June 1972, the "plumbers" broke into the national headquarters of the Democratic Party at the Watergate apartment complex in Washington, D.C. As evidence of wrongdoing began to implicate Nixon himself, he ordered his subordinates to commit perjury, or lying under oath. Unfortunately for Nixon, he had taped his own crime, and for reasons also still not clear, he had not destroyed all the evidence. The upshot was the preparation for an impeachment trial in the Senate. When it became obvious to Nixon that his removal from office was all but a certainty, he resigned; Vice-President Gerald Ford then became the nation's chief executive.

15. During the Vietnam War, the United States turned Saigon's Tan Son Nhut Airport into one of the busiest in the world and Cam Ranh Bay into one of the largest naval supply bases in the world, but, ironically, in the 1980s they were both used mainly by the Soviet Union to supply its needy ally.

16. McNamara, *In Retrospect*. McNamara's doubts about the war were not new; as early as 1967, he had begun to reevaluate the U.S. position in Vietnam. For that reason President Johnson replaced him with Clark Clifford who, too, eventually concluded (during the Tet Offensive of 1968) that the United States had reached a dead end and the time had come to find a way out of Vietnam.

Ironically, Johnson had doubted the wisdom of any involvement in Vietnam as early as May 1964. In a telephone conversation with his former Democratic colleague in the Senate, Richard B. Russell, Johnson questioned the wisdom of a continued involvement in Vietnam: "It is the damndest worst mess that I ever saw . . . and it's going to get worse." "How important is that [Vietnam] to us?" Russell wanted to know. Neither Vietnam nor Laos, so important to the Kennedy administration, according to Johnson were worth "a damn." The Republican Party, however, would make political hay of a withdrawal. "It's the only issue they've got," Johnson told

Russell. Johnson's telephone conversation with Russell, May 27, 1964, Lyndon B. Johnson Library, Tape WH6405.10, Side A.

17. Nate Thayer, "The War Party: Khmer Rouge Intransigence Threatens Peace," *Far Eastern Economic Review,* June 25, 1992, p. 12. UNTAC head Yasushi Akashi stated that there was no evidence of Vietnamese "formed units" in Cambodia and accused the Khmer Rouge of trying to sabotage the UN agreement.

10

Détente and the
End of Bipolarity

Ironically, the years of direct U.S. involvement in Vietnam, 1965–1973, which represented a crusade against international Communism, saw a gradual improvement in relations between Washington and the two great Communist states. Toward the end of that period, the Cold War took on several unexpected turns. First, détente eased, if only for a short time, the tensions between Moscow and Washington. Second, the early 1970s saw the normalization of relations between the United States and the People's Republic of China. In the end, President Richard Nixon, the quintessential anti-Communist who had always urged strong measures against the Vietnamese Communists (commonly perceived as proxies of the Soviet Union and Communist China), visited Moscow and Beijing. The bipolar world, with Moscow and Washington at center stage, was no more.

■ THE UNITED STATES AND CHINA:
THE NORMALIZATION OF RELATIONS

The split between the Soviet Union and the People's Republic of China gave the United States a golden opportunity. Monolithic Communism, or "international socialist solidarity" as its proponents frequently called it, proved to be an ideological quest that ran aground on the shoals of nationalist interests. A succession of governments in Washington, tied down to the principle of an international Communist conspiracy, had been slow in taking advantage of the falling out between the two most important of Communist states. But by the early 1970s, the time had come to cash in on what clearly had become a windfall for Washington.

Rapprochement between the United States and the vast Chinese empire could only give the Soviets a headache. At first, it had been Moscow that had been able to play the "China card." With it, the Soviet Union's first line of defense in the East had been on the shores of the Yellow Sea.

225

Washington's ability to play the same card promised to pay immeasurable dividends. The Chinese in their turn, a proud and ancient people, had no intentions of playing the pawn and instead sought to carve out their own niche as a major player in the superpower game. When Beijing and Washington took the first steps toward the normalization of relations in the early 1970s, the result was an end to great-power bipolarity and a renewed complexity in international relations.

For more than twenty years the United States and the People's Republic of China (PRC) had no official relations; instead, they were hostile adversaries. Successive U.S. presidents denounced "Red China" as a menace to the peace-loving peoples of Asia, as a reckless, irresponsible, aggressive regime, unworthy of diplomatic recognition or United Nations membership. The United States maintained relations instead with the Nationalist regime on Taiwan, adhering to the fiction that it was the only legitimate government of China and pledging to defend it against "Communist aggression." It did not immediately commit itself to the defense of the government on Taiwan, but it did so in 1954, after having engaged Chinese Communist forces in battle for three years in Korea. Beijing denounced the U.S. military alliance with Jiang's Nationalist government and the U.S. military presence on Taiwan as "imperialist aggression" and as interference in the internal affairs of China. Meanwhile, the United States effectively blocked the PRC from gaining admission into the United Nations, contained it with a ring of military bases, maintained a rigid embargo on all trade with China, and permitted no one from the United States to travel to China.

Nor was this merely a bilateral feud, since both antagonists called upon their respective Cold War allies for support. Supporting China, at least in the first decade of the Beijing-Washington clash, was the Soviet Union, its satellite states in Eastern Europe, and Communist parties in other parts of the world. The Soviet Union had supported from the outset the PRC's bid to replace the Republic of China (as Jiang's government was called) in the United Nations. The United States, which perceived itself as leading and speaking for the "free world," applied diplomatic pressure on its allies for support of its uncompromising China policy. Washington realized that a trade embargo against China would not be effective unless most, if not all, of the allies of the United States adhered to it. And Washington also pressured its friends to stand united against diplomatic recognition of the PRC and against its entry into the United Nations. The United States reacted negatively, for example, when in 1964 the independent-minded French government decided to break ranks and extend formal recognition to the PRC.

While Washington tirelessly denounced "Red China" and condemned Mao and the Chinese Communists for their brutal enslavement of the Chinese people, Beijing regarded the United States, the most powerful capitalist nation in the world, as its "Number One Enemy" and argued persistently that U.S. imperialism was the major threat to world peace. The United States pointed to the Chinese intervention in the Korean War and China's border war with India in 1962 as examples of Chinese aggression. But Beijing (and some observers in the West) countered that in both cases China acted legitimately to protect its borders. The Chinese pointed to the ring of U.S. military positions on China's periphery—from Japan and Korea in the northeast, through Taiwan and the Philippines to Vietnam and Thailand in the south—as proof of the aggressive imperialism of the United States. So intense was this ideological conflict between the two countries that any reduction of tensions seemed impossible.

The Sino-Soviet split that became manifest in the late 1950s did not bring about an improvement in Sino-U.S. relations. Instead, relations worsened since it was China, not the Soviet Union, that argued for a stronger anti–United States line. When the United States and the Soviet Union began to move toward détente in the late 1960s, Beijing's anti-imperialist, anti–United States rhetoric became even more shrill as it sought to make its point: the Soviet Union had grown soft on capitalism, while China had not. China complained bitterly of Soviet "socialist imperialism," arguing that it was linked with U.S. "capitalist imperialism" to encircle China. Mao spoke fervently of China's support for the revolutionary peoples of the world and support for wars of national liberation such as that waged by the Communist forces in Vietnam. He even taunted the United States to make war on China, saying that the atomic bomb was merely a "paper tiger" and that China would prevail in the end. Mao's inflammatory rhetoric made it easy for both superpowers to condemn China as a reckless warmonger and as the major threat to world peace.

The seemingly interminable hostility between China and the United States ended quite suddenly in the early 1970s, in one of the most dramatic turnabouts in modern diplomatic history. On July 15, 1971, President Richard Nixon made an unanticipated announcement that stunned the world. He stated that he intended to travel to China within six months, at the invitation of the Chinese government, for the purpose of developing friendly relations with that government. He revealed that his secretary of state, Henry Kissinger, had just returned from a secret trip to Beijing where he and Chinese Premier Zhou Enlai had made arrangements for this diplomatic breakthrough.

The Nixon administration had begun making subtle overtures to the PRC in the previous year. In Warsaw, Poland, where the U.S. and Chinese ambassadors had periodically engaged in secret talks, the U.S. side intimated its desire for improved relations. In his State of the World speech before Congress in February 1971, President Nixon referred to the Beijing government as the People's Republic of China, instead of the usual Red China or Communist China, and Chinese leaders took note of the fact that for the first time the U.S. government had publicly used the proper name of their government. This opened the door to what became known as "ping-pong diplomacy." A U.S. table tennis team was invited to play an exhibition tournament in Beijing, and Premier Zhou gave them a warm reception and noted that their visit "opened a new page in the relations between the Chinese and U.S. peoples."[1] President Nixon responded by announcing a relaxation of the U.S. trade embargo with China, and this was followed by Kissinger's secret trip to Beijing in early July 1971 that prepared the ground for President Nixon's dramatic announcement.

The following February, President Nixon made his heralded two-week visit to China. He was welcomed by Chinese leaders with great fanfare. At the Beijing airport he extended a hand to Premier Zhou, the same Chinese leader whom John Foster Dulles had pointedly snubbed eighteen years earlier by refusing to shake hands. In addition to his own large staff, Nixon was accompanied by a large retinue of journalists and television camera crews who recorded the historic event and gave the U.S. people their first glimpse of life in Communist China. For two weeks the United States was treated to pictures of China and its friendly, smiling people. And they were treated to the spectacle of the U.S. president, a man known for his trenchant anti–Chinese Communist pronouncements in the past, saluting the aged and ailing Chairman Mao Zedong and toasting the new bond of

U.S. President Richard Nixon and Chinese Premier Zhou Enlai at a reception banquet in Beijing, Feb. 21, 1972. (*National Archives*)

friendship with China's most able diplomat, Premier Zhou Enlai. For the United States and China alike, it was a mind-boggling 180-degree turnabout.

It was ironic that Nixon, a conservative, Communist-hating Republican, would be the one to go to China and establish friendly relations with its Communist government. But the task required just such a politician. A Democratic president would have found it impossible to do so, because the Democratic party still carried the scars of allegedly having "lost China" to Communism in the first place. But a Republican president like Nixon, whose anti-Communist credentials were beyond question, would encounter much less opposition for reversing U.S. policy toward Communist China.

In any case, the normalization of U.S.-PRC relations was an event whose time had come. Indeed, it was long overdue. Both sides finally came to the realization that they had much more to gain by ending their mutual hostility than by continuing it. The Chinese needed to end their isolation in the face of a growing Soviet threat after the Ussuri River border clash in March 1969. The Soviets had greatly increased their ground forces along the Chinese border and equipped these forces with tactical nuclear weapons. Menaced by a superior Soviet force on their border, the Chinese leaders came to view closer ties with the United States as a means to decrease the possibility of a preemptive nuclear attack on China by the Soviet Union. By ending its isolation and reducing tensions between itself and the United States, the PRC stood to gain greater security against becoming engaged in a war with either of the two superpowers, much less with both of them in a two-front war. Normalization of relations with the United States was also seen as a means to finally gain entry into the United Nations and to solve the Taiwan question. China's international prestige would be greatly enhanced by its new relationship with the United States, while that of its rival, the Nationalist government on Taiwan, would be undermined. In addition, China had much to gain economically from the new trade opportunities that would come with normalization of relations with the United States and its allies.

The United States stood to benefit from normalization as well. President Nixon and his ambitious secretary of state, Henry Kissinger, had developed a grand design for achieving a new global balance of power. They postulated that the bipolar world dominated by the two opposing superpowers was giving way to a world with five major power centers: the United States, the Soviet Union, Western Europe, Japan, and China. In order to achieve an international power balance it was necessary to end the isolation of one of those new centers of power, the PRC. Détente with the Soviet Union was already well under way, but now the United States sought to "play the China card" when dealing with Moscow. By cautiously drawing closer to China the United States sought to gain greater leverage in its diplomacy with Moscow. The Nixon administration saw that détente with the Soviet Union and normalization of relations with China were possible at the same time and that together these policies would constitute giant steps toward ending the Cold War and attaining world peace. The result would be greater national security for the United States at a reduced cost. Nixon and Kissinger also calculated—incorrectly it turned out—that Beijing could bring influence to bear on Hanoi to negotiate an end to the Vietnam War. The opportunity for trade with China was also a motivating factor, but not as important as the diplomatic factors.

The major obstacle to improvement of relations between the two countries was—as had always been the case—Taiwan. The United States had stood by the Nationalist regime on Taiwan, recognizing it as the sole legitimate government of China, and had made a commitment to defend it. The only compromise solution to the Taiwan question that U.S. leaders had ever been willing to discuss was the so-called two China formula, which called for formal diplomatic recognition of two separate Chinese governments, one on the mainland, the other on Taiwan. But this proved to be an impossibility since both Chinese governments firmly refused to accept that formula. Neither would give up its claim as the sole legitimate government of the whole of China.

When President Nixon first communicated his desire for talks aimed at improving relations with the PRC, Zhou Enlai replied that he was ready to join in that effort on the condition that the United States was prepared for serious negotiations on the Taiwan issue. Beijing was not willing to bend on that question, but the U.S. government was finally willing to do so. The first step toward a solution of this issue came with the U.S. government's ending its objection to the PRC's entry into the United Nations.[2] In October 1971, the PRC was admitted to the United Nations on its terms, namely, as the single legitimate government of China and as the rightful claimant of the seat that had been occupied by the Republic of China in that body.

It was a test of the diplomatic skills of Henry Kissinger and Zhou Enlai to arrive at an agreement on Taiwan that would recognize the PRC's claim to Taiwan and yet would be less than a complete sell-out of the Nationalist government on Taiwan by its U.S. ally. A tentative agreement on the Taiwan issue was reached in the carefully worded Shanghai Communiqué at the end of Nixon's visit to China in February 1972. In it, the United States acknowledged that all Chinese maintain "there is but one China and that Taiwan is part of China" and that the United States does not challenge that position. In the communiqué, the U.S. side reaffirmed "its interest in a peaceful settlement of the Taiwan question by the Chinese themselves." The United States also agreed to reduce its military forces on Taiwan "as tension in the area diminishes." (This was in reference to the war in Indochina from which U.S. forces were gradually withdrawing.) The PRC obtained important concessions on the Taiwan issue—namely, the U.S. acknowledgment that the island is part of China proper and a U.S.

promise to withdraw its military force from that island. The United States, which seems to have conceded more than it gained, came away with an understanding that the PRC would not attempt to take over Taiwan by military means and with the satisfaction that its new friendship with China would serve to enhance stability in Asia.

This was not the end, but the beginning of the normalization process. Full normalization of relations, involving the formal recognition of the PRC by the United States and the breaking off of U.S. diplomatic ties with Nationalist China was yet to be achieved. However, in accordance with the Shanghai Communiqué, the two countries respectively established liaison offices in each other's capital, began a series of exchanges in the fields of science, technology, culture, journalism, and sports, and initiated mutually beneficial trade relations that grew steadily in subsequent years.

It was not until January 1979 that full diplomatic relations between the two countries were achieved. There were two main reasons for the seven-year delay: the political leadership problems in both countries in the mid-1970s, and the still unresolved Taiwan issue. In the United States, President Nixon was suffering from the Watergate scandal and finally resigned in disgrace in August 1974. And in China, both Chairman Mao and Premier Zhou died in 1976, leaving a succession problem that was not resolved until Deng Xiaoping consolidated his leadership in 1978. It was left to new political leaders, Deng and President Jimmy Carter, to settle the Taiwan question. Deng came to the view that establishing diplomatic ties with the United States was of greater importance than liberating Taiwan and that a formula could be found to achieve the former by postponing the latter. Secret negotiations produced an agreement in December 1978, the terms of which included restoration of full diplomatic relations between the two nations and termination of the United States's official relations and defense pact with the Republic of China. It did allow, however, for continued U.S. commercial and cultural ties with Taiwan and continued U.S. arms sales to Taiwan. On the latter point, the Chinese government agreed to disagree, which is to say that it did not formally agree to such arms sales, but would set aside that issue so that the normalization agreement could be made without further delay. In effect, the U.S. government now recognized the PRC's title to Taiwan even though the island remained in the hands of the anti-Communist Nationalist government now headed by Jiang Jingguo (Chiang Ching-kuo), son of Jiang Jieshi, who had died in 1975. The U.S. government attempted to soften the blow to Taiwan by passing the Taiwan Relations Act, which affirmed the resolve of the United States to maintain relations with the people (not the government) of Taiwan and to consider any effort to resolve the Taiwan issue by force as of "grave concern to the United States." To further strengthen the new diplomatic relations, Deng Xiaoping accepted an invitation to visit the United States, and he was given a warm reception during his nine-day visit that began less than a month after the normalization agreement went into effect on January 1, 1979.

The consequences of the normalization of Chinese-U.S. relations were immense. The United States ended the anomaly of recognizing a government that ruled only 17 million Chinese in favor of one that governed over 900 million. Normalization resulted in a significant reduction of tension between the two nations and it provided greater stability in Asia. Both countries attained greater security, and at the same time they gained greater maneuverability in dealing with other powerful nations, notably the Soviet Union. Normalization opened the way to a vast increase in trade, which provided China with much-needed capital and technology for its ongoing economic modernization. In the United States it was hoped that China's large market might serve to offset the mounting U.S. trade deficit in other world markets.[3]

One of the most important consequences of the normalization of Sino-U.S. relations was the ending of China's diplomatic isolation. Not only did the PRC gain a permanent seat in the UN Security Council, but many nations of the world that had formally withheld formal ties with the PRC now followed the U.S. lead by breaking off official ties with Taiwan and recognizing the PRC instead. In 1969, sixty-five countries recognized Taiwan as the legal government of China, but by 1981 only twenty countries did so.

The breakthrough in Sino-U.S. relations brought in its wake an equally abrupt turnaround in Sino-Japanese relations, which was of great significance to both countries and for peace and stability in Asia. Initially, the Japanese were stunned by President Nixon's surprise announcement in July 1971, not because they opposed the move but because they were caught off guard by it and felt that they should have been consulted beforehand.[4] But once they got over the "Nixon shock," as they referred to it, the Japanese hastened to achieve their own rapprochement with China. Japan's prime minister, Tanaka Kakuei, responded to mounting public pressure within Japan for normalization of relations with China by arranging a visit to Beijing at the invitation of the Chinese government. His trip to China, which took place in September 1972, was also of great historical importance, being the first visit to China ever made by any Japanese head of state and coming after almost a century of hostile Sino-Japanese relations. In Beijing, the Japanese prime minister contritely expressed his regret over the "unfortunate experiences" between the two nations in the past and stated that "the Japanese side is keenly aware of Japan's responsibility for causing enormous damage in the past to the Chinese people through war and deeply reproaches itself."[5]

The product of Tanaka's talks with Zhou Enlai in Beijing was an agreement on the restoration of full diplomatic relations between the two countries on the following terms: Japan affirmed its recognition of the PRC as the sole legal government of China and agreed to the claim that Taiwan was an inalienable part of the territory of the PRC. China waived its claim to a war indemnity amounting to several billion dollars and agreed to discontinue its protest against the U.S.-Japan Mutual Security Pact and to drop its insistence that Japan end its trade relations with Taiwan. The two countries also agreed to negotiate a new treaty of peace and friendship in the near future. (It was implicitly understood that Japan would then abrogate its existing peace treaty with the Republic of China.) Japan was thus able to achieve full normalization of relations with China much more rapidly than the United States, which had initiated the process. Both China and Japan reaped enormous benefits from their improved relations, particularly from the huge volume of two-way trade that developed between them in the following years. The two countries are natural trading partners. China had various raw materials to offer resource-poor Japan in exchange for Japan's technology, machinery, and finished goods. The diplomatic rewards of the Sino-Japanese détente were probably even greater, for relations between these two major Asian nations had never been better than this since the nineteenth century, and the new friendship between these once hostile neighbors brought an era of stability and security to this previously inflamed part of the world.

The government most disaffected by the PRC's new diplomatic achievements was, of course, the Republic of China on Taiwan. It bitterly denounced its former allies—the United States, Japan, and others—for abandoning a friend and argued that leaders in Washington and Tokyo had been duped by the Communist government in Beijing, toward which Taiwan leaders directed their strongest attacks. Although it was becoming isolated diplomatically, Taiwan carefully sought to retain ties with the United States, Japan, and other Western nations with whom it still maintained a lucrative commercial trade. And despite its diplomatic setback, Taiwan continued to maintain a high rate of economic growth, which produced a much higher standard of living for its people than the Chinese on the mainland achieved. Stubbornly, its government, still dominated by the Nationalist Party, rebuffed every overture by the PRC for a peaceful reunification. Meanwhile, the PRC, careful not to risk damaging its good relations with the United States, patiently refrained from forceful gestures toward Taiwan and waited for a softening of Taiwan's position. But, insofar as the very *raison d'être* of the Nationalist government on the island was to overthrow the Communist rulers of the mainland, it neither wavered in its resolute anti-Communist policy nor moderated its strident anti-Beijing propaganda. The spirit of the Cold War remained very much alive on the island of Taiwan until the late 1980s.

■ DÉTENTE BETWEEN EAST AND WEST

The rapprochement between Washington and Beijing took place in an era of thawing of frozen relations across a wide front. It pointed to significant changes in the Cold War mentality in both camps. Originally, both sides had taken the position that there could be no improvement of relations until such grievances as Taiwan, Germany, and the like had been resolved. In the mid-1960s, however, the belligerents backtracked when they took the position that a normalization of relations—such as in the areas of trade, international travel and contact, and arms limitations—could contribute ultimately to resolving the greater issues—the unification of divided nations, the nuclear arms race—and perhaps even put an end to the Cold War. The result was a period of lessening tensions in international relations.

*   *   *

As described previously, the Cold War of the late 1940s had created two German states—a West German state aligned with the West and ultimately with the North Atlantic Treaty Organization (NATO), and an East German state whose government had been installed by the Red Army and which later joined the Soviet Union's military organization, the Warsaw Pact. The conservative anti-Communist West German governments of the 1950s and the early 1960s, particularly that of Chancellor Konrad Adenauer, considered the Soviet creation of East Germany as illegitimate and refused to recognize and deal with it. The West German leaders insisted that only they spoke for all Germans, in East Germany as well as in West.

Adenauer stated his position forcibly when his government issued the Hallstein Doctrine (named after the state secretary of the West German Foreign Office) in 1955. The Hallstein Doctrine made it clear that West Germany would not recognize any state (with the exception of the Soviet Union) that had diplomatic relations with East Germany. In practical terms it meant that West Germany would have no dealings with the Soviet client states of Eastern Europe. It would make no attempt to raise the Iron Curtain.

But in 1966, Willy Brandt, West Germany's new foreign minister, reversed Adenauer's stand when he took the first steps to establish contact with the socialist nations of Eastern Europe. He was willing to recognize the political realities now that more than two decades had elapsed since the Red Army had rolled into the center of Europe. The president of the United States, Lyndon Johnson, anticipated Brandt's new position when he stated that the reunification of Germany could only come about as a result of détente. In other words, Brandt and Johnson took the position that détente was a precondition for a unified Germany, whereas Adenauer and Hallstein had earlier argued that there must first be a unified Germany before there could be talk of improved relations with the Soviet bloc. Brandt and Adenauer sought the same end; they only differed over the means.

Brandt's departure from Adenauer's stance also meant that he was willing to grant de facto recognition to the existence of East Germany, as well as to the new borders of the two Germanies resulting from Germany's defeat in World War II. To achieve the normalization of relations between East and West, Brandt's government was willing to recognize the Oder-Neisse Line as the border between East Germany and Poland. The new border had been in existence since the end of the war, when the Soviet Union moved Poland's western border about 75 miles (into the region of Silesia, which before the war had been German territory) to the Oder and Western Neisse rivers. Of the 6 million former German inhabitants of the area lost to Poland, many had been killed during the war, others had fled before the advancing Red Army, and the remaining 2 million were expelled. The Germans also had lost East Prussia, the easternmost province of the German Reich, to the Soviets, who took the northern half, and to the Poles, who took the southern. And in Czechoslovakia, the Germans had lost the Sudetenland, which the British and the French had granted Hitler in 1938. The Czechs, of course, wasted little time after the war in expelling what was left of the 3 million Sudeten Germans.[6]

The Adenauer government had been most adamant in its refusal to accept the loss of German territory to Poland. Willy Brandt, however, acknowledged that the Oder-Neisse Line had existed as the new German boundary for over twenty years and had few Germans living east of it. Brandt also stopped believing that his government could ever hope to reclaim East Prussia. Any attempt to do so would lead to another war in Europe and only drive Poland and the Soviet Union into each other's arms. (In 1945, the Poles and the Soviets had been able to agree on only one thing, that Germany must pay for the war with the loss of territory.) Brandt also abandoned all claims to the Sudetenland. This was the least controversial of the steps Brandt was willing to take, for the region had been Czechoslovakia's before the war and its transfer to Hitler's Reich was generally seen as one of the most significant events leading to World War II. That the Sudetenland would be returned to Czechoslovakia after the war had been a foregone conclusion.

The Soviet Union and East Germany, however, wanted more than a mere West German recognition of what after all had been a reality for two decades. They wanted a West German recognition of the East German government, which, of course, would legitimize the Soviet Union's creation of and the permanence of two Germanies. Such recognition would also undermine the West German government's claim that it spoke for all Germans. This, however, Brandt—or any other West German leader—was not willing to do.

But the two German governments did begin to talk to each other. On March 19, 1971, a historic meeting took place in Erfurt, East Germany, between Willy Brandt, who by then was West Germany's chancellor, and the head of the East German Communist Party, Walter Ulbricht. This event led to the Basic Treaty of 1972 between the two German states. East Germany did not obtain full diplomatic recognition from West Germany. But the treaty did call for "good neighborly" relations and it led to increased contacts of a cultural, personal, and economic nature. The Iron Curtain was therefore partially lifted.

Brandt's attempts to establish contacts with Eastern Europe became known as *Ostpolitik* (an opening toward the East, literally "eastern politics").

It included a partial thaw in relations with the Soviet Union and other East European countries. In 1968, West Germany established diplomatic relations with Yugoslavia. In 1970, the governments of West Germany and the Soviet Union signed a nonaggression treaty in Moscow. Later that year, Brandt went to Warsaw to sign a similar treaty with the Polish government and his government accepted the Oder-Neisse Line.

But Brandt's recognition of that line merely meant that he would not permit it to stand in the way of better relations with the East. A central feature of the West German position—one spelled out during the early 1950s—had not changed. There could be no adjustment of Germany's borders until Germany signed peace treaties with the nations involved. The Helsinki Agreement (see below) was not a legally valid substitute for such treaties and until such treaties were ratified there could be no de jure recognition of the postwar borders. With the later deterioration of East-West relations, West German conservatives, including Chancellor Helmut Kohl, dusted off this argument. They refused to consider Germany's borders a closed issue.[7]

Détente and Brandt's *Ostpolitik* made possible a series of U.S.-Soviet arms limitation talks, including SALT I and SALT II (of which more later), which led directly to the European Security Conference of August 1975 in Helsinki, Finland. The Soviets had proposed such a conference as early as 1954 and again in the late 1960s to ratify the consequences of World War II. The Soviet proposals were to no avail. Since no formal treaty or conference had recognized the redrawn map and the new governments of Eastern Europe, the Soviet leaders continued to press for such a conference. At Helsinki in 1975, thirty years after the fact, they hoped to obtain such recognition.

The participants at Helsinki included all European states (except Albania) as well as the United States and Canada. The agreement signed at Helsinki recognized the postwar borders of Europe, but it left open the prospect that the borders could be changed, although only by peaceful means. West Germany renounced its long-standing claim as the sole legitimate German state. East and West agreed to observe each other's military exercises to avoid the misreading of the other's intentions. Lastly, all signatories of the Helsinki Agreement promised greater East-West contact and to guarantee the human rights of their citizens. In Eastern Europe, however, the rights of citizens were defined differently than in the West, and this point later become a central issue when détente was shelved by the United States during the late 1970s.

Détente between East and West also produced the first steps on the road to limit the unchecked nuclear arms race. Until 1972, there were no limits on the nuclear arsenals of the United States and the Soviet Union. Both had more than enough firepower to destroy each other several times over and there was little point in adding to stockpiles already of grotesque

West German Chancellor Willy Brandt after placing a wreath at the Tomb of the Unknown Soldier in the Polish capital of Warsaw, Dec. 1970. (*German Information Center*)

Soviet leader Leonid Brezhnev and U.S. President Richard Nixon at the White House Washington, D.C., June 19, 1973. (*AP/Wide World Photos*)

proportions. By 1970, the Soviet Union had concluded its concerted effort to catch up with the United States and had achieved a rough sort of parity. The U.S. nuclear arsenal consisted at that time of 3,854 warheads; the Soviet total was 2,155.[8]

The year 1975 with its Helsinki Agreement saw the high point of détente. After that, relations between the United States and the Soviet Union began to deteriorate, and by 1980, détente was a thing of the past. A number of factors contributed to the new climate.

Détente had never set well with a number of U.S. policymakers. To them, détente was always a snare and a delusion. One cannot do business, they warned, with an ideological system that professes world revolution. They wasted no time seizing every opportunity to sabotage détente. Eventually, a number of liberals joined their chorus.

With the intensification of the Cold War came a reassessment of Soviet military strength and intentions. In 1976, George Bush, as the head of the CIA, brought in a group of Cold War warriors (better known as the B Team) who overruled a CIA estimate of Soviet military spending. The professionals in the CIA, the B Team declared, had misunderstood the nature of the Soviet threat, for according to the B Team's interpretations, the Soviets were spending nearly twice as much on their military as the CIA had reckoned. These ominous interpretations placed Soviet intentions and capabilities in a new light. The new figures were quickly accepted by reporters and editorial writers and became part of the new orthodoxy of the latest phase of the Cold War.[9]

With these new estimates of Soviet military spending came a reevaluation of the nuclear arms race and the charge that the Soviets had opened up a lead on the United States. Between 1976 and 1980, presidential candidate Ronald Reagan got considerable mileage out of this argument. He also promised to restore U.S. military might, a pledge that, probably more than anything else, gained him the presidency in 1980 after the incumbent Jimmy Carter proved impotent in gaining the release of the U.S. hostages in Iran (see Chapter 18). Most of the U.S. public had taken the defeat in Vietnam stoically; it had been clear for a number of years that Vietnam was a losing proposition. The seizure of the hostages and the burning of U.S. flags in full view of television cameras had a more profound effect. A new militancy set in.

The Soviets, in their turn, appeared to be doing everything in their power to scuttle détente. Their definition of détente had always been different than that of the West. They insisted on the right to continue to conduct their foreign and domestic affairs as they had in the past. For example, what they did in Africa, they insisted, had nothing to do with Soviet-U.S. relations. But many in the United States perceived the Soviet activities in Africa differently. In 1975, the Soviet Union began sending arms to clients in Angola, Somalia, Ethiopia, and Mozambique, and Cuban soldiers arrived in Soviet planes in Angola and Ethiopia to train African soldiers. In the early 1970s, the Soviet Union had established close ties with the Marxist leader of Somalia, Siad Barre. Then, in late 1976, the Soviet Union began to send arms shipments to the Marxist head of Ethiopia, Mengistu Haile Miriam. In 1978, the governments of Somalia and Ethiopia went to war over a stretch of desert in the Somalian border province of Ogaden. The Soviets had to choose, and they decided to stay with Ethiopia. The United States then became the supplier of weapons to Siad Barre. In addition, Moscow had a client in Vietnam who, in 1979, marched into Phnom Penh, the capital of Cambodia. And in December 1979 the Soviet Army moved into Afghanistan to prop up a bankrupt and brutal Communist government. Then, in 1981, the head of the Polish state invoked martial law in an attempt to destroy the only independent labor union in the Soviet bloc. To many in the West, Moscow and its surrogates appeared to be on the march. In reality, until the Soviets invaded Afghanistan in late 1979, most major conflicts during the second half of the 1970s were between contending Marxist factions. In Angola, the Horn of Africa, and in Cambodia, the Soviet Union supported one Communist side, the United States the other.

At home, the Soviets also undermined the spirit of détente. Jewish emigration from the Soviet Union was drastically curtailed. Jews who wished to leave the Soviet Union had always been bargaining chips in East-West relations during the 1970s. In all, about 270,000 Jews emigrated. The numbers rose steadily between 1975 and 1979, when over 50,000 Jews were granted permission to leave. Afterwards, emigration slowed to a trickle. Dissidents, the most famous of whom was the nuclear physicist Andrei Sakharov, were either jailed or exiled in violation of the Helsinki Agreement. Under these conditions, détente had little chance of survival.

RECOMMENDED READINGS

Bueler, William M. *U.S. China Policy and the Problem of Taiwan.* Boulder, Colo.: Colorado Associated University Press, 1971.
  An analysis of the Taiwan issue on the eve of Nixon's visit.
Fairbank, John K. *The United States and China.* 4th ed. Cambridge, Mass.: Harvard University Press, 1981.
  A standard work that provides a historical account of Sino-U.S. relations as well as a survey of Chinese history.
Garthoff, Raymond. *Détente and Confrontation: American-Soviet Relations from Nixon to Reagan.* Washington, D.C.: The Brookings Institution, 1985.
  The most detailed and best analysis of the topic to date.
Griffith, William E. *Peking, Moscow, and Beyond: The Sino-Soviet Triangle.* Washington, D.C.: Center for Strategic International Studies, 1973.
  Discusses the implications of Nixon's visit to Beijing.
Hersh, Seymour M. *The Price of Power: Kissinger in the Nixon White House.* New York: Summit Books, 1983.

A devastating analysis of Kissinger's foreign policy.
Schaller, Michael. *The United States and China in the Twentieth Century*. New York: Oxford University Press, 1979.
   A useful study that takes the story well beyond the Nixon visit to China.
Ulam, Adam B. *Dangerous Relations: The Soviet Union in World Politics, 1970–1982*. New York: Oxford University Press, 1983.
   Discusses the problems of and the end of détente.

NOTES

1. Immanuel C. Y. Hsu, *The Rise of Modern China*, 3d rev. ed. (New York: Oxford University Press, 1983), p. 373.
2. In fact, the United States voted against the PRC replacing the Republic of China in the United Nations but made it known that it would not block this move as it had for over two decades. The U.S. vote was essentially a face-saving gesture.
3. By 1996, that hope vanished when China (overtaking Japan) ran up the largest trade deficit of any nation with the United States for that year.
4. The Japanese prime minister, Sato Eisaku, had for years stressed the mutual trust between his government and Washington, and, in order not to jeopardize the strong ties with the United States, he had consistently resisted the popular pressure within his own country for normalization of relations with China. For the United States to suddenly reverse its China policy without consulting its major Asian ally was considered by the Japanese as a diplomatic slap in the face and was referred to as the "Nixon shock."
5. As quoted in Hsu, p. 751.
6. For a map of the transfer of land after World War II, see the one on p. 36 in Chapter 2, "The Cold War Institutionalized."
7. Bernt Conrad, "How Definite Is the Oder-Neisse Line?" *Die Welt,* December 24, 1984; reprinted in *The German Tribune: Political Affairs Review* (a publication of the West German government), April 21, 1985, pp. 15–16. See also *The Week in Germany,* a weekly newsletter of the West German Information Center, Washington, D.C., June 21, 1985, p. 1.
8. For details of negotiations between Washington and Moscow, see Chapter 23, "The Nuclear Arms Race."
9. In 1983, the professionals in the CIA, in a report to a congressional committee, cast off the shackles of Bush and the B Team when they restated the validity of their original estimates of Soviet military spending. They cut the B Team's estimates by more than half. While the B Team's findings had received much publicity, the CIA's declaration of independence from meddling outsiders received scant attention. In January 1984, a NATO study concluded that Soviet military spending since 1976 had been at less than 2.5 percent of the nation's GNP, as compared to 4–5 percent during the early 1970s.

PART 4

THE THIRD WORLD

The East-West confrontation was surely the dominant theme in international relations in the postwar period, but since the 1970s another cleavage, the North-South divide, has become increasingly important. "North" refers to the modern industrialized nations, most of which happen to be located in the temperate zones of the Northern Hemisphere, and "South" signifies the poorer nations, most in the equatorial region or in the Southern Hemisphere. Many of the nations of the South are scattered throughout Asia, Africa, and Latin America. They are sometimes euphemistically called "developing countries," even though some have hardly been developing at all, and are sometimes called "underdeveloped countries." More commonly, they are referred to collectively as the "Third World."

During the 1950s, French journalists first referred to a Third World to describe nations that were neither part of the industrialized world nor of the Communist bloc. In 1955, the leaders of these nations met for the first time at an Afro-Asian conference in the Indonesian city of Bandung. Among the leaders were Jawaharlal Nehru (India), Gamal Abdel Nasser (Egypt), Kwame Nkrumah (Ghana), Achem Sukarno (Indonesia), and Zhou Enlai (China). They had much in common; all had participated in the struggle for independence from colonial control and led poverty-stricken countries seeking to resolve their economic dilemmas. They tended to reject capitalism, the economic model of the former colonial powers, and tended to lean toward some variant of socialism. Some sought a third economic model but, ultimately, with little success. Officially, they were nonaligned in the Cold War, although some leaned toward the Soviet bloc and some to the Western bloc. Genuine neutrality, particularly as the superpowers constantly bid for the loyalty of these nations, was impossible, however.

The principal identifying characteristic of Third World nations is poverty. In the dispossessed nations of the Third World live more than three-quarters of the world's population, but they possess less than one-quarter of the world's wealth. The economic dilemma of the Third World is a major theme of Chapter 11, in which we examine the reasons for the relative lack of economic progress and point out that the gulf between the prosperous North and the impoverished South has been growing, especially in Africa.

After forty years, however, the bonds that had tied these nations had all but disappeared. The Soviet-led Communist bloc had dissolved and, perhaps more significantly, Third World nations had taken different economic roads. Some—such as Nigeria, Ghana, Nicaragua, the Philippines, and Bangladesh—remained mired in poverty. Others—South Korea, Singapore, and Turkey, for example—had achieved remarkable material progress and showed an ability to function in the competitive global economy. In short, at the end of the twentieth century, the Third World as a large, non-Western, poverty-stricken entity had largely ceased to exist. The phrase, however, continued to be deployed to describe nations that lack economic development, notably in the area of industrialization.

Economic development and political development are interrelated, one being a function of the other. It is necessary, therefore, to seek political reasons for the economic problems in the Third World and economic reasons for its political problems. In the first section of Chapter 11, we examine the gap between North and South and the various reasons for the retarded economic development of the latter. We particularly discuss the population factor and problems in agricultural and industrial development. In the remainder of the chapter, we focus on the postindependence political patterns of sub-Saharan Africa, where the demise of fledgling democratic governments and the increase in political instability went hand in hand with economic difficulties. After noting the rise of militarism on the continent, we look at specific cases: Nigeria, Angola, Somalia, and Rwanda. We also take note of a new push for democracy in the early 1990s that ultimately bore little fruit.

South Africa stood apart from its northern neighbors, not so much because it was more prosperous but because it alone among African nations continued to be ruled by a white minority (until 1994). The policy of apartheid in South Africa and the resistance to that racist policy are treated in Chapter 12. Here we relate the story of abolishing apartheid, the political resurrection of Nelson Mandela, and his role in the creation of a nonracial democratic South Africa. We also relate the darker side of the story—the violence that attended this transformation.

The militarization of politics, new to Africa after independence, had long been a reality in Latin America. In South American countries, large and small, postwar economic development was disappointing, and the disaffected classes in these countries—mainly laborers and landless farmers—continued to be victimized by an elitist system that has endured for centuries. In Chapter 13, we examine the patterns of politics—the swings between democratic rule and militarism in South America, particularly in Argentina, Brazil, Chile, and Peru. We also take up in this chapter the issue of Latin American narcotics trade, centering on Colombia.

Economic problems and political struggle in Central America have been even more acute than in South America, especially in the 1980s. Several Central American nations became hotbeds of revolution, and in Chapter 14 our attention is directed toward them, particularly Nicaragua and El Salvador. We also treat the U.S. intervention in Panama here.

In Chapter 15, we turn to Asia to study the twists and turns of the Communist government of the People's Republic of China as it attempted to put that huge Third World nation on the track of economic development. China, the world's largest nation—with over 1 billion people in 1990—was faced with problems of feeding and sheltering a burgeoning population and maintaining political order and industrialization. China is unique not only because of its great size but because for almost three decades, while under the rule of Mao Zedong, the political goal of creating a Communist society was given higher priority than the economic goal of industrial development. From the late 1970s, however, China's new leader, Deng Xiaoping, reversed the two goals and gave priority to economic modernization. We chart this course in Chapter 15, as well as relate the crushing of the pro-democracy demonstration in Tiananmen Square in Beijing in 1989.

In great contrast to China were the smaller nations on its periphery, specifically the "four tigers"—South Korea, Taiwan, Hong Kong, and Singapore—whose success in economic modernization was phenomenal. In Chapter 15, we treat the economic policies and the politics of these four countries. We also trace the ongoing Cold War between North and South Korea and between Taiwan and China.

In Chapter 16, the focus shifts to South Asia and Southeast Asia where the trials and tribulations of India—the world's second-largest nation—Pakistan, and Bangladesh are given primary attention. In contrast to China, India sought solutions to its manifold problems of overpopulation and poverty with a democratic form of government and a mixed economy (a mix of capitalism and state planning). In the same chapter, we relate briefly the recent economic surge of three Southeast Asian countries—Thailand, Indonesia, and Malaysia—and examine the problems of the Philippines, where the corrupt Marcos dictatorship was overthrown in 1986.

In Chapter 17, our focus is on a global economic problem that became acute in the early 1990s: the world debt crisis. Many of the nations of the Third World—even those with relatively industrialized economies such as Brazil, Mexico, and Argentina—amassed foreign debts so large that they have been unable to pay either the principal or the interest on their loans. Their precarious position has threatened not only the economic structures of these nations but the international monetary system as a whole.

11

Africa:
Political and Economic Disasters

In the early 1960s, when most African nations gained their independence, proud African leaders heralded the dawn of a new age for their continent. Freed from the shackles of European colonialism, they looked confidently to a new political and economic order that promised an end to the continent's economic backwardness and dependence on the West. But the euphoria of the early 1960s soon gave way to a more somber reality, for as years went by the leaders' shared goals of economic growth, of national self-reliance and dignity, and of African unity remained elusive. Indeed, thirty years later those dreams were in shambles, as most African countries had become increasingly impoverished and more dependent on foreign aid than ever before. Across the continent one found declining economies, grinding poverty, civil strife, corruption, crop failures, starving and hungry people, spreading disease, overcrowded and deteriorating cities, massive unemployment, and growing numbers of desperate refugees. Many of those leaders of Africa's new nations who had been filled with hope did not live to see the dashing of their dreams, for they became victims of military revolts, which were common throughout the continent.

The plight of Africa must be understood in terms of the larger context of global economics. Therefore, we will first examine the growing disparity since the early 1960s between the developed nations of the North and the underdeveloped nations of the South, as well as the reasons for the disparity. Most of the various obstacles to industrialization discussed here were present in Africa, especially in sub-Saharan Africa. The economic problems of African nations were particularly acute, and they were exacerbated by the political turmoil that became common throughout Africa. In one African country after another, democratic rule gave way to military rule, and several countries experienced a series of military coups.

■ THE DISPARITY BETWEEN NORTH AND SOUTH

Among the nations of the world, a gulf has always existed between the rich and the poor, but never has that gulf been as wide as it became in the postwar era. Most of the world's wealth is produced and consumed by a relatively small proportion of its people, those of the North. Conversely, the large majority of the earth's people, those in the South, produce and consume but a small proportion of the world's wealth. This disparity in wealth between the North and the South is revealed by the figures on per capita GNP (gross national product)[1] in Table 11.1.

The alarming increase in the gap between the impoverished South and the more prosperous North was the focus of an international conference in Cancún, Mexico, in September 1981. Figures presented at this conference indicated that the 140 countries that classified themselves as "developing nations" comprised 75 percent of the world's population but had only 20 percent of the world's income. Still, the gap between the North and South continued to grow larger in the 1980s. (See Table 11.2.)

The statistical average of $700 annual per capita GNP for the Third World in 1985 masked the great disparity in wealth among Third World nations. In fact, per capita GNP for most sub-Saharan African countries was far below $700. According to World Bank figures, in 1984 Ethiopia had a per capita GNP of only $110—the lowest among African nations—followed by Mali ($140), Zaire ($140), and Burkina Faso ($160).[2] Moreover, most of

Table 11.1   Per Capita Gross National Product, 1990

North	
United States	$21,790
Switzerland	32,680
Japan	25,430
West Germany (before unification)	22,320
OECD members	21,170
South	
Sub-Saharan Africa	340
East Asia and the Pacific (without Japan)	600
South Asia	330
Middle East and North Africa	1,790
Latin America and the Caribbean	2,180
World	4,200

Source: World Bank, *World Development Report 1992*, pp. 196, 218–219.

Table 11.2   North Versus South, 1985

	North	South
Population	1.18 billion	3.76 billion
Annual per capita GNP	$9,510	$700
Life expectancy	73 years	58 years
Annual rate of population growth	0.6%	2.0%

Source: Population Reference Bureau, *1986 World Population Data Sheet.*

the nations of Africa had very low economic growth rates. Indeed, at least fourteen African nations registered "negative growth," or decline of per capita GNP. World Bank figures revealed that Zaire, for example, had a negative growth rate of –1.2 percent and Uganda one of –3 percent for the decade between 1972 and 1982. This meant that in those countries the population grew faster than the economy. And in real terms, this meant continued dismal poverty, hunger, and misery.

Within each impoverished nation of the South, a great disparity existed between the relatively wealthy and the poor. The maldistribution of wealth in the underdeveloped nations of the Third World was greater than that in industrialized nations of the North.[3] The majority of the people in Third World nations, mainly peasants but many city dwellers as well, had far less than the national average per capita income. Taking this fact into account, as well as considering the increasing population and low per capita income figures for the poorest nations, we can begin to fathom the dimensions of poverty and hunger in the Third World. Perhaps as many as one-fifth of the earth's inhabitants lived in dire poverty and suffered from chronic hunger and malnutrition.

■ THE POPULATION FACTOR

Unquestionably, population growth was a major factor in the persistence of poverty. The population of the world grew at an increasing rate and at an especially alarming rate in the twentieth century. It took about 5 million years for the world's population to reach 1 billion, around 1800. The second billion mark was reached in about 130 years, by 1930; the third billion in 30 years, by 1960; the fourth billion in 15 years, by 1975; and the fifth billion in only 11 years, by 1986. The *rate* of population growth, however, has decreased since the mid-1960s, as witnessed by the fact that the sixth billion was reached after 14 years. (See Figure 11.1.) The rate of growth of world population peaked at 2.4 percent annually in 1964 and by the mid-1990s had fallen to about 1.5 percent, a drop attributable mainly to the population controls instituted in China and other developing countries.

The pressure of overpopulation was much greater in the Third World, where population growth rates remained very high compared with the developed nations of the North. After World War II, Third World population grew at a historically unprecedented rate. During the late 1980s, Third World nations, especially in Africa, had growth rates of more than 3 percent, and some rose to more than 4 percent. In contrast, the industrialized nations had a much lower rate of growth, and—notably East Germany, West Germany, and Austria—attained a stable population (no growth at all) or even a negative growth rate. (See Figure 11.2.)

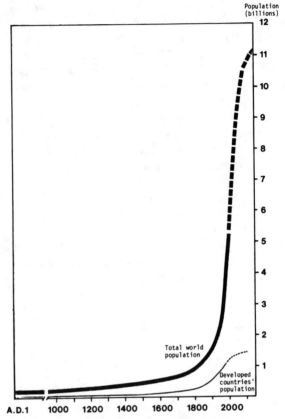

Figure 11.1   Past and Projected World Population, A.D. 1–2150

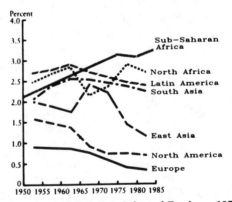

Figure 11.2   Population Growth Rates, Selected Regions, 1950–1985.
(Source: *Population Growth and Policies in Sub-Saharan Africa,*
World Bank, 1986.)

Because of their huge population growth rates, many Third World nations were on a treadmill. Africa was a case in point. The increase in its economic output, never large to begin with, was all too often swallowed up by the relentless growth in population. During the 1970s and 1980s, Africa's population growth rate, at just under 3 percent, was about nine times that of Europe and about three times that of the United States and Canada. These ominous statistics meant that unless the trend was reversed, the continent's population of 450 million would double in only twenty-three years. The growth rate in Kenya throughout the 1970s stood at 3.5 percent, and by the mid-1980s it had risen to 4.2 percent. Kenya's fertility rate (the average number of children born to a woman) was 8.0. These figures were among the highest in recorded history. But Kenya was not alone, for all of these African countries had population growth rates approaching 4 percent: Rwanda, Burundi, Zimbabwe, Tanzania, Uganda, Ghana, and Libya.

How is the population explosion in the Third World to be explained? In briefest terms, the death rate fell while the birth rate either rose or remained constant. Demographers explained that the introduction of modern medicines, the eradication of communicable diseases (such as smallpox), and improved public health and education all contributed to a reduced rate of infant mortality and an increased life expectancy. But there was no corresponding decrease in fertility. In most developing countries, most families had at least four children and in rural areas often more than five. In these countries—similar to the developing European countries in the nineteenth century—the larger the number of children in a family, the greater the number of hands in the fields or in the factories, where they were able to earn an income to supplement their parents' meager salaries. For this reason, having a large family was a means to escape poverty and was therefore considered economically rational. The responsibility for overpopulation in the Third World is often attributable to men, who tended to disdain all artificial birth control methods and for whom having many children was a sign of virility and moral rectitude. Yet, it was the women who bore the children and wound up caring for the large families. But it was also true that in most of the Third World, women also typically shared the men's desire for many children.

Programs of local governments and international agencies to control population growth in the Third World met with mixed success. The most dramatic reduction of the birth rate occurred in China, where the Communist government instituted a stringent birth control program including paramedical services, free abortions (even at near full term), public education, social pressure, and economic sanctions. Government-supported family planning programs were moderately successful in other Third World countries, notably South Korea, Colombia, Mauritius, Sri Lanka, Argentina, Uruguay, and Egypt. In many other countries governments were less active in, or were slow to begin, birth control efforts. In India, birth control programs had mixed results but were generally more effective in regions where public education was more widespread. Until the 1960s, birth control programs, whether those of Third World governments or international agencies, had little impact on many countries in Latin America (especially Central America) and in sub-Saharan Africa.

The problems of overpopulation in the Third World were compounded by an ongoing exodus of people from the surrounding countryside migrating into the city. Where land could not support large populations, millions flocked to the already overcrowded cities in quest of a better life.[4] The result was a phenomenal growth of Third World cities, many of which became the largest in the world—for example, Mexico City, São Paulo, Buenos Aires, Seoul, Calcutta, and Cairo. In Africa, only three cities had a population of 500,000 in 1950; thirty-five years later there were twenty-nine cities of at least that size. The urban population of Kenya doubled in a decade. The population of Lagos, Nigeria, grew incredibly from 300,000 in 1970 to over 3 million in 1983.

Although the cities typically offered more and better employment opportunities, medical services, and education than the villages, they could not accommodate the massive numbers of newcomers. It was impossible for these cities to provide adequate employment, housing, sanitation, and other services for the numerous new inhabitants—many of whom remained unemployed, impoverished, and homeless. Mexico City was the most extreme case. Its population doubled in a decade to over 18 million. More than one-third of these people lived in squatter settlements in the world's largest slum. This scene was duplicated in most other Third World cities, such as Cairo, where many thousands lived in the city's refuse dump, and Calcutta, where nearly 1 million of the city's 10 million inhabitants lived in the streets. The concentration of such huge numbers of disaffected peoples, living in the shadows of the edifices of the more opulent class and often within marching distance of the centers of political power (many of the largest Third World cities are capital cities), heightened the potential for massive political revolts.

One of the most critical problems associated with overpopulation was how to feed the people. In the 1960s, television began to bring home to people in the North the tragedy of mass starvation in Ethiopia and Somalia, but most viewers remained unaware that hundreds of thousands of people in other African countries—Sudan, Kenya, Mozambique, Chad, Mali, Niger, and others—also suffered from starvation. Estimates of the extent of world hunger varied greatly, depending in part on how hunger was defined, but there was little doubt that an enormous number of Third World people—perhaps 1 billion—were chronically malnourished.

In the late 1980s, a number of international agencies began to single out overpopulation as a leading factor threatening the quality of life in the twenty-first century. The UN Population Fund, in its Amsterdam Declaration of November 1989, urged a recognition of responsibility to succeeding generations. It stressed that societies—that is, men in control—must recognize that "women are in the center of the development process" and that their freedom to make choices "will be crucial in determining future population growth rates." Without rights for women—legal, social, educational, and reproductive—there would be little hope of solving the problem of rapid population growth.[5]

Similarly, the Development Assistance Committee of the Organization for Economic Cooperation and Development (OECD), at its annual conference in 1989, argued that "women must be fully involved in the planning and implementation of population programmes" because thus far they "have often been designed in a way which takes insufficient account of women in their reproductive role and as decision-makers, producers and beneficiaries."[6] The committee concluded that one of the priorities for international assistance should be the slowing of population growth. The World Bank's fifteenth annual *World Development Report* (1992) emphasized for the first time the link between unchecked population growth and environmental degradation, slow economic growth, declining health care, and declining living standards.

These international organizations understood that the implementation of effective family planning programs would not be easy because they frequently clashed with deeply entrenched cultural and religious values held particularly (but not exclusively) by adherents of Islam, Hinduism, and Roman Catholicism. Pope John Paul II, for instance, in his encyclical "On the Hundredth Anniversary of Rerum Novarum" (May 1991), denounced, as he had done before, all measures "suppressing or destroying the sources of life." "Anti-childbearing campaigns," he argued, rested "on the basis of a distorted view of the demographic problem." The pope went on to restate his position that new birth control techniques were responsible for "poisoning the lives of millions of defenceless human beings, as if in a form of 'chemical warfare.'"[7]

Since 1945, the world has witnessed a veritable population explosion unprecedented in history. By the mid-1960s, the world's population was increasing by 2.4 percent each year. But the world also witnessed a second historic trend, a considerable decline in population growth since that time. By the mid-1990s, the rate had slowed to 1.5 percent. The world was slowly moving toward the zero-growth fertility rate of 2.1 infants per female.

Conventional wisdom declared that a falling birth rate was necessarily tied to prosperity, but the increasingly wider availability of birth control in many poorer countries upset this theory. One example was Bangladesh, which not only ranked among the poorest nations but was also overwhelmingly Muslim. The tenets of Islam prohibit family planning, yet 40 percent of that country's women used some sort of birth control. This trend produced a shift from the view that "development is the best contraceptive" to "contraceptives are the best contraceptives."[8] In addition, Third World feminists stressed that birth control alone was insufficient. At a UN conference on population control in April 1994, they produced statistics pointing to the correlation between higher female education and a lower fertility rate.[9]

■ THE AGRARIAN DILEMMA

Food production in the South actually increased at about 3.1 percent annually from the late 1960s to the late 1980s, but population growth ate up this increase almost entirely. Although most Asian nations made considerable progress in agricultural production, fifty-five Third World nations—again most of them in Africa—registered a decline in food production per capita after 1970. In the early 1970s, the nations of the South were collectively net exporters of agricultural produce, but by the early 1980s they were net importers of food.

Why were the nations of the Third World, almost all of which were agrarian, unable to increase their agricultural production to a level of self-sufficiency? This complex question defies a simple explanation, but there are several major causal factors.

1. Natural causes. Most Third World nations are in the tropics, close to the equator, where the climate is often very hot and where both extended droughts and torrential rainstorms occur. Desertification is a major problem in Africa, where the Sahara Desert has pushed its frontier southward into West Africa and eastward into Sudan. Indeed, much of that continent has suffered from prolonged drought. Other Third World areas have also suffered from drought and various other natural catastrophes such as excessive heat, flooding, cyclones, and earthquakes.

2. Abuse of the land. Great amounts of topsoil were lost to wind and water erosion every year, in part because of human causes such as deforestation and overcultivation. In Africa, the problem was often one of overgrazing, that is, too much of the land was devoted to herd animals. Also, land was overcultivated, and its nutrients were exhausted.

3. Primitive farming methods. Most Third World peasants worked with simple tools, many with nothing more than a hoe, and most plowing was still done with draft animals. Peasants were usually too poor to afford modern equipment. In some instances, intensive farming with traditional methods and tools was very efficient, especially in the case of paddy farming in Asia, but in many other areas—especially in Africa—toiling in parched fields with hand tools was an ineffective mode of production. In some parts of Africa, much of this toil was done exclusively by women.[10]

4. *Inequality of landholdings.* Throughout the Third World, agricultural production suffered because the majority of the peasants had too little land to farm and many were tenants burdened with huge rent payments. The impoverished, debt-ridden peasants were often forced to become landless laborers. According to one international study reported in 1984, in Latin America 80 percent of the farmland was owned by 8 percent of landowners, and the poorest peasants—66 percent of all owners—were squeezed onto only 4 percent of the land.[11] Land reform, that is, redistribution of land, paid off with significantly increased agricultural output for nations such as Japan, and it would no doubt benefit many Third World nations.

5. *Lack of capital for agricultural development.* Third World food-producing farmers needed irrigation works, better equipment, chemical fertilizers, storage facilities, and improved transport. Yet all too often, their governments were unwilling or unable to supply the capital needed to provide these essentials.

6. *One-crop economies.* In many Third World nations, the best land with the best irrigation belonged to wealthy landowners (and sometimes to multinational corporations) who grew cash crops—peanuts, cocoa, coffee, and so on—for export rather than food for domestic consumption. Generally, Third World leaders accepted the dogma that the progress of their countries depended on what they produced for sale to the developed countries. Dependence on a single cash crop for export placed the developing nations at the mercy of the world market, where prices fluctuated greatly. This situation has proven disastrous for Third World countries in recent years, when prices of their agricultural exports dropped sharply while prices of necessary imports (especially petroleum, fertilizers, and finished goods) rose. Meanwhile, Third World leaders neglected the needs of the majority of the farmers, that is, the food-producing peasantry, in favor of support for the cash crop farmers. In many cases, these leaders deliberately kept food prices artificially low to the benefit of the growing number of city dwellers and to the detriment of the food-growing peasantry.

This list could be extended with still other reasons for the lack of growth of agricultural output in the Third World, some of which were peculiar to specific regions, but it was apparent that many of the problems were caused by the political leaders rather than the farmers. The solution to these problems consisted of land reform, diversification of agriculture, and the building of irrigation systems, roads, storage facilities, fertilizer plants, and agricultural schools. But these efforts required a large amount

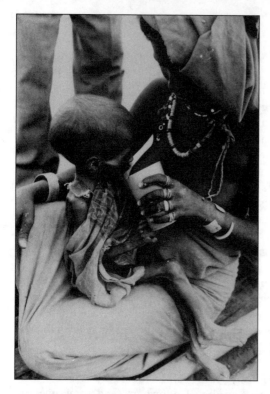

Ethiopian famine victims,
1984. (*AP/Wide World
Photos*)

Cambodian children receiving relief food at a refugee camp in Trat, Thailand,
June 4, 1979. (*AP/Wide World Photos*)

of capital, political stability, and strong and able political leadership—all of which were frequently lacking.

A number of Third World nations obtained relief in the form of large shipments of food to feed starving people. Although such aid was beneficial and humane, it did not go to the root of the problem (and, in fact, it often did not reach those who needed it most). Subsequently, donor nations and international financing institutions increasingly channeled their aid into long-term agricultural development programs for which they provided expertise, training, and incentives, as well as capital.

■ PREREQUISITES FOR INDUSTRIALIZATION

Upon gaining independence from Europe, Third World nations tended to blame their economic backwardness on their former colonial masters. They looked forward to rapid progress as independent nations, hoping to close the gap that separated them from the economically advanced nations of the world. The leaders of these nations usually viewed industrial development as the primary road to economic modernization. By giving priority to industrial growth, however, these countries tended to neglect agriculture and its role in economic development. Moreover, their efforts at rapid industrialization were often met with frustration and failure. They expected the dynamics of change to bring them rapid progress, but they have found, to their dismay, that industrial development is a difficult process. Economists have long argued over the prerequisites for industrial development, but the following are generally considered minimal necessary conditions.

1. Capital accumulation. Money for investments to build plants and buy equipment has to come from somewhere: the World Bank, foreign powers (which usually sought to gain political or military influence), heavy taxation (often falling upon people who could least afford it), or the export of cash crops or raw materials. This last method of capital accumulation often led to an anomaly: the agrarian nations of the Third World found themselves importing food, often from the developed nations, in ever-increasing amounts and at ever-increasing cost; thus, money tended to flow out of their economies rather than in.

Third World nations were in great need of foreign aid, but such aid was not necessarily the answer to their problems. They received vast amounts of aid from abroad for many years, but too often the money was mismanaged, misdirected, squandered on unproductive projects, or simply siphoned off by corrupt leaders. Moreover, hazards were involved in over-reliance on outside financial aid. Third World leaders were wary of political strings attached to foreign loans, which they saw as intrusions into their national sovereignty or as threats to their personal power. The loans also produced excessive indebtedness (see Chapter 17). After having struggled to win political independence from the developed nations of the North, the leaders were loath to become economic dependencies of those same nations.

2. Technology. To compete with the highly sophisticated industries of the economically advanced nations, developing nations must rapidly incorporate new technology. But technology transfer is a complicated matter, and its acceptance and implementation in tradition-bound societies has at best been a slow process. Meanwhile, technological change in developed nations has been rapid, and the developing countries, even when making progress, have fallen further behind.

3. Education. Technology, even when borrowed from abroad, requires educated technicians and workers. An industrialized society requires a literate working class, as well as educated managers and engineers. Industry needs skilled labor, and literacy is essential for training such a work force. The attainment of mass education is a long-term and costly undertaking.

4. Favorable trading conditions. In general, the system of free trade erected by the industrially advanced nations of the world after World War II served both developed and developing nations well, but the latter needed preferential treatment to compete with the former in the international marketplace. The Third World nations sought new trade agreements that would, in some manner, underwrite their exports with guaranteed minimum purchases at prices not to fall below a fixed level. They wanted to maintain higher tariffs on imports to protect their native industries.

5. Political stability. Capital accumulation and the conduct of business require safety and stability. Domestic strife and international wars are disruptive and costly, draining off the meager resources for industrial development. (Nearly all of the wars since 1945 have been fought in Third World countries. The list is endless: China, Korea, Vietnam, Iran, Iraq, Ethiopia, Angola, Chad, Nigeria, Lebanon, India, Pakistan, El Salvador, Nicaragua, and so on.) Even those developing nations not engaged in external or civil wars have spent an extraordinary amount on sophisticated weapons, which they were ill able to afford and which were purchased from the industrialized powers—primarily the United States and the Soviet Union.

6. Capital investment. The economies of the Third World tended to be exploitative of their own people. Available capital from whatever source was often spent on luxury imports for the elite, the building of showcase airports and hotels, and the like, and not on the development of the economic substructure for industrial and agricultural growth—an activity that would benefit the population as a whole. Thus, we see in Third World cities great contrasts of wealth coexisting with grinding poverty—elegant mansions in one part of town and tin-roof hovels in another.

After independence, the hard realities of economic development began to set in as Third World countries struggled to overcome their economic deficiencies and to come to terms with the problems of feeding their people and improving the quality of life. In this endeavor, some countries, mainly in Asia, met with considerable success, but others, mainly in Africa and Latin America, continued to find themselves in a perilous condition.

■ AFRICA'S ECONOMIC PLIGHT

Africa had the world's worst poverty, lowest economic growth rates, highest infant mortality rates, and highest rates of population growth. The population of Africa grew at about twice the rate of increase in food production in the 1970s. Chronic malnutrition and starvation became more common in subsequent years. Perhaps as many as 200,000 people succumbed to starvation in the Ethiopian famine in the early 1970s,[12] and another famine a decade later—more publicized than the earlier one—took an equally large toll. Media attention focused on Ethiopia diverted attention from the hundreds of thousands of people malnourished and on the verge of starvation in Sudan, Chad, Niger, and Mali. These nations were the most affected by the relentless expansion of the Sahara Desert. Further south, countries such as Kenya, Uganda, Gabon, and Mozambique were also drought-stricken. The Economic Commission for Africa, a UN agency, reported that from 1960 to 1975 there was no significant improvement in most African nations' economies, and it suggested that if trends continued, Africa would be even worse off in the year 2000 than it had been in 1960. In 1960, Africa had been about 95 percent self-sufficient in food, but twenty-five years later every African country except South Africa was a net importer of food.

The nations of sub-Saharan Africa were not equally impoverished. By far the most prosperous nation on the continent was South Africa, which stood as an exception to the economic decline characteristic of the remainder of sub-Saharan Africa.[13] Nigeria, burdened with Africa's largest population and yet blessed with large deposits of oil, prospered greatly following independence, only to find its economy in collapse as a result of political corruption and plummeting world oil prices in the early 1980s. An examination of per capita GNP growth rates in the decade after 1973 reveals that black African nations were either struggling to maintain marginal economic progress, marking time, or actually declining. According to World Bank figures on these growth rates, only Benin, Botswana, Cameroon, the People's Republic of Congo, Ivory Coast, and Rwanda had marginal growth. Fourteen countries had a decline in per capita GNP.[14] Most tragic were those states that had displayed the potential for economic growth and actually made progress in the first decade of independence only to slide backward since then. Ghana, Nigeria, Kenya, Uganda, and Zaire particularly come to mind.

■ POLITICAL INSTABILITY
IN SUB-SAHARAN AFRICA

The miseries of Africa have been both economic and political. Indeed, an interrelationship existed between economic and political problems. Political chaos often followed economic disaster; conversely, political problems often contributed to the economic woes of African nations.

Following independence, Africa witnessed the steady erosion of democratic institutions and the steady militarization of politics. After initial trial runs in parliamentary democracy, elected governments often retained power by eliminating the electoral process and political opposition. Subsequently, military coups—not popular elections—were the primary vehicle for the transfer of power. Authoritarianism became common throughout Africa, where about three-quarters of the governments were controlled either by one-party regimes or militarists. Only about half a dozen states in sub-Saharan Africa permitted opposition parties to engage in the political process, and no African head of state was voted out of office until 1990. Political repression became the order of the day, especially in countries such as Uganda, Zaire, and Guinea, where political leaders massacred many thousands of opponents. And more often than not, African leaders were as corrupt as they were repressive.

How and why did the political chaos in Africa come about? Many African leaders were quick to answer that a century of European colonialism was responsible for many of Africa's problems. Colonialism was exploitative and disruptive, and its impact on Africa was enormous, but the nature of the impact is not easily determined. This is not the place to reexamine the legacy of European colonialism in Africa, the mix of positive and negative aspects of that long experience on African society. Still, it is possible to discern certain consequences of colonialism that left Africans ill-prepared for the task of nation building. One may question whether the political and economic models Europeans provided Africa and which many westernized African elites adopted were suitable for African society. In retrospect, it might also be argued that the Europeans left too abruptly, leaving the Africans with political institutions that few, beyond a small circle of educated elites, appreciated or understood. The colonial powers did little to develop national economies in their colonies; instead, they had

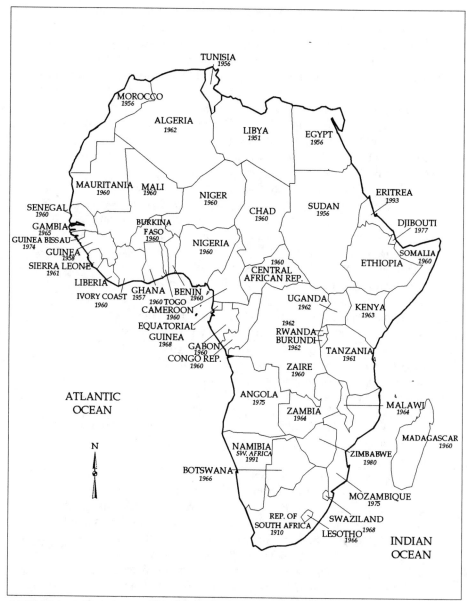

AFRICA AFTER INDEPENDENCE

mainly built up enterprises focused on a single export product, whether agricultural products such as coffee or raw materials such as copper. The economic system inherited by the new African nations was hardly designed for delivery of goods and services to the people. Moreover, the export-oriented economy of each colony was directly linked with the former colonial power instead of to its African neighbors, and this remained a major obstacle to regional trade and economic development.

Perhaps the most baleful legacy of European colonialism was the artificiality of the national boundaries it had created. In the nineteenth century, the European imperialists often hastily drew straight-line boundaries as they divided Africa into colonies, and these arbitrary boundaries—drawn with little or no recognition of the ethnic makeup of Africa—remained the root of many of Africa's problems after independence. It was not so much that the new African nations disputed the boundaries, for border conflicts were not as serious a problem as ethnic conflicts and secessionist wars within the new African nations. As a result of the political boundaries created by the Europeans, most African states were much larger than the precolonial political units and contained within them many ethnic groups. Only two countries in sub-Saharan Africa—Lesotho and Swaziland—had ethnic uniformity. All others had populations made up of several ethnic groups. The most extreme cases, such as Nigeria and Zaire, include within their borders over 100 distinct ethnic groups. The new nations of Africa were in many instances artificial constructs, and their rulers had the task of superimposing a new national identity over the existing ethnic configuration. In most instances, however, tribalism prevailed over nationalism—a relatively new and foreign concept—to the detriment of the process of nation building. The result was frequent ethnic conflict ranging from political contention to bloody civil wars, secessionist wars, and even genocide.

The first and one of the most tragic instances of postcolonial ethnic warfare was the Katangan separatist movement in the Congo (now Zaire) just as independence was attained in 1960. Tribalism also claimed a frightful toll of lives in the two small Central African nations of Rwanda and Burundi in the 1960s and 1970s. Even more lives were lost in Nigeria in the 1960s in ethnic strife known as the Biafran War.

Tribalism is a legacy not of colonialism but of African history. It persisted through the colonial era—in some places strengthened by colonial policy, in others diluted—and remained strong after independence. Typically, an African's strongest loyalties were to family and ethnic group. Given the relative lack of geographic mobility in Africa, people of one ethnic group maintained local roots and mixed little with people of other ethnic groups. Governments in Africa often represented one dominant ethnic group to the exclusion of others, and the discontent of the excluded ethnic groups was often the source of both political instability and political repression. In countries ruled by political leaders from a minority ethnic group, such as Kenya, Uganda, and Zambia in the mid-1980s, the ruler maintained political order only as long as the country's largest ethnic groups were satisfied.

Tribalism relates to another aspect of African heritage that plagued African politics: corruption. In kinship-based societies such as those in Africa, communal elders were entrusted with authority not only to make decisions binding for the group but also to divide the wealth among its members. This situation entailed a communal sense of property with little distinction between personal and public possession, which gave rise to a pattern of self-indulgence by leaders and public acceptance of the same. It also entailed a patronage system whereby gifts and favors were parceled out by the leader, who expected to be favored with gifts in return; this, too, lent itself to practices that elsewhere were viewed as graft and corruption. Once an ethnic leader attained rulership of a nation and gained access to its wealth and control of its instruments of power, self-aggrandizement and corruption on an immense scale were often the result. There was usually little dissent, except from members of other ethnic groups whose opposition to the corruption was based more on jealousy than on morality. Thus, African politics often degenerated into ethnic contests for the spoils of power.

The combination of unbridled corruption and the cult of personality in Africa produced some of the world's most outrageous displays of extravagance. Not a few African rulers lived in regal splendor in fabulous palaces, owned fleets of Mercedes-Benz cars, and stashed vast amounts of money in Western banks. Many were excessive, but for bizarre extravagance none exceeded Col. Jean-Bedel Bokassa, erstwhile emperor of the Central African Republic. He spent about $20 million—one-quarter of his nation's revenue—on his coronation ceremony in 1977. For that occasion, this dictator of a country that had no more than 170 miles of paved roads wore a robe bedecked with 2 million pearls that cost $175,000 and donned a $2 million crown topped with a 138-carat diamond. Two years later, Bokassa was deposed.

The demise of democratic government and the militarization of African politics did not happen overnight but evolved in several stages. Most of the newly independent nations of Africa began with an inherited parliamentary system of government in which executive power was in the hands of a prime minister who was elected by and responsible to a popularly elected legislative body. The challenges of rapid nation building were such that strong political leaders were called for. Moreover, many of the new rulers had affected a charismatic style of leadership prior to becoming prime ministers of the new nations. Typically, the African prime ministers revised the constitutions to allow themselves to become presidents with broadened executive powers and longer terms of office. (A prime minister is elected by and responsible to the parliament and may be called to resign at any time by a vote of no confidence in the parliament. But a president is elected by the people for a fixed, usually longer, term and is not so easily expelled from office.) Without an effective check on their new powers, the presidents began exercising them in a dictatorial manner and no longer tolerated political opposition. They argued that opposition parties were divisive, a threat to political stability, even unpatriotic; on these grounds the presidents abolished them, thus creating one-party states. The notion of the "loyal opposition," an out-of-power political party opposed to the party currently in power but loyal to the nation and qualified to govern if elected, was still foreign to Africans, especially to those in power.

Thus, the African presidential dictators entrenched themselves in power by eliminating parliamentary procedures and political opponents. They also took steps to strengthen the central governments by bringing local administration and all levels of civil service under their direct control. They replaced local officials with ruling party members and cronies loyal to themselves. The dictators made use of state wealth, especially foreign loans, to buy off or secure the loyalties of others. To win popular support, they used other instruments of modern state power, such as media control and propaganda, in which loyalty to nation and loyalty to the ruler were equated. They also relied on military force to guard their power, to suppress dissent, and sometimes to terrorize the population.

■ THE MILITARIZATION OF AFRICAN POLITICS

Presidential dictators in Africa, however, could not be certain of the loyalty of the military, and this proved to be the Achilles heel for many of them. In many African nations, military revolts supplanted presidential dictators with military dictators. Many of Africa's first line of rulers were overthrown by their own armies.[15] The forceful overthrow of Ghana's Kwame Nkrumah in 1966 gave rise to a wave of military coups across Africa, and by 1980 no fewer than sixty successful coups had taken place. In Benin (formerly Dahomey), there were five military coups and ten attempted coups between 1963 and 1972. Military officers with their own esprit de corps and political ambitions had little difficulty in finding cause to overthrow corrupt rulers who had destroyed democratic institutions and wrecked the economy. Some of the new military rulers promised to restore rule to civilian politicians, but few actually did so. Some, like Zaire's Joseph Mobutu, retired their military uniforms and became presidents, whereas others became victims of later military coups. Most of the earlier coups were carried out by high-ranking officers, but as time went on, lower-ranking officers and even noncommissioned officers thrust themselves into power using the barrel of a gun. In Sierra Leone, army generals took power in 1967 but were overthrown several months later by other army officers, who in turn were soon ousted by a sergeants' revolt.

New military regimes were often welcomed by a disillusioned people, but because the military rulers were usually less prepared than the ousted politicians to cope with the problems of poverty, economic stagnation, and political unrest, they seldom succeeded. As their regimes became more tyrannical and as corrupt as those of the civilian rulers they had overthrown, they quickly lost popular support and became ripe for overthrow by still other ambitious military officers.

The process of militarization in African politics was demonstrated by the experience of Ghana, a nation once looked upon as the pacesetter in Africa's drive for modernization. The charismatic Kwame Nkrumah, who had led the fight for independence, provided vigorous leadership as prime minister of the hopeful nation, which in the early 1960s had the second-highest per capita income in Africa. As the most outspoken champion of pan-Africanism, Nkrumah was involved in the struggle to liberate other African colonies as he was simultaneously guiding his own nation's progress. He adopted a socialist program for Ghana that entailed nationalization of industries and state planning, but he did not attempt a social revolution involving land redistribution. Nkrumah was an inspirational nationalist who placed special emphasis on education as a vehicle for Ghana's development. But before his reorganization programs produced significant economic progress, Ghana was victimized by a drastic decline in the world price for cocoa, its principal cash crop and source of earnings. In the decade following independence, the price fell to a third of its previous level. The declining economic fortunes of the country in combination with the rising expectations of its people stirred discontent. Nkrumah's own corruption and extravagance were also targets of criticism. As president, Nkrumah did not tolerate dissent and became increasingly repressive. With the pressures of a bankrupt economy and popular unrest mounting higher, the volatile Nkrumah, now a dictator, jailed the opposition and silenced dissent. Finally, in February 1966, when he was away on a visit to China, his regime was toppled by the army.

In the years that followed, Ghana became the epitome of political instability as coup followed coup. The officers who grasped power in 1966 made good on their promise to restore civilian rule, but after a brief period of democratic government a group of junior officers staged another coup in 1969, eliminating former government leaders with firing squads. After still another coup in 1972, Ghana remained under military rule through the 1970s. In 1979, a youthful flight lieutenant named Jerry Rawlings shot his way into power and carried out another wave of executions. In 1980, however, he made good on his promise to give democracy another chance in Ghana. This, too, proved short-lived, for at the end of 1981 Rawlings once again took power. Like others before him, he promised an end to corruption, sweeping political and economic reforms, and a brighter future for the blighted country. All the while, however, Ghana's economic and social woes continued to worsen.

Many of Africa's military leaders have been brutal, but few have exceeded the brutality of Idi Amin of Uganda. In 1971, Amin—an army officer—staged a coup, overthrowing the government of Milton Obote. Soon Amin found scapegoats for the economic and social ills of Uganda in several minority tribes and in the community of Asian (mainly Indian) residents of the country. In 1972, Amin forcefully expelled some 50,000 Asians from Uganda, an act that hurt the economy. As conditions worsened in the country, Amin resorted to torture, public executions, and assassinations to enforce his rule. He meanwhile launched an attack on neighboring Tanzania and used the pretext of war to further terrorize his own people. After surviving a number of plots on his life, he was finally overthrown in 1979 by a force from Tanzania, which then installed a civilian government of native Ugandans. Before his removal from power, Amin—the crazed dictator—had massacred an estimated 250,000 of his own people, caused about as many to flee the country as refugees, and left Uganda in shambles. In 1980, Milton Obote returned to power as dictator of Uganda. His regime continued military "cleanup operations" but never succeeded in restoring order. Instead, he eventually killed almost as many people as Amin had and caused another wave of refugees to flee the stricken country.

■ THE BIAFRAN WAR

Nigeria provides another case of militarization and offers an example of the consequences of ethnic conflict. During the early years of independence, no country made greater efforts to overcome ethnic disunity, yet none spilled more blood in ethnic strife. At the time of independence, Nigeria, Africa's most populous nation and one of its wealthiest, was a federal republic of three self-governing regions, each dominated by a major ethnic group—the Hausa-Fulani in the Northern Region (approximately 15 million strong), the Yoruba in the Western Region (15 million), and the Ibo in the Southeastern Region (10 million). But tensions remained high among these groups since each feared domination by the other. The first census in independent Nigeria only added to the suspicion that the Northerners were about to abolish the federal system of power sharing. The census, manipulated by Northerners, declared that the Northern Region contained an absolute majority of the population and thus could create a government dominated by Hausa and Fulani. The census upset the balance of power, charged the political atmosphere, and set the stage for the political crisis that followed.[16]

In January 1966, military officers—mainly Ibos—staged a coup and established a military regime under Gen. J. T. Ironsi. The Northerners, who were mainly Muslims, feared and resented the largely Christian and better-educated Ibos, who had enjoyed commercial and political privileges under British rule and during the early years of independence. The Northerners saw the coup as an attempt to destroy the power of the Hausa-Fulani oligarchy.

At the end of May 1966, the Northern general, Yakubu Gowon, staged his own coup and kidnapped (and later murdered) Ironsi and members of his government. It was at this point that the first wave of assaults against the Ibos took place, first in the north where tens of thousands were massacred and 2 million were driven to flight. In July 1966, Ibo soldiers in the Nigerian army were massacred. Additional attacks on Ibos followed. An Ibo brotherhood called upon Ibos throughout the country "to come home." On May 30, 1967, at the regional capital of Enugu, an Oxford-educated lieutenant colonel, C. O. Ojukwu, issued the declaration of independence of the Republic of Biafra. The declaration denounced the "evils and injustices"—not the least of which were the "premeditated and planned" pogroms—carried out by the military government.[17] Now came the difficult task of defending the independence of Biafra.

The Biafran rebels quickly found out that they stood alone. Only four of Africa's fifty-odd nations and one European state, France, recognized Biafra. France did so because Biafra was located in the oil-rich southeastern corner of Nigeria and contained the nation's largest oil field and its only refinery. The African nations, even though they had denounced repeatedly the arbitrary borders the European colonialists had carved out,[18] did not want to see a dangerous secessionist precedent take place. Nearly all of the countries had numerous ethnic minorities chafing under the control of corrupt and oppressive governments.

General Gowon treated the rebellion as a Nigerian matter that was not the business of others. The United Nations and the rest of the world accommodated him. When the great powers did become involved, notably Britain and the Soviet Union, they did so in support of a united Nigeria. Britain sought to maintain its political and economic influence in Nigeria. Moreover, within a week after the Biafran declaration of independence, the Six Day War in the Middle East closed the Suez Canal, and Nigeria's oil suddenly became more important for Britain. The Soviets, in turn, sought to increase their influence in Africa and thus provided Gowon's army—the likely winner—with modern weapons. This was the first time in modern history an African nation fought a war using weapons provided by outside powers, but it would not be the last. Civil wars and secessionist movements armed by outside powers were later responsible for the destruction of much of Angola, Mozambique, Ethiopia, and Somalia.

Biafra's resistance ended after thirty months. Defeats on the battlefield, bombing raids, and widespread starvation took their toll. In January

1970, the Ibos surrendered. Gowon insisted that no retribution be taken and that the Ibos be reintegrated into Nigerian society. A Nigerian colonel described the aftermath to a U.S. reporter: "It was like a referee blowing a whistle in a football game. People just put down their guns and went back to the business of living."[19]

■ FOREIGN INTERVENTION

The political instability and widespread economic disaster following independence made African nations ripe for exploitation and intervention by outside powers. From the outset of independence, African leaders sought to eliminate dependence on foreign powers and insisted on "African solutions to African problems." It was largely in quest of this ideal that the Organization of African Unity (OAU) was formed in 1963. This body never achieved a meaningful concert of Africa, as the individual nations tended to pull apart rather than together and most maintained closer ties with their former colonial masters in Europe than with their neighbors. They continued to rely on the Europeans for economic aid and sometimes military assistance as well, and the Europeans continued to invest in Africa and to protect their investments. France, in particular, maintained a military presence of more than 15,000 troops, including its highly mobile *force d'intervention*.[20] As the gap between African economic development and that of the industrialized nations widened, especially after the oil crises in the 1970s, the Africans were forced all the more to depend on foreign aid and became even more vulnerable to meddling by outside powers. These powers were not limited to the former colonial powers of Europe but came to include the superpowers, which, in their global struggle, were eager to make themselves indispensable to new African friends and to check the spreading influence of the other. In addition to the East-West rivalry, the Soviet Union and China competed for influence as well.

China's boldest undertaking in Africa was the building of the 1,200-mile Tanzam "Great Freedom" railroad in the mid-1970s, linking landlocked Zambia with the Tanzanian port city of Dar es Salaam. The $500 million project—which employed some 20,000 Chinese and 50,000 African workers—was undertaken after Britain, Canada, and the United States declined the project. The United States had earlier missed an opportunity to expand its influence in northern Africa when, in 1956, it rejected Egypt's request for financial backing to build the Aswan Dam on the Nile River. The Soviet Union moved in within a year to build the dam and temporarily won Egypt as a client state.

East-West power rivalry on the African continent was relatively mute during the 1960s, when the two superpowers contended mainly for influence over the newly independent nations but without direct military involvement. The United States sought to extend its sphere by offering security arrangements and arms, as well as economic aid, to needy African clients, and the Soviet Union sought to pull African states into its orbit by generously supplying weapons, especially to those nations whose leaders espoused Marxism. Although the United States provided much more developmental aid to African nations than did the Soviet Union, it did not win more friends. Nowhere was this more evident than in the United Nations, where African nations and the Soviet Union—sharing an anticolonialism viewpoint—often voted the same way, whereas the United States was seldom able to count on the votes of these nations.

Advocacy of Marxism by an African leader did not necessarily signify successful Soviet intervention, however. To some extent, Marxism-Leninism was in vogue in the early postindependence years, as new African leaders were attracted to the ideology for its explanation of past colonial exploitation and neocolonialism (continuing economic domination by the capitalist nations). They also found in Marxism-Leninism a model for political organization and state planning for economic modernization. But nations that adopted Marxism and established close ties with Moscow, such as Guinea and Angola, found developmental aid from the Soviet Union to be disappointingly meager. Some African leaders, such as Nkrumah of Ghana and Nyerere of Tanzania, conjured up their own brands of "African socialism," a blend of Marxist ideas and indigenous African notions, which were usually fuzzy and had little resemblance to either Marxism or the Soviet system. In actuality, it was difficult to distinguish between those African states that were nominally socialist and those that claimed to be capitalist, for in them all state planning and control of the economy were common, and none shed elitism for genuine egalitarian reforms. "The distinction between socialist and capitalist states in Africa," two noted African specialists have explained, "has often proved to be more one of rhetoric than reality. . . . In the last resort, the socialist or capitalist jargon employed in any individual state is often a reflection of where external aid was coming from at a particular time."[21]

It was not until the mid-1970s, with the end of Portuguese colonial rule in southern Africa, that a direct confrontation between the superpowers occurred in Africa. The departure of Portugal created a volatile situation across southern Africa, not only because power was up for grabs in Portugal's former colonies but also because the buffer between black African nations and the white supremacist regime of South Africa had been removed. South Africa previously had the support of a white minority government in Rhodesia. It also provided valuable trade and aid, as well as employment opportunities, to its black-ruled northern neighbors. But South Africa found itself threatened by the accession of a Marxist regime in Mozambique in 1975, the transfer of power to a black government in Zimbabwe (formerly Rhodesia) in 1980, and the increasing resolve of Botswana, Zambia, and other black African nations to oppose its racist policies. As a consequence, South Africa resorted increasingly to military force, intervening in Angola, Mozambique, and Lesotho.

In defiance of the United Nations and the major powers of the world—East and West—South Africa continued to dominate Namibia, occupying it militarily and thwarting its demand for independence.[22] South Africa installed a puppet black government in Namibia in 1975 and promised to grant it independence, but the left-leaning South-West Africa People's Organization (SWAPO), the largest Namibian party, was left out of the government. SWAPO, which was supported by black African nations, continued guerrilla resistance in its fight for Namibian independence.

The focal point of international struggle in sub-Saharan Africa between 1975 and 1990 was Angola, where the largest buildup of foreign military forces in Africa in postcolonial times took place. The outside forces were from nations such as the United States, the Soviet Union, the People's Republic of China, Cuba, and Zaire, in addition to South Africa. When Portugal withdrew in April 1975, three separate Marxist Angolan revolutionary groups rivaled each other for power. The Popular Movement for the Liberation of Angola (MPLA), a group founded in 1956 and the one longest engaged in the fight for independence, was in control of the capital city of Luanda. The National Front for the Liberation of Angola (FNLA), established in 1962, held control of the mountainous region in the north. And the National Union for the Total Independence of Angola (UNITA), founded in 1966, representing the Ovimbundu—the largest ethnic group in Angola—ruled in the central and southern regions. The transitional government established by the Portuguese collapsed in June 1975, and foreign powers, instead of supporting the accords drawn up by Portugal for the transfer of power, intervened in support of rival revolutionary groups.

Typically, the United States and the Soviet Union accused each other of intervention in Angola and claimed their own involvement was justified by the aggression of the other. By the time fighting began in mid-1975, the MPLA had received Soviet financial support and was assisted by Cuban advisers and a Zairean military unit, and the FNLA and UNITA were receiving financial support and covert military assistance from the CIA. By September, the MPLA had won a decisive victory against the FNLA, and it then battled a UNITA force backed by South African troops. The South African entry into the conflict led to stepped-up CIA action in Angola, as well as a huge increase in Soviet and Cuban assistance for the MPLA. In November 1975, the scales were tipped heavily in favor of the MPLA with the arrival of a massive amount of Soviet and Cuban armaments and several thousand Cuban troops. By the end of the year, the MPLA's victory appeared complete, and it formed a new Angolan government.

Continued U.S. military aid to UNITA rebels and South African military involvement in the years that followed served to keep the Angolan situation alive as an international issue. Indeed, this inflamed issue was one of several that brought an end to the era of détente between the United States and the Soviet Union.

■ THE WORSENING ECONOMIC PLIGHT OF SUB-SAHARAN AFRICA

The 1980s saw in general an increase in the living standard throughout much of the globe, except for nations at war such as Afghanistan, Nicaragua, El Salvador, and certainly Cambodia, Iran, and Iraq, for which no figures are available. The most important exception, however, was sub-Saharan Africa (SSA), the region that covers all of Africa with the exception of the Arabic-speaking belt along the shores of the Mediterranean Sea in the north and South Africa and Namibia in the south. In this rather heterogeneous region, some nations were doing relatively well (Botswana and Mauritius), whereas others clung to the bottom rung of the world's economic ladder (Ethiopia, Chad, and Zaire).

From 1965—that is, shortly after independence—through the 1980s, per capita income in SSA grew a mere 0.6 percent. Overall, economic growth averaged 3.4 percent per year, only a fraction above the increase in population. From independence until 1973, SSA's economies saw slight improvement and grew along the lines of other developing countries but then began to fall behind. Between about 1973 and 1990, thirteen SSA countries with one-third of the region's population became poorer per capita than they had been in 1960.

The 1980s in particular saw the further deterioration of an already bleak picture. In November 1989, the World Bank published a detailed account of SSA's economic performance.[23] Per capita income and food production had decreased; the share of SSA's exports in world markets had declined from 2.4 percent in 1970 to 1.3 percent in 1987; and the region had witnessed, in the terse language of the World Bank report, "accelerated ecological degradation." Several countries—among them Ghana, Liberia, and Zambia—had slipped from the middle-income to the low-income group. In 1987, SSA's population of 450 million produced only as much as Belgium's 10 million. The world's per capita GNP in 1987 stood at $3,010; for SSA, the figure was $330,[24] a ratio of over nine to one.

The causes for the miserable economic performance are many. For one, the newly independent governments sought to industrialize as rapidly as possible. In the process, they neglected the agricultural sector. In the 1960s, farm production increased by nearly 3 percent, thus generally keeping up with population growth. From 1970 to 1987, however, the rate of growth of agricultural production declined; it grew at a pace of less than half of the rate of population growth, 1.4 percent against 3.3 percent. Droughts and the increasing drying up of the Sahel, the belt directly south of the Sahara, were in part to blame for the decline in agricultural production. Whatever economic gains SSA had enjoyed during the preceding thirty years were eaten up by the phenomenal rise in population. "Never in human history has population grown so fast," the World Bank concluded. By the year 2010, SSA's population was expected to more than double, to over 1 billion. Often the result of such growth is hunger. Nearly one-quarter of the population faced "chronic food insecurity." Family planning was necessary not only to reduce the threat of hunger but also to improve health care. SSA had the highest rates of maternal and infant mortality in the world. In the poorest countries (Burkina Faso, Ethiopia, and Mali), one-quarter of the children died before they reached age five.

Another problem that went back to the 1960s was the high level of public expenditures for government, schools, and the military. A direct link existed between low military spending and good economic performance, as in Botswana and Mauritius. The World Bank addressed for the first time the question of official corruption, although only briefly and gingerly. "Bad habits," it noted, "are hard to undo," such as the siphoning of millions of foreign aid dollars into private accounts outside of SSA. An unfettered and vigilant press, which could play the role of a watchdog, was all too rare. The two nations with the best economic performance—Botswana and Mauritius—had parliamentary democracies and a free press.

Meanwhile, SSA was increasingly unable to pay off its mounting debt. The region was overburdened by an external debt that totaled nearly $106 billion in 1987, up from $5.3 billion in 1970 and $41.2 billion in 1980. It had to reschedule its foreign debt payments, and several lenders wrote off debts.

■ AFRICA IN THE EARLY 1990s

☐ The Call for Democracy

In the early 1990s, a number of factors came together that had a considerable impact on sub-Saharan Africa. For one, the Cold War had ended, and the countries of that region were no longer considered important since the superpower rivalry had come to an end. It was no longer necessary for either Moscow or Washington to prop up African dictators. Second, it had become possible, therefore, for political factions to try to resolve their problems without outside interference. Third, the world's leading international financial institutions, notably the International Monetary Fund (IMF) and the World Bank, had come to the realization that the region's economic plight could not be resolved without governments becoming accountable for their actions. Britain's foreign secretary, Douglas Hurd, declared in mid-1990 that "governments which persisted with repressive policies, corrupt management and wasteful, discredited economic systems should not expect us to support their folly with scarce aid resources which could be used better elsewhere."[25] French President Mitterand delivered the same message at a Franco-African summit meeting when he asserted that there could be "no development without democracy and no democracy without development."[26]

The year 1990 saw the rise of protest from below as political discontents—students and scholars, labor unions (often including government employees), and the impoverished masses—railed against oppressive government, corruption, and deprivation. Strikes, protest marches, and riots suddenly had an effect on dictators who for many years had been intolerant of opposition and impervious to criticism. The main instrument for political change in Africa in the early 1990s was the "national conference." Opposition leaders demanded the convening of these conferences, where the political future of the nation was to be deliberated and political groups could present their demands and proposals for multiparty elections. In 1991, almost three-quarters of the forty-seven countries south of the Sahara claimed to be undertaking programs of political liberalization. In the euphoric words of one African diplomat, "What you are really seeing now is an anti-despot movement. What people want most of all is to get rid of those dictators who refuse to change."[27]

One of the first nations to undergo such a political transformation was Benin. In 1990, Benin's President Mathieu Kerekou—military dictator for seventeen years—bowed to political pressure and convened a national conference, which proceeded to strip him of his powers, appoint an interim president, call for a presidential election, and draft a new constitution. Kerekou accepted the decisions of the national conference, and, after being defeated by his opponent by a two-to-one margin in the March 1991 election, he became the first African ruler to be voted out of office. Benin's national conference became a model for political change in Africa, particularly in the former French colonies. Another outstanding success in the new prodemocracy movement occurred in Zambia. In December 1990, Zambian President Kenneth Kaunda, dictator since independence, signed a constitutional amendment legalizing opposition parties. When Kaunda was soundly defeated in the October 1991 election, he relinquished power to the leader of the opposition party.

Not all of Africa's strongmen readily succumbed to the demands for democratic change, nor did all those promising to hold free elections keep their promises or abide by their results. A case in point was Mobutu Sese Seko, the heavy-handed dictator of Zaire since 1965. As early as April 1990, he announced an end to one-party government and promised to accept the verdict of a free, multiparty election, but he then hedged on these pledges and by the mid-1990s was still resisting free elections. In the Central

African Republic, strongman President André Kolingba authorized opposition parties and scheduled an election in October 1992 but then abruptly halted the election in process and suppressed the opposition. Another holdout was President Daniel arap Moi of Kenya, who denounced the movement for multiparty elections as "garbage" and an invitation for chaos. He first answered political protesters with bullets.[28] After a year and a half of continued political agitation and after Western governments had terminated aid to his country, arap Moi finally consented to legalize opposition parties in December 1991 and to call an election a year later. He then worked to manipulate the election to make certain he remained in power.

Most of these dictators had no intention of relinquishing power. They had ulterior motives for participating in "democratic" reforms: to legitimatize and extend their own rule, to pacify the opposition and foreign critics, and to avoid economic retribution at the hands of aid-granting nations. Despite their professed acceptance of political reforms, the dictators retained the means to subvert their implementation. Not all of the widely proclaimed elections, therefore, were free or fair. Several erstwhile rulers, including Ivory Coast's President Félix Houphouët-Boigny, one of Africa's more benevolent dictators, were not beyond rigging elections to stay in power. In October 1990, demonstrations forced this aged ruler, whose one-party rule dated back to the early 1960s, to legalize opposition parties and call an election, which, however, he took every precaution to win decisively.

In many African countries, declarations of democratic progress proved premature. Even when the elections were relatively free, they did not of themselves constitute democracy; nor did they guarantee that either political stability or social justice, much less economic recovery, would necessarily follow. The democratic movement in Africa, which began with much fanfare in 1990, faltered for various reasons—not the least of which was that dictators, by their very nature, are loath to relinquish power. Other reasons included the lack of democratic experience in the African tradition, the lingering effects of past colonial rule, the weakness and inexperience of political parties, the persistence of ethnic separatism, the continued rejection of the concept of "loyal opposition," and the fact that after the Cold War interest in Africa among Western nations declined sharply. Although the lock of one-party monopoly of power was broken in several nations, more dictators remained in power by the end of 1992 than had been removed.

☐ **Namibia, Angola, and Mozambique**

The impact of the end of the Cold War was felt quickly and unmistakably in three war-torn countries in southern Africa: Namibia, Angola, and Mozambique. Soviet ruler Mikhail Gorbachev withdrew financial support for the leftist government in Angola and for the maintenance of Cuban troops deployed in that country and in neighboring Namibia against the white South African forces. U.S.-sponsored and Soviet-supported negotiations produced an agreement signed by Angola, South Africa, and Cuba in December 1988 calling for the evacuation of Cuban troops within two years in exchange for Namibian independence from South Africa. As foreign forces withdrew from Namibia, opposing revolutionary groups were brought together by UN negotiators (again with U.S. and Soviet support) to draft one of Africa's most democratic constitutions and to hold one of Africa's freest and fairest elections. Namibia's newly elected government, formed by SWAPO leader Sam Nujoma, presided over the proclamation of independence in March 1990, marking the end of seventy-five years of colonial rule and twenty-three years of guerrilla warfare.

Gorbachev's withdrawal from Third World Cold War engagements affected Angola as well, but the impact was delayed because of the unrelenting civil war in that country. The war pitting the Soviet/Cuban–supported MPLA government headed by José Eduardo dos Santos against the U.S./South African–supported UNITA guerrilla forces of Jonas Savimbi persisted even after the superpowers cut off military support. But dos Santos's government was piling up foreign debts as well as casualties, and Savimbi's exhausted guerrilla forces had no prospect of victory without supplies of U.S. weapons. With Portugal, the former colonial ruler, serving as peace broker and Washington and Moscow cooperating in applying pressure on the two sides to resolve their differences, a negotiated settlement was finally signed in Lisbon in May 1991. In addition to ending the war, the agreement called for the dos Santos government to remain in power until elections were held in late 1992, the adoption of market-oriented economic reforms, and steps to be taken to demobilize and integrate the two military forces. The breakthrough promised to end the sixteen years of continuous and crippling warfare that had devastated the country, claimed over 300,000 lives, and given Angola the morbid distinction of having the world's highest per capita population of amputees.[29]

The new armistice held as both sides prepared for the impending elections. In quest of support both at home and abroad, dos Santos ardently touted his conversion from Marxism to free-enterprise economics. This transition and the disappearance of Soviet advisers and Cuban soldiers made Savimbi's anti-Communist cause less compelling. Angola's first free multiparty presidential election took place in September 1992 and was relatively free of irregularities. The apparent victor was dos Santos, but Savimbi, charging election fraud, disputed the election even before the results were in. Gunfire once again rang out in the streets of Luanda. The United States, the United Nations, and African leaders urged the recalcitrant revolutionary to lay down his arms and accept the election's verdict. Savimbi, however, remained defiant, and his armed resistance soon claimed another 1,000 lives.

At the same time, a similar sequence of events was unfolding in Mozambique, another former Portuguese colony in southern Africa. There, too, a long-enduring bloody civil war between a Soviet-backed Marxist government and a South African–supported right-wing rebel force, Renamo (the Mozambique Nationalist Resistance), ended with a negotiated settlement. The peace agreement between Renamo and the government in September 1992 terminated an extraordinarily brutal war that had claimed nearly a million lives. It also set the stage for UN-supervised elections and opened the way for desperately needed foreign aid to reach the people of this blighted country, where about one-quarter of the population of 15 million had become refugees, over 3 million people faced starvation, and the standard of living was one of the world's lowest. After fifteen years of civil war, Mozambique produced but one-tenth of the food needed to feed its 15 million inhabitants.[30] The violence had taken place in what was already one of the world's poorest nations. In 1990, Mozambique had a per capita GNP of $80, and one of the world's lowest life expectancy rates (forty-seven years).[31]

☐ Sudan, Ethiopia, and Somalia

The demands for change affecting most of sub-Saharan Africa in the early 1990s were hardly relevant to the most war-ravaged and famine-stricken region of the continent. In Sudan, Ethiopia, and Somalia, starvation, disease, and the displacement of peoples were exacerbated by the relentless and fierce warfare raging there. In 1990, drought returned to Sudan and Ethiopia, causing crop failures and famine and forcing farmers to eat their remaining animals and seed grain.

In Sudan, war between the government in the north and the Sudan People's Liberation Army in the south had deep-seated ethnic and religious roots. In the heavily Muslim north, Arab and Egyptian Mamluk influence was strong; in the south, darker-skinned Africans, many of them Christians, resisted northern domination. Prospects for a peaceful resolution of the conflict were set back in 1989 when a military junta took power in the capital of Khartoum and announced plans for establishing an Islamic state. As the fighting continued, some 8 million Sudanese were in desperate need of food, many becoming wandering refugees in regions beyond the reach of overland food shipments.

In Ethiopia, superpower competition was largely responsible for the ceaseless civil war (the longest in Africa), as the Soviet Union provided over $11 billion in military and economic aid to prop up the brutal Marxist regime of President Mengistu Haile Miriam. Arrayed against him were various ethnic-based rebel armies including the People's Revolutionary Democratic Front, representing mainly Tigre Province, and the Eritrean People's Liberation Front. The Eritrean fight for independence began in

1952 shortly after the United Nations had transferred Eritrea (previously an Italian colony) to Ethiopia. Ironically, the Eritrean rebel leaders were Marxists who fought the Marxist regime in the capital of Addis Ababa, and many of the Tigre rebels were also Marxist.

In 1990, the Soviet Union shut off military aid to the Ethiopian government, and soon thereafter the rebel forces in Ethiopia gained the upper hand. In April 1991, as rebel armies closed in on Addis Ababa and Eritrean forces liberated their homeland in the north along the coast of the Red Sea, Mengistu fled the country. Down came the statues of Lenin in Addis Ababa. Meles Zenawi, leader of the Democratic Front—formerly a Marxist organization—headed a transitional government that pledged to stabilize the country, implement sweeping economic reforms, protect human rights, and, ultimately, hold free elections. With the restoration of order, urgently needed international food relief and developmental aid began to arrive.

The new Ethiopian government and the Eritrean People's Liberation Front agreed to accept the results of an internationally supervised referendum on independence held in May 1993. The Eritreans, whose long war for independence was finally crowned with victory, were flush with nationalism; thus, the outcome of the referendum was a foregone conclusion.

In neighboring Somalia, the superpower rivalry left behind a devastated nation. Its ruler, Mohammed Siad Barre, had maintained a semblance of order in that country for twenty-one years by force of arms (supplied first by the Soviet Union and then by the United States), but in January 1991 he was forced by opposing clans to flee the capital of Mogadishu, taking refuge in his home region in the western part of Somalia. What followed was armed anarchy, as various rebel forces fought for control of the capital. It was a clan feud, a fight for power by forces armed with a wide array of U.S. and Soviet weapons. Somalia quickly became an utterly lawless land filled with savage fighting, fear, looting, and starvation. Jeeps roamed the streets of Mogadishu mounted with recoilless rifles manned by teenage soldiers. In a three-month period at the end of 1991, an estimated 25,000 people—mostly civilians—were killed or wounded in the fighting, and a quarter of a million residents of the capital were forced to flee the city.

The combination of drought and warfare produced a famine as severe as any in modern times. Nongovernmental relief agencies such as the Red Cross, CARE, and Save the Children (a British-based charity) managed to deliver thousands of tons of food a day, but many interior areas of Somalia and even some sections of Mogadishu were beyond reach. Warring forces often blocked shipments of relief food from reaching the starving people and stole the food. In mid-1992, the UN Security Council sent emergency food airlifts into Somalia protected by a token UN force of 500 armed guards. The UN relief missions frequently came under armed attack at the airport outside the capital, and ships laden with UN relief food were denied permission to unload at the docks. Finally, in December 1992, the United Nations sanctioned a request from U.S. President George Bush to send a military operation led by 28,000 U.S. troops to ensure the distribution of international food, medicine, and supplies. By the time the world's largest armed humanitarian rescue mission was launched, an estimated 300,000 Somalis had died of starvation, and as many as one-third of the 6 million people of Somalia were in immediate danger of death by starvation.

After the first U.S. marines had landed, a disagreement broke out between President Bush and UN Secretary-General Boutros Boutros-Ghali over the nature of the mission. Bush envisioned a purely humanitarian mission of short duration; Boutros-Ghali, however, proclaimed a larger mission: to disarm the Somali warlords and establish political stability in the country. The new U.S. president, Bill Clinton, accepted this expanded mission to eliminate the primary source of mayhem and famine in Somalia.

Initially, the U.S.-led intervention in Somalia was an admirable success, making possible the delivery of life-saving food to hundreds of thousands of starving people, but this achievement was soon overshadowed by military failure. Even as UN forces from various nations replaced U.S. troops, Clinton authorized U.S. soldiers to engage in a manhunt for the Somalian warlord considered the person most responsible for the continued violence, Gen. Mohammed Farah Aidid. His capture was deemed all the more important after his troops ambushed and killed twenty-four Pakistani UN soldiers in June 1993. Meanwhile, opposition to the extended military operations in Somalia was mounting in Washington, and this opposition became a furor several months later when an unsuccessful U.S. helicopter attack on Aidid's headquarters led to a furious day-long firefight that left eighteen U.S. soldiers dead and eighty wounded. Worse yet was the spectacle of Aidid's troops dragging the corpse of a U.S. soldier through the streets of Mogadishu. Despite all this, the Clinton administration eventually decided that instead of fighting Aidid the United States would accept him as a political leader who held one of the keys to restoring peace and order in Somalia.

Peace and political order remained elusive, however. Sporadic warfare between Aidid's clan and various rivals continued during the remaining year and a half of the UN operation in Somalia. In the end, the operation— which cost over $2 billion (30 percent of which was borne by the United States) and hundreds of casualties—was a political failure. But thanks in part to a plentiful harvest in 1994, the operation did bring an end to the famine and saved hundreds of thousands of lives.

☐ **Ethnic Violence in Burundi and Rwanda**

The bloodiest confrontations between blacks in postcolonial Africa took place between the Tutsis and the Hutus in the center of the continent, in the Great Lakes region in Burundi and Rwanda. Widespread violence, the consequence of ethnic and class divisions, began as the Belgians granted independence to their colonies in 1960.

The origins of the two peoples are not clear. The Hutus arrived in the Great Lakes region well before the Tutsis, who came from around the Horn of Africa, perhaps from Ethiopia, 400–500 years ago. The Tutsis were cattle herders, the Hutus were cultivators. By the mid-nineteenth century, when the first reliable records were kept, the two groups had developed a common culture (spirit faiths, cuisine, folk customs) and languages. Occasionally, they also intermarried. At that time, there were so few ethnic distinctions that one could not readily call them two different tribes or ethnic groups; the division was made mainly on the basis of class, of social stratification.

The Europeans helped to intensify the class and particularly the ethnic divisions between the Tutsis and the Hutus. The Belgians, who were these peoples' colonial rulers, stressed the differences between them and issued ethnic identity cards. The Belgians treated the minority Tutsis (15 percent of the population) as a separate, superior ethnic entity and favored them for educational, professional, and administrative opportunities. The majority Hutus (85 percent) were treated as an inferior group.

By the time the Belgians withdrew in 1962, the ethnic divisions were deep. The colonial system of using ethnic identity cards remained in force. Ever since, the history of Rwanda and Burundi has been marked by Hutu uprisings and massacres of Tutsis followed by brutal Tutsi repression. In Rwanda in 1965, after Tutsi extremists had assassinated the Hutu prime minister three days after he had been appointed, Hutu military officers attempted a coup. Tutsi reprisals were extremely brutal in an attempt to wipe out the first generation of postcolonial Hutu political leaders. In 1972, following another Hutu rebellion—this one in Burundi—the Tutsis responded with what can only be called a genocidal fury. In a span of three months, they killed approximately 250,000 Hutus and purged the army, the government, and the economy of Hutu elements. In fact, both sides practiced murder and ethnic cleansing in a way that was unambiguously genocidal in nature. The event was a watershed in Tutsi-Hutu relations. By this time, the Belgian myth of two different tribes had been turned into reality. The Tutsis and Hutus feared each other and began to construct their own mythical versions of their past, which only further solidified the divisions, fear, and hatred.[32]

In Burundi in 1987, Tutsi Gen. Pierre Buyoya ousted sitting President Jean-Baptiste Bagaza and then tried to bring about a reconciliation between the two groups. But suspicion ran so deep that reconciliation proved impossible. In August 1988, a confrontation between Tutsi administrators and Hutu civilians in northern Burundi sparked a renewal of violence. Hutu and Tutsi mobs once again began to slaughter each other indiscriminately.

Extremist forces on both sides had an interest in maintaining instability. Many anticipated violence and responded with preemptive violence.

Tutsi control of Burundi continued until June 1993, when the country elected its first Hutu president, Melchior Ndadaye. Six months later, in December 1993, the Tutsi military assassinated him. This event touched off another round of bloodletting. In the first six months alone, the estimated death toll was between 50,000 and 100,000, and 600,000 refugees fled into neighboring countries.

The ethnic violence in Burundi was soon overshadowed by a far greater massacre in neighboring Rwanda. Under the banner of "Hutu Power," President Juvenal Habyarimana, who had ruled Rwanda since 1973, oppressed the Tutsi minority and forced many Tutsis into exile in neighboring Zaire. In 1990, exiled Tutsis in Zaire formed the Rwandan Patriotic Front (RPF), whose aim was to reclaim power in Rwanda. An RPF invasion of Rwanda in October of that year provoked the government to step up its Hutu Power campaign of violence against the Tutsis. The Hutu-Tutsi warfare in Burundi in 1993 had a similar effect, as Rwandan Hutus became ever more vigilant against a resurgence of Tutsis in Rwanda. The immediate cause for the outbreak of violence was the assassination of President Habyarimana in April 1994, when his plane was shot down over Kigali, the Rwandan capital. Hutu soldiers blamed the incident on Tutsis and began immediately to avenge Habyarimana's death with indiscriminate massacres of any and all Tutsis, as well as moderate Hutus—particularly those who had married Tutsis. The militants forced other Hutus to join in this melee of murder or be killed themselves. Mobs conducted a house-to-house search, hunting down and killing their victims with whatever weapons they had at their disposal—machine guns, machetes, spears, knives, and clubs. People were herded into buildings, including churches, which were then set ablaze.

In the end, the Tutsis, true to their military tradition, fought back and took revenge. They rallied to the RPF, which fought its way into the capital and in a brief civil war drove out the Hutu government and its army. In July 1994, RPF leader Paul Kagame set up a new government with a moderate Hutu as president and himself as vice-president and defense minister. Kagame, who retained actual power, took effective measures to halt the violence—including Tutsi crimes of vengeance against the Hutus—and before long assured the Hutu refugees that it was safe to return home. When the carnage ended in Rwanda, a country of 8 million people, between 800,000 and 1 million Rwandans lay dead. In the capital city of Kigali alone, 100,000 had been slaughtered.

The refugee problem generated by the bloodletting in Rwanda was also of immense proportions. Between 1.1 and 1.5 million refugees—mainly Hutus, fearing for their lives—streamed into neighboring Zaire, and another 350,000 poured into Tanzania. Besieged relief workers were overwhelmed. Donor nations and international relief agencies sent food and medicine, but even though a total of over $1.4 billion in aid was sent (one-fourth of all international relief aid in 1994), it proved insufficient and tardy. Thousands of refugees died from hunger and disease in refugee camps. The UN High Commissioner for Refugees negotiated a repatriation agreement with the new government of Rwanda, which gave assurances to the Hutu refugees that it was safe to return home, but few were persuaded to do so. They feared not only retribution at the hands of Tutsis but also bloody reprisals closer at hand by armed Hutu militants, including rene-gade soldiers of the defeated Hutu Rwandan army who menaced the refugee camps in Zaire. Two years later, more than a million Hutu refugees were still living (and dying) in the same overcrowded camps.

In 1996, the Hutu-Tutsi war spilled beyond the borders of Rwanda and Burundi. By this time, the Rwandan Hutu militants in Zaire had linked up with the Zairean army in an effort to oust Tutsis indigenous to that region of Zaire. The Zairean Tutsis, in turn, were armed by Tutsis from Rwanda, who also entered the fray. The chaotic fighting caused many Hutu refugees to take flight from their camps into the surrounding bush in search of safety. As a UN rescue mission was being planned in November 1996, large numbers of desperate Hutu refugees were finally persuaded—apparently by Tutsi military superiority over the Hutu-Zairean forces in the area—to re-turn to Rwanda. Once again, roads were clogged with hundreds of thou-sands of refugees, balancing on their heads bundles containing their only belongings—this time heading home to Rwanda and an uncertain future.

The French government (which in the past had intervened in that part of Africa), the Organization of African Unity, the United Nations and the United States all were wary about becoming involved (other than provid-ing food and other humanitarian relief) in a war of unbridled savagery. Eventually, the United Nations set up an international tribunal commis-sioned to undertake the herculean task of trying some 92,000 genocide suspects in Rwanda.

By the end of 1996, the rising of Zairean Tutsis, known as the Banya-mulenge, became a full-scale civil war in Zaire. Laurent Kabila, the leader of the rebel forces, disclaimed intentions of Tutsi sepratism but pro-nounced as his objective the overthrow of the corrupt regime of Mobuto Sese Seko. The ailing and aged Mobuto returned in December 1996 to Zaire from a four-month stay in Europe where he had been recovering from cancer surgery, but his presence failed to rally his army to victory. In March 1997, the rebel forces took Kisangani, the Zairean army's head-quarters in the war zone. By this time political leaders from South Africa and other African nations were engaged in diplomatic efforts to end the war, which threatened to spread beyond the heart of Africa. Mobuto him-self expressed interest in a negotiated settlement, but Kabila and his rebel forces, smelling victory, would not be swayed.

RECOMMENDED READINGS

Third World—General

Barnet, Richard J. *The Lean Years: Politics in the Age of Scarcity.* New York: Simon and Schuster, 1980.
A study of the political factors involved in sharing limited global resources.

Brown, Lester R., et al. *State of the World, 1986.* New York: W. W. Norton, 1986.
An up-to-date reference on food and environmental issues around the globe.

Ehrlich, Paul E., and Anne H. Ehrlich. *The Population Explosion.* New York: Simon and Schuster, 1990.
In this sequel to Paul Ehrlich's *The Population Bomb* (1968), he and his wife declare that the "population bomb has detonated," with the focus on the environmental damage caused by population pressures.

George, Susan. *Ill Fares the Land: Essays on Food, Hunger and Power.* Rev. and expanded ed. London: Penguin, 1990.
A sociological inquiry into what went wrong with agricultural planning in the Third World.

Harrison, Paul. *Inside the Third World.* 2d ed. New York: Penguin, 1984.
An excellent comprehensive description and analysis of the dilemmas of the Third World.

Kapuscinski, Ryszard. *The Soccer War.* New York: Alfred A. Knopf, 1991.
A Polish journalist's explanation of the political problems of the Third World.

World Bank. *World Development Report: Development and Environment.* New York: Oxford University Press, 1992.
Fifteenth in an annual series, this report discusses the link between economic development, population pressures, and the environment.

Africa

Crowder, Michael. *The Story of Nigeria.* New York: Frederick A. Praeger, 1978.

Finnegan, William. *A Complicated War: The Harrowing of Mozambique.* Berkeley: University of California Press, 1992.
An analysis of the reasons for and consequences of the civil war between the Marxist Frelimo Party and the rebel Renamo movement following Mozambique's independence.

Gavshon, Arthur. *Crisis in Africa: Battleground of East and West.* New York: Penguin, 1981.

Lamb, David. *The Africans.* New York: Random House, 1982.
An eye-opening account of today's Africa and its various problems by a journalist who spent four years in Africa visiting and reporting from forty-eight of its countries.

Leys, Colin. *Underdevelopment in Kenya: The Political Economy of Neo-Colonialism.* Berkeley: University of California Press, 1975.

Mazrui, Ali A. *Africa's International Relations: The Diplomacy of Dependency and Change.* London: Heinemann, 1977.
A study by a noted specialist who presents his case from the Africans' viewpoint.

Neuberger, Ralph Benyamin. *National Self-Determination in Postcolonial Africa.* Boulder, Colo.: Lynne Rienner Publishers, 1986.
A theoretical and comparative analysis of the impact of colonial experience on postcolonial African nationalism and secession.

Oliver, Roland, and Anthony Atmore. *Africa Since 1800.* 3d ed. New York: Cambridge University Press, 1981.

Soyinka, Wole. *The Open Sore of a Continent: A Personal Narrative of the Nigerian Crisis.* New York: Oxford University Press, 1996.
By the Nigerian Nobel laureate for literature.

NOTES

1. GNP, or gross national product, is the wealth—the total goods and services—a nation produces per year. The per capita GNP is calculated by dividing the figure for wealth generated (calculated in U.S. dollars) by the nation's population.

2. World Bank, *World Development Report, 1986* (Washington, D.C.: World Bank, 1986), p. 180. Actually, the African nation with the lowest per capita GNP is Chad. No GNP figures were available for war-torn Chad in this report, but an earlier World Bank report indicated that in 1982 it had a mere $90 per capita GNP.

3. See Paul Harrison, *Inside the Third World,* 2d ed. (New York: Penguin, 1984), pp. 414–415. Harrison provides figures to illustrate that the gap in income between the richest and the poorest people in Third World countries is, on average, greater than the income gap between rich and poor in the world's developed countries.

4. Ibid., p. 145, notes that 185 million people lived in Third World cities in 1940, but by 1975 the number had risen to 770 million. In the early 1970s, 12 million people a year—33,000 a day—were arriving in these cities.

5. For the text of the Amsterdam Declaration, see *Population and Development Review,* March 1990, pp. 186–192.

6. For the text of the OECD's statement, see "Population and Development—DAC Conclusions," *Population and Development Review,* September 1990, pp. 595–601.

7. "Pope John Paul II on Contemporary Development," *Population and Development Review,* September 1991, p. 559; the citations are from Chapter 4 of the encyclical.

8. The statement was made by Bryant Robey of the Johns Hopkins School of Hygiene and Public Health and the editor of *American Demographics,* cited in William K. Stevens, "Poor Lands' Success in Cutting Birth Rate Upsets Old Theories," *New York Times,* January 2, 1994, p. 8.

9. Susan Chira, "Women Campaign for New Plan to Curb the World's Population," *New York Times,* April 13, 1994, pp. A1, A12.

10. Traditionally, African men were primarily hunters and herdsmen, and women were left to work in the fields. The tradition has changed only to the extent that with the depletion of wild game, few men still hunt. But too proud to toil in the fields, men either supervise women who do that work, seek other employment, or loaf in the towns. Exact figures are difficult to obtain, but a UN report, *State of the World's Women, 1985,* estimated that between 60 and 80 percent of farm work in Africa was still done by women. Barber Conable, president of the World Bank, at a joint World Bank–International Monetary Fund meeting, stated that women do two-thirds of the world's work, earn 10 percent of the world's income, and own less than 1 percent of the world's property. "They are the poorest of the world's poor" (Clyde Farnsworth, "World Bank Chief Outlines Strategy," *New York Times,* October 1, 1986, p. D23).

11. Harrison, *Inside the Third World,* p. 455.

12. Ethiopia's aged emperor, Haile Selassie, did little to avert the earlier famine and instead went to great lengths to suppress news of it. After he was overthrown in

1974, a new Marxist regime attempted to carry out an extensive land reform program, only to reap another agricultural disaster that was the consequence not so much of the reforms as of past years of deforestation, overcultivation, and the hostile forces of nature. In 1984, Ethiopia's plight was given broad television coverage around the world, resulting in a great outpouring of food relief from various nations, with the United States alone providing several hundred thousand metric tons of emergency food.

13. Since 1980, South Africa has had a per capita income of more than $12,650, far higher than that of any other African country. It should be pointed out, however, that blacks, who outnumber whites by five to one, earn only about one-sixth of what white workers are paid. In contrast to the standard of living of South African whites, which is among the highest in the world, that of the blacks is substantially lower.

14. *The World Bank Atlas, 1985* (Washington, D.C.: World Bank, 1985).

15. The most notable exceptions include such rulers as Léopold Senghor of Senegal, Félix Houphouët-Boigny of the Ivory Coast, Jomo Kenyatta of Kenya, Julius Nyerere of Tanzania, Kenneth Kaunda of Zambia, Sekou Touré of Guinea, and Seretse Khama of Botswana—all of whom remained in power for fifteen years or more.

16. Moyibi Amoda, "Background to the Conflict: A Summary of Nigeria's Political History from 1919 to 1964," in Joseph Okpaku, ed., *Nigeria: Dilemma of Nationhood: An African Analysis of the Biafran Conflict* (New York: Third Press, 1972), p. 59.

17. "Proclamation of the Republic of Biafra," Enugu, May 30, 1967, in Arthur Agwuncha Nwankwo and Samuel Udochukwu Ifejika, *Biafra: The Making of a Nation* (New York: Praeger, 1970), pp. 336–340.

18. One British commissioner later joked: "In those days we just took a blue pencil and a rule, and we put it down at Old Calabar, and drew that blue line up to Yola. . . . I recollect thinking when I was sitting having an audience with the [local] Emir . . . it was a very good thing that he did not know that I . . . had drawn a line through his territory." Cited in ibid., p. 11.

19. David Lamb, *The Africans* (New York: Random House, 1982), p. 309.

20. Arthur Gavshon, "French Troops in Africa," in *Crisis in Africa: Battleground of East and West* (New York: Penguin, 1981), p. 175.

21. Roland Oliver and Anthony Atmore, *Africa Since 1800* (New York: Cambridge University Press, 1981), p. 330.

22. Namibia had been a German colony known as South-West Africa until World War I when it was conquered by South African forces. After the war, it was placed under a League of Nations mandate administered by South Africa. The mandate was assumed by the United Nations after World War II, but by that time the South African presence in Namibia was deeply entrenched politically and militarily.

23. *Sub-Saharan Africa: From Crisis to Sustainable Growth: A Long-Term Perspective Study* (Washington, D.C.: World Bank, 1989). All data are from this source.

24. The figures are for all "reporting countries," which excluded the Soviet Union and most of its bloc—the inclusion of which, however, would not appreciably change the figures. See World Bank, *World Development Report, 1989* (Washington, D.C.: World Bank, 1989), p. 165.

25. Cited in "Democracy in Africa," *The Economist,* February 22, 1992, p. 21.

26. Cited in "Under Slow Notice to Quit," *The Economist,* July 6, 1991, p. 43.

27. Cited in Kenneth B. Noble, "Despots Dwindle as Reform Alters Face of Africa," *New York Times,* April 13, 1991, pp. 1A, 3A.

28. "Lion's Den," *The Economist,* July 4, 1990, pp. 36–37. In July 1990, Kenyan police opened fire on several hundred dissidents during a peaceful demonstration for the legalization of opposition parties, killing at least 26 and jailing over 1,000.

29. "Angola Moves to Put Aside the Devastation of War," *U.S. News and World Report,* May 13, 1991, p. 50. During the sixteen-year war, Moscow had poured in 1,100 advisers, 50,000 Cuban troops, and between $500 million and $1 billion annually to prop up the leftist government; the United States provided at least $60 million a year to support Savimbi's guerrillas. Christopher Ogden, "Ending Angola's Agony," *Time,* June 3, 1991, p. 22.

30. William Finnegan, *A Complicated War: The Harrowing of Mozambique* (Berkeley: University of California Press, 1992). For a summary of Renamo's "ultraviolence," see pp. 23–26.

31. World Bank, *Sub-Saharan Africa,* p. 221; World Bank, *World Development Report, 1992,* pp. 211, 218.

32. Philip Gourevitch, "The Poisoned Country," *New York Review,* June 6, 1996, pp. 58–60.

12

Apartheid in South Africa

■ THE ORIGINS OF APARTHEID

From 1949 to 1994, South Africa stood apart from the rest of Africa, not only as the most economically developed nation on the continent but also as one ruled by a white minority. In defiance of world opinion, the expressed will of the remainder of Africa, and the demands of the black majority within the country, the rulers of South Africa maintained political power by means of a racist policy known as apartheid. Literally, "apartheid" means apartness; in reality, it was a legal system that demanded the most rigid form of racial segregation to be found anywhere. The laws forbade the most elementary contact among the four racial groupings in South Africa: the blacks (also known as Bantus), the whites (mostly of Dutch, French, and English descent), the coloureds (of mixed black-white parentage), and the Asians (largely Indians).

In 1948, the whites of Dutch (and in part of French)[1] origin replaced another group of European settlers, the English, as the dominant political force in shaping the destiny of a country they considered to be theirs. The Dutch, having settled on the South African coast as early as 1652, considered it their native land. In fact, they called themselves "Afrikaner," Dutch for Africans. (They also called themselves "Boers," or farmers, and are often referred to by that name.) They argued that their claim to the land rested on discovery, conquest, economic development, and, ultimately, on the will of God.

Apartheid was steeped in the teachings of the Dutch Reformed Church, which saw the Afrikaner as God's chosen people, destined to dominate the land and others who inhabited it. Apartheid, the Afrikaner argued, was the word of God and was specifically sanctioned in the Bible. The most fervent defenders of apartheid were frequently ministers of the Dutch Reformed Church. Apartheid was also based on the primitive principle of racial superiority. The Bantus, the Afrikaner argued, contributed nothing to civilization; their existence was one of savagery. The twin pillars of apartheid—religious determinism and racial superiority—were the consequence of the Afrikaner's long struggle against heresy, Western liberalism, and the black, native population of South Africa.

By the end of the eighteenth century, the Dutch had deep roots in the South African soil. In 1795, however, the British gained control of the South African cape. The result was a struggle for political and religious supremacy between the established Dutch and the newly arrived, victorious English who had settled largely around the Cape of Good Hope. It was a contest the Afrikaner could not win, and it brought about their decision to move into the hinterlands to escape the discriminatory English laws. Moreover, the Afrikaner opposed the English ban of slavery, which in 1833 became the law of the empire. In 1835, the Boers set out on the Great Trek northward into the high plains of Natal and Transvaal. The journey was filled with bitterness and determination, coupled with a religious fervor seldom matched. The trek became a dangerous, triumphant religious procession by which God's elect, a people with a very narrow view of salvation, set out to build a new Jerusalem. And God's favor clearly seemed to shine on the "righteous" when, on December 16, 1838—in a scene straight out of the Old Testament—470 Boers decisively defeated a force of 12,500 Zulu warriors, killing 3,000 of them, on the banks of what became known as the Blood River.[2] After the Afrikaner came to power, December 16 became a national holiday, the Day of Covenant between God and the Afrikaner.

Later in the century, when the British once again encroached on Boer territory, the Boers stood and fought two wars; however, by 1902 the British emerged victorious. This was a bloody and brutal struggle in which the Afrikaner were defeated in what they considered to be their own country. From that day, they prepared for the day of liberation to redress their defeat and to reestablish the social and religious principles of the Great Trek. That day came in 1948, when their party, the National Party, under the leadership of D. F. Malan—a former minister of the Dutch Reformed Church—won a narrow electoral political victory.

At this juncture, British efforts to maintain racial harmony in South Africa were abandoned, and the South African segregation laws came into being. The Afrikaner, driven by an intense sense of religious and cultural self-preservation, rejected all previous proposals for social and racial integration. Instead, at a time when Hitler's brutality and defeat in World War II had thoroughly discredited once respected racial theories, the Afrikaner insisted that the races must be kept apart by law and that no one had the right to cross the color line. The upshot of this militant position in the wake of World War II was the political isolation of South Africa. Yet, such isolation only bred defiance and strengthened and reinforced the outlook of a people long accustomed to adversity and determined to go it alone. A stiff-necked people, the Boers had stood up to the British, the blacks, and now the world.

The first of the segregation laws, enacted in 1949, forbade miscegenation—the marriage or cohabitation of persons of different color. Another law, passed in 1953, barred interracial sex, and other segregation laws followed in rapid succession. Schools, jobs, and pay scales were all determined by the segregation laws. The Population Registration Act listed individuals on the basis of race; another law demanded residential segregation and limited the rights of blacks to remain in designated cities. Political organizations and strikes by nonwhites were outlawed. All public facilities—from hospitals to park benches and beaches—became segregated. Whites and nonwhites were not permitted to spend the night under the same roof. Every aspect of sexual, social, religious, and economic intercourse between the races was regulated, among both the living and the dead—even the cemeteries were segregated. The number of apartheid laws ran well over 300.

The issue of race and segregation became an obsession in South Africa. But to separate the races, a classification board first had to assign a category for every individual. In many cases that was not an easy task. Deliberations took months and years, for the science of distinguishing facial features, skin color, and hair texture is not exact. Ultimately, however, the board rendered its verdict. Often the result was as follows:

> In one typical twelve-month period, 150 coloreds were reclassified as white; ten whites became colored; six Indians became Malay; two Malay became Indians; two coloreds became Chinese; ten Indians became coloreds; one Indian became white; one white became Malay; four blacks became Indians; three whites became Chinese.[3]

The laws of apartheid were designed to preserve both the dominant position of whites and racial purity. They turned the once oppressed Afrikaner into oppressors of the majority of the population. In 1980, in this nation of 28 million, blacks outnumbered whites by a ratio of three to one, 18 million to 6 million. The coloureds numbered about 3 million, the Asians nearly 1 million. It was little wonder that a siege mentality permeated white society. And, in fact, white settlements were frequently referred to as *laagers,* literally "camps," a term taken from the Great Trek of the 1830s.

The segregation laws were also the linchpin of economic exploitation. The laws excluded nonwhites from the better-paying jobs and positions of authority. In the construction industry in the late 1980s, for instance, whites earned twice the salary of Asians, three times that of coloureds, and five times that of blacks. A white miner earned $16,000 a year, a black miner $2,500. The combination of rich natural resources, industrial planning, and cheap labor provided by the black work force turned the nation into the African continent's only modern, industrialized state—but only for the white population. The defenders of apartheid pointed out that the wealth of the nation also trickled down to the black population, whose standard of living was the highest of any blacks in Africa. Blacks regarded this argument as irrelevant.

Apartheid was a philosophy of psychological oppression, economic exploitation, and political domination. It was a way of life that only force could maintain. And the white minority showed time and again a willingness to go to any length to maintain the status quo. Political observers, both in South Africa and abroad, frequently asked how long such conditions could prevail. Black activists repeatedly called for the repeal of all apartheid laws, insisting that nothing short of equal pay for equal work, equal political representation, and equal protection under the law would do.

■ THE SHARPENING OF TENSIONS, 1959–1961

In 1959, the National government set aside ten regions (Bantustans, or "homelands") for the black population that constituted 13 percent of the nation's land. The Bantustans became the centerpiece of apartheid, for they denied native blacks unrestricted access to the rest of South Africa. They were designed to establish the legal principle that blacks merely enjoyed temporary residence in South Africa proper. This was part of what the government euphemistically called "separate development" or "plural democracy," words that sounded more appealing than apartheid, which had acquired a stigma throughout the world. The Bantustans were the sole legal residences for the nation's black population. That population, the nation's essential work force, thus consisted of transients who had no right to be in, say, the city of Johannesburg. It also meant that although black fathers could find work in areas set aside for whites, their families had to remain behind. Thus, not only were blacks and whites divided but black families as well, frequently for eleven months at a stretch. Blacks were but visitors at the pleasure of the host, the whites of the city. The blacks of South Africa were aliens in their native land.

The creation of the "homelands" signaled the completion of the system of apartheid. The South African government hoped to obtain international recognition of the Bantustans as the national homes of the blacks of South Africa, yet no country ever recognized them as independent and sovereign. They acquired no legal international standing, for none of the "homelands" was ever viable. The arid soil made farming difficult, and the "homelands" remained financially dependent on the South African government. One writer called them an "archipelago of misery." The Bantustans, however, did create the correct impression that the South African government had no intention of retreating from the experiment of apartheid.

Nelson Mandela, leader of the
African National Congress and
first non-white president of the
Republic of South Africa *(Courtesy
of the Embassy of the Republic of
South Africa)*

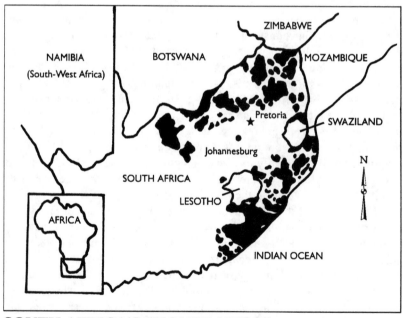

SOUTH AFRICA'S "HOMELANDS"

The government's position became clearer still in 1960, the UN's Year of Africa during which a number of sub-Saharan African nations gained independence. In February, British Prime Minister Harold Macmillan went to Capetown to address the South African parliament. He delivered his "wind of change" speech in which he warned that black nationalism was a force that had to be recognized or the newly independent African nations would be drawn into the Communist camp. The government of Hendrik Verwoerd ignored whatever winds were blowing through Africa and made clear that there would be no accommodation with African nationalism in South Africa. Six weeks later, on March 21, Verwoerd's government replied to Macmillan with the Sharpeville massacre in which the police killed sixty-nine demonstrators who had protested the creation of the Bantustans and the pass laws that required them to carry documents granting them permission to be in places reserved for whites.

The Sharpeville massacre had an extraordinary psychological impact on black Africans, who viewed it as a watershed; the time had come to move from peaceful agitation to armed revolution. The laws of South Africa left them two choices: accept the status of second-class citizenship or rebel. In addition to Sharpeville, highly publicized disturbances also took place in Soweto (short for South-West Township), a black ghetto of 1 million people thirty minutes from Johannesburg, the elegant financial capital of South Africa. In April 1960, the government banned the still moderate African National Congress (ANC) and the militant Pan-Africanist Congress. And in May 1961, South Africa, in defiance of the other members of the British Commonwealth, "resigned" from that organization.

It was at this juncture that South Africa's oldest and most influential civil rights organization, the African National Congress—an umbrella organization of blacks, whites, Asians, coloureds, liberals, and Communists—reassessed its strategy. Since its formation in 1912, the ANC had sought the peaceful establishment of a nonracial democracy. As its leader, Nelson Mandela, explained at his trial in 1964, until the advent of apartheid the organization had "adhered strictly to a constitutional struggle."[4] But the events between 1959 and 1961 made clear that this approach had reached a dead end.[5]

In 1961, the ANC, having concluded that all legal venues were now closed, adopted armed struggle as one of the means to bring an end to apartheid. It formed its armed wing, *Umkhonto we Sizwe*—the "Spear of the Nation"—because as Mandela, one of the founders of *Umkhonto*, explained, "fifty years of nonviolence had brought the African people nothing but more and more repressive legislation, and fewer and fewer rights."

On December 16, 1961, *Umkhonto* responded with acts of sabotage throughout South Africa. On that day, it also issued its manifesto, which explained that the struggle against apartheid had reached a new stage:

The people's patience is not endless. . . . The time comes in the life of any nation when there remain only two choices: submit or fight. . . . The choice is not ours; it has been made by the Nationalist government, which has rejected every peaceable demand by the people for rights and freedom. . . . The Nationalist government has chosen the course of force and massacre, now deliberately, as it did at Sharpeville.[6]

Appropriately, *Umkhonto*'s opening shots took place on the Day of Covenant that commemorated the defeat of the Zulus by the Afrikaner at the Blood River in 1838. Before the National Party came to power in 1948, this day had been known simply as Dingaan's Day, after the defeated Zulu king. But in the days of apartheid, it became a national holiday symbolizing the covenant between God and his people that had made the victory possible. The ANC, in an act of defiance, marked December 16 as Heroes' Day to honor those who had lost their lives in the struggle against apartheid.

The armed struggle between *Umkhonto* and the government had precisely the effect Macmillan had feared. The ANC made common cause with the country's Communist Party, and South Africa was drawn into the global Cold War. The Soviet Union provided money and weapons to the ANC, and the United States tilted toward the South African apartheid regime. In the eyes of many Westerners, the fact that the ANC included some Communists in its ranks made it a Soviet front organization. The ANC, however, did not espouse Marxist economic theory; in fact, it advocated a capitalist South Africa but one in which private property was more equitably distributed.

As the South African police began to look for Mandela in the early 1960s, the U.S. Central Intelligence Agency (CIA) joined in the search, and it was because of a tip from the CIA that the police arrested Mandela in 1963. At his trial in 1964, Mandela justified the formation of *Umkhonto* by pointing to the repeated acts of violence by the government against the black population. In August 1996, thirty-five years after the founding of *Umkhonto*, Gen. Constand Viljoen, the former head of the South African defense forces, acknowledged that the South African government had "invited" the ANC to create *Umkhonto,* to forge an alliance with the Communists, and take up the armed struggle.[7]

■ BLACK CONSCIOUSNESS AND ZULU NATIONALISM

The early 1970s saw the emergence of the "black consciousness" movement, a phenomenon influenced in part by the U.S. civil rights movement. Its leading advocate was Steve Biko, who insisted that South African blacks must no longer have liberal whites speak for them but must deal with all whites on an equal basis. As "whites must be made to realize that they are *only* human, [and] not superior," he declared, blacks "must be made to realize that they are *also* human, [and] not inferior."8 The very thought of a black man demanding racial equality as his birthright made Biko a dangerous and a marked man. He died in police custody in September 1977, his skull fractured in many places.

After Biko's death, the radical Azanian People's Organization (Azapo), the militant wing of the Pan-Africanist Congress, declared itself the heir of Biko's "black consciousness" and then went further than the position he had taken. The group demanded the expulsion of all whites and declared war on them under the slogan "one settler, one bullet." Azapo also became engaged in an ideological—and soon bloody—conflict with the ANC and its allies who promoted a nonracial democracy.

At the same time, the ANC faced opposition from still another black organization, the Inkatha Freedom Party, the political base of Zulu chief Mangosuthu Buthelezi. In their younger days, Buthelezi and Mandela had been comrades in their opposition to apartheid, but over the years Buthelezi had become the champion of narrow Zulu, rather than national, interests. He became a defender of the Zulu "homeland," KwaZulu, located in the province of Natal. An integrated South Africa threatened Buthelezi's base of power, and thus he sought to perpetuate the continued existence of KwaZulu or the creation of an entirely independent Zulu state. Biko had expressed the hope that all black organizations could work together to abolish apartheid, but he also understood the deep splits among them. He described Buthelezi in this fashion:

> He has a *tribal* following among the Zulus. He has managed to combine many elements as a *traditional* chief in a *nonurban* setting. He speaks up strongly against apartheid, but today he is the governmentally paid leader of the Zulus. . . . We oppose Gatsha [Buthelezi]. He dilutes the cause by operating on a governmental platform. Because of this I see the danger of division among blacks.9

But Buthelezi did more than merely "dilute" the anti-apartheid cause. He was responsible for one of the many splits leading to black-on-black violence, which began in earnest in September 1984 and eventually eclipsed the white terror. A South African reporter described it thus:

> Chief Gatsha Buthelezi's Inkatha movement was trying to crush the Mandela Charterists [the ANC], and the Charterists were reciprocating. . . . All the blacks were killing each other and atop the boiling roil sat the Afrikaner tyrants, playing the various forces against one another and killing anyone who survived to challenge them.10

■ THE DISMANTLING OF APARTHEID

In the mid-1980s, the government began to reassess its policy. Slowly, a number of its members, once staunch defenders of apartheid, began to question the wisdom of continuing with this policy. The financial, psychological, and human costs were becoming too high. June 1976 saw an uprising in Soweto that the police put down by killing several hundred residents. In 1985, during demonstrations commemorating the twenty-fifth anniversary of the Sharpeville massacre, the police killed 19 people at one demonstration alone, and scores of others died in separate clashes. The funeral processions for those killed served as protest demonstrations and brought more violence. The summer of 1985 saw the deaths of over 700 blacks, as well as several whites. At summer's end, for the first time white residential areas became the scenes of racial confrontations. There were 1,605 outbreaks of political violence in January 1986, and the numbers kept climbing in subsequent months. The anti-apartheid uprising of the mid-1980s claimed 1,650 lives and nearly 30,000 detainees.[11]

Neither the arrests nor the shooting of demonstrators brought a semblance of order to South Africa. In 1985, the government began to consider the unthinkable: the establishment of a political dialogue with the banned ANC and its leader, Mandela, who had been sentenced to life imprisonment in 1964. But in early 1985 Mandela refused a deal whereby he would have been granted freedom on the conditions that the ANC pledge to refrain from violent activity and that he live in the "homeland" for the Xhosa, the Transkei.

At the same time, another voice in opposition to apartheid came to international attention, that of Episcopalian Bishop Desmond Tutu, who in 1984 received the Nobel Peace Prize in recognition of his attempts to work out a peaceful solution to his country's political dilemma. The Botha government began to understand that eventually it would have to deal with both Mandela and Tutu.

In early 1985, President P. W. Botha took the heretical position of acknowledging the reality of the permanence of blacks in "white" South Africa, a permanence that ultimately would have to be granted legality. Demographics alone, in a nation where the black population was growing more rapidly than the ruling white population, demanded such a concession. With this position, Botha brought into question the very essence of apartheid.

Botha's statements reflected a split in his government between the *verligte,* or "enlightened," ministers and the conservatives, who were fearful of any change. At stake was the very survival of Afrikaner society. Botha's slogan in early 1985 was "adapt or die," but his Afrikaner opponents vowed not to take a single step backward. After the widespread riots in the summer of 1985, Botha succumbed to pressures from his right. The wave of unrest in South Africa, in which 700 blacks died by summer's end, provoked the traditional response by the Boers. They retreated to their *laager* in defiance of the black majority and world opinion.

The anti-apartheid movement was not silenced, however, and in 1986 blacks continued to defy government restrictions against protest marches. Time and again, they were met by police equipped with a vast arsenal of riot control weapons. Determined to quell the racial disturbances and to put an end to worldwide press and television coverage of the carnage occurring in its streets, the Botha government imposed a nationwide state of emergency on June 12, 1986. Under this decree, a black protester could be imprisoned without trial for up to ten years for statements interpreted to "weaken or undermine" confidence in the government. Botha also scrapped the hated pass laws; with that move he abandoned the Boer fiction that a purely white South Africa was a possibility. Botha made clear that the old days were over without having a clear idea of what would come next.

Under persistent pressure at home and from abroad, the Botha government continued efforts to seek solutions to the racial unrest in the country. International pressure began to have a telling effect. Under the aegis of the United Nations, the United States and most European governments imposed trade sanctions, and many foreign corporations began withdrawing capital from South Africa. Between 1986 and 1988, the country suffered a net capital outflow of nearly $4 billion; consequently, unemployment, inflation, and interest rates all increased and economic growth declined from 5 to 2 percent. The price of apartheid had become too high.[12] In reaction, a growing number of whites, especially in the business community, began urging a change in the apartheid program. Many whites also felt a sense of isolation from the world community. Since the late 1960s, South Africa, a nation proud of its world-class athletes, had been banned from the Olympic Games and other venues of international competition, such as the World Cup in soccer.

In response to these pressures, Botha began gradually to moderate the apartheid system in 1988 and 1989. Some of the more superfluous apartheid restrictions were lifted. Certain public facilities—such as drinking fountains, movie theaters, and public parks and swimming beaches—were desegregated, and mixed residency was permitted in certain previously segregated urban residential areas.

In 1989, Botha was outmaneuvered in his own party by a more flexible leader of the moderate faction, Frederik W. de Klerk, who was sworn in as South Africa's president in September of that year. In his inauguration speech, de Klerk pledged to work for "a totally changed South Africa . . . free of domination or oppression in whatever form."[13] He went on to declare his intentions of bridging the deep gulf of distrust and fear among the races and finding a "completely new approach" to negotiations with black leaders.

A major sign of the changing attitudes in the country under the leadership of de Klerk was his remarkably conciliatory policy toward the outlawed ANC. He released several leaders of the ANC from prison and began negotiations for the release of Nelson Mandela, the seventy-one-year-old titular leader of the organization. Anti-apartheid protesters were permitted to hold a mammoth rally in Soweto at which the released ANC leaders were allowed to address a throng of some 60,000 people. Even more surprising were the lifting of the ban of the ANC and the unconditional release of its heralded leader, Mandela, in February 1990. At the same time, de Klerk promised to free all political prisoners and ended the state of emergency Botha had declared in June 1986—a tacit admission that more than forty years of apartheid had not worked.

De Klerk gave hope to anti-apartheid leaders, but they awaited more substantial reforms necessary to bring an end to apartheid. Meanwhile, international investors lost no time in making money available to the South African economy. The Johannesburg Stock Exchange industrial index rose 7.2 percent in two days.[14] But at the same time, the right wing within de Klerk's party promised demonstrations and strikes to bring him down.

As the newly freed Mandela began to take the first tentative steps to negotiate an end to apartheid with the de Klerk government, old issues came to the fore. One was the continued political rivalry between Mandela's ANC and the ethnic Zulu-based Inkatha movement, led by its chief, Buthelezi. In contrast to Buthelezi, Mandela, although a descendant of Xhosa kings, had long since moved beyond ethnic politics and was committed to the abolition of all Bantustans.

Mandela's release from prison had no impact on the violence between the ANC and Inkatha. Between 1985 and 1996, the Inkatha-ANC bloodletting cost 10,000–15,000 lives. Much of the violence was carried out by young radical blacks, the "Young Lions," who sought to establish bases of economic and political power in the townships. The Young Lions had gained notoriety by "necklacing" their victims (placing tires around their necks and setting them on fire). Many were still unemployed, and they continued to face the consequences of decades of legal, social, and economic discrimination. They were beyond the control of, and were impervious to, the pleas for moderation by all of the established leaders, as well as the radical Zeph Mothopeng, the head of the Pan-Africanist Congress. Even Mandela, upon his release from prison, was unsuccessful in his appeal to the Young Lions to throw their guns and knives into the sea.

White society, too, became polarized between the diehards who defied the winds of change blowing out of Pretoria and those who wanted to rid the nation of apartheid. De Klerk's problems thus went beyond the abolition of apartheid laws. His first order of business after Mandela's release was to end South Africa's civil violence. De Klerk and Mandela shared the general objective of a nonracial and democratic South Africa, but neither trusted the other with shaping the country's future. In 1991, de Klerk took decisive steps to abolish the apartheid laws (including the Population Registration Act, the legal underpinning of apartheid) to clear away obstacles to the negotiation of a new constitution. The ANC signed a tenuous peace agreement with the Zulu Inkatha.

The ANC continued to insist on "one man, one vote"—that is, majority rule.[15] Such a solution would mean the election of a black majority government and, therefore, would produce a strong reaction from the Afrikaner right-wing groups, such as the Conservative Party and the Afrikaner Resistance Movement. De Klerk decided by means of a referendum to confirm support from the nation's white population for his policy of abolishing apartheid and negotiating a constitution with the nation's black leaders. In March 1992, he won a resounding victory by garnering over 68 percent of the votes of the all-white electorate.

Negotiations, however, were repeatedly halted by outbursts of violence. The ANC charged that the government was deliberately stirring up anti-ANC violence, particularly by the Zulus, to discredit blacks and sabotage the negotiating process. In July 1991, revelations surfaced that members of de Klerk's cabinet, in fact, had secretly financed the rival Zulu Inkatha Party. Soon afterward, Inkatha launched an offensive that resulted in over 800 deaths in a three-month period. The ANC sharply rebuked the government for complicity in the killing of ANC supporters, demanded the resignation of specific cabinet members responsible for security and justice, and called for investigations of the conduct of security forces. In June 1992, a band of Zulus stabbed and bludgeoned their way through Boipatong Township near Johannesburg, leaving over 40 dead, again apparently with the complicity of the police.

The ANC, which accused de Klerk of wrecking the talks, walked out of the negotiations and resorted to a different strategy. It launched a nationwide mass movement featuring protest marches, strikes, and sit-ins to pressure the government into meeting its terms for a new constitution. The ANC also unleashed a tirade against de Klerk, calling him a "dangerous criminal" and a "murderer" and likening his regime to that of the Nazis. The ANC took its fight to the streets, hoping for a victory in the manner of the mass protest movements that had toppled the Communist regimes of Eastern Europe in 1989. The policy was confrontational and fraught with peril, since it threatened to drive the white population away from de Klerk and into the arms of the rightists.

In 1992, the last remnant of the apartheid laws, the ten "homelands," became a focal point of the ANC's political agenda. Pretoria still considered four of them—Ciskei, Bophuthatswana, Transkei, and Venda—independent entities even though they were a creation of, and were financially dependent on, South Africa. The ANC did not recognize the "homelands'" independence and insisted they be reincorporated into South Africa and that they participate in the political process. The leaders of KwaZulu, Ciskei, and Bophuthatswana, where elections and opposition parties (including the ANC) had been banned, insisted on maintaining their autonomy and made clear that they would defend that autonomy by force if necessary.

In September 1992, the ANC launched a mass campaign in an attempt to eliminate the black "homelands" once and for all. It first targeted the "homeland" of Ciskei, where the ANC had considerable popular support. The ANC felt a massive demonstration could topple the government of the military dictator Joshua Oupa Gqozo. Gqozo announced, however, that he would not permit the ANC to enter the "homeland" and would shoot Mandela if he did so. The ANC's tactic proved to be a reckless gamble. When 80,000 unarmed ANC supporters entered Ciskei's capital of Bisho, Gqozo immediately ordered his troops to open fire, killing 28 people and wounding 200.

Another challenge to the ANC came in December 1992, when Azapo rejected the ANC's vision of a multiracial society and the political principle of "one man, one vote." Under its slogan "one settler, one bullet," Azapo declared war on all whites, murdering several. In response, white groups that opposed the dismantling of apartheid once again began to murder black South Africans.

In 1993, the ANC was engaged in intense negotiations with the National Party and other political parties, attempting to settle such issues as holding South Africa's first free multiracial election, planning the transition from white minority rule to government by majority rule, and dismantling the "homelands." By September 1993, negotiators had produced a general agreement. They established April 27, 1994, as the date for nationwide elections for a 400-seat National Assembly. At this point, Mandela joined de Klerk in calling for an end to international economic sanctions, stating that they had served their purpose.

But not all parties were on board. Zulu leader Buthelezi had boycotted the negotiations that produced the transition plans and continued to hold out for the independence of KwaZulu, with its population of 7.5 million. Not until the very eve of the April elections did Buthelezi finally direct his Inkatha Freedom Party to participate. Another holdout was Lucas Mangope, president of Bophuthatswana, but he, too, was won over at the eleventh hour.

Mandela's ANC was, as expected, the big winner in the historic elections—the first free multiparty and multiracial elections in South Africa. The ANC garnered 62 percent of the vote and won 252 seats in the National Assembly, whereas the National Party obtained 20 percent of the vote and 82 seats. On May 27, 1994, the seveny-five-year-old Mandela, who had spent twenty-seven years of his life as a political prisoner, was elected by the National Assembly as the first nonwhite president of his country. In a speech two weeks earlier, Mandela marked the profound historical importance of the accomplishment of South Africa in these words: "The time for the healing of wounds has come. . . . Never, never, and never again shall it be that this beautiful land will again experience the oppression of one by the other. . . . Let freedom reign. God bless Africa!"[16]

This remarkable turn of events was the result of five coinciding factors: the South African government's inability to produce a stable society under apartheid; the enactment of effective international economic sanctions; the end of the Cold War, which ended direct outside meddling by the superpowers; and the roles of de Klerk and Mandela. For their efforts, de Klerk and Mandela shared the Nobel Peace Prize in 1993. Nor should the roles of old-guard National Party leaders, who began behind-the-scenes initiatives for change a decade earlier, be overlooked. At the time of the 1994 elections, several members of the former Botha government revealed that they had become convinced in the 1980s that apartheid could not be sustained for long and that they should strike a deal with leaders in the ANC to work out a peaceful transition to majority rule.

To reach an agreement on a permanent constitution took another two and a half years after the election. When the time came to sign this document in December 1996, it was only appropriate that the signing should take place at Sharpeville in the presence of survivors of the 1960 massacre.

Mandela's inauguration could not disguise the hard realities of unresolved divisive political issues and persistent economic and social inequalities. The dismantling of apartheid and the changing of the guard did not miraculously erase the miserable living conditions for the bulk of the black population or provide the education needed for their advancement.

One of the most difficult tasks was determining how to deal with those who were guilty of political violence since 1960 (the year of Sharpeville and the banning of the ANC). Under Mandela's persistent demands, South Africa, which had one of the world's highest rates of capital punishment, abolished the death penalty. In July 1995, the government set up a Truth and Reconciliation Commission, which sought—as its name implied—not to punish the guilty but to try to bring about national reconciliation between peoples who only recently had been killing each other. The commission could only be established because the new leadership genuinely believed in reconciliation. The head of the commission was retired Episcopalian Archbishop Desmond Tutu, the recipient of the Nobel Peace Prize for 1984—a man whose entire life had been dedicated to the idea of peaceful reconciliation.

The commission operated on the principle of granting amnesty to all who acknowledged their past crimes. The families of the victims—understandably—were generally opposed to amnesty, but there appeared to be no workable alternative to the commission's solution. If punishment were to be meted out, then to whom? The current defense minister, Joe Modise, who had been the head of the *Umkhonto?* Former Defense Minister Magnus

Malan, who had organized anti-ANC death squads manned by Zulus? The guilty parties in the ANC-Inkatha violence that had claimed as many as 15,000 lives in a ten-year span and who continued to kill each other even as the commission was holding its hearings? Could the state, even if it wanted to, bring some of the Inkatha leaders—not to mention Buthelezi— into the dock? And what was one to do about the charges that directly implicated P. W. Botha in acts of violence?[17] If Tutu succeeded in bringing about anything even resembling national reconciliation, he would be first in line for a second Nobel Peace Prize.

RECOMMENDED READINGS

Breytenbach, Breyten. *The True Confessions of an Albino Terrorist.* New York: Farrar, Straus, Giroux, 1984.
    An autobiographical account by a poet from a well-known Afrikaner family who became a revolutionary activist.
Lelyveld, Joseph. *Move Your Shadow: South Africa, Black and White.* New York: Times Books, 1985.
    A *New York Times* reporter explains the racial realities of South Africa.
Malan, Rian. *My Traitor's Heart: A South African Exile Returns to Face His Country, His Tribe, and His Conscience.* New York: Atlantic Monthly Press, 1990.
Mandela, Nelson. *The Struggle Is My Life.* New York: Pathfinder Press, 1986.
    Collection of Mandela's speeches and writings.
Thompson, Leonard. *The Political Mythology of Apartheid.* New Haven, Conn.: Yale University Press, 1985.
    An account of the origins of, and a justification for, that racial policy.
Woods, Donald. *Biko.* New York: Paddington Press, 1978.
    A white South African's sympathetic account of the racial issue in his country, focusing on the role of Steve Biko, founder of the black consciousness movement, who died in police custody in 1977.

NOTES

1. In the late 1680s, French Calvinists, the so-called Huguenots, left France after their government revoked in 1685 the Edict of Nantes of 1598, a decree of religious toleration. The Huguenots were shortly absorbed into the Dutch Afrikaner community.

2. C. F. J. Muller, ed., *Five Hundred Years: A History of South Africa* (Pretoria: Academia, 1969), pp. 166–167.

3. David Lamb, *The Africans* (New York: Random House, 1982), pp. 320–321. The official absurdity knew no end. Chinese were classified as a white subgroup, and Japanese, mostly visiting business representatives, were given the questionable title of "honorary whites."

4. This and other statements by Mandela later in the chapter are from his defense from the dock in Pretoria Supreme Court, April 20, 1964, cited in *Nelson Mandela: The Struggle Is My Life* (New York: Pathfinder Press, 1986), pp. 161–181.

5. The Nobel Peace Prize committee acknowledged the peaceful nature of the ANC when in 1960 it awarded its medal to Chief Albert J. Luthuli, the ANC's president since 1952.

6. "Manifesto of Umkhonto we Sizwe," December 16, 1961, in Mandela, *The Struggle Is My Life*, pp. 122–123.

7. Reuters, "De Klerk Takes Blame for Apartheid Crimes," *Baltimore Sun*, August 20, 1996, p. 11A.

8. Biko cited in Donald Woods, *Biko* (New York: Paddington Press, 1978), p. 97.

9. Cited in ibid., p. 98.

10. Rian Malan, *My Traitor's Heart: A South African Exile Returns to Face His Country, His Tribe, and His Conscience* (New York: Atlantic Monthly Press, 1990), p. 333. For black-on-black violence, see pp. 323–334.

11. For details, see ibid., pp. 264–266.

12. World Bank, *World Development Report, 1989* (Washington, D.C.: World Bank, 1989), pp. 165, 167, and 179, has the following figures: the percentage of average annual growth rate, 1965–1987, stood at a mere 0.6 percent; the average rate of inflation, 1980–1987, was 13.8 percent. During the years 1980–1987, there was a decline in average annual growth rate in industry and manufacturing of –0.1 and –0.5, respectively. Gross domestic investment, 1980–1987, declined by 7.3 percent.

13. Peter Honey, "De Klerk Sworn In, Promises 'Totally Changed' S. Africa," *Baltimore Sun*, September 21, 1989.

14. Floyd Norris, "Hopes Run High for South Africa," *New York Times*, February 6, 1990, p. D10.

15. Between 1980 and 1992, the black population increased from 18 million to 28 million, whereas that of whites declined from 6 million to 5.5 million. The black-white ratio was more than five to one; by the late 1990s, it was six to one.

16. "Mandela's Address: 'Glory and Hope,'" *New York Times*, May 11, 1994, p. A8.

17. Tina Rosenberg, "Recovering from Apartheid," *The New Yorker*, November 18, 1996, pp. 86–95.

13

South America: Oscillation Between Military and Civilian Rule

Latin America embraces the thirteen countries of the South American continent, the seven countries that make up Central America, and the various islands that dot the Caribbean Sea. In the first part of this chapter, generalizations are made about the entire region of Latin America; then the focus shifts to South America specifically. Central America is taken up in Chapter 14.

Latin America is a part of the Third World and shares many of its features: economic underdevelopment, massive poverty, high population growth rates, widespread illiteracy, political instability, recurrent military coups, dictatorial regimes, intervention by outside powers that seek to further their own causes, and fervent nationalistic pride. A wide range of economic development exists, however, within Latin America. For example, several large nations such as Mexico, Brazil, and Argentina have sustained impressive industrial growth and have attained gross national product (GNP) and standards of living that qualify them as middle-income nations. The causes of Latin American economic and political problems are similar to those of other Third World nations. But unlike most other parts of the Third World, the nations of Latin America are not newly independent states struggling to meet the challenges of nationhood after World War II. On the contrary, most won their independence from Spain early in the nineteenth century and had experienced almost a century and a half of nationhood by the post–World War II period.

■ THE COLONIAL HERITAGE

But if Latin America's colonial experience lies in the distant past, it still conditions the present, much as other Third World nations are conditioned by their colonial past. The legacy of Spanish rule has persisted over the centuries and is still embodied in the culture and social fabric of Latin

American countries. They inherited from their distant Spanish past complex multiracial societies with pronounced social cleavages between a traditional aristocracy and the underprivileged lower classes. The prosperous and privileged elite, mainly the white descendants of the European conquerors, preserved for themselves vast wealth and power and have thoroughly dominated the remainder of the population—which consists mainly of mestizos (racially mixed peoples), native Indians, descendants of black slaves imported from Africa, and newer immigrants from Europe. The traditional social structure continued to influence political and economic patterns, even in the post–World War II period.

The great gulf between the privileged class, whose tight aristocracy may be thought of as an oligarchy, and the dispossessed lower classes is best seen in the landholding patterns in Latin America. Nowhere in the world is the disparity in land ownership as great. Traditionally, in Latin America over two-thirds of the agricultural land was owned by only 1 percent of the population. The *latifundio,* huge estates owned by the elite, are so large—often over a thousand acres—that they cannot be fully cultivated; as a result, much of that land lies fallow. One 1966 study revealed that in Chile and Peru, for example, 82 percent of the agricultural land was *latifundio,* and that the average size of the *latifundio* was well over 500 times larger than the *minifundio,* the small farms of most farmers.[1] *Minifundio* were often too small to provide subsistence even for small families. In Ecuador and Guatemala, for example, nine out of ten farms were too small to feed a family with two working adults. Moreover, in many Latin American countries the majority of the rural population owned no land; they were peons whose labor was exploited by the owners of the *latifundio.*

Even after years of land reform efforts, the imbalance remained. Another study of the 1960s showed that on the one hand, about 70 percent of the land was owned by the mere 1.5 percent of landowners whose farms were over 2,000 acres; on the other hand, only 3.7 percent of the agricultural land was in the hands of that 73 percent of farmers whose farms were smaller than 8 acres.[2] Among Latin American countries, only Mexico (after the revolution of 1910) and Nicaragua (after the Sandinistas came to power in 1979) carried out anything resembling genuine land reform. Some of the other countries enacted modest land reform programs, but they were hardly implemented; consequently, very little agricultural land was redistributed.

Many of Latin America's persistent economic problems stem from this inequity of land ownership and its inherent inefficiencies. The inequity is the direct cause of the dreadful poverty throughout rural Latin America, and the wastefulness of the *latifundio* is a major cause of the failure of Latin American agriculture to meet the food needs of its people. Other reasons include the primitive methods of farming and use of the best land to raise crops for export. Consequently, Latin America imported an increasing amount of foodstuffs, and the high cost of such imports had a baleful effect on the economies of the region. Moreover, the depressed state of agriculture and the impoverishment of the rural population militated against industrial development because the majority of the people were too impoverished to be consumers of manufactured products.

■ "YANQUI IMPERIALISM"

The colonial heritage is but one of two major outside influences on the economic and political life of contemporary Latin America; the other is the "Colossus of the North," the United States. Ever since Spain left the continent in the early 1800s, the United States has cast its long shadow over its neighbors to the south and has especially been a dominant force in Latin American affairs in the twentieth century. In many ways, the role played by United States in Latin America has been analogous to that played by European colonial powers in other parts of the Third World. Whereas the nationalism of Asian and African countries has been directed against their former European colonial masters, nationalism in Latin America has characteristically focused on "Yanqui imperialism," an emotive term referring to the pattern of U.S. (Yankee) domination and interference in Latin America.

With the Monroe Doctrine of 1823, the United States claimed for itself a special role in the Western Hemisphere as the protector of the weaker countries to the south. Early in the twentieth century, Washington extended its claim with the Roosevelt Corollary, by which it asserted the right to intervene in Latin American countries to maintain political order. By the 1920s, the corollary had been invoked several times, and a pattern of military intervention to prop up tottering regimes and protect U.S. investments was firmly set. Inevitably, Latin American leaders bristled with fear and resentment at "Yanqui" interventionism. The strains in U.S.–Latin American relations were somewhat ameliorated, however, by President Franklin Roosevelt's "good neighbor" policy and by the exigencies of World War II during which the two cooperated as allies.

After the war, Washington sought to strengthen its bonds with Latin American countries by plying them with military and economic aid, taking the lead in forming an organization for regional collective security, and making bilateral defense agreements. Latin leaders welcomed U.S. aid but were disappointed at being left out of the generous Marshall Plan, which pumped far greater amounts of aid into European allies of the United States. Meanwhile, Washington's increasing preoccupation with the Cold War gave its hemispheric relations a distinct anti-Communist ideological cast; consequently, it pressured Latin American governments to cut ties with the Soviet Union and outlaw local Communist parties, and it altered its aid program to give greater priority to bolstering the armies in Latin

American countries than to economic development. Whereas Latin American military leaders stood to gain by this shift, politicians, who were generally more interested in economic assistance—especially in modern technology—had misgivings. The United States, however, became all the more vigilant in its Latin American policy as a result of Cuba's turn to Communism in 1959 under Fidel Castro.

Thus, Latin American leaders were placed in a bind; although they sought to reduce their dependence on their powerful neighbor to the north, they still needed its economic assistance. The United States readily exploited that need, for it had long understood the utility of economic aid as an effective tool for achieving political ends. The dollar dangled before needy governments was more effective and less likely to prompt outcries than military intervention. Political use of economic aid caused friction only when the political aims of the United States were contrary to those of Latin governments. Generally, democratic leaders in Latin America were willing to accept U.S. aid programs directed at fostering democracy as well as economic growth, and generally, Washington professed such aims. And when an economic aid package was as generous as President Kennedy's 1961 Alliance for Progress program, Latin leaders were eager to accept it, even with its political and military components.

The Alliance for Progress offered $20 billion to Latin American governments over ten years if they instituted fundamental social and economic reforms, including land reform, and developed counterinsurgency programs designed to thwart Cuban-type revolutionary movements. Despite the initial enthusiasm for this program, it eventually proved a failure. The Alliance produced increased financial dependency and indebtedness of Latin American countries, confusion over priorities (social reform, relief to the poverty-stricken, industrial projects, and others), and political and administrative confusion (would aid be administered before, during, or after a reform program was undertaken?).

Direct governmental aid was but one level of increased U.S. influence in the Southern Hemisphere. In addition, corporate U.S. business interests continued to invest heavily, buying Latin American land, mines, and oil fields; establishing industries (exploiting cheap labor); and selling arms. As a consequence, in Brazil, for example, in the 1960s thirty-one of the fifty-five largest business firms were owned by foreigners, mainly from the United States. In the 1970s, eight of the ten largest firms and 50 percent of the banks in Argentina were foreign-owned.[3] U.S. business interests assumed that, as in the past, the U.S. flag followed the dollar, and they lobbied for and expected U.S. diplomacy to protect their investments. Business interests usually coincided with Washington's ideological and strategic interests insofar as both gave priority to the maintenance of political stability and the suppression of revolutionary movements that threatened their investments. If support for military dictators were deemed necessary to achieve these ends, the dictators would be supported. If political intervention—overt or covert—were deemed necessary, intervention would occur.

■ ECONOMIC AND POLITICAL PATTERNS

Industrialization became an obsession for many Latin American countries after World War II, and the postwar industrial progress of several of the larger countries was indeed impressive. Governments began playing an important role in this endeavor, investing in heavy industry, erecting high import tariffs, and fostering industrialization in other ways. Argentina particularly exhibited a strong economic nationalism aimed at ending foreign dependency. Industrial progress was, however, limited to only a few countries (Argentina, Brazil, and Mexico accounted for 80 percent of Latin America's industrial output in the late 1960s) and to just a few cities in those countries, with most industry concentrated in Buenos Aires, São Paulo, and Mexico City.

In addition to the problems incurred by this imbalance, the postwar industrial surge was stymied by a number of serious problems. In general, the new industries were mainly import-substitution industries, designed to produce consumer goods that had once needed to be imported; as such, they depended on a growing domestic market, which failed to develop—mainly because the majority of the population lacked purchasing power. Moreover, even the larger industrializing countries lacked sufficient capital and soon found themselves again relying heavily on foreign investments. By the early 1960s, they had become even more dependent on outside sources—mainly the United States—for capital, technology, and markets.

Although industrial growth did produce higher GNP figures and contributed to a modest increase in the standard of living, it also produced frustration as it failed to meet expectations. It contributed to the growth of the middle class and an urban working class, both of which sought a larger share of the nations' wealth and a larger role in the political process. The middle class, which found political expression through political parties, provided support for democratic governments. The growth of the middle class was stunted, however, by lagging industrial growth, and it remained too weak politically to challenge the traditional landowning elite. The attempts of the middle class to institute meaningful social and political change—for example, land reform—through democratic reforms were frustrated by the entrenched oligarchy and the military; nor was it able to protect democratically elected governments. Indeed, the middle class could often do little better than to acquiesce to the status quo and ape the social status of the traditional elite.

SOUTH AMERICA

The new urban working class grew in size but remained largely impoverished. It sought to advance its cause for higher wages through both trade unions and political parties. The growing radicalism of organized labor, however, tended to arouse fears of the middle class and caused it to side with the more conservative elements: the traditional oligarchy and the military.

Given the frailties of the middle class, the entrenchment of the oligarchy, the lack of political involvement of the impoverished rural masses, and the potential radicalism of the growing labor class, it was little wonder that democratic governments never became firmly rooted in Latin America. They became all the more vulnerable when they failed both to achieve promised economic development after World War II and to lift their countries from economic dependency. Thus, having proved unable either to meet the rising expectations of their people or to quell growing unrest, democratically elected governments were often ripe for military takeover.

Military intervention in politics has a long history in Latin America. Since World War II, there have been scores of military coups, and in one short span of less than three years (1962–1964) eight countries fell victim to military takeovers. The military in Latin America, with few foreign wars to fight, tended to assume a domestic role as the guardian of the state. Officers, traditionally nationalistic and conservative, could be counted on to defend the status quo and maintain order. Military rule was reinforced by still another enduring legacy: authoritarian rule by a strongman. Latin America saw a number of powerful, charismatic demagogues such as Getulio Vargas of Brazil and Juan Perón of Argentina.

The political pattern of postwar Latin America, with its pendulum swings from civilian to military rule, begs certain questions: Is social revolution a necessary condition for the achievement of democracy and economic development? Or to put it another way, can democratic government and economic modernization occur without causing a degree of social and political disruption unacceptable to the stubborn oligarchy and the military? And what of the middle class, which has yet to exhibit either the will or the power to bring significant social change to Latin American countries? Or is the military itself capable of being the agent of social reform? By examining more closely the postwar political experiences of selected South American countries—Argentina, Brazil, Chile, and Peru—we see variations of the pattern of alternating civilian and military rule in particular national settings.

☐ Argentina

Postwar Argentina went through four distinct political phases: a decade of the dictatorship of Juan Perón, a decade-long experiment in democratic government, seventeen years of military dictatorship, and a new period with the return to democracy in 1983. The rule of Perón was rather distinctive, for it simultaneously contained elements of populism, dictatorship, capitalism, and national socialism. Perón, a former army officer, was elected to the presidency of Argentina in 1946 largely on the strength of the votes of the working class, whose support he had cultivated in his previous post as labor minister. Perón's nationalistic policies aimed at ridding his country of foreign domination and attaining Argentine self-sufficiency were initially fairly successful; as a result, his popularity soared. He bought out foreign businesses, created a government board for marketing agricultural produce, subsidized industrial development, extended social services, expanded education, and strengthened labor's rights. Meanwhile, he took steps to greatly increase his personal power by impeaching the Supreme Court, enacting a new constitution that broadened the powers of the president, and purchasing the support of the army by vastly increasing the military budget. He also benefited from the immense popularity of his wife, Eva Perón, who was given a large budget for building hospitals and schools and dispensing food and clothing to the needy.

Perón's economic program, however, began to sputter by 1950, and within a year he was confronted with an economic crisis marked by falling agricultural and industrial production, wage reductions, worker layoffs, and runaway inflation. In response to the economic woes and protests, Perón became more dictatorial, silencing the press and political opposition. Frustrated by his loss of public support (occasioned in part by the death of Eva in 1952) and the mounting economic chaos, he became more erratic. Perón feuded with the Roman Catholic Church, which caused him a still greater loss of support.[4] Finally, in September 1955, the military, too, abandoned him and forced him into exile.

The army made good its promise to restore democracy but only after struggling for over two years to root out Peronistas from the government, the army itself, and the powerful General Confederation of Labor (CGT). The Peronista constitution was scrapped, the Peronista Party was outlawed, and its leaders were arrested. Elections were held in February 1958, and a democratically elected president, Arturo Frondizi, took office. His government inherited a politically fragmented country with a still bankrupt, inflation-ridden economy. Although Perón himself remained in exile in Spain for the next seventeen years, he continued to cast a shadow over Argentine politics, and his Peronista Party—although officially outlawed—remained a force to be reckoned with, as did the CGT, which was still dominated by Peronistas. So strong were the Peronistas that only by wooing them was Frondizi able to stay in power. But Frondizi's economic policies, specifically his invitation to foreign interests to take control of the stalled oil industry, provoked a nationalistic outcry, especially from the Peronistas. All the while, his relations with the military were strained, and when he began to look to the left for support, a section of army leaders known as the *gorillas* began to stir. In desperate need of support during the 1962 election, Frondizi tried once again to enlist Peronista support by legalizing the Peronista Party. The result was a smashing electoral victory for the Peronistas. The army, however, rejected this verdict, seized power once again, arrested Frondizi, and again banned the Peronistas.

A similar round of events followed. A newly elected president found it necessary to curry favor with the Peronistas, ultimately legalizing their party, only to be unseated by them in the next election (1965); this was followed by the inevitable military coup in June 1966. Thus began an extended period of military dictatorship in Argentina. The military regime—headed first by Gen. Juan Carlos Ongania—ruled by fiat, arrested the Peronistas and other political dissenters, muzzled the press, controlled the unions, and imposed an economic austerity program to curb inflation and stabilize the economy. This time there were no promises of a return to democracy. But as the economic malaise continued and political disorders broke out, General Ongania was forced aside by other generals, who proved no more successful.

The parade of military rulers was broken in 1972 by none other than Juan Perón, whose regenerated party once again won an electoral victory. Perón's return was triumphant, but the Perón spell was insufficient to remedy the country's economic ills. He died in office in July 1974, leaving power in the hands of his third wife, Isabel, who was also his vice-president. But she, too, proved unequal to the immense task of governing this troubled nation, and in 1976 her government was overthrown when the army again stepped in.

The new military regime, headed by Gen. Jorge Rafael Videla, was more ruthless than any of its predecessors. Determined to force compliance with its dictates and to eliminate terrorism and political disorders caused mainly by leftists, the regime imposed a reign of terror that not only filled the jails but also took many lives. The army engaged in a witch-hunt against its political enemies, rounding them up by the thousands and killing them—sometimes pushing them off airplanes over the Atlantic Ocean. Nearly 10,000 Argentines were killed or simply "disappeared." Meanwhile, inflation continued, and the standard of living declined. As if to draw people's attention from their woes and arouse their patriotism, in 1982 the militarists took the nation to war in defense of Argentina's historical claim to the Falkland Islands (a British possession known in Argentina as the Malvinas), located some 300 miles off its coast. The costly defeat suffered by the Argentine forces at the hands of the British further discredited the military; consequently, it was forced to call elections and relinquish power to a new civilian government in October 1983.

Argentina's new president, Raul Alfonsín, head of the Radical Party, was the first to defeat the Peronistas in an open election, and his election was considered a mandate to restore order and civility to the country. Cautiously, Alfonsín set in motion criminal proceedings against his military predecessors. He put the junta leaders on trial, and those convicted of various crimes committed in the "dirty war" were sentenced to long jail terms. In one stroke, Alfonsín succeeded in retiring fifty generals. Several years later, however, in what he called an "act of reconciliation," he declared a general amnesty. Alfonsín's successor, Carlos Menem, had initially opposed the amnesty, but once in power, Menem went so far as to side with the military when the courts decided the state must pay compensation to the relatives of the victims the military had murdered. The military clearly remained a force to be reckoned with.

Alfonsín had to face an even greater challenge, one that had doomed all of his predecessors—to reverse the downward slide of the Argentine economy. In this effort he was less successful. He inherited an economy with one of the world's highest rates of inflation and highest debts. At the end of Alfonsín's presidency in 1989, the inflation rate was far worse—estimated at an incredible 7,000 percent annually—and the debt crisis remained unresolved. A dramatic economic turnaround came under Menem, who was elected in July 1989. The primary cause of this change in fortunes was the convertibility plan instituted in April 1991 by Menem's economic minister, Domingo Cavallo. This plan, in which the Argentine currency would be backed by the nation's U.S. dollar reserves, together with government retrenchment and the sale of government property (the telephone system, airlines, and so on) brought fiscal solvency, economic stability, a restructuring of Argentina's foreign debt, and new credit from the International Monetary Fund (IMF). By the mid-1990s, Argentina was registering a growth rate of 7 percent.

☐ Brazil

Brazil stands out among the nations of South America in part because of its Portuguese background but even more because of its immense size. In both population (150 million in 1990) and size (one-third of the continent), it dwarfs the other nations of South America. Brazil's vast resources and economic potential make it a giant among them. The political pattern in Brazil, however, has been strikingly similar to that of other South American countries. Its problems are also similar: the quest for industrialization while trying to meet the demands of militant workers for higher wages; and the flagrant inequality of land ownership, with its inherent waste and oppression of the peasantry.

Brazil, like Argentina, experimented with democracy (after a long rule by a charismatic dictator); when democratically elected governments proved unable to cope with economic decline and popular unrest, they gave way to military leaders who used harsh methods to tackle these problems.

In both Argentina and Brazil, military rule lasted from the mid-1960s to the early 1980s and finally yielded to popular pressure for the return to democracy. The major difference between the two countries' experiences was that the Brazilian military regimes proved somewhat more successful in dealing with economic problems.

Brazil was led by the paternalistic dictator Getulio Vargas from 1930 to 1945. Vargas had done much to centralize political power in the nation and to promote industrial growth, and under his rule the middle class grew in size. His regime became increasingly dictatorial as he sought to quash both rightist and leftist movements; by the end of World War II, the nation—especially the middle class—demanded liberalization. In October 1945, the military ousted Vargas and scheduled elections. Most of the candidates for president were former officials in the Vargas regime, and the most conservative of those candidates, Gen. Eurico Dutra, was elected. His five-year administration hardly represented a clean break with the past; it enacted a conservative constitution and made no attempt to institute social reform. The administration's economic policies of heavy government borrowing and spending were ruinous, causing a huge trade deficit and serious inflation. An election victory in 1950 returned Vargas to power, but his presidency proved no more successful in solving the economic problems. His austerity program slowed inflation only slightly, and it did so at the cost of the support of the urban workers whose wages were held down. But the main opposition to his government came from the military. In August 1954, when the army demanded that Vargas step down, he committed suicide.

The new president, Juscelino Kubitschek, aggressively pursued the goal of economic modernization in Brazil with lavish spending programs. His most extravagant project was the founding of a spectacular new capital city, Brasilia, located in the interior of the country. This project was designed to spur the development of the interior region, stimulate national pride, and divert attention from the ever more serious problems of high inflation and national debt. Kubitschek was defeated in the 1960 election largely because of the worsening economic conditions, but his successor, Janio Quadras, fared no better. After only seven months in office, Quadras resigned when his austerity measures met bitter opposition from many groups, including the military, who railed against the budget cuts.

Brazil's new president, João Goulart, brought a fresh approach to the nation's problems, for unlike any of his predecessors, he attempted fundamental reforms. Goulart proposed extensive land reform, election reform to enfranchise the nation's illiterate (40 percent of the population), and a tax reform to increase government revenues. When Congress blocked his reforms, he tried to achieve them through presidential decree. In March 1964, Goulart ordered the expropriation of certain types of the nation's largest estates. Such programs earned him the support of the peasantry and the working class but incurred the wrath of the landowning elite, the middle class, and the military. Goulart also proclaimed a neutralist foreign policy, established diplomatic relations with the Soviet Union, legalized the Brazilian Communist Party, and began to woo that party's support. This shift to the left in both domestic and foreign policy placed him in even greater difficulty with conservative elements. He overplayed his hand when he supported efforts of enlisted personnel in the armed services to unionize and granted amnesty to several who had been found guilty of mutiny. Goulart's free-spending policies, like those of Kubitschek, caused runaway inflation, and this, too, resulted in an erosion of support from the middle class. Army leaders, who had secured U.S. support in advance, forced his resignation in April 1964.

This time the military came to stay; military officers governed Brazil with a heavy hand for the next twenty years. Blaming civilian politicians (especially the cashiered left-leaning Goulart) for all of Brazil's ills, the military was determined to purge them from the government, silence all opposition, and force its austerity program on the nation. The new ruling junta (a military group in power after overthrowing a government) banned the Communist Party and carried out mass arrests of suspected Communists. The junta then issued a series of "institutional acts" that incrementally restricted the powers of the Congress, arrogated greater powers to the presidency, disenfranchised politicians and their parties, repressed political freedoms, and crushed the labor unions. Brazil moved steadily toward totalitarian government; the strong-arm methods were relaxed only slightly in the 1970s.

Repression tends to breed revolutionary violence, for when legal opposition is suppressed, only illegal and violent means of opposition are possible. The polarization of Brazilian politics began before the military came to power, but with military rule the struggle between the entrenched right and the outlawed left became nasty and brutal, as in Argentina. (To the extent that the military rulers were engaged in a battle to quash Communist terrorism, they had the blessings and material support of the United States.)

Still, the Brazilian economy responded to the stringent austerity program, and, in fact, during this phase Brazil realized its highest economic growth rates. In 1966, Brazil's annual rate of growth of GNP was 4 percent, but this rate rose steadily and reached 10 percent in the early 1970s— a rate higher than any other Latin American country had ever achieved. The growth of both agricultural and industrial production made possible a favorable balance of trade for the first time since World War II. But this economic success story had a dark side. On the one hand, it could not be sustained, partly because of the severe impact of the oil crises of the 1970s and partly because of the gigantic foreign debt the military leaders ran up (a problem discussed in Chapter 14). On the other hand, the growth of the GNP had not produced a higher standard of living for the Brazilian people.

Industrial growth was made possible by keeping wages low, and the rise in the cost of living continued to exceed the growth in wages. In addition, no land reform was undertaken, and nothing was done to improve the lot of the rural poor.

Brazil's first free election in three decades, held in March 1989, was won by a young, winsome, articulate politician who promised democratic reform and economic prosperity, Fernando Collor de Mello. But what he brought to Brazil instead was the largest scale of corruption the country had ever seen. In 1992, his jealous younger brother, Pedro, revealed that the president was involved in a multimillion dollar influence-peddling operation orchestrated by his campaign treasurer. Investigations produced sufficient evidence to warrant impeachment proceedings, which were begun in December 1992. Collor immediately resigned and was succeeded by Vice-President Itamar Franco. The new president put together a multiparty cabinet that instituted reforms aimed at restoring public confidence, warding off the military's intrusion, and stimulating the economy—which was in recession in the early 1990s. Finance Minister Fernando Henrique Cardoso engineered successful monetary reform in 1994 that stopped inflation in its tracks. He also reached an accord with the IMF for a $2.1 billion loan and a rescheduling of Brazil's debt payments, which, in turn, produced a return of capital flow from abroad. In October 1994, Cardoso handily won the presidential election, which was generally considered a referendum on his economic policy.

☐ Chile

In Chile, we see still another variation on the theme of oscillation between civilian and military governments. Military rule in Chile resembled that of Argentina and Brazil in its conservatism and strong-arm methods. Unlike those two countries, however, Chile did not succumb to military rule until the 1970s. Until then, democracy had prevailed; the army had stayed out of politics until 1973, when it entered with a vengeance. As historian Arthur Whitaker pointed out, "Chile's political system was the most orderly and democratic in Latin America from World War II to 1970," and until then "the Chilean armed forces were exceptionally apolitical by Latin American standards."[5]

Chile also stood out as one of the most flagrant examples of U.S. interference in South America to further the ideological and strategic objectives of the United States, not to mention its business interests. Nowhere in South America were U.S. business interests more substantial. Since early in the twentieth century, Chile had been the main source of copper for the United States, and its copper mines and many of its industries were owned by U.S. firms. Thus, when Chilean politics moved further to the left, more than conservative elements within Chile were alarmed. Washington would not sit still as another Latin American country, especially one as economically and strategically important as Chile, edged closer to Communism.

In 1964, the presidential election in Chile was a contest between two left-of-center candidates who sought to succeed Jorge Alessandri. Eduardo Frei, head of the Christian Democratic Party, campaigned for extensive reforms and defeated the Marxist Salvador Allende, the candidate of a leftist coalition. Frei's campaign was supported by the United States (which employed the CIA to that end) and Chilean conservatives, both of which sought to head off an electoral victory by Allende. Frei's administration instituted moderate agrarian reform, fostered industrial development, expanded the education program to reduce illiteracy, and advanced the government's social services. Under Frei, Chile received generous amounts of Alliance for Progress aid, which financed industrial expansion but also greatly increased the nation's indebtedness. Frei's gradualist reform program was opposed as too radical by the Chilean elite and conservative parties, and it drew fire from the working class and the parties on the left for being too modest. Only the middle class and Washington seemed happy with the plan.

The polarization of Chilean politics was evident in the 1970 election. The battle lines were drawn between the conservative Alessandri on the right and Allende, who again headed a leftist coalition known as Popular Unity. (Frei was ineligible for a second six-year term, and his party's candidate was not a strong contender.) Allende squeaked by with a narrow victory and became the world's first freely elected Marxist head of state. Allende, whose cabinet consisted mainly of socialists and Communists, called for a peaceful transition to socialism. He went right to work to achieve that end, nationalizing both U.S. and Chilean copper and nitrate companies, many other industries, and banks; extending the land reform begun by Frei; and placing a ceiling on prices while raising workers' wages. These measures were immensely popular with the great majority of people in Chile, but they alarmed Allende's opponents, as well as policy makers in Washington. Spurred by his initial success and by the Communists in his government, Allende pushed on to even more radical reforms. Initially, Allende had the tentative support of the military, but his efforts to retain its loyalty were frustrated by the worsening economic problems and the political strife stirred by his policies.

Ultimately, Allende's regime failed for both economic and political reasons. Chile was already in a depression caused by declining copper prices when Allende took office. By the second year of his term, the economy was in a tailspin, with inflation running out of control. To a considerable extent, Allende's policies had contributed to these problems, but the major blow to the Chilean economy was a drastic fall in the international price of copper. By mid-1972, the economy was in dire straits, and Allende's base of support had dwindled to little more than the working class and the poor. The middle class and other conservative elements began organizing in opposition to Allende and carried out such actions as a crippling nationwide trucking industry strike, an action that was secretly supported with CIA funds. The polarization of the nation became extreme, and a violent clash seemed imminent. Allende and his Communist supporters began arming workers, and the army began plotting a coup. That coup took place in September 1973 when the air force bombed the presidential palace, where Allende was gunned down.

The United States was not an innocent bystander in the overthrow of Allende's government. It was involved in efforts to prevent Allende from coming to power in the first place, and, having failed that, it participated in the efforts to destroy his government. President Nixon and National Security Adviser Henry Kissinger treated Allende as a pariah and regarded his regime as a Communist threat to the entire region. The Nixon administration used two levers to force his downfall: it funneled some $8 million through the CIA to Allende's opponents, and it took steps to cut off all loans, economic aid, and private investments to Chile. The administration argued that this was justifiable retaliation for Allende's nationalization of U.S. properties, but these measures clearly amounted to an attempt to economically strangle Allende's government. Some have argued that there was direct U.S. involvement, or at least complicity, in the military coup. But although this appears likely, it is still unproven. The Chilean military officers who led the coup—like many others from Latin American countries—*had* received training at the School for the Americas, a facility in Panama established by the U.S. Army to train Latin American military officers. Washington was, of course, delighted by the coup and quickly came to the support of the new military regime.

The new government, headed by Gen. Augusto Pinochet, swiftly carried out a relentless campaign against leftists and anyone suspected of having been associated with the deposed regime. The military killed thousands and crammed the jails with political prisoners. Pinochet invited back U.S. copper companies, halted the land reform program, broke up labor unions, banned all leftist parties, dissolved Congress, and in general conducted a wholesale attack on civil liberties in the name of national reorganization. His regime steadily became more savage in crushing political opposition as the years went by. Through the 1980s, there was no letup in the strong-arm tactics and no indication of when the military intended to return the country to civilian rule. All the while, the Pinochet government continued to enjoy the support of the United States, which preferred the secure climate for investment and the anti-Communist partnership that government provided over the political instability its overthrow might bring.

Pinochet's authoritarian rule outlawed antigovernment demonstrations, but in the late 1980s thousands of protesters went into the streets to demand political change. Finally, in 1990, Pinochet relented by allowing

Chilean President Salvador Allende, who was slain in the presidential palace during the Sept. 1973 coup. (*Organization of American States*)

Gen. Augusto Pinochet, who led the military coup against Allende in 1973 and remained in power in Chile afterward. (*Organization of American States*)

a referendum on whether military rule should continue. The people voted overwhelmingly to restore civilian rule. The new president, Patricio Aylwin, became Chile's first elected head of state in twenty years. Pinochet, however, remained army commander by virtue of a clause in the constitution he had written preventing the elected president from dismissing him until 1997. The constitution made the armed forces the "guarantor of institutionality";[6] in other words, it gave them the right to step in whenever they felt Chile's interests were threatened.

Aylwin's economic policy, which hewed closely to that of the Pinochet regime by maintaining tight government controls—especially on labor—continued to pay dividends, with increased economic growth and stability. The nation's volume of foreign trade increased steadily, partly as a result of a reevaluation of the Chilean peso and partly because of product diversification. Consequently, Chile boasted one of the highest economic growth rates in the Western Hemisphere in the 1990s.

☐ Peru

Military rule in South America usually meant the reinforcement of the status quo and the forceful suppression of reformist or revolutionary political movements, as seen in the cases of Argentina and Brazil. But Peru was somewhat of an exception. In the 1960s, Peruvian military rulers were the instruments, not the opponents, of social reform and actually took the lead where politicians had failed in combating age-old inequities in Peruvian society.

Perhaps nowhere in South America were those inequities as flagrant as in Peru. A very small, very wealthy elite kept the Peruvian masses—mainly of native Indian stock—in dismal poverty. About 80 percent of the land was owned by a mere 1 percent of landowners, and the richest owned over 1 million acres. Landless Peruvian peasants sporadically rose in revolt seeking to grasp some of the largely unused lands of the elite, only to be crushed by the Peruvian army, which did the elite's bidding. Neither the early postwar military regime in Peru (1946–1956) nor the two civilian administrations that followed (Manuel Prado, 1956–1962, and Fernando Belaunde, 1963–1968) attempted land reform. All the while, the country was seething with peasant unrest, and a rural-based Communist movement began to spread. In October 1968, President Belaunde's government was floundering amid economic chaos, corruption scandals, and political unrest when the military interceded and expelled him from power.

The new military government, headed by Juan Velasco, rapidly set about introducing state planning and social and economic reforms that were enforced by the army. Most noteworthy was land reform, which within seven years expropriated and redistributed some 25 million acres—about 72 percent of Peru's arable land. The government also undertook a program of land reclamation to increase agricultural output and meet the needs of the land-starved Indians. The Velasco regime also nationalized foreign properties, including U.S.-owned copper, petroleum, and sugar companies. Private enterprise was maintained, but industries were required to share profits with their workers. Although a modest increase in agricultural production resulted from the agrarian reforms, the economy slumped badly, especially after the 1973–1974 oil crisis.

With the economy failing, Velasco was removed from power in a bloodless coup in 1975 and was replaced with a leading member of his cabinet, Gen. Francisco Morales. Morales reversed the government's leftward direction and struggled for the next five years to revive the economy and maintain political order. Finally, the military responded to public pressure for an end to military rule by voluntarily returning power to civilians. The presidential election held in 1980 was won by Belaunde, who had been overthrown in 1968. The political and economic problems he faced were as severe as those he had contended with twelve years earlier. During the military interlude, the reformist military rulers had failed to achieve either a fundamental social transformation or a significant improvement in the standard of living for most Peruvians.

Not until the early 1990s did new leadership emerge to take on the nation's ills—economic stagnation, corruption, political instability, drug traffic, and insurrection. The unlikely winner of the July 1990 presidential election was Alberto Fujimori, an inexperienced politician of Japanese ancestry. When he took office, Peru had not made a payment for two years on its $23 billion debt; the inflation rate was over 40 percent a *month;* political parties had lost credibility; and the central government was unable to govern outlying areas, where hostile guerrillas stalked the countryside. Fujimori first attacked the economic problem. Through such stringent measures as slashing government payrolls and subsidies and overhauling the tax system, he managed to break the inflationary cycle within six months.

The unorthodox Fujimori, who lacked political party backing, formed an alliance with the military. In April 1992, he carried out a stunning political coup—suspending the constitution, closing the assembly, and assuming emergency executive powers. For this he was denounced not only by unseated Peruvian politicians but also by governments throughout the hemisphere. But Fujimori's bold housecleaning measures were popular with most Peruvians, even though they cost the country much-needed foreign aid and slowed economic progress.

Fujimori won greater acclaim at home and abroad by winning a surprising victory in Peru's twelve-year war against the *Sendero Luminoso,* the "Shining Path," a Maoist-Marxist movement that had combined violent revolution with drug trade. His government arrested and sentenced to life in prison the leaders of the Shining Path including its charismatic founder, Abimael Guzman Reynoso, a former philosophy professor. This tenacious insurrectionist movement had organized poverty-stricken peasants to protect them against brutality at the hands of the police and the military and, ultimately, to bring down the government. The result was a civil war with extraordinary brutality on both sides. The guerrilla war had threatened to bankrupt the government, causing an estimated $22 billion in damages and costing 25,000 lives. Fujimori's stunning victory against the revolutionaries, combined with a measure of economic progress, restored Peru's standing internationally and won him considerable popularity within Peru. He handily won reelection in 1994.

Fujimori's restoration of economic and political order came at a price, however. His austerity program benefited only small segments of the population—among them the financial sector and international investors. For the majority, poverty increased dramatically. Two-thirds of Peruvians continued to live in poverty, and real wages fell by 10 percent in 1995. The residents of a desolate slum on the edge of Lima contemptuously named their place of residence "Susana Higuchi," in honor of Fujimori's wife.[7] Fujimori's first task, however, was to meet Peru's financial obligations as spelled out by the IMF and the World Bank, one of the pillars that sustained his regime.

Fujimori had not been the choice of the military generals in the July 1990 election, but the two soon struck a bargain by which the military became Fujimori's other pillar of support. He granted the army broad powers that included a system of "faceless" martial courts to try suspects who were guilty until proven innocent. Throughout, Fujimori continued to present himself as the champion of "true democracy," the spokesman for the common man.[8] In May 1991, the army established a base on the campus of La Cantuta, Peru's leading teacher training university just east of Lima. In December of that year, Fujimori legalized the presence of security forces there. In July 1992, a military death squad operating under the direct orders of government officials and the commander in chief of the army, Gen. Nicolas Hermoza, abducted and murdered nine students and a professor. When the courts convicted and sentenced twelve soldiers, Fujimori, in June 1995, pushed through a pliant Congress a blanket amnesty for those convicted of human rights crimes between May 1980 and June 1995. Among the first to walk free were Hermoza's men who had been convicted of the La Cantuta murders.[9] The amnesty cemented a symbiotic relationship between the president and the chief of the armed forces. Hermoza used Fujimori to assert his authority within the army, and Fujimori used Hermoza to shore up his political power. It was no wonder Hermoza was popularly known in Peru as "the other president." The road to "true democracy" promised to be long and hard.

In December 1996, yet another leftist organization, the Tupac Amaru, which Fujimori claimed had been defeated, resurfaced when it took approximately 400 hostages at a Christmas party hosted by the Japanese ambassador at his residence in Lima. Tupac Amaru aired its grievances against the Peruvian government and demanded the release of its imprisoned comrades, many of whom had been engaged in acts of violence and had been sentenced by Peruvian military tribunals. The hostage crisis continued unresolved into the spring of 1997, in part because the Japanese government insisted on a negotiated settlement. Peruvian commandos ended the standoff in April 1997 when they stormed the building killing all members of the Tupac Amaru who were inside and in the process losing one hostage and two commandos.

■ **LATIN AMERICAN DRUG TRAFFIC**

In the late 1980s, the increasing volume of illicit drugs flowing from South America—particularly to the United States and Western Europe—and the rising level of violence attendant to this drug traffic became a major issue in relations between Washington and several South American countries. In 1989, President Bush proclaimed an all-out war against drugs to be waged both within the United States and in Latin America, aimed at eliminating demand in the former and supply in the latter. Despite the resounding fanfare with which the plan was proclaimed, it had very little success.[10]

The heart of Latin American drug traffic was in Colombia, where several powerful drug cartels managed operations responsible for about 80 percent of the cocaine entering the United States in the late 1980s. Coca plants, from which cocaine is extracted, and marijuana grew abundantly in the equatorial climate of Colombia, Bolivia, and Peru. The farmers on the slopes of the Andes Mountains and in the Amazon Valley were paid far more to grow and harvest these plants than they could possibly have earned from growing food crops. The infusion of drug money was the salvation of farmers and a windfall for local police and politicians, who pointed with pride to the new houses and newly paved roads in their once poverty-stricken towns and villages.

The largest drug operation, the Medellín cartel, was founded in 1981 in the Colombian city of Medellín. The cartel operated like a large multinational corporation with a multibillion dollar business. U.S. Drug Enforcement Agency officials estimated that its profits were as high as $5 billion a year and that tens of thousands of people were on its payroll. It was rivaled by another cartel based in the smaller city of Cali.[11] Both cartels were well prepared to offer enormous bribes to Colombian military, political, and judicial officers to protect their operations; when bribes failed to achieve their purpose, they readily resorted to intimidation and violence.

The Colombian government launched its own war on the drug cartels in August 1989, shortly after presidential candidate Luis Carlos Galán, who had pledged to eradicate the drug cartels, was assassinated by drug thugs. Colombian President Virgilio Barco Vargas ordered military forces into action against the drug cartels, setting their crops ablaze, destroying production facilities, and seizing the homes and properties of several major drug kingpins. The drug cartels, particularly the Medellín, responded with a counteroffensive of terrorism. They carried out hundreds of bombings and gunned down opponents in cold blood. Among their victims were judges and elected officials. In December 1989, they bombed the headquarters of the Department of Security, the agency most involved in the effort to destroy the drug operations. Half a ton of dynamite destroyed the six-story building, killing 52 people and injuring 1,000. The Medellín cartel also claimed responsibility for the bombing of a Colombian jetliner ten days earlier, killing all 107 people aboard. In terms of property and lives lost, the drug cartels appeared to be winning the war in Colombia. Barco's government was, however, able to claim some success, as the flow of drugs from Colombia was reduced—at least temporarily— by about 30 percent in 1990. Also, in January 1990, Colombian security forces killed José Gonzalo Rodríguez Gacha, reputed to be the principal Medellín leader responsible for the recent violence.

A central issue in the drug war within Colombia was the extradition treaty signed with the United States in 1979, according to which a captured Colombian drug boss would be sent to the United States to stand trial. Extradition was the main weapon of the United States and the Colombian government in fighting the drug cartels and it was therefore what the drug lords feared most. In February 1987, Carlos Lehder, a major drug figure, was captured and extradited to the United States, where a year later he was found guilty of drug smuggling and sentenced to life plus 135 years. The drug lords exerted enormous pressure on judges and politicians to overturn the extradition law, in some cases offering them a choice between fantastically large bribes or death. They also attempted to persuade politicians to legalize the drug trade by promising an end to further violence.

In February 1990, U.S. President Bush met with the leaders of Colombia, Peru, and Bolivia at Cartagena on the coast of Colombia. This "Andean Summit" produced a five-year cooperative strategy and provided $2.2 billion in aid to assist these three countries in their fight against the drug cartels. The plan called for raiding cocaine-producing laboratories, destroying airstrips used by drug lords, and seizing their shipments by land, air, and sea.

The war on drugs was stepped up, especially in Colombia, but with mixed results. In a shootout in August 1990, Colombian police killed the Medellín cartel's second in command, Gustavo de Jesús Gaviria Rivero. But his cousin, Pablo Escobar, the most powerful Medellín kingpin, remained at large. In June 1991, Colombian authorities happily announced they had taken Escobar into custody. But all was not what it seemed, for Escobar had surrendered on his own terms. He had accepted the government's offer to surrender in exchange for both immunity against extradition to the United States, where he was under indictment, and a greatly reduced prison sentence. Moreover, he was allowed to select his own "jail"—a comfortable rural villa in his home province replete with Jacuzzis, fax machines, cellular telephones, computers, and even guns—and to dictate the security arrangements, including selecting his own guards. This arrangement protected Escobar from Colombian police and U.S. prosecutors and allowed him to continue to run his drug empire from "prison."

Then in July 1992, an embarrassed Colombian government reported that Escobar had escaped from prison. For the next year and a half, the renegade drug lord sought desperately to restore his cocaine empire, resorting to attempts to kidnap his former partners, but Colombian police finally cornered and killed him in a shoot-out in December 1993. Escobar's drug-trafficking competitors viewed his death as the elimination of a worthy rival.

The pattern of one step forward and one step back continued in Colombia's drug war. In 1992, the government struck a deal with the Medellín cartel whereby the cartel disbanded its military organization, which had been responsible for killing several hundred civil and police officers and three presidential candidates, and the government rescinded the law for extradition of arrested drug traffickers. Meanwhile, the Cali cartel had moved in to fill whatever void Medellín's problems had created. By the time of Escobar's death, Cali controlled three-quarters of Colombia's cocaine trade with the United States. The size of that trade had not diminished, for in 1993 drug profits in Colombia rose to an estimated $20–$25 billion. Drug trafficking had also increased in neighboring countries, and the drug traffic had a new center of operations in Venezuela, where drug money laundering was masked by a huge oil export business. By 1993, as much as 200 metric tons of cocaine was funneled through Venezuela annually.

In 1994, Colombia elected as president Ernest Samper, a reformist politician who pledged a renewed war on drugs. During his first eighteen months in office, Samper—under increased pressure from the United States—vigorously pursued the war on drugs, arresting six of the seven leaders of the Cali cartel and conducting the most extensive cocaine crop destruction to date. But the drug-busting president was confronted in July 1996 with charges that he had taken some $6 million from the Cali cartel during his presidental campaign in exchange for leniency for arrested traffickers. His accuser was the treasurer of his campaign, and the main evidence consisted of tape recordings confiscated by U.S. drug enforcement officers. Further evidence uncovered by Colombian police in drug raids revealed that the cartel had dispensed a total of $25 million to hundreds of politicians, police officers, and journalists. Samper's defense minister, who had been his campaign manager, was arrested, and a number of other cabinet members and legislators were indicted. Samper, who denied knowledge of money received from drug lords, was eventually exonerated for lack of sufficient evidence by the congressional committee investigating the matter. The crisis continued, however, as an independent chief prosecutor courageously continued the investigation of the charges against the president. Samper persisted in his denials, but with his credibility damaged, his antinarcotics policy—although vigorously pursued—was undermined.

Meanwhile, through the mid-1990s the flow of drugs from Latin America into the United States continued unabated despite the U.S. government's stepped-up interdiction efforts, and drug abuse in the country relentlessly continued to rise.

RECOMMENDED READINGS

Latin America—General

Burns, Bradford. *Latin America: A Concise Interpretive History.* 3d ed. Englewood Cliffs, N.J.: Prentice-Hall, 1982.
Lewis, Paul H. *The Governments of Argentina, Brazil, and Mexico.* New York: Crowell, 1975.
Rosenberg, Tina. *Children of Cain: Violence and the Violent in Latin America.* New York: Penguin, 1991.

Skidmore, Thomas E., and Peter H. Smith. *Modern Latin America.* New York: Oxford University Press, 1984.
Wolf, Eric R., and Edward C. Hansen. *The Human Condition in Latin America.* New York: Oxford University Press, 1974.

South America

Alexander, Robert J. *The Tragedy of Chile.* Westport, Conn.: Greenwood Press, 1978.
    The tragedy is the overthrow of Allende by the militarists.
Alexander, Robert J. *Juan Domingo Perón: A History.* Boulder, Colo.: Westview Press, 1979.
    An authoritative biography of the most important political figure in modern Argentine politics.
Blanco, Hugo. *Land or Death: The Peasant Struggle in Peru.* New York: Pathfinder Press, 1972.
    A longtime revolutionary strongly argues his case for radical land reform.
Burns, E. Bradford. *A History of Brazil.* 2d ed. New York: Columbia University Press, 1980.
Valenzuela, Arturo. *The Breakdown of Democratic Regimes: Chile.* Baltimore: Johns Hopkins University Press, 1978.
    Strongly critical of the militarist intervention in Chile.
Wesson, Robert. *The United States and Brazil: Limits of Influence.* New York: Frederick A. Praeger, 1981.
Whitaker, Arthur P. *The United States and the Southern Cone: Argentina, Chile, and Uruguay.* Cambridge, Mass.: Harvard University Press, 1976.

NOTES

1. Paul Harrison, *Inside the Third World: The Anatomy of Poverty,* 2nd ed. (New York: Penguin, 1984), cites a survey by the Inter-American Commission for Agricultural Development, pp. 108–109.

2. Richard P. Schaedel, "Land Reform Studies," *Latin American Research Review,* Fall 1965, p. 85.

3. E. Bradford Burns, *Latin America: A Concise Interpretive History,* 3d ed. (Englewood Cliffs, N.J.: Prentice-Hall, 1982), p. 214.

4. Perón was angered by the Catholic Church's refusal to canonize Eva as a saint. The church, in turn, opposed his efforts to require the teaching in schools of his ideology, which deified the state and himself as its head. Perón accused the church of organizing a mass movement against him and responded by censoring Catholic newspapers, arresting priests, and forbidding church processions. Pope Pius XII retaliated by excommunicating Perón.

5. Arthur P. Whitaker, *The United States and the Southern Cone: Argentina, Chile, and Uruguay* (Cambridge, Mass.: Harvard University Press, 1976), pp. 301, 309.

6. Tina Rosenberg, "Force Is Forever," *New York Times Magazine,* September 24, 1995, p. 46.

7. Simon Strong, "Where the Shining Path Leads," *New York Times Magazine,* May 24, 1992, p. 16.

8. Guillermo Rochabrun, "The *De Facto* Powers Behind Fujimori's Regime," *NACLA Report on the Americas*, July–August 1996, pp. 22–23. For the impact of economic reform on the population at large, see Manuel Castillo Ochoa, "Fujimori and the Business Class: A Prickly Partnership," in the same publication, pp. 25–30.

9. Enrique Obando, "Fujimori and the Military: A Marriage of Convenience," in ibid., pp. 31–36; also "Anatomy of a Cover-Up: The Disappearances at La Cantuta," a summary of a report by Human Rights Watch/Americas, in ibid., pp. 34–35.

10. For a scorching criticism of President Bush's war on drugs, see Lewis H. Lapham, "A Political Opiate: The War on Drugs Is a Folly and a Menace," *Harper's*, December 1989, pp. 43, 48.

11. Medellín was the main supplier of drugs to Miami, and Cali had control of the cocaine traffic in New York City until the fall of 1988 when the Medellín dealers invaded the drug market in New York City, touching off an underground drug war.

14

Revolution and Counterrevolution in Central America

The twentieth century has been one of extraordinary violence, death, and destruction. It has witnessed the most devastating wars in history; it has also been an age of unmatched revolutionary upheavals, often produced by a leftist challenge to the status quo.

Central America was no exception to this pattern of revolutions. Political struggles, recurrent since the days of colonial occupation, resurfaced with a vengeance during the 1970s and attracted worldwide attention. The conflicts in Latin America between the left and the right became a focus in the global struggle between the United States and the Soviet Union. Deep social divisions fueled Central America's revolutions. On one side were the landowners, who enjoyed political power and had the backing of the army. Opposing them was the majority of the population, which owned little land, had few political rights, and was generally impoverished.

Students of revolutionary movements are well aware that the side that commands the loyalty of the army will ultimately hold power. In Central America, those in power have generally been able to call on the army. A notable exception took place in Cuba in the late 1950s, when the dictator Fulgencio Batista found that at the end he had little support in the army—not to mention among the population—and in 1959 Fidel Castro took Havana by default. The army, from whose ranks Batista had risen to power, ultimately had no desire to save his corrupt regime. But this case was the exception to the rule. In El Salvador in 1932, General Hernández massacred 30,000 campesinos (field workers) and effectively eradicated whatever revolutionary movement existed in that country. More recent instances of intervention by the military in Latin America took place in 1954 in Guatemala, when the army overthrew the reformist government of Jacobo Arbenz, and in 1973 in Chile, when Augusto Pinochet murdered Salvador Allende. In each case, the armed forces determined the political fate of the nation. And in the cases of Chile and Guatemala, the armies overthrew democratically elected governments.

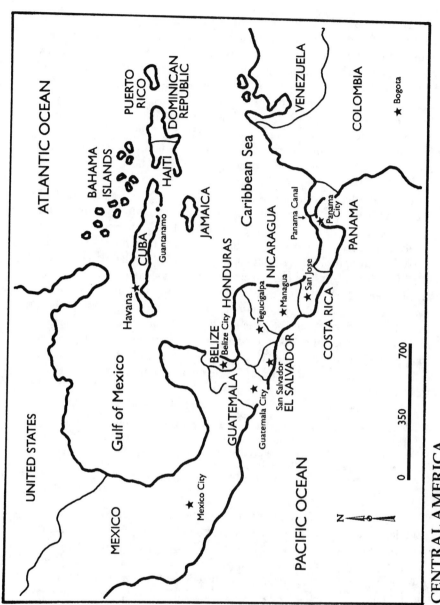

CENTRAL AMERICA

Direct U.S. involvement in Central America began in the 1890s and increased after the Spanish-American War of 1898, when the United States took on the role of police officer of the Western Hemisphere, especially the Caribbean. The United States, in the words of Teddy Roosevelt, would not permit "chronic wrongdoing" in a region many in the United States considered its "backyard."[1] Successive U.S. administrations repeatedly intervened to suppress political unrest and prop up governments tolerant of a U.S. presence in Central America. The region became a U.S. sphere of influence where the protection of U.S. interests—political, economic, and military—became of paramount concern.

On the official level, the U.S. goal in Central America was always to introduce the local populations to the blessings of democracy. In 1913, President Woodrow Wilson commented that he would "teach the South American republics how to elect good men."[2] But democracy has generally been defined differently in Central America than in the United States. In the United States, the outcome of an election is final, and no one, least of all the military, has the right to circumvent the electoral process. Yet, no one has been able to teach the Central American military to stay out of political affairs. Thus, military dictatorships, rather than democracies, have been the rule there. Also, U.S. attempts to champion the cause of democracy tended to take a back seat to what became the primary quest: political stability and the protection of U.S. interests. In the early 1960s, President John Kennedy, in describing the U.S. dilemma in Central America, offered this explanation:

> There are three possibilities in descending order of preference: a decent democratic regime, a continuation of the Trujillo regime [a right-wing dictatorship in the Dominican Republic] or a Castro regime [a left-wing dictatorship in Cuba]. We ought to aim at the first, but we really can't renounce the second until we are sure that we can avoid the third.[3]

Washington's problem, therefore, was the absence of Kennedy's "decent democratic regimes" in Central America. Successive U.S. administrations had to choose between the likes of a Trujillo or a Castro. The trick, however, was to reconcile the official U.S. creed of political liberty with its support of right-wing dictators who had come to power with the help of the military. Washington, in its quest for stability in the region, justified its support of military regimes by labeling them "democracies." And contrary to its official stance, the U.S. government did little to assist democratically elected, reformist governments such as that of João Goulart in Brazil in the 1960s.

The first significant change in Latin America came with the Cuban revolution of 1959. Fidel Castro, unlike other revolutionaries in Latin America, refused to accept the unequal relationship between his country and the United States, one that dates back to 1898 when the United States seized Cuba from Spain. A large portion of the Cuban economy was in U.S. hands, and the U.S. ambassador to Havana wielded great power. To rectify this condition, Castro insisted on the nationalization (governmental takeover) of U.S. property—with compensation[4]—and the reorganization of the Cuban economy along socialist lines. In addition, Castro worked out a trade agreement with the Soviet Union, trading Cuban sugar for Soviet oil and machinery.

The United States, unaccustomed to such a brazen show of defiance, initiated economic warfare against the Castro regime and broke off diplomatic relations. It then moved to overthrow Castro, which resulted in the fiasco at the Bay of Pigs in 1961 (see Chapter 4). Other attempts followed, but Castro survived and, with the help of the Soviet Union, consolidated his power. The Cuban missile crisis in 1962 led to a U.S. pledge not to invade Cuba, but successive U.S. governments, whether Democratic or Republican, were in no mood to tolerate other radical regimes in their "backyard." One Cuba was enough.

■ NICARAGUA

The next serious outbreak of revolutionary violence in Central America began in Nicaragua during the early 1970s. It came in the wake of a devastating earthquake in 1972 that leveled Managua, the nation's capital. Nicaragua was ruled by the Somoza family, which had come to power in the early 1930s with the help of U.S. marines (an occupation force in Nicaragua, off and on, from 1911 to 1932). President Franklin Roosevelt once remarked that Anastasio Somoza García, the founder of the dynasty, was an "s.o.b., but [he is] our s.o.b."[5] The greed of the Somozas became legendary. Exact figures of their wealth are not available, but when Anastasio Somoza said "Nicaragua is my farm," he was stating a fact. When the last of the Somozas, Anastasio Jr. ("Tachito"), fled the country in 1979, he took with him an estimated $100–$400 million, most of it from the national treasury.

The 1972 earthquake brought into sharp focus the greed of Anastasio Somoza Jr. and the National Guard, his private army. Both had long been involved in the seizure of land and the control of many sectors of the economy—construction kickbacks, prostitution, gambling, taxation. When the devastation hit the capital, all discipline in the National Guard broke down. Rank-and-file soldiers looted publicly; Somoza and his officers did so in private. They handled the foreign contributions for the relief of the earthquake victims, siphoning off large sums of money and selling relief supplies.

By 1974, Somoza had created powerful enemies, including the Roman Catholic Church and the middle class, neither of which had forgiven him for his conduct after the earthquake. In January 1978, Somocista killers assassinated Pedro Joaquín Chamorro, an outspoken critic and the editor of the newspaper *La Prensa*. This act sparked the first mass uprising against Somoza. After Jimmy Carter became president in 1977, the U.S. government officially became the champion of human rights throughout the world. Somoza now stood alone; he could no longer count on the United States to bail him out (although it continued to sell him arms). The National Guard systematically executed thousands, but it was too late. The rebellion gathered in strength; no amount of bloodshed could save Somoza's regime.

The violence in Nicaragua was brought home to the U.S. public in June 1979 when the National Guard arrested ABC newsman Bill Stewart, forced him to kneel, and executed him. Stewart's camera crew recorded the murder on film, and hours later the scene was reproduced on U.S. television screens. Only then did the Carter administration cut off arms sales to Somoza's government.

A month later, in July 1979, Somoza fled, leaving behind a devastated country. The death toll was between 40,000 and 50,000, 20 percent of the population was homeless, and 40,000 children were orphaned. The industrial base was in ruins. The Somocistas had plundered the country, leaving behind a foreign debt of $1.5 billion.

In Somoza's place, the Sandinistas, a coalition of revolutionaries, seized power. The Sandinistas had taken their name from the revolutionary Augusto Sandino, whom the first Somoza had murdered nearly fifty years previously. The United States did not intervene in the civil war, despite the fact that the administrations of Presidents Gerald Ford and Jimmy Carter did not like the leftist orientation of the Sandinistas. In the late 1970s, the U.S. public, after the withdrawal from Vietnam, had no inclination to attempt the suppression of another revolutionary movement. Eventually, Carter provided a modest amount of foreign aid to the Sandinistas to retain a bit of leverage in the internal politics of Nicaragua. But the Nicaraguan revolution, to the dismay of Washington, continued to shift to the left and came into conflict with its own middle class. Shortly before he left office in January 1981, a disillusioned Carter suspended all economic aid to the Sandinistas.

The Sandinistas then proceeded to solidify their position and established a new order that included the nationalization of land, press censorship, political prisoners, the nationalization of segments of industry, a militarized government, and a restricted electoral process. But it also included extended health care for the population, a fair measure of freedom of speech, a literacy campaign, the redistribution of land, and an economy of which half remained in private hands. In short, the Sandinista government became a typical example of a revolution seeking to consolidate its power while at the same time seeking to resolve the nation's most pressing social and economic problems.

The war of nerves between Washington and Managua escalated in 1981, after President Ronald Reagan was sworn in. Reagan canceled all aid to Nicaragua and launched an ideological war, as well as covert CIA actions, against the Sandinistas—who had become an affront and an obsession to him and his first secretary of state, Alexander Haig. The Sandinistas had committed the unpardonable sin of becoming recipients of aid from the Communist states of Eastern Europe, notably the Soviet Union (but also from West European states such as France and West Germany). In this fashion, the Sandinistas had reversed Nicaragua's traditional dependence on Washington. And prior to March 1981, they had even sent a small amount of arms to the leftist rebels in neighboring El Salvador. In the eyes of the Reagan administration, the Sandinistas had become a spearhead of Soviet expansionism in the Caribbean.

The CIA then proceeded to organize and arm the Contras, the counterrevolutionary opponents of the Sandinistas. Headed by former members of the National Guard—Somoza's army—the Contras were tainted by their past association with Somoza and, therefore, had little support in Nicaragua. Reagan had a difficult time selling his assistance of the Contras to Congress and the U.S. public, who were leery of being drawn into another civil war in a land of which they knew little. But when Daniel Ortega, the dominant figure in the Sandinista government, flew to Moscow seeking economic aid, the links between Moscow and Managua became closer. Up to that point, the Soviets had provided only military aid. Congress reacted to Nicaragua's tightening of its ties with Moscow by approving financial assistance to the Contras, but that aid was to be used only for "humanitarian"

Daniel Ortega, Sandinista leader and one-time president of Nicaragua. (*Organization of American States*)

rather than military purposes. As Reagan had promised earlier in the year, the screws were going to be tightened until the Sandinistas "cried uncle."

In reaction to the Reagan administration's military solution, the so-called Contadora group—Mexico, Panama, Colombia, and Venezuela—called for a political settlement. The Contadora group, which was named for an island off the coast of Panama where its representatives initially met in September 1983, called for a mutual disengagement of all foreign advisers and soldiers—Cuban, Soviet, and U.S.—from Central America. In short, the group sought the political neutralization of the region. The Contadora group pointed out the counterproductive nature of Washington's Central American containment program: the Salvadoran revolutionaries had tripled their forces since 1981, and the Sandinista army had doubled in size. Cuban advisers in Nicaragua had increased from 2,000–3,000 in 1983 to over 7,000 three years later, and they had been joined by military advisers from the Soviet Union, East Germany, Libya, and the Palestine Liberation Organization (PLO). Washington had conducted its own escalation when it directed the CIA to arm and assist the Contras, increased the number of military advisers in El Salvador, and began to conduct military exercises in Honduras. Central America was becoming another Third World battleground in the East-West confrontation.

The Sandinistas proclaimed their willingness to abide by the Contadora solution. The Reagan administration, however, rejected this solution because it would permit the Sandinista regime to remain in power and because it contained an implicit understanding that the time-honored U.S. interpretation of the Monroe Doctrine—the right to intervene in Central America—had become an anachronism.

The Reagan administration repeatedly invoked the specter of U.S. security and credibility being at risk. In his address to Congress in April 1983, President Reagan tied the fate of the Nicaraguan revolution to the global Cold War:

> If Central America were to fall [to Communism], what would be the consequence for our position in Asia and Europe and for alliances such as NATO? If the United States cannot respond to a threat near our own border, why should Europeans and Asians believe we are seriously concerned about threats to them? . . . Our credibility would collapse, our alliances would crumble.[6]

Here, Reagan tied events in Nicaragua to the very survival of the United States. Once again, events in a small and distant land were linked to the existence of the United States. It was little wonder that many in the United States heard the echoes of Vietnam. Secretary of State George Shultz, too, compared Nicaragua to Vietnam: "Broken promises. Communist dictatorship. Refugees. Widened Soviet influence, this time near our very borders. Here is your parallel between Vietnam and Central America."[7] Shultz's remarks touched a responsive chord among the convinced, those who had defended the U.S. role in Vietnam. But for many they reawakened the memory of a divisive and costly war of dubious import to U.S. interests.

To complicate matters for the Reagan administration, the Contras had made no significant military progress, had no base of popular support in Nicaragua, and had virtually no prospect of defeating the Sandinista army. When Congress, in response to the public's distaste for becoming involved in Nicaragua, suspended further military aid to the Contras in 1984 and again in early 1985, Reagan resolved to find other ways to support the Contras and win a proxy war against the "Communist" regime in Nicaragua.

Thus began what came to be known as the "Iran-Contra affair." Officials in the president's National Security Council worked out a complex scheme whereby profits from the covert and illegal sales of arms to Iran through intermediaries would be turned over to the Contras. Col. Oliver North, who conducted this operation from the basement of the White House, also sought money for the same purpose from political donors within the United States and from friendly foreign governments—all in violation of congressional laws prohibiting further military aid to the Contras. These illegal and covert operations, detected in November 1986, remained the national focus for several years—much like the Watergate scandal in the Nixon era—for they raised many questions about ethics, law, and power, as well as foreign policy. Where Nicaragua was concerned, the Iran-Contra affair had a ruinous effect on Reagan's policy. Congress, which earlier had vacillated on the issue of Contra aid, now firmly rejected any further military support despite Reagan's persistent pleas. Another setback for the Reagan administration's Nicaraguan policy came in June 1986, when the World Court (the International Court of Justice in The Hague, Netherlands) ruled that the United States had violated international law by mining Nicaraguan harbors in 1984 and in providing military support to the Contras for the purpose of overthrowing the government of Nicaragua.

The Contadora peace process, begun in 1983, expired in 1987, but Costa Rica's president, Oscar Arias, launched a new peace initiative that won the endorsement of the rulers of all five Central American nations—including Sandinista leader Daniel Ortega. The Arias plan committed the Central American nations to a cease-fire, a general amnesty, a dialogue with civilian political opposition, freedom of the press, free elections, the suspension of all foreign military aid, and a reduction in the level of arms.

Ortega's unconditional acceptance of the Arias peace plan offered him a diplomatic victory over Washington and spelled doom for the Contras, who now stood isolated in Central America. In February 1989, the presidents of the five Central American nations agreed to a plan calling for the disbanding of the Contras and their expulsion from their bases in Honduras. They had lost their reason for existence and could expect scant additional financial support from the United States.

But Ortega's problems were by no means over. The Sandinista regime now had to deal with a crisis more threatening to its survival than either the Contras or the United States: the failing economy. The looting of the treasury by Anastasio Somoza before he fled in 1979, the war against the Contras, the U.S. trade embargo, the loss of foreign credit, and its own mismanagement had caused an economic disaster. Nicaragua's per capita gross national product (GNP) had fallen from over $1,000 in 1980 to $830 in 1987; in 1993, it sank to $340.[8] Even more ruinous was hyperinflation, which by 1989 was beyond the control of the government. At the end of the 1980s, the fate of the Sandinista government hung in the balance as the nation languished in poverty.

In 1989, the Sandinistas took a calculated risk when they agreed to hold and abide by free elections in February 1990. They reasoned that not only would they win but that an election would make it even more difficult for Washington to continue to arm the Contras. The Sandinistas, however, lost the gamble when a coalition of anti-Sandinista parties led by Violeta Chamorro—the widow of the publisher of *La Prensa* whom Somoza had murdered in 1978—won fifty-two of the National Assembly's ninety seats. Nearly a dozen years of war and deprivation had taken their toll on the Sandinista revolution when the voters cast their ballots for a change. Ortega grudgingly accepted the electoral defeat and agreed to transfer his movement's base of power, the 70,000 troops of the army, to the authority of the new government. The army, however, remained under the command of the Sandinista military leader, Umberto Ortega, the brother of Daniel.

The Chamorro government in Nicaragua adopted a centrist and reconciliatory position, keeping a wary eye on both the Sandinista-led army and the former Contras. Although peace—or at least the end of overt warfare—had its benefits, the new government was unable to reverse the fortunes of the exhausted nation. The economy continued to decline each year in the 1990s as it had in the previous decade. There were no effective reforms, and neither production nor the standard of living increased. The country remained heavily dependent on external financial aid, which remained meager.

By 1993, many Nicaraguans had lost faith in the political system and in the ability of Chamorro's government to maintain order. Chamorro had retained Sandinista military leader Umberto Ortega as commander of the army, and in doing so she raised the ire of the conservative elements who had brought her to power. She pointed out that Ortega had in good faith reduced the size of the Sandinista-led army from over 70,000 troops down to 15,000. But an explosion in Managua of a huge cache of weapons secretly stored by the Sandinistas proved to be not only an embarrassment for both Ortega and Chamorro but the beginning of a wave of incessant political violence. Rightists demanded that Chamorro sack Ortega. At this point, bands of retread revolutionaries—former Contras on the right and ex-Sandinista soldiers on the left—engaged in retaliatory acts of violence, notably hostage takings and political killings. Without effective government or external assistance, Nicaragua remained a blighted country in the mid-1990s with a level of political violence bordering on armed anarchy.

When Chamorro's six-year term ended, the October 1996 presidential election was won by Arnoldo Aleman, the candidate of the rightist Liberal Alliance, who defeated the Sandinista candidate, Daniel Ortega. The election was a referendum not only on the future of the country but also on its past.

When the votes were counted, Aleman—a wealthy lawyer and businessman who had five farms that had been confiscated by the Sandinistas and who as mayor of Managua had frequently clashed with them—was declared the winner.[9] During the campaign, Aleman had spoken of reversing the land reforms of the Sandinistas. Much of the land had gone to campesinos, but other properties wound up in the hands of Sandinista officials—including Ortega—for private gain. After the election, to avoid civil strife Aleman suggested a program he called "Buying Peace," whereby the state (with the help of international aid) would compensate those who had lost property.

Aleman's main task, however, remained the economy. In 1996, parts of Managua still had not rebuilt from the 1972 earthquake. The long wars had ruined the economy, and Nicaragua was now the second-poorest country (after Haiti) in the Western Hemisphere—an estimated 60 percent of its people lived in poverty.

■ EL SALVADOR

In El Salvador, a repetition of the Nicaraguan scenario appeared to unfold in the early 1980s. A rebellion in the countryside threatened to oust the oligarchy that governed the country. This oligarchy was composed largely of *las catorce familias,* the Fourteen Families. Jorge Sol Costellanos, an oligarch and a former minister of the economy, defined the class structure in El Salvador as follows:

> It's different from an aristocracy, which we also have. It's an oligarchy because these families own and run almost everything that makes money

in El Salvador. Coffee gave birth to the oligarchy in the late 19th century, and economic growth has revoled around them ever since.[10]

Sol went on to say that, in fact, the Fourteen Families (or, more accurately, clans) controlled 70 percent of the private banks, coffee production, sugar mills, television stations, and newspapers. In contrast to the wealth of the Fourteen Families were the landless poor. The impoverished peasantry of El Salvador made up the bulk of the population but received a disproportionately small share of the nation's meager wealth. In 1984, the annual per capita GNP of El Salvador was around $710, about 6 percent of the U.S. figure.

The revolutionary violence that broke out in El Salvador in the early 1970s had its roots in the events of the early 1930s. In 1932, deteriorating economic conditions—brought about by the Great Depression and falling farm prices—and Communist activities under the leadership of Augustín Farabundo Martí led to peasant uprisings. A lack of organization and arms proved to be fatal for the peasants, for machetes were no match against a well-equipped army. In a matter of days, the armed forces, led by Gen. Maximiliano Hernández, slaughtered 30,000 campesinos. Martí was captured and executed. The revolution was over, but its impact remained deeply etched into the collective memory of the nation. Hernández became the symbol of both deliverance and oppression, and his ghost continued to haunt El Salvador.

The 1932 massacre produced an uneasy stability in El Salvador until the 1972 national elections, when the candidates of the Christian Democratic Party (PDC)—José Napoleón Duarte and his running mate, Guillermo Ungo—defeated the military candidate. The PDC had called for reforms to forestall a revolution, but the oligarchy and the military shrank from the prospect of reforms, particularly the redistribution of land and wealth. The military, therefore, arrested Duarte, tortured him, and sent him into exile; it then terrorized the country. These acts, in turn, spawned left-wing terror. The 1973 oil crisis added to the nation's economic problems. Duarte, in exile, continued to hold out hope for electoral reforms. Others in the PDC, notably Guillermo Ungo, joined the revolutionary cause.

Violence reached a new level when right-wing death squads went on a rampage of indiscriminate killings. These assassination squads summarily killed thousands of men, women, and children. In March 1980, the Roman Catholic archbishop of San Salvador, Oscar Arnulfo Romero—a critic of the right-wing government—was gunned down at the altar while saying mass. The assassins were members of a death squad under the command of Roberto d'Aubuisson. The CIA informed the Reagan administration that d'Aubuisson was the "principal henchman for wealthy landowners and a coordinator of the right-wing death squads that have murdered several thousand suspected leftists and leftist sympathizers during the past year."

The agency went on to say that he was also involved in drug trafficking, arms smuggling, and the death of Romero—even providing details of how the men were selected to carry out the murder. The CIA also told Richard Allen, Reagan's national security adviser, that "d'Aubuisson is egocentric, reckless and perhaps mentally unstable."[11] The Reagan administration did not condone d'Aubuisson's activities, but it continued to work with him as part of its strategy to deal with the insurgency.

The assassination of Romero put into focus a major change in the political life of Latin America that had been occurring during the previous decade. The Roman Catholic Church, traditionally the champion of the status quo, had begun to reexamine its mission. Many of its clergy had moved toward a renewed commitment to improve the lot of the faithful on this earth. Village priests in particular found they could not preach eternal salvation and at the same time ignore the violence visited upon their parishioners. The upshot was a split between the traditional wing of the clergy and those, such as Romero, who championed what became known as Liberation Theology.

☐ Liberation Theology

The origins of Liberation Theology can be traced to the encyclicals of Pope John XXIII (*Pacem in Terris,* 1963) and that of Pope Paul VI (*Populorum Progressio,* 1967) and the Second Vatican Council (1963–1965), all of which stressed the need for human rights and a decent living standard for all. The encyclicals and the council had a profound impact on the Roman Catholic Church in Latin America. At the Second General Conference of Latin American Bishops in 1968 in Medellín, Colombia, the 150 bishops in attendance focused their attack on the "institutionalized violence" that condemned the lower classes to poverty and hunger. They denounced the Alliance for Progress by which Latin America had become increasingly more dependent on foreign-controlled investments that primarily benefited foreign investors at the expense of the local population. The church thus combined its spiritual mission with one for social change and justice. "Salvation is integral—of the whole man," explained Marcos G. McGrath, archbishop of Panama; the church's mission was to "integrate eternal salvation and revolutionary action for a just order in this world into one."[12] One of its tasks became to raise the consciousness of the campesinos; the poor, with the help of the church, were to change their own condition.

At Medellín, the bishops denounced both capitalism and Marxism and looked for a third way. In their eyes,

> The liberal capitalist system and the temptation of the Marxist system appear as the only alternatives in our continent. . . . Both these systems are

affronts to the dignity of the human person. The first takes as a premise the primacy of capital, its power, and the discriminating use of capital in the pursuit of gain. The other, although ideologically it may pretend to be humanist, looks rather to the collective man, and in practice converts itself into a totalitarian concentration of state power.[13]

Eventually, the church found a third way. It began to work on the local level to establish base communities and cooperatives in an attempt to ameliorate the consequences of police and army brutality, poverty, illiteracy, and the lack of medical facilities. Not all clergy, however, were ready to join the ranks of what was becoming a revolutionary movement. In El Salvador in particular, the church was split on this issue. But when the Third Conference of Latin American Bishops convened in Puebla, Mexico, in 1979, a radicalized church was already a fact of political life in much of Latin America. Church leaders repeatedly condemned state and guerrilla violence—that is, both the capitalists and the Marxists. But as they had done in Medellín earlier, they directed their harshest attacks toward multinational corporations whose interpretation of the "stages of growth" stressed that poverty in the Third World was a temporary phenomenon and that capitalism would eliminate poverty. "Poverty is not a transitory stage," the bishops countered, but is "the product of economic, social, and political situations and structures."

Maryknoll Sister Ita Ford, shortly before she and three others were murdered in El Salvador in 1980, stated that "the Christian base communities are the greatest threat to military dictatorships in Latin America," a view the military dictatorships—particularly that of El Salvador—readily shared. As early as 1972, Salvadoran death squads began to murder members of the clergy, at times leaving their bodies dismembered as warnings. The Jesuit Rutilio Grande, for example, was murdered because of his work in the village where he had proclaimed the equality of all—peasants, priests, and oligarchs. The oligarchs, in turn, denounced the clergy as Communists and urged citizens "to be patriotic—kill a priest!" In the years between the Medellín and Puebla conferences (1968–1979), military governments or their henchmen murdered, tortured, arrested, or expelled an estimated 850 nuns, bishops, and priests in El Salvador. The murder of Archbishop Romero was but the most dramatic act of violence visited on the champions of Liberation Theology.[14]

* * *

Unlike the Latin church, Washington continued to be more concerned about violent left-wing revolution in El Salvador than about right-wing violence. U.S. policy makers continued to insist that revolutionary violence was inspired from the outside, by Nicaragua, Cuba, and, ultimately, the Soviet Union.

The Reagan administration's stance on El Salvador rested on three pillars. First, it provided much-needed economic aid to a nation wracked by civil war. Second, it became the source of the military hardware the Salvadoran army employed in its attempt to suppress the revolution. Third, it emerged as the champion of Salvadoran electoral democracy. Under U.S. supervision, elections returned Duarte to power in 1979 but clearly at the pleasure of the military who needed him, because without Duarte the Reagan administration could hardly justify its support of the Salvadoran military. Duarte's election enabled Washington to argue that reforms were taking hold and that the army's human rights record was improving. The violence, however, continued after the election of Duarte, who was powerless to stop it.

By 1989, after nine years of fighting, some 70,000 Salvadorans had been killed. Despite $3.3 billion in U.S. economic and military aid, little had changed. The guerrillas, regarded by one observer as "the best trained, best organized and most committed Marxist-Leninist rebel movement ever seen in Latin America,"[15] controlled about one-third of the country and made their military power felt through periodic attacks in the remainder. President Duarte remained Washington's best hope for political reform, but he was never able to control the army. Duarte's U.S.-backed Christian Democratic Party lost ground to the right-wing ARENA (Nationalist Republican Alliance), which had won control of the legislative assembly in elections in March 1988. ARENA staunchly opposed political change, and its paramilitary death squads continued to work with the army, murdering political opponents and terrorizing the nation. Duarte, whose health was deteriorating, prepared to step down after elections scheduled for March 1989.

In anticipation of the elections, the rebels, known as the FMLN (Farabundo Martí National Liberation Front), announced in February 1989 that they were willing to take part in the election but requested that it be postponed for six months to give them time to prepare. The FMLN also proposed a cease-fire and declared its willingness to recognize the army as the sole legitimate military force in the country, but only on the condition that the army officers responsible for massacres such as the murder of Archbishop Romero and four U.S. nuns be tried and punished. This condition was critical; no senior military officer had ever been brought to trial, even though many had been linked to the killings. At the urging of Washington, leaders of Duarte's party and ARENA held talks with FMLN leaders, but although the atmosphere was peaceable, ARENA and the army ultimately rejected the rebels' proposals. The army argued that the 1987 Amnesty Law absolved the security forces of all past crimes. It was plainly unwilling to submit to civilian and judicial authority.

ARENA candidate Alfredo Cristiani won the election and took office on June 1, 1989. The presidential elections and a peaceful transfer of power brought a semblance of political progress, but violence soon returned to El Salvador. In November 1989, the FMLN even briefly took the war into the capital, San Salvador.

As the battle still raged, the army committed yet another atrocity. Right-wing death squads burst into the rooms of six Jesuit priests who taught at the Catholic University and brutally beat and murdered them, their cook, and the cook's daughter. Cristiani, whose government still received U.S. military aid, was pressured by Washington to conduct a thorough investigation and bring the killers to justice.[16] In mid-January 1990, his government arrested and officially charged eight military men, including a colonel who allegedly had ordered the murder of the priests.

Peace finally came to El Salvador, but it was not the result of Washington's policy of military support for the right-wing ARENA government and its army. The FMLN offensive in November 1989 had taught the Bush administration that military victory was beyond reach. The main factor in ending the proxy conflict in El Salvador was the end of the Cold War. ARENA could count on U.S. military aid only as long as its army was seen as holding Communism at bay. With the global Communist menace suddenly gone, Washington's threat to discontinue aid to El Salvador became more credible, which made ARENA more amenable to compromise. It also meant ARENA could no longer ignore demands for human rights reform and for prosecution of the suspected death squad killers.

In May 1990, Moscow and Washington agreed to back UN-arranged Salvadoran peace talks, which, after twenty months of difficult negotiations, produced a peace agreement in January 1992. This treaty, brokered by UN Secretary-General Javier Pérez de Cuéllar in his final days in office, ended a brutal war that had claimed approximately 80,000 lives over twelve years. In exchange for an agreement to dissolve their military forces, the rebels secured government pledges to legalize the FMLN as a political party, to reduce by one-half the number of troops in the Salvadoran army within two years, and to strip from the army its control over internal security forces. The treaty also included agreements to implement land reform, as well as judicial and electoral reforms.

Nine days after the peace accords were signed, the two leading officers convicted of slaying the six Jesuit priests were sentenced to thirty years in prison. Moreover, a three-member UN Truth Commission investigated other major human rights cases, such as the December 1981 massacre of more than 700 peasants by the U.S.-trained elite Atlacatl Battalion in the remote village of El Mozote. In 1982, the Reagan administration had angrily and repeatedly denied that such a massacre had taken place. But in El Salvador, for over a decade El Mozote remained a metaphor for the army's ability to avoid responsibility for human rights abuses.[17] The conviction of the murderers of the priests represented an important first, for no military officer had ever been charged with—let alone convicted of—a human rights abuse crime in the Salvadoran civil war. Only by breaking the army's death lock on the country and asserting civilian control of the military could Cristiani (or any ruler in Central America) put an end to political violence and war, for only then could the roots of revolution—poverty, despair, and social injustice—be dealt with effectively.

It was an uneasy peace in El Salvador. The demobilization of the FMLN forces fell behind the timetable established by the January 1992 peace accords, but when it was completed in December of that year a ceremony was held marking the formal end of the twelve-year civil war. Meanwhile, progress was made on another goal of the peace agreement: building a national civilian police force independent of the army that included former FMLN troops. Friction occurred, however, between the rightist ARENA government and the former rebels in 1993 when the FMLN delayed the scheduled destruction of its anti-aircraft guns because the government refused to carry out the purge of army officers involved in atrocities. In response to a UN-appointed commission's report calling for the resignation of accused officers and the dismissal of the Supreme Court, irate ARENA legislators passed an amnesty law granting full immunity to all army officers—despite allegations of incontrovertible proof of the El Mozote massacre in 1981. ARENA went on to hold presidential and National Assembly elections in May 1994. ARENA and its presidential candidate, Armando Calderon Sol, the ideological heir of the El Mozote assassins, handily defeated the leftist opponent, Ruben Zamora, leader of the FMLN. This free election, in which the former rebels were given the opportunity to unseat the conservative regime through the ballot, did signify, however, that the 1992 peace was holding and that a degree of reconciliation had been achieved.

■ MEXICO

The roots of many of the problems Mexico faced at the end of the twentieth century can be traced to the political and economic consequences of the revolution of 1910–1917. This revolution, as is the case with most revolutions, disintegrated into a bloody civil war in which 1.5 million people—approximately 10 percent of the population—lost their lives. Not until the late 1920s did the country began to enjoy a measure of stability. It was then that a new party, the Partido Revolucionario Institucional (the Institutional Revolutionary Party, or PRI), was able to end the continuing fratricide. The party began to organize diverse groups in support of the state. It encouraged workers, peasants, bureaucrats, big-business executives, owners of small enterprises, teachers, and other groups to bargain with the state, which then acted as the arbiter for these various interest groups. The PRI also skillfully formed political alliances, doled out patronage jobs, co-opted its opponents, occasionally carried through reforms within the party, controlled the media, and, when necessary, resorted to fraud and violent repression. Thus, the PRI-dominated Mexican government produced a surface calm that did not address the underlying causes of social discontent that periodically became visible.

The revolution of 1910 began as a liberal challenge to the dictatorship of Porfirio Díaz, but it soon became more radical when the campesinos, under the slogan "Land and Liberty," and leaders such as Emiliano Zapata demanded the redistribution of land. At the time, 96 percent of the rural households owned no land, and fewer than 850 families owned 97 percent of Mexico's arable land.[18] The 1917 constitution promised a redistribution of land, but prior to the reign of Lazaro Cárdenas (1934–1940), only about 10 percent of the rural population had benefited from the land reform.

Cárdenas tried to divert the class struggle endemic to Mexico into safe channels under state regulation. Yet, he was also a populist, a champion of the campesinos, who carried out the first serious land redistribution at a time when the *latifundistas* tried to limit redistribution as much as possible. Cárdenas distributed much more land than any other Mexican president; during his tenure, the campesinos' irrigated landholdings increased fourfold.[19] But even under Cárdenas, land distribution came to a halt after 1937.

Cárdenas's populist program had put him out on a limb. His fellow army generals thought his populist reforms had gone too far. He had to find a new focus of attack. In March 1938, his target became "imperialist intervention," that is, foreign—U.S. and European—corporations that controlled certain sectors of the Mexican economy, notably oil. The time was ripe for the nationalization of these companies, which were widely seen as the enemy of Mexico.[20] There was a massive outpouring of support; millions of Mexicans contributed to a national indemnity fund to help pay off the $200 million the oil companies had received in compensation. Cárdenas's "anti-imperialist" measures, however, did little to free Mexico from foreign control. The country remained dependent on foreign investments, and in 1940, 87 percent of its trade was with the United States.[21]

One of the PRI's functions was to oversee the development of state capitalism, which gave Mexico decades of sustained growth during the mid-twentieth century. Between 1940 and 1960, manufacturing rose by 365 percent, steel production by 934 percent, motor vehicle production by 451 percent, and agricultural output by 218 percent; during the same period, the population increased by 78 percent. Per capita government expenditures increased from 31 to 114 pesos, nearly a fourfold increase.[22] Yet, despite the land reform and a growing economy, the gap between the rich and the poor grew after World War II. Economic growth, raised expectations, a pattern of rising social inequalities, and dissent went hand in hand.

An economic downturn in the late 1960s had severe social and political repercussions, as by that time Mexico had a steadily growing and better-educated middle class. On October 2, 1968, tens of thousands of demonstrators—mostly young students—congregated on Mexico City's Tlatelolco Plaza to protest police brutality, political corruption, and economic hardship. The army promptly put an end to this new challenge to the PRI's power by fatally shooting at least 300 civilians in the square. Ten days later, the Mexico City Olympic Games began, the first and only such showcase in a developing country. As the torch was lit in Aztec Stadium, troops and tanks were deployed outside the view of television cameras. The massacre did not solve the PRI's problems. Instead, the repression triggered a crisis of legitimacy for the PRI.

In 1970, Luis Echeverría, the interior minister during the 1968 massacre, became president of a country in turmoil. Dissidents—among them students, guerrillas, and practitioners of Liberation Theology—sought to build grassroots social bases in the barrios and among the campesinos. The press became increasingly more critical. Echeverría, under pressure to create more jobs, borrowed both time and money. He felt it was better to have inflation than social conflict. The government bought bankrupt enterprises in an attempt to save jobs, and the legislature passed even more restrictive laws against foreign investors. It then began to borrow increasing amounts of foreign money—without the revenue to finance the borrowing binge. When Echeverría took office in 1970, the nation's foreign debt stood at $5 billion; by the time his successor, José López Portillo (1976–1982), took office in 1976, the debt had risen to $20 billion.

López came to power in the midst of the oil boom of the 1970s, which made it possible for Mexico—which was sitting on top of vast oil reserves—to borrow still more money. During López's presidency, the public and private sectors borrowed another $60 billion. His government borrowed $20 billion in 1981 alone to keep it solvent, at a time when tax revenues were falling and international interest rates were rising. By August 1982, Mexico was unable to pay off its massive foreign debt, a condition that triggered a Latin American debt crisis. From this point on, Mexico's financial dilemma was no longer its own.

Elections in northern Mexico in the early 1980s—free of the usual tampering by PRI functionaries—showed the weakness of the PRI, which lost several local races to the National Action Party (PAN), a center-right, business-based party. In the mid-1980s, an environmental protest movement responded to the ecological emergency that was the result of Mexico City's horrendous air pollution. Then came the massive earthquake of September 19, 1985, which buried more than 10,000 people. The government scarcely responded during the first forty-eight hours; it was civic groups that first tried to cope with the disaster. In the aftermath of the earthquake, Cuauthemoc Cárdenas (the son of the revered Lazaro Cárdenas) broke with the PRI and became the candidate of a center-left coalition; in the 1988 presidential election, he challenged the PRI candidate, Carlos Salinas de Gortari. Cárdenas gained a substantial following, but two days before the election two of his key aides were murdered (crimes that were never solved), and a few hours after the voting ended the computerized ballot counting came to a halt. When the computers came back on-line, Salinas had won the election by gaining officially just over 50 percent of the vote. A few months later, the ballots were destroyed.

By now, Mexico's economy was treading water during what became the country's worst recession in sixty years. Between 1980 and 1993, annual output declined by an average of 0.5 percent. Salinas, in an attempt to revive the stagnant economy, continued Mexico's venture into the minefields of the global economy, which his predecessor, Miguel de la Madrid, had begun. Under the auspices of the Brady Plan of 1989, Mexico worked out agreements with multilateral international lending institutions (such as the World Bank and the International Monetary Fund [IMF]) that gave it access to much-needed foreign credits; simultaneously, it negotiated with Canada and the United States the terms of the North American Free Trade Agreement (NAFTA).[23] Lozaro Cárdenas's "anti-imperialist" campaign of the 1930s was now but a dim memory.

The social price of admission into the global economy was high. It consisted of deep structural adjustments to satisfy the creditors—the elimination of tariffs, deregulation of the economy, privatization of state enterprises, and labor *flexibilizacion* (literally, making labor more flexible, more amenable to the demands of factory owners) with the object of increasing productivity and international competitiveness. Labor flexibility meant, in short, that workers were expected to work harder for lower wages. The state feared worker mobilization, and it took steps to deny unions the right of free association and repeatedly used police and the army against workers and their unions. With economic restructuring and *flexibilizacion,* the unions lost both economic and political power.

☐ **Chiapas**

On January 1, 1994, Mexico faced yet another crisis. In the state of Chiapas, in the southeastern corner of the nation along the border with Guatemala, campesinos, mostly Indians, suddenly rose in rebellion. They called their organization the Zapatista National Liberation Army in memory of Emiliano Zapata, one of the heroes of the revolution of 1910. The group seized control of a number of cities and *latifundio,* which they turned into communal farms, or *ejidos,* and insisted that the land they worked had been granted to them by the 1917 constitution.

The 1994 Zapatistas saw land as the core issue. Since the move toward privatization of the economy during the mid-1980s, the campesinos—who had little land to begin with—had been losing land to the *latifundistas*. When the Zapatistas seized the courthouse in San Cristobal de las Casas, they promptly burned the municipal archives that contained the land titles. They denounced the government's electoral fraud;[24] demanded regional autonomy; and declared that they would no longer endure abuse at the hands of the police, the army, and the terrorist *guardias blancas* ("white guards") deployed by the owners of the *latifundio*.

Chiapas was the poorest state in a poor country. The federal government spent less than half the amount of development money per capita in Chiapas than it did in the nation as a whole. Chiapas needed paved roads, adequate schools, electricity (the state contained large dams that exported energy to other states), and health facilities. A large percentage of the population was of Indian origin (26.4 percent, compared to the national average of 7.5 percent), and a third of the people did not speak Spanish. The national minimum daily wage of workers in 1990 was $3.33; in Chiapas, nearly 60 percent earned less than that amount. Nineteen percent of the labor force had no income, working as peasants and existing at a bare subsistence level. Food production had barely kept up with a population that had doubled over the past two decades,[25] the result of a high birth rate and the migration of Indians from war-torn Guatemala and other parts of Mexico. Prices for the main cash crop, coffee, had fallen drastically.

The rebellion broke out the very day NAFTA went into effect—the final indignity, according to the rebels. They saw the treaty with the United States as a "death certificate" for the Indians in Mexico, who would not be able to compete with manufacturers and food producers in the United States and Canada. Led by the charismatic and mysterious Subcomandante Marcos, his face hidden by a ski mask,[26] the Zapatistas declared that they spoke for all of Mexico in a struggle for democracy, land, economic change, and autonomy. The Salinas administration, hamstrung by repeated scandals and mistrusted by the majority of its people, deployed the army in an attempt to end the rebellion. Estimates of fatalities varied widely, from 145 to 400. Within the context of Mexican history, however, the government showed remarkable restraint. In the end, President Salinas agreed to negotiations with the rebels, who were poorly armed yet were able to find refuge from the well-equipped army in the vast Lacandon Forest and whose strength lay in their manifestos, through which they rallied public support.

In the past, radical movements in Mexico had often stood alone, but the Zapatistas were hardly alone in venting their anger against the system. Two million members of the middle class—small shopkeepers, merchants, and farmers—hard hit by the recession in the mid-1990s, had already formed their own resistance movement, *El Barzon*. They, too, had a program of legal action and civil resistance. They showed up in large numbers at foreclosure hearings to halt the legal proceedings and make sure no one bid on the property; they also carried coffins into banks to dramatize their descent into poverty. Yet another group, the Civic Alliance, sent election observers to polling stations to attempt to stop the PRI's rampant electoral fraud. And the National Episcopal Conference expressed its support for the role of the Roman Catholic Church in Chiapas, headed by Bishop Samuel Ruíz García, who not only worked with the poor but also played the role of intermediary in the talks between the rebels and the authorities.

* * *

PRI candidate Ernesto Zedillo Ponce de Leon won the 1994 election. At the time, the PRI still had considerable influence, notably in terms of patronage jobs. Yet, it no longer fulfilled the functions for which it had been created—to arbitrate disputes among competing interest groups. The PRI's political monopoly was crumbling. In 1996, PAN, the right-center party, elected four state governors and ruled about one-third of the population. Unresolved political murders in 1994 and 1995 further undermined the legitimacy of the PRI. The assassination of Luis Donaldo Colosio Murietta, the original PRI presidential candidate, in March 1994 was apparently carried out by other PRI functionaries. The investigation into the murder of PRI Secretary-General José Francisco Ruíz Massieu in September 1995 led to the arrest of Raul Salinas de Gortari, the brother of the former president. While the former languished in jail under suspicion of both murder and the theft of approximately $100 million from the national treasury, the latter escaped to Ireland, which did not have an extradition treaty with Mexico.

■ THE NORTH AMERICAN FREE TRADE AGREEMENT

The roots of NAFTA can be traced back to the mid-1980s, when Mexico decided to join the global economy and began to open its economy to foreign goods and investors. The movement toward that end began when Mexico accrued the staggering foreign debt of over $100 billion. At that point its creditors, such as U.S. banks, urged the privatization of Mexico's state enterprises, some of which were sold off to the creditors. In 1986, Mexico applied to join GATT (the international General Agreement on Tariffs and Trade); as a result, protective tariffs as high as 100 percent dropped to 20 percent or less. Foreign investments in Mexico began to increase. U.S. investments increased from $5 billion in 1986 to $11.6 billion in 1991, and U.S. exports to Mexico rose from $12 billion to $33.2 billion during the same period.

This situation set the stage for NAFTA, through which all tariffs among Mexico, the United States, and Canada (which already had a free trade agreement with the United States, effective January 1, 1989) were scheduled to be eliminated by the year 2008. Investors would be able to operate freely in a market that combined the manufacturing and purchasing potential of more than 360 million people. Among the main goals of NAFTA were to protect the rights of North American investors in Mexico, open Mexico to foreign capital, lock it into the global economy, and foreclose radical options in the future.

Presidents George Bush of the United States and Carlos Salinas de Gortari of Mexico first proposed NAFTA in June 1990, hailing it as a "powerful engine for economic development, creating new jobs and opening new markets." An intense debate ensued over NAFTA's pros and cons. The business elites in all three countries, as well as all five former U.S. presidents and all former secretaries of state, favored the agreement. Three hundred of the best-known U.S. economists signed a letter of support. In corporate boardrooms across Mexico, the United States, and Canada, support for NAFTA was nearly unanimous. President Clinton, to obtain congressional ratification of the agreement,[27] needed to persuade the U.S. public of its benefits. He repeatedly promised that NAFTA would immediately produce hundreds of thousands of new jobs in the United States—and high-skilled, well-paying ones at that.

Those nearer the bottom of the economic ladder, however, had misgivings. The rebellion in the state of Chiapas in Mexico began on the very day NAFTA went into effect, in part because the agreement made it possible for foreigners to purchase even more Mexican lands. Canadian and U.S. workers expressed concern that competing with lower-paid Mexican workers could lower their standards of living. Even before NAFTA, the free trade agreement with Mexico had cost more than 360,000 U.S. manufacturing jobs between 1989 and 1993. The American Federation of Labor–Congress of Industrial Organizations (AFL-CIO) estimated that the United States would lose 500,000 manufacturing jobs to Mexico, where the average wage was one-seventh of that in the United States. An AFL-CIO official put it bluntly:

> What is unstated . . . is that you are adding 50 million low-wage Mexican workers, many of them skilled, to the United States labor force. They are not located across the Pacific, but in a country that is attached to ours, as if it were another state.[28]

The concerns of U.S. workers were not alleviated when, in October 1993, President Clinton asked large corporations to pledge that they would not take jobs to Mexico and found he had no takers. This came when the Mexican state of Yucatan advertised that workers there could be hired for less than $1 an hour (including fringe benefits), a savings of $15,000 per worker annually.

NAFTA went into effect on January 1, 1994, at a time when the Mexican economy already suffered from the effects of a deep recession. At the same time, the government of President Ernesto Zedillo introduced drastic measures to pay off Mexico's obligations. Society had to swallow a very bitter medicine. Zedillo raised taxes; clamped down on wages to make Mexican goods more competitive in the world economy (labor unions meekly accepted an 8 percent cut in real wages); raised interest rates to retain the capital of foreign investors; cut back on state-subsidized prices for basic items such as food, bus transportation, and gasoline; cut spending on social programs (such as pensions); and sold off state-owned enterprises—often at bargain prices to cronies of politicians. These measures went a long way to address the concerns of international investors. When Zedillo raised taxes in March 1995, for example, Wall Street received the news enthusiastically; the U.S. stock market rose, and the peso gained 18 percent in value. The measures had their intended effect, but they also produced a deeper recession during which 1 million workers lost their jobs. Unemployment, fiscal austerity, and the decline of the value of the peso drove down the purchasing power of many Mexicans by as much as 50 percent. The middle class, which had hoped for a better day, was particularly hard hit.

In December 1994, matters turned worse when the value of the peso dropped sharply. Previously, the Mexican government had shored up the peso when it bought excess pesos with U.S. dollars. But when its dollar reserves declined, the government was forced to let the peso float freely. The peso plunged over 40 percent in a single day (from 39 cents to 22 cents to the peso and to 13 cents by November 1995), and drove up consumer prices overnight.[29]

NAFTA also drove down even further the wages of workers in the *maquiladores,* the assembly plants established by foreign companies across the Mexican border. The *maquiladores* were "restructured"—that is, wages were lowered and workers were dismissed—to become more competitive in the global economy. Mexican farmers, too, felt the impact of NAFTA when they suddenly found themselves facing competition from the efficient farmers in the United States and Canada who sent large volumes of processed meat, powdered milk, corn, and other commodities across the border.

NAFTA was an experiment that had never been tried. It marked the first time fully developed economies had agreed to eliminate all barriers with a low-wage, developing country that had a minimum wage of $3 a day. It became evident that whatever benefits NAFTA brought in the long term, there would be not only winners but also losers. The bulk of the casualties would be among the workers, because in the global free market employers could purchase labor as a commodity at the lowest possible price.

In December 1994, the three original members of NAFTA agreed in principle to permit Chile to join the organization as the next step in creating a free market zone from the Arctic Ocean to Tierra del Fuego. The march toward the globalization of the national economies continued without missing a step.

■ PANAMA'S NORIEGA

The first year of the Bush presidency saw a puzzling war of words with Manuel Noriega, the military strongman of Panama. It was a strange spectacle because only a few years previously Noriega had been an ally of the United States. In fact, he had been on the payroll of the CIA, which paid him $250,000 a year for Caribbean intelligence. As head of intelligence in Panama during the 1970s, Noriega had risen rapidly through the ranks of the National Guard of Panamanian dictator Omar Torrijos. After the death of Torrijos in 1981 and after Noriega had consolidated his hold on power, the United States used him in the war against the Sandinistas in Nicaragua. Throughout, the Reagan administration had turned a blind eye to human rights abuses by Noriega. Torture, murder,[30] rape, plunder, prostitution, drug trade, and the theft of elections—such as that in 1984—did not faze Washington. It continued to fund the army, now renamed the Panamanian Defense Forces (PDF), as it contemplated the military withdrawal from the Canal Zone by the year 2000 as stipulated by the treaty of 1979. Under Noriega, the PDF grew from 10,000 to 21,000 troops.

But in 1987, Washington became aware that Noriega had transgressed the bounds of propriety when it learned he was also offering intelligence to Castro's Cuba. Noriega's military headquarters had become a brokerage house where intelligence was bought and sold as just another commodity. Ambler Moss, President Carter's envoy to Panama, explained that Noriega was "dealing with everybody—us, the Cubans, other countries. We used to call him the rent-a-colonel."[31] The betrayal became too much for President Bush to bear. He accused Noriega of being part of the international drug cartel. But the episode was reminiscent of Claude Rains's discovery of gambling in Rick's place in the movie *Casablanca*. After all, knowledge in Washington of Noriega's drug connections went all the way back to the Nixon administration.[32]

Noriega resisted U.S. pressure to step down and presented himself instead as the champion of small Latin American nations once again bullied by the "Colossus of the North." In 1987, grand juries in Tampa and Miami indicted Noriega on drug trafficking charges. Just before Christmas 1989, Bush sent a posse of 20,000 U.S. soldiers to bring Noriega to justice. Operation "Just Cause," as Bush chose to call the U.S. military intervention, got its man, but the cost was high. Several hundred Panamanians—mostly civilians—and twenty-three U.S. soldiers died in the fighting. In addition, the collateral damage of property and subsequent looting of stores in Panama City resulted in losses to small businesses totaling $1 billion.

The invasion may have served the cause of democracy, but the Bush administration appeared well on its way to repeating the mistakes of the past when it insisted on rebuilding the shattered Panamanian army. When the new president of Panama, Guillermo Endara, visited President Oscar Arias of Costa Rica in January 1990, Arias urged him to forgo an army. Instead, Arias advocated the Costa Rican solution of 1948, when that country abolished its army and became the only viable democracy between the Rio Grande and the Straits of Magellan.

The invasion of Panama was also perhaps the first instance of U.S. military intervention abroad since 1945 in which the anti-Communist theme was not central. As such, it was a sign of the times that the Cold War was winding down. Bush defended his action as part of his war on drug dealers, as his duty to defend the Panama Canal, and as his obligation to protect the lives of U.S. citizens. But as another sign of the times, he stood in direct contrast to Soviet leader Mikhail Gorbachev, who declared at about the same time that no nation had a legal or moral right to interfere in the internal affairs of another.

In Miami, before a federal judge, Noriega—dressed in his general's uniform—presented himself as a "prisoner of war." The judge, however, held that he was dealing with a common criminal. U.S. foreign policy was acquiring a new focus—the international drug connection—and Noriega's arrest became Exhibit A of the federal prosecution's commitment to a new war. In April 1992, when Noriega was found guilty after a seven-month trial, he became the first head of a foreign state convicted of criminal charges in a U.S. court. In July 1992, he was sentenced to forty years in prison (eligible for parole in twenty-five years) on eight counts of drug trafficking, money laundering, and racketeering—specifically for accepting millions of dollars in bribes from the Medellín cartel in Colombia to ship large amounts of cocaine through Panama.

The unprecedented sentencing of Noriega took place shortly after the U.S. Supreme Court upheld the federal government's right to kidnap a Mexican national who had participated in the torture murder of a U.S. narcotics agent. In doing so, the court ignored international law and the extradition treaty between the United States and Mexico. The governments of Mexico and Canada, with which the United States had a similar extradition treaty, protested that the Bush administration had violated the sovereignty of a neighboring nation.

RECOMMENDED READINGS

Berryman, Phillip. *Inside Central America: The Essential Facts Past and Present on El Salvador, Nicaragua, Honduras, Guatemala, and Costa Rica.* New York: Pantheon, 1985.

The observations of a man who for four years served as the Central American representative of the American Friends Service Committee.

Chace, James. *Endless War: How We Got Involved in Central America and What Can Be Done.* New York: Vintage, 1984.
Offers a brief, popular but insightful historical analysis.

Danner, Mark. *The Massacre at El Mozote.* New York: Random House, 1993.

Diedrich, Bernard. *Somoza and the Legacy of U.S. Involvement.* New York: Dutton, 1981.

LaFeber, Walter. *Inevitable Revolution: The United States in Central America.* Expanded ed. New York: W. W. Norton, 1984.
By a well-known revisionist historian of the role of the United States in the Cold War.

Langley, Lester D. *Central America: The Real Stakes, Understanding Central America Before It's Too Late.* New York: Crown, 1985.

Montgomery, Tommie Sue. *Revolution in El Salvador.* Boulder, Colo.: Westview Press, 1982.

Schlesinger, Stephen, and Stephen Kinzer. *Bitter Fruit: The Untold Story of the American Coup in Guatemala.* Garden City, N.Y.: Doubleday, 1982.
The best seller on the CIA's 1954 coup in Guatemala.

NOTES

1. Theodore Roosevelt, "Annual Message to Congress," December 1904, in Robert H. Farrell, *American Diplomacy: A History* (New York: W. W. Norton, 1959), p. 251.

2. A conversation with Sir William Tyrell, a representative of Britain's Foreign Office, November 13, 1913. Wilson explained his position on the civil strife in Mexico with this comment: "I am going to teach the South American republics to elect good men!" Arthur S. Link, *Wilson, II, The New Freedom* (Princeton: Princeton University Press, 1956), p. 375.

3. Kennedy, quoted in Arthur M. Schlesinger Jr., *A Thousand Days: John F. Kennedy in the White House* (Boston: Houghton Mifflin, 1965), p. 769.

4. Castro offered to pay for U.S. property, but only on the basis of a low assessment the companies themselves had submitted for tax purposes. The U.S. companies insisted on full value. Stephen E. Ambrose, *Rise to Globalism: American Foreign Policy, 1938–1970* (New York: Penguin, 1971), p. 269n.

5. "I'm the Champ," *Time* (cover story on Somoza), November 15, 1948, p. 43.

6. Ronald Reagan to a joint session of Congress, reported in the *New York Times,* April 28, 1983, p. A12.

7. Don Oberdorfer, "Central America Could Share Vietnam's Fate, Shultz Warns," *Washington Post,* April 26, 1985, pp. A1, A16; and George P. Shultz, excerpts from a speech to State Department employees on the tenth anniversary of the fall of Vietnam, "The Meaning of Vietnam," ibid., p. A16.

8. World Bank, *World Development Report: Workers in an Integrating World* (New York: Oxford University Press, 1995), p. 162.

9. Aleman won 48.4 percent of the vote in the first round, to 38.6 percent for Ortega; 45 percent was needed to win the presidency outright in the first round.

10. Paul Heath Hoeffel, "The Eclipse of the Oligarchs," *New York Times Magazine,* September 6, 1981, p. 23.

11. Clifford Krauss, "U.S. Aware of Killings, Kept Ties to Salvadoran Rightists, Papers Suggest," *New York Times,* November 9, 1993, p. A9.

12. Marcos G. McGrath (archbishop of Panama and former vice-president of the Council of Latin American Bishops), "Ariel or Caliban?" *Foreign Affairs,* October 1973, pp. 85, 87.

13. From the bishops' *Document on Justice,* as quoted in ibid., p. 86.

14. Walter LaFeber, *Inevitable Revolutions: The United States in Central America* (New York: W. W. Norton, expanded ed., 1984), pp. 219–226; Tina Rosenberg, *Children of Cain: Violence and the Violent in Latin America* (New York: Penguin, 1992), pp. 219–270.

15. James Le Moyne, "El Salvador's Forgotten War," *Foreign Affairs,* Summer 1989, p. 106.

16. One month later, a witness to the murders complained to church officials of "coercive interrogation" by Salvadoran and U.S. officials, who were allegedly attempting to get her to change her story. Neither Cristiani nor the Bush administration wanted the Salvadoran army to be found responsible for this atrocity, which threatened to bring about congressional suspension of further military aid to the country.

17. Mark Danner, "The Truth of El Mozote," *New Yorker,* December 6, 1993, pp. 50–133 (eventually published in book form as *The Massacre at El Mozote* [New York: Random House]). El Mozote was but one of many massacres carried out by the Salvadoran army.

18. Judith Gentleman, "Mexico: The Revolution," in Barbara A. Tenenbaum, ed., *Encyclopedia of Latin American History and Culture,* vol. 4 (New York: Charles Scribner's Sons, 1996), p. 15; Alma Guillermoprieto, "Zapata's Heirs," *New Yorker,* May 16, 1994, p. 54.

19. The census of 1940, the year Cárdenas left office, showed that 41.6 percent of the population engaged in agriculture had seen the fulfillment of the promise of the revolution; James W. Wilkie, *The Mexican Revolution: Federal Expenditure and Social Change Since 1910* (Berkeley: University of California Press, 1970), pp. 193–194.

20. James D. Cockcroft, *Mexico: Class Formation, Capital Accumulation, and the State* (New York: Monthly Review Press, 1983), p. 135, who cites Jesus Silva Herzog, *El petroleo mexicano* (Mexico: 1941), p. 5.

21. Cockcroft, *Mexico,* pp. 136–138.

22. Wilkie, *The Mexican Revolution,* pp. 222–225, 128–129, 195–197. The expenditures are calculated in constant 1950 pesos.

23. Philip L. Russell, *Mexico Under Salinas* (Austin, Tex.: Mexico Resource Center, 1994), p. 179.

24. The government's figures for the past three presidential elections—1976, 1982, 1988—gave the PRI 97.7, 90.2, and 89.9 percent respectively, of the vote in Chiapas; Paco Ignacio Taibo II, "Images of Chiapas: Zapatista! The Phoenix Rises," *The Nation,* March 28, 1996, pp. 407– 408.

25. "The Mexican Rebels' Impoverished Home," *New York Times,* January 9, 1994, p. 6E, based on the 1990 Mexican census and the president's report to Congress, November 1, 1993.

26. The government eventually identified the leader of the largely Indian uprising as a man of Spanish origin, Rafael Sebastian Guillen Vicente, a university graduate who issued his manifestos before television cameras and posted them on the Internet.

27. NAFTA was not a treaty (which only the Senate would have to ratify by a two-thirds vote) but a "trade agreement," which needed a majority vote from both houses of Congress.

28. Clyde N. Farnsworth, "What an Earlier Trade Pact Did Up North," and Louis Uchitelle, "Nafta and Jobs: In a Numbers War, No One Can Count," *New York Times,* November 14, 1993, p. 1E.

29. After having made sweeping predictions about the benefits of NAFTA, President Clinton and Congress wound up allocating $20 billion in loan guarantees to shore up the peso. Canada, the World Bank, and the IMF added additional sums, bringing the bailout to about $50 billion.

30. Guillermo Sánchez Borbùn, "Hugo Spadafora's Last Day: A Murder in Panama Undoes a Regime," *Harper's,* June 1988, pp. 56–62.

31. Quoted in Tim Collie, "Noriega Played All Angles in Ascent," *Tampa Tribune,* December 25, 1989, p. 22A.

32. Ibid., pp. 22A, 25A.

15

The People's Republic of China and the Four Tigers of Asia

In the mid-1990s, many of the countries of Asia were Third World nations, and several—such as Bangladesh, Cambodia, Myanmar (Burma), and Laos—were among the world's poorest. The two giant Asian nations, the People's Republic of China and India, each with a per capita gross national product (GNP) under $400 in 1990, definitely qualified as Third World nations. Other countries in Asia, however, all on the rim of China, had far higher GNPs and growth rates and were by no means Third World or underdeveloped nations. Japan immediately comes to mind, but some other Asian countries were following Japan's footsteps in the 1970s and were rapidly becoming highly industrialized nations.

The twentieth century was an age of social experimentation and upheavals, and China, the world's largest nation, had its share of both. The Chinese Communist government's efforts to transform and modernize China warrant an examination, not only because of the magnitude of the task but also because of the great lengths to which the Chinese Communists went to apply Marxism. The endeavor to put Marxism into practice in this huge country, however, caused enormous political and economic upheavals. Only after the death of Mao Zedong in 1976 did China attain a significant measure of both political stability and economic growth.

India, the other Third World giant in Asia, maintained a democratic form of government and enjoyed a greater degree of political stability than China, but its economic performance was no better. India, too, engaged in social and economic experimentation, mixing elements of capitalism and socialism while avoiding radical shifts in policy. In their own ways, India and China struggled to come to terms with a massive population and massive poverty. Not until the 1980s were they able to register substantial economic gains, and since then China has outpaced India.

In stark contrast with China and India were Japan and four other East Asian countries that had remarkable economic development between 1960 and the early 1990s. In this chapter, our attention will be on the "four tigers of Asia"—namely, South Korea, Taiwan, Hong Kong, and Singapore (leaving Japan for Chapter 19). South Korea, Taiwan, and Singapore were poor Third World countries in the 1950s, but they later achieved spectacular growth and economic modernization, and, like Hong Kong (a British colony rather than a nation), they became newly industrialized countries (NICs).

■ MAO ZEDONG'S QUEST FOR A COMMUNIST UTOPIA

The enormity of China is the starting point of any inquiry into China's economic progress, for its size alone sets it apart. Never before in history has there been a nation of over a billion people. China has always been an agrarian nation with a mass of poor peasants, but throughout the twentieth century the nation struggled for economic development. The Communist government of China stressed industrialization, economic growth, and improvement of the standard of living. At the same time, it gave priority to building a revolutionary Communist society. The interplay of the economic and political objectives and the issue of priorities are the keys to understanding revolutionary China and its efforts to achieve economic growth.

First, one must note the objective conditions in China and the country's past efforts to deal with those conditions. China's overriding problem in modern times (for at least the past two centuries) has been how to feed itself. The population continued to grow rapidly both before and after the Communists came to power in 1949. At that time, it was about 535 million; by 1970 it was 840 million; and in the early 1980s, it passed the 1 billion mark. Traditionally, over 90 percent of the people were peasants engaged in subsistence agriculture. Despite the country's great size, there was barely enough land to support the people. Only about 20 percent of the land is arable, with the remainder either too mountainous or too arid for agriculture. China's huge population, therefore, was heavily concentrated in the areas with arable land, mainly the coastal regions. But even in these areas there is a scarcity of land. And because of the unequal distribution of land, in the past the bulk of the peasants either owned too little land or none at all. This set of conditions—the plight of the impoverished peasants and their exploitation by the landowning class—gave rise to Mao Zedong's Communist movement, which was committed to putting an end to these conditions.

China had made very little progress toward industrialization prior to Communist rule. The Nationalist regime in the 1930s attempted to industrialize, but this endeavor was cut short by the eight-year-long war with Japan. In 1949, the Communists inherited a country that had suffered the destruction of that war, as well as three subsequent years of civil war. The country had only very meager industrial development, was wracked with uncontrolled inflation and economic chaos, and had an impoverished and illiterate peasantry and cities swollen with jobless, desperate people. Moreover, China lacked many of the basic elements for modernization: capital, technology, and an educated working class.

Under the rule of Communist Party Chairman Mao, politics—which is to say Marxist revolution—had greater priority than did economic growth. Mao's often quoted dictum "politics take command" meant that every activity in China was to be defined politically in Marxist terms. Thus, to study economic development in Mao's China is to study the Marxist politics of Mao and his comrades in the Chinese Communist Party (CCP).

Initially, upon coming to power in 1949, the Communists stressed economic rehabilitation and postponed their socialist objectives. In the first three years, they managed to establish economic and political order, control inflation, and restore production in the existing industries to their prewar level. Major industries were nationalized, foreign enterprises were confiscated, and private enterprise was eliminated gradually as state control of the economy was increased. The new regime also addressed the peasant question—an issue that could not wait—by instituting wholesale land reform. The redistribution of land was carried out swiftly and ruthlessly, resulting in the transfer of millions of acres to over 300 million peasants and the elimination of the "landlord class." Estimates of the loss of life vary greatly, but no doubt several million Chinese met their deaths during this revolutionary process.

By 1953, the Chinese government was ready to institute the First Five-Year Plan, which was modeled on that of the Soviet Union and guided by Soviet economic advisers. Economic assistance from the Soviet Union was of great importance to China—the technical aid more than the monetary loans, which were rather meager (although more than China obtained from anywhere else). As in the Soviet Union, the First Five-Year Plan stressed rapid development of heavy industry. It was implemented successfully, and as a result China's production of steel, electricity, and cement increased remarkably.

☐ The Great Leap Forward

As the Second Five-Year Plan was about to be launched, Mao questioned the effect this method of economic modernization was having on the Chinese revolution; he feared it would result in the entrenchment of a powerful bureaucracy, a new elite that would exploit the Chinese masses. In early 1958, Mao suddenly called a halt to the Second Five-Year Plan, thereby rejecting the Soviet model for development, and called instead for a "Great Leap Forward." This plan called for tapping the energies of the masses of people—China's greatest resource—to industrialize and collectivize at the same time. In the countryside, the agricultural collectives, which had been formed in the mid-1950s, were to be reorganized into larger units (communes) that would embody the basic Marxist principle "From each according to his abilities, to each according to his needs." Mao's approach was to mobilize the masses through the use of ideology to develop a revolutionary fervor. This frenzied pace could not be maintained, however, and the excess of zeal, lack of administrative ability, and poor planning produced an economic disaster. The economic collapse was made worse by Soviet Premier Nikita Khrushchev, who withdrew all Soviet technicians from China in 1960, and by three consecutive years of crop failures (1959–1961). The Great Leap Forward was, in fact, a disastrous leap backward, and it cost China dearly—causing untold hardship, crippling the economy, and taking a huge toll in lives. It is impossible to know the number of Chinese who died as a result of revolutionary violence, political upheavals, and famine during Mao's rule, but an estimate of such deaths attributed to the Great Leap Forward is 10 million.[1]

From this point on, we can clearly detect the contention between two conflicting strategies in Communist China. The one we can label Maoist, or radical, the other moderate. The radical approach was reflected in the manner in which Mao built the Communist movement in China in the 1930s, in the Great Leap Forward, and later in the Great Cultural Revolution. This approach stressed the "mass line," meaning the power of the people and their active engagement in the revolution. It called for intense ideological training of the CCP cadre, the dedicated party activists who stimulated and served as a model for the masses. The cult of Mao was also an important tool for politicizing the masses. It was not an end in itself but a means to an end: a thoroughly revolutionary society that was egalitarian and free of exploitation of the masses.

The moderate line de-emphasized ideology and revolutionary zeal and instead stressed state planning, bureaucratic leadership, and development of the skills and expertise necessary for the advancement of China. Its main feature was pragmatism—a rational, problem-solving, do-what-works approach. This approach was, therefore, less political, ideological, and emotional than the Maoist line, and it gave higher priority to bureaucratic management and economic modernization than to ideology.

☐ The Great Cultural Revolution

After the Great Leap Forward fiasco, the moderates took charge of cleaning up the mess Mao had made. Gradually, during the first half of the 1960s, the economy recovered under the guiding hand of such moderate leaders as Liu Shaoqi (Liu Shao-ch'i) and Deng Xiaoping (Teng Hsiao-p'ing). But once again, Mao became disturbed about the trend toward bureaucratic elitism. Using his immense prestige as "the Great Helmsman,"

Mao bypassed the Chinese Communist Party structure and in July 1966 initiated a new political movement aimed at purging the CCP of its elitist leaders: the "Great Proletarian Cultural Revolution."

Chairman Mao was determined once and for all to eradicate bureaucratism in the Chinese revolution. He charged his opponents not only with elitism, meaning they were guilty of selfishly guarding and advancing their own personal power and privilege, but also with revisionism, meaning they were guilty of revising (distorting) Marxism-Leninism, just as Mao felt recent Soviet leaders had. He claimed many party leaders were taking the "capitalist road" and thus destroying the Communist revolution. Mao enlisted the active support of the youth of China—who were dismissed from colleges and schools—organized them into the "Red Guards," and instructed them to go out and attack all those who were guilty of selfish elitism. "Serve the people" was the slogan, and Mao's writings were the guidelines. Throughout China, the Red Guards pressured all people high and low—officials, soldiers, peasants, and workers—to reform themselves through arduous study of the thought of Mao Zedong as presented in capsule form in the "Little Red Book," and they severely abused all who they found wanting.

Mao's Cultural Revolution was a unique event—a revolution within a stagnant revolution, a people's revolt against the revolutionary party ordered by the head of that party. Mao called upon the masses to purge their leaders—even in his own Communist Party—to put the revolution back on track. This upheaval was an embodiment of Mao's theory of "permanent revolution"—that is, continuing class struggle and use of revolutionary violence to purge the enemies of the revolution and prevent backsliding toward capitalism.

Coercion, Mao contended, was necessary to rid people of wrong ideas, just as "dust never vanishes of itself without sweeping." Mao's own Revolutionary Committee was to do the sweeping. Even though his Cultural Revolution was proclaimed in the name of lofty ideals, to bring about a utopian, egalitarian society utterly free of class exploitation, it would produce unimaginable mayhem—terror, death, and destruction. Mao's Red Guards, pumped up with Mao's revolutionary charge, rampaged throughout the country as on a crusade—wreaking havoc, destroying property, and capturing, condemning, brutalizing, and sometimes killing those deemed to be less than ideologically pure. Their excessive fervor soon rendered the Cultural Revolution a terrifying witch-hunt that not only destroyed the political order in China but disrupted the economy and caused untold torture, suffering, and death for countless people—probably in excess of 1 million.[2] When the Red Guard radicals met resistance, clashes occurred. In time, opposing bands of Red Guards, each claiming to have the correct Maoist line, engaged in pitched battles fought with weapons secured from the police or army units. As the violence and disruption mounted, Mao had to call in China's military forces, the People's Liberation Army (PLA), to quell the storm and restore order.

Two other victims of Mao's Cultural Revolution were the economy and education. Unchecked political violence caused disruption of the economy: work stoppages, decreased production, shortages, and inflation. In the long run, however, education, science, and technology may have suffered the greatest damage. High schools and universities were shut down for about five years, teachers and professors were taken to the countryside for political re-education (forced labor and study of Mao's writings), and books and laboratory equipment were destroyed. When schools reopened, academic standards were replaced with ideological standards—that is, students and teachers were evaluated not on the basis of measurable knowledge but on their dedication to Communism à la Mao. This was political correctness to the extreme. The disruption in Chinese higher education probably retarded China's economic development by more than a decade.

It took several years for the Cultural Revolution to wind down. It was never repudiated or terminated until after Mao's death in 1976, but, in fact, it was being quietly abandoned by the beginning of the 1970s. By then, Mao was aged and ill, and leadership passed into the hands of the very able Zhou Enlai. Zhou was actually a moderate, but he managed to dodge an attack by the Maoists as such, and now, more than ever, Mao trusted and relied on him. Gradually, Zhou reinstated moderates who had been expelled from the CCP and put China back on the track toward economic development. It was Zhou who engineered the new foreign policy of rapprochement with the United States in the early 1970s.

But the tensions between radicals (Maoists) and moderates were mounting under the surface of calm maintained by Zhou and Mao. These tensions erupted in 1976, the eventful "Year of the Tiger," when both Zhou and Mao died. Mao's designated successor, Hua Guofeng (Hua Kuo-feng), was able to quash an attempt by the radicals to gain control of the CCP and the government. Hua arrested the ringleaders, who collectively were labeled "the Gang of Four." One of the principal culprits was none other than Mao's wife, Jiang Qing (Chiang Ch'ing). For the next several years, Hua and resurrected moderate leader Deng Xiaoping conducted a political campaign of denunciation of the Gang of Four as a means of attacking the radicalism the Gang (and the departed Mao) had stood for. By the end of the 1970s, Deng was in full control of the party, having gently nudged Hua aside, and the Gang was put on trial for its crimes. Cautiously, the new leadership undertook the de-Maoization of China, as even Mao was denounced for his "mistakes" during the Cultural Revolution. Clearly, the moderates were back in the saddle again. It was their turn to reorganize Chinese society.

■ DENG XIAOPING'S MODERNIZATION DRIVE

Under Deng's leadership, the march toward economic development gained momentum. China normalized relations with the United States and Japan with the objectives of developing trade relations, attracting foreign capital, and purchasing technology. These and other programs, such as providing bonuses as material incentives for production and restoring a capitalistic market mechanism, stimulated economic growth and modernization. In their drive to close the technology gap, Chinese leaders welcomed foreign visitors—especially scientists, technicians, and industrialists—and began sending large numbers of Chinese students abroad, especially for study of science and technology.

In an effort to increase agricultural production in China and thus increase surpluses for investment in the industrial sector, in 1979 the new leadership instituted a new agrarian program called the "responsibility system," or "contract system." Under this new system, the peasants contracted for (or rented) land, seeds, and tools from the state; at harvest time, they met their contract obligations (paid their rent) and were allowed to keep as personal income all they had earned over and above what they had contracted for. They then sold their surplus production on the open market. The incentive for personal profit led to efficient farming and served to increase overall agricultural production. A very able farmer could rent a large amount of land and even hire other workers, and thus become an entrepreneur.

The new system, which worked rather well, struck observers as more like capitalism than Communism. It surely represented a radical departure from Mao's brand of Communism, with its emphasis on egalitarianism. But Deng, the dauntless pragmatist, remained determined to pursue whatever course would speed China's modernization and strengthen its economy. The new pragmatism was guided by Deng's two slogans: "Practice is the sole criterion of truth" and "Seek truth from facts."[3] Deng also said, "It doesn't matter what color the cat is, as long as it catches mice." Soviet leaders, who once had criticized Mao for moving too far to the left, condemned Deng's programs as going too far to the right. A Soviet visitor to China is said to have remarked, "If this is Marxism, I must reread Marx."[4] The following commentary, which appeared in the authoritative *People's Daily* in December 1984, made it abundantly clear that the Chinese leaders had indeed adopted a new view of Marxism:

[In addition to Marx] we must study some modern economic theories, as well as modern scientific and technological know-how. We can never rigidly adhere to the individual words and sentences or specific theories. Marx died 101 years ago.

His works were written more than 100 years ago. Some of his ideas are no longer suited to today's situation, because Marx never experienced these times, nor did Engels or Lenin. And they never came across the problems we face today. So we cannot use Marxist and Leninist works to solve our present-day problems. . . . If we continue to use certain Marxist principles, our historic development will surely be hampered.[5]

Deng's regime put a new face on China. Economic liberalization transformed China almost overnight from a drab proletarian society in which individual expression was suppressed into a lively new consumer society in which individuality was expressed much more freely. This transformation was even more dramatic than the one instituted by Mao's revolution. In Deng's China, private enterprise, profit seeking, capital investment, consumerism, and the pursuit of private wealth were no longer taboo but instead were encouraged. Enterprising Chinese became extremely successful in business ventures and displayed their newfound wealth in conspicuous ways, purchasing large homes and automobiles and taking trips abroad. Although authorities were concerned about the jealousy this behavior caused, they nonetheless encouraged people to seek their fortunes in the belief that doing so was for the betterment of both the individual and the economic development of the nation. Deng went so far as to proclaim as a new credo for the Chinese people "to get rich is glorious," an utterly outlandish notion by Maoist standards but one welcomed by the new entrepreneurs.

Deng's economic reform program represented a bold attempt to restructure the economy of the world's largest nation, and it proved to be remarkably successful. By 1987, eight years after Deng's ascent to power,

Chinese leader Deng Xiaoping, chairman of the Chinese Communist Party Central Advisory Commission, Dec. 14, 1985. (*Embassy of the People's Republic of China*)

the nation's GNP had grown substantially; rural incomes had tripled and urban incomes had doubled; foreign trade had doubled, reaching $10 billion; and direct foreign investment in China had risen dramatically.

Between 1980 and 1994, China sustained an average annual growth rate of nearly 8 percent.[6] The rapid rise in agricultural output in the first half of the 1980s resulted in self-sufficiency and even a modest surplus in food production. This feat, previously considered impossible for this nation of 1.1 billion people, was the result of both the new profit-motivated farming system and new population control measures enacted by the government.

The great, persistent problem of modern China remained overpopulation, but the Communist regime addressed this problem effectively. The regime instituted a stringent birth control program that rewarded families with no more than one child (with increased food rations and employment and education benefits, for example) and penalized families with more than one child (through decreased food rations, increased taxes, and other penalties). This policy and its related family planning program, including coerced abortions, had a significant effect on reducing the rate of population growth. The program served to hold in check a population explosion that threatened to swallow up any increased economic output. One of its social consequences, however, was an increase in infanticide—that is, parents killing unwanted children.

The economic modernization program, so successful in the early 1980s, began to falter by 1987 when it encountered new problems. Agricultural output fell in the mid-1980s, as many farmers sought enrichment in other, more profitable economic enterprises now open to them. The resulting grain shortage caused havoc for the economic modernization program.

Moreover, the efforts to institute price reforms resulted in sharply rising inflation. Deng and his protégé, Premier Zhao Ziyang, the most vigorous of the economic reformers, regarded price reform as the key to the continued success of the economic reform program. Heretofore, prices of consumer goods had been rigidly controlled and kept artificially low by government subsidies. When the government began removing price controls on such basic commodities as food and fuel, prices soared. By 1988, the inflation rate had reached about 30 percent. Only those whose income had increased significantly as a result of new business opportunities or those able to take advantage of Communist Party connections could afford the new prices. The vast majority of people whose incomes were fixed and relatively low—factory workers, intellectuals, lower- and middle-level government workers—were less fortunate. The new inflation inevitably brought an increase in corruption and resentment.

Inflation also brought a government decision to slow the economic modernization program. Li Peng, newly appointed as premier in early

1988, emerged as the leading proponent of retrenchment. Under his influence, in September 1988 the government called for a two-year program of austerity, renewed centralized planning, reinstatement of state trading monopolies, and postponement of further price reform. The aim was to curb inflation, cool off the "overheated" economy, and maintain a "reasonable" economic growth rate.

■ THE TIANANMEN SQUARE MASSACRE AND ITS AFTERMATH

The program of economic liberalization represented a significant departure from Marxism, a rejection of the Stalinist-type economic system, and considerable ideological flexibility, but it was not attended by a program of political liberalization. Deng's regime, however, did embark on a program of cautious political reform, which gradually offered a greater degree of openness and accountability in reporting governmental affairs, permitted freer access to information and ideas, reduced censorship, and allowed greater freedom of personal expression. The reform plans drawn up by Deng and Hu Yaobang, head of the Communist Party since 1981, specifically called for (1) administrative reforms that decentralized decision making and made individual political leaders more accountable for their decisions, (2) legal reforms aimed at replacing arbitrary and personal power with the rule of law, (3) election reforms offering more than one candidate in National People's Congress elections, and (4) a greater role for public opinion in the governing of China through such means as opinion polling and encouragement of suggestions and criticism in letters to editors of newspapers.

These political reforms were attended by considerable rhetoric about "democratization." Deng and his fellow reformers employed this term loosely in reference to reforms they had enacted to make the political system less arbitrary and more accountable. These reforms were never intended to introduce a democratic political system characterized by free elections contested by rival political parties vying for power. Deng strongly rejected the notion that "bourgeois liberalism" was appropriate for China. Instead, he consistently reaffirmed China's "four cardinal principles": (1) the socialist road, (2) rule by the Chinese Communist Party, (3) the "people's democratic dictatorship," and (4) Marxist-Leninist and Maoist thought. By invoking these principles, Deng made it clear that there were limits to "democratization" and to dissent in the People's Republic.

If Deng's regime, reformist though it was, had no intention of power sharing, its rhetoric of democratization, as well as the greater political and personal freedoms it had already permitted, whetted the appetites of many

Chinese for a greater measure of political liberalization. The new freedoms permitted in the economic sector could not, of course, be neatly limited to that sector, and the call for creativity, resourcefulness, and unrestricted inquiry in scientific and technological fields could not help but influence people's thinking on social and political matters. Since the early 1980s, hundreds of thousands of Chinese had gone abroad to study and had been exposed to democratic institutions and ideas and to social values that gave greater rein to individual rights and liberties. The increased knowledge of democratic societies, together with new economic liberalization, contributed to the emergence of a freer, more individualistic life in China— characterized by greater pursuit of pleasure and privileges, as well as profit. By the mid-1980s, however, the government began condemning the new, Western-influenced thinking and behavior (such as rock music) as "spiritual pollution" and cracked down on the more vocal proponents of democratic reform.

The growing demand for democratic change was suddenly made manifest by university students in large political demonstrations in December 1986 and January 1987. First in Shanghai and then in Beijing, students turned out by the hundreds of thousands to register their demand for political reforms. These demonstrations, by far the largest to date in the People's Republic, continued for almost two weeks before being broken up by the government, which had shown considerable restraint and offered vague promises of addressing the students' concerns. In reprisals that followed, however, Deng underscored the Communist Party's position as the final arbiter of all political matters. And more conservative party leaders, such as Li Peng, attacked party chief Hu Yaobang—the most outspoken advocate of political reform—as being too radical and reckless in the pursuit of democratization. Deng was willing to accept Hu's dismissal from his post for the sake of protecting the economic reform program.

The movement for democratic reform in China remained silenced until it suddenly erupted again in the spring of 1989. In the interim, students and intellectuals in China chafed not only at the growing repressiveness of the regime but also by the increased economic hardship caused by inflation. They were also rankled at the increasing evidence of widespread corruption, especially on the part of high-ranking government officials and their families. Further, they were repulsed by a ruling Communist Party that, in effect, had abandoned Marxism and the ideals of Mao and offered nothing worthy of commitment in their place. For many disillusioned youth, state ideology had become irrelevant. Some looked back to Mao's era with nostalgia, not because it had been democratic but because it had at least inspired people with high ideals and a sense of purpose. Many felt the party had lost its moral authority to govern China. At a minimum, the students who rallied in 1989 demanded accountability on the part of government leaders and an unfettered press, without which accountability could not be achieved.

The occasion that triggered the student demonstrations in late April 1989 was the death of Hu Yaobang. Students from several Beijing universities defied government orders by marching on Tiananmen Square in the heart of Beijing—first to commemorate Hu, whom they heralded as a champion of the democratic cause, and then to demand political reforms. On their posters they demanded increased respect for human rights, the release of political prisoners, a new democratic constitution, greater freedom of speech and press, and the right to hold demonstrations.[7]

The student leaders exploited Western press coverage, deluding themselves that the government would not risk its international prestige by using force against unarmed demonstrators. They also made excellent use of opportunities presented by the calendar. The first important anticipated date was May 4, the seventieth anniversary of the student uprising in 1919 that gave birth to the Chinese Communist Party. The students of spring 1989 laid claim to being the rightful heirs of that hallowed movement. By May 4, their numbers in Tiananmen Square had grown to over 100,000, and the movement had spread to other cities. Government leaders, recognizing the powerful symbolism of the date, considered it too dangerous to stop the demonstrations.

Another reason the government did not move to suppress the movement was the scheduled arrival of Soviet leader Mikhail Gorbachev on May 15. Gorbachev's visit had enormous diplomatic significance in its own right. Chinese leaders were eager to ratify the end of the Sino-Soviet feud, and they were determined not to allow the students to interfere with this important diplomatic objective. Nor could Deng's government afford to jeopardize good relations with the Soviet leader by using brutal force against the students on the eve of, much less during, his visit. Two days before Gorbachev arrived, 2,000 student protesters began a public hunger strike on Tiananmen Square; the next day, hundreds of thousands flocked to the square in support, ignoring the deadline the government had issued for clearing the area. The students hailed Gorbachev as a true champion of democratization and lampooned Deng, the dauntless author of the post-Mao reforms, as a stodgy old hard-liner. Gorbachev deftly managed neither to support nor discourage the students, and he gave faint praise to Chinese leaders for "opening a political dialogue with the demonstrators."[8]

There would be no dialogue, however. No sooner had Gorbachev left Beijing than the government declared martial law. Over the next three weeks, the drama unfolding on Tiananmen Square gripped the nation and the worldwide viewing public. Student demonstrators were emboldened by the fact that the government had not taken action to enforce the martial decree and that large numbers of workers in Beijing and other cities had openly embraced their movement. It was precisely this fact that caused the government to crack down on the demonstrators, for it could not afford to allow the antigovernment agitation to spread to the general public. The protesters took heart when the troops who assembled to suppress the movement seemed disinclined to use force against the students. Emotions were fired all the more by the erection of a "goddess of democracy" statue (resembling the Statue of Liberty in New York harbor) on Tiananmen Square as a symbol of their cause. Meanwhile, as the protesters became more defiant in their demands—no longer merely calling for dialogue but demanding the overthrow of the government—other army units were brought into position to crush the revolt. Finally, under the cover of darkness in the early hours of June 4, columns of tanks rumbled into the square, and a terrible massacre began. The extent of the carnage is still not known and may never be known, but estimates vary from as many as 3,000 deaths to the government's preposterous claim that no students were killed on Tiananmen Square.[9]

Much remains unclear regarding the objectives of the protesters, the discord within both the government and the army, and the facts regarding the massacre itself. But it is clear that despite its denials, the government used deadly force to end a popular movement that, on the one hand, had threatened the political stability of the country and the continued rule of the Communist Party and, on the other, had captured the hopes of millions of young Chinese and the sympathy and support of millions of people outside of China.

The June 4 Tiananmen Square massacre was not the end but only the beginning of the government effort to suppress political opposition and restore its own authority. No sooner was the shooting over than the Chinese government employed a second tool of repression—a controlled media—to communicate to the entire nation its version of what had taken place. First came the denial of the massacre and the rationalization of the crackdown. The Chinese were told that the army had heroically defended the nation against an armed counterrevolutionary rebellion. Then came the reprisals, as leaders of the "rebellion" were hunted down, arrested, pronounced guilty of treasonous acts, and, in some cases, executed. Thousands of others were imprisoned. Cowed by state power, Chinese citizens who had witnessed the events on Tiananmen Square completely denied having witnessed anything at all.

In the year that followed, the old guard was steadfastly determined to stay the course by cracking down on "counterrevolutionary offenders," silencing dissent, intensifying ideological education, and warding off international criticism. By the first anniversary of Tiananmen, their success was limited to the suppression of opposition and the maintenance of political stability. The government's effort to renew ideological fervor was met only with the sullen compliance of a demoralized society. Rather than accept the party leaders' campaign for ideological purity, many Chinese reverted to the style of mutual self-protection they had learned in earlier Maoist times. Of the thousands arrested after the massacre, about forty were executed and eighteen were given long prison sentences. When a U.S. State Department official inquired into possible violations of the dissenters' human rights, Beijing countered with charges that such inquiries constituted a violation of China's sovereignty and lectured foreign observers that those in jail were not "dissidents" but "offenders."[10]

In its diplomacy, Beijing sought to repair the damage caused by Tiananmen and to induce foreign investors and buyers to continue to do business with China. The Tiananmen crackdown had cost China an estimated $2–$3 billion in investments and developmental assistance, but by the second anniversary of that event, Beijing had succeeded in wooing most major industrial democracies back into normal diplomatic and economic relations. A major reason for the return to business as usual was the pull of China's own economy, which in the first half of 1991 grew at a rate of 13.7 percent. Meanwhile, China gained international respectability through diplomatic moves, such as supporting UN resolutions against Iraq, signing the Nuclear Non-Proliferation Treaty, terminating military aid to the Khmer Rouge, and supporting the UN peace plan in Cambodia.

* * *

At the same time, Beijing faced another challenge: the demise of Communism in Eastern Europe and the Soviet Union. Chinese leaders had opposed Gorbachev's political reforms and were distressed by the dismantling of the East European bloc and the unraveling of the Soviet Union itself. Still, Beijing cautiously sought to maintain relations with the new Russian Federation and the other successor states of the former Soviet Union. The collapse of the citadel of Communism was an ideological blow to the Chinese rulers, but their response was to hunker down, intensify ideological training, and tighten party control of the media and the military.

■ DENG'S LAST STAND

Within China, a long-festering debate among the Communist leaders over economic policy and ideology came into the open in early 1992. Chief among the ideological hard-liners was Li Peng, who remained critical of the market system reforms Deng Xiaoping had instituted in the 1980s. Li Peng was clearly in ascendance among Chinese leaders in the post-Tiananmen period, despite the widespread public view of him as "the most hated man in China." But suddenly, the eighty-seven-year-old Deng reemerged from retirement to tour China's most advanced economic zones and reissue the call for stepping up economic reform.[11] Within a month, party leader Jiang Zemin and the Politburo jumped on Deng's bandwagon, publicly endorsing his campaign for accelerated economic liberalization and vigilance against leftist extremism. The *People's Daily* trumpeted Deng's command: "Firmly grasp the party's basic line and do not waver for 100 years. . . . Seize the opportunity to speed up reform and opening up to the outside world to improve the economy."[12]

Deng's dictum remained in force through the mid-1990s, during which time China's economy registered an unprecedented growth rate of 10 to 13 percent annually. China's progress was indisputable: its people were wealthier, freer, and better fed, dressed, and housed than at any time in the past. But the economy was dangerously overheated, for it had been built mainly through foreign investment, speculation, and deficit spending. Li Peng's consistent call for cooling the economy was reflected in a new five-year economic plan in October 1995 that called for measured growth, a return to centralized controls, and a return to price controls to curb inflation—which was running at a rate of about 25 percent. Beijing feared continued unrestrained growth would trigger "social instability," meaning such things as corruption, gross inequality in wealth, and discontent among the restless youth. Another matter of great concern was the flood of an estimated 100 million rural migrants to China's cities. The government's renewed crackdown on political dissent reflected its anxiety over its ability to maintain control and to stave off an upheaval such as Tiananmen Square or the collapse of Communism, as had happened in the Soviet Union.

As long as Deng lived, a precarious stability held, but by 1996 he was ninety-two years old and rather feeble. A cautious tug-of-war was taking place for leadership in anticipation of the old patriarch's passing—reminiscent of the situation prior to Mao's death two decades earlier. Deng's designated successor, Jiang Zemin, who held the offices of president and general secretary of the CCP, was a compromise candidate, characterized as cautious and colorless. Striving to maintain order and ensure his succession, Jiang attempted to steer a safe course between Deng's drive for economic liberalization and growth and Li Peng's fiscal conservatism and toughness against dissent.

In the mid-1990s, China's leaders were also confronted with several persistent foreign policy issues, especially the worsening of its relations with its largest trading partner, the United States. Ever since Tiananmen Square, Washington had pressured China about its deplorable human rights record. The United States threatened to deny China most-favored-nation treatment (trade terms equal to those enjoyed by other nations), thus denying continued access to the huge U.S. market unless China took measures to safeguard human rights, particularly in regard to its treatment of political dissenters. Beijing contended that this threat constituted unwarranted encroachment on China's sovereignty. In 1993, President Bill Clinton granted most-favored-nation status to China and thereby separated the economic and human rights issues, but international rebuke of China on the latter issue persisted. Beijing, however, rebuffed criticism on this and on issues such as its suppression of Tibet, its atmospheric testing of nuclear weapons, and its sale of missiles and nuclear technology to Pakistan and certain Middle Eastern countries. Trade relations with the United States remained contentious, as China built up an enormous trade surplus at U.S. expense and came under attack for pirating intellectual property (computer software, videos, compact disks, and the like) and for other alleged violations of trade agreements. Finally, Beijing was rankled by continued U.S. military support for the rival government (the Republic of China) on Taiwan, including its sale of 150 advanced jet fighters to Taiwan in 1992. (For Taiwan-PRC relations, see the last section of this chapter.)

* * *

After a long illness, Deng Xiaoping died in March 1997, at the age of ninety-two. He had retained authority even in infirmity as China's "paramount leader," even though the top party, government, and military posts had already been awarded to his designated successor, Jiang Zemin. Because the transfer of power was firmly set, Deng's death caused no struggle for power in Beijing or abrupt changes in its policies—at least in the short run.

■ THE FOUR TIGERS OF ASIA

By the 1980s, along the Asian shores of the Pacific Ocean were five prospering nations: Japan, South Korea (the Republic of Korea), Taiwan (the Republic of China), Hong Kong, and Singapore. Foremost among them as an economic power was Japan, whose "economic miracle" was launched in the early 1960s. The others, sometimes referred to as the "four tigers of Asia," followed in Japan's footsteps in the 1970s and 1980s to produce their own economic miracles. Their economic performance, especially their vigorous export-oriented industrial development, together with that of Japan gave rise in the 1980s to such notions as the coming "Asian-Pacific century" and to the concept of the "Pacific Rim" as the arena of the world's fastest economic growth and largest international trade flow. The "four tigers" became the source of a flood of imports into the United States and a major source of its mounting trade deficit. The U.S. trade gap with the four countries grew from $3.6 billion in 1980 to over $35 billion in 1987, an imbalance that caused strains in the relations between them and Washington.

The "four tigers" all shared with Japan certain common features that accounted for their remarkable economic performance (see Table 15.1). They shared a Chinese historical and cultural heritage, particularly an ingrained Confucian value system. It appears that this philosophy—long ridiculed by the West (and by westernized Asians) as antiquated and a barrier

Table 15.1   Growth Rates of the Four Tigers (by percentage)

	1977–1981	1982–1986	1987	1988
South Korea	7.3	8.5	12.2	10.3
Taiwan	9.0	6.9	12.3	7.4
Hong Kong	10.8	5.9	13.5	7.1
Singapore	7.1	4.4	8.8	9.1

Sources: Bank of Japan, *Comparative International Statistics, 1988;* International Monetary Fund, *International Financial Statistics, 1988,* Tokyo; and *Wall Street Journal,* Washington, D.C., November 1, 1988, p. A24.

to modern progress—was a major source of traits and attitudes that accounted for the high productivity of Asian workers and the efficiency of Asian management. Inculcated in the youth of countries that share the Confucian heritage are such traits as discipline, loyalty, respect for authority, paternalism, desire for harmony, sincerity, a strong sense of duty, and respect for education. The Confucian legacy seemed to have been a vital ingredient for making capitalism work in these Asian nations.

Other factors were no doubt involved in the economic success of the "four tigers," including the model of Japan and the investments and technology flowing from Japan. Still another major cause of the growth of these countries was their ready supply of relatively cheap labor. Moreover, each of these countries had authoritarian governments that curbed democratic development but made economic development their highest priority and marshaled the power of the state toward that end. Their rulers centralized power and economic planning, enforced political stability (except for South Korea, as noted later), and mobilized human resources effectively. Like Japan, all four of these Asian nations, as newly industrializing countries, stressed export-oriented industrial development and took advantage of the global free trade system established by the industrialized nations of the West after World War II. They also emphasized public education, the development of technology, and birth control.[13]

The two most successful of the "four tigers," South Korea and Taiwan, had several common characteristics that set them apart from the other two, Singapore and Hong Kong, which were city-states. Both South Korea and Taiwan thrived on adversity. Both countries were highly militarized, with each facing threats to its security—from Communist North Korea and from the Communist mainland, respectively. The maintenance of large military establishments and the burden of large military budgets may have been seen as a drag on economic development, but it seemed they also had the effect of spurring economic modernization. Moreover, the presence of a threat to the nation produced a sense of national urgency and national purpose that was useful to these governments and government-supported industrialists as well. One can detect in the recent historical experience of

South Korea and Taiwan a similar pattern whereby authoritarian governments began to give way to democratization after the achievement of prosperity. Economic modernization gave rise to an affluent middle class, which, in turn, demanded political liberalization and representation in the political process.

Before examining the economic performance and politics of each of the "four tigers," it should be noted that in the early 1990s they were joined by three other rapidly advancing Asian nations: Thailand, Malaysia, and Indonesia. (For these three nations see Chapter 16)

☐ South Korea

South Korea catapulted from the level of a miserably poor Third World nation in the 1950s to the status of a rapidly industrializing nation. South Korea had suffered from the division of the Korean nation after World War II because most of the minerals and industries in the peninsula were located in North Korea, and it suffered still more from the devastation of the Korean War in the early 1950s. Although at that time it had more paved roads and railroads (built by the Japanese before World War II) than most Third World countries, South Korea was an extremely impoverished nation. Gradually, living standards improved in the 1960s, and in the early 1970s the nation began its economic takeoff. Its annual rate of economic growth rose to over 14 percent in the early 1970s; after a brief slowdown in the early 1980s, it climbed again to the rate of 12 percent in 1986 and 1987. In 1964, the per capita GNP of South Korea was a mere $103, but by 1994 it had soared to $8,260. Only Japan and Taiwan matched this phenomenal record of economic growth.

South Korea's rise to economic prominence occurred during the rule of the military regimes of Gens. Park Chung Hee and Chun Doo Hwan. General Park, who came to power as a result of a military coup in 1961, dissolved the National Assembly and established military rule. Three years later, he resigned from the army and was elected president, but this hardly changed the character of his military dictatorship. With the help of generous economic aid from the United States and Japan, Park's government embarked on an industrialization drive led by giant state-supported industrial firms. Economic development was concentrated largely in Seoul, the capital, and Pusan, the southern port, where living conditions improved; poverty in the rest of the country, however, remained endemic. Political unrest in the country continued, and in 1979 his own intelligence agency chief shot and killed Park.

After a brief power struggle, army Gen. Chun Doo Hwan emerged as the new ruler of the country. Following the model of Park, Chun took off his military uniform for his inauguration as president in September 1980 and continued military rule in civilian clothes. Korean students protested vehemently against the continuation of dictatorship, and in an uprising in the city of Kwangju in May 1980, as many as 2,000 student protesters were gunned down by security forces. Through the 1980s there was no letup in student demonstrations—which at times became violent—although political repression diminished somewhat. All the while, as the generals cracked down on dissenters, South Korea continued to grow and prosper economically.

The showcase of South Korea's emergence as a modern nation was the summer Olympic Games in Seoul in September 1988. In anticipation of the event, there was great concern over the possible disruption of the games by either mounting political student demonstrations or acts of terrorism by the jealous North Koreans.[14] When President Chun rejected the pleas of opposition parties for new election rules to allow the direct election of the president, he was faced with still larger political demonstrations spearheaded by university students but now joined by many of the country's new middle class. Finally, to head off a bloody confrontation that might result in the cancellation of the Olympics, Chun suddenly backed down. In June 1987, he appointed his military academy classmate, Roh Tae Woo, as his successor, and Roh announced a general election to be held in December in which he would run as the ruling party's candidate for president. In that election, the first free presidential election in South Korean history, Roh won a narrow victory but only because the two popular opposition candidates, Kim Dae Jung and Kim Young Sam, had split the opposition vote.

A political lull prevailed in summer and fall 1988 while South Korea basked in the international limelight of the Olympics. But the political rancor resumed soon afterward as Roh's opponents attacked his predecessor for corruption and demanded that he be put on trial. Meanwhile, students returned to the streets protesting the continued presence of U.S. military forces in Korea. Roh strengthened his grip on power in 1989 when his ruling party merged with that of Kim Young Sam, his leading opponent in the 1987 election, and a third party. The new party created by this merger, the Democratic Liberal Party, commanded an unassailable 70 percent majority in the National Assembly and seemed securely in power for the long haul. But university student activists—who regarded themselves as guardians of Korean democracy—protested relentlessly against the new regime, denouncing Roh as a militarist and Kim as an opportunist and a traitor. Student protest escalated in the spring of 1991 when, in reaction to one student demonstrator having been beaten to death by riot police, nine separate incidents of protest through self-immolation occurred.

Although President Roh achieved some startling breakthroughs on the diplomatic front, establishing diplomatic and economic relations with both the Soviet Union and China, he encountered many problems on the home front. In addition to increased student agitation, a series of political scandals and an economic downturn occurred in the early 1990s. With Roh's single five-year term coming to an end, the presidential elections in December 1992 pitted the inveterate opposition candidate Kim Dae Jung against Kim Young Sam, formerly an opposition leader but now the nominee of the ruling party.

The winner of South Korea's first presidential contest between two civilian politicians was Kim Young Sam, who, as president, took bold steps to reform South Korean politics—purging corrupt politicians from the legislature, curbing the power of the internal security agency, and arresting military officers charged with corruption. He also sought to pacify the student protesters by pledging a full-scale investigation of the 1980 Kwangju massacre and compensation for its victims. The students, however, kept the pressure on; 50,000 marched in May 1993 demanding that former Presidents Chun Doo Hwan and Roh Tae Woo be punished for having ordered the bloody massacre. Both men were already under investigation for massive bribery that occurred during their administrations.

In November 1995, Roh was arrested after admitting he had received huge contributions from leading business tycoons and operated a $653 million slush fund. Not only the two former presidents but leading military officers and captains of industry—heads of the most powerful business groups (Hundai, Samsung, and others)—were brought to heel. President Kim finally bowed to student and public demand to bring indictments against Chun and Roh for their role in the Kwangju massacre. At the sensational trials of the two former presidents in 1996, Chun was sentenced to death (subsequently commuted to a lengthy prison term) for his role in the 1979 military coup and the 1980 Kwangju massacre, whereas Roh was sentenced to a twenty-two-month prison term for accepting half a million dollars in bribes. Meanwhile, Kim himself was implicated in past corruption and met with declining credibility and diminishing public support.

☐ Taiwan

Since the 1960s, the economic development of the Republic of China on the island of Taiwan has been as spectacular as that of South Korea. The GNP of Taiwan rose from $8 billion in 1960 to $72.5 billion in 1986, and for most of the 1970s it maintained double-digit growth rates. Taiwan's annual volume of foreign trade increased from $2.2 billion to $100 billion between 1969 and 1988. By virtue of its burgeoning exports, by 1988 Taiwan had accumulated a foreign exchange reserve in excess of $70 billion, second in the world only to Japan. Within Taiwan, wealth was relatively evenly distributed.

Taiwan's economic success can be attributed to many factors, including (in addition to those discussed earlier) the infrastructure the Japanese built in Taiwan before 1945, a quarter century of U.S. economic aid and an open U.S. import policy for Taiwanese goods, the influx of highly educated Chinese from the mainland in 1949, the growth-oriented economic policies of the Nationalist government, and, its industrious people.

In the 1950s, a sweeping land reform was carried out, and agricultural production grew steadily, paving the way for capital accumulation and investment in industrial development. By the 1960s, Taiwan's industries began shifting emphasis from production of goods for domestic consumption to export-oriented production. Lured by Taiwan's cheap, high-quality labor, U.S. and Japanese companies began making substantial investments, and Taiwanese industrialists and workers rapidly absorbed modern technology. In the late 1970s, Taiwan began making the shift to capital-intensive and knowledge-intensive industries, a shift that paid huge dividends in the 1980s. By the end of the 1980s, electronics had replaced textiles as the leading export, and Taiwan became one of the world's leaders in microcomputers and computer parts.

As with South Korea, Taiwan's economic growth was not accompanied by political modernization; only later did significant liberalization occur. Although lauded for many years by the United States as the "democratic" alternative to the oppressive Communist regime on the mainland, the "Free China" under Nationalist ruler Jiang Jieshi (Chiang K'ai-shek) was anything but free or democratic. When Nationalist officials wrested control of Taiwan from the Japanese after World War II, they were met with resistance by the native Taiwanese, and this resistance was brutally suppressed by the Nationalist Army.[15] After arriving on the island in 1949 with almost 2 million soldiers and civilian supporters, Jiang created the political myth according to which the Nationalist government (the Republic of China), now situated on the island of Taiwan, remained the only legitimate government of China. The National Assembly, for example, was made up entirely of Nationalist Party politicians who had been elected on the mainland in 1948, and it remained without Taiwanese representation until the 1980s. In this manner, Jiang and his Nationalist Party maintained thorough domination of the Taiwanese majority (about 13 million people in the 1950s) for four decades. Over the years, until his death in 1975, Jiang maintained the Nationalist myth and ruthlessly suppressed all opposition. The regime remained stridently anti-Communist and ever vigilant against both Communist subversion and the outlawed Taiwanese independence movement.

Democratization finally came to Taiwan in the mid-1980s under Jiang Jingguo, son of and successor to Jiang Jieshi. This was made possible by the new prosperity in Taiwan, social change, the spread of education, and the Nationalist government's increased confidence in domestic security. In 1986, a newly formed opposition party, the Democratic Progressive Party (DPP)—although not yet legalized—was permitted to run candidates in the National Assembly election and won a surprising 25 percent of the vote.[16] In

July 1987, the government lifted the martial law decree that had been in effect for thirty-eight years, legalized opposition parties, and granted freedom of the press. It also dropped the ban on travel to Communist China, for the first time permitting its citizens to visit families on the mainland. Ten of thousands of residents quickly took advantage of this new opportunity.

President Jiang Jingguo died in January 1988, thus ending the sixty-year Jiang dynasty. His successor was his vice-president, Lee Teng-hui, who was not from mainland China but from Taiwan. Although Lee did not advocate independence for Taiwan, the fact that a native Taiwanese was now president encouraged those who did. Moreover, Lee, without a strong power base of his own, could hardly revert to the strongman type of rule characteristic of the Jiang dynasty. Instead, he continued the political liberalization begun by Jiang Jingguo. The first signal event in Taiwan's democratization under Lee was the December 1989 National Assembly election, which was the first free, multiparty election in Chinese history. The result of this election, in which 78 percent of eligible voters cast ballots, was an assembly far more representative of the people of Taiwan than the previous assembly, which was made up entirely of mainland Chinese. Another major step on the road to democracy was the first direct election of the president of the republic, held in April 1996. In these elections, the Nationalist Party held on to its ruling power, but its share of the vote decreased and opposition parties made substantial gains.

☐ Hong Kong

The British crown colony of Hong Kong has long been a mecca of capitalism, and it, too, experienced phenomenal economic growth in the post–World War II era. Britain's "gunboat diplomacy" had pried Hong Kong away from China in the nineteenth century, and it remained in British control even after the Communists came to power in China. In its early years, the PRC was too weak militarily to attempt to recover Hong Kong by force, and Beijing eventually took a pragmatic, rather than a doctrinaire, view of the British presence there—deciding it represented not a threat to China but an opportunity to maintain profitable economic relations with the West.

The British governors of Hong Kong maintained political stability and presided over a docile populace (only 6 million in 1990) and a prospering economy. Hong Kong steadily developed as a major financial, trade, and insurance center, and in the 1980s it also became highly industrialized. The thriving business environment attracted huge investments from Western countries and Japan, further stimulating economic growth. Hong Kong's average annual rate of growth was 5.5 percent between 1980 and 1992, but it rose as high as 13.5 percent in 1987. Although Hong Kong had a large number of poor people, mainly recent arrivals from the PRC, its per capita GNP reached $15,360 in 1992. The central section of the city-state became resplendent with wealth, with gleaming skyscrapers soaring above Mercedes-Benz automobiles and free-spending shoppers crowding the streets below.

The single threat to Hong Kong's continued economic stability and prosperity was the fact that it was scheduled to revert to Chinese rule in 1997. As early as the 1970s, when that target date was still twenty years away, the British and Chinese governments began to plan for the reversion. International business interests became nervous about their investments, and to head off a flight of capital and financial chaos the British government was eager to secure an early agreement with the Chinese government for an orderly transition. Similarly, it was in the PRC's interest to maintain the financial strength of Hong Kong, since the city-state played an important role in China's economic growth.

After long negotiations, London and Beijing signed a joint declaration in 1984 that provided a framework for the Chinese takeover, still thirteen years away. The agreement stipulated that Hong Kong would retain its capitalist system while maintaining "a high degree of autonomy" as a "special administrative region" of the People's Republic for fifty years after the reversion in 1997. With this formula, the Chinese and British sought to preserve political and economic stability through 1997 and beyond. The agreement also stipulated that the ethnic Chinese citizens of Hong Kong (98 percent of the population) would become citizens of China at the time of reversion but that they were free to leave the colony prior to that time.

The reversion agreement had mixed results as the years ticked away. Economic growth did not decline appreciably, and, in fact, foreign and domestic investments increased dramatically. Even in 1996, with reversion to China only a year away, the Hong Kong government was pumping record amounts (U.S.$21 billion) into a series of twenty-first-century investments, including a new international airport, a high-speed rail line to link the airport to the inner city, new superhighways, vast new housing projects, a new harbor tunnel, and the world's longest suspension bridge.

But if investors remained confident about Hong Kong's future, many of its residents were less so. In the late 1980s, about 50,000 people emigrated from Hong Kong annually (mainly to Canada, Australia, and the United States). This exodus of residents—largely wealthy, well-educated elites—reflected fear of Chinese rule.[17] The exodus caused consternation in Beijing, which sought to reassure the people in the colony and avert the hemorrhage of wealth and talent. The bloody suppression of the prodemocracy movement in Tiananmen Square in June 1989 and the subsequent political repression carried out by the Chinese government further damaged its credibility in Hong Kong and caused even greater emigration. Within five years, however, the annual rate of emigration had leveled off again at about 55,000, and by this time about 12 percent of those who had emigrated had returned. Many Hong Kong residents sought to leave open the possibility of emigrating after the reversion by securing a British passport beforehand. The PRC at first said no to this plan but later agreed to allow passports to be issued up until a year prior to reversion.

After Tiananmen, mutual distrust and suspicion lingered between the British and the Chinese. London took the position that Beijing—its promises notwithstanding—had already taken too many steps to curtail Hong Kong's autonomy. Shortly after arriving as the newly appointed governor of Hong Kong in July 1992, Christopher Patten abruptly announced a plan to substantially broaden the voting franchise for Legislative Council elections and thus to strengthen democracy and autonomy in the crown colony before its transfer to China. Beijing lost no time in venting its indignation, arguing that London had shown little interest in promoting democracy in the colony in the past and was now violating the spirit of the transfer agreement. When talks on this issue reached an impasse, the PRC declared in 1996 that Hong Kong's elected legislature would be abolished after reversion and replaced with an appointed one.

As the date neared for handing China the keys to Hong Kong, the latter's economy was still booming (growing at a steady 5 percent annually), and plans for the transition were being worked out with improved cooperation. All involved—the Chinese, the British, and the residents of Hong Kong—seemed to recognize the importance of Hong Kong's future as the dynamic economic capital of southern China and the Southeast Asian region. Yet, apprehension and uncertainty remained palpable, especially for its residents, because of the enormous gulf between Hong Kong's system—said to be the freest economic system in the world—and the centrally planned, politically controlled economy of the PRC.

☐ Singapore

Singapore is also a city-state and a former British colony, which won its independence in 1964. Located at the southern tip of the Malay peninsula in the South China Sea, Singapore was a member of ASEAN (the Association of Southeast Asian Nations), but unlike the other ASEAN nations its population was mainly ethnic Chinese. (For ASEAN see Chapter 16.) Singapore was also far more wealthy than the other ASEAN nations. Under its authoritarian ruler, Lee Kuan Yew, Singapore became one of the most prosperous countries in Asia, with a per capita GNP of $22,500 in 1994. A combination of political stability, population growth control, high standards of education, a disciplined and skilled work force, efficient economic management, export-oriented planning, and a free market system worked miracles for its 2.8 million people. Strategically situated at the center of the Southeast Asian sea-lanes, Singapore became a conveyor belt for the shipment of goods from outside the region to neighboring ASEAN countries, as well as a major regional financial center.

Singapore's remarkable economic development was also largely a result of the leadership of Prime Minister Lee Kuan Yew, whose authoritarian rule extended well beyond conventional bounds of politics and economics. Lee endeavored to make Singapore a spotless, crime-free, morally upright, and austere society; toward that end, he took it upon himself to dictate social and moral standards and to enforce them with strict laws and strong penalties. He decreed, for example, that men could not grow their hair long, and offenders were subject to arrest, fines, and even imprisonment. Possession of drugs, even small amounts, was punishable by death. Nor did Lee, who had exercised unlimited authority in Singapore since the late 1950s, allow dissent. He maintained that the curbs on individual freedoms was not regimentation but produced guidance that led to a more disciplined and productive people whose work habits contributed to even higher productivity and the betterment of all members of society.

■ THE UNFINISHED COLD WAR IN EAST ASIA

□ Divided Korea: North Versus South

For decades after the Korean War, Korea remained the site of the Cold War's most intense confrontation, as South Korea and North Korea each sought reunification of the nation on its own terms and armed itself against an attack by the other. All the while, a propaganda war continued with each region making bristling rhetorical attacks on the other. In the North, Kim Il Sung consolidated his power over a Stalinist regime, which by the early 1960s had achieved an impressive economic and military recovery. Kim created an ideologically based militarist society that served as his "revolutionary base" for reunifying Korea. In the 1960s, Kim resorted mainly to insurgency to achieve that objective, sending commandos across the demilitarized zone (DMZ). In 1968, he sent agents to assassinate President Park. They were within a mile of their target when South Korean security forces captured them. By the early 1970s, détente in the global Cold War had created an atmosphere for inter-Korean talks. Several meetings between Red Cross representatives and low-level diplomatic officials from both countries were held in 1973, but before any substantial progress was made toward peaceful reunification, Pyongyang abruptly ended the talks that year.

North Korean policy toward the South was marked by bewildering fluctuation between threats and provocation and renewed appeals for talks. Examples of the former are building tunnels under the four-mile-wide

DMZ wide enough to infiltrate large numbers of North Korean troops into the South; attacking U.S. border guards and killing two of them with hatchets at Panmunjom in 1978; and in 1983, bombing a South Korean airliner out of the sky over Burma, killing seventeen South Korean cabinet ministers and officials. Such reckless provocations brought talk of war in the South and assurances of support from Washington. One of North Korea's major objectives had always been to remove U.S. forces from South Korea. These forces, about 40,000 strong in the 1970s, were armed with tactical nuclear weapons, which Washington made clear would be used in the event of a North Korean attack on the South.[18] The North viewed periodic joint U.S.–South Korean training maneuvers as proof of aggressive intentions and denounced them as dangerous provocations.

With the appearance of Mikhail Gorbachev and his Cold War–ending peace initiative in the late 1980s came new opportunities for resolving the Korean conflict. By this time, both the Soviet Union and the People's Republic of China were interested in lowering tensions and were less willing to support the pesky Communist regime in Pyongyang and more willing to do business with the prosperous South. South Korean President Roh met with Gorbachev in June 1990 and secured an agreement to establish diplomatic and trade relations with the Soviet Union; he also won Gorbachev's support for South Korea's admission to the United Nations.[19] Roh then increased diplomatic pressure on Kim to join negotiations for the peaceful reunification of Korea. Later in 1990, the two governments initiated a series of ministerial conferences, the fifth of which produced some surprising results. The two sides signed a nonaggression pact and an agreement banning nuclear weapons from the Korean peninsula.

The latter agreement was especially remarkable, since North Korea's clandestine nuclear bomb project had become the major bone of contention. Kim had engaged Roh (whose country had been blocked by the United States from developing nuclear weapons) and Washington in a guessing game. Both Washington and Seoul insisted that Pyongyang submit to inspections by the International Atomic Energy Agency (IAEA), but Kim steadfastly denied that he was building a bomb and refused to comply.[20] Kim played his nuclear card for all it was worth in an attempt to buy time and to wring concessions from Seoul and Washington.

But time was not on Kim Il Sung's side. North Korea's diplomatic isolation and economic stagnation worsened, and the economic disparity between it and the South greatly increased.[21] In April 1992, Kim's government finally agreed to open its nuclear facilities to IAEA inspection, which reported that although North Korea had built a large plutonium reprocessing plant, it had probably not produced enough nuclear material to make an atomic bomb. Pyongyang, however, refused to allow the inspectors to see all of its nuclear facilities and was thus able to perpetuate uncertainty and continue to cause worries in Seoul and Washington. Not until 1994, after the United States had threatened North Korea with UN economic sanctions, was the nuclear weapons issue resolved, but even then the wily North Korean regime continued to hedge and win major concessions from its foes. (For more on the North Korean nuclear bomb issue see "Nuclear Proliferation" in Chapter 23.)

All the while, in North Korea the tightly controlled Communist regime faced no internal political challenge until its cultlike ruler, Kim Il Sung, died. The end finally came in July 1994 for this stalwart eighty-two-year-old dictator, the longest surviving leader who had come to power in the 1940s. Secrecy shrouded "the Great Leader's" death as it had his rule, and secrecy likewise hid the facts of the succession to power of his little-known son, fifty-two-year-old Kim Jong Il. (Father-son succession in a Communist system is ideologically absurd.) Kim Jong Il, too, was the object of the state-promoted cult, which dubbed him the "Dear Leader." Although his actual role in the Communist regime remained unclear, the Pyongyang regime persisted in its policies, particularly the use of the nuclear threat in quest of concessions from both Washington and South Korea.

But North Korea's worsening economy caused it to become more pragmatic. In July and August 1995, North Korea was inundated by a deluge of floods that were biblical in scope. Torrents of water destroyed reservoirs, farms, farm animals, roads, bridges, schools, and more than a million metric tons of food reserves. UN officials declared the food situation the worst in the world. Rations were set at 450 calories a day, but not everyone had access to even that meager amount.[22] North Korea was reduced to accepting a donation of 150,000 tons of rice from South Korea to deal with its acute food shortages (but it took pains not to reveal to its people the source of the handout). By the end of the year, the UN-based World Food Program issued an appeal for $8.8 million in food. In the spring of 1996, the United States, South Korea, and Japan provided an additional $15 million in food. Swallowing its pride, Pyongyang accepted these badly needed food shipments, even from its erstwhile capitalist enemies.

But North Korea was not ready to abandon its belligerence toward South Korea, for even as it received shipments of food it created a new border incident at the DMZ. In yet another test of wills, North Korea declared in April 1996 that it would unilaterally scrap the 1953 truce agreement and send military forces into the DMZ. Once again, tensions mounted dangerously. President Clinton, who was on a visit to South Korea, responded with a new initiative calling for unconditional four-way negotiations of the North-South conflict that would involve both China and the United States. Pyongyang denounced the idea without rejecting it but staged yet another provocative military incursion into the DMZ two months later. Persisting in its cat-and-mouse diplomacy and well-timed acts of provocation and conciliation, North Korea continued to keep the far more prosperous South on edge. Although remaining militarily alert, Seoul demonstrated remarkable patience in its dealings with the North—anticipating the day when peaceful reunification might come but, at the same time, dreading its enormous financial cost.

☐ Divided China: Taiwan and the People's Republic

Democratization in Taiwan not only carried the risk of the Nationalist Party being voted out of power, but it also raised serious questions about the very status of the Republic of China and its relations with the People's Republic of China. The native Taiwanese people, who made up over 80 percent of the population, increasingly favored independence for Taiwan; having gained voting power, they could now elect a government that would proclaim Taiwan a sovereign nation. This would mean abandoning any claim to being a part of China and rejecting the Nationalist regime's policy of seeking peaceful reunification with China. The Democratic Progressive Party (DPP), which advocated holding a binding referendum on Taiwanese independence, won 40 percent of the vote in the 1989 National Assembly election.

Taiwan's liberalization movement, especially the growing independence movement it unleashed, was of great concern to the People's Republic of China, which was vehemently opposed to the permanent separation of Taiwan from China. The PRC had consistently taken the position that Taiwan was merely a renegade province of China that sooner or later must be reunited with the mainland. Prior to the deaths of Jiang Jieshi and Mao Zedong in the mid-1970s, relations between the PRC and Taiwan had remained extremely hostile, but the 1980s had brought a thaw in those relations—especially because Deng Xiaoping eagerly sought Taiwanese investments. Trade (through third parties) and contact between the two Chinas increased vastly. In 1993, over 1.5 million Taiwanese traveled to the mainland. That same year, the two contending regimes cautiously opened a formal channel, the so-called cross-straits talks, for negotiating economic and social issues. Although both governments professed the goal of peaceful reunification, they remained far apart on the terms. Beijing offered assurances that upon reversion Taiwan would become an autonomous region within the PRC retaining its capitalist economy. The Nationalist government refused to accept such assurances and insisted that as a first step the PRC must renounce the use of military force to bring reunification.

The growth of the Taiwanese independence movement brought a new sense of urgency to these talks. In fact, it tended to bring the two sides closer together, since both opposed Taiwanese independence. As the expression goes, politics makes strange bedfellows. But Beijing worried that Lee, as a Taiwanese, might succumb to political pressure to endorse the independence policy. It remained wary of any action or policy of the Nationalist government that suggested an assertion of Taiwan's independent status, such as Taiwan seeking membership in the United Nations. Beijing even protested when President Lee made a personal visit to the United States in mid-1995 to receive an honorary doctorate from his alma mater, Cornell University.

Beijing was not content merely to register protests; it attempted to intimidate Taiwanese voters by issuing threatening statements and engaging in military exercises near the coast of Taiwan. In April 1996, just before Taiwan's first presidential election, the PRC carried out large-scale military maneuvers—including tests of missiles with live ammunition—dangerously close to Taiwan's main port cities. It was not clear whether this show of force had the desired effect on Taiwan's voters, but President Lee was reelected by a comfortable margin over the proindependence candidate. Soon afterward, the cross-straits talks, which had been suspended, were resumed. Beijing's objective was to secure a settlement with Taiwan similar to that for the reversion of Hong Kong to China and thereby to head off the Taiwanese independence movement before it necessitated military intervention.

RECOMMENDED READINGS

China

Copper, John. *A Quiet Revolution: Political Development in the Republic of China.* Lanham, Md.: University Press of America, 1988.

Evans, Richard. *Deng Xiaoping and the Making of Modern China.* London: Penguin Books, 1995.

Hinton, William. *Fanshen: A Documentary of Revolution in a Chinese Village.* New York: Monthly Review Press, 1966.
    An enthusiastic report on Maoism at work in the countryside in the early years of the revolution.

Hsu, Immanuel C. Y. *China Without Mao: The Search for a New Order.* New York: Oxford University Press, 1982.

Meisner, Maurice. *Mao's China and After: A History of the People's Republic.* New York: Free Press, 1986.
    Assesses Chinese politics on its own Marxian terms.

Perkins, Dwight. *China: Asia's Next Economic Giant.* Seattle: University of Washington Press, 1986.

Schell, Orville. *In the People's Republic.* New York: Random House, 1977.
    A lucid eyewitness account of the PRC shortly after Mao's death.

Wilson, Dick, ed. *Mao Tse-tung in the Scales of History.* New York: Cambridge University Press, 1977.
    A composite view of Mao's leadership by various scholars; among the best books on Mao.

East Asia

Hofheinz, Roy, Jr., and Kent Calder. *The Eastasia Edge.* New York: Basic Books, 1982. A comprehensive account of the surging economic growth of the various East Asian countries.

Keon, Michael. *Korean Phoenix: A Nation from the Ashes.* Englewood Cliffs, N.J.: Prentice-Hall, 1977.

Vogel, Ezra. *The Four Dragons: The Spread of Industrialization in East Asia.* Cambridge, Mass.: Harvard University Press, 1991.

NOTES

1. R. J. Rummel, *China's Bloody Century: Geonocide and Mass Murder Since 1900* (New Brunswick, N.J.: Transactions Publishers, 1994). The author arrives at the estimate of 10,729,000 deaths caused by the Great Leap Forward and its aftermath by averaging the highest and lowest estimates available.

2. After the death of Mao in 1976, the CCP condemned his Cultural Revolution and its excessive violence and encouraged the Chinese people to testify to its cruelty, but the party remained reticent to reveal the number of lives the violence had claimed.

3. Immanuel C. Y. Hsu, *The Rise of Modern China* (New York: Oxford University Press, 1983), p. 804.

4. Quoted in John F. Burns, "Canton Booming on Marxist Free Enterprise," *New York Times,* November 11, 1985, p. A1.

5. Deng Xiaoping quoted in "China Calls Rigid Adherence to Marxism 'Stupid,'" *New York Times,* December 9, 1984. This piece is based on an article that appeared as a front-page commentary in the December 7, 1984, edition of *People's Daily,* the official organ of the Chinese Communist Party, and we can assume it was written or approved by Deng.

6. Economic statistics here and elsewhere in this chapter are from various editions of the World Bank's annual *World Development Report.* The 1994 figures are from the Bank's 1996 edition.

7. John Schidlovsky, "Strike Gains Momentum in China," *Baltimore Sun,* April 25, 1989.

8. Scott Shane, "Gorbachev Praises China for Dialogue with Demonstrators," *Baltimore Sun,* May 18, 1989.

9. The Chinese government would later take the position that no unarmed students were killed on Tiananmen Square but that a total of 300 people died in the clash between the soldiers and the rebels and that most of the dead were soldiers.

10. Robert Benjamen, "China Reiterates Hard-line Views of Human Rights," *Baltimore Sun,* December 21, 1990, p. 4A. China's foreign ministry spokesman stated: "We should not impose our own views on others, much less interfere in the internal affairs of other countries under the pretext of human rights. China will never do this, and we will never allow any other country to do the same."

11. "China's Economy: If It Works, It's Private," *The Economist,* November 30, 1991, p. 25. The private sector of the economy grew at a far faster rate and accounted for a greater proportion of exports than did state enterprises that produced shoddy goods piling up in warehouses.

12. Cited in the *Baltimore Sun,* March 13, 1992, p. 3.

13. The World Health Organization rated Taiwan's birth control program first among developing nations in 1989, and Singapore rated second, South Korea third,

and Hong Kong fifth. The PRC was fourth. "ROC Rated Top for Birth Curbs by World Group," *Free China Journal,* December 21, 1989.

14. The Communist regime of Kim Il Sung in North Korea had resorted to terrorist attacks on South Korea, the most shocking of which was the killing of several South Korean cabinet members in a bomb attack in Rangoon, Burma, in October 1973. Speculation was rife in the South that North Korea might even demolish a dam upstream on the Han River and flood Seoul prior to or during the Olympic Games.

15. In February 1947, an anti-Nationalist uprising occurred that was suppressed with enormous violence, leaving between 5,000 (the Nationalist figure) and 20,000 (the Taiwanese figure) native Taiwanese dead. Over the years, Jiang's government forbade anyone from speaking of this massacre on punishment of death.

16. The platform of the new party, the Democratic Progressive Party, called for full implementation of democracy, welfare, and self-determination for Taiwan.

17. "New Record Set in Exodus," *Free China Journal,* December 22, 1988.

18. David Rees, *A Short History of Modern Korea* (New York: Hippocrene Books, 1988), p. 168. In 1975, U.S. Secretary of Defense James Schlesinger stated explicitly that in the event of a North Korean attack, the United States would not become involved in "endless ancillary military operations" but would "go for the heart" of its opponent.

19. North Korea had consistently opposed the entry of either of the two Koreas into the United Nations and had been able to count on a Soviet veto, but now it had to acquiesce. In September 1991, both Koreas were admitted.

20. North Korea said it would permit inspections only if U.S. nuclear weapons were completely removed from South Korea. In 1991, Washington announced its intention of pulling out all of its nuclear weapons from the South.

21. "Placing Bets on a New Korea," *The Economist,* December 21, 1991, pp. 27–28. In 1990, South Korea had over five times higher per capita income and twenty times more foreign trade than the North; the latter spent more than 20 percent of its meager GNP on its military, whereas the South spent only 4 percent of its burgeoning GNP on its military.

22. Walter Russell Mead, "More Method Than Madness in North Korea," *New York Times Magazine,* September 15, 1996, p. 50.

16

The Indian Subcontinent
and Southeast Asia

■ THE POPULATION AND POVERTY OF INDIA

The Himalayan Mountains separate the two Third World giants—China and India. India shares many of China's problems, not the least of which is a burgeoning population. About one-fifth of the world's population lives on the India subcontinent, which consists mainly of India, Pakistan, and Bangladesh. Many of these people live in poverty. In the postwar era, India and the other heavily populated nations of this region struggled to hold population growth in check and to elevate the standard of living, but only recently have they met with moderate success. Although they shared many of the same problems, these nations have not lived in peace with one another. Hostility between India and Pakistan has flared up several times, and both countries have confronted violent internal disorders. The maintenance of large armies to deal with these problems has drained the limited resources of each of these quarreling neighbors.

To speak of India is to speak of population and poverty. At the time of the partition in 1947, India's population was about 350 million, and it has grown steadily ever since at a rate of almost 3 percent a year. This meant an average annual increase of about 5 million people in the 1950s, 8 million in the 1960s, and 13 million in the 1970s. In the mid-1990s, the population was over 960 million—more than double that of 1947. Moreover, about 40 percent of the Indian people were concentrated in the Ganges River basin, where the population density was among the highest in the world. Although in the mid-1980s India had eight cities with over 1 million inhabitants, over 80 percent of the people still lived in rural villages, and most were dreadfully poor.

India's primary task was to feed its huge population. The twin aims of the Indian government, therefore, were population control and increased food production. Although the government tried to implement a birth control program, it had minimal effect in rural areas. The largely illiterate villagers were suspicious of the purpose and methods of birth control, and they clung to the age-old ideas that a large family was a blessing and that it represented wealth and security. Moreover, one way Indians combated the high infant mortality rate was simply to have more children in the hope some would survive. But even where birth control had some effect, it did not produce an immediate decrease in population growth. Offsetting the slight decrease in the birth rate was a declining death rate; thus, the pressure of overpopulation on India's economy remained undiminished. An electronic display in New Delhi reminded Indians that in mid-July 1992 the country's population stood at 868 million and was increasing by 2,000 people per hour, 48,000 per day, or 17.5 million per year.[1]

Indian food production increased steadily following independence, but it remained barely adequate. In general, the rate of increase of output was slightly higher than the rate of population growth, but this was offset by occasional years of crop failure caused by droughts or flooding. Moreover, the increased food production was unevenly distributed. Indian agriculture consisted largely of subsistence farming and was one of the world's least efficient in terms of yield per acre. Among the reasons for this inefficiency were the small size of farms, the lack of sophisticated tools and machinery, a general lack of irrigation, a tradition-bound social system, and widespread malnutrition. The last of the reasons suggests a cruel cycle of cause and effect: malnutrition and disease contributed to low agricultural productivity, which in turn led to greater poverty and hunger.

In India, as in the other agrarian nations in this part of the world, a wide gulf existed between the wealthy landowners and the more numerous poor peasants, many of whom were landless. This great discrepancy between well-to-do farmers and the rural poor was an age-old problem that was inherent in the traditional society and the farming system. The practice of dividing land among sons contributed to making the average family farm so small that it did not support the family; thus, the farmer was often forced to borrow money at high rates of interest to make ends meet. All too often, he was unable to repay the loan without selling what little land he had. The result was a steady increase in the number of landless peasants.

More recent developments—the so-called Green Revolution and agricultural mechanization—produced an increase in agricultural output in India, but they also made the gulf between rich and poor even wider and increased rather than diminished the poverty of the majority of peasants. The Green Revolution refers to the introduction of newly developed plants—high-yield varieties of wheat and rice—and new farming techniques to grow the new types of grain.[2] In certain areas of India, wheat production doubled between 1964 and 1972, and the new rice strains had a similar effect when introduced in the late 1960s. The Green Revolution, however, turned out to be a mixed blessing at best. It benefited only the minority of India's farmers—the wealthy landowners who could afford the new seeds and the additional irrigation works, fertilizers, and labor required to grow the new high-yield grain. The majority of the rural population—small landholders, landless peasants, and dry-land farmers—lacked the capital or the means to borrow enough money to grow the new crops. Not only were they unable to reap the benefits of the increased food production, but they were actually hurt by it; the increased yield lowered the market price for grain crops, which meant a lower income for peasants who still used the traditional mode of farming. The Green Revolution thus made the rich richer and the poor poorer.

The mechanization of farming, meaning primarily the increased use of tractors, had a similar effect. On the one hand, it contributed to a rise in food production; on the other hand, mechanization benefited only those who could afford the expensive new equipment, and it brought greater hardship to the poorer peasants. Specifically, the use of farm tractors greatly reduced the need for farm laborers and, by eliminating many jobs, increased the ranks of the unemployed. More and more impoverished villagers of India were reduced to collecting firewood and animal droppings to sell as fuel. Even progress sometimes breeds poverty.

One of the consequences of the dislocation of the landless in the countryside was the overcrowding of Indian cities. Many of those who migrated to the cities joined the ranks of the unemployed and found life little better there than in the villages they had left. Large cities such as Calcutta and Bombay were teeming with hungry and homeless people, many of whom literally lived and died in the streets. In the mid-1980s, in Calcutta—which had a population of about 11 million—around 900,000 people were living in the streets without shelter.

■ INDIA'S ECONOMIC DEVELOPMENT

India's efforts to modernize its economy and increase industrial production met with moderate success. India opted for a mixed economy, whereby major industries such as iron and steel, mining, transportation, and electricity were nationalized—that is, owned and operated by the government. The government instituted its First Five-Year Plan for economic development in 1951. The plan's relatively modest goals for increased industrial output were attained, and it was followed by a sequence of similar five-year plans. In 1961, at the conclusion of the second plan, Prime Minister Jawaharlal Nehru admitted that his country "would need many more five-year plans to progress from the cow dung stage to the age of atomic energy."[3] Although some impressive large-scale, modern industrial plants were built, most of India's industry remained small in scale and lacked modern machinery.

The overall growth rate of India's economy was steady but insufficient. Following independence in 1947, India maintained an average annual growth rate of GNP of between 3 and 4 percent.[4] A large gap also existed between the incomes of the educated elite, technicians, and skilled laborers in the modern sector and the unskilled laborers and peasants in the traditional sector—not to mention the many unemployed or underemployed city dwellers.

India was handicapped by most of the problems of Third World countries: a lack of capital, difficulty in attracting foreign capital, illiteracy, and a lack of technology. To this list one might add social conservatism—the weight of tradition, especially a Hindu religious tradition around which much of Indian life is centered. The remnants of the ancient caste system militated against social mobility and the advancement of all members of society. Ethnic and linguistic diversity was also an obstacle to economic modernization. Still another factor retarding India's economic growth was the continual "brain drain" the country experienced. Many of India's best foreign-trained scientists and engineers chose not to return and remained in Western countries, which provided career opportunities and creature comforts unattainable in their native land.

One important prerequisite for economic development is the existence of a market, either domestic or foreign. In India, the poverty of the masses meant a lack of purchasing power and, thus, the lack of a strong domestic market. India strived to increase its exports of raw materials and manufactured goods to pay for its large volume of imports—a substantial portion of which consisted of petroleum, foodstuffs, and industrial equipment. The impact of the oil crisis and global inflation and recession made it virtually impossible to maintain a favorable balance of trade. India was unable to match the increased cost of its imports with its substantially increased exports. Over the years, its trade deficit, its need of capital to finance continued industrialization, and its periodic food shortages forced India to rely heavily on foreign loans. In the 1950s and 1960s, India received huge shipments of food grains, mainly from the United States. After that time, however, India needed less food relief, and, in fact, it became a net exporter of food in the early 1980s. After U.S. developmental aid was terminated in 1971, the Soviet Union became India's primary source of foreign aid. India also received substantial amounts of developmental aid and assistance from other sources, such as Japan, the World Bank, and the Asian Bank.

Political stability is a very important asset for developing nations, and this was one asset India generally possessed. The nation retained a functioning parliamentary system, an institution inherited from the British. It also had prolonged rule by one dominant party—the Congress Party—and continuity of leadership in the persons of Jawaharlal Nehru, who ruled from independence (1947) until his death in 1964; his daughter, Indira Gandhi, who ruled (except for one brief interlude) from 1966 to 1984; and her son, Rajiv Gandhi, who ruled until 1989.

Political stability in a country with widespread poverty and ethnic diversity was quite a feat. After gaining independence, India's leaders were confronted with the monumental task of binding together in nationhood the numerous subgroups of diverse ethnic and religious backgrounds. They pacified, for example, the separatist movement of the Dravidian language–speaking peoples of southern India. The mid-1980s, however, witnessed considerable violence between Hindus and Sikhs, a large religious minority group in northern India that launched a separatist movement. The secessionist cause was dramatized by the assassination of Prime Minister Indira Gandhi in October 1984 by Sikhs, who then suffered bloody retaliation at the hands of angry Hindu mobs.

■ INDIA, PAKISTAN, AND BANGLADESH

India's foreign relations were not peaceful, despite the "live and let live" neutralist policy proclaimed by Prime Minister Nehru in the 1950s. Nehru's efforts to exert the moral influence of India as a neutral peacemaker in the early Cold War years were noteworthy and gained him considerable international prestige, but they did little to help the country in its troubled relations with its neighbors. India's conflicts with Pakistan and China served to undermine its neutralist diplomacy and necessitated large military expenditures that drained its meager resources.

Indian-Pakistani relations were strained from the time of partition and became rapidly worse as the two countries feuded over disputed territory. Both countries claimed the remote mountainous state of Kashmir. In both 1948 and 1949, despite UN efforts to keep peace, Indian and Pakistani forces clashed over this issue. India managed to secure control of Kashmir and turned a deaf ear to Pakistan's continual demands for a plebiscite there. The Pakistani claim to sparsely populated Kashmir was based on the fact that the majority of its people were Muslim, which explains why Pakistan wished to settle the matter with a plebiscite. India's claim rested mainly on the expressed will of the local ruler of Kashmir to remain within India.

India was confronted by a more formidable foe in Communist China over still another territorial dispute in the Himalayas. Both China and India laid claim to the southern slopes of the Himalayan Mountains north of the Assam plain, each staking its claim on different boundaries drawn by nineteenth-century British surveyors in this remote mountainous area. India took the position that its claim was non-negotiable and turned down repeated diplomatic efforts by Beijing to settle the issue. In 1962, India's forces suffered a humiliating defeat by China in a brief border war.

While India was still recovering from this setback, and not long after the death of its highly revered ruler, Prime Minister Nehru, Pakistan decided to seek a military solution to the Kashmiri issue. Tensions mounted as skirmishes along the disputed border occurred with increasing frequency. Pakistan's forces then crossed the cease-fire line in August 1965, and the conflict quickly escalated into a brief but fierce war. India rallied to defeat the Pakistanis. Both sides had been fortified with modern weapons purchased mainly from the United States. U.S.-built jet fighters battled each other—some bearing Pakistani insignia and flown by Pakistani pilots, the others bearing Indian insignia and flown by Indian pilots.

At this point, Indian-Pakistani conflicts began to take on important global dimensions, because both sides had lined up the support of the superpowers. India rebuked the United States for supplying arms to its enemy. (The United States had been selling modern weapons to Pakistan since 1954 under terms of the Baghdad Pact, and it increased its military aid to Pakistan after the 1965 war.) Consequently, India increasingly turned to the Soviet Union, which was only too willing to provide support to a new client and extend its influence in the region. Pakistan, meanwhile, found another friend, the People's Republic of China (PRC). Ironically, the supporters of Pakistan—the United States and the PRC—were bitter Cold War foes during these years.

Before turning to the next round of conflict, we need to note Pakistan's progress and problems. During the 1960s, Pakistan was worse off than India in terms of economic development, overpopulation, and poverty. Much of what we have said about India's plight and the causes for its problems generally applied to Pakistan as well. But Pakistan was beset by additional problems stemming from its peculiar situation as a nation with two separate parts. West Pakistan, where the capital was located, was separated from East Pakistan by nearly 1,000 miles of Indian territory. The distance between the two parts was even greater culturally and politically. The people of East Pakistan are Bengalis who, except for their Muslim religion, had little in common with the West Pakistanis, who are made up of several ethnic groups—the largest of which is the Punjabi.

The two parts of Pakistan were unbalanced politically in favor of West Pakistan, which produced a sense of grievance in East Pakistan. Political and military power was concentrated in the West, despite the fact that the more densely populated East contained over half of the nation's population. Constitutionally, East Pakistan comprised only one of the nation's five provinces and thus had only 20 percent of the seats in the Pakistani parliament. Moreover, only about 35 percent of the national budget was earmarked for East Pakistan. The Bengalis also argued that East Pakistan was treated as a captive market for West Pakistan. For these reasons, the Bengalis in overcrowded East Pakistan felt victimized by their own government.

Bengali frustration mounted until it erupted in late 1970, when East Pakistan was hit first by a terrible natural catastrophe and then by a manmade disaster. In November of that year, a powerful cyclone was followed by an enormous tidal wave and widespread flooding, leaving approximately 200,000 people dead and 1 million homeless. The lack of effective government relief measures provided irate Bengalis with further evidence of their government's indifference toward the problems of East Pakistan, thus feeding the flames of Bengali separatism. While still suffering the prolonged effects of the flooding, East Pakistan fell victim to a disaster of an entirely different kind: an assault by the military forces of West Pakistan.

The military regime of Gen. Yahya Khan had called for an election in December 1970 for a National Assembly to draft a new constitution for Pakistan and thus end thirteen years of military rule. In the election, Sheikh Mujibur Rahman, the Bengali leader and head of the Awami League—a political party that stood for elevating the status of East Pakistan—won a large majority. General Khan and Zulfikar Ali Bhutto, head of the leading West Pakistan–based party, were shocked by the election results and conspired to block the scheduled convening of the National Assembly. Consequently, the Bengalis of East Pakistan began to stir, but their protest demonstrations were met with a military crackdown and the imposition of martial law. Sheikh Mujibur, who was solidly supported by the Bengali people, met with General Khan and Bhutto in an attempt to resolve the political crisis, but he refused to yield to their demands. As a showdown approached in March 1971, General Khan unleashed a military attack on East Pakistan, striking first at the leaders of the Awami League and placing Mujibur under arrest. Thus began the bloody suppression of the Bengali people in which, ultimately, some 3 million people of East Pakistan met their deaths at the hands of a Pakistani army of 70,000 troops. This indiscriminate brutality, in turn, caused more violent resistance by the Bengalis, who now demanded independence. Meanwhile, around 10 million of the terrorized Bengali people began fleeing their ravaged homeland and crossed the borders into India.

The military assault on East Pakistan was met by Bengali armed resistance, mainly in the form of guerrilla warfare, and the conflict soon escalated into a full-fledged civil war. In December 1971, India entered the fray and, after two weeks of intensive combat, forced Pakistan's surrender in the East. India had seized an opportunity to deliver a blow to its longtime foe by intervening on the side of the Bengalis, whose cause for independence the Indian government supported. The result, after nine months of bitter struggle and approximately half a million casualties (on all sides), was another victory for India over Pakistan and the birth of a new nation: Bangladesh.

This South Asian struggle, like most wars in the Third World, had an important Cold War dimension. The United States felt obliged to stick by its ally, Pakistan, despite the latter's widely reported brutality; therefore, the United States opposed the independence movement that created Bangladesh. During the war, Washington had denounced India for its aggression

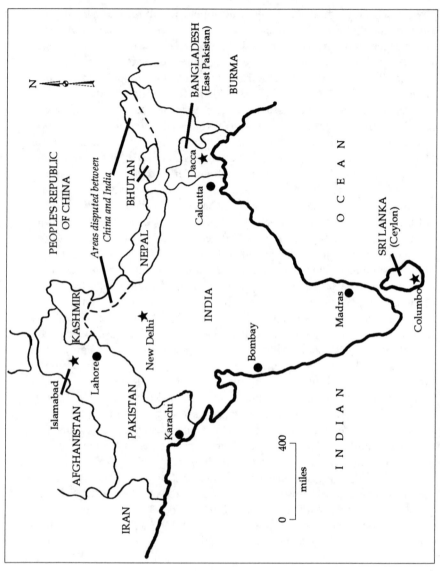

THE INDIAN SUBCONTINENT

and terminated economic aid to India. This fact combined with PRC support of Pakistan caused India to strengthen its ties with the Soviet Union, with which India signed a twenty-year pact of friendship in August 1971. In effect, the United States had lost ground to its Soviet adversary in a regional Cold War battle. The United States delayed recognizing the new state of Bangladesh until May 1972 and delayed for almost as long sending shipments of economic aid, which Bangladesh desperately needed. For its part, the PRC withheld recognition of the new nation until 1975 and continually vetoed Bangladesh's efforts to gain admission to the United Nations.

The impact of the 1971 war was even more profound on the nations directly involved. India's victory was more decisive than victories in previous wars with Pakistan, and its national security was greatly enhanced by the severity of Pakistan's loss, as well as by India's new ties with the Soviet Union. Within India, Prime Minister Indira Gandhi's popularity was strengthened immensely by the country's success in this war, and this served her well in upcoming elections.

For Pakistan, the 1971 war had a sobering effect. Now limited to what had been West Pakistan and with a population reduced by more than half, Pakistan turned to the tasks of rehabilitation and reorganization. Military government was ended when Gen. Yahya Khan resigned and transferred power to Bhutto, whose Pakistan People's Party had come in second in the December 1970 election. One of Bhutto's first acts was to release Sheikh Mujibur from prison and arrange his return to Bangladesh, where he was to become president of the new country. Bhutto also saw the wisdom of reducing tensions in his country's relations with India, and for that purpose he agreed to meet with Indira Gandhi in 1972. Indian-Pakistani relations were substantially improved through the diplomacy of the two leaders, at least until May 1974, when India successfully tested a nuclear device. By demonstrating its nuclear capacity, India established even more conclusively its position as the dominant power in South Asia, but at the same time it aroused Pakistani fears.

Bangladesh, born of disaster, learned that independence produced no miracles. After the war, India ordered the return of the 10 million refugees; when they began pouring back into their ravaged homeland, they found little that could support them. The catastrophic flood damage and war destruction had left the country devastated and unable to cope with the continuing wave of starvation, disease, and death that followed. Mujibur's government confronted not only a destitute people but also crime, corruption, and general disorder. The government declared a state of emergency in 1974, and in 1975 the once popular Mujibur was killed in a military coup. In the years that followed, political instability was prolonged by feuds between military factions contending for power.

The grinding poverty of this overpopulated land seemed beyond remedy. No larger than the state of Georgia, Bangladesh was the homeland of over 90 million people (118 million by 1994, with a per capita GNP of $220). There was simply too little land to support the swollen population. About 90 percent of the people lived in the countryside, and about half owned less than an acre of land—an amount insufficient to feed the average household of six. To make matters worse, the monsoons dump such heavy amounts of rain on this delta country that it is virtually impossible to farm the flooded land for about four months of the year. And at times, the land is hit by cyclones, whose winds and torrential rains cause flooding and enormous death and destruction. Floods and famine, year after dismal year, appear to be the fate of Bangladesh. It is little wonder that many of the desperate people of Bangladesh fled their harsh homeland in quest of a more secure life in neighboring India. But India was also overpopulated, especially in the state of Assam bordering Bangladesh, and could not support the unwanted refugees.

■ SOUTH ASIA SINCE 1980

☐ India

The 1980s brought to the Indian subcontinent a measure of economic growth and a slight improvement in the standard of living. In both India and Pakistan, one could witness the steady growth of industry, increased urban construction, greater agricultural output, and the expansion of the middle class. Yet, because of continued population growth, both countries remained among the poorest in the world in terms of per capita GNP, which in 1994 was $320 for India and $430 for Pakistan. The abysmal poverty of peasant villagers and many city dwellers remained unaffected by economic growth. Both countries needed to control their population growth rates, which threatened their economic futures. Family planning programs in past years had witnessed scant success. As a result, family planners were hoping for a feminist revolt against the grain of societies dominated by men.[5]

Soon after coming to power in 1984, Indian Prime Minister Rajiv Gandhi nudged his country away from the system of state economic planning established over three decades earlier by his grandfather, Jawaharlal Nehru. The new policy meant a freer market, the growth of light industry, and the growth of the middle class. A new consumerism contributed to the slight but sustained rise in the nation's economic growth rate, which during the 1980–1992 period averaged about 3 percent annually. Yet, India was still beset by persistent problems, such as a gross maldistribution of wealth and an equally disproportionate distribution of land. More than 300 million people—over one-third of the population—still lived below the

Indian Prime Minister Rajiv Gandhi, former pilot who succeeded his mother, Indira Gandhi, as prime minister in Oct. 1984. (*Embassy of India*)

poverty line. Wealthy landowners did not farm their land intensively, and because no thorough land reform was attempted, the productive potential of the countryside was not fully realized.

Another problem was the separatist movement of the Sikhs in the northern state of Punjab and the repressive measures Indira and Rajiv Gandhi used in response to that movement. The Sikhs, whose religion is a mixture of Hinduism and Islam, made up about 2 percent of India's population, but they constituted the majority in Punjab. The brutal raid by government security forces on the Sikhs' Golden Temple in Amritsar in June 1984 left 1,200 dead and as many taken prisoner. The Sikhs became unrelenting in their demand for an independent state—to be called Khalistan—and the Indian police became overzealous in their effort to ferret out Sikh militants, sometimes taking the law into their own hands by torturing and even murdering suspects. Thousands of Sikhs became political prisoners held with neither charges nor trials. An immediate consequence of these events was the assassination of Indira Gandhi by two of her Sikh bodyguards and the subsequent massacre of an estimated 1,000 Sikhs by Hindus. Rajiv Gandhi, who succeeded his mother, continued to deal with the Sikhs with a heavy hand. In May 1987, after four months of escalated violence during which over 500 Sikhs were killed by security officers, Gandhi imposed direct federal rule over Punjab and ousted the elected state government of the Sikh moderates.

In November 1989, the Congress Party was narrowly defeated in the parliamentary election, and Rajiv Gandhi resigned as prime minister. He was succeeded by V. P. Singh, an experienced politician who ran his campaign as a populist crusade against the arrogance and corruption of Gandhi's government. Singh's experience as finance minister in Gandhi's cabinet in the mid-1980s augured well for continued economic growth under his rule, but the fragile coalition on which his administration was based limited his power. Singh's government proved too weak to deal effectively with either India's faltering economy or its divisive religious disputes. He was succeeded as prime minister in October 1990 by Chandra Shekhar, a rival in the same party, but Shekhar's government was no stronger. It was dependent on the tacit support of former Prime Minister Rajiv Gandhi, whose Congress Party controlled the lower house. Gandhi cajoled Shekhar into resigning in March 1991, and parliament called for new elections.

On May 21, 1991, while campaigning, Rajiv Gandhi was assassinated, the victim of a terrorist bomb attack. The attack was indicative of ethnic strife in India, for Gandhi was killed by members of the Tamil Liberation Tigers who felt Gandhi had betrayed them in their war for independence against the Singhalese majority in the island nation of Sri Lanka. Initially, Gandhi had intervened on behalf of the Tamil minority, but he later backed away because he became uncomfortable supporting a secessionist movement. He died as his mother had, the victim of an ethnic movement seeking independence.

From the ranks of the Congress Party, which won the parliamentary election, P. V. Narasimha Rao, an elderly veteran politician, was selected to form a cabinet to govern India—a nation in shock and in great need of effective leadership. Prime Minister Rao crafted an economic reform program aimed at stimulating India's slumping economy. India had limited options; it was burdened with a foreign debt of $71 billion and dwindling foreign reserves. Moreover, India could no longer count on the Soviet Union for support, as the latter itself was disintegrating at that time (1991). It became necessary to abandon India's centrally planned economy to open the country to foreign investment and provide incentives for private business and technological development. The first step was to reverse India's balance of payments crisis by securing emergency loans from the International Monetary Fund (IMF) and the World Bank. Rao slashed government spending and red tape, cut import duties, invited foreign investment, and loosened interest rates to encourage private business and increase exports.

The economy showed signs of responding to Rao's reforms, but no economic miracle was in the making. The dead weight of India's economic structure and its bureaucracy continued to impede rapid restructuring, and foreign investors did not rush to India's rescue. By mid-1992—a full year after the reform program was instituted—the momentum of Rao's reform program was spent, and India was still struggling to modernize its moribund economy.

To make matters worse, in December 1992 India suffered a renewal of religious violence. Fighting between Hindus and Muslims erupted in Ayodhya when Hindu zealots tore down a Muslim mosque built in 1528 at the birthplace of the Hindu god Ram. This was the first time Hindus had razed a mosque since the 1947 partition. The violence spread to numerous Indian cities.[6] Before order was restored, the casualty toll reached over 1,200 dead and 4,600 wounded in the worst Hindu-Muslim clashes since 1947. The destruction of the mosque and the ensuing attacks on Indian Muslims provoked anti-Indian protests in Pakistan and many other Islamic nations.

Rao's government continued to limp along in the 1990s until it was upended in the general election of May 1996. His administration and the Congress Party had become stagnant and unresponsive, and his reforms had failed to improve the lives of the rural poor; nor was he able to curb corruption and cabinet infighting. The election, which was the most indecisive in India's history, clearly reflected the country's diversity and political polarization. Voters turned to parties on both the right and the left. On the right was the Hindu extremist Bharatiya Janata Party (BJP), which won the most seats; on the left was the National Front–Left Front alliance (led by the Communist Party). The BJP, headed by Atal Bihari Vajpayee, stood for making India a Hindu state and curbing the rights of India's Muslims and other religious minorities. Vajpayee and his party also advocated restricting foreign investment, maintaining a tougher line against Pakistan, and declaring openly that India possessed a nuclear arsenal—something all previous Indian governments had refused to do. A BJP cabinet would surely mean a break with the political tradition established by early Congress Party leaders—Gandhi and Nehru—which held that India must remain a secular state tolerant of religious and ethnic diversity.

The BJP's margin of victory in the election was not large enough for it to form its own cabinet, and both the Congress Party and the leftist alliance refused to enter into a coalition with the BJP, viewing it as anathema. The political deadlock was broken when Vajpayee was finally able to form a cabinet, but it lasted only twelve days before it was forced to resign by a vote of no confidence. A little-known politician, H. D. Dewe Gowda, leader of one of the parties in a newly formed "United Front," was named prime minister of a coalition cabinet. Gowda's cabinet relied on the support of the Congress Party, now in a kingmaker role—support that was promised only as long as Gowda retained Rao's economic reform program.

☐ **Pakistan**

Pakistan, too, witnessed swings of the political pendulum in the late 1980s and the 1990s. Until 1988, it remained under the rule of military strongman Gen. Mohammed Zia ul-Haq. Zia disregarded critics who called for a return to civilian rule, citing the national emergency caused by the ongoing war in Afghanistan on Pakistan's western border. The influx of thousands of refugees from that war-ravaged country strained the economy and threatened internal security. Zia also pointed to the persistent threat of Indian aggression, which remained a Pakistani obsession.

Military rule ended abruptly in August 1988, however, when General Zia died in an airplane explosion—an apparent assassination—and parliamentary elections were held in November to return the country to civilian rule. The result of those elections was a stunning victory for Benazir Bhutto as the new prime minister. The thirty-five-year-old Bhutto became the first female head of government of a predominantly Muslim nation. She was the daughter of Zulfikar Ali Bhutto, Pakistan's last civilian ruler, who had been deposed in 1974 and executed in 1979 by the same General Zia she now succeeded. After returning from extended exile early in 1988, the British-educated Bhutto had led a national movement against Zia.

Bhutto's grip on power was tenuous from the beginning because she had only a slight parliamentary plurality and the opposition parties, the military, and the conservative clergy were watchful lest she make a slip. Her task was nothing less than ruling a nation beset with all the problems of the Third World and at the same time satisfying its military leaders, who remained distrustful of her efforts to govern without them. Bhutto endeavored to steer a careful course between delivering promised increases in social spending and implementing an austerity program required by international lending agencies for desperately needed loans. During her first year in power, Bhutto's government played a key role in negotiating the terms by which the Soviet military withdrew from neighboring Afghanistan while officially maintaining Pakistani support for Afghan rebels based in Pakistan.

Although Bhutto appeared on Pakistan's political scene like an angel of democracy and enjoyed popular support among younger Pakistanis, she was confronted by formidable political foes. Military leaders were suspicious of her appeal to the masses and were eager to find a pretext for her removal, lest she become too popular. Corruption and ethnic violence, although not new to Pakistan, proved cause enough to overthrow Bhutto in August 1990. She was charged with misconduct and abuse of power, but the attack on her was focused mainly on her husband, a businessman accused of using his wife's office for illegal financial gain. The real force behind her demise was Gen. Mirza Aslam Beg, who resented Bhutto's attempts to rein in the military. Since she represented an effort to establish a democratic tradition and improve relations with India, Bhutto's loss was Pakistan's loss.

An interim government was formed until the parliamentary elections in October 1990. The winner of the elections was Nawaz Sharif, who immediately set out to make good on his campaign pledge to establish an Islamic state in which the Koran became the supreme law and all aspects of life were subjected to its ultimate authority. Sharif's government, however, was ineffective in dealing with endemic corruption, recurrent violence (such as kidnapping for ransom), a mounting foreign debt, and worsening relations with India. Moreover, Pakistan suffered a major diplomatic and economic setback when the United States withdrew an annual $500 million in aid in protest of Pakistan's development of nuclear weapons. Military interference continued. The deployment of the army in the southern province of Sindh to restore order in June 1992 raised the prospect of another military takeover.

Meanwhile, Benazir Bhutto was again waiting in the wings. In November 1992, she planned a mass demonstration in the capital to demand Sharif's resignation but was blocked by police and expelled from the capital. When elections were held in 1993, however, Bhutto narrowly defeated Sharif in a bitter contest. As had been true during her previous stint as prime minister, Bhutto's government was shaky, largely because of her precarious relations with the nation's military leaders. Although she defended Pakistan's position on the two key foreign policy issues (the territorial dispute over Kashmir and Pakistan's development of nuclear weapons), Bhutto, unlike the military and her predecessor, showed signs of diplomatic flexibility. But her position was made more difficult when opposition party leader Sharif declared publicly in August 1994 that Pakistan had produced nuclear weapons and even threatened their use against India in another war over Kashmir. In doing so, Sharif broke Pakistan's long-held silence regarding its nuclear capability and inflamed relations with India and with the United States—its erstwhile ally—which had long sought to dissuade Pakistan from building the bomb.

By October 1996, Bhutto had again lost favor and was forced to resign. Corruption was so rampant in her regime that even her vehement denials, her personal charisma, and the power of her family name were insufficient to save her from the wrath of her political opponents and the general public.

■ ASSOCIATION OF SOUTHEAST ASIAN NATIONS

Southeast Asia, the region stretching from Burma in the west to the island countries of Indonesia and the Philippines in the east, was made up of nations that emerged from colonialism in the 1950s. Each faced a host of problems common to Third World nations, particularly the lack of economic development. The struggle for independence had fostered nationalism, which, on the one hand, abetted the nation-building cause and, on the other, created contention among ethnic minorities within nations and animosity among the nations in the region. Moreover, the region was made insecure by the continuing Cold War struggle at the center of the region in Indochina, where the United States had committed half a million troops to stop the spread of Communism. In quest of greater security and particularly in response to the perceived threat of Communism, five of the region's non-Communist nations—Indonesia, Malaysia, Thailand, Singapore, and the Philippines—formed the Association of Southeast Asian Nations (known by its acronym, ASEAN) in 1967. ASEAN's founders proclaimed that its purpose was "to promote regional peace and security," as well as to foster regional economic and social cooperation.

From the outset, ASEAN was a loosely organized group of nations that did not envision economic, political, or military integration. In ASEAN's early years, its leaders talked ardently of regional cohesion and cooperation, but nationalism remained an inhibiting force as each of ASEAN's member states tended to be preoccupied with its own national interests and internal affairs. Antipathy toward Communist Vietnam was the glue that kept ASEAN together and gave it meaning in the 1970s. The U.S. withdrawal from Indochina in 1973 and the Communist victories in Vietnam and Cambodia in 1975 increased the members' fears of the Communist menace and served as the impetus for building stronger diplomatic ties among them and strengthening their respective armies, albeit without taking steps to establish a regional military alliance. The ASEAN members acted in concert in denouncing Vietnam for taking power in Cambodia in 1979 and in steadfastly turning down both Communist Hanoi's overtures for better relations and economic support and the Khmer Rouge's bid for support.

In the 1980s, ASEAN diplomatic solidarity served as a platform on which to seek greater regional economic coordination. With the exception of the Philippines, each of the ASEAN nations had registered steady economic growth in the 1960s and 1970s. The countries were making substantial progress toward industrializing their economies while shifting to an export-oriented pattern of economic growth. But the mid-1980s brought an economic downturn caused largely by the contraction of the U.S. market. The result was a sharp drop in exports and production. GNP growth rates fell in 1985 and 1986. (Indonesia's GNP growth rate of 6 percent in 1984 fell to −1 percent in 1986, and Thailand's rate fell from 6 percent to 4 percent during the same years.)

The downturn engendered not only corrective economic policies within the respective ASEAN countries but new cooperative ventures among them. The members took action to implement an earlier agreement on regional tariff reduction and agreed to new initiatives for ASEAN economic cooperation, such as joint industrial ventures, increased intra-ASEAN investment, and coordination of the allocation of major new industries in the region. Not all these plans were carried out, but increased cooperation and new national initiatives contributed to remarkable new economic growth for the region, especially in Indonesia, Thailand, and Malaysia. The progress and problems of each of these three rapidly advancing nations are discussed briefly. (Singapore, whose economic takeoff came earlier, was treated in Chapter 15. The Philippines, which lagged behind the rest, is treated separately in the next major section. Brunei, which had joined ASEAN in 1968, is a singular case because of its vast oil reserves.)

☐ Indonesia

After a long and difficult struggle for independence in the 1940s, Indonesia faced the daunting task of bringing its large, ethnically diverse population (the fifth-largest in the world), which is spread over many islands, into a functioning national entity. Its revolutionary leader and new president, Achem Sukarno, continued to provide nationalistic and charismatic leadership in the first two decades after independence. After experimenting with parliamentary democracy for several years, in the 1950s Sukarno turned to "guided democracy," which was a barely disguised dictatorship. His regime failed to stimulate economic growth, but he sought to quiet the growing discontent by harping on the theme of nationalism. When the new nation of Malaysia was founded in 1965, Sukarno proclaimed a "Crush Malaysia" campaign through which he sought to divert attention from his own woes. Meanwhile, many disenchanted Indonesians joined the rapidly growing Communist Party of Indonesia (PKI). Before long, Sukarno himself turned to the PKI for support of his faltering government.

It was then, in September 1965, that a military coup d'état led by General Suharto brought the army into power. The army claimed that its action was actually a countercoup that crushed an attempted coup plotted by leftist army officers and the PKI. The army's primary target was the Communists. Suharto's determination to completely exterminate the PKI resulted in one of the greatest bloodbaths in modern times. Hundreds of thousands of Indonesians—Communists and suspected Communists—were slaughtered within a year. In the process, the discredited Sukarno was pushed aside and later placed under house arrest. Suharto went on to firmly establish a military regime that ruled Indonesia for the next three decades.

(Washington was curiously silent during the Indonesian military's rampage of slaughter. Although some analysts speculate on U.S. complicity in the crushing of the Indonesian Communists, its actual role in the affair remains unclear. It is of course noteworthy that earlier in the same year the United States had launched its massive military intervention in the war in nearby Vietnam to crush the Communist movement there. In any case, Washington welcomed the destruction of the largest Communist Party in Asia outside China.)

To legitimatize his rule, Sukarno created a "government party," which leading military and administrative officers were required to join, and an election system in which his party always managed to handily defeat the only two opposition parties allowed. Having settled into his own pattern of "guided democracy," Suharto decreed that Western-style liberal democracy was inappropriate for a nation with Indonesia's traditions, diverse makeup, and needs.

Suharto dropped Sukarno's campaign against Malaysia. (It was Suharto's reconciliation with Malaysia that had paved the way for the formation of ASEAN in 1967.) But in his quest for national integration, Suharto readily resorted to armed force to suppress the Timorese independence movement on the island of East Timor. In point of fact, East Timor had not been part of Indonesia, but had been a Portuguese colony for over 400 years and had been granted independence by Portugal in 1974. In December 1975, as rival leftist revolutionary groups were fighting for power there, Suharto—with the apparent support of Washington—sent his army in to claim the territory as Indonesian. The result was a long and bitter war. The resilience of the revolutionaries and the massive force applied by Suharto's army to defeat them resulted in a death toll of over 200,000 during the next two decades. Insofar as this was about one-third of the population of East Timor and most of the dead were noncombatants, the slaughter may well be considered genocide.

East Timor aside, Suharto was more successful in achieving national integration and in generating economic development, the twin goals of the "New Order" he proclaimed in 1966. With the help of his Western-educated bureaucrats he embarked on an ambitious program of economic growth. He courted foreign investment, especially from oil companies, which greatly increased Indonesia's production of petroleum. Oil export earnings increased still more with the international increase in oil prices in the 1970s, and this windfall fueled continued economic development. By the early 1980s, oil accounted for 78 percent of the country's export earnings. Steady, though not spectacular, economic growth continued until oil prices tumbled in the mid-1980s. The government then introduced reforms that called for a reduction in government expenditures, diversification, less reliance on oil revenues, and even more foreign investment and joint ventures. These reforms were generally successful, and Indonesia's GNP continued to climb upward. The stability and legitimacy of the authoritarian regime were in turn enhanced by the nation's economic performance. Although the standard of living of Indonesia's people improved substantially, regional disparities remained a problem. Moreover, many lower-class, unskilled laborers still worked in sweatshop conditions at dreadfully low pay and without job security.

☐ Thailand

Having escaped colonization, Thailand was spared the pains of a revolutionary fight for independence in the postwar period and was more receptive than neighboring countries to free trade incentives. This situation, together with the political stability provided by military regimes, accounts for Thailand's earlier and steady economic growth. Benefiting from increased agricultural production and foreign investment, Thailand built up an infrastructure for industrial development and diversification. The country sustained an average annual GNP growth rate of 7 percent for over two decades until a brief slowdown in the mid-1980s, after which it rebounded with a growth rate of about 11 percent for three years (1987–1989)—the highest in the world at the time.

But, as in Indonesia, the new prosperity was by no means enjoyed by all elements of society; indeed, the hard-suffering, underpaid working class saw precious little of the national earnings its labor helped to generate. Such assertions as "Thailand has become an exemplary case of how Third World countries can develop successfully"[7] must be tempered with an evenhanded assessment of social realities in that country.

Thailand's political development, however, did not keep pace with its economic development. Its political tradition of authoritarian rule, deference to authority, and patron-client relationships was more conducive to military rule than to democracy. In the 1930s, the military had entrenched itself in power and only occasionally gave way to civilian rule, which usually proved unstable. In 1973, a popular revolt succeeded in ousting a military regime, but three years later another military coup ended a brief interlude of democratic rule. The military returned power to elected politicians in 1988.

When the military high command took control of the government in February 1991, it was following a traditional pattern. The leader of the 1991 coup and strongman of the new regime, Gen. Suchinda Kraprayoon, arrested the prime minister, abolished the constitution, dissolved parliament, and established the National Peace Keeping Council, which had powers of martial law. But to reassure the Thai public and international investors, Suchinda appointed as prime minister a highly respected businessman and diplomat, Anand Panyarachun, and promised elections within a year. Anand, who enjoyed popular support, was given considerable leeway in governing, particularly in introducing economic reforms. But in April 1992, Suchinda and his generals reclaimed ruling power. This time, however, they overreached themselves. The "second coup" touched off angry antimilitary demonstrations in Bangkok, the capital. Soon, over 100,000 protesters—mainly students—took to the streets demanding a return to civilian rule and constitutional revisions to prevent military rule. As the demonstration grew larger and more riotous, the highly revered Thai

King Bhumibol Adulyadej, who had occupied the throne since 1946, intervened, calling on leading parties to amend the constitution as the protesters demanded.

But Suchinda refused to give in to the protesters and decided instead on a military solution to the political crisis. On May 17, 1992, the army unleashed a ruthless assault on the demonstrators. For three days, 50,000 troops scattered the unarmed protesters, firing live ammunition and killing over 100. The bloody spectacle was seen on television news around the world except in Thailand, where the military controlled the media. Once again, King Bhumibol interceded to put an end to the massacre.[8] He summoned the general and the leader of the opposition movement for an audience. As they knelt before him, he rebuked them and instructed them to restore peace and order immediately—a scene also seen on television screens around the world and this time in Thailand as well.

Suchinda soon resigned, but not before securing cabinet approval of amnesty for the army generals and appointing a military successor to form a cabinet. Again King Bhumibol intervened, rejecting Suchinda's hand-picked successor in favor of former Prime Minister Anand—who, as head of a caretaker government, was charged with putting the country on the path to a democratic government. The king had read the public mood correctly, for the antimilitary movement had gained broad public support—including that of the well-educated and affluent middle class. Business leaders condemned the army's recent resort to brute force, warning that such measures damaged Thailand's international image and might drive away much-needed foreign investors.

Prime Minister Anand, bolstered by the king's mandate and public support, set out to break the military's sixty-year control of power. He commissioned an investigation of the recent massacre and, on the basis of its findings, sacked four leading military officers. Meanwhile, the parliament enacted amendments to the constitution intended to ensure civilian rule and strengthen democracy. The parliamentary election held in September 1992 signified the new public enthusiasm for democratic rule. The election had the largest voter turnout and was the freest election in Thai history. The Democratic Party won a plurality, and its leader, Chuan Leekpai, formed a coalition government with other parties that opposed military rule.

It remains to be seen whether the dramatic turn of events in 1992 and the new burst of enthusiastic support for democratic rule will end the cycle of military coups. The military influence was curtailed but by no means eliminated, for it retained control of many levers of power, including the police and important state industries (e.g., telecommunications, airlines, shipping, and trucking). Yet, the military seems to have learned that it can no longer dominate Thai politics without incurring strong rebuke. The military also understood the importance of political stability for sustaining the nation's prosperity. Gradually, in the 1990s a consensus emerged among political party, military, bureaucratic, and business elites on the priority of keeping the nation on its course toward economic prosperity and democracy. Thai leaders recognized that the former depended on the latter.

☐ Malaysia

With a per capita income of $3,000 in 1995, Malaysia had become one of the most economically successful Third World nations. The manufacturing share of the economy had grown from less than 10 percent in 1960 to 27 percent in the mid-1990s. Malaysia's economic development was all the more remarkable in light of its ethnic and geographic diversity. The population of Malaysia is about 50 percent Malay, 36 percent Chinese, and 9 percent Indian. The main part of the nation is on the Malay peninsula to the south of Thailand; the other two parts, Sabah and Sarawak, are on the island of Borneo, which is over a thousand miles from the peninsula. Malaysia began in 1963 as a federation composed of those three parts and Singapore, but in 1965, Singapore—with its Chinese population—became independent. The remainder of the federation, renamed Malaysia, now had a dominant Malay population.

With the exception of a two-year interval (1970–1972) of military rule, Malaysia has maintained stable civilian rule under a peculiar form of parliamentary democracy. It was a system designed to maintain the Malays in power and to keep the Chinese and other ethnic minorities satisfied with limited representation in parliament and thus a lesser role in the government. The country's paramount ruler, Taunku Azlan Muhibbudin, established the Malay-dominated Alliance Party, which secured governing power by winning successive elections. But in the 1969 election, the Alliance Party lost its majority. The resultant celebration by the mainly Chinese supporters of the opposition parties touched off four days of violent communal clashes. In response to the rioting—which exploded into ethnic warfare and threatened a loss of Malay political control—the government proclaimed a state of emergency, disbanded parliament, and created a National Operations Council to restore order. The government then enacted the New Economic Policy, which granted special rights, privileges, and quotas to Malays—only to Malays—for advancement in education and business. One of the policy's aims was to achieve 30 percent ownership by Malays of the nation's industrial firms by 1990. The government also enacted "sedition acts" prohibiting discussion of "sensitive issues," meaning the special rights granted to Malays.

During the 1970s, the economy grew at a rate of nearly 8 percent annually. The economic growth, driven largely by petroleum and natural gas exports, provided resources to cushion the nation's ethnic tensions. Although pockets of poverty remained, the people's living conditions improved tangibly during the decade. By the mid-1980s, the majority of the population benefited from electricity, piped water, paved roads, telephone service, and television.

Malaysia, however, as with other export-oriented Southeast Asian nations, was hit by an economic downturn in the mid-1980s. Datuk Mahatir bin Mohamad made policy adjustments to revitalize the economy, including privatizing public utilities and expanding state-owned heavy industries through more foreign investment and joint ventures. He also initiated a "Look East" policy that stressed emulating the Japanese and Korean industrial model and attracting more investments and technology from those countries. The result of these policies was a renewed burst of economic growth (8 percent annually) in the late 1980s. By the 1990s, manufactured goods accounted for half of the country's exports, and Malaysia became the world's largest exporter of semiconductors. Yet again, it must be noted that as in the other rapidly developing ASEAN countries, many in Malaysia—even in the gleaming capital city of Kuala Lumpur (which boasts the world's tallest building)—did not share in the nation's new economic prosperity.

■ DICTATORSHIP AND REVOLUTION IN THE PHILIPPINES

As the "four tigers" prospered and several ASEAN nations registered impressive economic growth in the 1970s and 1980s, the Philippines fell behind. This island nation, once a Spanish dominion (1571–1898) and then a U.S. colony (1898–1946), struggled to sustain economic growth and maintain a semblance of democratic institutions after gaining independence in 1946. Under a succession of dictators, the Philippines lost ground on both fronts, especially during the twenty-year rule of Ferdinand Marcos. When Marcos came to power in 1965, the country was developing at a pace with South Korea, Taiwan, and Singapore. When Marcos was driven from power in 1986, those nations had per capita incomes three or four times higher than that of the Philippines. By then, the country had a foreign debt of $27 billion and had been unable to make a payment on the principal of that debt since 1983. The GNP had fallen by over 25 percent since 1982, unemployment had risen to over 20 percent, and inflation had reached 70 percent.[9] Corrption was rampant.

At the center of mismanagement and corruption was Marcos himself. He had been elected president in 1965 as a social reformer, but he soon succumbed to the pattern of patron-client corruption common to Philippine political tradition, and he proved to be a master at it. Governing the Philippines became so lucrative for Marcos that he made certain he would stay in power despite a constitution that permitted only two four-year terms for the president. As the end of his second term approached, Marcos declared martial law, citing a mounting Communist insurgency and an economic crisis as the justification for canceling elections, suspending the constitution, and writing a new constitution that gave him a new term and broad powers. He also rounded up and jailed political opponents and critical journalists. Marcos then stole the nation blind, raking off protection payments from wealthy sugar growers and pocketing foreign aid.

Marcos—who promoted himself as the nation's indispensable leader—claimed to be a lawyer who had never lost a case, a heroic military officer who had never lost a battle, a lover who had won the heart of the nation's beauty queen, a great athlete and marksman, a good father, a good Catholic, and an honest and modest man. His wife, Imelda, was a former Miss Philippines, and her popularity was an added attraction in her husband's cult of power. Successive administrations in Washington turned a blind eye to what was taking place in Manila and honored Marcos as a stalwart opponent of Communism and a champion of democracy.[10] Washington remained tolerant as long as Marcos provided the political stability considered necessary to protect substantial U.S. financial investments in the Philippines and to retain the two mammoth U.S. military installations on the islands—Subic Bay Naval Station and Clark Air Base—considered vital to U.S. strategic interests in East Asia. Marcos skillfully traded assurances regarding the military bases for ever larger economic and military aid from Washington.

In the early 1980s, Marcos's regime began to unravel. In 1981, he released his foremost political opponent, Benigno Aquino, from prison to allow him to go to the United States for heart surgery. Aquino, the likely winner of the 1973 presidential election (had it taken place) decided to end his exile in August 1983 to return home and lead a movement to unseat Marcos. Upon arriving at the Manila airport, he was shot to death before even setting foot on the tarmac. Responding to the outrage of the Filipinos, Marcos appointed a commission to investigate the murder. After lengthy deliberations, the commission reported that evidence pointed to a military conspiracy reaching all the way to Chief of Staff Gen. Fabian Ver, a cousin of Marcos. The verdict of the eight-month trial that followed was predictable: Ver and the twenty-four other military defendants were acquitted. Meanwhile, a vigorous opposition movement developed that regarded the fallen Aquino as a martyr and his wife, Corazon, as a saint. While Marcos was losing credibility at home and abroad, the economy was deteriorating rapidly, largely because of the flight of capital triggered by Aquino's assassination. In the hinterlands, a Communist-led New People's Army stepped up its war.

In response to mounting pressure, in November 1985 the undaunted dictator, who had won every election he had entered thus far, announced his decision to hold a presidential election in February 1986. Aquino's wife, Corazon, had already stated she would run against Marcos should he allow an election. The stage was set for an election that had all the makings of a morality play. Although the sixty-eight-year-old Marcos was visibly ill, suffering from kidney disease, and was roundly attacked by the press, he remained confident of victory and appeared unfazed by the enormous throngs of people who rallied in support of his opponent. Aquino, who presented herself as Cory, a humble housewife, sought to redeem the legacy of her murdered husband and called for a return to democracy, decency, and justice.[11] As election day approached, it appeared Cory's "people power" would surely sweep her to victory—if the elections were fair. Big business and the middle class were abandoning Marcos, and the Roman Catholic Church openly supported Aquino. Many feared, however, that the cagey Marcos, who resorted to paying people to attend his political rallies during the campaign, would find ways to rig the voting to ensure his reelection.

No clear winner emerged from the election, as each side claimed victory and charged the other with fraud. Despite indisputable evidence of election interference and fraudulent vote counting by the Marcos-appointed election commission, Marcos proceeded to declare himself the winner and plan for inauguration ceremonies.[12] Meanwhile, at the encouragement of Roman Catholic leader Jaime Cardinal Sin, hundreds of thousands of people went into the streets to assert their support of Aquino and demand that Marcos step down. At this point, Marcos's defense minister and high-ranking army officers decided to change sides. The climax came when the pro-Marcos troops, advancing toward the rebel encampments, were stopped by the human wall of Aquino supporters and Catholic nuns knelt in prayer in front of the stalled tanks. At that juncture, the Reagan administration, which had steadfastly supported Marcos, bowed to the manifest will of the majority of the Filipino people and arranged for the fallen dictator to be airlifted to Hawaii. Marcos and his wife fled the country with millions—possibly billions—of dollars they had stolen from the Filipino people. With the help of people power, the church, and her new military allies, Cory Aquino proclaimed victory for the democratic revolution.

After the exultation over her triumph against dictatorship, the hard realities of governing the nation and restoring its shattered economy had to be faced by the new, inexperienced president. Aquino moved swiftly to restore civil rights, free political prisoners, eliminate pro-Marcos elements from the government, and enact political reforms. Aquino, whose family possessed large stretches of land, had promised land reform during her campaign, but afterward she showed little interest in the problem. The power of the old oligarchy and the old economic system remained intact. Instead of "reprofessionalizing" the army, as U.S. advisers called it,

Aquino promoted officers who were personally loyal to her.[13] This policy proved to be a major cause of several coup attempts staged by disgruntled forces. During a December 1989 coup attempt, U.S. forces intervened on Aquino's behalf.

The Philippines were still saddled with a $27 billion foreign debt, the payment of which consumed about one-third of the country's export earnings. In 1988, the country was granted a $10 billion developmental grant from the combined sources of the IMF and several European and Asian nations but to little avail. Affluence for the few and misery for the many remained the dominant theme. On the eve of Aquino's fourth anniversary in power in February 1990, people power was but a distant memory. She had lost support in virtually all segments of the population.

The status of the two large U.S. military facilities, Subic Bay Naval Station and Clark Air Base, remained controversial. Many nationalist groups saw them as an affront to Philippine sovereignty, a social blight, and potential targets in a nuclear war. Aquino promised not to abrogate the agreement on the bases, which was due to expire in September 1991, but she placed clauses in the new Philippine constitution that called for no nuclear weapons on Philippine territory and required that any extension of the lease agreement beyond 1991 be approved by a two-thirds majority of the Philippine senate.[14] Meanwhile, Aquino accepted an interim agreement in October 1988 in which the United States boosted its annual military and economic aid to the Philippines to $481 million a year—two-and-a-half times the amount pledged in the 1983 agreement.

Two events in 1991 intervened to cause an unanticipated resolution of the issue of U.S. military bases in the Philippines: the sudden end of the global Cold War and a powerful volcanic eruption. The former caused the United States to reconsider its Asian security needs, and the latter provided sufficient cause to terminate prolonged U.S. efforts to retain the two bases. In June, Mount Pinatubo, a volcano dormant for 600 years, erupted, sending a towering plume into the air and blanketing the surrounding region—including the two bases—with a thick layer of powdery ash. With Clark Air Base buried under volcanic ash, U.S. authorities decided to abandon the base rather than spend the estimated $500 million to dig it out. U.S. and Philippine negotiators initialed a treaty extending for ten years the lease of the naval base at Subic Bay—which, too, was heavily damaged by Pinatubo's ash—but the Philippine senate rejected the treaty by a twelve-to-eleven vote. The United States decided to pull up stakes at Subic Bay as well and in November 1992 hastily completed the evacuation of its largest overseas military base. The U.S. military presence in the Philippines, which had existed since the Spanish-American War of 1898, was at an end.

The combination of the disastrous volcano eruption and the loss of the two foreign bases dealt a severe blow to the Philippine economy, which was already stagnant and debt-ridden. The eruption and the mud slides that followed caused over 600,000 people to lose their livelihood. The closing of the U.S. bases cost another 80,000 Filipinos their jobs and resulted in a considerable loss of currency spent by the tens of thousands of U.S. military personnel and their dependents.

The country remained in need of fundamental social reform and was still confronted with insurrections from both the right and the left. It is little wonder that the weary but still personally popular Aquino decided against running for reelection in spring 1992. Instead, she endorsed Gen. Fidel Ramos, who had helped her stay in power. He ran against a host of candidates—including Imelda Marcos, who had been permitted to return home after six years of exile. After an unusually long delay in announcing the results of the hotly contested election, Ramos was declared the winner. The burden of pulling the Philippines out of its morass of poverty, stagnation, and political corruption was now his.

RECOMMENDED READINGS

South Asia

Ali, S. Mahmud. *The Fearful State: Power, People, and Internal War in South Asia*. London: Zed Books, 1993.
    A study of insurrection in South Asian separatist groups, such as the Sikhs and the Tamils.
Barnds, William J. *India, Pakistan and the Great Powers*. New York: Praeger, 1972.
Bhatia, Krishan. *The Ordeal of Nationhood: A Social Study of India Since Independence, 1947–1970*. New York: Atheneum, 1970.
Brecher, Michael. *Nehru: A Political Biography*. London: Oxford University Press, 1959.
Brown, W. Norman. *The United States and India, Pakistan and Bangladesh*. 3d ed. Cambridge, Mass.: Harvard University Press, 1972.
Kangas, G. L. *Population Dilemma: India's Struggle for Survival*. London: Heinemann, 1985.

Southeast Asia

Ali, Anuwar. *Malaysia's Industrialization: The Quest for Technology*. Singapore: Oxford University Press, 1992.
Crouch, Harold A. *The Army and Politics in Indonesia*. Ithaca, N.Y.: Cornell University Press, 1988.
Diamond, Larry, Juan Linz, and Seymour Martin Lipset, eds. *Democracy in Developing Countries: Asia*. Boulder, Colo.: Lynne Rienner Publishers, 1989.
Kulick, Elliot, and Dick Wilson. *Thailand's Turn: Profile of a New Dragon*. New York: St. Martin's Press, 1992.
Neher, Clark D. *Southeast Asia in the New International Era*. 2d ed. Boulder, Colo.: Westview Press, 1994.
Palmer, Ronald D., and Thomas J. Reckford. *Building ASEAN: 20 Years of Southeast Asian Cooperation*. New York: Praeger, 1987.

Taylor, John G. *Indonesia's Forgotten War: The Hidden History of East Timor.* London: Zed Books, 1991.
An exposé of Indonesia's ongoing effort to suppress with brutal violence the Timorese nationalist movement.

Wurfel, David. *Filipino Politics: Development and Decay.* Ithaca, N.Y.: Cornell University Press, 1988.

NOTES

1. "Population Commentary," *Baltimore Sun,* July 12, 1992, p. 2A.

2. The development of these new plants that produce more grain and less stem per plant was the result of years of scientific work financed by the Rockefeller and Ford Foundations. The new high-yield variety of wheat was developed in the 1950s, and the high-yield variety of rice was produced in the 1960s. Under ideal conditions, the new rice plants produced twice as much grain per acre as the old variety and reduced the growing period in half, so two crops could be grown in one growing season.

3. Jawaharlal Nehru quoted in Stephen Warshaw and C. David Bromwell, with A. J. Tudisco, *India Emerges: A Concise History of India from Its Origins to the Present* (San Francisco: Diablo Press, 1974), p. 132.

4. World Bank, *World Development Report, 1984* (New York: Oxford University Press, 1984). India's average annual rate of growth of GNP between 1955 and 1970 was 4.0 percent; during the 1970s, it fell to 3.4 percent. The rate of growth of GNP per capita for these two periods was 1.8 percent and 1.3 percent, respectively.

5. Steve Coll, "Burgeoning Population Threatens India's Future," *Washington Post,* January 21, 1990, p. H7.

6. According to India's constitution, it is a secular state in which 83 percent of the people are Hindu and 11 percent, about 100 million, are Muslim.

7. Clark T. Neger, *Southeast Asia in the New International Era,* 2d ed. (Boulder, Colo.: Westview Press, 1994), p. 25.

8. According to the British ambassador to Thailand, the king learned about the massacre from his daughter, who was in Paris at the time and saw it on the news there. "Months of Grace," *The Economist,* June 20, 1992, p. 32.

9. Rnajit Gill, *ASEAN Coming of Age* (Singapore: Sterling Corporate Services, 1987), pp. 126–127.

10. When U.S. Vice-President George Bush visited the Philippines in 1981 after nine years of martial law, he told Marcos, "We [the United States] love your adherence to democratic principles and to the democratic processes." Cited in William J. vanden Heuvel, "Postpone the Visit to Manila," *New York Times,* September 8, 1983, p. A23.

11. Aquino did not hestitate to point the finger of blame at Marcos, charging that "Mr. Marcos is the No. 1 suspect in the murder of my husband." "A Test for Democracy," *Time,* February 3, 1986, p. 31.

12. Marcos was emboldened by U.S. President Ronald Reagan who, although noting concern about charges of election fraud, accepted Marcos's claim to victory and stated that his administration wanted "to help in any way we can . . . so that the two parties can come together." Cited in William Pfaff, "The Debris of Falling Dictatorships," *Baltimore Sun,* February 17, 1986, p. 9A. Pfaff criticized Reagan's view as "a preposterous proposition, wholly irrelevant to what was happening on the scene."

13. Richard J. Kessler, "The Philippines," in Peter J. Schraeder, ed., *Intervention in the 1980s: U.S. Foreign Policy in the Third World* (Boulder, Colo.: Lynne Rienner Publishers, 1989), pp. 231–233.

14. The constitutional provision outlawing nuclear weapons on Philippine territory begged the question of enforcement, because the U.S. government maintained its standard position that it would neither confirm nor deny the presence of nuclear weapons on its bases.

17

Third World Debt: Africa and Latin America

The 1970s saw the emergence of a phenomenon with potentially serious international repercussions: the increasing indebtedness of the Third World to the industrial First World. Traditionally, nations seeking to develop their economies rely upon capital from abroad. This was true, for example, of the industrial revolutions in England, the Netherlands, the United States, and Russia.[1] Foreign capital—in the form of profits from sales abroad, loans, or capital investments—has long been a catalyst for speeding up the difficult process of industrialization.

It is little wonder that the emerging, developing economies of the Third World sought this shortcut after World War II. But until the oil crises of the 1970s, the reliance on foreign money had been kept in bounds. The money borrowed from the First World was doled out in reasoned, and at times sparse, amounts—until the surfeit of "petrodollars" (that is, money invested in Western banks by the oil-rich nations) created a binge of lending by these same banks and an orgy of borrowing by the nations of the Third World. There appeared to be no limit to the banks' willingness to extend credit and the recipients' willingness to take it. Foreign capital seemed to promise the road out of the wilderness: rapid economic development and, with it, the ability to repay the loans. By the mid-1980s, the consequence was a staggering debt of Latin American and African nations in excess of $500 billion, a sum far beyond the capacity of most of the debtor nations to repay.[2] Many were staring bankruptcy in the face, and if they defaulted, they threatened to take the lending institutions and the international banking system itself down the road to ruin.

■ AFRICA

The African debt had its roots in the political instability that followed independence, which resulted in frequent government turnovers, secessionist

411

movements, and civil wars. Among the first casualties were the budding democratic institutions. Military coups became the order of the day. Political and military considerations quickly began to take precedence over economic development, for the first priority of dictatorships has always been the retention of power. As such, precious resources were diverted to the military, whose main task was not so much the defense of the nation against a foreign foe, but the suppression of domestic opposition.

One consequence of political instability in Africa was the flight of Europeans, who took with them their skills and capital. This was the case particularly in the new states where independence was won by force and where a legacy of bitterness and mistrust remained after the violence had subsided. Algeria, Mozambique, Angola, Zimbabwe (formerly Southern Rhodesia), and Kenya readily come to mind. South Africa, too, saw the flight of whites as racial tensions were beginning to mount during the early 1980s. The result of this exodus left many African nations with a badly depleted industrial base and a continued reliance on the agricultural sector. Yet, Africa's agriculture remained the world's most primitive. Most of it consisted of subsistence farming in which women did most of the work.

Not only did the continent's agricultural sector suffer from inefficiency but it also suffered from two additional defects that produced catastrophic consequences: desertification and a burgeoning population. The growing deserts of Africa were the result of two factors: (1) the lack of rainfall—at times over a period of several years; and (2) overgrazing and the cutting of trees in marginal lands by the rapidly growing population. The first condition was caused by nature and was thus beyond anyone's control; the second was caused by people.

The Sahara steadily pushed its southern frontier into West Africa. Much of the Sahel, the steppe region of the southern Sahara, was claimed by the desert during the 1970s and 1980s. The desert also pushed toward the east, particularly into Sudan. The lack of rainfall plagued nearly all of East Africa—from Somalia in the north to the Cape of Good Hope in South Africa. In these and other parts of Africa, droughts lasted for years; and land lost to the desert is not readily reclaimed.

Until the late 1970s, the African economies limped along, but then the roof began to cave in when a number of conditions came together. The result was that much of the continent was bankrupted. First came the oil crisis with its accompanying rise in the cost of crude oil. The crisis had a greater impact on the poorer nations than on the industrial West, which had the means of meeting the higher payments. (Although several oil-producing nations of sub-Saharan Africa, such as Nigeria and Cameroon, benefited from the new higher price tag on oil, most suffered greatly. And when oil prices began to fall in the early 1980s, Nigeria was among the hardest hit and became saddled with mounting debts and attendant political instability.)

In the West, the oil crisis contributed to a global recession, which in turn lessened the demand for raw materials. The prices for copper, bauxite (aluminum ore), and diamonds fell. Prices for agricultural exports, the result of a worldwide surplus, fell similarly. The glut in agricultural commodities played havoc with the African economies. Cacao, coffee, cotton, peanuts, and such no longer brought the prices African exporters had been accustomed to. After 1979–1980, prices for commodity exports declined by as much as 30 percent. Yet, the prices for crude oil and for goods manufactured in the West—such as machinery, tools, electronics, and weapons—continued to rise.

Appreciation of foreign currencies, particularly the U.S. dollar, added to the dilemma. Because the debts of nations were calculated in U.S. dollars, the increasing purchasing power of the dollar in the early 1980s played havoc with the pay rate of debtor nations. Debts now had to be repaid in dollars with greater purchasing power; this meant that Third World nations had to export more. In effect, this condition forced African governments to repay more than they had borrowed.

Africa's indebtedness to the industrial world increased considerably during the first half of the 1980s. The poorest continent became a net exporter of capital. In 1985 alone, African nations were required to pay $7 billion to banks and governments of the developed world. On average, African nations used 25 percent of their foreign currency earnings to repay their foreign debts. They were reaching the point where they were dismantling their social and economic development plans in order to meet their debt obligations. They were, in effect, cannibalizing their economies to meet their interest payments. Hope for a future resolution of the continent's dilemma faded.

By 1990, the following African nations had amassed the largest foreign debts. Each showed an increase in indebtedness after 1987.[3]

	Increase in Debt Between 1987 and 1990		Percentage of Increase Between 1987 and 1990
Nigeria	$28.7	$36.1 billion	26
Ivory Coast	13.5	17.9	33
Sudan	11.1	15.4	39
Zaire	8.6	10.1	17
Zambia	6.4	7.2	13
Kenya	5.9	6.8	15
Tanzania	4.3	5.9	37

Africa's foreign debt in the mid-1980s stood between $150 billion and $170 billion. As such, Africa's debt was about half that of Latin America's, which was over $360 billion. But Latin America's condition, as grim as it was, was not as hopeless as Africa's because of its stronger economic base. Africa reached a point where it could no longer repay its debt nor borrow any appreciable sums of money. (Not surprisingly, Nigeria, a major oil-exporting nation, ran up the largest debt on the basis of its projected ability to repay its obligations.) On top of this, there was no significant foreign investment in Africa after 1980. The continent was on a treadmill, pledged to come up with interest payments over an indefinite period to the industrialized West and its banks. Under such circumstances, the indebtedness to the West remained indefinite, since there was no question of making a dent in the principal (i.e., the debt itself). Predictably, African leaders were pointing an accusing finger at the international banking system.

In July 1985, the African heads of government met under the aegis of the Organization of African Unity (OAU) in Addis Ababa, Ethiopia's capital, to address this bleak situation in the hope of finding economic and political solutions. The meeting ended with a surprisingly frank declaration that most African countries were on the brink of economic collapse. The declaration placed part of the blame on an "unjust and inequitable [international] economic system," but it also acknowledged that natural calamities such as droughts, as well as "some domestic policy shortcomings," had contributed to Africa's problems.

The chair of the OAU, Tanzanian President Julius Nyerere, hinted at the creation of a defaulter's club, which promised to seek, among other things, the cancellation of government-to-government loans and the restructuring of interest rates—all for the purpose of avoiding default (national bankruptcy).

■ LATIN AMERICA

Latin America experienced problems similar to those of Africa. The economies took sharp downward turns during the late 1970s, and the reasons were not unlike those that caused problems in Africa. Latin American nations, too, remained heavily dependent upon agricultural export. The rapid increase in oil prices in the 1970s and the drop in agricultural commodity prices produced a sharp decline in the standard of living.

Latin America has long been a region of economic promise. This has been especially the case with Brazil, a land of seemingly unlimited potential, resources, and workers. On the basis of future earnings, the Brazilian government was able to borrow huge sums of money during the 1970s, an action that later came back to haunt it. By 1987, the foreign debt of Brazil stood well over $120 billion, an amount that appeared to be beyond the country's capacity to repay. The best that Brazil could do was merely make the interest payments and in this fashion avoid a declaration of bankruptcy. The country's potential bankruptcy threatened the international banking system, and for this reason, despite its staggering debt, Brazil was able to demand additional loans until the time—sometime in the distant, nebulous future—when it would be able to begin to repay the principal. In the meantime, Brazil, like many of the African countries, remained beholden to the Western banks and governments.

Argentina was another Latin American nation that accumulated a large foreign debt. Argentina had traditionally been a nation with a strong and vigorous economy, which made it relatively easy for its governments to borrow money from abroad. But a succession of military regimes (1976–1983) contributed to the ruination of the nation's economy. The regimes' brutality (most notably the disappearance of thousands of political suspects) and a losing war with Great Britain over the Falkland Islands in 1983 brought about the return to civilian rule in 1983. At that time, Argentina's foreign debt was thought to have been at about $24 billion—a large sum by anyone's yardstick. The new civilian government discovered, however, that the military had in fact run up a debt of twice that figure. Argentina held the dubious distinction of having the third-largest foreign debt (after Brazil and Mexico) among the developing countries, an obligation of $48 billion.

Mexico was yet another case in point. In contrast to most Third World nations, the oil shortages of the late 1970s did not initially harm Mexico's economy. Instead, the shortages appeared to work to its benefit, for Mexico's oil reserves were potentially the world's largest. It was oil that promised to solve Mexico's economic problems, caused in part by its large and rapidly growing population, weak industrial base, and inefficient agricultural system. Mexico, like Brazil, was able to borrow large sums of money in the expectation that oil shortages and high oil prices would make it possible to repay the loans. In short, Mexico borrowed against future income. At the end of 1981, Mexico's foreign debt was at about $55 billion. Four years later, that figure had risen to well above $100 billion.

By 1990, Latin America's leading debtors, unlike those of Africa, had a measure of success in reducing their debts—by a combination of increasing exports, selling off equity, and debt cancellation by lenders.[4]

	1987	1990
Brazil	$124 billion	$116 billion
Mexico	108	97
Argentina	57	61
Venezuela	37	33
Chile	21	19
Peru	18	21
Colombia	17	17

■ OPEC

The reason for the rapid rise of Mexico's debt was that, by the early 1980s, a global oil glut was in the making and the bottom of the market began to drop out. The surplus was the result of conservation, a worldwide economic recession (which lessened the demand for all fuels), the discovery of new deposits (on the North Slope of Alaska and in the North Sea, as well as the Mexican contribution), a worldwide increase in production once prices rose, and the cold, hard fact that even during the shortages at the pump there was always a surplus of oil.

The oil shortages had been artificially created in the 1970s by OPEC (the Organization of Petroleum Exporting Countries), led by Saudi Arabia, the shah of Iran, and the Western oil companies. The thirteen members of OPEC included all of the oil-exporting states of the Middle East—Saudi Arabia, Iran, Iraq, the United Arab Emirates, Qatar, and Kuwait. The rest were the African states of Algeria, Libya, Nigeria, and Gabon; two South American nations—Venezuela and Ecuador; and Indonesia. Equally important as oil-exporting nations that did not belong to OPEC were the Soviet Union (among the world's leading exporters of oil in the 1970s and 1980s), Mexico, Great Britain, the United States, and Canada.

In 1973, OPEC conspired to limit the supply of oil available to the rest of the world; the result was a fifteen-fold increase in prices for crude oil by the end of the decade. During the 1970s, OPEC managed to dictate the price of oil by virtue of its dominance of the market and with it its ability to create shortages. In 1979, its members controlled 63.4 percent of the world's oil market. But all this began to change during the 1980s. By 1984, the figure had dropped to 42.8 percent; by 1985, it had fallen to 30 percent.

In 1985, as their world market share continued to decline, OPEC members, desperate for oil revenues, began to break ranks by surreptitiously selling more than their allotted quotas. The most important task before OPEC in the mid-1980s, therefore, was to reestablish discipline among its members and thus to regain the means to set the price for crude oil. But this proved to be a difficult task.

The early 1980s brought renewed competition for the petrodollar, an end to the oil shortages, and a return to the laws of the marketplace. The laws of supply and demand ruined not only OPEC, but also the prospects of several nations that had banked on a prosperity based on the sale of a scarce commodity to a world addicted to the consumption of gasoline products. As an overabundance of supply drove down the price of oil, such countries as Mexico, Venezuela, and Nigeria became saddled with large foreign debts.

For years, Mexico (although not a member of OPEC) sought to follow OPEC's pricing levels, but in the summer of 1985 it began to establish its own pricing policy in direct confrontation with OPEC. It lowered the price of a barrel of crude oil to about $24. The Soviet Union followed Mexico's example as it too lowered its price, thus placing additional pressures on OPEC. OPEC, in its turn, tried to cut back on production to reestablish an artificial scarcity, but with little impact on prices. Instead, OPEC output declined to about 14.5 million barrels per day, the group's lowest level of production in twenty years. Saudi Arabia, the linchpin of OPEC, in order to maintain the level of the price of oil, dropped its production to 2.3 million barrels a day (almost half of its quota allotted by OPEC), its lowest level since 1967. By the end of summer 1985, however, Saudi Arabia had joined the price-cutting war. At the meetings of OPEC oil ministers that summer, the debates centered on a Hobson's choice, the question of whether to cut prices or production. In the end, OPEC wound up doing both.

No event underscored OPEC's dilemma as sharply as Ecuador's defection in September 1992, when it became the first member to leave the organization. For Ecuador, membership in OPEC, with its quotas for its members, became pointless. Without OPEC restraints, the nation's oil industry hoped to double its output.

■ INSURMOUNTABLE DEBTS

In 1985, the combined Latin American debt stood at more than $360 billion; together, Brazil, Mexico, and Argentina owed in excess of $250 billion. Africa and Latin America combined owed more than $500 billion. A default by any one of the major nations of these regions threatened to trigger an economic crisis with worldwide repercussions. At the least, such action promised bank failures and the slowdown of international trade. At its worst, such a development threatened to cause the most severe economic crisis in history, one certain to produce an extraordinary political fallout, particularly in the regions the hardest hit, namely the Third World.

Third World countries at times raised the specter of default, but they were at pains to avoid such a drastic measure. Instead, they sought to meet their obligations. When in early 1987 Brazil announced a halt in its foreign debt payments, its government was careful to spell out that this was a temporary emergency measure by which it hoped to find a solution eventually. Similarly, in March 1987, after Ecuador was hit with a devastating earthquake that cut its main oil pipeline from the interior to the coast, this oil-exporting nation also suspended temporarily its foreign debt payments. Third World leaders well understood that a declaration of bankruptcy was no solution. It would cut their nations adrift, incapable of borrowing additional funds and subject to economic retaliation. The consequences promised additional economic dislocation and the specter of political violence.

Debtor nations, therefore, took steps necessary to meet their obligations. Yet, these measures demanded putting one's economic house in order. In essence, it meant the raising of taxes, which can be achieved by various means: the elimination of subsidies on food, sales taxes on fuel, a limitation on imports (particularly luxury items), and the devaluation of money. Such steps, however, promised inevitable political repercussions, for they entailed the lowering of the standard of living for large segments of the population. This was especially the case whenever an increase in the cost of food was the price for meeting international obligations. Public outbursts and riots in the streets shook governments that sought to administer such bitter medicine. Sudan, Tunisia, the Dominican Republic, Jamaica, Bolivia, and Argentina all experienced the politically dangerous consequences of such actions.

The Third World was thus caught between two unpalatable choices: (1) default and with it the potential of economic ruination, which in turn threatened to produce political unrest; or (2) compliance and political unrest. Either way, the Third World was not a place to look to for political stability, which can only exist hand-in-hand with economic progress.

The international agency that sought to maintain the precarious balance between compliance and political stability was the International Monetary Fund (IMF). The IMF, an organization of 181 nations,[5] was the lender of last resort. It was the result of a conference at Bretton Woods (New Hampshire) in July 1944, at which representatives of 44 Allied nations gathered for the purpose of bringing about the resumption of international trade upon the conclusion of World War II. The specific purpose for the creation of the IMF was the restoration of the system of multilateral international payments that had broken down during the Great Depression of the 1930s.

The Fund consists of a pool of money contributed by the member states, of which the United States is the largest contributor. When a debtor nation proves unable to meet its international obligation, the IMF takes on the role of a financial St. Bernard and steps in to eliminate the specter of "non-performing" loans and with it the breakdown of the international system of payments. The IMF lends money and lines up the banks that will lend money. Without this program, the poorest nations are cut off from the credit needed to purchase imported necessities such as food and fuel. But the IMF also insists that the recipients remain in compliance with the lending terms. The Fund here performs two functions. It lends money to shore up the international system of obligations and trade, and at the same time it holds a most powerful weapon over the heads of many governments: the threat of withholding additional funds necessary to keep impoverished societies afloat.

This second aspect of IMF involvement in a nation's economy created much resentment in the Third World, for the Fund sometimes appeared to be more interested in bailing out the private lending institutions than in helping the desperate recipients. The IMF was not alone in dealing with

Third World nations, but it was the most visible and thus served as a lightning rod for the ire of people who felt they were victimized by the developed, capitalist First World. The defenders of the IMF replied that the institution provided, first of all, much-needed capital, and second, it merely demanded a proper, although painful, treatment to restore the patient to health. The result of this arrangement was a love-hate relationship between desperate nations that needed assistance and a Western, capitalist agency that provided aid and as part of the bargain insisted on interfering in the internal affairs of nations. For the IMF, it was all too often but a short step from the welcome mat to becoming the target of political violence.

In September 1986, the World Bank responded to a U.S. request to play a leading role in managing the Third World debt crisis, especially in Latin America. The World Bank responded by pledging to double by 1990 the loans available to Third World nations. Officially known as the International Bank for Reconstruction and Development, the World Bank came out of the conference at Bretton Woods and began its operations in 1946. Its purpose is to provide financing for specific projects throughout the world. Its original working capital came from its members' contributions, which put it on its feet, but the bulk of its capital comes from borrowing in the world's money markets. It operates as any bank; it has to borrow money (frequently at high rates), and it lends money at a markup. In fiscal 1986, the Bank approved loans totaling $13.2 billion, a figure that rose to over $20 billion for fiscal 1990 to meet the Third World's debt crisis. But, as Barber Conable, the president of the World Bank explained, this would be done in a measured way, not merely to "shovel money out for the sake of shoveling money out." The main criterion for granting new loans was increased accountability.[6]

The mid-1980s witnessed another phenomenon that compounded the debtors' plight, the flight of Third World capital. A case in point was Mexico, where a high rate of inflation undermined the value of money in Mexican banks. Depositors, therefore, sought safer havens—Western Europe and the United States—where the rate of inflation had been brought under control. In a decade and a half, the Third World changed from a net importer of capital to a net exporter, a trend that only served to widen the gap between the North and the South.

The staggering Latin American debt gave the Communist Fidel Castro of Cuba the opportunity to take center stage as the region's elder statesman. In 1985, Castro spoke several times of the need to create a "debtors' cartel" to resolve Latin America's debt obligations. Oddly, Castro, the revolutionary, urged a resolution of the crisis, with the help of the U.S. government and the Western capitalist banks, for the purpose of avoiding the repercussions of widespread unrest. Castro wanted the cancellation and the mitigation of debts to prevent revolution. He pointed to the example of the Soviet Union, which repeatedly had written off its assistance to Cuba.[7]

In the summer of 1985, Peru's newly elected president, Alan García, declared that his nation would limit its foreign debt payments to 10 percent of its export earnings. This was the first time a debtor nation had tried to link payments to the ability to export. When, in early 1987, Brazil and Ecuador suspended their payments, they took as their model Peru's argument. Other debtors were likely to find such a solution an attractive alternative to the impossible payments and domestic austerity measures demanded of them.

Donor nations were forced to begin to grapple with the prospect that some debts could not be recovered. In March 1989, U.S. Secretary of the Treasury Nicholas Brady called on the IMF and the World Bank to consider debt reductions as well as new financing for major developing countries. A number of nations (such as Canada, Finland, Germany, the Netherlands, Norway, Sweden, and Great Britain) converted loans to grants. France decided to write off the $2.4 billion in loans to the thirty-five poorest African countries, and Belgium cancelled the debts of $200 million to thirteen African countries. The amount of money involved, however, was quite small and affected only government-to-government loans.[8] Private banks, however, were in no position to write off the massive—and unrecoverable—loans to Third World nations.

The end of the Cold War made possible a reevaluation of what had gone wrong with international monetary lending practices, why some countries were showing little if any economic growth and were, therefore, unable to repay their debts. In 1991, the internal World Bank study "Managing Development: The Governance Dimension" concluded that dishonest and inefficient governments were at the core of the problem. Britain's Ministry of Overseas Development came to a similar conclusion and as a result began to shift substantial amounts of money to train efficient local officials in Commonwealth nations such as Zambia, Ghana, and India in an effort to eliminate widespread corruption, a by-product of the Cold War when officials were permitted to skim off aid in exchange for loyalty to the donor. The ministry also increased its funding of private organizations in an attempt to bypass corrupt government officials. It gave as an example the British Red Cross's contributions to health care on the local level. The World Bank called nongovernmental organizations "eyes and ears" capable of providing a system of checks and balances of corrupt governments and of monitoring the effective uses of aid.[9]

The reassessment of reckless lending practices brought the bankers back to the fiscal conservatism of the earlier days of the World Bank when its second president, Eugene Robert Black (1949–1962), insisted that in the struggle against Communist influence investments would have their greatest impact only if they made "the greatest possible contribution, raising living standards and opening opportunities for further investment." Black was not interested in providing money for questionable projects simply to bring a leader of a Third World nation into the Western ideological camp. He insisted above all that money must be lent for projects that created income, which then could be used to repay the loans. Black's fiscal conservatism made possible the lending of billions of dollars by the World Bank without a default, a basic lesson the lending spree of the 1980s forced international lending institutions to relearn.[10]

RECOMMENDED READINGS

Blair, John M. *The Control of Oil*. New York: Pantheon Books, 1976.
  An analysis of the large oil companies' control of supply and market.
Emerson, Steven. *The American House of Saud: The Secret Petrodollar Connection*. Danbury, Conn.: Franklin Watts, 1985.
  An account of the link between the U.S. oil companies and Saudi Arabia.
Harrison, Paul. *Inside the Third World: The Anatomy of Poverty*. 2d ed. New York: Penguin, 1981.
  A useful introduction by an English journalist to the realities of the Third World.
Lacey, Robert. *The Kingdom: Arabia and the House of Sa'ud*. New York: Avon, 1983.
  Another look at the oil crisis.
Sampson, Anthony. *The Sovereign State of ITT*. 2d ed. New York: Fawcett, 1974.
  By an English muckraking reporter who has written several popular books on the world of international finance, this book discusses ITT's foreign operations, particularly in Latin America.
Sampson, Anthony. *The Seven Sisters*. New York: Viking Press, 1975.
  A chronicle of the activities of the major international oil companies.
Sampson, Anthony. *The Money Lenders: The People and Politics of International Banking*. New York: Penguin, 1982.
  A look at the international banking community and its involvement in the Third World.

NOTES

1. Prerevolutionary tsarist Russia drew heavily upon foreign capital and foreign engineers to begin the industrialization process. Stalin's industrial revolution of the 1930s, in contrast, accomplished largely without foreign assistance, became in the early 1960s one of the models considered by a number of newly independent nations of the Third World. Their economic planners found out, however, that their economic base was so primitive, in contrast to what Stalin had inherited from the tsars, that they had little choice but to turn to economic assistance available from the industrialized First World.

2. All dollar amounts are in U.S. dollars.

3. World Bank, *World Development Report, 1989*, p. 205; *World Development Report, 1992*, p. 258.

4. World Bank, *World Development Report, 1989*, pp. 202–205; *World Development Report, 1992*, pp. 258–259.

5. All nations except Cuba and North Korea.

6. Hobart Rowen, "World Bank May Nearly Double Loans for Third World by 1990," *Washington Post,* September 22, 1986, p. A25.

7. Joseph B. Treaster, "Cuban Meeting Stokes Emotions on Latin Debt," *New York Times,* August 1, 1985, p. D1.

8. *Sub-Saharan Africa: From Crisis to Sustainable Growth: A Long-Term Perspective Study* (Washington, D.C.: World Bank, 1989), pp. 176–179.

9. Barbara Crossette, "Givers of Foreign Aid Shifting Their Methods," *New York Times,* February 23, 1992, p. 2E.

10. "Eugene R. Black Dies at 93; Ex-President of World Bank," *New York Times,* February 21, 1992, p. A19.

PART 5

THE END OF
THE POSTWAR ERA

During the 1980s, the Cold War took the world on a roller coaster ride, escalating in the first half of the decade and descending rapidly at the end. In the United States, the Reagan administration, which took office in January 1981, stepped up its confrontation with the Soviet Union. All the while, the pace of the nuclear arms race was quickening. The combination of the continued East-West conflict and the widening gulf between North and South produced a host of dilemmas for the world in the 1980s. Many Third World countries were politically unstable, and the superpowers continued to battle each other through proxies, as in Nicaragua and Afghanistan. The rise of militant Islam in Iran and other Islamic nations produced a powerful third ideological force in the Middle East. As the global standoff between East and West continued unabated, other power centers emerged. Japan and the European Community (EC) sustained remarkable economic growth and became new economic forces to be reckoned with.

At the end of the decade came a series of momentous events that, taken together, signified the disappearance of the forty-five-year postwar world order. The Soviet Union, under a dynamic new ruler, Mikhail Gorbachev, began a program of restructuring that not only resulted in the transformation of the Communist system of that nation but also had an explosive effect on the East European countries that were its former satellites. Gorbachev, however, proved unable to contain the forces he had unleashed in the Soviet Union. A stunning consequence of events unfolded in rapid succession in the early 1990s: the demise of Communist rule, the breakup of the Soviet Union, and the end of Gorbachev's *perestroika*—which gave way to an even more ambitious program, the restoration of capitalism in Russia and in other former republics of the Soviet Union.

The world felt the impact of the revival of Islam and its political militancy. Although long one of the world's great religions, Islam is little known by Westerners; for that reason, we have seen fit to devote the first

423

section of Chapter 18 to an exposition of the tenets of Islam and its political dimensions. It is necessary to see that in Islam, religion and politics are inseparable and that an Islamic state is not merely a country whose established religion is Islam but is rather a state where politics are rooted in that religion. The political power inherent in Islam became evident most dramatically in the Iranian revolution. In Iran, leaders of the Shiite branch of Islam led a revolt that overthrew a U.S.-supported autocrat, the shah of Iran, and brought a new order to the country—one extremely hostile toward the West, particularly the United States. In the wake of the Iranian revolution, U.S. embassy officials were taken hostage, which created a major diplomatic crisis for the United States on the heels of its setback in Vietnam. In Chapter 18, we also turn our attention to the Iran-Iraq War and the problem of Middle East terrorism. We conclude the chapter with an account of one of history's most unusual armed conflicts, the Gulf War, ignited by Iraqi ruler Saddam Hussein's attack on Kuwait in August 1990.

The emergence of Japan and the European Community as economic superpowers is the topic of Chapter 19. One of the premier postwar success stories is the rise of Japan from the ashes of war in the mid-1940s to become the world's second economic power in the 1980s. Japan's "economic miracle" is explained in this chapter, as is the friction that developed in its economic relations with the United States. In the 1980s, the nations of the EC made great strides in economic growth and toward the achievement of the goal of full economic integration (establishment of the European Union, EU) by 1992. In this chapter, we also examine both the competition and the growing interdependence among the three economic superpowers—the United States, Japan, and the EU.

In Chapter 20, we examine changes within the Communist bloc in the early 1980s. Our attention is focused initially on the crisis in Poland, where a dramatic showdown between Solidarity, the Polish labor movement, and the Communist government took place during 1981. The subsequent military crackdown in Poland aroused Cold War passions, as the United States charged not only the Polish government but Moscow as well with crushing Solidarity. We also discuss the contrasting case of Hungary, where a quieter but nonetheless substantial change took place.

In the same chapter, we examine the 1979 Russian invasion of Afghanistan, the impact of that action on international relations, and the subsequent full-fledged return of the Cold War. In response to the Soviet invasion, the Carter and Reagan administrations took a hard line toward Moscow. Tensions mounted rapidly as President Reagan charged the Soviet Union with an escalation of the arms race, expansionism, and intervention all around the world—in Angola, Poland, Nicaragua, Cambodia, and most of all Afghanistan.

We turn in Chapter 21 to the incredible cascade of events in the Soviet Union at the end of the 1980s. Our focus first is on Mikhail Gorbachev, the architect of the Soviet empire's radical transformation. We examine the various aspects of his program of restructuring (*perestroika*) and the resistance it encountered. Although Gorbachev's economic reforms had problems, his call for openness (*glasnost*) touched a responsive chord. Many took advantage of the new opportunity to air their grievances and rally for still greater liberalization. *Glasnost* also touched off a wave of nationalistic unrest among the non-Russian Soviet republics that soon disrupted the unity of the Soviet Union. We analyze the nationality issue and the other causes and events leading up to the collapse of Soviet Communism and the disintegration of the Soviet Union. The final topic in this chapter is Boris Yeltsin's endeavor to steer the new Russian Federation toward capitalism and democracy while struggling to maintain political and social order.

Chapter 22 examines the upheaval in the East European countries triggered by Gorbachev's call for the reform of Communism and his pledge of noninterference. For more than forty years, these countries had been ruled by Communist regimes that answered to Moscow; suddenly, in 1989, they were encouraged to undertake their own restructuring and told they were now on their own. When Communist rulers began loosening controls, the people rallied in huge throngs to demonstrate against Communist rule; when the retreating Communist rulers granted free elections, the people voted them out of office. We trace this parade of events first in Poland, then in Hungary and in the other former satellites. Included in this account of the dismantling of European Communism is the dramatic story of the reunification of Germany. Also in this chapter we describe the disintegration of Yugoslavia and the bitter fighting among Serbs, Croats, and Muslims in Bosnia.

Finally, we turn to what has been potentially the gravest issue facing mankind since 1945: the nuclear arms race. As both cause and effect of the Cold War, the nuclear arms race continued unabated for over forty years, but in the 1980s it became more menacing than ever. Each of the superpowers insisted on maintaining an arsenal sufficient to deter an attack by the other, and the deadly logic of deterrence compelled both sides to build ever more weapons and continually upgrade them. In Chapter 23, we briefly review earlier efforts at nuclear disarmament and then turn to the Strategic Arms Limitation Talks (SALT I and II), the controversy over the Strategic Defense Initiative (SDI, or Star Wars), and progress toward disarmament since the end of the 1980s. After SALT II was initialed in 1979, the United States and the Soviet Union made no progress toward nuclear arms reduction or arms limitations over the next six years. Meanwhile, President Reagan insisted the Soviets had gained a lead in the nuclear arms race and vowed to retake the lead. Reagan's reading of the arms race and his arms buildup gave rise to much debate over the question "who is ahead?" This question is discussed in Chapter 23, as is the controversy over the SDI program launched by President Reagan in 1983.

We also examine the Gorbachev peace initiative and Washington's positive response, which resulted in a substantial lowering of tensions and the first successful nuclear disarmament agreement, the intermediate nuclear forces agreement of 1988. The signing of the agreement, the continuation of disarmament talks since that time, and the events in Europe at the end of the 1980s signaling the end of the Cold War era all brought about the reversal of the nuclear arms race and made possible significant steps toward disarmament agreements in strategic weapons in the early 1990s. As the arms race scaled down and the likelihood of nuclear confrontation between the superpowers diminished, nuclear proliferation became the focus of attention in nuclear diplomacy.

18

Islam, Iran, Iraq, and the Gulf War

The Cold War after 1945 was largely a bipolar struggle between Western liberalism and the Soviet variant of Communism, with much of the world simply trying to stay out of harm's way. In the late 1970s, however, a new political force emerged, militant Islam. This new political movement, steeped in the religion of Islam, sought to resurrect the world of Islam, to free it from the debilitating and overbearing influence of such outside forces as Communism, secularism, and above all the pervading Western presence. Militant Islam has left its mark throughout Islamic societies in a region that stretches, with a few interruptions, from the Atlantic shores of Africa to the easternmost tip of the Indonesian archipelago in Asia.

■ ISLAM: THEORY AND PRACTICE

Islam is the third of the world's great religions to come out of the Middle East. It represents to Muslims the third and last of the "true revelations" by a divinity whom the Jews call Jehovah, the Christians call God, and the Muslims call Allah.

This final revelation came in the seventh century of the Christian era when Allah spoke to His Prophet Mohammed of Mecca, Islam's holiest city, located in what today is Saudi Arabia. Mohammed had been born into a society of idol worshipers, Jews, and Christians, and he quite naturally fell under the influence of Arabia's two dominant monotheistic faiths, Judaism and Christianity. In fact, these were the starting point of Mohammed's teachings. He was always at pains to acknowledge that God had revealed himself to his prophets of another age—Abraham, Moses, and Jesus Christ among them. But he also insisted that Christians and Jews had gone astray and had ignored God's commandments and corrupted the original scriptures. Mohammed held the view that uncorrupted Judaism and Christianity were early manifestations of Islam, literally "submission" to

God. Abraham, according to Mohammed, had been the first Muslim. But since Jews and Christians had strayed from God's word, God then revealed Himself to the last in the long line of prophets, Mohammed.

Islam in this fashion became an offshoot of Judaism. Its linear relationship to the earlier faiths resembles Christianity's link to Judaism. For this reason there remain numerous significant similarities among the three faiths. At one time, Muslims, including Mohammed, faced Jerusalem while in prayer. All three religions stress justice and compassion. Islam has a heaven and a hell; God spoke to Mohammed through the Archangel Gabriel; Islam has its Day of Resurrection and Judgment, "and the hour is known to no one but God." Believers who are created "from an essence of clay . . . shall surely die hereafter, and be restored to life on the Day of Resurrection," a "day sure to come."[1]

Arabs and Jews both claim Abraham as their ancestor. The Jews descended from Abraham's second son, Isaac, born of his wife Sarah; the Arabs from the first son, Ishmael, born of Hagar, Sarah's Egyptian maid. The Bible prophesied that great nations would descend from the two sons of Abraham. The biblical account, however, also stresses that God renewed with Isaac the covenant he had made with Abraham, while the Muslim account makes no distinction between the sons of Abraham. Islamic scholars have argued that it is inconceivable that God would favor one son over the other. In Islamic teachings, the conflict between Jews and Muslims, therefore, becomes a family divided against itself. Since both Muslims and Jews trace their religious ancestry to Abraham, it was not surprising that both sought to control the West Bank city of Hebron, which contains the tombs of Abraham and his family (notably his wife, Sarah, and his son, Isaac). Some Jews consider Hebron their second-holiest city.

The revelations to Mohammed were codified in the Koran, the holy, infallible book of the Muslims, which contains God's commands to the faithful. The Koran is God's word, last in time and the completion and correction of all that had been written before.

A deviation from established religions is no trifling matter; it is nothing less than an attempt to replace established faiths with one that claims to be the only true revelation from God. The consequences of such an attempt have been religious conflicts, which in the case of Islam began in Mohammed's day and have lasted centuries down to our time. Neither Judaism nor Christianity has ever recognized the validity of Islam. Western scholars have often used the insulting label "Mohammedanism" to describe Islam, the suggestion being that it is an invention of one man rather than God's final word to humanity. And Islam, in its turn, has denied the Holy Trinity, and thus the divinity of Jesus Christ, which amounts to a demand for "the unconditional surrender of the essence of Christianity."[2]

Islam means "submission" to Allah, and a Muslim is someone who has submitted to the will of God. It is thus a religion that encompasses the totality of one's existence. It is a complete way of life, both secular and religious. There can be no separation between one's spiritual and secular existence. In an Islamic nation, therefore, a believer cannot make a distinction between secular and religious law. All laws must be based on the Koran; they cannot be otherwise. And the rulers and their governments must reign according to the word of Allah. Islam is, after all, a religion of laws.

There is an elemental simplicity to the fundamental laws, the "five pillars," of Islam. They include, first and foremost, the affirmation that consists of one of the shortest credos of any religion in the world: "There is no god but God and Mohammed is the Prophet of God." All that a convert to Islam has to do is to state this credo in the company of believers. No other rite or ceremony is required. (The very simplicity inherent in the act of conversion explains in part why Islam was the fastest growing religion in Africa at the end of the twentieth century.) Second, a Muslim is obliged to pay an alms tax (the *zakat*) of around 5 percent. Islam emphasizes the importance of charity: "Whatever alms you give . . . are known to Allah . . . and whatever alms you give shall be paid back to you in full."[3] The alms tax also has become a source of revenue for the government. Third, a Muslim must say five daily prayers facing toward Mecca. The *muezzin* (crier) calls the faithful to prayer from the minaret (a slender tower) of a mosque (or temple) at various times during the day: at sunset, during the night, at dawn, at noon, and in the afternoon. Fourth, Islam demands abstention from food, drink, and sexual intercourse from dawn to sunset during the lunar month of Ramadan. Fasting here becomes a spiritual act of renunciation and self-denial. Last, a Muslim must attempt to make at least once a pilgrimage, or *haj*, to the holy city of Mecca.

In the seventh century, following the death of Mohammed, Islam spread quickly throughout the Middle East and North Africa. With the spread of Islam came the establishment of one of the world's great civilizations, centering on the cities of Damascus and Baghdad. Yet, ultimately, this golden age of Islam gave way to a European ascendancy, which may be dated to the Crusades of the Middle Ages. In more recent times, Western powers (notably Great Britain, France, and Italy) managed to establish their presence in the Muslim lands of the Middle East, only to find their grip weakening after World War II. Islam today seeks to free the Muslim countries from the centuries-old, overbearing influence of the Christian West and to reassert the sovereignty and dignity denied them in the past. Militant Islam is, therefore, a potent political and revolutionary weapon.

☐ The Shiites and the Sunnis

The most visible and radical advocates of resurgent, militant Islam are the Shiites, the smaller of the two main branches of Islam. The other wing, the

Sunnis, represents what is generally called the mainstream of Islam and, in fact, they make up approximately 90 percent of all Muslims. Shiites are little known in Africa among the Arabs in the north or among the blacks in sub-Saharan Africa. The same is true of southern Asia, in countries such as Indonesia, Malaysia, Bangladesh, India, Turkey, and Pakistan. The keepers of the holy places in Mecca and Medina, the Saudi family, and their subjects are mostly Sunnis. In Iran, however, nearly all Muslims belong to the Shiite branch; in fact, it became a state religion there. The majority of the Muslims of the former Soviet Republic of Azerbaijan and of Iraq are Shiites. Shiites may also be found in large numbers in all the other states of the Gulf, Syria, Lebanon, Yemen, and in Central Asia.

The split in Islam came two decades after the Prophet's death in 632. A line of *khalifa*, or caliphs, took Mohammed's place as his deputies and successors. The first four caliphs, the Rightly Guided, were selected from the ranks of Mohammed's associates, and after that the line became hereditary. From the very outset there were strains in the Muslim community over the question of succession. As the caliphs became more tyrannical they increasingly appeared as usurpers. There were those who insisted that Ali, the husband of Mohammed's daughter Fatima, was the true successor. The assassination of the reigning caliph in 656 set off a civil war from which dates the open split between the party of Ali (in Arabic, *shia* means party or sect), who also was assassinated, and the main branch (*sunna* in Arabic means practice or custom). The struggle lasted until the Battle of Kerbala in 681, when the Sunnis established their domination and the Shiite resistance went underground.

The struggle was both political and religious in nature. Its political content lay in the fact that the Shiites became the champions of the oppressed and the opponents of privilege and power. The Shiites found their inspiration in the actions of Mohammed in Mecca, where the Prophet first made his mark as the advocate of the downtrodden. As such, the Shiites in Iran, for example, have always been in conflict with the throne (the government) in their attempts to recreate a social and political order in line with the teachings of the Koran. Politics and religion, in the Shiites' eyes, cannot be separated. When in 1963, the shah of Iran offered his uncompromising critic, the Ayatollah Ruhollah Khomeini, his freedom on condition he leave politics to the politicians, Khomeini replied: "All of Islam is politics."[4] Khomeini was the shah's most vocal opponent, who charged the monarch with having sold his country into bondage on behalf of U.S. interests. In 1964, Khomeini was arrested for having publicly refused to recognize the government, its courts, and laws. Ten days after his release in 1964, Khomeini delivered the first of a number of political speeches. Later that year he was rearrested and then exiled.[5] (Obedience to civil authority has never been a hallmark of Shiite behavior. Shiites in their challenges to entrenched political power have time and again elevated political disobedience to a religious duty.)

After a quarter century of warfare between the Shiites and the caliphs, the Sunnis defeated Ali's son Hussein at the Battle of Kerbala (in present-day Iraq) in 681. Shiites still pray at Hussein's grave and mourn his death with passion plays that reenact his martyrdom. Suffering and martyrdom became part and parcel of the existence of the Shiites. Such an existence, however, cannot continue without hope of deliverance. Sunnis and Shiites both accept the Prophet's promise of the return of one of his descendants who will "fill the world with justice and equity."[6] For the Shiites, however, the spirit of messianism is central to their creed. They look to an imam, a divinely appointed descendant of Mohammed, whose purpose is the spiritual—as well as political and at times insurrectional—guidance of the faithful.

The Sunnis, the party of custom and practice, have always stood for the continuity of the social, political, and religious order. They have emphasized consensus and obedience to civil and religious authority. The Sunnis, in contrast to the Shiites, have looked for inspiration to Mohammed's work in Medina, where he created the first Muslim state and ruled as a military commander, judge, and teacher to whom Allah's word was revealed.

Radicalism in the name of Islam, however, is not a Shiite monopoly. The Shiites have a lower boiling point when it comes to dealing with corruption and oppression. The militant Muslims in Iran, Iraq, Lebanon, and Saudi Arabia were generally Shiites; the Islamic radicals in Algeria, the Hamas in Gaza, and the Taliban in Afghanistan were Sunnis. What militant Islam—whether Shiite or Sunni—sought to achieve was the elimination of foreign influences that humiliated and degraded their societies. The militants in Algeria fought a military dictatorship still heavily dominated by French culture, those in Iran combated Western (at first largely British and later U.S.) influence, and the Soviet Muslims (whether Shiite Azeris or Sunni Chechens or Uzbeks) sought to free themselves of Moscow's rule and dreamed of a restoration of their once glorious civilizations.

■ THE REVOLUTION IN IRAN

□ The Shah and the United States

From the end of World War II until the late 1970s, Iran stood in sharp contrast to its neighbors. Shah Mohammed Reza Pahlavi and his country appeared to be a rock of stability in the turbulent Middle East, a bulwark against political radicalism, Islamic fundamentalism, and Soviet expansionism. It was little wonder that, even after the shah's internal position had been shaken by violent protests, U.S. President Jimmy Carter could still praise him for his stabilizing influence in the Middle East. Surely, there was no solid reason to believe that the shah, still apparently a vigorous man in middle age, would not continue to rule Iran as he had in the past. Moreover, he was preparing his young son to succeed him on the Peacock Throne.

But Iran turned out to be another case of U.S. involvement in a foreign land of which few people in authority in Washington had an adequate understanding. The outward stability of the nation only masked the volatile undercurrents, which had deep historic roots. The shah had ruled for a long time, ever since 1941, but his reign had often been unstable, an uncomfortable fact that too many U.S. policy makers often conveniently overlooked. The militant clergy were a nuisance, they reasoned, but they certainly appeared to be no threat to the shah.

Successful resistance to Iran's shahs by the militant Shiite clergy over the centuries was a constant thread running through Iranian history. This was particularly the case with those shahs who made deals with foreigners granting them favorable concessions at the expense of the nation as a whole. In 1872, for example, Nasir ed-Den Shah granted Paul Julius de Reuter, a British subject, such comprehensive monopolies that the shah, in effect, had sold him the country. De Reuter received monopolies in the construction of railroads, canals, and irrigation works, the harvesting of forests, the use of all uncultivated lands, and the operation of banks, public works, and mines. The British leader Lord Curzon called this "the most complete and extraordinary surrender of the entire industrial resources of a kingdom into foreign hands that has ever been dreamed of, much less accomplished."[7] The clergy did manage, however, to bring about the cancellation of some of these concessions. In 1892, the shah faced an angry mob that had stormed his palace demanding the repeal of a monopoly granted to a British firm in the production, sale, and export of tobacco. This exercise of political power in the streets was sufficient to bring about the repeal of these concessions. But the shah's troubles persisted and, in 1896, he was assassinated. Nasir ed-Den Shah's reign points to a recurring pattern of Iranian politics: royal complicity with foreign powers, the power of the mobs in the streets, and the inability of most shahs to maintain their power. During the past 360 years, only four shahs died natural deaths while still in possession of the throne. The rest were either dethroned or assassinated. Iran is not a likely place to look for political equilibrium.

After Nasir en-Den Shah's assassination, the practice of selling favors to foreigners—British, French, and Russian—continued. In 1906, the Iranian parliament took away this privilege from the shah. But despite the prohibition, the practice continued, contributing to a legacy of bitterness and resentment directed toward the ruling Qajar dynasty (1779–1925) that ultimately led to its demise. In its place, a usurper pronounced the creation of his own ruling house. He was Colonel Reza Khan, who subsequently crowned himself Reza Shah Pahlavi.

Years later, Reza Khan's son, Mohammed Reza (1941–1979), attempted to identify his ruling house, the Pahlavi dynasty, with the glories of Persia's past. In 1971, he staged an elaborate ceremony in Persepolis, the ancient city of Cyrus the Great. Guests from far and wide attended the gala celebration. The shah then proceeded to date the calendar from the reign of Cyrus, symbolizing over 2,500 years of historic continuity.[8] He became the Shahansha (the King of Kings), the Light of the Aryans, who ruled by divine right, a man who claimed to have experienced religious visions.[9]

This spectacle impressed the world, but many Iranians, particularly the clergy, saw the shah in a different light. The Shiite clergy, Allah's representatives on this earth, demanded submission to their will, that is, the will of Allah. They considered the shah merely a usurper—only the second in the short line of the Pahlavi dynasty—who had been educated in the West and who had sent his own son to study there. Moreover, the shah's close relationship with the West, the United States in particular, was something that did not sit well with many Iranians.

Reza Shah did not act appreciably differently from the previous monarchs when it came to dealing with foreign powers. In 1933, he granted new favorable concessions to the Anglo-Iranian Oil Company, an enterprise that was largely controlled by the British. His close association with the British continued until World War II, when he shifted toward Nazi Germany at a time when it threatened to take the Soviet Union's oil fields north of the Caucasus along the western shores of the Caspian Sea, notably around the city of Baku. A successful German drive in that direction would have linked German-occupied territory with Iran. The upshot was the joint occupation of Iran by the Soviets (who took control of the northern part) and the British (who occupied the southern regions). The shah was then sent packing when the British and Soviets forced him to abdicate in favor of his young son, who turned out to be the second and last of the Pahlavi dynasty.

The greatest source of wealth for the Pahlavi dynasty was the country's oil. By 1950, Iran was the largest producer of oil in the Middle East. By that time Iran's own share of the oil profits had increased, but many nationalists, including many of the clergy, were not satisfied. For one thing, the Arab-American Oil Company, a U.S. concern operating in Saudi Arabia, had offered the Saudis more favorable terms. More important, the lion's share of the profits from Iran's natural resources still went to the foreign investors, who were mostly British.

The result was that in 1951, parliament, under the direction of Prime Minister Mohammed Mossadegh, challenged the shah and voted for the nationalization of the oil industry. The British, predictably, declared such an act illegal. U.S. President Truman sought to negotiate the dispute, eventually siding with the British. Mossadegh's challenge to the West struck a responsive chord in Iranian society. Anti-U.S. riots and attacks on U.S. consulates and libraries in 1952 led to reprisals by the Eisenhower administration, which came to power in January 1953. In May of that year, the U.S. government decided to put economic pressure on Mossadegh by cutting off aid and refusing to buy Iranian oil. The U.S. use of an economic weapon only inflamed the militants in Tehran, the Iranian capital. In August 1953, street riots forced the shah to flee to Rome. There he apparently came to the conclusion that his reign had ended.

But at this point, the CIA, which had already been involved in actions directed against Mossadegh, moved into operation. With the help of elements in the army and others opposed to Mossadegh, the CIA managed to return the shah after only three days in exile. Demonstrations in the streets had ousted the shah; counterdemonstrations in these same streets created a political climate permitting the shah to return.[10]

The shah now owed his throne to a foreign power, something he always resented. But his ties with the United States continued to grow. Oil production and export to the West continually increased, and in the process the shah became one of the United States's best overseas customers. He then took steps to modernize Iranian society, but such a transformation came at a price. Modernization created a gulf between a new privileged class, which benefited from the shah's close link with the West, and much of the rest of the country. The influx of Western technicians, engineers, military advisers, and sales representatives did not sit very well with many Iranians. The distribution of the country's enormous wealth and the attendant westernization and modernization led to a distortion of traditional Iranian social patterns. Too many were left out and it was inevitable that the shah's actions bred resentment. Traditional Iranian self-sufficiency became a thing of the past. By the 1970s, Iran became greatly dependent on foreign imports; it even bought food from abroad. And since Iran based much of its wealth on a one-product economy (80 percent of its export earnings coming from the sale of oil) its dependency on the West appeared to be total.

Much of the money the shah spent abroad went for the purchase of modern military equipment, most of it U.S.-made. Between 1972 and 1978, he ordered $19.5 billion in U.S. arms. And the greater the oil revenues, the more weapons he bought. After 1973, about one-third of the government's spending went for armaments. This proved to be a boon for U.S. arms manufacturers, for by the end of the 1970s, one-third of all U.S. arms sales went to Iran.

The U.S. government, particularly the Nixon administration, applauded such a course: Iran, armed to the teeth, would preserve stability in the Middle East, particularly in the Gulf, the waterway through which passed much of the oil on which the industrial powers depended. It was here that the "Nixon Doctrine" appeared to work best. Nixon had first formulated his doctrine toward the end of the war in Vietnam. It was designed to permit him to exit from that war without appearing to have lost it. According to the Nixon Doctrine, the United States would arm and support a client who would do the actual fighting in support of U.S. interests. In South Vietnam the doctrine collapsed like a house of cards in 1975 when its army took to its heels. In Iran the application of this doctrine seemed to be working to perfection.

In the early 1970s, it was not clear how Iran would pay for the massive military equipment the shah demanded. But good fortune intervened. October 1973 saw the fourth Arab-Israeli War conflict, the "Yom Kippur War," which led to an oil embargo by the Arab members of OPEC (the Organization of Petroleum Exporting Countries) and a doubling of oil prices. The shah took the lead in demanding this increase in the price of oil. The Nixon administration, however, saw a silver lining in all of this. The United States was now able to supply Iran with military equipment without raiding the U.S. treasury. As Henry Kissinger, Nixon's secretary of state, explained in his memoirs:

> The vacuum left by British withdrawal [from Iran during the early 1950s], now menaced by Soviet intrusion and radical momentum, would be filled by a power friendly to us [the shah's Iran]. . . . And all of this was achievable without any American resources, since the Shah was willing to pay for the equipment out of his oil revenues.[11]

But this scenario began to fall apart in a most unexpected way when militant Islam drove the shah, whom it denounced as a servant of the "great satan" (the United States), from power.

☐ The Return of Khomeini

The best-known practitioner of militant Islam was the Ayatollah Ruhollah Khomeini. He identified Western civilization as Islam's enemy; an Islamic society, therefore, must be purged of it. The shah, with the trappings of Western civilization all around him, was little different from the tens of thousands of Western technicians he had invited to Iran. In the eyes of the mullahs, the Muslim clergy, the shah stood in direct violation of the history and religion of Islam.

Khomeini's denunciations of the shah at first had little effect. They were regarded merely as the ravings and rantings of an old man in exile. But as dissatisfaction with the shah's rule increased, Khomeini's sermons on cassette tapes, smuggled into Iran, began to have an effect. By January 1979, it became apparent that the shah could only maintain his throne if SAVAK (the secret police) and the army were willing to suppress all manifestations of discontent with much loss of life. Civil war loomed on the

Shah Mohammed Rezi Pahlavi, monarch of Iran, with U.S. Secretary of Defense James Schlesinger, Washington, D.C., July 26, 1973. (*AP/Wide World Photos*)

Ayatollah Ruhollah Khomeini, Shiite leader of the Iranian revolution, 1979. (*Embassy of Iran*)

horizon. The shah, unsure of the loyalty of the army and unable to obtain a clear-cut U.S. commitment from the Carter administration, decided to leave the country. There was little else he could do. Opposition to his regime ran deep. The influx of oil money had only intensified the dissatisfaction felt by many. Corruption, favoritism, police brutality, poverty and luxury existing side by side, the lack of justice, the influence of foreigners—all contributed to the fall of the shah.

The events of 1978–1979 showed that the shah had merely maintained an illusion of power. In February 1979, the Ayatollah Khomeini returned in triumph from exile in Paris, where he had been the most visible symbol of righteous, Islamic resistance to a ruler who had betrayed both his religion and his people. Iran, under the leadership of the Muslim clergy, could now be expected to experience a spiritual and national rejuvenation. There was little doubt that the support for Khomeini's regime was massive in those heady days when the shah was put to flight.

But the shah had not officially abdicated. When he left in January 1979, he emphasized that he and his family were going abroad for an unspecified period. In effect, he promised to return.[12] It was clear that the United States preferred the shah over the anti-U.S. militants who now governed Tehran. The militants, for their part, feared a repetition of the events of 1953, when the CIA had returned the shah to power from his brief exile in Rome. Radicals, bitterly hostile to a U.S. government on which they blamed all of Iran's ills, were able to stir up deep emotions. Anti-U.S. street demonstrations became daily affairs, and two weeks after Khomeini's return from exile, the first attack by militants on the U.S. embassy took place. The organizers of the attack claimed that the embassy housed the CIA. Khomeini forces at this time dispersed the attackers.

The Khomeini government initiated a concerted attack on the U.S. presence in Iran. It repealed, for example, the 1947 law authorizing a U.S. military mission in Iran. Instead of concentrating on the consolidation of power, Khomeini thus sharpened the differences between his revolution and the United States. The crucial moment came in October 1979, when the shah arrived in New York for medical treatment. To the militants in Tehran, this marked the first step of what to them was a U.S. attempt to bring the shah back to power. They never believed the shah was in need of treatment.

On November 4, a group of radical students decided to take matters into their own hands. They climbed over the walls of the U.S. embassy compound and seized diplomatic personnel, demanding that the United States dissociate itself from the shah and extradite him to Iran to stand trial. Sixty-six U.S. citizens were captured, and after fourteen were released the remaining hostages were kept blindfolded in the embassy, which then became their prison. There was no evidence that Khomeini gave the order for this act, but it suited his political position since it drove political sentiments in Iran further to a radical extreme. As the symbol of the revolution, he had but little choice except to place himself at the head of it. And the extraordinary support for the students by the huge crowds who gathered daily in the square in front of the embassy ensured his open support for this radical action.

The hostage crisis came at a time when memories of helicopters lifting off the rooftop of the U.S. embassy in Saigon were still fresh in the U.S. public's eye. And, less than two months after the onset of the hostage crisis, the United States was hit with another jolt when the Soviet Union sent 80,000 troops into Afghanistan—to bail out a bankrupt Communist government (see Chapter 20). Together, the hostage crisis and the Soviet army's invasion of Afghanistan had a dramatic impact on U.S. public opinion. The United States had lost a sphere of influence in Iran, and the Soviets had sent troops outside their postwar sphere for the first time. The U.S. loss and what appeared to be the Soviet Union's gain gave President Carter a foreign policy headache that ultimately played a major role in his defeat in the presidential election of 1980.

The fifty-two U.S. hostages eventually came home, but only after the 1980 election and after 444 days of captivity. President Carter had punished the Soviets with a grain embargo and a U.S. refusal to attend the 1980 summer Olympic Games in Moscow. But Carter's actions were too little and too late. He could not shake the damaging public perception that he was indecisive and a "wimp." Voters decided to give the tough-talking Republican Ronald Reagan the chance to handle the nation's foreign policy.[13]

At home, the Khomeini government set out to transform Iran according to the strictures set down in the Koran. The Islamic revolution transferred sovereignty from the shah to the clergy. The secular parties, however, had a different vision of the future of the Iranian Republic. The upshot was a bloody conflict between the Shiite clergy and its opponents. The challenge to the revolution came mainly from the numerous splinter groups on the left—Marxists, Maoists, socialists—who feared the replacement of one dictatorship by another. When the bloodletting was over, the Islamic revolution had consolidated its power. Waves of revolutionary terror had brought about the execution of approximately 10,000 Iranians, and another half million, many of them of the professional classes, went into exile.

The revolution in Iran swept aside the Pahlavi dynasty and many of the Western influences it had introduced, and denied the United States a client in the Middle East. It also brought about a redistribution of land and gave the nation a new constitution based on Islamic laws. In addition, Khomeini's revolution threatened to spread beyond the confines of Iran. Large Shiite communities in Lebanon, Iraq, the Gulf states, and Saudi Arabia began to look to Iran for guidance. Khomeini's revolutionary message in support of the downtrodden masses and his virulent opposition to the West added a new and dangerous element to the Middle East. The shah, until the very end, had always felt that Communism posed the greatest danger to his throne. But with the Iranian revolution, the conflict in the Middle East ceased to be primarily a contest between Western democracy and Communism. Militant Islam, in direct challenge to the Soviet Union and the West, became another force to be reckoned with.

■ THE IRAN-IRAQ WAR

With Iran in the throes of a revolution, the government of Saddam Hussein of Iraq availed itself of the opportunity to invade Iran in September 1980. Hussein had three objectives. He sought (1) to destroy Khomeini's revolution, which he feared might spread to his subjects, most of whom, although Arabs, were Shiites; (2) to secure disputed territory at the confluence of the Tigris and Euphrates rivers, the Shatt el-Arab, to improve Iraq's access to the Gulf; and (3) to emerge as the paramount leader in the Arab world.

Hussein's plan called for securing the Shatt el-Arab, capturing Iran's oil ports on the other side of the river, and crippling Iranian forces in a drive eastward into Iran. He calculated that Iran was unprepared for war because of extensive losses to the officer corps and to its pilots due to

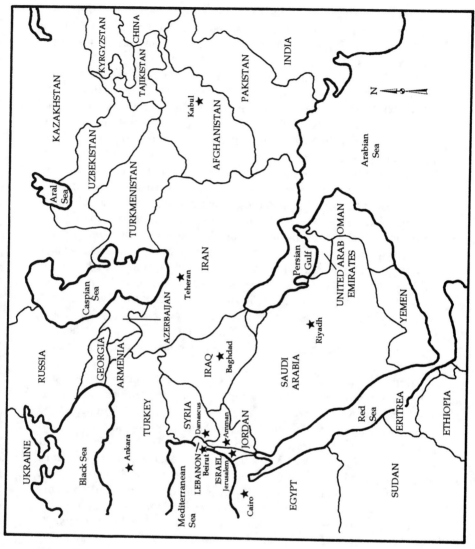

THE GULF STATES

purges and desertions during the revolution. Iran, however, still had many loyal middle-grade officers and pilots, and it rallied its people quickly to war. Iran saw the conflict as a resumption of the ancient wars between Persians and Arabs.

Because Iraqi invading forces moved too cautiously, Iran gained time to rapidly build up its Revolutionary Guard (its regular forces) from 7,000 to 200,000 men and to create a new militia of more than 350,000 men. The appeal by religious extremists in Tehran for volunteers to fight the "holy war" produced a rapid mobilization. Iran was thus able to offset Iraq's initial advantage of a better trained and better equipped army. With the two sides evenly matched, neither side was able to score a decisive victory. After Iran's counteroffensive in 1982 regained lost territory and captured almost 60,000 Iraqi troops on the battlefield, the war became a stalemate.

The United States and the Soviet Union as well as the European powers declared their neutrality in the conflict. But as the war dragged on, over forty nations supplied weapons to one side or the other, and several nations, including the United States, sold weapons to both sides. Israel and the United States both sold weapons covertly to Iran to keep the war going.[14] Israel's defense minister, Yitzhak Rabin, stated frankly, "We don't want a resolution of this war."[15] Iran was supported also by Libya and Syria. Iraq received financial support from Saudi Arabia and the other oil-exporting Arab states on the Gulf, all of which feared Iran's ideological revolution.

Both sides understood the importance of oil in financing the war, and each targeted the other's oil-producing and shipping facilities in the Gulf. The United States, however, was determined to keep the Gulf open as the passageway through which much of the Western world's and Japan's oil flowed. It accepted, in December 1986, a request of the Kuwaiti government to protect its oil tanker fleet. Kuwaiti tankers were then "reflagged"; that is, they were placed under the U.S. flag and escorted by U.S. naval vessels. This brought the United States into direct confrontation with Iran, which denounced this as U.S. intervention and threatened to attack such ships.

The war also saw the first extensive use of chemical weapons since World War I. In March 1988, Iraq launched a chemical weapons attack on its own city of Halabja, which was populated by Kurds, a non-Arab Islamic people hostile to Hussein's regime. The lethal chemicals killed as many as 5,000 of the city's residents, as well as many Iranian troops; thousands of others suffered excruciating burns. Iraq's use of chemical warfare brought strong worldwide rebuke, for it underscored the new potential danger the world faced, "the poor man's atomic bomb," as Third World nationals called it.

Iraq offered to negotiate an end to the long war many times. Hussein announced in the summer of 1987 his willingness to accept a UN Security Council resolution calling for an armistice, but Tehran rejected it. Khomeini had his own terms for ending the war: Hussein must step down and Iraq must pay $150 billion in reparations. But after suffering a series of military setbacks—air attacks on Tehran, loss of its naval force to the United States, and a serious decline in oil profits—the Ayatollah suddenly reversed himself, announcing on July 18, 1988, that he must take "the bitter drink of poison" and accept the UN peace formula.[16]

There was no winner of the absurd eight-and-half-year-long war. Each side suffered almost a million casualties and enormous economic losses. Iraq emerged from the war with the stronger military forces. But Iran was not defeated, and its Islamic revolution remained very much intact.

■ MIDDLE EAST TERRORISM

In the years following the 1982 Israeli incursion into Lebanon, the Arab-Israeli conflict became diffused. The central issue, the dispute between the Palestinians and the state of Israel, became but one of a host of Middle East conflicts. Moreover, it came to an impasse as neither the pro-Israelis nor the Palestinians were able to defeat the other. As a consequence of this deadlock, a new wave of terrorism became the order of the day.

Inspired by Islamic fundamentalism and frustrated by setbacks at the hands of Israel or outside forces supporting Israel, Arab and pro-Iranian extremists resorted to desperate, sometimes suicidal, acts of violence against the perceived enemies of Islam. To them the act of terrorism was a moral act, whatever the cost to themselves, their enemy, or for that matter, innocent parties. In some instances, they acted to redress specific grievances or to gain specific ends, such as the return of prisoners taken by Israel. Israeli defense forces responded in kind with bombing raids and kidnappings.

The United States, by its military intervention on behalf of the Phalangist government of Lebanon in 1983 and its naval bombardment of "enemy" strongholds in the mountains, made itself the target of terrorism. In retaliation, terrorists took Westerners in Lebanon as hostages. In March 1984, William Buckley, a CIA agent, was kidnapped in Beirut by the pro-Iranian Shiite group known as the Islamic Jihad and was later killed by them. In the following two years, at least twenty others—college teachers, journalists, businessmen, and priests from the United States, Britain, France, and several other countries—were taken hostage by the Islamic Jihad and other revolutionary groups in Lebanon. Lacking knowledge of the specific identity of the kidnappers or the location of the hostages, Western governments were unable to rescue them. In January 1986, Terry Waite, an envoy of the Church of England, went to Beirut in an effort to negotiate the release of foreign hostages, only to be kidnapped himself by the Islamic Jihad. Although several hostages were released, at least ten were killed.

Exasperated by the continuing wave of terrorism and determined to stop it, the Reagan administration vowed to retaliate. It found a likely target for retaliation in Muammar Qaddafi, dictator of Libya. Qaddafi, a strident Arab extremist, had already raised President Reagan's ire for his support of the PLO and for his brash threats against the United States for trespassing in what he proclaimed to be Libya's territorial waters, the Gulf of Sidra. Moreover, Qaddafi had maintained terrorist training camps in Libya and had provided financial support for Lebanese extremist groups suspected of terrorism.[17] In April 1986, a terrorist bomb ripped through a discotheque in West Berlin, killing two people, among them a U.S. soldier, and leaving 204 injured. Reagan blamed Qaddafi and ordered a punitive air attack on the Libyan cities of Tripoli and Benghazi, for the purpose of killing Qaddafi.[18] One bomb landed yards away from Qaddafi's residence, leaving him unharmed but, Qaddafi claimed, killing his adopted infant daughter. The U.S. attack, which was not supported by its European allies, was little more than an act of frustration and vengeance and was of questionable value as a deterrent to terrorism, which, in any case, continued unabated.

Two years later, in December 1988, one of the most savage of terrorist attacks occurred when a U.S. jetliner, Pan Am 103, exploded in flight while over Lockerbie, Scotland, killing all 258 people aboard and 58 on the ground. After three years of masterful detective work, investigators were able to identify two suspects, agents in the Libyan secret service. In the interim, Qaddafi sought improved relations with the West by renouncing and apparently refraining from terrorism. He refused, however, to hand over the suspects to be tried, no doubt fearing that in a trial the two defendants might point the finger at him. After Qaddafi ignored an April 1992 UN Security Council resolution demanding the extradition of his agents, the UN imposed economic sanctions and an international ban on air traffic and arms sales to Libya.[19] Amid rumors of another Reagan-like punitive attack on Libya, Arab nations, including moderates such as Egypt, came to Qaddafi's support in a rare display of Arab solidarity. Egypt's argument was that any such punitive action might be detrimental to the delicate Arab-Israeli peace talks then under way.

* * *

On August 8, 1991, in the wake of the Gulf War, John McCarthy, a British subject held hostage for five years by the Islamic Jihad in Lebanon, was released, carrying with him an important letter addressed to UN Secretary General Javier Pérez de Cuéllar. It indicated that his captors were interested in arranging the release of the remaining ten Western hostages in Lebanon. It became apparent that the long-held hostages had become a liability to the various Shiite Muslim factions that held them, and to their sponsors in Iran and Syria. Although the air was soon filled with rumors of the impending release of all remaining hostages, another five months passed before most were freed.

Finally, with the release of the last two hostages in June 1992, the ten-year ordeal of captivity for over seventy Westerners was over. Syria, Iran, and the Lebanese Shiites had come to realize that they stood to gain more by releasing the hostages than by keeping them. By granting them freedom, each reckoned to enhance the prospects for settling other Middle East issues and improving relations with the West.

■ THE GULF WAR

□ A War of Nerves

On August 2, 1990, Saddam Hussein, the dictator of Iraq, launched a full-scale invasion of neighboring Kuwait and quickly conquered this small, virtually defenseless, oil-rich nation. The ruler of Kuwait, the Emir Sheikh Jabir al-Sabah, his cabinet, and his family fled to Saudi Arabia. International reaction was swift. As early as August 6, the UN Security Council voted unanimously to impose a worldwide trade embargo and three weeks later approved the use of armed force to enforce the embargo. U.S. President George Bush responded to a request from Saudi Arabia for protection by ordering Operation Desert Shield, a massive airlift of U.S. ground troops, aircraft, and naval vessels, to guard that country and its oil fields from potential further Iraqi aggression. Meanwhile, Arab League nations held an emergency meeting at which twelve of its twenty-one members, including Egypt and Syria, voted to send troops to protect Saudi Arabia.

Hussein defiantly defended his conquest of Kuwait by word and deed. In speeches full of bravado, he promised a "holy war" against "aggressive invaders" who dared to attack his forces in Kuwait. In the weeks prior to the invasion, he had made clear to Kuwait his grievances. He had accused Kuwait of cheating on its OPEC-approved quota of oil production; of dumping large quantities of oil on the market to keep prices low, thus depriving Iraq of badly needed revenue; of stealing oil from the Ramaila oil field, which straddled the Iraqi-Kuwaiti border; and of refusing to cancel the billion-dollar loans it had granted Iraq during its long war against Iran. Hussein ordered his massed troops into action three days after Kuwait rejected Iraq's demands for some $14 billion compensation for lost oil revenue and for the cession of two Kuwaiti islands to Iraq. Hussein then revived old Iraqi claims to the entire territory of Kuwait and proclaimed it Iraq's nineteenth province. He ordered the foreign embassies in Kuwait closed, took many of their diplomatic personnel hostage, and removed his "foreign guests" to military sites in Iraq. Ten days after the invasion, Hussein made a bid for Arab support by suggesting a possible Iraqi withdrawal from Kuwait on the condition that Israel withdraw from its occupied territories. However, only the PLO and Jordan, which was economically dependent on Iraq and militarily vulnerable, expressed support for Hussein's policy.

Hussein found little international support. His "naked aggression," as Bush called it, was a quest for oil, the consequence of Iraq's fiscal bankruptcy brought on by the long and inconclusive war with Iran. The nations of the Middle East feared that Hussein sought not only Kuwaiti's oil but Saudi Arabia's as well, which together comprised a substantial portion of the world's known oil reserves. Hussein appeared to seek control over the entire oil-rich Gulf and power over the Arab world. Foreign critics also focused attacks on Hussein personally, on his unsavory past, his political beginnings as an assassin, his summary execution of political opponents, and his use of poison gas in his earlier war against Iran and his own Kurdish population. They charged him with violations of international law for annexing Kuwait, committing acts of brutality against its people, and taking diplomats hostage. Bush went so far as to equate him with Adolf Hitler.

Bush cultivated U.S. and international support for a forceful response, but the effect of personalizing the conflict ultimately made it harder to resolve. To the extent that he made Hussein the issue, Bush made his removal from power a political objective and gave rise to expectations that proved difficult to achieve. Bush, who saw an opportunity to turn the Gulf crisis into political advantage, took the lead in building a coalition of forces in the name of creating a "new world order." Bush noted that the invasion of Kuwait was the first major post–Cold War crisis and that the Soviet Union, no longer an adversary, supported the measures against Iraq. He projected a vision of a new era in which the United Nations—led by the United States—maintained international peace and order. Iraqi aggression thus became a test case for the "new world order." Bush also came to see the Gulf crisis as a means of restoring the honor of the U.S. military and of purging the United States of its "Vietnam syndrome."

Bush's shock and moral outrage masked concerns about the failure of his policies toward Iraq prior to its attack on Kuwait. In September 1990, Baghdad released a transcript of U.S. Ambassador April Glaspie's final talk with Hussein, on July 25, one week before he attacked Kuwait and several days before her departure for vacation. In the transcript, which the U.S. State Department confirmed as 80 percent accurate, she was quoted as having said in response to Hussein's threat of war against Kuwait: "I know you need funds. We understand that and . . . you should have the

Saddam Hussein, president of Iraq.
(*Iraqi Office, Embassy of Algeria*)

opportunity to rebuild your country. But we have no opinion on the Arab-Arab conflicts, like your border disagreement with Kuwait."[20]

The tenor of the verbal exchange revealed that the ambassador not only had failed to read Hussein's aggressive intentions, but also had failed to clearly object to his explicit threats against Kuwait, thereby placing no obstacles in the path of his invasion plans. This revelation did not, however, appreciably diminish public support for Bush's confrontational policy.

Revelations after the Gulf War also indicated that the Bush administration had been far less than candid about its pre-August 1990 relations with Hussein. It had consistently pursued a policy of providing substantial economic, military, and intelligence support to Hussein, a policy begun by the Reagan administration early in the 1980s when Iraq was at war with Iran. It had ignored Hussein's record of human rights violations, offered him U.S. intelligence secrets (while neglecting to gather Iraqi secrets), suppressed warnings regarding the Iraqi atomic bomb project, and granted Hussein substantial agriculture credits, which he used to rebuild his large army.

The road to war in the Gulf was itself a war of nerves. By early November 1990, when 200,000 U.S. forces were already deployed in the Gulf, President Bush ordered a doubling of the U.S. troop level in order to give the allies "an offensive option." He argued that economic sanctions alone would not suffice to expel Iraq from Kuwait and that a military offensive was needed. At Bush's urging the UN Security Council, on November 29, 1990, passed by a twelve-to-two vote Resolution 678 authorizing the use of military force if Iraq did not leave Kuwait by January 15, 1991. It now became a forty-eight-day countdown during which allied forces readied for a war already sanctioned by the UN. By the deadline, the thirty-one-member coalition massed in the Gulf area included over a half million U.S., 35,000 Egyptian, 25,000 British, 22,000 Saudi, 19,000 Syrian, and 5,500 French troops. Bush had placed himself in a no-retreat position. Hussein answered with increasing vocal vehemence. He responded to the UN Security Council that if war occurred, there would be "columns of dead bodies that may have a beginning but which would have no end."[21]

War commenced one day after the deadline set by the United Nations. It came because of each side's miscalculations. President Bush mistakenly expected the show of overwhelming force and firm resolution to cause Hussein to back down. He believed that the best chance for peace was to threaten war. Hussein miscalculated as well, believing that his own threats of a horrible "mother of all wars" would dissuade Bush from leading a frightened U.S. citizenry into war. He was also mistaken in his belief that the Arab masses would rise up against their governments and rally to him, and thus cause the coalition to collapse. War soon made clear another miscalculation: both sides greatly overestimated the ability of Iraqi forces to withstand an attack.

☐ A Most Unusual War

For the first six weeks, the Gulf War, code-named Desert Storm, was fought in the air. Iraqi pilots chose not to engage attacking allied aircraft in battle and instead flew their planes on a one-way trip to Iran, apparently for safekeeping. The allies, therefore, were able to strike at Iraqi targets at will. In the first fourteen hours they flew more than 2,000 sorties, and the round-the-clock bombing of Baghdad and other parts of Iraq continued day after day. Television coverage of the war provided viewers an impressive display of the new, seemingly pinpoint accurate high-tech weaponry used against defenseless Iraqi targets.

Iraq answered the air attacks with Scud missile attacks against Israel. On the first day of the war, it fired eight missiles, two hitting Tel Aviv, three exploding near Haifa, and the others falling harmlessly in open areas. Although no one was killed by the Scud attacks, they caused great fear and anger in Israel. Especially frightful was the prospect that the next Scuds might be armed with chemical weapons. Hussein hoped that this diversionary attack would draw a military response from Israel, which might cause Arab nations to withdraw from the coalition. Washington was able to restrain Israel with promises of destroying Iraqi Scud missile sites and providing Israel protection by U.S. Patriot antimissile missiles. Iraq aimed its Scud missiles at Saudi Arabian targets as well, but the inaccuracy of the missiles and the effectiveness of the U.S. Patriot missiles in intercepting the incoming Scuds limited the damage, with one exception. On February 25, two days before the end of the war, a Scud missile hit a U.S. barracks in Dhahran, Saudi Arabia, killing twenty-eight soldiers.

The air war produced only a small number of allied casualties, but the anticipated, potentially bloody ground war against Hussein's armies had yet to be fought. On February 22, Bush set a deadline of noon on the following day for the unconditional Iraqi withdrawal from Kuwait, and when Hussein ignored it, the ground assault on Iraq began.

The ground war lasted only 100 hours because the coalition forces, carrying out a well-laid battle plan under the command of U.S. Army Gen. Norman Schwarzkopf, met far less resistance than expected in liberating Kuwait and entering Iraq. Iraq's vaunted Republican Guard forces retreated from the battle leaving the weaker, poorly trained, poorly fed, and exhausted regular troops to absorb the brunt of the invasion. On February 27, Bush proclaimed that "Kuwait is liberated" and ordered a cease-fire. At the United Nations on March 3, Iraqi Foreign Minister Tariq Aziz stated that Iraq accepted the UN terms for a cease-fire, including the requirement that it make reparation payments for damage to Kuwait.

The Gulf War was a mismatch resulting in one of the great debacles in the history of modern warfare. Yet, despite the decisiveness of the allied military victory, the war's outcome was ambiguous. Before and during the war, Bush spoke not only of liberating Kuwait but also of removing Hussein from power, of trying him as a war criminal, and of completely destroying Iraq's military forces, including its weapons of mass destruction. Only the first of these objectives was achieved. Hussein remained in power and, despite the devastation to his country, continued to draw support from his people, proclaiming that he had stood up against the enemies of the Arabs.

Another unusual feature of the war was that the militarily powerful United States did not have to carry the entire cost of its military policy. For the first time, a superpower sought contributions from other nations to pay for the huge military operation it had already undertaken. Several Gulf nations and wealthy nonparticipants (Germany and Japan) ended up paying the greatest part of the bill. The United States argued that, for one, it protected the energy source upon which the industrialized world depended and, therefore, should not have to carry the entire burden. Second, it also provided security for not only the wealthy oil-producing countries of the Middle East, but also Turkey, Egypt, Syria, and Israel.[22]

The most bizarre features of the Gulf War were the means Hussein used. They include his peculiarly bombastic threats and taunts, his crude attempt to make use of captured diplomats and soldiers as bargaining chips in violation of international laws, his terrorist use of Scud missiles against a nation with which he was not at war, the deployment of his aircraft to a neighboring country (Iran) that actually opposed his war, his opening of oil pipeline valves to create in the Gulf the largest oil spill in history, and his torching of some 700 Kuwaiti oil wells, creating yet another environmental catastrophe.

Still another peculiar feature of the Gulf War was the sharp contrast between the jubilation produced by the swift and decisive coalition victory and the later, more sober assessments of the war. At war's end, as the people of the United States reveled in ecstatic patriotism, Bush's popularity soared to 87 percent approval of his performance, the highest ever attained by a U.S. president. The Bush administration and the press had trumpeted the triumphant claims of military leaders during and immediately after the war, but long after the celebrations were over, more accurate assessments of the war revealed that those claims had been greatly exaggerated. Far more of Iraq's armed forces and weapons remained intact after the war than expected. The highly acclaimed air attack, for example, had boasted of the near complete destruction of Iraq's Scud weapons and nuclear weapons facilities, but UN inspectors later found that at least 819 Scud missiles had escaped destruction and that only three of Iraq's thirty nuclear weapons facilities had been attacked.[23]

The costs to the United States of its short, victorious war were greater than first assumed when the delayed effects of exposure to chemical and biological agents by its soldiers were taken into account. Veterans of the Gulf War began complaining of chronic symptoms ranging from rashes, hair loss, aching joints, breathing problems, memory loss, nerve disorders, and so forth, and there were cases of crippling birth defects among their children as well. The Veterans Administration denied claims for compensation for the so-called Gulf War syndrome because the Pentagon held there was no evidence that these soldiers had been exposed to chemical or nerve agents during the war. But as cases of the syndrome mounted, the Pentagon finally—in September 1996, more than five years after the war—brought forward its findings that the demolition by U.S. troops of an Iraqi ammunition depot containing chemical weapons in March 1991 may have exposed as many as 5,000 U.S. soldiers to toxins. Two weeks later, the Pentagon further revealed that the same depot may have been hit by an aerial attack several weeks earlier and that the total number of ground forces affected may have been as high as 15,000. Speculation was rife that the estimates could rise much higher.

☐ **The Aftermath**

The single undisputable accomplishment of the Gulf War was the liberation of Kuwait, but this was no victory for democracy. Two weeks after the war, the ruling emir, his family and government, and the wealthy Kuwaiti elite returned from their seven-month exile to reclaim their devastated homeland, now darkened by the smoke from the oil well fires. The Iraqi occupation of that country had been a reign of terror in which 33,000 Kuwaitis had been killed or captured and many tortured or raped. But there would be no significant postwar political change. When the emir formed a new cabinet in April 1991, it included no members of political opposition groups; it was, as before, composed almost entirely of members of the ruling Sabah family. His government was mainly concerned about rehabilitation and security. Initial estimates for reconstruction costs ranged as high as $110 billion, with the most serious problem being the sabotaged oil wells, which took nine months to cap. In September 1991, Kuwait concluded a ten-year bilateral defense agreement with the United States, which allowed U.S. armed forces to keep equipment and conduct military exercises in Kuwait. The Saudis and the other Gulf states beefed up their own armed forces, purchasing ever larger amounts of arms from the United States.

For Saudi Arabia, the cost of the war was largely economic. So great were its financial outlays in 1991 that the oil-rich nation had exhausted its cash reserves and had to seek foreign loans.[24] During the war, the Saudi government came under pressure from Islamic clerics for allowing the infidels (Western soldiers—male and female) to defile the land of the Prophet Mohammed, and after the war they demanded their early departure.

The Gulf War left Iraq battered by the six-week-long aerial bombardment and left an area in the southern part of the country under temporary allied military occupation. More important, it left Hussein in power. His forces had suffered a humiliating defeat and he had to accept humiliating terms for peace. But he survived the war and, to the chagrin of his enemies, sought to turn defeat into victory. Hussein, protected by a tight internal security system, cranked up his propaganda machine to declare that he and his faithful people had been the victims of aggressors and of betrayal by fellow Arabs.

During the war, rebellion against Hussein's government broke out spontaneously in southern Iraq, where the Shiites, who made up 55 percent of the nation's population, briefly took control of the bombed-out city of Basra, and in northern Iraq, where the Kurds fought to take control of the region where they were the majority. During the war, Bush had openly encouraged rebellion by the Shiites and Kurds, only to betray the rebels when he stated on March 26 that he would not support or protect them.[25] Hussein then quickly defeated them because he still had sufficient strength to crush them, and no foreign forces came to their rescue. Hussein's troops extinguished the insurrection in the south by the end of March, causing as many as 30,000 Shiite casualties and the flight of over 1 million into Iran.

By that time, Kurdish leaders in the north claimed that the "whole of Kurdistan [in Iraq] had been liberated." But they spoke too soon, for in the following week, loyalist Iraqi forces using helicopter gunships and aerial bombardment drove Kurdish forces out of their strongholds. Ultimately, Hussein's forces crushed their uprising and around 50,000 Kurds were killed. The Kurds, in fear of Hussein's vengeance and defenseless against his superior force, fled in early April 1991 eastward into Iran or northward into the mountains along the Turkish border. There, more than 1 million Kurdish refugees suffered for lack of food and shelter and many died from exposure and disease. Bush followed the lead of British Prime Minister John Major in sending food and supplies and implementing a plan to create a "safe haven" in northern Iraq for the refugees, to be policed by U.S., British, French, and Dutch troops. Refugees then began settling in camps in the area guarded by the foreign forces. In June, the UN assumed responsibility for humanitarian aid and protection of the Kurds in their—for the time at least—safe haven.

The defeat of the Kurds was but another chapter in the long and tragic history of an ancient people whose Indo-European language and distinct culture sets them apart from their neighbors. In 1990, there were approximately 10 million Kurds in eastern Turkey, 5 million in western Iran, 4 million in northern Iraq (about 20 percent of the population), and 1 million in northeastern Syria. These nations were always able to agree on one thing, that there must be no independent Kurdistan. Since 1961, Kurds fought the authorities in Baghdad and Tehran whenever the opportunity availed itself, only to be defeated repeatedly by one or the other and sometimes both. In 1972, after Baghdad and Moscow had signed a Treaty of Friendship and Cooperation, the Nixon administration and the shah of Iran supported the rebellious Iraqi Kurds, only to drop them after the shah and Hussein worked out an agreement to bring the Kurds to heel. When the Kurdish leader Mustafa Barzani asked for continued U.S. aid, Secretary of State Henry Kissinger ignored the request. He later justified the abandonment of the Kurds by the remark that "covert action should not be confused with missionary work."[26] In 1991, Turkey, more than any other country, wanted no part of a successful rebellion of Kurds in Iraq. In the past, Turkish Kurds had been prevented from speaking their language in public and their very existence was denied by their government. Turkish politicians and newspaper publishers were sentenced to long prison terms for even mentioning the Kurds.

Predictably, Bush obliged Turkey, a NATO ally and participant in the Gulf War, by delivering the Kurds to the armies of Hussein. The Saudi government, in its turn, feared that a successful Shiite rebellion in Iraq would strengthen Shiite Iran's hand in the Gulf region. From a geopolitical view, it was better to have Hussein control Iraq's Shiites and Kurds than to destroy the political and military center in Baghdad and then have to face the unsettling consequences.

The Sunni Arabs of Iraq, who live mainly in the central region, fared only somewhat better than the Shiites and Kurds, for they, too, suffered from deprivation and disease. One study calculated that as many as 70,000 Iraqis died during the war as a result of allied bombing of electric power plants and transport facilities, which affected water purification, sewage treatment plants, and the distribution of food and medicine.[27] The continuing grief of the Iraqi people was partly the consequence of UN-imposed economic sanctions, which remained in effect after the war. But it was also the consequence of Hussein's refusal to accept a UN plan that would have allowed Iraq to sell $1.6 billion worth of oil over a six-month period, provided that 70 percent of the proceeds went to the purchase of food and medicine and the remainder was paid into a UN compensation fund for Kuwait's reconstruction.

Hussein remained a hardy survivor, continuing to sneer at the assemblage of nations that had stopped him and testing their will. The severe economic sanctions were to remain in effect pending Iraqi compliance with the UN cease-fire terms. Under the terms accepted by Baghdad, Iraq had agreed to destroy its chemical, biological, and nuclear weapons and their production facilities and to pay the cost of UN inspections of those facilities out of future oil revenues. But from the beginning, Hussein sought to stymie UN inspectors in an effort to save as much of his weapons facilities as possible. Iraqi soldiers repeatedly interfered with UN inspectors, even firing warning shots to prevent them from gaining access to certain facilities. These actions produced warnings from Washington of a renewal of the aerial bombardment of Iraq to force compliance with the UN resolutions.

A sequence of events in January 1993 demonstrated the pattern of Hussein's defiance. It began after U.S. jet fighters had downed an Iraqi warplane over the "no-fly zone" Washington had imposed over southern Iraq several months earlier to protect Shiite Muslims in that area from attacks by Iraqi forces. Hussein responded by moving anti-aircraft missiles into the zone, only to have U.S. planes attack them. A few days later, Hussein sent workers to dismantle a warehouse in an area the United Nations considered to be Kuwaiti territory. The UN Security Council passed a resolution condemning repeated Iraqi violations of the cease-fire terms, and the United States followed with a wave of air strikes, including firing forty cruise missiles at a suspected nuclear arms site near Baghdad.

Saddam Hussein's continued defiance of the peace terms remained a thorn in the side of the United States, the nation that had paid the heaviest price to defeat him and that now played the role of the unrelenting enforcer of the cease-fire. By 1994, Washington no longer had the full support of its erstwhile Gulf War allies; indeed, it sometimes stood alone in its wrathful chastisement of Hussein, who continued to twist dangerous confrontations to his political advantage. In October 1994, Hussein began marching several divisions of his Republican Guard—his best forces—toward the Kuwaiti border. Predictably, Washington scrambled to meet this new crisis with a rapid deployment of forces, including B-52 bombers and fighter jets, to head off what was seen as an impending second invasion of Kuwait. But no sooner had the Iraqi troops approached the border than they turned around. Hussein's brinkmanship, which won him acclaim at home, frayed the nerves of Washington and saddled it with the high costs of a rapid military mobilization.

UN officials responsible for monitoring Iraq's compliance with UN cease-fire terms told Hussein that although Iraq had finally complied sufficiently with the UN provisions for dismantling weapons production facilities, it would still have to meet a host of other UN resolutions—compensation for Gulf War damages, recognition of Kuwait, acknowledgment of no-fly zones, among others—before the UN-imposed embargo on Iraqi oil sales could be lifted. It had been over three years since the embargo had been enacted, and the continuing deprivation of Iraq's major source of earnings had kept the country in economic shambles. An enraged Hussein denounced the UN position as a policy of "moving the goal posts." Some nations—including some members of the UN Security Council, as well as some Arab states—began to sympathize with Iraq's position. In November 1994, Iraq declared its recognition of Kuwait's sovereignty, thereby abandoning its claim to Kuwait and meeting another of the cease-fire terms. At the Security Council meeting at which a UN response to this conciliatory gesture was formulated, the United States and Britain stood alone in rejecting a proposal favored by China, Russia, and France to partially lift the embargo on the sale of Iraqi oil. When the United Nations finally offered Hussein a partial lifting of the economic sanctions in April 1995, Hussein thumbed his nose at the offer and insisted upon the complete removal of all sanctions. Finally, in early 1997 the UN offered that concession and Iran was permitted to sell its oil.

Another flare-up between Washington and Baghdad occurred in fall 1996 over the Kurdish problem in northern Iraq. After the Gulf War, President Bush had created a no-fly zone north of the thirty-sixth parallel to protect the Kurdish population in northern Iraq. Five years later, that policy was challenged by Hussein when he marched his troops across the line into the city of Erbil (just north of the thirty-sixth parallel) and swiftly reconquered Iraq's portion of Kurdistan. The region in northern Iraq that the Kurds call Kurdistan was contested by two rival Kurdish parties backed by their respective armies. The Kurdistan Democratic Party of Massoud Barzani and the Patriotic Union of Kurdistan (PUK) of Jalal Talabani were engaged in a struggle over political power and control of a lucrative black market in cigarettes and Iraqi gasoline for sale in Turkey. The U.S. State

Department and the CIA attempted to broker a truce between the two groups but failed. In what became a Kurdish civil war, Barzani asked Hussein for assistance, and Talabani turned to Iran for support. The two arch-enemies, Iran and Iraq, now faced a showdown in Kurdistan. Hussein moved to quickly dislodge the PUK and announced that he had taken action at the invitation of Barzani and to prevent Iran from controlling northern Iraq.

The U.S. policy of protecting the Kurds from Hussein was now in shambles. President Clinton, who was in the midst of a presidential campaign, had no choice but to express his displeasure at Hussein's actions. Although he was unwilling to risk the life of a single U.S. soldier, Clinton deployed reinforcement troops in the Gulf region and launched a number of cruise missiles, which, however, caused negligible damage to Hussein's military capacity or to his prestige at home.

RECOMMENDED READINGS

Islam

Dawood, N. J., trans. *The Meaning of the Glorious Koran.* New York: Penguin, 1956.
    A translation of the Koran for Western readers, as well as a valuable introduction to the early history of Islam, by Mohammed Marmaduke Pickthall, an English convert to the faith.

Guillaume, Alfred. *Islam.* 2d rev. ed. New York: Penguin, 1956.
    The classic analysis of the theological basis of Islam by one of the West's recognized scholars in the field.

Jansen, G. H. *Militant Islam.* New York: Harper and Row, 1979.
    Explains to Western readers the philosophic foundations of Islam and the reasons for its militant form in Iran.

Kedourie, Elie. *Islam in the Modern World.* New York: Holt, Rinehart and Winston, 1980.
    Focuses on the link between Islam and Arab politics.

Iran and Its Revolution

Bakhash, Shaul. *The Reign of the Ayatollahs: Iran and the Islamic Revolution.* New York: Basic Books, 1984.
    A scholarly account of Khomeini's revolution.

Kapuscinski, Ryszard. *Shah of Shahs.* San Diego: Harcourt, Brace, Jovanovich, 1985.
    By a veteran Polish journalist, an eyewitness to the Iranian upheaval.

Rubin, Barry. *Paved with Good Intentions: The American Experience and Iran.* New York: Oxford University Press, 1980.
    An analysis of what went wrong with the U.S. scenario for Iran.

Said, Edward W. *Covering Islam: How the Media and the Experts Determine How We See the Rest of the World.* New York: Pantheon Books, 1981.

A critical analysis, by a U.S. citizen of Palestinian descent, of how the U.S. press handled the Iranian hostage crisis.

Salinger, Pierre. *America Held Hostage: The Secret Negotiations.* Garden City, N.Y.: Doubleday, 1981.
By a U.S. journalist who was directly involved in settling the crisis.

Sick, Gary. *All Fall Down.* New York: Random House, 1985.
A member of President Carter's National Security Council presents a first-hand account of the hostage deliberations.

Iraq and the Gulf War

Arnett, Peter. *Live from the Battlefield: From Vietnam to Baghdad: 35 Years in the World's War Zones.* New York: Touchstone, 1994.
Gordon, Michael R., and Bernard E. Trainor. *The General's War: The Inside Story of the Conflict in the Gulf.* Boston: Little, Brown, 1994.

NOTES

1. N. J. Dawood, trans., *The Koran,* 4th rev. ed. (New York: Penguin, 1974), p. 220, Surah 23:14–16; p. 375, Surah, 4:87.

2. Alfred Guillaume, *Islam* 2d rev. ed. (New York: Penguin, 1956), p. 38. Islam does, however, recognize Jesus as one of a long line of God's prophets.

3. *The Koran,* pp. 362–364, Surah 2:261–265, 270–277.

4. Khomeini in June 1963, when visited in prison by the chief of SAVAK, cited in Bernard Lewis, "How Khomeini Made It," *New York Review of Books,* January 17, 1985, p. 10.

5. His exile lasted for fourteen years. In one of his speeches Khomeini denounced a law that his country's parliament had passed in October 1964 by which U.S. citizens in Iran had been granted extraterritoriality, the right to be tried according to U.S., instead of Iranian, law. Khomeini called the law "a document for the enslavement of Iran" that "acknowledged that Iran is a colony; it has given America a document attesting that the nation of Muslims is barbarous." Bernard Lewis, "How Khomeini Made It," p. 10.

6. The basis of the Shiite creed, in Bernard Lewis, "The Shi'a," *New York Review,* August 15, 1985, p. 8; Shiites point to Allah's will "to favour those who were oppressed and to make them leaders of mankind, to bestow on them a noble heritage and to give them power in the land." *The Koran,* p. 75, Surah 28:5.

7. Robert Graham, *Iran: The Illusion of Power* (New York: St. Martin's, 1979), p. 33.

8. In March 1976, a dutiful parliament created the "monarchy calendar" (dating from the coronation of Cyrus the Great, 2,535 years ago) replacing the Islamic calendar based on the date of the hegira (flight) of Mohammed from Mecca to Medina in A.D. 622. Ibid., p. 61.

9. "Aryans" here is in reference to the Persian- (Farsi-)speaking peoples of Iran, originally from northern India. It was an attempt to identify the shah with the nation's earliest history.

10. The operation proved to be one of the CIA's greatest triumphs. It pointed to the agency's ability to topple and create foreign governments.

11. Henry Kissinger, *The White House Years* (Boston: Little, Brown, 1979), p. 1264.

12. After the shah's death in 1980, his son became the claimant to the throne and many Iranian exiles pinned their hopes on him.

13. It therefore came as a surprise to the U.S. public when in November 1986 it was revealed that Reagan, who for six years had bitterly denounced any and all terrorists and had vowed never to deal with any of them, was found in effect to have paid ransom to terrorists in Lebanon who were holding U.S. hostages. In the process, the Reagan administration had provided numerous shipments of weapons to the government of the Ayatollah Khomeini, which was engaged in a long and bloody war with Iraq.

14. The U.S. involvement was part of the Iran-Contra affair (see Chapter 14). The Reagan administration at first denied that it approved arms sales to Iran, which were illegal, but later admitted the sales, explaining that the purpose was nothing more than to strengthen "moderate elements" within Iran. Reagan, who had come to power because of the hostage crisis in Tehran during 1979–1981, had become deeply troubled by the fact that he was incapable of freeing U.S. hostages in Lebanon and hoped that somehow Iranian moderates could help him. He had vowed never to negotiate with terrorists, particularly Shiites and Iranians, yet he was now arming them.

15. Quoted in Mansour Farhang, "Iran-Iraq Conflict: An Unending War Between Two Despots," *The Nation,* September 20, 1986.

16. Graham E. Fuller, "War and Revolution in Iran," *Current History,* February 1989, p. 81.

17. In October 1989, Qaddafi admitted to having bankrolled terrorist groups but added: "When we discovered that these groups were causing more harm than benefit to the Arab cause, we halted our aid to them completely and withdrew our support." "Kadafi Admits Backing Terrorists, Says He Erred," *Baltimore Sun,* October 26, 1989.

18. Reagan provided no proof of Qaddafi's complicity. West German intelligence later stated that the evidence pointed to Syria.

19. Britain and the United States took the lead in pressing for extradition. They were joined by France, which demanded Libyan cooperation in an investigation of four Libyan suspects in the explosion of a French airliner over Niger in 1989, killing 404.

20. Cited in Jim Hoagland, "Transcript Shows Muted U.S. Response to Threat by Saddam in Late July," *Washington Post,* September 13, 1990, p. A33. In March 1991, before the Senate Foreign Relations Committee, Glaspie refuted the Iraqi version of her conversation with Hussein; the State Department, however, refused to make public its transcript of the meeting or its correspondence with Glaspie.

21. Cited in Robert Ruby, "Security Council OKs Military Force," *Baltimore Sun,* August 26, 1990, p. 1A.

22. To pay for the war, Saudi Arabia pledged (in billions) $21.4, Kuwait $21, the United States $15, Japan $13.8, Germany $6.8, the United Arab Emirates $2.9, and South Korea $0.56.

23. Jeffrey Record, "The Air War Missed Its Biggest Target," *Baltimore Sun,* November 21, 1991, p. 11A.

24. The cost to Saudi Arabia, including the quartering of foreign troops and fuel, was estimated at over $48 billion, over one-half of its annual income.

25. "President Reportedly Signed Orders Allowing CIA to Aid Rebels Within Iraq," *Baltimore Sun,* April 4, 1991, p. 3A.

26. Quoted in Raymond Bonner, "Always Remember," *New Yorker,* September 28, 1992, p. 48. At the end of World War I, U.S. President Woodrow Wilson

proclaimed in his Fourteen Points that the ethnic minorities of Ottoman Turkey should have "absolutely unmolested opportunity of autonomous development." The Treaty of Sèvres (1920), intended to deal with the consequences of the breakup of the Ottoman Empire, called for an independent Kurdish state, but the Turkish government of Kemal Ataturk refused to accept it.

27. "70,000 Postwar Civilian Deaths in Iran Laid to Bomb Damage," *Baltimore Sun*, January 9, 1992, p. 2A.

19

The New Economic Superpowers: Japan and the European Union

In the early 1940s, the United States and its allies were menaced by armed aggression by Germany and Japan. Less than a half century later, those two countries again posed a challenge to other nations—not a military challenge, but an economic one. After World War II, when the United States was the world's only economic superpower, it assisted West Germany and Japan in their economic recovery and provided them security. By the 1980s, however, the European Community (EC), in which West Germany was economically the strongest member, and Japan became economic superpowers, and the United States no longer stood alone. Before examining the relative economic strength of the three and the new economic relationship among them, we will examine the remarkable economic development of Japan, the strains in its economic relations with the United States, and the emergence of the EC as an economic giant.

■ JAPAN'S "ECONOMIC MIRACLE"

Between the late 1940s and the late 1970s, Japan underwent an incredible transformation. This nation, no larger than the state of California, gutted by bombs in World War II and lacking in virtually all the raw materials needed for modern industry, grew in the space of thirty years to become the second-largest economic power in the world.[1] Only the United States had a larger GNP. But Japan's industrial productivity, in terms of output per person, was already as large as that of the United States.

Japan's postwar economic recovery was rapid, but it did not occur immediately. Quite the contrary; after the war Japan's inflation-ridden economy was in shambles and it remained that way for about three years as the people of Japan endured great hardships. In 1948, the U.S. occupation policy shifted in the direction of assisting Japan's economic recovery, and the United States began providing aid and technological assistance. Still, it was not until 1953 that Japan's economic output reached its prewar level. This resulted from U.S. assistance, Japan's own assets and hard work, and some good luck as well. The luck was the timely occurrence of the Korean War, which provided the Japanese with opportunity to sell their light industry goods to the UN forces in Korea and thereby earn capital to pour into rebuilding Japan's industries.

U.S. economic aid and assistance to Japan came in various forms. In addition to a total of about $2 billion in direct economic aid (spread over a span of five years), the United States (1) persuaded its Western wartime allies to drop their demands for reparations from Japan, (2) pressured Japan to curb inflation and regain fiscal solvency, (3) provided Japan modern technology by making U.S. patents available cheaply, (4) opened the U.S. market to Japanese goods, (5) persuaded other countries to resume trade with Japan, (6) tolerated Japan's protective tariffs for its industries, and (7) took up the burden of Japan's defense. This assistance was not mere kindness to a former enemy, but the strengthening of a new, critically important and strategically located, Cold War ally. The Japanese appreciated the generous assistance and took full advantage of it. Without the diligent work of the Japanese themselves, however, the economic recovery would not have been possible. Moreover, the U.S. assistance was by no means the sole factor for the Japanese economic miracle that followed the recovery.

Japan's economy began its skyrocket growth in the late 1950s, and it kept on zooming upward through the 1960s. The average annual growth rate of Japan's GNP in the 1960s was about 11 percent, far higher than other industrialized nations. In the same period, a 3 percent growth rate was considered good for the United States and other developed countries. The double-digit growth rate continued into the 1970s, until Japan's economic drive was thrown off track in 1974 by the global oil crisis. Detractors were quick to point out the fragility of Japan's economic system because of its resource dependency, and some declared that Japan's miracle was ended. But the Japanese made adjustments, reducing their oil consumption and diversifying their energy sources, and were back on track by 1976. Until the late 1980s, Japan's average annual growth rate was about 4.5 percent, still the highest among the world's industrialized nations.

Japan surged past most European industrial leaders—Italy, France, and Britain—in the 1960s, and then in the early 1970s it surpassed West Germany, whose own postwar economic recovery was also impressive. By 1980, Japan ranked first in production in a number of modern industries. It had long been first in shipbuilding; in fact, it has built more than one-half of the world's ships by tonnage since the early 1970s. It outpaced the Germans in camera production and the United States in the production of electronic equipment such as radios, televisions, sound systems, and video recorders. Japanese motorcycles left their rivals in the dust, and Japanese automobiles captured an increasing share of the world's markets, so that Japan became the world's leader in automobile production in 1980. Although not the largest producer of steel, by 1970 it had the most modern and efficient steel industry. By 1980, Japan was poised to mount a challenge to U.S. leadership in the new, all-important high-tech industries, especially in the computer and microelectronic fields.

Many in the West tended to belittle Japan's success and explain it away with self-serving excuses or outdated, if not entirely erroneous, notions—for example, Japan's cheap labor. Japan, they argued, was competitive because its people were willing to work for very low wages. This assertion had some truth to it in the 1950s and early 1960s, but by the early 1970s, Japan's wage structure had reached the level of most industrial nations. Another notion was that Japan's prosperity was a consequence of its free ride on defense because the United States guaranteed its security. Japan surely benefited from having a much lower level of defense spending than the United States, especially in the first two decades after World War II.[2] Other internal factors, however, were more important in explaining Japan's economic growth in the 1970s and 1980s.

■ THE BASES FOR JAPAN'S ECONOMIC GROWTH

Following are seven major categories of domestic factors for the economic success Japan achieved by the mid-1970s.

1. *The government-business relationship in Japan was complementary and cooperative, rather than antagonistic.* The government, particularly the Ministry of International Trade and Industry (MITI), charted a course for the nation's economy and coordinated its industrial growth. Government and industrial firms engaged in long-term planning, and both made use of consensus decision making. The MITI bureaucracy in Japan, with its ties to political and business leaders, steered a steady course, thereby providing policy continuity. It guided industrial development not only by targeting specific industries for growth, but also by designating other declining industries to be scaled down or even dismantled. It also targeted foreign markets on which the Japanese would concentrate their attack. In sum, the Japanese government fostered a national consensus on the priority of economic growth and established industrial and trade policies.

2. *The labor-management system in Japan stressed mutual harmony between the workers and management, rather than confrontation.* Japan's "lifetime employment" system, with its built-in rewards for worker seniority, provided employment security to the workers who in turn developed strong identity with and dedication to their firms. This obviously benefited the firm, which could count on retaining the services of its well-trained and

loyal work force. Generally, management treated its work force as an investment. Worker morale and motivation were increased by various management programs, including a generous bonus system, educational benefits, housing, insurance, recreational facilities, and the like, and all this resulted in greater worker loyalty and productivity. There were labor unions in Japan, but they were organized locally (as opposed to national trade unions) and their relations with management tended to be cooperative rather than confrontational. Worker participation in management decision making and in quality-control circles also contributed significantly to the mutual benefit of employer and employee.

3. *The Japanese educational system, which is controlled by the central government, maintained uniform, high standards and was extremely competitive.* In Japan, university entrance examinations determine a person's entire future, and only the cream of the crop are admitted to the best universities, whose graduates get the best jobs. Therefore, students at all levels study intensely—incredibly so—in preparation for entrance examinations or, as they are called in Japan, "examination hell." The result is a highly educated society with well-developed work habits. (An unfortunate consequence of such a high level of pressure on young people was a relatively high rate of suicide.)

Quality of education may be difficult to compare from one nation to the next, but it is true that, on the whole, the Japanese student receives *more*, if not better, education than his counterpart in other countries. The Japanese school year is sixty days longer than in the United States, and Japanese schoolchildren typically study many hours a day after school with tutors or in private schools. About 33 percent of Japanese high school graduates enter universities, compared to over 55 percent in the United States, but in Japan a higher percentage of entering students graduate from universities. The education system is centralized under the Ministry of Education, which provides a uniform curriculum. Generally, it maintains high standards, especially in math and science. This and the fact that Japanese universities turn out more engineers (even in absolute terms) than the United States help to explain Japan's technological progress.

4. *The Japanese aggressively sought new technology in quest of industrial rationalization and greater productivity.* The Japanese were, for example, swifter than their foreign competitors to modernize their steel plants with the most recent, efficient, and cost-saving technology. When the oxygen-burning type of steel furnace was developed in Austria in the early 1960s, the Japanese quickly purchased the patents and invested a vast amount of capital to rapidly convert their plants to the new technology. They also adopted the new continuous casting process at about the same time, and the result was that within a decade they had in operation the world's most efficient and cost-competitive steel plants. This explains why the Japanese were able to compete with U.S.-made steel in the United

States, even though they had to import their iron ore and ship their finished steel across the Pacific Ocean. The Japanese did not hesitate to install the most recent technology in their plants to improve quality and increase production. Not surprisingly, Japan was far ahead of the rest of the world in robotics and the automation of the production line. Data show that by the late 1980s Japan had twice as many industrial robots in operation than the rest of the world combined.[3]

5. *The high rate of personal savings by the Japanese and Japan's financial and banking practices were beneficial to capital formation for economic growth.* The average Japanese saved a remarkable 18 percent of his salary, compared to about 6 percent for U.S. workers.[4] The banks in which their savings accounts were held invested in industry. Although Japanese firms were also financed by selling stock, a great portion of their capital came from banks, which, unlike stockholders, did not insist on quarterly profits. Instead, the banks financed long-term business enterprises, which at times operated in the red several years before they began to turn a profit. The availability of this risk capital made possible continuous plant modernization.

6. *Japan developed superior mechanisms for marketing its products abroad.* The Japanese government, mainly MITI, established a foreign trade policy. Also, there existed in Japan comprehensive trading companies that specialized in foreign commerce. These companies had branch offices all around the world collecting data, doing thorough market research, and in numerous ways facilitating Japanese trade. They also worked with MITI to arrange the most advantageous trade agreements, secure long-term supply of vital raw materials, and direct Japanese investment abroad. Although Japan was vulnerable because of its lack of natural resources, it made itself much less so by becoming indispensable to resource-supplying nations both as a reliable buyer and as a supplier of technology and capital. Other nations had nothing comparable to Japan's comprehensive trading companies for conducting a large volume of foreign trade. (In fact, foreign firms sometimes employed these Japanese trading companies to make their trade arrangements with other countries.)

7. *There were also certain intangible factors unique to Japan—or to East Asian countries—that contributed to economic growth.* The Japanese were served well by certain historically conditioned cultural traits, such as acceptance of authority, paternalism, a desire for harmony, loyalty to superiors, discipline, and a sense of duty and sincerity. Group consciousness prevailed over individualism. Without these traits, Japan's labor-management system would hardly have been possible. Additionally, there were certain historical circumstances that fortuitously benefited Japan, such as the timing of its industrial development during a period of global economic expansion. It may also be argued that Japan thrived on its own deprivation. Japan's dearth of raw materials, for example, necessitated hard

work to attain, conserve, and use them efficiently. By necessity, the Japanese came to excel in industry and foreign commerce.

There were, no doubt, other factors (such as industrial rationalization or efficient organization of the industrial workplace and the rapid growth of Japan's domestic market) involved in Japan's economic performance. Japan's relatively low level of defense spending and the openness of U.S. markets also worked to Japan's economic advantage. With regard to defense spending, Chalmers Johnson has pointed out that "the effect of low defense expenditures was negligible," because Japan had a very high rate of investment—capital formation exceeding 30 percent of the GNP.[5] Lower military spending may have been an important factor in the first decade or so after World War II (when the United States saw fit to protect the nation it had just demilitarized), but from the 1970s Japan's military spending steadily increased, and by 1990 it had the third-highest defense budget in the world. In any case, this factor was less important than those outlined above as explanations for Japan's economic success. As Japan's industrial competitiveness improved and its trade surpluses continued to increase in the 1980s, its trade partners across the Pacific added another explanation (more an accusation) for Japan's economic miracle: unfair trading practices. This charge against Japan became a recurrent theme in Japan's economic relations with the United States and other nations of the world.

■ STRAINS IN U.S.-JAPANESE ECONOMIC RELATIONS

Bilateral trade between the United States and Japan in the 1980s became the largest volume of overseas trade between any two nations in history. (Only U.S.-Canada trade, which is not overseas commerce, was larger.) Japan had a deficit in its commodity trade with the United States until 1964; that is, it exported less to the United States than it imported from the United States. From that point, it has been the reverse, with the U.S. deficit in the bilateral trade rising to $1 billion in 1972, $12 billion in 1978, $25 billion in 1984, and then soaring to an astronomical $56 billion in 1987. No nation ever had such a huge trade imbalance with its trading partner. Table 19.1 compares the U.S. trade deficits with Japan and other trading partners in 1987.

Only belatedly did the U.S. public begin to take the Japanese economic challenge seriously. In the late 1970s, people in the United States were caught by surprise by Japan's seemingly boundless economic growth and began to wonder about the contrast between Japan's economic success and the recession in their own country. Many of those disaffected by the

Table 19.1   U.S. Trade Deficits with Selected Areas, 1987 (in US$)

Total U.S. trade deficit	−153,035,000
with Japan	−56,326,000
with the "four tigers" of Asia	−34,117,000
with the European Community	−20,613,000
with OPEC	−12,895,000
with Latin America	−11,507,000

latter, especially the unemployed, began to blame their problems on Japan. In their minds the growing amount of Japanese imports and rising unemployment were directly related. In Washington, politicians were quick to respond to their plight and take up the cause of combating Japan's trade policies.

In the 1980s, "Japan bashing" became one of Washington's favorite pastimes, even though economists and government officials recognized that declining U.S. industrial competitiveness was an important cause of the trade imbalance. Consumers found Japanese products, especially cars and electronic equipment, superior and less expensive than U.S.-made products. But Japan was open to charges of unfair trade practices, such as "dumping" (selling its products abroad at a loss or at lower prices than in Japan) and protecting its own market from foreign imports by high tariffs, import quotas, and various nontariff barriers. Some found political hay to be made by calling for "get tough" trade policies and economic sanctions against Japan. If the Japanese did not lower their trade barriers, they argued, then the United States must erect barriers against the flood of Japanese products. In the 1980s, President Reagan, like his immediate predecessors in the White House, opposed taking this protectionist route, knowing that it could lead to a mutually damaging trade war; instead, he put pressure on Japan to open its markets to U.S. goods.

Generally, Washington joined Tokyo in accentuating the positive aspects in U.S.-Japanese relations, which the U.S. ambassador to Japan, Mike Mansfield, liked to call "the most important bilateral relationship in the world, bar none."[6] But despite the talk of partnership and cooperation, Washington maintained pressure on Tokyo, which grudgingly gave in to its persistent demands. On the one hand, Tokyo agreed "voluntarily" to various trade limitations and quotas on its exports to the United States; on the other hand, Washington endeavored to pry open Japan's doors to U.S. products by removing Japan's trade barriers. In the 1960s, Japan agreed to quotas on textiles, in the 1970s to limitations on steel exports to the United States, and in 1981 to a voluntary ceiling on U.S.-bound automobiles. Japan also began building automobile plants in the United States, partly to reduce the volume of Japanese automobile imports and partly to quiet the argument that Japanese cars robbed U.S. workers of their jobs. As Washington erected trade barriers against Japan, it demanded that Japan pull down its own barriers. Since the late 1960s, Tokyo had, in fact, gradually reduced its own tariffs and quotas to make foreign goods more competitive in Japan, and by the early 1980s it had agreed to a schedule of tariff reductions that would by 1987 make its tariffs on industrial imports lower, across the board, than those of the United States and the European Community nations.[7]

Washington then pointed to remaining tariffs and quotas on agricultural imports. This was a problem area, as Japan sought to protect its farmers from foreign suppliers of such foodstuffs as beef, oranges, and rice. After years of hard bargaining, the two sides managed only to achieve interim agreements gradually elevating the quotas on beef and oranges.[8] But Tokyo continued to hold out on rice, even if it meant that the Japanese would continue to pay seven times the world price for their precious home-grown rice. Still, Tokyo could respond to U.S. charges by pointing out that Japan was already by far the world's largest importer of U.S. agricultural exports.

Washington applied still more pressure on the Japanese for access to the Japanese market. It called upon Tokyo to remove various *nontariff* barriers to imports and to stimulate the domestic market in Japan in order to boost sales of imported goods. Japan was charged with keeping U.S. goods out of its market through such means as restrictive licensing, excessive inspection of imports and burdensome customs clearing procedures, rigid safety standards, a uniquely cumbersome distribution system, and nettlesome purchasing regulations. The charges were not groundless, but these were complicated matters involving peculiarities of the Japanese business system as well as cultural patterns, and in any case they would be difficult to change or adjust. Only after long and difficult talks were trade negotiators able to achieve limited progress in this area.[9]

Some analysts explained that the huge U.S. trade deficit with Japan was due less to trade policies than to such macroeconomic causes as an unfavorable monetary exchange rate, the increase of the U.S. budget deficit, and low spending in Japan's domestic economy.[10] In April 1986, a panel of economic advisers headed by Maekawa Haruo, former governor of the Bank of Japan, submitted to Prime Minister Nakasone Yasuhiro a report (the Maekawa Report) that called for the Japanese economy to shift from dependence on exports to greater reliance on domestic economic growth. To stimulate domestic consumption the panel recommended wage increases, reduction of work hours, income tax reductions, and removal of the tax exemption on personal savings accounts. The purpose of the proposed reforms was to enlarge the Japanese market for foreign goods, thereby deemphasizing export-led economic growth and reducing the trade imbalance between Japan and its trade partners. The Maekawa Report also said Japan should contribute more to resolving global problems, especially to relieving the debt burden of developing countries.

Prime Minister Nakasone endorsed the Maekawa plan, stating that "Japan's future depends on this transformation" and that Japan could no longer remain a "prosperous isolated island."[11] After a meeting with President Reagan in Washington at which he vowed to vigorously implement the Maekawa plan, Nakasone made a direct appeal on television to the Japanese people to "accept foreign manufactured products in order to make your lives richer and more affluent."[12] Implementation of the plan, especially increasing purchases of foreign imports, was slow, however, mainly because of resistance by the business community. Some of the recommendations of the plan were adopted (the shorter work week and increased foreign aid, for example), but one could still hear through the end of the decade, from foreigners and Japanese leaders alike, demands that still more be done to stimulate domestic spending in Japan and to increase the country's import of foreign manufactured goods.

The Reagan administration attempted another strategy to decrease the U.S. trade deficit with Japan. A monetary policy to lower the value of the dollar against the Japanese yen, it was thought, would lower the price tag on U.S. goods in Japan and raise the price tag on Japanese goods entering the United States. The dollar began its decline against the yen in 1985, when the exchange rate was 260 yen to the dollar, and continued falling until the rate leveled out at around 125 yen to the dollar in 1988. But for a variety of reasons, this strategy did not have the desired effect: the volume of Japanese exports to the United States did not decline; U.S. exports to Japan hardly increased;[13] and Japan's bilateral trade surplus zoomed to more than $56 billion in 1987. The strategy only enriched the Japanese because the yen suddenly doubled in purchasing power around the world and tripled by 1995.

The Reagan strategy had another unanticipated and undesired effect: the falling value of the dollar, in effect, lowered the cost of foreign investment in the United States, and this in combination with high interest rates in the United States attracted wealthy Japanese investors. As a result, the Japanese, who had accumulated a tremendous amount of capital from selling goods in the United States (and elsewhere), recycled these profits and went on a buying spree, purchasing U.S. banks, companies, and real estate. Most conspicuous were the highly visible real estate acquisitions of Japanese investors in Hawaii, California, and New York City. U.S. Senator Ernest F. Hollings, an advocate of retaliatory sanctions against Japan, noted that the effect of Reagan's monetary approach was to transform the United States "into a coast-to-coast yard sale, with our assets available to foreigners at cut-rate, foreclosure-sale prices."[14]

The trade conflict between Japan and the United States heated up in 1987 when the U.S. Congress demonstrated its "get tough" policy by passing an omnibus trade bill, and the Reagan administration placed a retaliatory tariff on $300 million worth of Japanese electronic products. The

1987 protectionist trade bill contained provisions requiring mandatory retaliation by the president against violations of U.S. trade agreements. Not
only did the Japanese denounce the bill, but the Reagan administration
also rejected the mandatory provisions in it. Finally, in 1988, Congress
passed a modified, slightly less protectionist version of the trade bill and
overrode the president's veto.

Despite the efforts made by both Japan and the United States, the bilateral trade imbalance was not reduced, and the Japanese made still
greater gains as an economic competitor. By 1982, Japan had won a crucial battle in the "high-tech wars" when it gained a decisive edge on U.S.
competitors in the production and sales of microchips (particularly the
64K RAM chips).[15] In the early 1980s, Japan found a booming market in
the United States for VCRs (video cassette recorders), a product that, ironically, had been invented in the United States but abandoned as commer-
cially impractical. The Japanese also won increased shares of the U.S.
market for other industrial products such as precision tools, musical instruments, and power tools. Meanwhile, Japan surpassed the United States
in nonmilitary research and development (R&D) expenditures, and its
technological research programs either gained the lead or challenged the
U.S. lead in a number of new and important fields, particularly in robotics,
magnetic levitation, superconductivity, fiber optics, and high-resolution
television.

Japan pulled ahead of the United States in several other ways during
the decade. In the mid-1980s, the United States swiftly fell from the status of the leading creditor nation in the world to the largest debtor. Japan
just as swiftly became the world's leading creditor. Japan's assault on the
money market in the United States in the late 1980s was breathtaking.
Japan's economic expansion was no longer limited to the industrial sector, but now extended into the fields of banking and finance. By the end of
the decade, eight of the ten largest banks in the world were Japanese; six
of the twelve largest California banks were Japanese-owned; 20 percent of
U.S. government bonds were placed by Japanese financial firms; 10 percent of the New York Stock Exchange was handled by four large Japanese
companies; the top four security companies in the world were Japanese,
with the largest, Nomura, being ten times larger than Merrill Lynch, the
largest in the United States; and the Tokyo Stock Exchange surpassed the
New York Stock Exchange in capital value, while the Osaka Exchange surpassed the London Stock Exchange.[16]

The dramatic elevation of Japan's economic status raised new questions about the relative wealth of the United States and Japan. Older
Japanese, clinging to outdated images, still worried about Japan's
"poverty," such as its paucity of natural resources, and still stood in awe of
the prosperity of the United States with all its land and resources. But

younger Japanese and many in the United States as well held that Japan had indeed become a rich nation and that the United States with its double deficits (trade deficit and budget deficit) and declining productivity had become a poorer nation by comparison.[17] U.S. leaders cited Japan's new wealth as the basis for insisting that Japan change its economic policies from those of a poor country, which limited access to its own market.

The rising tide of anti-Japanese feeling and the renewed calls for protectionism in the United States caused irritation in Tokyo, and the Japanese responded with a tough-talking counteroffensive of their own. Prime Minister Takeshita Noboru, at his first press conference in 1987, called upon the United States to first get its own house in order before making demands of Japan. Japanese political and business leaders became more outspoken in lauding Japanese economic superiority and pointing out U.S. economic inferiority. They argued that Japan was unfairly put on the defensive by Washington and made the scapegoat for the United States's own failings. They faulted the United States for such things as fiscal mismanagement, lack of long-term planning, low productivity of its workers, poor quality of its products, and deterioration of its industrial plant and technology. They argued that if Japan removed all remaining barriers to foreign imports, the imbalance in U.S.-Japan trade would scarcely be affected—a view shared by some U.S. observers as well.[18]

By the end of the 1980s, however, persistent effort by both sides did produce some progress in resolving the trade conflicts between the two countries. The bilateral trade deficit dropped from $56.3 billion in 1987 to $55.4 billion in 1988, and U.S. exports to Japan rose 34 percent in 1988 to $37.7 billion. Manufactured goods rose from 30 percent of Japan's total imports to 50 percent.[19] Japan now imported more from the United States than from West Germany, France, and Italy combined.

During the 1980s, Japan also built up a large surplus ($20 billion in 1987) in its trade with the European Economic Community, where the demand for protection against Japanese imports was even stronger than in the United States.

■ THE EUROPEAN COMMUNITY

In March 1985, the European Council, whose members included the heads of the governments of the twelve member states of the European Community (EC),[20] announced its intention of establishing a single market by the end of 1992, which would fulfill the goal set in 1957 when the EC was founded. The European Commission, the executive branch of the EC, published a White Paper that called for the removal of national rules and regulations, such as in banking, transport, and border controls, in favor of supranational regulations. It was a mammoth task encompassing 279 areas, from the rights of labor and women to banking and insurance, agricultural subsidies, border controls, immigration, air pollution and health standards, transportation, and communication. The EC went so far as to plan the issue of the common European Currency Unit to put an end to the twelve different currencies then in use.[21]

By the late 1950s, the EC had gone a long way toward breaking down many of the formidable barriers between the nations of Western Europe, but many had remained in place. Moreover, some nations—France in particular—had turned to "national solutions" to solve their economic problems, particularly those brought about by the oil embargoes of the 1970s. But in the early 1980s, several factors came together: the French and Spanish socialists, who in the past had favored governmental regulations and control of the economy, acknowledged the superiority of the market over a planned economy. They too began to extol the virtues of competition tied to deregulation of the economy. The EC of 1992 was the logical result of this trend to deregulation.

The first nation to take the road to 1992 was France, which at the time was no longer ruled by the nationalist Charles de Gaulle, but by the "European" François Mitterrand. In January 1984, Mitterrand became the president of the Council of Ministers of the EC, and in this capacity he became a convert to European unity. His term as president of the Council, a French diplomat noted, became his "road to Damascus."[22] Helmut Kohl, the chancellor of West Germany, supported this approach as he felt that the strong German economy could only benefit from the removal of national economic barriers. Margaret Thatcher, the prime minister of Britain, long an apostle of laissez-faire capitalism, had no reason to object to a free market. The main goal was to strengthen the competitiveness of Western Europe in the world market against the other great players—the United States, which in 1989 created its own free trade zone with Canada, and particularly Japan, the primary target. The Europeans resented Japan's aggressive economic expansion and its continued protection of its own domestic market. In European eyes, competition with Japan had turned into economic war.

The driving force behind European economic unification was the business elite; it was not a popular mass movement. Many, in fact, viewed the full integration process with misgivings. West Germans, for example, feared the influx of immigrants from the south. In the 1960s, West German industry had recruited a large number of workers from Turkey, Yugoslavia, and Greece, many of whom did not return home. European economic unification also fostered resentment of foreigners. The EC had its own North-South division. Northern workers feared competition from immigrants from southern countries such as Portugal, Spain, and Greece, where the standard of living was less than half that in the North. Labor also feared that the removal of barriers could mean relocation of businesses to countries with lower wages and social benefits. It was little wonder that "labor's sullenness contrasts with the frenzied activity of businessmen."[23]

The British journal *Economist* in July 1989 sought to answer the question, "What is the EC building?" Its answer was, "Grander than at first seemed likely." At the end of the 1980s, the EC's competitors, the United States and Japan, increasingly took notice of the emerging structure. In Japan, stated the article, industrialists "talk of little else when Europeans come to call." The EC sought to allay fears abroad that the EC was creating a "Fortress Europe." Its communiqué of June 1988 declared that the EC "should be open to third countries and must negotiate with these countries where necessary to ensure access to their market for [European] Community exports. It will seek to preserve the balance of advantages accorded, while respecting the identity of the internal market of the Community." The EC toughened its rules against dumping, tightened the "rules of origin" against suspected dumpers, and uncompromisingly demanded "reciprocity" abroad.[24]

At the same time, the EC also underscored its commitment to international trade. After all, the total exports of its member nations (including exports to each other) amounted to 20 percent of world exports, compared to the United States with 15 percent, and Japan with 9 percent. To forestall the impact of future protectionism, U.S. and Japanese companies invested heavily in EC countries. Toyota invested $1 billion in an automobile factory in Great Britain; AT&T bought into Italtel in Italy to circumvent the rules of origin. For the Japanese, the central problem was access. Should the walls go up, Japan's global companies hoped to qualify as insiders by building industrial plants within EC nations. For this reason their direct investments in EC countries increased from $1 billion in 1984 to about $9 billion in 1989.

After 1987, the EC cracked down on dumping by Asian firms, particularly against Japanese companies, but also against businesses operating in South Korea and Hong Kong. It drew up "rules of origin" and "local-content regulations" to determine the origin of an item of merchandise. They were meant to prevent the establishment of Asian "screwdriver plants" in Europe. The EC commission on dumping declared that "assembly is not enough to give origin" when it sought to prevent U.S.-assembled Japanese Ricoh copiers from avoiding antidumping rules.[25]

But the Europeans remained divided over the issue of Japanese investment. Margaret Thatcher's government particularly welcomed Japanese investment to shore up the economy of Britain, where in 1989 100 Japanese-owned factories employed over 25,000 employees. To lure Japanese investments into their countries, France and Italy, which had maintained notoriously high barriers to foreign imports and investment, began to reconsider their import barriers to Japanese cars produced in Britain. But many European industrialists feared the possibility that unrestricted Japanese investments might lead to Japan's domination of entire sectors of the European economy, as it had achieved in the United States.

In the early 1990s, the EC, whose aggregate economic power was second only to that of the United States, was one of the world's three economic superpowers. The four leading members of the EC—West Germany, France, Italy, and the United Kingdom—ranked third through sixth in the world in GNP. West Germany alone, with one-half the population of Japan and one-quarter that of the United States, had become the world's leading exporting nation in 1988, surpassing the United States for the first time and extending its lead in 1989. West Germany's 1989 commodity trade surplus of $61 billion equaled that of Japan and exceeded it in 1990.[26]

■ THE EMERGENCE OF A NEW GLOBAL BALANCE OF ECONOMIC POWER

The simultaneous rise of Japanese and European Community economic power and the relative decline of U.S. economic strength caused uncertainty in their relations and necessitated adjustments by all three to achieve a new economic balance. As recently as the 1960s, the United States alone accounted for 33 percent of the world's GNP, but by 1989 its share had slipped to 20 percent. By then, the U.S. current account deficit had reached $125 billion, while Japan's surplus had risen to $72 billion, Taiwan's to $70 billion, and Germany's to $53 billion. Japan and West Germany had taken on the role of the world's central bankers. Through the 1980s, Japan and the Asian NICs (newly industrializing countries) on the one hand and West Germany and the EC on the other were gaining momentum, while the United States was struggling. The latter's massive domestic debt was a symptom that the nation was living beyond its means, consuming too much and unable to pay its bills.

Although in relative decline, the United States was still economically strong at the end of the 1980s. Its GNP was still by far the world's largest,

Table 19.2　Comparative Data on the EC, the United States, and Japan, 1987

	Population	Per Capita GNP (US$)
European Community	322,871,000	10,730
West Germany	61,200,000	14,400
United States	243,800,000	18,530
Japan	122,100,000	15,760

and its per capita GNP was still among the highest. It had recovered from a recession at the beginning of the decade and had sustained a modest rate of growth during the decade. The rates of unemployment and inflation had been brought under control and, on the whole, the stock market remained robust. U.S. citizens continued to enjoy one of the world's highest standards of living, and immigrants from all over the world still came with their skills and talents looking for opportunity and a better life.

But there were economic woes. The strength of the stock market—normally a key barometer of the health of the economy—disguised serious problems. U.S. business was busier making money than making products that people used; it was moving money around laterally, rather than building an economy vertically. From the early 1980s to the end of 1992, the national debt soared from $1 trillion to $4.1 trillion. Linked to this burgeoning national debt was the vast increase in foreign lending to the United States as foreign investors were contributing substantially to keep the U.S. government solvent with their purchases of U.S. bonds.

The decline in U.S. economic strength was the product of many factors, including an imbalance between commercial and military priorities, lack of government planning, mismanagement by business leaders, executive greed, labor greed, lawyer greed, and other broader social problems such as declining education standards. While it is not possible to analyze all these issues here, something must be said about the impact of military spending on U.S. economic performance and about major failures on the part of U.S. business leaders. The U.S. effort to remain militarily invincible placed a great burden on the nation's economy. The U.S. defense budget, amounting to $300 billion in 1989, over 25 percent of the budget, was an enormous drain on capital and was the largest single factor contributing to the nation's crippling debt. Although military weapons projects such as the Strategic Defense Initiative (SDI; see Chapter 23) and the Stealth bomber provided employment for many workers and produced some "spin-offs" (commercial applications of defense-related R&D), they drew heavily from national resources, from the pool of capital, and from the pool of engineers and technicians.[27] Since the United States spent about 30 percent of its research money on defense projects, its spending on nonmilitary R&D was lower on a per capita basis than that of Japan and West Germany.

Among the major blunders by U.S. business leadership was Detroit's persistence in building large gas-guzzling automobiles when the global oil crisis created the demand for smaller, fuel-efficient cars; the failure of U.S. steel producers to modernize their plants in the 1960s when new technology became available; and the electronic industry's failure to meet consumer demands for electronic home entertainment systems—for example, the VCR—for lack of insight and research, both in design and in marketing. The consequences of such failures were damaging to the economic competitiveness of the United States. U.S. business leaders pursued shortsighted policies pitting labor against management and the long-term interest of companies against the financial gain of a few, as evident in a General Motors policy calling simultaneously for increases in the already absurdly high salaries for executives and pay cuts for and layoffs of workers.

Much of the discrepancy in the economic performances of Japan and West Germany on the one side and the United States on the other is to be explained by basic differences in their histories and cultures as well as their economic systems. In the United States, the "free enterprise" ideal was historically rooted and remained very much alive; business wanted as little government interference in the marketplace as possible. But in Japan and West Germany, which were both later developers, the government was directly involved from the beginning of the economic modernization process in the nineteenth century, and it continued, especially in Japan, to play a major role in determining industrial and developmental policies.[28] In the United States, the idea of government determination of industrial priorities remained an anathema to the business community. Also, Japan and West Germany, being smaller nations and more dependent on the world economy, both developed export-oriented economies that favored developing industries that produced for the international market.

Japan's emergence as an economic superpower became a concern not only to the United States but to West Germany and the other EC nations as well. In this regard, West Germany and the EC had greater affinity with the United States than with Japan. Like the United States, EC countries believed their finished goods were kept out of Japan by its nontariff barriers and demanded that Japan stimulate its domestic market and open it to foreign-made products. Unlike the United States, most EC nations maintained substantial tariff barriers and guarded against Japanese dumping. They were less tolerant of Japan than was the United States. Typical of European criticism of Japan's trade policy is a broadside in a 1989 article in *Der Spiegel,* the leading West German news weekly, which argued that the Japanese were not interested in trade but in ambushing their competitors, not merely to gain a share of the market but to dominate certain sectors completely—and all this by unfair means, such as dumping, stealing technology, and excluding foreign competitors from their shores. *Der Spiegel* also declared that MITI not only organized trade, it was the headquarters of an economic war machine, which sought to dominate the world.[29]

All three economic superpowers fretted about each other's protectionist policies. Both the United States and the EC berated Japan for its nontariff barriers; the United States and Japan feared that the fully integrated EC would close its doors to foreign competitors; and Japan and the EC both were apprehensive about protectionist rumblings in Washington. Yet, all three preached the gospel of free trade, for each knew that an all-out trade war would be devastating to all involved.

During the early 1990s, the principle of economic interdependence, however, clashed with economic nationalism. Interdependence had become a well-established fact of the industrial revolution by the end of the nineteenth century, and by the end of the twentieth it had become greater than ever before. Several examples illustrate the point. The U.S. Chrysler Corporation held 50 percent ownership in a joint venture with Mitsubishi Motors to produce cars in the United States and 15 percent interest in Mitsubishi of Japan, which produced cars in Japan for Japanese and foreign markets. General Motors, Ford, and several British corporations entered into similar joint ventures with Japanese car producers. Many "U.S.-made" or "British-made" cars had a large percentage of Japanese parts, produced in Japan. Honda, the Japanese car builder, shipped some of its cars manufactured in Ohio by U.S. workers to Japan.

Interdependence notwithstanding, international capitalism frequently resembled a zero-sum game, one of winners and losers. It sometimes produced nationalist backlashes, such as the protest in the United States against the rapid increase in foreign investment in the late 1980s, especially against the sharp rise in Japanese investments.[30] But foreign investment in the United States was hardly a new phenomenon. Foreign capital, mainly from Britain, had contributed substantially to the industrialization of the United States in the latter half of the nineteenth century. During World War I, it was the United States that became the world's leading foreign investor. But in the late 1980s, foreign financial assets in the United States rose sharply, leaving the country a net deficit in foreign investment transactions. Despite the increasing possibility of overdependency on foreign loans, the United States did benefit from the flow of foreign capital from abroad. On the one hand, it helped keep the U.S. government and banks solvent, and on the other, it was a benefit to both the investor, who obtained high returns on the investment, and to the United States, which obtained capital needed to revitalize its industries. Foreigners invested in the United States because they considered it a strong economy and viewed their investments in it as safe and profitable.

■ THE END OF THE COLD WAR AND THE THREE ECONOMIC SUPERPOWERS

The end of the Cold War and the collapse of Communism in Eastern Europe and in the Soviet Union had profound effects on each of the economic superpowers. Economic rather than military competition promised to become the order of the day. The Cold War had been the factor binding Japan and West Germany respectively to the United States for over four decades. To maintain its special security arrangements with Japan, Washington had been willing to tolerate Japanese trade policies detrimental to U.S. economic interests, and all the while Japan closely adhered to U.S. policy in foreign affairs. Similarly, throughout the Cold War, West Germany had hewed closely to U.S. foreign policy as it had remained dependent since the late 1940s on the United States for its security. A half century earlier—in the late 1940s—the unity of the Big Three (the United States, Britain, and the Soviet Union) had vanished after the demise of their common enemy, Nazi Germany, and in the 1990s the demise of the Soviet Union threatened to undo the bonds uniting its adversaries: the United States, West Germany, and Japan. The three economic superpowers now had to search for a new basis for cooperation and new international roles to play. No longer could the United States take Japan and Germany for granted; no longer could they be counted on to toe the U.S. line; and no longer could they count on U.S. favors.

Germany, after the fall of Communism in Eastern Europe and its own rapid reunification, became more assertive in its foreign policy. Even though Germany bore an enormous financial burden in absorbing East Germany, it responded most promptly to the needs of the Central and East European nations struggling for economic and political stability in their post-Communist period of strife. Meanwhile, Germany continued to speak with a strong voice within the EC, advancing the agenda of European unity. On the occasion of the Gulf War in 1991, Germany was constrained from sending combat forces by its constitution, but it answered the U.S. call for sharing the financial burden of the U.S.-led military operation with a hefty $6.8 billion.

It was the Gulf War as much as the collapse of the Soviet Union that provided an impetus for Japan's new assertiveness in world affairs. Unlike Germany, its constitution even barred it from having an armed force, but this did not shield Japan from rebuke in the United States, where many reacted with anger to its apparent unwillingness to provide support for a war fought to protect its own oil supply. After months of parliamentary debate, the Japanese government finally pledged $13 billion toward the war costs, and it offered a token contribution to the post–Gulf War peacekeeping effort by sending a fleet of minesweepers to clear the Gulf of mines after the war. The Gulf War touched off a heated parliamentary and public debate in Japan over the issue of permitting its Self Defense Forces (SDF) to participate in UN peacekeeping operations. Within a year the Japanese Diet passed legislation allowing its SDF to take part in such peacekeeping and disaster relief operations. This prepared the way for Japan to play a leading role in the UN operation in Cambodia aimed at ending the decade-long civil war there and establishing an elected government. The director of that extensive UN operation was a Japanese, the bulk of the financial support of the operation came from Japan, and SDF personnel participated in a noncombat role, marking the first time since World War II that Japanese military forces had been deployed abroad.

But Japan's contributions to the operations in the Gulf and in Cambodia were little noted in the United States, where in the wake of the Gulf War, a worsening economic recession served to increase resentment toward Japan. This occurred despite signs of progress in Washington-Tokyo negotiations on the ongoing trade disputes. Their "Structural Impediment Initiative" (SII) talks, begun in the late 1980s, produced an agreement to gradually eliminate or at least ameliorate certain features of the Japanese business system regarded by foreign firms as constituting nontariff trade barriers. The U.S. particularly set its sights on Japan's *keiretsu,* the informal but powerful corporate network that controlled the distribution system and excluded foreign suppliers, and won modest concessions.[31]

However, negative perceptions overshadowed the progress, and U.S. criticism of Japan triggered by the Gulf War persisted in the early 1990s, when polls showed Japan's popularity in the United States plummeting.[32] Contributing to the growing acrimony were media coverage of the fiftieth anniversary of Pearl Harbor in December 1991, President Bush's twice-postponed and inept visit to Japan in February 1992, and several tactless remarks by leading Japanese politicians critical of the U.S. work ethic. In the United States, a novel and motion picture by Michael Crichton, *Rising Sun,* painting a strongly unfavorable portrait of a Japan covertly seeking to destroy the U.S. economy, became a best seller. Moreover, a new "revisionist" view of U.S.-Japanese economic relations was finding favor in the United States. Writers such as Karel Van Wolferen, Lester Thurow, James Fallows, and Clyde Prestowitz argued that the Japanese political economy was fundamentally different from the Western market economies and operated in ways that gave it distinct advantages in international economic competition. Japanese international business activity, they argued, was driven by national considerations, as if in a war with the rest of the world. They maintained that Japan's behavior was the result of conditioning since the very beginning of its industrialization in the 1880s, when it began to see "foreign economic intrusion in colonialist terms." It was not enough for Japanese businesses merely to make a profit; they sought, instead, to control the market.[33] The revisionists argued that the SII talks were but a smoke screen behind which Japan's informal government-corporate structure continued resolutely to resist the opening of Japan to foreign goods and investment.[34] Predictably, the revisionists called for strong countermeasures against Japan. Such sentiments reinforced the impression that international trade was becoming national cutthroat competition.

Throughout the 1980s in Washington, the "white hats" (officials from the State and Defense departments and the National Security Council) had been dominant with their arguments that the Japanese-U.S. economic, and especially, military relationship should not be disturbed in the face of the continued Soviet threat. But the end of the Cold War brought about a reevaluation of this relationship and brought to the fore officials who called themselves the "realists" (mainly in the Commerce, Agriculture, and Labor departments), who argued for measures to prevent a repetition of Japan's undermining critical U.S. industries, such as the machine tool sector.[35] (The rise of China's trade surplus with the United States was a measure of how little the white hats and realists had accomplished in reducing the U.S. trade deficit with East Asia in general. Incredibly, in 1996, China surpassed Japan as the nation that had the greatest trade surplus with the United States. Another dispute over trade was in the making.)

The acrimony in U.S.-Japanese relations over trade, which was strident in the early 1990s, virtually vanished in the mid-1990s as Japan fell into an economic recession. The early signs of what was first termed a "downturn" were noted in late 1991, but by 1992 symptoms of a full-blown recession had become unmistakable, or as the Japanese put it, the economic bubble (the overheated economy) had burst. The annual growth rate of the GNP fell suddenly from over 5 percent to about 2 percent, where it remained for the next three years; industrial production and plant spending declined, as did savings and interest rates, and unemployment rose (up to 3 percent, which was unusually high in Japan).

As serious as the prolonged recession was for the Japanese, it had surprisingly little effect on Japan's trade imbalance with the United States. In fact, Japan's bilateral trade surplus crept further upward, mainly because of the recession-induced reduction in U.S. sales to Japan. The recession, however, resulted in a restructuring of the Japanese economy, which, in turn, had a stabilizing or maturing effect and resulted in a leveling of the growth rate at the new lower level. As one economist put it, "In terms of economic growth rates, investment, productivity and capital flows to the world, Japan is becoming a 'regular' country. It is certainly a country of stature but not quite the financial superpower proclaimed by those who were dazzled by the fireworks of the late 1980s."[36] The long-term effect of this transformation of the Japanese economy on Japan's economic relations with the other two economic superpowers is not to be pondered here, but initially the transformation—together with the concurrent upturn of the U.S. economy—seems to have caused trade friction to subside.

* * *

In Europe, the member states of the EC took unsteady steps in the 1990s toward the goal of economic integration. In December 1991, in line with the EC's White Paper of 1985, representatives of the twelve EC nations worked out a treaty in the Dutch city of Maastricht committing it to a "deepening" process: the creation, by 1999 at the latest, of an economic and monetary union with a single currency, and a common central bank. Border controls were to come down, and foreigners were to be cleared at whatever border (or airport) they arrived.[37] Maastricht also called for standard environmental, labor, and social laws such as the minimum wage, vacation days, and maternity leave. All citizens would be free to work and live anywhere they chose and even be able to vote in local elections. The treaty also contemplated the establishment of a European Political Union with a coordinated foreign and defense policy, but no timetable was set.

The Maastricht Treaty, before it could go into force, had to be ratified by the member nations. The governments of Denmark, Ireland, and France decided to submit the treaty to voters in the form of a referendum. In the remaining nations, ratification remained in the hands of legislatures. In June 1992, the voters of Denmark, the third-smallest member of the EC, rejected Maastricht by the narrow majority of just over 50 percent. The French voters ratified the treaty, but by a scant majority of the vote; the Irish ratified it by a comfortable margin.

The Danish vote underscored a general uneasiness throughout the EC with the Maastricht plan. As already mentioned, the deepening process had been the handiwork of the business and governing elites. In the public's mind, however, they had gone too far and too fast along the road to political, social, and economic integration by insisting to an unprecedented degree on the subservience of national sovereignty to a supranational community. The Danes were not necessarily against a unified Europe, but against granting bureaucrats in Brussels authority to decide on the maximum speed of a Danish moped.[38] There was also the danger of an EC dominated by a resurgent Germany, and on this, the Danes were not alone in their fear. The plans for 1992 had been drawn up before German unification, something no one had predicted, at a time when Germany was first among equals, but equal nevertheless, and not as dominant as it became during the early 1990s. Earlier, the French had used the metaphor of the French rider controlling the German horse. With unification, however, the horse threw its rider and galloped off toward the east in an attempt to reclaim its former sphere of influence.[39]

Many, particularly in Germany, wanted no part of a single monetary system, "esperanto money," as it was called derisively, preferring instead their national currency. Unexpectedly, sixty German professors of economics and finance produced a study critical of Maastricht by concluding that a common European currency was not needed and in fact could cause economic problems. The German finance minister, Theo Waigel, acknowledged that a common currency did carry with it the danger of regional unemployment.[40]

The deepening and broadening of the EC continued, but at a slower pace. In December 1992, Swiss voters rejected a proposal to join the giant European Economic Area, consisting of the twelve EC members and the seven members of the European Free Trade Association (EFTA), as a first step to full EC membership. Again, the fear of losing autonomy became a deciding factor in the vote. Events were moving too rapidly for the historically neutral and independent Swiss. These developments were clear signals to the EC directors that nationalist sentiments had to be taken into account before returning to the hard task of deepening and broadening the Community.

The Maastricht Treaty finally went into effect in November 1993 (after the voters of Denmark approved a modified version of the treaty in a second referendum in May 1993). At this juncture, the European Community took a new name that reflected its commitment to integration; henceforth, it would be known as the European Union, or EU.

Despite the ratification of the Maastricht Treaty, a measure of pessimism over the deepening process remained. How deep should integration become? Britain's leaders, in particular, were having second thoughts about further EU integration. Prime Minister John Major declared that his country would not join a single-currency union anytime soon. And the enlargement of the EU (to fifteen members in 1995) made the intergovernmental process more unwieldy. Since the implementation of the ambitious Maastricht Treaty, public expressions of "euro-pessimism" had become widespread. But for the politicians in Bonn, Paris, Madrid, and Rome, there was no alternative to further integration. The deepening of the EU would slow down, but it would continue nonetheless.

Even before the Maastricht Treaty's ratification, the EU had taken steps to widen its membership. The first to seek admission was Austria in July 1989—months before the Berlin Wall, the symbol of Europe's division, came down. Austria's 1955 treaty with its former occupying powers had prevented it from joining any sort of association with Germany—economic or military. The Western powers (the United States, Britain, and France) had no objection to Austria's membership in the EU. It was primarily the Soviet Union that did not want to see another German *Anschluss,* or annexation, of Austria, creating another *Grossdeutschland,* or Greater Germany. Earlier, however, Mikhail Gorbachev had spoken of a culturally and economically unified Europe, "our common home." He, too, raised no objections to Austrian membership in the EU.

Sweden asked for membership in July 1991, and Finland and Norway followed suit in March 1992. Finland, as with Austria, had a close trade and defense relationship with the Soviet Union, one based on the treaty of 1948. But Finland suffered from an unemployment rate of 20 percent—the highest since World War II—and it saw the EU as a potential life raft. Membership in the EU would also give Finland the window of opportunity to formally become a part of Western Europe. Again, Moscow did not object.

In May 1994, the EU parliament in Strasbourg, France, enthusiastically accepted the membership applications—subject to ratification by the voters of the applicant countries. In June 1994, Austrian voters said "yes" by a wide margin. In Scandinavia, however, the votes were much closer. There, the countryside remained wary of the EU. The farmers opposed the opening of their markets to imports from the south. Voters in Sweden and Finland ratified entry into the EU by narrow margins; in Norway, however, the voters (as they had done twenty years earlier) narrowly rejected EU membership, preferring to go it alone. The country was self-sufficient in agricultural products and energy (by virtue of North Sea oil), and its fishers did not relish the thought of fishing vessels from Portugal and Spain gaining entry into their coastal fishing waters.

When the three new members officially joined the EU on January 1, 1995, its population increased from 349 million to 370 million, and its GNP increased by 7 percent. The EU's economy was now 10 percent larger than that of the United States. And still more applicants were waiting in the wings: Malta (which applied in July 1990), Hungary and Poland (each of which applied in April 1994), the Czech Republic, Estonia, Latvia, Lithuania, and others.[41] And a trade pact between the EU and Russia envisioned the removal of nearly all trade barriers by 1997. The deepening and widening of the EU continued apace.

The impending realization of the EU single market raised far-reaching questions about the emergence of three competing trade blocs: the EU,

U.S. President Bill Clinton received by Jacques Delors, president of the EU's European Commission, Brussels, Jan. 1994. (*European Commission*)

North America, and Japan. To improve the U.S. global competitive position, Washington took the lead in negotiating with Canada and Mexico a North American Free Trade Agreement (NAFTA). Its aim was to eventually establish a free trade zone for the world's largest market, consisting of some 360 million consumers. In Europe, in October 1991, the EU and EFTA agreed to create the European Economic Area. Meanwhile, in Southeast Asia, ASEAN countries agreed to create the ASEAN Free Trade Association, and Malaysia pushed for expanding it into an Asia-wide free trade zone including Japan but excluding non-Asian countries. The Malaysian plan, however, was strongly opposed by Washington and met with a cool reaction in Tokyo, which did not wish to further antagonize its largest trade partner, the United States.

The key question was protectionism; how closed to outsiders would the trade blocs be? Member nations of the EU were themselves divided on this issue—Britain welcoming Japanese investments and others seeking to minimize the same. In 1991, French Premier Edith Cresson advocated strict reciprocity in dealing with Japan, restricting its imports and investments, but in 1992, the new premier, Pierre Beregevoy, reversed course by actively seeking Japanese investments.[42] For all the talk of "Fortress Europe," trade and investment data indicated that Asia's share in EU imports and investment actually climbed significantly through the late 1980s.[43] Joint ventures by Japanese, U.S., and EU companies were on the rise as Japan and the United States raced to get a foothold in the EU market before 1993.

In 1992, the protectionist debate focused on two particular types of imports: agricultural products and automobiles. The GATT Uruguay Round of negotiations aimed at eliminating trade barriers had stumbled on the rock of French resistance to opening European markets to U.S. grains and vegetable oils. Only after explicit threats of strong U.S. retaliation did the year-long talks produce a solution acceptable to Washington, but the French government, pressured by its farmers, still refused to accede to the terms accepted by EU negotiators. The Japanese sat nervously on the sidelines watching with great interest, because if the GATT agreement held, Japan might have to open its market to foreign rice. Japanese political leaders continued to assuage their rural constituents with the pledge of allowing not "a single grain of foreign rice" into the country, but in 1993 Tokyo finally agreed to a gradual and limited import of foreign rice.

The EU wavered on the issue of limiting imports of Japanese automobiles and on permitting joint ventures with Japanese car builders. However, in order to head off friction, Japan and the EU signed a joint declaration in July 1991 aimed at improving cooperation. In that spirit they negotiated in the following month an agreement to create a free automobile market by 1999 and to maintain in the interim an annual limit of

1.23 million cars through a voluntary export reduction plan. Japan was pleased to attain in this agreement a provision that cars produced in the EU by Japanese companies would be excluded from the regulation.

In the post–Cold War world, foreign economic policy, no longer a handmaiden to East-West competition, had become a matter of containing economic warfare between nations that had long been economic and political partners. The question had become one of whether the old rules for regulating economic competition, such as GATT, were still adequate or whether new rules had to be drawn up. The issues of foreign economic policy became more acute as the three economic superpowers proceeded with the creation of free trade zones. A debate was now joined between those who stressed economic competition and those who emphasized globalism and economic interdependence. The former accepted economic warfare as reality and offered little hope for containing the rivalry and contention among nations and economic blocs except through tough negotiation, insisting that international trade was a form of competition their nations could not afford to lose. The globalists contended that the economies of the three economic superpowers had become inextricably interdependent and that their economic health—and that of the rest of the world—depended in large measure on whether the three of them were able to remain constructively and cooperatively engaged in the maintenance of their interdependent partnership.

RECOMMENDED READINGS

Buckley, Roger. *US-Japan Alliance Diplomacy: 1945–1990.* London: Cambridge University Press, 1991.
  Provides a much-needed historical survey of the recently troubled U.S.-Japanese relationship.
Christopher, Robert. *The Japanese Mind.* New York: Fawcett, 1983.
  One of the most readable of the many books on Japan's "economic miracle."
Frost, Ellen L. *For Richer, For Poorer: The New U.S.-Japan Relationship.* New York: Council on Foreign Relations, 1987.
  An evenhanded analysis of the changing economic relationship and the perceptions the two nations have of each other.
Garten, Jeffrey E. *A Cold Peace: America, Japan, Germany, and the Struggle for Supremacy.* New York: Oxford University Press, 1992.
  Examines the potential for economic cooperation and conflict among the three nations as the world economy grew ever more interdependent.
Hofheinz, Roy, Jr., and Kent Calder. *The Eastasia Edge.* New York: Basic Books, 1982.
  A comprehensive account of the surging economic growth of the various East Asian countries in recent decades.
Johnson, Chalmers. *MITI and the Japanese Economic Miracle: The Growth of Industrial Policy, 1925–1975.* Stanford, Calif.: Stanford University Press, 1982.
  A superb analysis of the role of government in Japan's economic growth.

Kearns, David T., and David A. Nadler. *Prophets in the Dark: How Xerox Rein-vented Itself and Beat Back the Japanese.* New York: Harper Business, 1992.
By former Xerox CEO David T. Kearns and his business consultant, who took back market shares from the Japanese.

Kuttner, Robert. *The End of Laissez-Faire: National Purpose and Global Economy After the Cold War.* New York: Knopf, 1991.
Argues that since Japan and the EU have close government-business cooper-ation, strategic economic planning, and managed trade, the United States must also develop a national strategy.

McCraw, Thomas K., ed. *America Versus Japan.* Boston: Harvard Business School Press, 1986.
Topical essays offering a comparative analysis of economic policies and an excellent overview and conclusion by the editor.

Prestowitz, Clyde V. *Trading Places: How We Are Giving Our Future to Japan and How to Reclaim It.* 2d ed. New York: Basic Books, 1989.
A revisionist interpretation of the twin causes of Japan's rise to economic power: Japan's strategic, long-range program and the U.S. "flight from reality."

Reich, Robert B. *The Work of Nations: Preparing Ourselves for 21st Century Cap-italism.* New York: Knopf, 1991.
A provocative postulation of the seamless global economy in which the na-tional competition and the nationality of business no longer have importance.

Reischauer, Edwin O. *The Japanese Today: Change and Continuity.* Cambridge, Mass.: Harvard University Press, 1986.
A masterful survey of many facets of modern Japan by one of the foremost Japanists in the United States.

Thurow, Lester. *Head to Head: The Coming Economic Battle Among Japan, Eu-rope and America.* New York: William Morrow, 1992.
A revisionist treatment of the nature of the Japanese economy and the conse-quences of European economic integration.

Vogel, Ezra. *Japan as Number 1: Lessons for America.* Cambridge, Mass.: Harvard University Press, 1979.
Not only offers an explanation for Japan's economic success, but also suggests ways in which the United States can learn from the Japanese.

NOTES

1. The size of the GNP of the Soviet Union was not known for certain, but it was generally believed in the West that Japan's GNP was as large and probably larger by 1980. Its per capita GNP was certainly much larger.

2. From the 1950s, Japan steadily increased its defense spending, so that by the 1980s it was about 6 percent of the annual budget, or 1 percent of its GNP, compared to U.S. defense expenditure of approximately 6–8 percent of its GNP.

3. Robot Institute of America, *Japan 1989: An International Comparison* (Tokyo: Keizai Koho Center, 1988), p. 27.

4. This remarkably high rate of savings was accounted for in part by the gov-ernment taxation laws and the relatively low pensions for Japanese workers, but other causal factors included the huge lump-sum biannual bonuses Japanese work-ers received and traditional habits of saving for future security. Similar saving habits were found in other Confucian-influenced Asian countries such as South Korea and Taiwan.

5. Chalmers Johnson, *MITI and the Japanese Miracle: The Growth of Industrial Policy, 1925–1975* (Stanford: Stanford University Press, 1982), p. 15. Johnson points out that for a nation with a very low rate of investment, such as China, a large defense expenditure does retard economic growth, but for nations where investment rates were high, such as South Korea and Taiwan, "their very high defense expenditures have had little or no impact on their economic performance."

6. John E. Woodruff, "Veteran Envoy Mansfield to Retire from Tokyo Post," *Baltimore Sun,* November 15, 1988.

7. In accordance with the Tokyo Round of multilateral trade negotiations, Japan's average tariff on industrial products was, by April 1987, 3 percent, compared with 4.2 percent for the United States and 4.9 percent for the European Community. Japan Economic Institute, "Market Access Problems in Japan: Part II," *JEI Report,* February 12, 1982. Japan also reduced its import quotas from forty items in 1971 to twenty-seven in 1976, of which only five were industrial products.

8. *The United States and Japan in 1988: A Time of Transition* (Washington, D.C.: School of Advanced International Studies, The Johns Hopkins University, 1988). After bilateral negotiations had reached an impasse on agricultural imports, Tokyo offered to place all agricultural issues on the table at the GATT (General Agreement on Tariffs and Trade) conference so long as other nations would do so.

9. As early as January 1982, the Japanese government announced plans to take immediate steps to eliminate sixty-seven of ninety-nine nontariff barriers that had been registered by foreign governments, and nine others were still under consideration. Japanese Economic Institute, "Market-Access Problems in Japan: Part II," *JEI Report,* February 1982.

10. C. Fred Bergten and William Cline, "The United States–Japan Economic Problem," Institute for International Economics, Washington, D.C., October 29, 1985.

11. Japan Economic Institute, "Maekawa Commission Report Unveiled," *JEI Report,* April 11, 1986.

12. Joseph Kraft, "Bashing Japan," *Baltimore Sun,* April 11, 1986.

13. One reason for this was that while Japanese domestic spending increased in 1986 and 1987, the Japanese continued to prefer Japanese-made goods over U.S. imports. Also, as the dollar declined in value and the yen appreciated, all of Japan's imports—not only finished goods from the United States but also raw materials and components—became cheaper, and this lowered the cost of Japanese industrial production, keeping their products price competitive. Japan's industries also benefited by the fall in the price of oil in these years.

14. Ernest F. Hollings, "We're Winning the Cold War While Losing the Trade War," *Baltimore Sun,* December 17, 1989, p. 4N.

15. See Clyde V. Prestowitz, *Trading Places: How We Are Giving Our Future to Japan and How to Reclaim It,* 2d ed. (New York: Basic Books, 1989), Chapter 2. By August 1982, the Japanese captured 65 percent of the world market for microchips. In 1980, when the United States was still trying to get their 64K chip out of the lab, the Japanese had already produced prototypes of the 256K chip.

16. Richard W. Wright and Gunter A. Pauli, *The Second Wave: Japan's Global Assault on Financial Services* (New York: St. Martin's, 1987).

17. Prestowitz, *Trading Places,* pp. 98–113, expresses this view in a rather alarming way. Also see Ellen L. Frost, *For Richer, For Poorer: The New U.S.-Japan Relationship* (New York: Council on Foreign Relations, 1987).

18. The Japan–United States Trade Study Group, "Report of the Japan–United States Economic Relations Group," October 1981. This group consisted of the U.S. business community in Japan, the U.S. embassy, and several Japanese economic and business organizations.

19. Mike Mansfield, "The U.S. and Japan: Sharing our Destinies," *Foreign Affairs*, Spring 1989, p. 5; Takashi Oka, "Japan's Next Big Change," *World Monitor*, December 1989, pp. 30–31.

20. The twelve members of the EU and their years of admission, listed in order of size of GNP in the early 1990s: West Germany (1958), France (1958), Italy (1958), Great Britain (1973), Spain (1986), Netherlands (1958), Belgium (1958), Denmark (1973), Greece (1981), Portugal (1986), Ireland (1973), and Luxembourg (1958).

21. A citizen of an EU country on a journey to all member nations might lose 47 percent of his money changing it into local currencies. Stanley Hoffmann, "The European Community and 1992," *Foreign Affairs*, Fall 1989, p. 28. In December 1996, the EU introduced a common currency—the "euro"—in a trial test run to put an end to the fourteen different currencies in use. The new bank notes featured windows, doors, and bridges symbolizing the mission of the EU.

22. Andrew Moravcsik, "Negotiating the Single Act: National Interests and Conventional Statecraft in the European Community," Cambridge, Mass., Harvard University, Center for European Studies, Working Paper Series #21, n.d. [1989], pp. 14–15.

23. Hoffmann, "The European Community and 1992," pp. 35–37.

24. The EU commission on dumping received about 100 complaints yearly, investigated about forty, and convicted about fifteen by imposing duties. "A Survey of Europe's Internal Market," *The Economist*, July 8, 1989, pp. 36–37.

25. Steven Greenhouse, "Europe's Agonizing over Japan," *New York Times*, April 30, 1989.

26. The figures are those issued in December 1989 by the Organization for Economic Cooperation and Development (OEUD); Hobert Rowen, "Bonn Next in Line as Power Center," *Washington Post*, January 7, 1990, pp. H1, H8.

27. Daniel S. Greenberg, "Two Nations Striving to Be Best," *Baltimore Sun*, December 11, 1988. President Bush's proposed budget for 1990 called for $4.5 billion for continued work on SDI and $5.5 billion for the B-2 Stealth bomber. The price tag for each airplane was $500 million, and the estimated cost of the 132 airplanes the U.S. Air Force had originally requested (before the inevitable cost overruns) would have been $60 billion.

28. See Johnson, *MITI*, pp. 18–23. Johnson explained that in states that were late to industrialize, such as Japan, the state itself led the industrialization drive. He contrasts the Japanese pattern, where the role of government in the economy remained a developmental function, with that in the United States where the government's intervention in the economy was generally limited to a regulatory function. The U.S. government, for example, generally did not concern itself with what industries ought to exist and which were no longer necessary.

29. "Der Krieg findet längst statt" ("The War Has Begun Long Ago"), *Der Spiegel*, December 6, 13, 20, 1989.

30. Much of the alarm was focused on Japan, but it was a distant second to Britain as the largest investors in the United States. Japan had been rising swiftly, however, and in 1989 it overtook the Netherlands as the second largest.

31. Edwin Reischauer Center for East Asian Studies, *The United States and Japan in 1992: A Quest for New Roles* (Washington, D.C.: Johns Hopkins University, 1992), pp. 51–58.

32. Ibid., pp. 8–13. A *Washington Post–ABC News* poll on February 14, 1992, reported that U.S. respondents who felt that anti-Japanese feelings were increasing rose from 33 percent in November 1991 to 65 percent in February 1992.

33. The revisionists pointed to the Japanese rejection of the purchase of the U.S.-built FSX fighter plane despite the fact that, from the standpoint of defense

and economics, the purchase would have been a sound decision. The Japanese government, instead, insisted on a costly cooperative venture with the United States for the purpose of obtaining access to sensitive U.S. technology. All this was part and parcel of a Japanese strategy to target foreign competitors, in this case the U.S. aircraft industry. See Prestowitz, *Trading Places,* pp. 5–58, 253, 318, 382–390.

34. Karel Van Wolferen, "The Japanese Problem Revisited," *Foreign Affairs,* Summer 1990, pp. 44–46.

35. Prestowitz, *Trading Places,* pp. 382–390.

36. Douglas Ostrom, "Japan's Economy: A Transformation?" *Japan Economic Report,* no. 11A, March 20, 1992, p. 10. Also see Ostrom, "Lessons from Japan's Recession," *JEI Report,* no. 43A, November 11, 1994, p. 3.

37. In March 1995, seven states (Belgium, France, Germany, Luxembourg, the Netherlands, Portugal, and Spain) abolished immigration controls on travel among their territories.

38. *Berliner Zeitung,* June 5, 1992, in "Pressestimmen zum dänischen EG-Referendum," *Deutschland Nachrichten,* June 5, 1992, p. 3.

39. Coner Cruise O'Brien, "Pursuing a Chimera: Nationalism at Odds with the Idea of a Federal Europe," *Times Literary Supplement,* March 13, 1992, pp. 3–4.

40. "Wirtschaftsprofessoren kritisieren Maastricht," *Deutschland Nachrichten,* June 12, 1992, p. 5.

41. Turkey's application of April 1987 remained on hold, in part because the EU demanded that prospective members must have democratic governments.

42. Shada Islam, "Turning on the Charm: France Warms to Japanese Companies," *Far Eastern Economic Review,* October 8, 1992, p. 72.

43. "If You Can't Beat 'Em: Europe Tries Softer Approach to Asian Business," *Far Eastern Economic Review,* October 8, 1992, pp. 70–72. Japan's exports to the EU rose 23 percent to $59.2 billion in 1989–1991, and ASEAN exports rose 31 percent to $26.7 billion in the same period.

20

The Soviet Empire:
A Beleaguered Colossus

A cursory glance at the Soviet Union's position in the world in the early 1980s revealed a powerful presence in Europe and Asia. This presence was one of particular concern for the policy makers in Washington who had to confront the aspirations of the world's other superpower. Moscow's position in the arms race made it a most dangerous foe. At the same time, however, the Soviet Union was an empire with the traditional problems of an empire. It was racked by centrifugal forces threatening to cause its disintegration.

The Soviet Union's nationalities were still well under Moscow's heel. The same sort of acquiescence could not be found, however, in Moscow's empire beyond its borders. Eastern Europe showed no signs of coming to terms with its subordinate status. Everywhere, with the exception of Bulgaria, the East European governments sought to move toward a position somewhere in the middle between the West and the Soviet Union. They were attempting a most precarious balancing act and the motion had to be inch by inch, as was the case in the Hungary of János Kádár. A stampede, as advocated by some of the hotheads of Poland's Solidarity, was not something the Kremlin was likely to look upon with an indifferent eye. In short, the East European governments sought to find their own niche within the Soviet empire.

Along its other borders, the Soviet Union again had its hands full. A hostile China tied down approximately one-third of the Soviet Army along the Soviet-Chinese border, a costly political and financial problem the new Soviet leader Mikhail Gorbachev understood only too well. Elsewhere, other neighbors of the Soviet Union, Turkey and Norway, remained loyal members of NATO, an alliance that showed remarkable resilience as long as the Soviet threat remained plausible. The Ayatollah Khomeini's Islamic government in Iran did not hide its distaste for the secular, atheist government in Moscow. And Afghanistan, governed by a socialist regime since the early 1970s, remained torn asunder by a bloody civil war that threatened to topple the Kremlin's clients in Kabul.

In the mid-1980s, Moscow remained proud and defiant, strong and aggressive. But it was also beleaguered by a host of problems, from restless clients along its borders, to hostile neighbors; from an economy in need of modernization, to the political and nuclear fallout from the disaster at Chernobyl. Soviet strengths and weakness were but two sides of the same coin.

■ POLAND AND SOLIDARITY

The social unrest of 1956 in Poland had brought to power Wladyslaw Gomulka, who continued with the reforms the death of Stalin had put into motion. After the end of World War II, Gomulka had been the champion of Poland's right to travel along its own road to socialism, but his position, a deviation from that spelled out by Moscow, had earned him a lengthy prison term. After Stalin's death in 1953, it was inevitable that de-Stalinization would return Gomulka to power. When the Soviets accepted Poland's own "October Revolution" of 1956, Gomulka and his party proceeded to sort out the nation's problems. The collectivization of arable land was halted and then reversed when the party returned some of the land to its previous owners; the intellectuals continued their debates on Poland's past and future; the state worked out a *modus vivendi* with the Roman Catholic Church; and the lot of the workers began to improve. Within the context of Polish socialism, the reforms were significant, especially when compared to developments in neighboring socialist states. In this fashion, Gomulka became a politician with considerable public support.

Reform movements, however, are fed by rising expectations, and they invariably produce demands for additional reforms. But Gomulka and his party had no intention of taking the reforms to what some considered their logical conclusion, namely the abolition of the Communist Party. Whatever the reforms, the changes had to be within the limits of Polish socialism. The inevitable then took place: the party sought to halt the reformist impulse. As a result, after more than a dozen years in office, the once popular Gomulka had overstayed his welcome. As the years passed, he became more and more rigid. Critics found it increasingly difficult to express their ideas, and social experimentation eventually came to a halt. Also, his austere economic program, which favored the interests of the state over that of the workers, caused considerable discontent.

In December 1970, just before the Christmas holidays in this most Catholic of nations, Gomulka announced a steep increase in the price of food. Riots broke out in the "Lenin" shipyard in Gdansk and elsewhere. Security forces used strong-arm methods and restored order after they had killed many workers. It was clear to the Communist Party that Gomulka had become a liability; a change at the top was needed. The party then turned to Edward Gierek, who came from the ranks of the working class. Gierek, a former miner, caved in to the demands of the radicalized workers, particularly the miners of Silesia, and proceeded to grant them their economic demands.

Gierek's tenure coincided with Willy Brandt's *Ostpolitik*, which was marked by détente, the easing of tensions between East and West. With détente came a considerable increase in East-West trade underwritten by Western bankers. To make possible the purchase of Western goods, Western banks (which held increasingly larger amounts of "petrodollars," money deposited by the oil-rich nations) began to lend large sums of money to socialist countries. Gierek, unlike the frugal Gomulka, borrowed heavily from Western banks. In 1973, Poland owed $2.5 billion to the West; by 1982, the debt had risen to $27 billion. With the influx of Western capital and goods (machinery, grain, consumer items, and raw materials) the standard of living rose considerably during the 1970s. But the day of financial reckoning had to come.

That day came in July 1980, when the Gierek government, in order to help pay off Poland's large foreign debt, announced an increase in food prices. As in the past, such announcements produced political repercussions. This measure led directly to an unexpected and dramatic event—the birth of Solidarity.

The Communist Party of Poland in the postwar era was a Russian creation and it remained answerable to Moscow. For this reason, it lacked wide popular support. Economic mismanagement, police brutality, and corruption also diminished its moral authority. Resentment toward the party ran deep and it resurfaced periodically. Work stoppages led to negotiations between the government and workers. The traditional tactic by the government was to buy off individual groups of workers with economic concessions.

But this time the workers refused to take the bait. Instead, workers at the "Lenin" shipyard in Gdansk demanded a concession from the government that was nothing short of revolutionary. They demanded that a settlement would have to be with the country's workers as a whole, rather than merely with the "Lenin" shipyard workers where most of the radical activity had taken place. This tactical position gave rise to Solidarity, a union ultimately representing 10 million people in a country of 35 million. Lech Walesa, the head of Solidarity, became one of Poland's most powerful men.

Solidarity, with the support of the vast majority of the population as well as the church, was able to wring concession after concession from the government. The attention of the world was riveted on Poland, where an extraordinary spectacle was unfolding in the sixteen months following the birth of Solidarity. There, the impossible was taking place. According to Marxist ideology, Polish workers were striking against themselves, for, in theory at least, they were the owners of "the means of production," the factories. Strikes by workers against their places of employment were, therefore, both illogical and illegal. Yet, this right to strike was the first and most important concession Solidarity wrenched from the state. And with it, Solidarity established its independence from the state and thus became the only union in Eastern Europe not controlled by the state.

Solidarity established itself as a political power to be reckoned with. Many of its thirty-eight semiautonomous chapters frequently used the right to strike, generally to correct a condition peculiar to a particular plant. The economic fate of the nation appeared to be in the hands of Solidarity. As its power grew, its leadership moved into larger headquarters it had managed to obtain from the government. It proceeded to put out a daily, uncensored newspaper, set up book printing facilities, and run a telex operation. It then wrested from the state the materials necessary to establish monuments in honor of workers the state had shot to death in the riots of 1956 and 1970. It gained unrestricted access to radio air waves and limited access to television. Finally, Solidarity's pressures on the government produced free local parliamentary elections with a secret ballot. In sum, Solidarity could boast of extraordinary achievements, and many of its members began to believe that the Communist state had become irrelevant.

Observers in both the West and Eastern Europe had felt that these sweeping concessions were impossible in an East European Communist society. But the Polish Communist Party was paralyzed in the face of Solidarity's demands. It was also deeply split. Some members openly supported Solidarity; others even quit the party to join Solidarity. Clearly, Solidarity and not the party expressed the people's will.

The party, as in the past, began to look for a savior, a Napoleon Bonaparte capable of bringing the revolution under control. It turned to a member who possessed considerable moral authority, Gen. Wojciech Jaruzelski. Jaruzelski had risen rapidly in the ranks of the Polish army and in 1968 had become the minister of defense. In 1970, the government had placed him under house arrest for refusing to use force to suppress strikers. During disturbances in 1976, he had acted similarly and it was at that time that he made his famous remark: "Polish troops will not fire on Polish workers."[1] Here was a man who could perhaps gain the confidence of the nation. In rapid succession, the party promoted him to prime minister in 1980 and then to first secretary of the party in October 1981. He now held what in the context of European politics were the three most important posts: head of the government, defense minister, and head of the party.

Jaruzelski well understood the precariousness of his position. He held the three paramount positions in the nation and yet he was unable to govern effectively. Lech Walesa, the head of Solidarity, who held no government position, clearly shared power with Jaruzelski. Another base of power, the Catholic Church, supported Solidarity. On November 4, 1981,

Jaruzelski met with Walesa and Archbishop Joseph Glemp, primate of Poland, to discuss the creation of a "National Front." The successful creation of such a coalition could institutionalize the sharing of power among the party, church, and Solidarity. But it was not to be. The party and Solidarity were unable to define what constituted a "National Front."

Powerful forces in both the party and Solidarity were lining up against any attempts to share power. The hard-liners in the party had always resented the concessions granted to Solidarity and they sought to rescind them. Within Solidarity, the radicals felt there could be no coexistence with the party. One of them, Jacek Kuron, who had long been in bitter combat with the party, put it succinctly: "The essential thing is to understand that the regime has received a final blow: either it must die, or it must destroy Solidarity. There is no other solution."[2] There could be no compromises.

On Saturday, December 12, 1981, Solidarity met amid warnings by the government that "law enforcement agencies will oppose with determination any actions aimed against people's power [the Communist Party], in the name of peace for citizens and public order."[3] TASS, the Soviet news agency, charged Solidarity with an attempt to seize political power. The stage was set for a showdown. At the meeting the moderates were overridden by the radicals. Solidarity's leadership then called for a national

Polish Solidarity leader Lech Walesa, surrounded by supporters, Warsaw, Poland, Nov. 11, 1980. (*AP/Wide World Photos*)

Gen. Wojciech Jaruzelski, prime minister, defense minister, and first secretary of the Polish Communist Party, addressing the UN General Assembly, Sept. 27, 1985. (*AP/Wide World Photos*)

referendum on the future of the Communist Party and at the same time it declared its intention to reexamine Poland's military relationship with the Soviet Union (in other words whether to leave or stay in the Warsaw Pact). Solidarity appeared to be getting ready to test the Brezhnev Doctrine of 1968 by which the Soviet Union reserved the right of intervention to maintain its East European satellite empire.

Solidarity officials felt that the following week would be decisive. Parliament was scheduled to convene on Tuesday with the expectation that it would grant the government sweeping emergency powers. Solidarity's response to an emergency decree was to be a national strike. Thursday promised to bring about another confrontation when Solidarity expected to draw a quarter of a million people to a demonstration in Warsaw.

Over the previous sixteen months, Poland had been drifting inexorably toward this position. The threat of Soviet military intervention always hung in the air. The final triumph of Solidarity or its suppression by the Soviet Army, with extraordinary consequences for the Warsaw Pact, appeared to be the two most plausible alternatives.

In the West, speculation ran high that the Soviet Union would interfere. But Brezhnev and his party were undecided on what course to take. They knew that the cost of intervention would be high, because it promised a war between the two most important members of the Warsaw Pact. (The Soviet Union had trained and equipped the large Polish armed forces to fight NATO invaders, not the Soviet Army.)

In the middle of November 1980, the Soviet Politburo—led by an apparently reluctant Brezhnev—took steps to authorize the mobilization of Soviet Army troops along the Polish border. The mobilization proved to be a disaster. Reservists could not be found, others failed to answer the call, and so many deserted and went home that the authorities gave up trying to punish them. Lack of coordination and confusion added to the difficulties. All of this gave Brezhnev a chance to turn on the interventionists in the Soviet Army, and the result was a shake-up in the high echelon of the armed forces.[4] For the time being, at least, armed intervention was out of the question.

Until mid-December 1981, Solidarity continued with its challenge to what appeared to be an impotent and vacillating government that seemed to stand hopelessly against the nation and the embodiment of the nation's will. Only the Soviet Army, it seemed, could save the government of Poland. But, instead, the unexpected happened. On Sunday, December 13, the day after the Solidarity leadership had questioned the future of both the Communist Party and the Warsaw Pact in Poland, the government arrested the union's leadership and declared martial law—effectively outlawing Solidarity and reestablishing the primacy of the Communist Party.

The commonly held view in the West was that the Soviet Union bore direct responsibility for Jaruzelski's actions. But there was no clear proof of this. To be sure, he did precisely what the Soviet Union had demanded all along: he restored order. But as the head of the Polish government, the party, and the army, he had little choice. He was in no position to yield to Solidarity demands that his government and his party transfer political power to the union, for that would have meant political suicide. He also knew that either he would restore order or the Soviet Army would do it for him. Jaruzelski certainly did not relish the latter prospect.

Martial law in Poland, generally attributed in the West to the Kremlin, contributed greatly to the intensification of the Cold War, particularly as it came on the heels of the Soviet invasion of Afghanistan. But the Western charge that the Communist leaders of Eastern Europe were but puppets whose strings were pulled by their masters in the Kremlin ignored the realities of East European politics. Between 1945 and 1981, Eastern Europe witnessed four major crises: the Tito-Stalin split of 1948, the events of 1956 in Poland and Hungary, the reforms in Czechoslovakia in 1968, and the rise of Solidarity in 1980–1981. In each of the first three crises, the Soviet leaders had the same complaint: Why did Tito, Gomulka, and Dubček keep the "fraternal" Communist Party of the Soviet Union in the dark? The precedents established in the first three instances did not necessarily mean that Jaruzelski acted independently of Moscow when he declared martial law in December 1981. But they did raise the question whether in fact Jaruzelski was "a Russian general in a Polish uniform," a charge Jaruzelski bitterly rejected.[5]

The extraordinary gains of the previous sixteen months were now largely erased. Jaruzelski's security forces acted with remarkable efficiency in restoring order, which astonished most observers, including Solidarity itself.[6] But Jaruzelski and his ruling party did not manage to win the hearts and minds of the nation. This chapter of Polish history was far from closed.

■ HUNGARY IN FLUX

At the same time that Solidarity in Poland conducted its noisy and determined challenge to the Communist Party, events in Hungary, though quieter, proved to be no less important to the transformation of Eastern Europe.

In 1956, János Kádár had come to power after the Soviet Army crushed the Hungarian rebellion. For the next dozen years, Hungary experienced little change. The Communist Party (officially the Socialist Workers' Party) did not experience the sporadic challenges to its authority that its counterpart in Poland had. By the late 1960s, however, Kádár and his party began a cautious program of domestic innovation that, by East European standards, was just short of revolutionary. Throughout, however, Kádár made clear his unswerving allegiance to the foreign policy of the

Soviet Union. While gradually moving away from the Soviet model at home, Kádár remained at pains to assure the Soviets that his actions did not threaten the breakup of their East European empire.

Kádár's innovations were made possible by the détente of the late 1960s, which was accompanied by an increase in trade between East and West. The relaxation of tensions also made possible experiments in small-scale capitalism. The result was a mixed economy in which the socialist sector predominated, but one in which small private businesses were permitted. Western journalists referred to this phenomenon as "goulash Communism." Hungarians called it "Communism with a capitalist facelift."[7]

Not only did the state permit the existence of small private enterprises—such as small shops, restaurants, bars, food stands, artisan shops, garages—but it in fact encouraged Hungarians to become entrepreneurs by its selling off its small and unprofitable businesses. Yet, this by no means suggested a return to private enterprise as the dominant mode of economic behavior. The bulk of the economic sector—heavy industry, transportation, banking—remained in the hands of the state. Also, private businesses could not employ more than three persons. The Hungarian Communist Party was far from handing over the economy of the nation to what Marxists liked to call the "international bourgeoisie."

From a rigid Marxist point of view, the Hungarian innovations were acts of heresy. But at no time did Karl Marx waste his time discussing the malfeasance of the man who owned a small barbershop for private gain or the peasant woman selling flowers and fruit at a street corner. When Marx wrote his *Capital* he denounced what the poet William Blake called the "dark Satanic mills" of the early industrial revolution. Kádár and his party had no intention of putting the large factories into private hands.

During the heyday of Solidarity in Poland, local elections gave the voters choices among the candidates, only to have martial law end this experiment in electoral politics. Hungary saw a similar reform but with little fanfare, despite the revolutionary nature of the innovation. On June 8, 1985, Hungarian voters cast their ballots for representatives to parliament and local councils, in which at least two candidates ran for nearly all seats. This was the first election under a 1983 law that demanded a choice for the voters. The law, proposed by János Kádár, was unique in a Soviet-bloc country. It provided that each of 352 parliamentary seats must have at least two candidates, which did not include, however, the 35 seats held by "nationalist personalities," that is, ranking party and government leaders—such as Kádár himself. Kádár, the champion of parliamentary democracy, was not willing to go so far as to put up his own safe seat for reelection.

Hungary's Patriotic Popular Front, the Communist organization in charge of conducting the elections, nominated two candidates for each parliamentary seat in order to stay within the guidelines of the law, but in seventy-one districts people nominated third, and at times fourth, candidates and in several cases replaced a Front candidate with one of their own choosing. The election results showed that 25 of the independent nominees won seats in the 387-member parliament. The Communist Party, however, sought to make sure there would be no clashes between the independent legislators and the Communists. All candidates had to sign a pledge promising to abide by the rules of a socialist society. In short, the contest remained one essentially between two socialist candidates. But there was a crack in the door and someone was certain to try and push through it.

■ THE SOVIET UNION

The reforms in Poland and Hungary began during the reign of Leonid Brezhnev, who had come to power in 1964 after Nikita Khrushchev's ouster. Innovations in the economic sector Khrushchev had introduced were quickly shelved under the conservative Brezhnev. In the mid-1970s, the Soviet Union's economy and intellectual life had entered a period of stagnation that only a change in leadership could reverse. The Soviet Union's ministries ceased publishing statistics in order not to reveal the fact that the country was falling further behind the Western nations in productivity, technology, health care, and the standard of living. Brezhnev and the entrenched bureaucrats proved incapable of moving off dead center. Finally, after a long illness, Brezhnev died in November 1982. His successors, Yuri Andropov, who turned out to be mortally ill from cancer, and Konstantin Chernenko, who suffered from emphysema, merely served time until the Communist Party of the Soviet Union elected Mikhail Gorbachev in March 1985. Gorbachev immediately took a number of highly publicized steps to transform the Soviet Union.

Gorbachev's approach initially consisted of Western industrial productivity grafted onto the traditional Soviet system to give Soviet society much greater room to maneuver. Still, he advocated a new openness, *glasnost,* whereby Soviet citizens and officials alike would be free to discuss not only the strengths but also the weaknesses of their society. This approach was reflected in *Pravda,* the newspaper of the Communist Party, which began to cover disasters such as the nuclear accident at Chernobyl, floods, avalanches, and collisions between ships in the Black Sea. Shortly, the scope of discussion included official corruption, cover-ups, sloppy workmanship in factories, police abuse, Stalin's impact on society, and so on. A number of manuscripts, long refused by publishers in the employ of the state, were printed. Motion pictures never before shown to the public at large played to sell-out crowds. In January 1987, when a plenary session of the Central Committee refused to accept officially the principle of two candidates for Communist Party offices, Gorbachev took a highly publicized trip throughout the nation to drum up support at the local level. The Gorbachev revolution was on its way.

■ THE AFGHAN CRISIS

In December 1979, the Soviet Union sent 80,000 troops into Afghanistan. It was an act that stunned the world. For the first time since the end of World War II, the Soviet Union had sent troops into a territory that lay beyond its sphere of influence. The Soviet Union had in the past ordered its army into other nations—into Hungary in 1956 and Czechoslovakia in 1968—but the West, its rhetoric to the contrary, had tacitly recognized these nations to be within the Soviet socialist bloc. But Afghanistan was another matter.

Since 1973, the political orientation in Afghanistan had been toward the left, yet it was generally considered a neutral nation, a part of the Third World outside the spheres of any of the great powers. Until 1973, both the United States and the Soviet Union had jockeyed for influence in Afghanistan without anyone emerging a clear-cut winner. Moreover, Afghanistan ranked far down the scale among the brass rings up for grabs by the superpowers. It was among the poorest nations on earth, with an annual per capita GNP in 1979 of $170.[8]

☐ The U.S. Reaction

The Soviet invasion came at an unfavorable time for the United States. For one, the defeat in Vietnam did not sit well with many; it was, after all, the country's first defeat in war. Second, 1979 had seen the second oil shortage of the decade. Third, Soviet activities in Africa had already raised suspicion in Washington about Moscow's intentions. Finally, the traumatic hostage crisis had just begun in Iran. The takeover of the U.S. embassy in Tehran pointed to the limitations of U.S. power. With one setback following another, the result was frustration and belligerence.

The U.S. response to the Soviet invasion of Afghanistan was swift, but ineffective. President Carter had to do something; if only for political reasons at home, he would have to go through the motions of responding to this example of Soviet ambition. This is not to say that the expanded Soviet military presence did not pose a potential threat to U.S. strategic interests to the south of Afghanistan, particularly in the Persian Gulf, where the U.S. fleet sought to protect the shipping lanes of oil tankers. But on the eve of the 1980 presidential election, Carter's problem was primarily of a domestic, political nature. He could not afford to stand idly by and leave himself open to the charge of having done nothing to avert the "loss of

Afghanistan." A country of extraordinary poverty and industrial back-wardness, a country of little significance in the international balance of power, Afghanistan suddenly took on an importance unmatched in its modern history.

There was scarcely a debate in the United States of the implications and the motivation of the Soviet action. The CIA quickly explained that the Soviet Union faced an "extremely painful" decline in oil supplies and the move into Afghanistan was intended to move the Soviet Army closer to the lucrative oil fields of the Gulf. The Soviet motive seemed obvious. "Moscow is already making the point," said CIA Director Stansfield Turner, "that Middle Eastern oil is not the exclusive preserve of the West."[9] The CIA later retracted its statement when it declared that the Soviet Union was not likely to suffer from oil shortages in the near future. In September 1981, the CIA announced that the Soviet Union's energy prospects looked "highly favorable" for the rest of the century. Moreover, the CIA more than doubled its estimate of the Soviet Union's proven oil reserves, from 35 billion barrels to 80–85 billion.[10]

A Soviet thrust through Afghanistan directed at the oil refineries of the Gulf made little sense from a strategic point of view. Why take a 500-mile detour through rugged country with the prospect of getting bogged down and at the same time tip off your enemy? (In the late 1940s, when the strategic planners for the Joint Chiefs of Staff contemplated a Soviet attack on the oil-refining installations of the Persian Gulf, they envisioned a quick and decisive act, a Soviet parachute drop on Abadan, the site of the world's largest oil refinery.)

But the CIA's inflammatory statements had done their damage. There was little rational discussion of Soviet motives behind the invasion. The Soviet Union seemed to have chosen the right time to make its move, while the United States was preoccupied in Iran. It appeared to be a clear example of Communist aggression and expansion and unless something were done the pattern would continue elsewhere. Once again, the time had come to draw the line and contain the Soviet Union.

Carter's options were limited. A direct military challenge to the USSR was out of the question since it promised grave repercussions. Carter had to find, therefore, different ways by which to express U.S. displeasure with the Soviets. He wound up taking several steps. He refused to permit U.S. athletes to participate in the Soviet showcase, the 1980 summer Olympic Games in Moscow, unless the Soviets withdrew from Afghanistan. The Soviets were stung by Carter's boycott, for they had envisioned the Olympic Games as another stepping-stone toward legitimacy and final acceptance as one of the world's two great powers. But it was an ultimatum the Soviets ignored. They went on to hold the Olympic Games without U.S. participation, and the Soviet Army remained in Kabul. Carter also halted U.S. grain sales to the Soviet Union. But the glut on the world market in agricultural commodities meant that the Soviets shifted their orders to more reliable sources. Lastly, Carter began to look around for clients willing to help him contain the Soviet Union in Asia. Communist China and the United States were, as a result, drawn a bit closer, and both began in secret to provide weapons for Afghans fighting the Soviets. The United States also provided military assistance to Pakistan, a country situated along Afghanistan's eastern borders. All told, these measures had little effect on the Soviets, who continued to beef up their forces, which soon numbered over 100,000.

The Soviet invasion of Afghanistan finished off the détente of the 1970s. Neither Brezhnev nor his Politburo ever really understood the West's definition of détente, which linked improved relations with Soviet behavior. From the West's point of view, the Soviets could not expect a thaw in the Cold War and at the same time intervene in the internal affairs of another nation. In contrast, Soviet spokesmen always insisted that détente would not prevent the Kremlin from playing the role of a great power in international affairs. Détente and throwing one's weight around in the Third World, the Kremlin argued, were not antithetical.

☐ Soviet Objectives in Afghanistan

The chief reason the Soviet Union intervened in the internal affairs of Afghanistan was to bring order to a chaotic political situation in a neighboring socialist country. The Politburo, the guardian of Soviet interests and prestige, was unwilling to accept the defeat of a client. In the simple arithmetic of the Cold War, a setback for the forces of socialism would mean a victory for capitalism. (The reverse argument, after all, was well understood and often used in the West.) Such an argument is generally motivated by a sense of the loss of prestige and image rather than rational analyses of the needs of national security. It rests largely on what conclusions others might draw from one's own misfortune.

Political instability had long been the order of the day in Afghanistan; coups and countercoups have often followed in rapid succession. A case in point was the political instability of the 1970s. In 1973, the leftist Prince Mohammed Daoud, with the help of the military, overthrew in a bloodless coup his cousin, King Zahir Shah. In 1978, Daoud himself was ousted and killed in a second coup by the socialist People's Democratic Party under the leadership of Nur Mohammed Taraki, who established closer ties with the Soviet Union. Taraki in turn was ousted and murdered in a third leftist coup carried out by Hafizullah Amin, who was in power in Kabul at the time of the Soviet invasion. All this bloodletting took place in the Marxist party, the People's Democratic Party.

It is here that one can find another clue to the Soviet Union's decision to invade Afghanistan. Taraki and Amin had a falling out, with Taraki looking to Moscow for support and Amin apparently looking to Washington.

Amin met a number of times with the U.S. ambassador, Adolph Dubs. What exactly transpired between these two men is not clear, but the Soviets feared the worst. To them, Amin was at the threshold of following in the footsteps of Anwar Sadat, the Egyptian head of state, who had ousted in 1972 the 20,000 Soviet advisers in Egypt and then had invited in U.S. military personnel. It is possible that more than anything else the fear of an Afghan diplomatic revolution—from Moscow to Washington—prompted the Soviet invasion.[11] When, seven years later, Gorbachev sought an exit from Afghanistan, he insisted on a guarantee that no hostile power become entrenched along the Soviet Union's southern flank.

The publication of Soviet documents and the memoirs of KGB Colonel Alexander Morozov, the deputy of intelligence operations in Kabul during 1975–1979, put into focus Moscow's reasons for intervention. In March 1979, when Taraki initially asked for Soviet intervention to fight the Afghan rebels, Brezhnev and Kosygin were resolutely opposed to such a step. Brezhnev told Taraki: "I will tell you frankly: We must not do this. It would only play into the hands of enemies—both yours and ours." But after Taraki's murder at the hands of Amin, the Soviet leadership, against its own better judgment, sent its troops into Afghanistan in an attempt to restore order.[12]

After the Soviet invasion, opposition to the central government increased. Such opposition had long been a central feature of Afghan politics. Local rulers in outlying regions had always jealously guarded their authority and freedom of action. But this time they had other grievances. They resented the attempts at social and economic transformation of their tradition-bound society, untouched even by colonial rule. Resentment of reform, especially when carried out with force and in direct opposition to popular will, ran deep. Amin sought to introduce education (and even coeducation) for girls and the elimination of the veil and bridal dowries. The confiscation of land added fuel to the fire.

In the name of freedom, Islam, and anti-Communism, the *mujahidin*—as the rebels were called—rose against a succession of Marxist governments in Kabul, which found themselves increasingly isolated from the countryside where the rebels were gaining in strength. Amin's brutal regime only made things worse and the counterrevolution threatened to doom the socialist experiment in Afghanistan. Ultimately, Amin literally waved the red flag before his enemies when he replaced the national, traditional Islamic flag of green, black, and red with one similar to those of the Soviet Union's Central Asian republics. And with it, to use an expression favored by geopolitical strategists in Moscow and Washington, the "correlation of forces" in Afghanistan threatened to shift in the West's favor. The Politburo in Moscow decided to act. Invoking the Brezhnev Doctrine of 1968 (by which the Soviet Union had taken the right to save the Communist Party in Czechoslovakia from what it called a "counterrevolution"), Brezhnev and his associates sent the troops. Once again, the Soviet Army bailed out a bankrupt Communist regime. Amin was deposed and killed by Soviet commandos and replaced by his rival, Babrak Karmal. The Kremlin then proclaimed that it had acted upon invitation by the government of Afghanistan.

But the removal of Amin did not placate the *mujahidin*. If anything, the rebellion against socialist Kabul only increased in strength and intensity. The rebels regarded the new ruler of Afghanistan as a Soviet puppet who promised to subjugate his nation to the interests of a foreign power. Such a prospect did not sit easily with most Afghans, many of whom remembered Stalin's brutal collectivization drive and the purges of the 1930s. In those years, many Muslims of Soviet Central Asia had fled into neighboring Afghanistan, where they found refuge among the local population. To many Afghans, Soviet intervention promised the repetition of history. To them, Karmal was the creation of a foreign power bent upon the social, economic, and ideological transformation of the nation.

Another explanation for the Soviet invasion lay in the very ethnic makeup of the Soviet Union. It was an empire, conquered and controlled by the Russians, one that contained scores of nationalities openly hostile to the Russians. Half of the country's population consisted of Russians, the other half of non-Russians. The geographic division of the USSR pointed to this fact. Officially, the nation was a "union" of fifteen "Soviet, socialist republics," the largest of which was the "Russian Republic." The other "republics" contained Ukrainians, Belorussians, Lithuanians, Estonians, Georgians, and others, all with their different histories, cultures, languages, and, in many instances, religions. In the West, especially in the United States, these peoples were too often lumped together under the heading of "Russians," such as "Russian athletes," and they deeply resented this erroneous characterization. One of the largest ethnic groups in the Soviet Union was the Muslims of Central Asia, peoples with long histories who only a little more than a hundred years before had fallen under Russian domination.

The Soviet Union had one of the largest Muslim populations in the world. It contained approximately 50 million people of Muslim origin, an estimated 75 percent of whom were believers. Millions of Muslims never bothered to learn the Russian language. To make matters worse for Moscow, the birth rate among the Russians was extraordinarily low, while that among the Muslims of Central Asia was quite high. It was clear that by the year 2000, the Russians would no longer constitute a majority in their empire. All this posed several pressing questions for Moscow. What impact did the rise of militant Islam have on this large population? (The Ayatollah Khomeini never made much of a distinction between the atheist Brezhnev in the Kremlin and the born-again Christian Carter in the White House. He condemned them both.) Dare the Kremlin, therefore, permit a successful

Muslim insurgency against a Communist regime along the borders of the Soviet Union?

As the Soviet Army crossed the border into Afghanistan, it mobilized a sizable percentage of recruits from Central Asia. This step was in line with standard procedure of using the most readily available reserves. The use of such troops appeared to have an added virtue: officially, the Kremlin declared that its army had been "invited" by a beleaguered Afghan government. The Central Asian Muslim recruits, therefore, became *prima facie* evidence of "fraternal" Soviet assistance to the Afghan government. But this policy soon ran into trouble when these soldiers found out that their task was the pacification of the country. The Soviet Muslims showed little inclination to fight their ethnic and religious counterparts. Some even went over to the rebels; others deserted. Within three months, Soviet authorities began to change the composition of their forces. The Soviet Army in Afghanistan began to consist largely of politically more reliable Slavic troops.

The invasion of Afghanistan was designed to eliminate a source of potential trouble. Unfortunately for the Soviet Union, Afghanistan did not prove to be another surgical operation as had been the case in Hungary in 1956 and Czechoslovakia in 1968. The Soviet Army was unable to restore order, but neither was it defeated.

Unlike guerrilla movements in other parts in the world, the Afghan rebels had no program of social, political, and economic reform. There was no literacy campaign (in 1979, primary school enrollment stood at 30 percent, mostly in the cities; the adult literacy rate was 15 percent), no declaration of the rights of women, no medical programs (life expectancy at birth was thirty-six years; in the industrial nations of the West it was twice that), no political experiments such as elected village councils, and no economic enterprises such as cooperatives or shops. In short, the rebels offered no political alternative to the Marxist program of Kabul. Moreover, the rebels were deeply split into contending factions. Gérard Chaliand, a French specialist on Third World guerrilla movements, concluded:

> The current Afghan resistance movement looks [more] like a traditional revolt [against the capital] . . . than like modern guerrilla warfare. Among contemporary guerrilla movements only the Kenyan Mau Mau [of the early 1950s] are less sophisticated in their strategy and organization.[13]

The nature of Afghan resistance and its foreign supporters proved once more that politics make strange bedfellows. Some of the rebel factions were financed by Libya's Muammar Qaddafi, the Ayatollah Khomeini of Iran, and the United States government under Ronald Reagan. This story becomes even stranger when one takes into account that the Reagan administration supported Islamic/Marxist rebels who in 1979 had kidnapped U.S.

Ambassador Adolph Dubs, who then died in a rescue attempt by the pro-Soviet Taraki government. The Islamic world faced the choice between a modern, secular society or the reinvigoration of Islam's traditions. The Afghan mujadihin represented neither alternative. They sought instead the preservation of a traditional society to the exclusion of the industrial revolution and all it entailed. Yet, in a strange twist of fate, the United States, the standard-bearer for the industrial revolution and parliamentary democracy, became the main arms supplier for the Afghan rebels.

■ SOVIET EXODUS FROM AFGHANISTAN

□ Gorbachev's Role

Shortly after Gorbachev came to power in March 1985, he found out that it was easier to start a war than to end one. He took a number of steps in an attempt to extricate his armed forces from Afghanistan. He sought to establish a dialogue with the resistance forces, only to be rebuffed. He wanted a coalition government of Communists and members of the resistance, but too much blood had been shed to make such a solution a possibility. The Afghan rebels were not interested in sitting down with either the Soviets or their clients, against whom they had been waging an uncompromising war.

The Gorbachev policy of establishing normal relations between the Soviet Union and the West demanded the withdrawal of Soviet troops from Afghanistan. At first, however, Gorbachev was unwilling to accept a military defeat along the southern flank of the Soviet Union, and for that reason he escalated the war. But the rebels were too well equipped, having received arms from a variety of sources, among them the effective U.S.-made Stinger ground-to-air missiles, which brought down numerous Soviet aircraft and helicopters. Gorbachev soon realized that only a massive increase in blood and treasure would bring victory. Yet, such a move was certain to undermine his position abroad, particularly in his dealings with the United States and China. For that reason, he shifted gears and announced that he sought the withdrawal of his army. He added that the invasion of Afghanistan had not been merely another mistake of the Brezhnev administration, but also a sin.

But the Soviet withdrawal would not be unilateral. Gorbachev would accept a defeat of his client provided that the new government of Afghanistan not be allied with the West. The superpowers would have to cease to conduct their wars by surrogates on the fields of Afghanistan. Those were the terms of the settlement between Moscow and the Reagan administration finally signed on April 14, 1988. On February 15, 1989, the last Soviet troops marched out of Afghanistan, leaving a client government, led by President Najibullah, in power in Kabul.

The war demanded a heavy toll from Afghanistan's population of 15 million people. Approximately 1 million died during the years 1979–1989, and between 5 and 6 million became refugees in Pakistan and Iran. Another 2 million became refugees within Afghanistan. The estimated physical damage—to agriculture, industry, power stations, schools, hospitals, and communication facilities—was $20 billion.[14]

☐ The Aftermath: Civil War

Old habits were hard to break. Both Washington and Moscow continued to prop up their clients. Firepower at the cost of billions of dollars and rubles continued to pour into Afghanistan. Many in the West had expected the rapid demise of the government in Kabul, which, however, showed remarkable staying power. It managed to survive the withdrawal of the Soviet Army because of the extraordinary fragmentation of Afghan society and the resistance movement in particular. In the 1950s, Prime Minister Mohammed Daoud (at that time still serving the king, Zahir Shah) had taken effective steps to form a modern, centralized state, which the civil war of the late 1970s, however, tore apart. During the 1980s, rural Afghanistan reverted to a state of fragmentation in which traditional kinship and religious affiliation took precedence over any attempt to create a national identification. Local leaders emerged who derived their legitimacy from the fighting men and territories they controlled. They tended to be loosely allied with one of the seven parties based in Peshawar, Pakistan. In May 1985, these parties created a wider front, the Islamic Union of Mujahidin of Afghanistan. But only hatred of the men in Kabul held this tenuous front together. Among the leaders of these groups one could find Pushtuns, Tadzhiks, and Arabs. The alliance was dominated by Shiite fundamentalists who previously had played only a minor role in national politics; most of the *mujahidin*, however, were Sunnis. Thus, one side was supported by Shiite Iran, the other by Iran's mortal enemy, the keeper of the Islam's holiest of shrines, Sunni Saudi Arabia. Inevitably, they turned against each other.[15]

The rebels hoped to seize the city of Jalalabad and establish a government there. But they made a major tactical error. By their indiscriminate shelling of Kabul and Jalalabad and the massacres of defectors, they left the government forces no choice but to fight to the bitter end. Although many in Afghanistan rejected the Marxist ideology of the Najibullah regime, they also rejected the policies of the Shiite fundamentalists.

The beginning of the end of the civil war between the Marxists and rebels came in December 1991, when Moscow stopped supplying arms to Najibullah and Washington ended its arms deliveries to the *mujahidin,* who, however, were still able to obtain weapons from Iran, Pakistan, and Saudi Arabia. Najibullah was on his own, and when in January 1992 he proved unable to suppress a local army mutiny, his own generals sensed his vulnerability and began to switch sides. By April 1992, Najibullah negotiated the transfer of political power to the *mujahidin* and then took refuge in a UN compound in Kabul.

In the meantime, the *mujahidin* fought among themselves for control of Kabul. In April 1992, a relatively moderate coalition led by the ethnic Tadzhik, Ahmad Shah Masoud, entered Kabul from the north and expelled another coalition, led by the militant Islamic fundamentalist Shiite, Gulbuddin Hekmatyar, who had been the chief recipient of U.S. aid in the war against the Soviets. Masoud benefited from the fact that most Afghans were Sunni Muslims and wanted no part of Hekmatyar's goal of a fundamentalist Islamic republic. But Hekmatyar, now supported by Iran, was by no means finished and continued to fight from his entrenched position in the hills south of Kabul. In August 1992, he launched a deadly artillery barrage against Kabul in which over 1,200 residents lost their lives. The attack gave notice that the political struggle for Afghanistan was by no means over.

Warfare was endemic and fierce in Afghanistan, but it became all the more so after the evacuation of Soviet forces in 1992 because of the increased firepower of the rival forces and the absence of external forces to place limits on that power. Observers in Kabul in 1993 noted that the city had suffered greater death and destruction in the single year after the fall of the Communist government than it had over the previous fourteen years of revolution and civil war. Continued bombardment over the next three years turned Kabul—a city of 1 million inhabitants—to rubble, killed as many as 10,000, and sent over half the population to flight.

Between January 1992 and September 1996, Afghanistan saw three successive Islamic governments, the last a coalition established in June 1996 between President Burhanuddin Rabbani, a clergyman, and the zealot Hekmatyar. The Afghan civil war appeared to be over when the country witnessed the emergence of yet another Muslim movement, the Taliban, in a bid to become the fourth—and most extreme—Islamic government since 1992.

The Taliban ("student" in Pushtun) was created by former Islamic Sunni seminary students (many from across the border in Pakistan) in August 1994, led by its supreme leader, the one-eyed, young (believed to be in his thirties) Mullah Mohammed Omar. The group had become disgusted with the corruption and factional fighting and demanded an Afghanistan governed by the laws of the Koran. Soon, the Taliban gained widespread popular support and began to rule large stretches of the country, where it applied stern measures against those it accused of having transgressed against the laws of Islam. It closed girls' schools, confined women to their homes, and punished thieves by cutting off their hands.

In September 1996, the Taliban—already in control of more than half of Afghanistan—began its final push toward Kabul, which was defended by forces loyal to Rabbani. After it had seized Kabul, the Taliban's first act was to beat and fatally shoot former Communist ruler Najibullah, who had been hiding in a UN compound, and hang him and his brother from a traffic post as a warning to any and all who opposed it; and it then began to look for Rabbani.

The Taliban's second act in Kabul was to forbid women to work in offices and to demand they don *burqas,* which cover the wearer from head to toe. It also ordered government officials to grow beards, closed down Kabul's sole television station (because Islam equates the reproduction of images of humans with idolatry), and banned Western music.

The Taliban now controlled approximately three-quarters of Afghanistan, but the fighting was not over. Forces from the ousted government regrouped and withdrew to the valleys north of Kabul. The history of Afghanistan—a struggle between the center and the outlying provinces—was repeating itself. The Taliban now had to deal with both regional and ethnic divisions, as well as with those who had a more secular vision of the future. When Taliban forces moved into the Panjshir Valley ninety miles north of Kabul (to catch up with President Rabbani and the forces of former Defense Minister Ahmad Shah Masood), the powerful northern Uzbek chief Gen. Abdul Rashid Dostum blocked their way.

Although Afghanistan was an Islamic state, neighboring Iran (controlled by Shiites) supported the ousted Rabbani government and mistrusted the Sunni Taliban movement, which had received much of its assistance from Pakistan (which, in turn, received support from the United States, which did not mind playing off a theocratic Afghan Sunni Muslim state against the ambitions of the theocratic state of Iran). The Taliban was not helped by the fact that many Afghans saw its victory as that of foreign powers (Pakistan and the United States) meddling in the affairs of Afghanistan. The military struggle for political control continued to play havoc with a country that had been at war against both itself and foreign interventionists for over two decades.

RECOMMENDED READINGS

Ascherson, Neal. *The Polish August: The Self-Limiting Revolution.* New York: Viking Press, 1982.
    A survey of the political climate in Poland that set the stage for the rise of Solidarity.
Ash, Timothy Garton. *The Polish Revolution: Solidarity.* New York: Charles Scribner's Sons, 1984.
    Discusses the rise and fall of Solidarity.
Bradsher, Henry S. *Afghanistan and the Soviet Union.* 2d ed. Durham, N.C.: Duke University Press, 1985.
    A detailed account of the events leading up to the Russian invasion.

Brumberg, Abraham, ed. *Poland: Genesis of a Revolution.* New York: Random House, 1983.
A collection of essays by Polish activists, intellectuals, workers, party officials, clergymen, dissidents, and loyalists; the stress is on political and cultural pluralism in Poland.
Carrère d'Encausse, Hélenè. *Decline of an Empire: The Soviet Socialist Republics in Revolt.* New York: Harper and Row, 1978.
An introduction to the ethnic complexity of the Soviet empire.
Chaliand, Gérard. *Report from Afghanistan.* New York: Penguin, 1982. A useful introduction to the history, geography, and politics of Afghanistan.
Garthoff, Raymond L. *Détente and Confrontation: American-Soviet Relations from Nixon to Reagan.* Washington, D.C.: The Brookings Institution, 1985.
A military historian discusses the Soviet intervention in Afghanistan; he argues that the Soviets feared that Amin would expel their advisers and bring in U.S. personnel as Sadat had done a few years earlier in Egypt.

NOTES

1. "Another Bloody Sunday," *Baltimore Sun,* December 18, 1981, p. A22.
2. Michael Dobbs, K. S. Karol, and Dessa Trevisan, *Poland, Solidarity, Walesa* (New York: McGraw-Hill, 1981), p. 70.
3. John Darnton, "Leaders of Union Urge Polish Vote on Form of Rule," *New York Times,* December 13, 1981, p. 1.
4. Andrew Cockburn, *The Threat Inside the Soviet Military Machine,* 2d rev. ed. (New York: Random House, 1984), pp. 111–114, 178–180; Michael T. Kaufman, "Bloc Was Prepared to Crush Solidarity, a Defector Says," *New York Times,* April 17, 1987, p. A9.
5. Vladimir Solovyov and Elena Klepikova, "Kudos for the General," *Baltimore Sun,* July 2, 1986, p. A15.
6. During the heady days of Solidarity, a reporter asked Walesa for his reaction should the government resort to force in an attempt to deal with Solidarity. Walesa replied: "We would ignore it."
7. Stuart H. Loory, "New Kid on the Bloc: Gorbachev's Reforms Spill into Eastern Europe," *The Progressive,* June 1987, p. 22; John Kifner, "A New Ingredient Spices 'Goulash Communism,'" *New York Times,* November 11, 1983, p. A2.
8. The last year for which the World Bank had figures for Afghanistan was 1979. Afghanistan's level of income put it among what the World Bank called "low-income developing countries, that is, countries with incomes below about a dollar per person per day." The Soviet intervention and the accompanying destruction brought only greater poverty.
9. AP, "Soviets Facing Oil Crunch, CIA Director Says," *Baltimore Evening Sun,* April 22, 1980, p. A5.
10. Bernard Gwertzman, "Soviet Is Able to Raise Production of Oil and Gas, U.S. Agency Says," *New York Times,* September 3, 1981, pp. A1, D14.
11. For details, see Raymond L. Garthoff, *Détente and Revolution: American-Soviet Relations from Nixon to Reagan* (Washington, D.C.: The Brookings Institution, 1985), pp. 887–965.
12. Michael Dobbs, "Secret Memos Trace Kremlin's March to War," *Washington Post,* November 15, 1992, pp. A1, A32; Aleksandr Morozov's memoirs, "Kabul'skii rezident," *Novoe vremia,* nos. 36–41, 1991; and "KGB i afganskie lidery," *Novoe vremia,* no. 20, 1992, pp. 30–31.

13. Gérard Chaliand, *Report from Afghanistan* (New York: Penguin, 1982), p. 49.

14. "Spravka 'NV,'" *Novoe vremia*, no. 17, 1992, p. 26.

15. For the politics of the Afghan resistance, see Bernard R. Rubin, "The Fragmentation of Afghanistan," *Foreign Affairs*, Winter 1989/1990, pp. 150–168.

21

Gorbachev and the Consequences of Perestroika

After the death of Konstantin Chernenko in March 1985, the Communist Party of the Soviet Union turned to Mikhail Gorbachev as its leader. The Soviet public and the West knew little about Gorbachev, although in December 1984 he had made a successful appearance on the world stage during his visit to London where he had behaved unlike previous Soviet visitors. Khrushchev's visit in 1955 had turned sour when he reminded his hosts ominously of his country's potentially devastating nuclear arsenal. Gorbachev spoke instead of the need to disarm and reminded the British of their wartime alliance with the Soviet Union and their losses at Coventry. Instead of the customary visit to Karl Marx's grave at Highgate Cemetery, Gorbachev visited Westminster Abbey. Margaret Thatcher, Britain's conservative prime minister, concluded: "I like him. We can do business with him."

■ GORBACHEV'S "NEW THINKING"

Gorbachev soon caused another stir with his speech in February 1985, in which he declared that the Soviet Union was in need of a radical transformation. "Paper shuffling, an addiction to fruitless meetings, windbaggery and formalism" will no longer do, he stated.[1] But at the outset he proved to be a careful reformer who understood that politics is the art of the possible. The party's 307-member Central Committee and the influential 12-member Politburo, which guided the party on a day-to-day basis, had come to power under the conservative Brezhnev. In his first speech as general secretary of the party, Gorbachev placated the right wing with his reaffirmation of the old values. But as time went by, he showed that he intended to reorganize the system inherited from his predecessors; the Soviet Union, he insisted, must undergo a radical *perestroika,* or restructuring.

In the long run, Gorbachev's program was nothing short of revolutionary. Among his targets were the centrally planned industrial system and the collective farms Joseph Stalin had introduced in the late 1920s. Gorbachev ended the rigid censorship of public opinion when he gave non-Communists a public voice. He ended the long and debilitating conflict between the state and organized religion, ended the isolation of his country's intellectuals, invited those who had been expelled from the Soviet Union to return to their native soil, sent an unprecedented number of Soviet citizens abroad, permitted the sale of Western publications, forced the Soviet Union's conservative historians to come to grips with their history, and broke down the power of the party. He also redefined the Soviet Union's position vis-à-vis China, Eastern Europe, the West, and the Third World and took the Soviet Army out of Afghanistan. In sum, Gorbachev turned the science of Kremlinology on its head; he did what had been thought no leader in the Kremlin could or would even try to do.

Gorbachev, in a sharp break with Soviet history, demanded an open and honest discussion of society's problems. To this end, he had to give society, not just the party, a voice. *Glasnost,* from the Russian for "voice," therefore, became the first order of business. The severest test of *glasnost* came early. In April 1986, an atomic reactor in Chernobyl, in the north of the Ukrainian Republic, suffered a meltdown and an explosion, spewing radioactive matter into the Belorussian Republic, Scandinavia, and then down into Germany and as far south as Italy. Soviet technology was contaminating what Gorbachev had earlier called "our common European home." In his New Year's address a few months earlier, he had promised "to call things by their name." The recognition of mistakes, he said, was the "best medicine against arrogance and complacency."[2] But for the first nineteen days after Chernobyl, no acknowledgment of the disaster came out of Moscow. When Gorbachev finally spoke on national television, he admitted that a nuclear plant had burned out of control.

During those nineteen days Gorbachev made the point that the old ways would no longer suffice. Instead, "new thinking" was required. Problems must no longer be denied, and officials had to be made responsible not only for their successes but also for their failures. Gorbachev used Chernobyl to weaken the conservative wing of the party, the chief obstacle to *perestroika.* At this point, the differences between Gorbachev and Nikita Khrushchev became apparent. When Khrushchev tried to implement his reforms, he always shrank back from the consequences. The result was a zigzag course, Khrushchev's famous "hare-brained schemes." Gorbachev, in contrast, repeatedly used political, natural, and man-made disasters—on the surface, setbacks—to his advantage. After Chernobyl, Gorbachev continued with the reorganization of the party, which he had begun as early as May 1985. He fired members of the old guard and replaced them with his people. Under Gorbachev's encouragement, the Soviet press began a remarkably open discussion of the causes and consequences of the Chernobyl disaster.

Artists and writers quickly tested the limits of *glasnost*. The consequence was the appearance of a veritable flood of works that had been created years before "for the drawer," waiting to see the light of day; some had waited more than twenty years. Among them were Anatoli Rybakov's *Children of the Arbat*, a novel set in 1933–1934 at the beginning of Stalin's terror; and films such as *Our Armored Train*, a critical analysis of the legacy of the Stalin era. Periodicals openly began to discuss society's ills—poor medical care, the high incidence of traffic accidents, alcoholism, official corruption, anti-Semitism, shoddy workmanship, and the lack of quality consumer goods.

A number of observers in the West and the Soviet Union insisted, however, that the acid test of *glasnost* would be how the Kremlin treated the writings of the exiled Alexander Solzhenitsyn, whose novel *One Day in the Life of Ivan Denisovich* had been the literary sensation of Moscow in 1962. Khrushchev had used this exposé of the prison system to further discredit Stalin. But Solzhenitsyn had refused to stop at this point. In his three-volume *Gulag Archipelago*, he laid the blame for the prison system squarely at the feet of the revered founder of the Soviet state, Vladimir Lenin—whose stature in the Soviet Union was no less than that of a saint. Gorbachev and his Politburo initially opposed suggestions to allow *Gulag Archipelago* to be published. Vadim Medvedev, the Politburo member in charge of ideology, explained that the book undermined "the foundation on which our present life rests." But public pressure, expressed in thousands of letters and telegrams, had an unprecedented impact on Soviet cultural history. In June 1989, Gorbachev told his Politburo that the decision of whether to publish Solzhenitsyn should be made by editors, not the party. After an absence of twenty-five years, Solzhenitsyn was reintroduced to Soviet readers.[3]

Gorbachev also insisted that Soviet society come to grips with its past. Journalists and dissident historians were quick to subject the Brezhnev "era of stagnation" (1964–1981) and in particular the Stalin legacy to close scrutiny. The professional historians, however, dragged their heels. Too many had become comfortable with the established formulas of writing history and wanted no part of Gorbachev's "new thinking." Early 1988, however, saw the purge of the old editorships of historical journals, among them the Soviet Union's most prestigious, *Voprosy istorii* (Problems of History). The lead article in the February 1988 issue declared that the journal's new task was to participate in the *perestroika* of the country. Articles began to discuss persons and events hitherto considered taboo—Stalin's purges of the party, the "tragedy" of collectivization in Kazakhstan by historians from that republic, the nationality problem, and the like. The journal participated in the political rehabilitation of Khrushchev and victims of Stalin's purges, such as Nikolai Bukharin, and went so far as to publish Leon Trotsky's essay "The Stalin School of Falsification of History." In the huge Lenin Library in Moscow, "new" books were made available to readers—books that had been published decades before and suppressed by Stalin.[4]

Most writers and historians, freed from the constraints of the past, expressed distinctly liberal, Western values. They supported *Memorial,* an organization in remembrance of those who had fallen victim to Stalin's purges. But *glasnost* also gave writers of an anti-Western, antiliberal persuasion a voice and showed that the nativist tradition still ran deep. Another organization, *Pamiat* (Remembrance), remembered history differently from *Memorial.* The Russian National-Patriotic Front Memory, *Pamiat*'s formal name, did not consider the Stalinist legacy to be the nation's main source of difficulty; instead, it blamed Zionists and cosmopolitans.[5] In *Pamiat*'s view, Stalin had played the role of the good tsar, terrible but righteous, who had punished the wicked and brought the nation to its military and industrial power. The debate was reminiscent of that in the nineteenth century between the Westerners and the Slavophiles—the former seeking the salvation of the nation in Western ideas, the latter in Russian institutions.

■ **INDUSTRY**

When Gorbachev first began to speak of *perestroika,* he intended a rapid process. Thus, for a time the third watchword was *uskorenie,* or acceleration. It became clear, however, that the process of reconstruction was one of extraordinary dimensions, compounded by the fact that many managers of factories and collective farms looked upon the Gorbachev revolution with skepticism or resentment. Their opposition was largely passive. Managers and workers had learned to fulfill the plan on paper and saw few reasons to embrace a new approach that promised to punish those who failed. In the mid-1960s, Premier Alexei Kosygin had sought to reorganize the economy so that factories would have to sink or swim on their own. In 1965, *khozraschet,* or accountability, became the new slogan as Kosygin introduced with much fanfare the Liberman program, named for the economist who had proposed it in an article in *Pravda* in 1962. The conservatives, who had their hands on the political and economic levers, soon brought this experiment to a halt.

The majority of the population expected the state to solve their problems; this was an attitude that had seeped into their blood. Gorbachev sent many people to the West to show them that an alternative to the Soviet system existed—one, however, that demanded hard work and competition in the marketplace. He also suggested that government subsidies come to an end. Gorbachev began to speak of closing down inefficient factories and raising the prices of certain goods. Much of what the state provided for its citizens it did at a financial loss: bread, milk, apartments, education, transportation, and other commodities. Gorbachev's statements hit a raw nerve, producing a resistance to an economic *perestroika* that promised not only higher prices but also unemployment. One of the consequences of *perestroika* was the hoarding of goods that promised to cost twice as much tomorrow. The relative security of the past began to give way to an uncertain future. By early 1988, talk in Moscow of an accelerated *perestroika* had become a thing of the past; the question now was whether Gorbachev could reconstruct the top-heavy economy by the year 2000. *Uskorenie,* unlike *glasnost* and *perestroika,* did not make it into English-language dictionaries.

■ FARMING

Gorbachev came no closer to resolving the agricultural problem. Agriculture, as with industry, had been directed from the top since the late 1920s. Private farming, except that on certain plots made available to collective farmers, had all but disappeared in the Soviet Union. Stalin had created the collective farm system and then had neglected it.

In his speech on November 3, 1987, at the seventieth anniversary of the October Revolution, Gorbachev still defended—under pressure from his opponents on the right—the necessity of Stalin's collectivization. In October 1988, however, in a televised address, he proposed radical changes. The farmers of the Soviet Union, he insisted, must once again become "masters of their land." Five months later, in March 1989, Gorbachev took his case to the party's decisionmaking body, the Central Committee, where he summarized the failure of Soviet agriculture. Between 1946 and 1953, Stalin had transferred 105 billion rubles from the agricultural sector to industry. Khrushchev and Brezhnev, subsequently, had spent huge sums to improve the productivity of the collective and the state farms but to little avail. Low productivity and an extraordinary amount of waste because of carelessness, poor transportation, and inadequate storage facilities had forced the government to purchase vast amounts of grain from capitalist farmers in the West. The time had come to abandon decision making at the top and to learn from experimentation, from the United States, China, India, and the Green Revolution.[6] One of Gorbachev's advisers, economist Leonid Abalkin, declared, "We are ready to borrow the best from all lands."[7]

Gorbachev did not manage, however, to abolish the collective farms. His conservative opponent in the Politburo, Yegor Ligachev, was strong enough to prevent a 180-degree turn. But on April 9, 1989, the Supreme Soviet—that is, the government—did pass a law permitting private individuals and collectives to lease land, buildings, mineral deposits, small factories, and machines from the state "for up to 50 years and more." TASS, the Soviet news agency, underlined that the law was intended to promote private initiative, such as the establishment of family farms. The difficulty lay in finding adventuresome entrepreneurs, *kulaks* as it were— a class Stalin had characterized as "enemies of the working classes" and had liquidated by the early 1930s.

At the end of 1989, voices made themselves heard in Moscow, complaining that Gorbachev's program lacked focus and that he did not really know in which direction to march. Many officials, who previously had known nothing but orders from the top, found his *perestroika* unsettling. Gorbachev was quick to reply in *Pravda*. "Ready-made schemes," he declared, "were the characteristic of the Stalin era with which we have parted ways."[8] In the past, mistakes had been made precisely because the top-heavy bureaucracy had decided that success was measured by how well the directive was fulfilled; whether it made any sense had not been the issue.

■ THE ROLE OF THE PARTY

What Gorbachev sought was a discussion of the ills of society and the potential remedies. But this could not be done within the party alone. He needed a wider forum, which, in turn, would whittle away the authority of the party. The result was a new legislature, the Congress of People's Deputies,[9] which held its first session in May 1989. Not only were the majority of the delegates freely elected but many were non-Communists, and Communists themselves had to compete for their positions. The weakness of the party became glaringly apparent when numerous party candidates failed to receive a majority of votes, although they ran unopposed. The old guard, the nomenklatura,[10] was shaken by this innovation. During debates before the Congress, officials were now held responsible for their actions.

Gorbachev, however, did not go so far as to support the abolition of Article 6 of the 1977 Soviet constitution, which granted his party a monopoly of political power. At the end of 1989, he lacked the votes in both the party's Central Committee and the Congress of People's Deputies to contemplate the abolition of Article 6.[11] But Gorbachev did not commit himself in stone. "At the present complex stage," he stated, "the interests of the consolidation of society and . . . of *perestroika* prompt the advisability of keeping the one-party system."[12]

Many radicals supported Gorbachev's policy as the only way to defend *perestroika* from the conservatives. But sentiment to scrap Article 6 ran deep. During his January 1990 visit to Vilnius, Lithuania, where the republic's Communist Party had already legalized a multiparty system and elections, Gorbachev stated, "We should not be afraid of [a multiparty system], the way the devil fears incense."[13] The evolution of Gorbachev's position on Article 6 was completed during the extraordinary plenum of the party's Central Committee in early February 1990. After three days of debates, the party did the unthinkable when it accepted the existence of opposition parties. Lenin's legacy, the Communist Party as the sole driving force in the Soviet Union, became the casualty of the "February Revolution" of 1990.

In the arena of foreign affairs, Gorbachev's initiatives were no less pathbreaking. His presence on the world stage overshadowed that of all other statesmen. He ended the seventy-year conflict with the West, withdrew the Soviet Union from the battles in the Third World, led the drive for nuclear and conventional disarmament (see Chapter 23), and discarded the Brezhnev Doctrine of unilateral intervention in the affairs of other Communist nations. Gorbachev insisted instead that the Soviet Union must live with its neighbors according to the norms of international law. In October 1989, Gorbachev went to Finland to underscore this point specifically by stating that the Soviet Union had "no moral or political right" to interfere in the revolutionary process in Eastern Europe.

■ THE NATIONALITY QUESTION

When Gorbachev declared that things should be called by their proper names, he set into motion a discussion of the Soviet Union's nationality question. By the end of the 1980s, the Russians made up 145.3 million of the total population of 281.7 million people; of the other Slavs, 51.2 million were Ukrainians, and 10.1 million were Belorussians. Thus, 206.6 million people, or 73 percent of the population of the Soviet Union, were of Slavic origin. Over the past two centuries, Ukrainians and Belorussians, however, had developed their own national consciousness, and many among them sought independence from Moscow.

The first successful Marxist revolution had taken place in an empire that consisted of well over 100 nationalities. Many had only one thing in common: they had been conquered by the dominant Russians. The 1917 revolution, so ran the official interpretation, had forged a new society of peoples who now voluntarily resided in the new Soviet Union. The fact that none had requested to secede from the Soviet Union—as permitted under the constitution—was proof that the new Communist consciousness had obliterated national antagonisms. The Soviet Union was one happy family of diverse nations, a point restated in Soviet publications *ad infinitum.*

Glasnost blew the official theory apart. The discussions revealed deep-rooted grievances among all national minorities, and they were directed not necessarily against the dominant Russians but often against each other. The national intelligentsia challenged the extreme centralization of the Moscow-imposed system and demanded greater cultural, economic, and political autonomy. An awareness that industrialization was destroying the environment became a major factor in publicizing nationalist grievances. Estonians complained that Moscow was polluting their land; Armenians argued that the air in their capital, Yerevan, had become a health hazard; and Uzbeks and Kazakhs charged that cotton irrigation had drained Lake Aral in Central Asia.

The discussions produced two approaches. The first was the reorganization of the relationship between the republics and Moscow. The fourteen non-Russian republics should be granted substantial economic and political autonomy; they should become, for example, the guardians of their own environment. This solution envisioned strong republics with a strong center, something on the order of the Swiss model—a nation of four nationalities with four official languages. Gorbachev favored this approach, as it would keep the nation together and fit into the framework of his plan for "democratization." The difficulty lay in convincing long-suffering peoples that their best prospects were in a future democratic Soviet Union.

The second solution called for the dismemberment of the empire. The republics should have the right to exercise their constitutional right of secession. This plan would mean a 180-degree reversal of Russian history. It was no coincidence that the Russian monarchs who were granted the appellation "Great"—Ivan III, Peter I, and Catherine II—had earned it by virtue of expanding their empire's borders.

The most serious challenge came from the Baltic states—Lithuania, Latvia, and Estonia—where so-called popular fronts began to test the limits of Gorbachev's "democratization." First, they demanded economic autonomy, stating they were merely supporting *perestroika*—that is, the decentralization of the top-heavy economy. Then they insisted on—and gained—the right to fly their old flags, openly practice their religions, and rewrite their histories. Their native languages gained official stature, they spoke of fielding their own teams for future Olympic Games, and they declared their Communist parties to be independent of the party in Moscow. But then came the inevitable talk of secession from the Soviet Union.

The reason for the radicalism in the Baltic states can be found in their recent history. They had been part of the Russian empire for over 200 years, but after the 1917 revolution they had managed to establish their independence—which, however, lasted only until 1940. On the eve of World War II, Hitler and Stalin agreed on a nonaggression pact and for good measure decided, on the basis of a secret protocol, to divide Eastern Europe. The Baltic states fell into the Soviet sphere of influence, and in spring 1940 Stalin incorporated them into the Soviet Union, deported or murdered hundreds of thousands of suspected nationalists, and forbade the symbols of independence—such as the flags. Officially, however, the Baltic peoples had joined the Soviet Union of their own free will.

As *glasnost* produced a critical reassessment of the Stalin era, the infamous Hitler-Stalin pact could not be ignored. After much soul-searching and hesitation, official Soviet historians finally admitted that, yes, there had been a secret protocol in violation of international law. In December 1989, the Communist Party of Lithuania voted to establish its independence from Moscow, a move that spawned a four-point proposal by the mass movement *Sajudis* demanding (1) "freedom and independence" on the basis of the repeal of the Hitler-Stalin pact, (2) removal of the "occupant Soviet Army," (3) compensation for "the genocide of Lithuanian citizens and their exile" and environmental destruction, and (4) the establishment of friendly relations on the basis of the 1920 peace treaty between Lithuania and the Soviet Union.[14] Gorbachev was put into a very uncomfortable position between *glasnost* and the breakup of the Soviet Union. His supporters warned that the Lithuanian radicals could wreck *perestroika*.

In January 1990, Gorbachev took a highly publicized trip to Lithuania to convince the population of the dangers of secessionism. He pleaded, cajoled, and issued thinly veiled threats, all to no avail. As his limousine departed for the airport, the crowd jeered him. In Moscow, the spokesman for the foreign office, Gennady Gerasimov, remarked that the divorce between Lithuania and Russia must follow an orderly course; it could not occur on the basis of Lithuania's unilateral action. Lithuanians quickly replied that there had been no marriage, only an abduction and a rape, and that there was nothing to negotiate. On March 11, 1990, the newly and freely elected parliament of Lithuania unilaterally declared its independence. Gorbachev demanded that Lithuania rescind its declaration; Lithuanian independence, he insisted, could be discussed only within the context of Soviet law.

Not all nationalist grievances were directed against the Russians. As Lithuanians demonstrated against the Russians, the Polish minority in Lithuania demonstrated for incorporation into Poland. Nearly every Soviet republic had territorial claims against a neighbor. The Muslim Abkhazians in the western region of the Georgian Republic demonstrated against the heavy hand of the Christian Georgians, who had curbed the Abkhazians' cultural autonomy. Oddly, Georgians and Abkhazians are related; centuries ago, however, the Abkhazians fell under Turkish influence and became Muslims. They nevertheless resorted to killing each other. The highly publicized anti-Russian rally in Tbilisi, the capital of Georgia, in April 1989, in which Soviet soldiers killed twenty demonstrators, began initially as an anti-Abkhazian demonstration.

The most violent clash among Soviet nationalities was the bloody conflict between the Christian Armenians and the Shiite Muslim, Turkic-speaking Azeris. When Gorbachev gave the Armenians a voice, they immediately demanded the return of a piece of their historical territory, which Stalin had placed under Azeri administration as far back as 1923. To appease the Turks, Stalin had decreed that the region of Nagorno-Karabakh, although its population was three-quarters Armenian, should be in Azerbaidzhan. Nagorno-Karabakh was officially an "autonomous" district, but the Armenians there were denied their civil rights by their ancient enemies.[15]

The history of Armenia has been marked by wars against invaders who have threatened to destroy it. Armenian national consciousness is deeply affected by the 1915 massacre at the hands of the Turks in which 1.5 million Armenians died.[16] The Turks then drove the Armenians from their historic territory in what today is eastern Turkey. As a result, the symbol of Armenian nationalism, biblical Mount Ararat, is in Turkey, just across the border from the Armenian capital, Yerevan.

Tensions rose in February 1988 when up to 100,000 people demonstrated in Yerevan over a period of several days against Azerbaidzhan but also against Moscow and Communism. At the end of the month, Azeris staged a pogrom in Sumgait, a city just north of the capital of Azerbaidzhan, Baku, in which 32 Armenians were murdered. Moscow deployed its army and internal security troops to keep continued sporadic violence at a minimum.

In June 1988, the Communist Party of Armenia voted to regain Nagorno-Karabakh, and the Communist Party of Azerbaidzhan voted to retain it.[17] For the first time, Communist parties of the Soviet Union split along national lines.[18] Only Moscow's intervention minimized further bloodshed, but the fear and hatred remained. When an earthquake destroyed much of one region in Armenia in December 1988, a number of Azeris rejoiced over the misery of their neighbors and prevented relief supplies from crossing their territory.

On January 13, 1990, a few days after Gorbachev's visit to Lithuania, the Azeri-Armenian violence erupted anew—this time in Baku, where Azeris murdered at least 60 Armenians in a replay of the Sumgait pogrom. This massacre marked the resumption of violence between Azeris and Armenians in and around Nagorno-Karabakh. Gorbachev decreed a state of emergency in the Transcaucasus; when it had no effect, he sent the Soviet Army and troops of the Interior Ministry into Baku. In a televised address, he explained that he had no choice because "neither side listened to the voice of reason."[19] In the ensuing violence, about 100 Azeris were killed. Azeris berated Gorbachev for his action; Armenians complained because he had not acted sooner. This time, Armenians rejoiced at the deaths of Azeris.[20]

* * *

The Gorbachev revolution was the product of a historical process. The social conditions that had produced support for Lenin and Stalin had undergone significant changes since 1917. The number of Soviet citizens, for example, who had a high school education or better had increased since 1964 from 25 million to 125 million in the mid-1980s.[21] When de-Staliniation began with Khrushchev's 1956 speech, more than half of the nation's population still lived in the countryside; that figure was down to about one-quarter by the late 1980s. Gorbachev inherited a nation with a sizable and largely urbanized middle class. Soviet citizens had no personal memory of the glorious October Revolution of 1917, and increasingly fewer remembered World War II—the Great Fatherland War, the last great age of heroism and sacrifice. Gorbachev's generation (he was born in 1931) came to political maturity during Khrushchev's "thaw" and his attacks on Stalin. They understood that their nation's ideological, intellectual, military, and economic isolation had to come to an end. *Perestroika* became a battle between reformers and the dead weight of history, the legacy generations of tsars and commissars had bestowed on the nation.

Gorbachev's *perestroika* and "new thinking" fostered one previously unthinkable reform after another. In December 1988, the West German newsweekly *Der Spiegel* named Gorbachev its "Man of the Year: Man of the Hour"—the first time it had bestowed such recognition on anyone. It compared him to the westernizer Peter the Great, the Protestant reformer Martin Luther, and the emancipator Abraham Lincoln. In January 1990, *Time* named him the "Man of the Decade." But the applause was for a tightrope walker who had not yet reached the other side.

■ THE END OF THE SOVIET UNION

Gorbachev's *perestroika* alienated both those on the right, who thought he was irrevocably disrupting Soviet society, and those on the left, who felt the reforms were not going far enough, that too much of the old power structure—the nomenklatura and its institutions—remained intact. By autumn 1990, the left and the right both wanted Gorbachev's ouster.

Perestroika had begun as an attempt to restructure Soviet society within the context of the existing social and political order. Gorbachev's feet, however, were never set in stone. The central feature of his "new thinking" was an insistence upon learning and experimentation. Gorbachev and his economic advisers eventually concluded that the freeing of prices (determined by supply and demand) and the right to make a private profit were not merely necessary evils but positive economic forces. By autumn 1990, he moved to the verge of accepting a radical proposal by Stanislav Shatalin, an economist long opposed to the Soviet centralized economy. The Shatalin Plan called for a sudden transition during a period of a scant 500 days from a centralized to what was still called a "market" economy, a pseudonym for capitalism. But Shatalin was unable to answer questions regarding the social and political consequences of his bold proposal, which was bound to disrupt the distribution system on which enterprises depended and to create rapid inflation and high rates of unemployment.

At this juncture, Gorbachev moved to the right. He feared the so-called democratic opposition[22] on the left, led by Boris Yeltsin, who sought to topple him and dismantle the Soviet Union. Gorbachev had initially brought Yeltsin to Moscow from Sverdlovsk (now Ekaterinburg) in Siberia to participate in *perestroika,* but the two men eventually had a bitter falling out over personality and political differences. In July 1990, Yeltsin staged his dramatic exit from the party. Gorbachev began to surround himself with conservatives who had become uncomfortable with the course of *perestroika.* In December 1990, he appointed Gennadii Yanaev as vice-president and, in January 1991, Valentin Pavlov as premier. When Foreign Minister Eduard Shevardnadze—one of the architects of *perestroika*—came under fierce attack by the right, he resigned in December 1990 and warned that the nation was drifting toward a dictatorship. In January 1991, Soviet paramilitary forces attacked border guards in Lithuania as a bloody object lesson to that country's independence movement. A rightist coup appeared to have taken place in the Kremlin, marking the end of the reforms.

But Gorbachev, in danger of becoming a prisoner of the right, now moved to the left. In April 1991, he and Yeltsin worked out the "9-plus-1" formula, which called for a decentralized Soviet Union and would leave its president with greatly diminished powers. The republics would be able to exercise virtually unlimited power on the local level, whereas the Soviet government would continue to handle matters such as currency, diplomacy, and the military. In June 1991, Yeltsin won a historic victory at the polls as Russia's first popularly elected head of state. Gorbachev returned to a version of the Shatalin Plan when he commissioned another economist, Grigorii Yavlinskii, with the help of economics professors from Harvard and MIT, to assemble the so-called grand bargain—which drew heavily on the Shatalin Plan but was also linked to Western aid to soften the inevitable economic shocks. This was the program Yeltsin inherited after the August 1991 coup.

These developments, as well as Yeltsin's demand that the Communist Party in Russia cease its traditional control of institutions (such as schools, universities, collective farms, factories, and army units) and Gorbachev's renewed attempt to reorganize the party at the highest levels, triggered a military coup by desperate men who saw their power slipping away. On August 19, 1991, as Gorbachev vacationed in the Crimea, the leaders of Soviet military and paramilitary organizations—Defense Minister Dmitrii Yazov, KGB chief Vladimir Kriuchkov, and Minister of the Interior Boris Pugo—sent tanks into the streets of Moscow and declared a state of emergency. Their front men were Gorbachev's recent appointees, Yanaev and

Pavlov. They declared that Gorbachev had taken ill and Vice-President Yanaev was assuming the position of president. At a live news conference later that same day, Yanaev stated that "his good friend Gorbachev" would some day return to political life in another capacity. Virtually no one believed his account, particularly as neither Gorbachev nor his physician was present to attest to it. Instead, a subversive camera operator focused on the trembling hands of Yanaev.

Since the days of Lenin, Communist ideology had always stressed unity of action. During the coup, however, there was none. The conspirators had acted in desperation and haste, without planning or coordination.[23] They never managed to enlist a unified military or KGB. Some commanders were deeply unhappy with the state of affairs to which *perestroika* had brought them, but even they were unwilling to use force against fellow citizens. Other commanders openly opposed the coup. A similar division was apparent in the press and television, the diplomatic corps, the KGB, and the party. The longer it took the conspirators (now labeled a junta in some Soviet publications) to restore order, the weaker they became. The coup collapsed with scarcely a shot fired. The three civilians who died did so needlessly, killed by soldiers who had panicked after being bombarded with stones, pieces of lumber, and Molotov cocktails.

The conspirators had but one hope: that Soviet society would tacitly accept the transfer of power. In 1964, when the party changed leadership, the KGB was surprised to find out that not a single demonstration or voice of support was heard on behalf of Khrushchev. This time it was different. The Russian parliament and its president (Yeltsin, standing on top of a renegade tank) denounced the *putsch*[24] and insisted upon the return of Gorbachev. The conspirators had gone after Gorbachev, the head of both the party and the Soviet government, without taking into account the fact that political power had already become diffused throughout the Soviet Union. Yeltsin's election as president of Russia had already created a situation of "dual power": Yeltsin and Gorbachev were co-equals. Had Yeltsin been arrested and had Gorbachev accepted the transfer of power (as he was pressured for three days to do), the coup might have succeeded. As it was, Yeltsin was able to take a defiant stand in front of the Russian parliament, Moscow's "White House." Anatolii Sobchak, the mayor of Leningrad, was able to make his way to Moscow's Sheremetovo Airport under KGB guard, fly home, and threaten the local military and KGB commanders with criminal prosecution if they obeyed the plotters. Leningrad never saw armed soldiers in the streets and celebrated the defeat of the coup with massive demonstrations in its historic squares.

When Gorbachev returned to Moscow, he was unable to regain his political power. The first casualty was the Communist Party, even though it had not staged the coup. On the contrary, the conspirators had bypassed the party, but since the coup had been staged for the express purpose of restoring a one-party system, the party was blamed for it. At first, Gorbachev continued to express his faith in the possibility of a reformed, democratic Communist Party; then, belatedly, he quit the party. Yeltsin held the party—and indirectly Gorbachev, the party's general secretary—responsible for the coup and suspended the party indefinitely. The conspirators had hoped to preserve the Soviet Union; the *putsch* instead hastened its demise. The 9-plus-1 formula no longer served a purpose. Yeltsin and the radicals dissolved the Soviet Union. By the end of 1991, the red flag with its golden hammer-and-sickle, the symbol of the Bolshevik seizure of power in 1917, came down from the buildings of the Kremlin and was replaced with the old flag of imperial Russia.

Gorbachev's historic role—as great as it had been—had suddenly come to an end. He had brought about the impossible—the demise of the Communist Party, the end of the Soviet Union, and the dismemberment of an empire numerous tsars and commissars had assiduously created. And all this was achieved with relatively little violence. Gorbachev left behind the rule of law and a transformed society. He had begun a free discussion of the Soviet Union's social and economic problems that eventually led to the adoption of a market economy, ended the political monopoly of the Communist Party, greatly reduced the arbitrary powers of the police, set the stage for multiparty competition for political power, decentralized political power among the republics, eliminated the Soviet Union's offensive capabilities in the heart of Europe, took the lead in ending the Cold War and the nuclear arms race, and put into motion the withdrawal of Soviet forces from Eastern Europe. Gorbachev had also set the stage, however, for the dissolution of the Soviet Union.

Yeltsin and the presidents of the now independent republics inherited a disintegrating economy that had once been Gorbachev's headache. By 1991, the Soviet Union had already been plunged into a depression as severe as that the West had experienced in the 1930s. The *putsch* removed all restraints on the economic *perestroika*. Yeltsin, who had criticized the gradual nature of Gorbachev's reforms, committed Russia to the full embrace of capitalism. The movement toward a market economy, however, further disrupted the network of resource allocation, and factories had to fend for themselves to obtain the necessary supplies. Once the market began to determine prices, they rose drastically. Suppliers, moreover, were asking for hard—that is, Western—currency, which factories simply did not have. Ethnic tensions contributed to the economic chaos. Armenians no longer provided parts to machine tool factories in Moscow, and Russians refused to deliver steel to the huge truck factories of independence-minded Tatarstan on the Volga River. The result was increased idleness in factories, empty stores, and a steep decline in the standard of living.

The collapse of the Communist regimes in Eastern Europe brought an end to COMECON (see Chapter 4). It also meant, for instance, that the former Soviet Union, which had obtained about half of its medicines from COMECON trading partners, saw a drastic decline in its health care facilities. Soviet commuters had relied heavily on the sturdy, reliable Hungarian "Ikarus" buses, which the Hungarians were still willing to provide but only for hard currency. The Hungarians learned that the former Soviet republics could no longer purchase the buses and that the West would not do so because its travel bureaus could not compete successfully unless they provided customers with the comfort found in, say, Mercedes-Benz or Volvo buses.

Yeltsin, however, no less than Gorbachev, could not ignore the political consequences of a capitalist system created at breakneck speed. To cushion the shock of higher prices, his government printed ever more money. The result was a rate of inflation of 2,000 percent and a government budget deficit of 25 percent in 1992. The government felt it had no choice but to print money to raise wages, provide for social services, subsidize agricultural products, and service the previous Russian debt. Still, wages declined relative to the newly freed prices to the point that during winter 1991–1992, 90 percent of Russians lived below the official subsistence level.[25]

By the first anniversary of the August 1991 coup, the former Soviet republics were mired in a deep recession accompanied by inflation, unemployment, shortage of consumer goods, and loss of confidence. Yeltsin and his economic advisers were committed from the outset to a market economy and to joining the International Monetary Fund (IMF). The "grand bargain" was predicated on obtaining aid from the capitalist nations, which were basking in the glow of their ideological victory over the Soviet Union. Unfortunately for Yeltsin, the money markets had dried up. President Ronald Reagan's push for military superiority had produced a binge of borrowing of capital, driving the U.S. national debt from approximately $1 trillion to over $4 trillion by the end of 1992. A worldwide economic recession and the collapse of the Japanese stock market—a decline of approximately 60 percent of its value since 1986—ended the era of relatively cheap capital. The German government provided more assistance to the former Soviet Union than did any other nation, but it, too, had little money to spare because of the heavy cost of German reunification. A cynical Russian political analyst noted that "as long as we pretend that we are carrying through reforms . . . the West will pretend to help us."[26]

The former Soviet republics turned to the IMF for assistance of $44 billion in 1992, with $24 billion to be earmarked for Russia alone.[27] The purpose of the IMF, however, was not so much to provide development money as to ensure that the borrower followed the strict principles of capitalist development: a balanced budget, the repayment of debts, a convertible currency to permit foreign investors to take their profits out of the country, the freeing of prices (notably of energy), provision for permitting unprofitable businesses to fail, and the sanctity of foreign investments. This meant the IMF would determine an economic policy bound to bring hardship to the public. The raising of the price of a barrel of oil from $3 to the world market's price of $19 stimulated Russia's oil industry, brought in Western investments and technology, and facilitated the repayment of the nation's foreign debts; it also made driving a car very expensive, undermined the farmers' ability to raise food cheaply, and shut down factories unable to pay the drastically higher price for energy. According to Sergei Stankevich, deputy mayor of Moscow, the economic choices were "between bad, very bad and awful."[28] Public opinion polls showed that a high percentage of former Soviet citizens viewed the capitalist experiment with considerable pessimism.

Yeltsin had to assure the Russians that he would not permit the IMF to "force us to our knees for this loan, no! Russia is still a great power." At the same time, however, his economic advisers sought to obtain aid by assuring Western lenders and the IMF that Russia would follow its international economic obligations in exchange for a "minimum" two-year moratorium on the repayment of Russia's foreign debt of $68 billion.[29]

The road to a market economy proved difficult and dangerous. It produced a class of private entrepreneurs (who only recently had been called capitalist exploiters) but also an impoverished, humiliated, and increasingly embittered mass of people who could not understand how their great nation had reached this juncture in its history. When the Communist Party went on trial in fall 1992, the Russian people were more concerned with their economic lot. A political commentator remarked that even to dream of such a trial during the past seven decades could have led to one's arrest—but now no one cared.[30] In November 1992, the voters in neighboring Lithuania gave the Communist Party (renamed the Democratic Labor Party) a majority of the seats in parliament precisely because the nationalist and anti-Communist politicians now in power proved incapable of dealing with the economic depression gripping the country. Yeltsin's own popularity plummeted. In December 1992, parliament forced him to drop acting Prime Minister Egor Gaidar, the leading proponent of capitalism, for Victor Chernomyrdin, minister of the state oil industry under the old regime, who favored a more cautious reform program. With the economy in shambles and the empire dissolved, the euphoria of 1991 had given way to deep pessimism by the end of 1992.[31]

■ THE FRAGMENTATION OF THE SOVIET UNION

The demise of the Soviet Union had no impact on the ethnic conflicts. Four former Soviet republics—Estonia, Latvia, Lithuania, and Georgia—declared their independence outright, whereas the remaining eleven republics insisted upon full sovereignty as members of a Commonwealth of Independent States (CIS). All of the republics inherited a host of ethnic problems, exacerbated by the fact that a center no longer existed. All had claims against other nationalities that too often were based on a dubious reading of history.

Armenia and Azerbaidzhan became members of the new CIS, but their war continued. By the end of 1992, the death toll had reached approximately 2,000, mostly civilians caught in the crossfire. Moreover, the conflict threatened to draw in other nations. Muslim Turkey, with its long record of hostility toward Christian Armenians, leaned toward the Turkic-speaking Shiite Muslims of Azerbaidzhan.

The nationality problems of the former Soviet Union were the consequence of historical processes. Eastern Europe was settled over centuries by peoples moving west out of Asia, from around present-day Mongolia and the southern regions of the Himalayas. They brought with them the Finno-Ugric, Turkic, and Indo-European languages, which remained the basis of national identity. The Slavic branches of the Indo-European root include the Russian, Ukrainian, and Belarus languages. To complicate matters, peoples of different ethnic backgrounds were scattered across the Soviet empire. Armenia had the most homogeneous population, as approximately 90 percent of its citizens were Armenians. But in Latvia, 34 percent were Russian, as were 38 percent in Kazakhstan and 13 percent in Ukraine; in Moldova, 14 percent were Ukrainian and 13 percent Russian.[32]

With the end of the Soviet Union came struggles for political power in the successor states. Georgia witnessed the most serious political problems of any of the former Soviet republics. In May 1991, the anti-Communist Georgian nationalist Zviad Gamsakhurdia became the first democratically elected president of a republic of the Soviet Union; he was also the first dissident to come to power. He had worked with the Georgian Helsinki Union—a body monitoring civil rights violations—expressed admiration for Western political ideals, and translated some of the classics of the English language into Georgian. Within months, however, Gamsakhurdia began to arrest political opponents, whom he denounced—in language reminiscent of his countryman Joseph Stalin—as spies, bandits, and criminals, "enemies of the people" all. In a fit of chauvinism and paranoia, he sought to ban interracial marriages in Georgia, which the Russians had used "to dilute the Georgian race."[33] In September 1991, he declared a state of emergency. The resultant civil war between Gamsakhurdia loyalists and the renegade National Guard reached its climax at the end of the year. Two weeks of heavy fighting destroyed the center of the capital, Tbilisi, and forced Gamsakhurdia to flee. The victorious faction then turned to Eduard Shevardnadze, Gorbachev's former foreign minister and one of the architects of *perestroika,* to bring political stability to Georgia. Throughout, Yeltsin refused to be drawn into the conflict.

Yeltsin, however, was not able to ignore the civil strife in Moldova (formerly Moldavia), a republic Moscow had seized from Romania as part of the Hitler-Stalin pact of August 1939. The Slavic minority, Russians and Ukrainians, feared above all Moldova's annexation by Romania and insisted on autonomy—something Moldova's President Mircea Snegur categorically rejected. Separatist Slavs then created their own breakaway Dniester Republic on a strip of land between the left bank of the Dniester River on the west and the Ukrainian border to the east. The escalating violence drew in the previously neutral Russian Fourteenth Army, led by Gen. Alexander Lebed, on the side of the separatists. The events in Moldova underscored a problem Yeltsin could not ignore: the status of approximately 25 million ethnic Russians scattered throughout the former Soviet Union.

The most publicized ethnic issue Moscow faced, however, was its dispute with the government of Ukraine over the Black Sea fleet and the status of the Crimean peninsula. Ukraine laid claim to a portion of the Soviet Black Sea fleet, with headquarters in the Crimean port of Sevastopol. Since 1954, the Ukrainian Soviet republic had administered the Crimea, and a glance at the map gives the impression that it is a natural appendage of Ukraine. The conquest of the Crimea and the establishment of the Russian Black Sea fleet, however, were the culmination of a Russian drive to the sea of several centuries' duration. Ukraine, therefore, demanded the reversal of Russian history when its president, Leonid Kravchuk, asserted his authority over the fleet. Yeltsin responded in April 1991 by putting the fleet under Russian jurisdiction. Moreover, the majority of residents in the Crimean peninsula were ethnic Russians, who called upon Moscow to defend them against Ukrainian encroachment. In August 1992, both sides agreed to postpone the final division of the fleet for three years, keeping it in the meantime under joint Russian-Ukrainian command.

Yeltsin had frequently criticized Gorbachev for refusing to grant the Baltic states independence. When the Soviet empire broke up, however, he began to face similar problems. The Muslim Chechen-Ingush (in November 1991) along the Georgian border and the Tatars (in March 1992) along the Volga River declared their independence. The Tatars, claiming to be victims of Russian imperialism as a result of Tsar Ivan the Terrible's conquest of Kazan in 1552, held a referendum in which 61 percent voted to separate from Russia—an act the Russian Constitutional Court declared unconstitutional even before the referendum was held. In Estonia, Russians and others not of Estonian extraction, who made up 42 percent of the population, suddenly found themselves second-class citizens.

Independence from Moscow and the reclaiming of territory were but one side of the equation. An even more ominous development began to appear: a demand for "ethnic cleansing." Russians demanded the expulsion of Jews and Azeris from Moscow, Chechen-Ingush were driven out of

Volgograd, and in Stavropol attempts were made to force out Armenian families that had lived there for thirty-five years. In the Kuban, north of the Caucasus Mountains, Russian cossacks appeared in their traditional dress insisting upon the ouster of Turkish-speaking Meskhetians, in line with the demand that all non-Slavs who had settled there after January 1, 1985, be expelled.[34] The demand for racial purity and the threat of pogroms were threatening to test the strength of Russia's fledgling democratic institutions.

■ THE YELTSIN PRESIDENCY

Once in power, Yeltsin and his advisers—prodded by the United States and the IMF—introduced a radical program to privatize the Russian economy. Much of the state's property went into the hands of those who had connections to the Yeltsin government. Regional politicians began to milk state-owned properties, and managers paid themselves generous salaries. The situation was corrupt even by Soviet standards.[35] As Russia entered the global economy, many of the old enterprises were unable to compete in the international marketplace and faced bankruptcy. Russian industrial productivity eventually declined by about 50 percent. Prices were permitted to float, to be determined by the iron law of supply and demand. Those left behind found the former Soviet safety net contained increasingly larger holes as state subsidies were eliminated. The gap between the rich and the poor increased steadily. The state operated at a 20–30 percent budget deficit, necessitating the printing of more and more money to meet its obligations. The result was hyperinflation[36] and with it the drastic decline of the ruble. The life savings of many citizens were wiped out. Capitalist "shock therapy" devastated the majority of the population.

The consequence of this economic disaster was a split among the politicians who ran the successor states to the Soviet Union. Alexander Rutskoi, Yeltsin's vice-presidential running mate in 1991, favored a mixed economy and broke with Yeltsin as the former tried to slow the rush toward privatization, which he began to describe as "profiteering." He was joined by Ruslan Khasbulatov, the speaker of Russia's parliament, the Congress of People's Deputies. The result was a deadlock between the legislative and executive branches of the Russian government.

By early spring 1993, Yeltsin began to talk of dissolving the Congress and holding new elections. He argued that since the Congress had been elected in March 1990, it was an anachronism, a holdover from the Communist past; some of its members were not democratically elected and thus did not represent the Russian people.[37] The Congress countered with an attempt to impeach Yeltsin.[38] In April 1993, Yeltsin went over the head of the Congress by staging a referendum, which showed that over 50 percent of the population supported his program. But the referendum also lacked juridical consequence. Eventually, this issue was settled with violence.

On September 22, 1993, Yeltsin—already accustomed to ruling by fiat—issued Decree No. 1,400 ordering the dissolution of the Congress, even though the Constitutional Court had ordered him to obey rather than rip up the constitution. Congress refused to go quietly, and its building—the so-called White House—soon became a defiant, armed camp surrounded by concertina wire. There, armed deputies voted to impeach Yeltsin and appointed a parallel government. Yeltsin ordered the Congress to disarm. In early October, 10,000 pro-Congress demonstrators overwhelmed the police when they tried to disperse them; then, at the urging of Rutskoi and Khasbulatov, the protesters marched on the state television complex (which was heavily biased in favor of Yeltsin) in an attempt to seize it. At the same time, Rutskoi and Khasbulatov appealed to army units and the general public to join them in an insurrection. Yeltsin declared a state of emergency, and troops soon joined the fray, eventually shelling the White House—the same building that had served as a symbol of democracy and resistance to the Communists in August 1991.

In the end, Yeltsin disbanded the Congress, suspended the Constitutional Court, and banned the opposition press and television. A total of 144 Russians lay dead, and the top half of the once gleaming White House was charred by tank artillery fire. Throughout, the Western powers refused to condemn Yeltsin and continued to refer to him as a "democrat," declaring that the actions by congressional radicals had forced his hand. Still, Yeltsin's actions (as well as those in the streets) had seriously compromised the principles of legitimate government and the rule of law.

The new constitution promulgated later in 1993 gave the president a measure of power that made it possible for Yeltsin to rule virtually without the legislature. But the parliamentary elections in December 1993 produced a surprise. The Liberal Democratic Party headed by Vladimir Zhirinovsky gained a plurality of the 450 seats in the new parliament, the State Duma. This party, as its critics pointed out, was neither liberal nor democratic; instead, it was highly chauvinistic and called for the reestablishment of the Soviet Union. Zhirinovsky presented himself as the only defender of the rights of Russians and the interests of the state. His support came from former Communists and nationalists, as well as those who had not benefited from the recent changes, such as members of the military and workers in the state enterprises.

The economy continued to decline. Unemployment in 1993 was still low, around 3 percent, for no major factory had yet been permitted to go bankrupt because of the dangerous social and political consequences. But in spring 1994, unemployment began to rise considerably. Inflation destroyed the ruble. At the beginning of 1991, the rate of exchange was around 25 rubles to the dollar; by July 1994, it was nearly 4,000 rubles to the dollar.[39] One-third of the population lived below the official poverty line. Organized crime appeared to control the economy; much of the wealth came from shady deals and laundered money. The nation faced a health care crisis; males born in 1994 were estimated to have a life expectancy of fifty-seven years (nearly twenty years below that of males in the industrialized West). The incidence of suicides was up. Then came the war in Chechnya.

The war in Chechnya began at the end of 1994, when Yeltsin decided he could no longer tolerate claims of independence on the part of Chechnya, one of Russia's eighty-nine territorial subdivisions. Yeltsin had been the champion of the dissolution of the Soviet Union—primarily to bring down his rival Gorbachev—but once in power he declared there could be no more talk of a further breakup of the Russian Federation.

Chechnya is located along the northern slopes of the Caucasus Mountains, a region that contained a number of other nationalities. The Muslim Chechens had been brought officially under Russian control in the mid-nineteenth century, but it took another quarter century for the imperial Russian army to finally subdue them. During World War II, as the German army pushed into the Caucasus, a number of Chechens—acting on the time-honored principle that "the enemy of my enemy is my friend"—collaborated with the Nazi government. The Chechens paid a heavy price for doing so. Stalin meted out collective punishment and deported the Chechens in 1943–1944 (along with other ethnic groups in that region) to Central Asia and Siberia. Nikita Khrushchev permitted the Chechens to return to their ancestral home in 1957,[40] but they never forgot what the Soviet state had done to them, and at the first opportunity they declared their independence.

For three years, Yeltsin ignored the Chechen claim to independence, as it had no practical consequences. The Chechen leadership practiced a great deal of autonomy, but the situation there was only marginally different from that in other provinces of Russia. It did not help when Dzhokhar Dudayev, the leader of the Chechen rebels and a former Soviet Air Force general, reminded the Russians that the northern Caucasus is one of the great fault lines where the Christian and Muslim worlds meet. He predicted that all Muslims in the Caucasus would rebel, Siberia would also secede, and the Russian Far East would align itself with East Asia.[41]

Why Yeltsin decided to act in December 1994 is not clear. Apparently, he wanted to exercise his strength in Chechnya to divert attention from domestic woes. Moreover, the majority of his citizens considered Chechnya an inviolable part of the Russian state. But instead of quickly reasserting control, Russian troops walked into deadly ambushes set by Chechen rebels, particularly in the capital city of Grozny. The heavy-handed Russian response reduced the city to ruins. By the end of 1996, an estimated 45,000 people had died in Chechnya, and almost 2 million had become refugees.[42] The television images from Grozny reminded Russians of the utter devastation World War II had brought to cities such as Stalingrad.

In spring 1996, the time had come to try to settle the dispute, if only because it had become a liability for Yeltsin in the upcoming presidential campaign. In April, he suspended hostilities, but as soon as he was re-elected he resumed the war. The conflict quickly turned into another embarrassment for Yeltsin when the seemingly defeated rebels retook Grozny. When Russian forces proved unable to oust the Chechens, who this time were more deeply entrenched than ever, Yeltsin sent his security adviser, Alexander Lebed, to negotiate a solution. The best Lebed was able to achieve by the end of August 1996 was a five-year cease-fire during which both sides would negotiate the political future of Chechnya.

Lebed's accomplishment played to mixed reviews in Russia. Many Russians wanted to see an end to a useless war in which too many young Russian soldiers, as well as Russian civilians who lived in Grozny, had been killed. Others, particularly Lebed's political rivals, accused him of betraying the fatherland for having granted the Chechens seemingly full independence. Prime Minister Victor Chernomyrdin, speaking for the government (and presumably for the ailing President Yeltsin), proclaimed that the "territorial integrity of Russia" must not be violated.[43] It took Yeltsin more than five weeks to give his support to the agreement. The situation was not helped when at that very moment Aslan Maskhadov, the Chechen chief of staff who had signed the agreement with Lebed, flatly declared, "no Chechen has ever signed any kind of document saying that Chechnya is part of Russia and there will never be such a Chechen."[44]

■ THE 1996 PRESIDENTIAL ELECTION

Early in 1996, on the eve of the Russian presidential election, few gave Boris Yeltsin much chance of winning. Opinion polls showed that a scant 10 percent of voters planned to cast their ballots for him in the first election round in June. During Yeltsin's first term (1991–1996), economic output had fallen by 50 percent; inflation was barely under control; an unpopular and inconclusive war in Chechnya continued; unemployment and income inequality, as well as crime, had grown vastly; and money and political power appeared to be in the hands of the *nouveaux riches,* commonly known as the "mafia." Many, particularly the elderly on fixed pensions, looked back to the days when life had been more stable and secure. The Communist Party candidate, Gennadi Zyuganov, appeared the likely winner of the election. Still another reason Yeltsin was considered a long shot for reelection was his poor health; during the election campaign he suffered a severe heart attack.[45]

But in April 1996, Yeltsin overtook Zyuganov in the polls and in the end won the election by a comfortable margin. The reasons for the drastic turnabout of Yeltsin's political fortunes were many. For one, voters—even those who suffered hardships because of the new economic order—ultimately proved reluctant to place their future in the hands of a Communist who unabashedly praised Stalin and promised a return to economic policies that had been tried and had failed. Unlike the former Communist candidates in Eastern Europe who had won political office after the first round of reformers had been rejected by the voters, Zyuganov offered no new ideas; he did not even bother to change the name of his party.

But another element was at work. In the ten weeks before the election in June, Yeltsin unabashedly used the power of the incumbent to its fullest measure. He issued decrees that doubled the minimum pension—effective immediately—and compensated those who had lost their savings because of the hyperinflation of the past years. Six days before the election, the first payments were made to pensioners over age eighty. Students, teachers, war veterans, single mothers, small businesses, and the agro-industrial, military, and aviation complexes all benefited from Yeltsin's directives. He singled out one region after another for special treatment and subsidies—from the heart of Russia to the farthest reaches of the land across Siberia.

Yeltsin also tackled the pressing issue of unpaid wages ($4.9 billion), paying workers a portion of their long overdue compensation. A woman who worked for a coal mine in Vorkuta asked Yeltsin for a car and received it in a highly publicized event on national television. Yeltsin's aides blatantly handed out cash to individuals who approached him. In all, this policy cost the hard-strapped Russian treasury the astonishing sum of $11 billion.[46] The spending spree was underwritten by a new $10.2 billion loan from the IMF, which had a stake in keeping the capitalist reforms of Yeltsin on track. It was no wonder that Yeltsin's pork barrel spending binge also produced a drastic increase in the federal deficit. As soon as the election was over, however, Yeltsin's largesse quickly came to an end, and he canceled all spending commitments.[47]

The hallmark of democracy does not consist of a first, free election. The test comes when the party in power acknowledges its defeat at the polls. Yeltsin and his advisers, however, showed no intention of accepting an electoral defeat. In March 1996, when prospects for a victory were still dim, they leaned toward what they called the "forceful option." Under the pretext of a bomb threat, they would dissolve the Duma and cancel the election. But they were unsure of the loyalty of the troops in the Internal Affairs Ministry and thus put this alternative on hold. They decided instead to try the "softer option": television controlled by the government (running footage of Communist atrocities and disasters), money spent in fantastic sums to curry favor with the voters, and a president who was obviously ill kept away from the public while television commentators spoke of his "firm handshake." The Yeltsin strategy in the last days before the election consisted of getting out the vote, buying the vote, hiding the president, and scaring the population. And if this plan failed, there was still the forceful option. As one of Yeltsin's advisers bluntly declared, "If Yeltsin loses, he will not give power to the Communists. He has said that more than once."[48] Either way, Zyuganov would not win, and Yeltsin would cling to power.

During the first round of presidential elections in June 1996, neither Yeltsin nor Zyuganov obtained an absolute majority of votes. The surprising third place finisher was retired Gen. Alexander Lebed, who garnered 15 percent of the vote. In the hope of attracting Lebed voters, Yeltsin offered Lebed the post of security adviser. With that position came the power to dismiss some of Lebed's political and personal opponents, notably Minister of Defense Pavel Grachev. The forty-five-year-old ambitious Lebed had become the rising star of the Russian political firmament.

Opinion polls in September 1996 showed that the blunt-speaking Lebed was by far the most popular politician in Russia. He had brought an end to the fighting in Chechnya (although the old issue of Chechnya's status remained unresolved), he openly discussed the problems of society (particularly in the armed forces), and he appeared to be the only honest man in a den of thieves who had set up residence in the Kremlin. He also made no bones about his political ambitions to become president. When a German weekly asked him whether he saw himself as president following the next election in 2000, he replied "possibly earlier."[49]

But as long as Yeltsin was still able to wield power, Lebed had no legal or moral authority. He hovered around Yeltsin's sickbed acting as if he were the man of destiny, the Napoleon of the Russian revolution of 1991, with a mandate to save Russia. Lebed's enemies, which included most of the country's political establishment, began to sharpen their knives.

The showdown came in October 1996, after Lebed had repeatedly blamed Interior Minister Anatoly Kulikov, who headed the nation's police, for the defeat in Chechnya and demanded his ouster. Kulikov, in turn, accused Lebed of plotting a military mutiny, of a "maniacal striving for power,"[50] of "high treason," and of signing the peace accord with Chechen separatists. He then put his own forces on alert.

The next day, Yeltsin ended the dispute when he signed a decree on live television dismissing Lebed. Lebed denied that he had planned a coup, affirmed his continued support for democracy,[51] and declared his candidacy for the next presidential election.

■ THE NON-RUSSIAN SUCCESSOR STATES

The dissolution of the Soviet Union brought the hope that its successor states would emerge into democratic nations. There were a number of success stories in which diametrically opposed parties replaced each other according to the laws of democratic transition of power, including Ukraine, Estonia, Latvia, and Lithuania.

But in many instances, the road to democracy was more difficult. Much of the Caucasus and Central Asia were plagued by ethnic strife and wars for political supremacy. When elections were held, they were often conducted fraudulently. The president of Uzbekistan, Islam Karimov, for instance, was reelected in September 1996 with an approval rate of 99.6 percent—in a country that had neither freedom of speech nor freedom of the press.

Belarus was another case where things did not go according to plan. Initially, Belarus appeared well on its way to reform, but in July 1994 its voters elected a conservative, Alexander Lukashenko. It was primarily economic discontent, as well as his pledge to fight corruption, that had brought Lukashenko his victory. After three years of independence, inflation was running at a rate of 500 percent annually, the average monthly wage was $25, and the majority of citizens lived below the poverty level.

It soon became clear that Lukashenko had no taste for change. He was the only deputy in Belarus who had voted against independence and who had supported the anti-Gorbachev conspiracy in 1991. He quickly rejected any economic reform and called for a return to the not-too-distant past. Lukashenko, a former head of a state farm, saw privatization as stealing from the state and insisted on the retention of collective farming and state control of factories. Within two years, the troubled economy of Belarus had declined another 40 percent.

Lukashenko also tried to turn back the political clock. He fired the editor of the country's largest newspaper and demanded that citizens seeking to travel abroad register with the proper authorities. He called demonstrators "enemies of the people" and blamed a strike by subway workers in the capital of Minsk on the U.S. Department of State. He sought to eliminate the parliament (in which all parties opposed him) and to amend the constitution, giving him virtually unlimited powers. Belarus, he stated, should be ruled by "one strong man." (Among his heroes were Felix Dzherzhinski, the legendary founder of the Soviet secret police, and Yuri Andropov, another head of that police.) Lukashenko then attempted to reestablish the former economic, political, and military ties with Russia.[52]

RECOMMENDED READINGS

Brown, Archie. *The Gorbachev Factor.* New York: Oxford University Press, 1996.
Goldman, Marshall I. *Gorbachev's Challenge: Economic Reform in the Age of High Technology.* New York: W. W. Norton, 1987.
    A discussion of the magnitude of Gorbachev's economic problems.
Gorbachev, Mikhail. *Perestroika: New Thinking for Our Country and the World.* New York: Harper and Row, 1987.
Gorbachev, Mikhail. *The August Coup: The Truth and the Lessons.* New York: HarperCollins, 1991.
    Gorbachev's account of the coup.
Matlock, Jack F., Jr. *Autopsy of an Empire: The American Ambassador's Account of the Collapse of the Soviet Union.* New York: Random House, 1995.

Medvedev, Zhores A. *Gorbachev*. New York: W. W. Norton, 1986.
  A discussion of Gorbachev's background by a dissident Soviet historian.
Morrison, John. *Boris Yeltsin: From Bolshevik to Democrat*. New York: Dutton, 1991.
Schmidt-Häuer, Christian. *Gorbachev: The Path to Power*. Boston: Salem House, 1986.
  A Moscow-based West German journalist's account of how the party elected Gorbachev as its chief.
Smith, Graham, ed. *The Nationalities Question in the Soviet Union*. London: Longman, 1990.
  Various authors analyze the historical development and claims of twenty nationalities of the former Soviet Union.
Tarasulo, Isaac J., ed. *Gorbachev and Glasnost: Viewpoints from the Soviet Press*. Wilmington, Del.: Scholarly Resources, 1989.

NOTES

1. "On a Course of Unity and Solidarity," *Pravda*, February 21, 1985; in *Current Digest of the Soviet Press*, March 20, 1985, p. 7.

2. "In Tschernobyl 'eine glühend aktive Zone,'" *Der Spiegel*, May 19, 1986, p. 128.

3. David Remnick, "Solzhenitsyn—A New Day in the Life," *Washington Post*, January 7, 1990, p. B3.

4. B. Minonov, "Otkryvaia dver' v 'spetskhran,'" *Pravda*, September 10, 1988, p. 6.

5. Its publications dredged up, for example, the nineteenth-century Russian forgery *The Protocols of the Elder of Zion*, alleging a Jewish conspiracy.

6. "On the Agricultural Policies of the Communist Party of the Soviet Union Under Present Conditions," *Pravda*, March 16, 1989.

7. Interview with Leonid Abalkin, *Der Spiegel*, April 10, 1989, p. 191.

8. M. S. Gorbachev, "Sotsialisticheskaia ideia i revoliutsionnaia perestroika," *Pravda*, November 26, 1989, pp. 1–3.

9. The old legislature, the Supreme Soviet, which traditionally had rubber-stamped the party's decisions, became irrelevant.

10. Literally, nomenklatura means the slate of names of party officials who were accountable only to the party and often served for life.

11. In December 1989, the Congress of People's Deputies, by a vote of 1,138 to 839, voted not to put this question on the agenda.

12. Gorbachev, "Sotsialisticheskaia ideia i revoliutsionnaia perestroika."

13. Cited in Ester B. Fein, "Gorbachev Hints He Would Accept Multiparty Rule," *New York Times*, January 14, 1990, p. 1.

14. The Moldavian Republic, along the Soviet-Romanian border, suffered a fate similar to the Baltic states. It, too, was brought back into the Soviet Union by the Hitler-Stalin pact. The Moldavians, ethnically related to the Romanians, also took to the streets—without, however, demanding a return to Romania as long as the Romanian dictator Nicolae Ceausescu was alive.

15. Armenian-Azeri violence was nothing new. During previous internal upheavals in the Russian empire, as in 1905 and 1918–1920, they had also fought against each other.

16. The exact number is unknown. In fact, the Turkish government bitterly resented any mention of a massacre, denying it ever took place. It merely admitted to Turkish-Armenian violence in which both sides suffered fatalities.

17. Gorbachev decided to maintain the status quo. If he had changed the status of Nagorno-Karabakh, he would have had to consider claims from nearly all other "autonomous" republics, provinces, and regions—eighty-nine in all—all multinational in composition.

18. "The Battle Lines of the Republic," *The Economist*, September 23, 1989, p. 58.

19. Transcript of address, "Soviet Chief's Address on Azerbaidzhan Fighting," *New York Times*, December 21, 1990, p. 12.

20. Esther Schrader, "Baku Refugees Celebrate Deaths of Azerbaijanis," *Baltimore Sun*, January 23, 1990, p. 4A.

21. Jerry F. Hough, "Gorbachev's Politics," *Foreign Affairs*, Winter 1989–1990, p. 30.

22. A catchall phrase suggesting that Gorbachev's opponents on the left were the sole champions of democracy. Although a good number were genuine democrats, many were anything but that.

23. See the interrogations of the conspirators in V. A. Zatova and T. K. Speranskaia, eds., *Avgust-91* (Moscow: Politizdat, 1991), pp. 253–271.

24. From the German, a botched, illegal attempt to seize political power.

25. Leslie Gelb, "The Russian Sinkhole," *New York Times*, March 30, 1992, p. A17; Steven Greenhouse, "Point Man for the Rescue of the Century," *New York Times*, April 26, 1992, section 3, pp. 1, 6.

26. Nina Plekina, "Posle Miunkhina, v chetverg," *Novoe vremia*, no. 30 (1992), p. 24.

27. Russia sought $100 billion over four years, a sum Michel Camdessus, president of the IMF, thought was far from adequate. Greenhouse, "Point Man for the Rescue of the Century," p. 1.

28. *ABC Evening News*, August 14, 1992.

29. Gelb, "The Russian Sinkhole."

30. Aleksandr Pumpianskii, "Sud na partiei, kotoraia byla pravitel'stvo," *Novoe vremia*, no. 42 (1992), p. 5.

31. For the dark mood, see Walter Laqueur, "Russian Nationalism," *Foreign Affairs*, Winter 1992–1993, pp. 103–116; Peter Reddaway, "Russia on the Brink?" *New York Review of Books*, January 28, 1993, pp. 30–35; and Andrew Kopkind, "What Is to Be Done? From Russia with Love and Squalor," *The Nation*, January 18, 1993, pp. 44–62.

32. *Baltimore Sun*, April 28, 1991, p. 11A; based on *Europa World Yearbook*, 1989 Soviet Census, and *World Almanac*.

33. Joe Murray in an interview with Gamsakhurdia, "Outside the Stronghold," *Baltimore Sun*, October 30, 1991, p. 9A.

34. Galina Kovalskaia, "Kavkaztsam v Stavropole doraga zakazana," *Novoe vremia*, no. 28 (1992), pp. 8–9.

35. Zhores A. Medvedev, "Property Rights," *In These Times*, April 19, 1993, p. 29; Stephen F. Cohen, "American Policy and Russia's Future," *The Nation*, April 12, 1993, p. 480.

36. It was, in fact, a case of "stagflation"—that is, stagnation and inflation simultaneously.

37. Yeltsin's critics compared his argument to that of Vladimir Lenin in 1918 when he dissolved the elected Constituent Assembly. Lenin, too, had argued that the Assembly no longer represented the will of the people.

38. It took a two-thirds vote to remove Yeltsin; his opponents managed only 60 percent (617 of 1,033 deputies voted for his ouster).

39. At the end of 1996, it stood at 5,600 rubles to the dollar.

40. In his "Secret Speech" of 1956, Khrushchev listed the deportation of the Chechens as one of many crimes Stalin had committed.

41. Dudayev declared: "I know the people of the Caucasus are with us. Russian racism in the Caucasus will not go unpunished." Cited in Michael Specter, "From Mother Russia with Brute Force," *New York Times,* January 21, 1996, p. 6E.

42. The estimates of fatalities varied widely. Among the highest, 80,000, is that of Michael Specter, "The Wars of Aleksandr Ivanovich Lebed," *New York Times Magazine,* October 13, 1996, p. 44.

43. Michael R. Gordon, "Moscow Move Casts Doubt on Accord in Chechnya," *New York Times,* September 15, 1996, p. 10.

44. "Chechnya Will Never Be Part of Russia, Top Rebel Leader Says," *Baltimore Sun,* October 7, 1996, p. 7A.

45. In November 1996, Yeltsin underwent open-heart surgery.

46. David Remnick, "The War for the Kremlin," *New Yorker,* July 22, 1996, p. 49.

47. Daniel Treisman, "Why Yeltsin Won," *Foreign Affairs,* September–October 1996, pp. 64–77. This was not the first Russian election in which the pro-government parties promised the voters aid. That had also been the case in the parliamentary elections of 1993 and 1995.

48. Comment by Sergei Karaganov to Remnick, "The War for the Kremlin," p. 50.

49. Interview, "'Ordnung schaffen—sofort,'" *Spiegel,* June 24, 1996, p. 131.

50. It was no secret that Lebed sought control of Russia's "power ministries," including Kulikov's Interior Ministry and its tens of thousands of troops, as well as the troops of Russia's elite paramilitary forces.

51. Previously, Lebed had pronounced that a parliamentary democracy did not suit Russia and that he was a "half-democrat"; "Lebed lehnt parlamentarische Demokratie ab," *Süddeutsche Zeitung,* July 3, 1996, p. 1.

52. Committee on Security and Cooperation in Europe, "Report on the Belarusian Presidential Election," July 1994; Galina Koval'skaia, "Fenomen Lukashenko: Belorussia, ty tozhe odyrela?" *Novoe vremia,* no. 26 (1994), pp. 10–11.

22

Eastern Europe:
The End of the Soviet Empire

In the annals of the British empire, 1759 is known as *annus mirabilis,* the "year of miracles," when the British army—seemingly doomed to suffer certain defeat—rallied to defeat the French and thus rearranged the map of the colonial world. The changes in Eastern Europe in 1989 were no less surprising and miraculous. When the year began, all of Moscow's satellite Communist parties appeared to be firmly in its control. By year's end, however, the ring of Communist states along the Soviet Union's western borders, which Stalin had created in 1945, was no more.[1]

In 1951, Hannah Arendt declared that the Communists had found a way to stay in power forever. More recently, Jeane Kirkpatrick, who served as President Reagan's ambassador to the United Nations, restated a variation of this thesis: authoritarian governments, meaning right-wing dictatorships, were capable of reform, but totalitarian regimes, namely Communist governments, were incapable of either change or abandoning their hold on power. The events of 1989 proved them both wrong.

The events of 1989 underscored the obvious fact that the governments of Eastern Europe had little popular support. Whenever a Communist party had shown signs of being overwhelmed by its own people, Moscow had always intervened—in East Germany in June 1953, in Hungary in 1956, and in Czechoslovakia in 1968. In both 1956 and 1981, the Polish Communist Party made it clear that it could maintain control without Soviet intervention and kept Soviet troops at bay. Intervention and threats had maintained a deceptive calm.

But early in his reign, Mikhail Gorbachev announced that the Brezhnev Doctrine was dead, that no one had the right to impose his will on another people. He restated this position several times, as in his address to the United Nations in December 1988. The Communist parties in Eastern Europe now stood alone, and they had to face their people without Moscow's support.

Economic factors played a large role in the events of 1989. The economies of Eastern Europe had done tolerably well in the first decade or so of Communist rule, when large factories were organized and surplus labor from the countryside was used to run them. The test was whether the Communist system could raise productivity, absorb new technology, and produce a wider range of products. When it could not, the result was that in 1989 every East European country was much poorer compared to the West than it had been in the 1970s. For nearly twenty years, the gap between Eastern and Western Europe had been widening. According to World Bank figures, the 1987 per capita gross national product (GNP) for Poland and Hungary was 14 percent of that of either West Germany or Sweden.[2] Moreover, the Iron Curtain had long ceased to be a barrier to the flow of information. Many East Germans, for example, regularly watched West German television—via cable, no less. The steady flow of visitors from the West gave the East Europeans a clear picture of how far they had fallen behind.

■ POLAND

The dam began to crack in Poland first. The events of the early 1980s showed that the vast majority of workers had supported Solidarity. It had been Solidarity and the Roman Catholic Church that spoke for the Polish nation, not the party—the creation of Poland's archenemy, the Russian empire. In 1981, *Pravda* had made it abundantly clear that Solidarity could not replace the party as the guiding force in society in Poland. Wojciech Jaruzelski and his party had been willing to grant Solidarity numerous concessions, such as the right to strike against the state, which amounted to the de facto sharing of power between the party and Solidarity. What the party could not grant, however, was its own dissolution as Solidarity demanded. Either Jaruzelski or Leonid Brezhnev would make certain that the party would maintain its power. Jaruzelski chose the lesser of two evils when he proclaimed martial law.

Jaruzelski found out that although he could keep the party in power, he could not rule his nation without Solidarity, particularly as the economic situation continued to deteriorate. In January 1989, the party agreed to resume talks with Solidarity. The lengthy discussions led to the legalization of Solidarity in April and to elections in June 1989.

The Polish Communist Party, however, was in no mood to simply hand over power to people it had only recently jailed. It sought to retain control of the Sejm, the parliament, and with it the election of the prime minister and thereby salvage what could be salvaged. The opposition, Solidarity, would be limited to 35 percent of the seats in the parliament. Solidarity balked at this proposal. The deadlock in the negotiations was broken only after the government agreed to create an upper house, or Senate, that would be elected democratically.

EASTERN EUROPE (1995)

The promise of a free and competitive election outside the Communist Party's control sealed the fate of the party. The Senate elections on June 4, 1989, gave Solidarity 99 of the 100 contested seats and became what Poles termed "the only known crucifixion in which the victim has nailed himself to the cross."[3] Solidarity's success in the lower house would have been scarcely less impressive except that the Communists and their allies were still guaranteed a majority in that body. But the Communists miscalculated. After Solidarity's smashing victory in the Senate elections, the Peasants' Party, which over the past forty years had been little more than a front for the Communists, suddenly bolted and joined the opposition. The opposition now controlled a majority of the seats and became the government.[4] It elected Tadeusz Mazowiecki as prime minister in August 1989, the first non-Communist leader in Eastern Europe since shortly after the end of World War II. His twenty-two-member cabinet contained nine Solidarity members and four Communists.

The legislature then elected, by the margin of one vote, Jaruzelski as president, a largely ceremonial post. Solidarity engineered the election of the Communist Jaruzelski to make it clear to Moscow that Poland henceforth was a non-Communist but not an anti-Communist or anti-Soviet state. Mazowiecki flew to Moscow to assure the Soviet leaders that his non-Communist government did not plan to leave the Warsaw Pact, as the Hungarian Communist Party had attempted to do in 1956. Moreover, Solidarity would not make the mistake it had made in 1981; it refrained from any language suggesting the abolition of the Communist Party, which, in any case, was on its way to becoming irrelevant. Gorbachev had no intention of invoking the Brezhnev Doctrine; instead, he welcomed the political developments in Warsaw.

Solidarity's main responsibility became the economy, a daunting task it was hesitant to tackle. Poland's foreign debt had risen from $27 billion in 1982 to $38.5 billion in 1988, an increase of nearly 50 percent in six years. Moreover, an inflation rate of several thousand percent annually had destroyed the country's currency. The consequences were a thriving black market, the smuggling of consumer goods, and the widespread circulation of Western currencies—notably the U.S. dollar and the West German mark. Solidarity now endeavored to introduce a market economy and integrate it into the economy of the West.

Unlike 1981, when Solidarity was eager to seize power, many of its members showed little enthusiasm for doing so in 1989. In fact, after the June elections, they were willing at first to allow Gen. Czeslaw Kiszczak—the same man who, as minister of the interior, had jailed them in 1981—to form the government and, as prime minister, to sort out the economic mess. Solidarity began to understand that playing the opposition was easier than tackling an economy run aground on the shoals of central planning. But it was the Mazowiecki government that had to bite the bullet. It did so on New Year's Day 1990, when it announced that numerous subsidies to which Poland's citizens had long become accustomed no longer existed. Immediately, the price of bread rose by 38 percent and that of coal, which many used for heating, went up 600 percent. A drastic increase in gasoline and automobile insurance prices forced some Poles to turn in their license plates, as they could no longer afford to drive their prized possessions.[5] The primary movers in this drastic step were Western banks and governments, as well as the International Monetary Fund (IMF), all of which insisted that Poland must put its fiscal house in order to justify additional aid.

Poland's plan for dismantling its centralized economy was the boldest in Eastern Europe. But by summer 1991, the government began to roll back some of its free market policies to stave off a popular rebellion. It intervened to check the rising rate of unemployment by preventing state-owned factories from going bankrupt and introducing protective import tariffs on certain goods. The man in charge of economic reform, Finance Minister Leszek Balcerowicz, became a casualty of this new policy when he announced he would not seek a parliamentary seat after the October 1991 elections. Economists who had envisioned a "big bang" transformation to capitalism began to speak of an evolution taking place over ten years. Opinion polls showed that the public had as little trust in the new government as it had previously had in the Communists.

The government of the new Prime Minister Jan Olszewski, citing the high social and political cost, began to search for a middle ground between a market and a planned economy. The reforms initiated on January 1, 1990, had immediately brought hyperinflation. One of the chief aims of the government, therefore, was to bring inflation under control by refusing to print more money, thus leaving workers with sharply reduced purchasing power. In February 1992, the government backtracked when it guaranteed minimum prices for farmers and eliminated wage restrictions on state-run enterprises. This could only be accomplished, however, by printing more money and running a budget deficit—all in direct contradiction of the IMF's austerity program for Poland.[6]

Poland's problems were but a microcosm of those facing all East European economies that sought a break with the centrally planned systems of the past. The developments in Eastern Europe clashed with textbook solutions proposed by IMF officials and Western academics, who argued that economic miracles take time—that it took Germany, Japan, and Spain twenty years to turn things around. It was simply a matter of letting the invisible hand of capitalism sort things out, a matter of "getting the prices right" in a capitalist market—but this also meant rising unemployment and lower wages. Many Polish politicians and economists, however, soon began to lose faith in capitalist orthodoxy and began to look for practical models from the past.

In the 1995 elections, after an interim of six years (1989–1995), the Communists reclaimed the presidency, the executive branch, and the parliament from the reformers. Aleksander Kwásniewski, former Communist minister of youth affairs, was elected president of Poland, defeating the bitterly disappointed incumbent, Lech Walesa. The reasons for this turn of events were many, including incompetence, economic difficulties, corruption, and disillusionment. Even 60 percent of Polish entrepreneurs voted for the Communists (renamed the Social Democrats), who continued the reforms Solidarity had initiated.[7] It was now up to the Communists to defend their record.

Gorbachev had looked to the tried and tested model of Sweden, only to witness a rejection by the radicals of any and all planned socialist models. By 1992, however, in Russia and elsewhere in Eastern Europe, the revolutionary pendulum had begun to swing back to the center. East European economists began to take into account that Germany, Japan, and Spain had not relied solely on the market—that they all had comprehensive industrial policies, government intervention, and targeted protection. The economists also began to examine the examples of South Korea and Taiwan, where governments had intervened extensively and deliberately by subsidizing and protecting domestic industries until they could compete in the international market. But the question was not only what did these governments do but also what did they not do. There were, after all, many instances of failed government intervention, such as in Argentina, Brazil, India, and Pakistan. Moreover, the South Korea–Taiwan analogy posed a danger, since these countries achieved economic success under military dictatorships and thus were not auspicious models for Eastern Europe to emulate.[8]

■ HUNGARY

In Hungary, a reform wing of the Communist Party took control in 1988 and set out to complete what party chief János Kádár had put into motion—a mixed economy and tentative political reforms. In May 1988, the reformers gently nudged Kádár aside as the party leader. The party, taking a cue from Gorbachev, began to come to grips with its own recent history. The political demise of Kádár paved the way for the political, posthumous rehabilitation of his victims. For the first time since 1956, it became possible in Hungary to mention the names of Imre Nagy, Hungary's party chief at the time of the 1956 revolution, and Pal Maleter, the general who had fought the Soviet Army. They had been among those Kádár had executed and dumped face down, with their hands still tied behind their backs, in an unmarked mass grave in Budapest. Their names had disappeared from the official histories but not from the collective memory of their nation. Their rehabilitation culminated in the solemn reinternment of Nagy and his associates, a ceremony broadcast live on television throughout Hungary in June 1989.

The reform process in Hungary, similar to the one in Poland, was controlled by the party. Other political parties were legalized, and Hungarians once again began to reevaluate their place in the Warsaw Pact. They began to insist that their nation had always been part of Western, not Eastern, Europe. In September 1989, the Communist Party renamed itself the Socialist Party, and parliament rewrote the constitution to permit a multiparty election scheduled for March 25, 1990. On October 23, the thirty-third anniversary of the demonstrations that had touched off the 1956 uprising, parliament declared Hungary no longer a "People's Republic." It became the Republic of Hungary, and the red star on top of the parliament building came down. (Earlier, Lenin's statue in Budapest had been taken from its pedestal, ostensibly for repairs.) The newly renamed Socialist Party hoped to obtain 40 percent of the votes in the March 1990 election and form a coalition government and, should it fail, to go into the opposition.

The two rounds of elections, in March and April 1990, shattered whatever illusions the party still had of clinging to political power. The voters gave the Hungarian Democratic Forum, a populist nationalist umbrella organization with a right-of-center orientation, a plurality of 165 of parliament's 386 seats, and its leader, Jozsef Antall, set out to create a coalition with the conservative Independent Smallholder and Christian Democratic parties. The Socialist Party won only 33, or 8 percent, of the 386 seats. The Communist experiment in Hungary was over.

■ EAST GERMANY

In the summer of 1989, Hungarian soldiers went to work to dismantle the fortifications along Hungary's Austrian border, the first example of the physical demolition of the Iron Curtain. The Hungarian government also guaranteed its citizens the right to a passport and freedom of travel and emigration. In March 1989, the government had also signed a UN protocol on refugees, which obligated it not to force East Germans who sought to continue to travel to Austria to return home. This protocol, however, ran counter to the 1968 treaty with East Berlin, which committed Budapest to return East Germans. In August 1989, Hungary's Communist Foreign Minister Gyula Horn sided with the UN protocol and against the treaty with East Germany. Hungary would no longer prevent East Germans from leaving for the West. Hungary, officially still a Communist country, became a hemorrhaging wound that threatened to bleed Communist East Germany, which for the first time since 1961—when the Berlin Wall was put up—was losing tens of thousands of its citizens.

The Hungarian foreign minister knew he was pulling the rug out from under Erich Honecker, the party boss in East Germany, when his nation opened its borders on September 10, 1989. In three days, 12,000 East Germans had crossed into Austria.[9] Other East Germans began to leave through Czechoslovakia and Poland. Honecker's own Warsaw Pact allies had become the road by which his people abandoned what they considered a sinking ship.

Throughout much of 1989, Honecker had made it clear that he would ride out the storm. Just because a neighbor was hanging new wallpaper, he said, was no reason he should do the same. Article I of the East German constitution, which granted the party the leading political role, was written in granite. But in May 1989, after the party had rigged the results of local elections, the voices of protest grew louder. Church leaders, in particular, grew increasingly critical of the regime; they were joined by civic groups such as the New Forum. Then came the summer's exodus. But more important, the summer saw repeated demonstrations in many cities, notably in Leipzig, where increasingly larger crowds demanded change and insisted "we're staying here." Honecker promised "another Beijing" (in reference to the massacre of protesters there in June 1989) and ordered the security police, the despised and dreaded Stasi, to use "any means" to put down the "counterrevolution."

Germans from East and West "occupy" the Wall at Berlin's Brandenburg Gate to demonstrate for the opening of the Iron Curtain. (*German Information Center*)

The showdown came in Leipzig on the night of October 9, 1989, one month after Hungary had become an unimpeded escape road and one day after Gorbachev's visit to East Berlin to commemorate the fortieth anniversary of the creation of the East German republic. Gorbachev had come not to support Honecker but to say good-bye to him. He reminded the East German Politburo that a leadership that isolates itself from its people loses the right to exist. During the demonstration on October 9, the party backed down and did not use force.[10] Nine days later, the Politburo forced Honecker, who continued to insist there was no problem to resolve, to step down in favor of his protégé, Egon Krenz.

Krenz's first trip as head of the party was a visit to Moscow, where he took pains to describe himself as a disciple of Gorbachev's "new thinking." Mass protests, Krenz now insisted, were a healthy sign of change. The demonstrators, he stated, wanted "better socialism and the renovation of society." His government then lifted a one-month ban on visa-free travel to Czechoslovakia, which essentially made the Berlin Wall—and the approximately 900-mile-long German-German border—an anachronism. On November 3, East Germans were granted the right to drive through Czechoslovakia directly to the West German border. Eight thousand East German citizens went to Czechoslovakia immediately. It was an end run around the Berlin Wall.

But the demonstrations continued. On November 6, 1989, 500,000 people demonstrated in Leipzig on a cold, rainy night. There were also rallies in Dresden, Erfurt, Schwerin, Halle, Cottbus, and Karl-Marx-Stadt. The Dresden march was sanctioned by authorities and led by the mayor, Wolfgang Berghofer, and the reformist local party chief, Hans Modrow. The march was the first officially approved antigovernment demonstration in the city. What only a short time previously would have been sensational concessions by the government were no longer enough. On November 8, approximately 350 East Germans per hour crossed the border into West Germany by way of Czechoslovakia. On November 9 came the historic announcement that East Germans wishing to emigrate to the West could do so by applying for passports at local police stations. East Germans who wanted to walk into West Berlin through the checkpoints at the Berlin Wall were free to do so. The reasons for the Berlin Wall had ceased to exist.

But the logic of revolution always demands that once changes are set into motion, halfway measures are no longer enough. The main demand now was for the abolition of Article I of the constitution, which granted the party its political monopoly. The party caved in to continued public pressure and scuttled Article I on December 1, 1989. This cleared the way for free elections, originally scheduled for May 1990. Krenz had done his historic duty, but he suffered from a reputation of having once been a Honecker loyalist. His days at the top were clearly numbered, and the party turned to a reformer, the party chief of Dresden, Hans Modrow, as the nation's provisional prime minister until the elections. Gregor Gysi became the new head of the party, which for the first time played a subordinate role to the government. Still, Modrow was a party functionary, and he tried to save as much of his party's political power as possible. The situation turned tense, as people began to become weary of the continued presence of Communists at the helm of the government and of the continued existence of the Stasi. A mob in East Berlin went so far as to storm and ransack the Stasi headquarters.

The exodus continued. In early 1990, 2,000 people left daily to seek their fortunes in West Germany, where the new immigrants strained the nation's social net. Plants in East Germany found themselves depleted of workers. Modrow's provisional government proved incapable of dealing with these problems; as a result, the elections were moved up to March 1990. The demise of the Berlin Wall also put the issue of the unification of Germany on the agenda. Washington, Moscow, and the nations of Europe were bracing themselves for the inevitable.

■ GERMAN REUNIFICATION

After the creation of the West German government in May 1949 and that of East Germany in October 1949, the division of Germany took on an aura of permanence. Officially, however, the West German government always considered the issue open. It treated Germany as whole, claimed to speak for all Germans, and automatically granted citizenship to any East German who made it across the border. West Germany considered the borders of the two Germanies, as well as its own existence, to be provisional. Officially, it did not even have a constitution, merely a temporary "basic law." Bonn was the provisional capital city of a provisional state; the true political heart of Germany was Berlin, which, for the time being, remained under the control of the victors of World War II. Lastly, according to the official West German position, the nation had been divided not merely into two but into three parts; there was still the issue of Silesia, Pomerania, and East Prussia—under Polish and Soviet "administration" since 1945.

When West German Chancellor Helmut Kohl began to speak of unification in November 1989, Moscow declared that just because East Germans had been granted unrestricted access to West Germany, this did not indicate the automatic unification of the two Germanies. Kohl's statements received a similar cool reception in the West. The wartime allies and Europeans generally did not relish the recreation of a strong and unified Germany in the heart of the continent. Such an eventuality dredged up unpleasant memories of Germany's past.

The question remained of the eastern border of a unified state. Officially, the war was not over because Germany had never signed a peace treaty accepting the loss of territory to Poland and the Soviet Union. Bonn had never officially accepted the border between East Germany and Poland, the Oder-Neisse Line. Legally, the Third Reich's territories as of December 31, 1937, still existed. With the emergence during the late 1980s of the new conservative West German Republican Party, which spoke openly of regaining the lost regions, many in West Germany and the rest of Europe wanted to know the future territorial, political, and economic composition—and ambitions—of a unified Germany.[11]

The sudden German reunification and the drastic changes in Eastern Europe had a number of consequences. With the disappearance of the threat from the east, the need for the U.S. presence in Western Europe declined. The Europeans, particularly the suddenly more powerful Germans, were able to pursue their own goals without having to take into account U.S. wishes. The unification of Germany in October 1990 and the decision to move the capital from Bonn to Berlin was taken by the West German government without much consultation with its allies, who were not enthusiastic about this development. Germany did, however, calm the fears of its neighbors, particularly Poland, when it officially accepted the borders the victors of World War II had drawn up and, concomitantly, the loss of East Prussia and the lands beyond the Oder and Neisse rivers. At the same time, Germany rediscovered Eastern Europe as its traditional sphere of influence. While the Bush administration was trying to make up its mind over what to do, Germany moved quickly, providing massive sums of money to prop up the crumbling East European economies. By September 1991, it had provided over $50 billion in assistance—32 percent of all Western aid to Eastern Europe and 56 percent of all Western aid to the Soviet Union.[12]

Once German unification had taken place, many Germans expressed a widely held—and correct—view that "we are once again somebody." The first symbolic act was the 1990 reinternment in Potsdam, outside Berlin, of the remains of Frederick the Great, a symbol of past German greatness. With the decline of the Russian empire, Germany became the most powerful nation in Europe and was ready to initiate action outside the European Community (EC) and the North Atlantic Treaty Organization (NATO), particularly in the East. Immediately after the failed coup in Moscow in August 1991, Germany took the lead in recognizing the independence of the Baltic states. In Yugoslavia, Germany broke ranks with the EC and the United States when it recognized the breakaway republics of Slovenia and Croatia and convinced its reluctant partners to do the same. During the Gulf War, Germany sent troops abroad for the first time since 1945, an air squadron to Turkey in case the war embroiled Germany's NATO partner. In summer 1992, the German navy showed its flag in the Adriatic Sea off the coast of Yugoslavia to help the United Nations enforce its embargo against Serbia, an action the government did not even deem worth discussing in the parliament.

The early 1990s also witnessed the beginning of the restoration of the German language as the lingua franca of Eastern Europe. The Goethe Institute—the cultural arm of the German Foreign Office and the champion of German language and culture abroad—established new branches in Moscow, Kiev, Riga, Krakow, and Bratislava and made plans for Minsk, St. Petersburg, and even Alma Ata, the capital of Kazakhstan near the border with China. In June 1992, a German-Russian university was founded in Samara on the banks of the Volga River, the former center of a large German community established there in 1764–1774, during the reign of Catherine the Great.[13]

German aid to Eastern Europe had more than an economic component. It was also designed to prevent the dreaded consequences of a collapse of the East European economies—a flood of refugees westward. The government was already grappling with the unpopular fact that approximately 10 percent (6 million of 61 million) of West Germany's population consisted of foreigners. Some were political refugees, but most were foreign workers, nearly half of whom had lived in Germany for at least fifteen years.[14] As residents, they were entitled to social services from a government whose resources were stretched to the limits because of the expense of German unification, aid to Eastern Europe, and a lingering recession. The result was an antiforeign backlash, particularly demonstrations in 1992 that saw 2,000 assaults—including a number of fatalities—against Turks, black Africans, and Jews.[15] The attackers were generally young males who unabashedly and openly proclaimed themselves neo-Nazis. By the end of 1992, the euphoria and promise of German reunification had given way to bitterness, violence, and economic stagnation.

After unification, nearly all physical traces of the Berlin Wall were immediately erased. But the psychological gulf between the *Ossis* (Easterners) and the *Wessis* (Westerners) remained. The *Ossis* had lived since 1933 under two consecutive dictatorships, first the Nazis and then the Communists. Their past experience was different from that of the *Wessis*. Many recoiled from the open democratic political discourse. Unification also meant the East German economic enterprises were thrown into a marketplace in which they had no chance of surviving. West German businesses appeared determined to show the superiority of their economic system, and they quickly destroyed their Eastern competitors. Economic progress under capitalism came slowly, despite the infusion of massive sums from the West German government to reconstruct the Eastern states. These sums were raised largely through higher taxes in the cash-strapped West.

The euphoria of unification did not last long. *Ossi* resentment of being swallowed up by their more powerful, arrogant Western cousins, already evident in 1990, became more and more pronounced. A German poll taken nearly six years after unification showed that 89 percent of the *Ossis* felt life had gotten worse, and only 1 percent thought it had improved. Among the *Wessis*, 91 percent thought the government had spent either the right amount or too much on the *Ossis*, whereas 84 percent of the *Ossis* thought they were neglected. The infusion of Western capital was not enough to prevent the stretching of the once tight East German social safety net. In the East, *Wessihass* (hatred of Westerners) became fashionable, and *Wessis* spoke contemptuously of the *Jammerossis* (whining Easterners).[16]

■ CZECHOSLOVAKIA

The fourth Communist domino to fall in 1989 was Czechoslovakia, a nation ruled by men who had been put into power by Brezhnev's tanks after the crushing of the Prague Spring in August 1968. With the demise of the hard-liners in East Berlin, it became clear to the ruling Communist Party that its days were numbered. As in East Germany, the party could not rely on Soviet intervention to prop it up.

The revolutionary vanguard against the old Communist regime was made up of intellectuals and students. As long as the crowds remained relatively small—2,000 in January 1989 and still only 10,000 at the beginning of November 1989—the police were able to maintain a measure of order through arrests and occasional beatings. The workers were slow to join, mainly because they enjoyed a relatively high standard of living—something the party had concentrated its attention on since 1968. When the workers joined the demonstrators on St. Wenceslas Square in Prague, however, the end had arrived for the Communist regime. It folded like a house of cards at the end of November 1989.

In the center of the opposition stood Charta 77, a loose union of 1,600 individuals who in 1977 had signed a petition demanding civil rights. Their spokespersons were Jiri Hajek, the country's foreign minister during the Prague Spring, and the writer Vaclav Havel. Other opposition groups emerged in 1989. Since June of that year, a petition demanding the release of all political prisoners, freedom of expression and assembly, and an independent news media had circulated throughout the nation, and 40,000 citizens had signed it.

The events in Czechoslovakia followed the script written in East Germany. Demonstrations and arrests were the order of the day until it finally became apparent that nearly the entire nation stood in opposition to the rulers. As in East Germany, it became clear that not even a bloodbath could save the old order. Once the party agreed to abandon its ruling monopoly on November 29, 1989, however, events in Czechoslovakia moved much more quickly and in a different direction. Havel and others took immediate steps to ensure a transformation to a new government without allowing the Communist Party a continued, or even a temporary and provisional, hold on power—as in the case of East Germany and, later, Romania.

The party, they insisted, no longer had the right to govern the nation. Backed by crowds of 200,000 demonstrators, they demanded—and obtained—a provisional government dominated by the opposition until the voters could choose the country's first freely elected government since 1948.

Havel, who earlier in the year had been arrested and jailed for antistate activities,[17] became the new prime minister as the representative of the new Civic Forum movement. Alexander Dubček, one of the architects of the Prague Spring, became the country's new president. The formation of the new Czechoslovak government set that nation apart from East Germany and Romania, where demonstrators wondered whether the Communist parties were, in fact, willing to abandon their hold on political power.

At a Warsaw Pact meeting in December 1989, the five participants in the 1968 invasion of Czechoslovakia—the Soviet Union, East Germany, Poland, Hungary, and Bulgaria—formally declared that the invasion had been "illegal" and pledged strict noninterference in each other's internal affairs in the future. This declaration marked the formal repudiation of the Brezhnev Doctrine. The Soviet government issued a separate statement admitting that the reasons for intervention had been "unfounded" and that its decision to do so had been "erroneous."[18]

After Egon Krenz became the head of the East German Communist Party, his first official state visit was the traditional call on Moscow. Havel, however, in a pointed reminder that Czechoslovakia was a part of Central, not Eastern, Europe, went to Berlin—both East and West—and then to Warsaw. "It's not good-bye to Moscow," a foreign ministry official explained, "but it's a new orientation toward West and Central Europe."[19] Havel then set out to negotiate the withdrawal of Soviet troops from Czechoslovakia.

The Czechoslovak "velvet revolution" immediately faced a host of problems. The economy was privatized with a measure of success. This came as little surprise, since before World War II the country had a flourishing private and national industrial and commercial base. The political picture, however, was more troublesome. Not only did Havel soon lose his majority in parliament, which ended his short career as prime minister, but he also found himself overseeing the breakup of Czechoslovakia.

In summer 1992, militant Slovaks in the eastern part of the country decided to form an independent state. Czechoslovakia had come into existence in 1918 as a federation of Czechs and Slovaks under the leadership of the Czech Thomas Masaryk. From the outset, Slovaks resented Czech domination, particularly the fact that they never received the autonomy the Czechs had promised. The nation finally split over the definition of autonomy when Slovak Premier Vladimir Meciar rejected the formula of his Czech counterpart, Vaclav Klaus.

The call for Slovak autonomy began in 1990 with the demand by nationalists that the Slovak language be recognized as the only official language in Slovakia. This measure was directed not so much against Czechs (since Czech and Slovak are mutually comprehensible) but against minorities—who made up 20 percent of the 5 million inhabitants of Slovakia—such as the reviled 570,000-strong Hungarians. At this point, Czechoslovakia's history intruded in the debate. In 1939, Hitler had taken advantage of friction between Czechs and Slovaks by creating a separate fascist Slovak puppet state under Josef Tiso, a Catholic priest, whose government participated in the deportation of Slovak Jews to Nazi death camps. In 1990, extreme nationalists tried to rehabilitate the memory of Tiso, a "hero of the Slovak nation," whom the Czechs had hanged in 1947 as a war criminal.[20]

Moreover, after Meciar threw his lot in with the nationalists, his government took on an increasingly dictatorial character. He built a new security apparatus using former Communist secret police agents; cracked down on the press, radio, and television; and fired government officials and replaced them with his people. The breakup, which became official on New Year's Day 1993, added to the economic woes of what had once been Czechoslovakia. The new state of Slovakia especially, with its weak industrial base and unemployment rate of 12 percent, found it difficult to compete in the European market.[21]

■ BULGARIA

Next in line was Bulgaria, the most loyal member of the Warsaw Pact. The seventy-eight-year-old boss of the Communist Party, Todor Zhivkov, in power since 1954, showed no signs of stepping down. But his rule, particularly in the last few years, had bred widespread opposition. He was responsible for reviving the ancient quarrel between Bulgarians and Turks in 1984 when he forced the 1-million-strong Muslim Turkish minority to adopt Slavic names. In May 1989, he encouraged approximately 310,000 Turks to emigrate. By doing so, not only did he damage Bulgaria's international standing, but the exodus also wrought havoc with the nation's economy. When Zhivkov promoted his son to the Central Committee's Department of Culture in 1989, even his old allies deserted him. In the end, Defense Minister Dobri Dzurov, Foreign Minister Petar Mladenov, and Prime Minister Andrei Lukanov forced a meeting of the Politburo and demanded the resignation of Zhivkov.

The charges against Zhivkov consisted of corruption, nepotism, and the ruination of the economy. But since Zhivkov's once loyal lieutenants had deposed him, the question was whether any meaningful changes had taken place. The new leadership promised radical changes: economic reform plus *glasnost*. But to the increasingly larger crowds of demonstrators, Mladenov, the new party chief, had not addressed the central issue—the party's monopoly on power. Five days before Zhivkov fell, 4,000 members of a green movement, called *ecoglasnost,* staged a demonstration in the capital city of Sofia and gave notice that Bulgarians had become aware of the trends in neighboring countries. In subsequent weeks, as the crowds grew larger and more defiant, it became clear that the overthrow of Zhivkov was too little and too late.

On January 15, 1990, Mladenov and his party caved in to popular pressure and announced the concession Communist parties in Warsaw, Budapest, East Berlin, and Prague had granted: the party agreed to give up its leading political role and hold free elections. In September 1992, after an eighteen-month trial, the now eighty-one-year-old Zhivkov was found guilty of economic crimes—including the embezzlement of nearly $1 million—and sentenced to seven years in prison. Zhivkov hereby became the first former Soviet bloc leader to be judged by a post-Communist court.

■ ROMANIA

The last and least likely of the Communist dictators to be toppled in 1989 was Nicolae Ceauşescu, who had come to power in 1965. Ceauşescu soon began to carve out a foreign policy independent of Moscow but without leaving the Warsaw Pact. He became known as the maverick in the Warsaw Pact, as he reserved Romania's right not to participate in the pact's annual war games, continued to recognize Israel after the 1967 Six Day War, and refused to participate in the invasion of Czechoslovakia in 1968. In 1984, he refused to join the Moscow-led boycott of the Olympic Games in Los Angeles, where the Romanian team received a standing ovation at the opening ceremonies. The West rewarded Romania with most-favored-nation treatment, and U.S. Presidents Richard Nixon and Jimmy Carter paid highly publicized visits to Bucharest, where they spared no words in heaping praise on Ceauşescu.

The West ignored the fact that the Ceauşescu regime was by far the most repressive in the Warsaw Pact and that he governed with his police force, the dreaded *securitate*. His position appeared secure. In fact, Ceauşescu was able to achieve what few strongmen dared contemplate: he decided that his country must pay off its foreign debt, never mind the economic consequences of his austerity program for the Romanian people. The result was a sharp drop in the standard of living. Large amounts of food were exported, the work week consisted of six days, the price of gasoline was raised, apartments were kept at about 50 degrees Fahrenheit in the winter, electricity was strictly rationed, and hospitals were unable to purchase medicines from the West. The 24 million people of Romania, an agrarian land, were reduced to a meager diet. Pigs' feet, commonly known as "patriots," remained in abundance; they were the only parts of the pig that stayed behind when the rest was exported.

Ceauşescu's style was a combination of that of Stalin and that of the fascist Benito Mussolini of Italy. He dropped the label "comrade" and began to call himself the *conducator,* the leader. Unlike the other leaders of Communist parties installed by the Soviet Union after World War II, Ceauşescu ruled not through his party but, similar to Stalin, through the police. The party existed merely to legitimize Ceauşescu's rule. The most prominent feature of Romanian television was the glorification of Ceauşescu and his wife, Elena, the nation's second-most-powerful figure. Their son, Nicu, was groomed to follow in his father's footsteps. Forty other relatives were on the government payroll. Ceauşescu made it clear that he intended to follow his own course and that he would defy the changes taking place in the Soviet Union and elsewhere in Eastern Europe.

In January 1989, as the Polish Communist Party initiated a dialogue with the opposition, Ceauşescu—who in 1968 had refused to participate in the Warsaw Pact's invasion of Czechoslovakia—now urged that the Warsaw Pact put an end to the dangerous political experiment in Warsaw. In June 1989, he sent a congratulatory message to Deng Xiaoping for crushing the Chinese student demonstrations. He made it clear that he would use force to deal with his dissidents should they take to the streets. In a nation where no more than three people were allowed to gather outdoors without government approval, the prospects for street demonstrations seemed slight. As one party official explained the Ceauşescu system: "All the systems of the world are based on reward and punishment. Ceauşescu works only with punishment. It is a reward that there is no punishment."[22]

When the foreign debt had been largely repaid, the conditions in Romania did not change. Ceauşescu continued to bleed his people when he initiated a massive building program designed to eradicate many of the symbols of Romania's past and replace them with monuments to the megalomania of the *conducator.* Fifteen thousand workers erected the thirteen-story, 1,000-room House of the Republic, made of white marble, on the Avenue of Socialist Victory. To make room for this palace, between 40,000 and 50,000 people were moved, and many historic buildings were destroyed—among them the sixteenth-century Monastery of Michael the Brave, the ruler who in 1600 had unified Wallachia, Moldavia, and Transylvania into modern Romania. Ceauşescu personally supervised the project, visiting it two or three times a week. Among Ceauşescu's other projects was the razing of entire towns, many inhabited by ethnic Germans and Hungarians in Transylvania. Germans, whose ancestors had built the towns 700 years before, left for West Germany, and Hungarians fled across the border into Hungary. Ceauşescu went so far as to begin to build his own iron curtain to seal off Communist Hungary, but he eventually abandoned this project.

The city of Timisoara, in Transylvania, lit the spark that brought down the seemingly impregnable Ceauşescu dictatorship. In early December

1989, the government decided to deport from Timisoara a little-known Hungarian Protestant priest, Laszlo Tokes. The decision touched off demonstrations, forcing the government to reconsider. The concession was a victory of sorts for the people in the streets and produced an even greater demonstration on December 16. Economic considerations also played a part. In October 1989, additional food items had been rationed without a guarantee that the scarce items could be found in the stores—this in a city that contained the largest pork-processing plant in central Europe, as well as bread bakeries and other food-processing plants. Workers who knew nothing of Tokes but who handled the food destined for export joined the ranks of the demonstrators.

The fall of the Communist parties in Poland, Hungary, East Germany, Czechoslovakia, and Bulgaria took place without a single fatality; Romania was destined to be different. Ceauşescu, who had made it clear he would follow the Chinese example, sent the *securitate* into Timisoara to gun down the demonstrators. The *conducator,* the "hero of the nation, the brilliant son of the people," began murdering his own people.[23] The uprising might have been contained by the police, had it not continued the practice of refusing to return the bodies of those killed, such as those shot to death while trying to escape into Hungary. The dead of Timisoara were dumped into a mass grave on the outskirts of the city. "Give us our dead," the demonstrators demanded.

Ceauşescu lost control of Timisoara but vowed in a public speech to win the war against the "terrorists and hooligans" of that city. That speech—before what appeared to be a traditionally docile crowd assembled by the authorities—became a disaster, as it turned into an anti-Ceauşescu demonstration. Ceauşescu never finished the speech and fled the presidential palace. At that point, Ceauşescu also lost control of the army. He had never trusted the armed forces, for good reason. After initially firing into the crowd, soldiers turned their guns on the police. Ceauşescu and his wife attempted to flee, only to be captured.

The new provisional government was headed by Ion Iliescu. Iliescu, Gorbachev's classmate in Moscow in the 1950s and party boss in Timisoara in the late 1960s, had become popular with many party members for speaking out against Ceauşescu's economic measures. (Gorbachev had done his part for the revolution during his visit to Bucharest in 1987, when he spoke out against nepotism and called for reform.)

The Ceauşescus were put before a military tribunal and charged with genocide, the murder of 60,000 Romanian citizens, theft, and the creation of Swiss bank accounts. Elena Ceauşescus termed the last accusation a "provocation." The unrepentant *conducator* denied all charges and claimed still to be the leader of his nation. A firing squad ended the discussion on Christmas Day 1989. Romanian television showed a tape of the trial and the elegantly dressed corpses of the Ceauşescus.

On the surface, the new government followed the precedents established in other East European countries. It declared that Romania was no longer a socialist state, stocked the stores with food, reduced the work week to five days, cut the price of electricity by more than half, permitted each farm family an acre of land for private cultivation, abolished the death penalty after the Ceauşescus' execution, abolished the *securitate,* and promised free elections for April 1990. The government also arrested Ceauşescu's closest associates, including the entire Politburo and ranking officers of the *securitate,* promising punishment for "all evildoers from the old regime."

What took place in Romania, however, was neither a political nor a social revolution. The Ceauşescus were executed by their own henchmen, among them Iliescu and First Deputy Defense Minister Victor Stanculescu, who now tried to save their own necks. Their aim was to eliminate the dictator but not the dictatorship. The "red aristocrats," as the Romanian nomenklatura was known, then made sure to stress the myth of a political revolution.[24]

The conspirators produced the trappings of parliamentary democracy yet continued Ceauşescuism without Ceauşescu. Their task was facilitated by the fact that Romania never had known a modern party system, a responsible political intelligentsia, or an autonomous church. Romania's political culture was steeped in intrigue, conspiracy, and subservience to authority. If Romania were to undergo a political transformation, the demise of Ceauşescu was but the first act.

Six months after the death of Ceauşescu, the political "red-brown" fusion[25] was complete when the Marxist Iliescu, following in the footsteps of Ceauşescu, found solace in fascism. He announced the formation of a National Guard—reminiscent of the Iron Guard of the 1930s that had brought the dictator Gen. Ion Antonescu to power in 1940—and proceeded to arrest opposition leaders, insisting all along that he was defending democracy.[26] The Romanian road to democracy promised to be long and hard.

■ ALBANIA

The Communist state of Albania, the creation of Enver Hoxha in 1944, became the next casualty. Hoxha's regime, a fusion of the worst features of Stalinism and Maoism, was perhaps even more oppressive than that of Ceauşescu. Poverty-stricken and isolated, Albania was the world's only official atheist state. Defendants were often executed without trials or simply disappeared, and their relatives were also punished for good measure. After Hoxha's death in April 1985, Ramiz Alia continued his policies. After 1989, however, Alia introduced reforms to an increasingly restless population. He rescinded, for example, the "crime" of religious propaganda and granted free elections, which ended Communist rule in March 1992. But the reforms came too late; they were unable to save either Alia or his party. In September 1992, he was put under house arrest to be tried for stealing state property.

* * *

As 1989, the year of popular uprisings, gave way to 1990, the year of elections, the mood in Eastern Europe changed. Euphoria gave way to apprehension about the future. All states faced serious problems. Whatever democratic institutions had come into being after World War I had been destroyed by indigenous strongmen (Poland, Hungary, Bulgaria, Romania) and then by Hitler (Germany, Czechoslovakia) and Stalin. These leaders had done nothing to teach lessons of political tolerance. The demonstrators in the streets demanded rights for themselves; the quality of East European democracy, however, depended on how they reacted to the rights of others.

■ YUGOSLAVIA

The most serious ethnic problems existed in Yugoslavia, a nation with eight major ethnic regions—Slovenia, Croatia, Bosnia-Herzegovina, Macedonia, Montenegro, Kosovo, Vojvodina, and Serbia. After World War II, the Croat Joseph Tito sought to establish a federation in which no one people would dominate another, particularly not the numerically and historically dominant Serbs. After Tito's death in 1980, the new Communist Party leader, the Serb Slobodan Milosević, however, overturned Tito's handiwork in the early 1980s when he stripped the Albanian majority in Kosovo Province of their autonomy. In summer 1989, Milosević added fuel to the fire when he led a massive Serbian demonstration of 1 million people into Kosovo to commemorate the 600th anniversary of a battle in which the Muslim Turks (and Muslim Albanians) had defeated the Christian Orthodox Serbs. The demonstration turned the ancient Serbs' defeat into a triumphant victory and called for the restoration of a Greater Serbia at the expense of its enemies.

Milosević gave notice by his action that he rejected the Yugoslav federation Tito had put together. Tito had understood the potential danger ethnic strife posed for Yugoslavia—literally "South Slavia," an artificial creation formed in 1918 after the collapse of Ottoman Turkish control of the Balkan peninsula. For that reason, the 1974 constitution granted the nationalities a measure of autonomy. The Serbian nationality, because of its great size, remained first among equals but an equal nevertheless. After Tito's death in 1980, however, Milosević began to pursue the dream of a greater Serbia dominating the other nationalities.

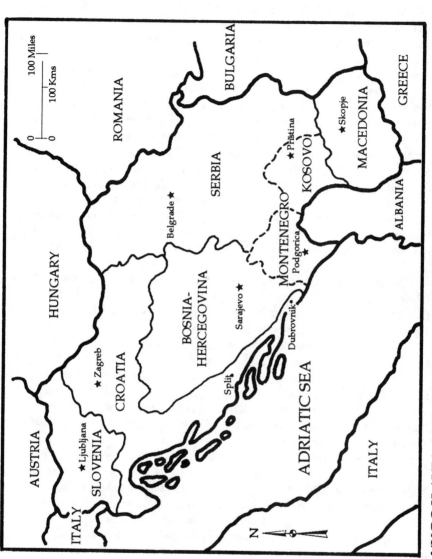

YUGOSLAVIA AND ITS SUCCESSOR STATES
(Serbia, Montenegro, and Kosovo consitute what remains of Yugoslavia as of 1997)

Although most of the citizens of Yugoslavia were of Slavic origin, there were serious divisions among them. For one, their historical experiences differed. Slovenes and Croats in the west had fallen under the influence of Roman Catholicism, whereas the Slavs further to the east, such as Serbs and Macedonians, belonged to the Eastern Orthodox Church. The country, moreover, contained a sizable Muslim population, such as the Albanians and Bosnians—the legacy of centuries of Turkish control. To complicate matters, the diverse population was interspersed. Yugoslavia was thus a fusion of Western and Eastern Christianity and Islam. It was little wonder that the Balkan peninsula was known as the "powder keg of Europe."

Assertive Serbian nationalism produced a fearful reaction from other nationalities in Yugoslavia. Taking a cue from the independence movements in the Soviet Union, they began to demand their own independence. The 1990 multiparty elections showed that political affiliation primarily followed ethnic lines, and the elections brought nationalists to power. The nationalists then took steps to declare the independence of their respective republics.

The first to do so, in June 1991, was Slovenia—with a population of 2 million—in Yugoslavia's northwestern corner. At the same time, the larger (4.8 million people) and more powerful Republic of Croatia also seceded. These events triggered a bloody conflict (the first on the European continent since 1945) when the Serbian-dominated Yugoslav army invaded Croatia. Milosević sought at a minimum to regain what he considered ethnic Serbian territory. That was the reason for the destruction of Vukovar, a city of 45,000 inhabitants (43 percent Croat and 37 percent Serbian) along the Danube River. In November 1991, after months of heavy fighting, Serbian forces "liberated" the city, which was now in ruins, its Croat population largely driven out.

At this point, the United Nations intervened. Cyrus Vance, the former U.S. secretary of state, acting in the capacity of special UN envoy to Yugoslavia on behalf of the new UN Secretary-General Boutros Boutros-Ghali, brokered a cease-fire that took effect in January 1992. Blue-helmeted UN troops—14,400 from thirty-one nations (including 900 Russians)—became the first such deployment on the European continent. But unlike the Korean and Gulf wars, the troops did not have a combat role; they merely served to keep the belligerents apart. Germany became the first nation officially to recognize Slovenia and Croatia in January 1992, and the other members of the European Community followed suit. The United States continued to hold out hope that a united Yugoslavia could somehow remain a viable option. But in April 1992, the Bush administration came into line with the EC when it simultaneously recognized Slovenia, Croatia, and Bosnia.

The violence between Serbs and Croats was not merely over territory; it was also fueled by the memory of World War II. Between 1941 and

1945, Yugoslavia—more than any other nation involved in the war—witnessed a bloody, almost genocidal civil war. That war pitted pro-Hitler Croat fascists—the *Ustashi*—against the Serbian, monarchist—*Chetnik*—resistance led by Draza Mihailović. (The winner in this civil war was a third force, Tito's Communists, who defeated both the *Ustashi* and the *Chetniks*.) When the fighting began in July 1991, it again became a battle between *Ustashi* and *Chetniks*—both sides decked out in their historical garb, flags, and religious symbols.[27] Under these conditions, atrocities against civilians soon became the norm.

In March 1992, the freely elected leaders of Bosnia-Herzegovina declared the republic's independence. The ethnic makeup of Bosnia was the most complex of all the Yugoslav republics—92 percent of its people were of Slavic origin, but 44 percent were Muslim, 31 percent were Serbian and Orthodox, and 17 percent were Catholic Croats.[28] Milosević, stymied in Croatia, turned against Bosnia ostensibly to protect the threatened Serb minority. Milosević's Yugoslav forces provided weapons for Serbian militia forces and proceeded to lay siege to the capital of Bosnia, Sarajevo. The siege lasted more than 1,000 days, one of the longest in history. For good measure, Croat forces joined the fray in an unholy alliance with Serbia to dismember Bosnia on the very day the United Nations managed to enforce the cease-fire that kept the two groups apart in Croatia. This cooperation at the expense of Bosnia did not, however, prevent Serbs and Croats from killing each other in Bosnia. The United Nations extended its peacekeeping forces to Sarajevo but they had no impact, as again they had no combat role.

The conflict in Bosnia became a war of extraordinary brutality. Serbs established concentration camps and undertook the "ethnic cleansing" of parts of Bosnia—that is, torturing, massacring, and forcibly deporting civilians in freight cars. These actions were reminiscent of crimes last committed in Europe by Stalin and Hitler. Serbian perpetrators were well aware that they faced potential charges as war criminals, and for that reason some wore masks to prevent identification. The violence in Yugoslavia produced a flood of refugees, approximately 2.5 million by the end of 1992—the first on such a massive scale in Europe since 1945.

What had once been Yugoslavia was reduced in 1992 to five separate entities: a rump state of Yugoslavia (consisting of Serbia and the once autonomous provinces of Kosovo and Vojvodina and the Republic of Montenegro), Slovenia, Croatia, Bosnia, and Macedonia. The Serbian chauvinist Milosević became the destroyer not only of Yugoslavia as a political entity but also of its cities and villages, its economy, its currency (inflation ran at 25,000 percent per year, which rendered the Yugoslav dinar worthless), and its people. As recently as 1989, many Europeans had exulted in the spiritual rebirth of the continent. Yet in 1992, the EC, the United Nations, and the United States all were reluctant to deal with Serbian chauvinism and Milosević, who represented the worst aspects of European history.

The Muslims in Bosnia were able to obtain little help from the outside world because of a UN embargo on weapons coming into the former Yugoslavia. The Bosnian Serbs, however, obtained large quantities of weapons from their kinsmen in Serbia proper, led by Milosević—the man primarily responsible for the violence. The Serbs in Bosnia, led by their president, Radovan Karadžić, and the commander of the Serb forces, Gen. Radko Mladić, proclaimed the establishment of a Serbian Republic. As the Serbs attacked from the east, Croat forces sent by President Franjo Tudjman drove into Bosnia from the west.

The Serbs and Croats were driven by their peculiar interpretation of the past. The homicidal Mladić saw himself as the vindicator of Serbian history. To him, there was hardly a difference between the past and the present; the violence of the 1990s was part of the continuum of Serbian history. Serbs were again fighting to save Europe from an Islamic tide, as well as from a German state once more seeking the conquest of the Balkans. But this time, Serbia's enemies were assisted by another imperial power, the United States.[29] Tudjman's reading of history was little different. His aim was to divide up all of Muslim Bosnia between Croatia and the Serbs. Bosnian President Alija Izetbegović was "an Algerian and a [Muslim] fundamentalist," whereas at least Milosević was "one of us"—meaning he was a Christian.[30] The history of Mladić and Tudjman produced a straight line to "ethnic cleansing" and a program of exterminating unwanted peoples—that is, genocide.

It became increasingly difficult for the United Nations and NATO to stand by idly as the evidence of atrocities, particularly by Serbs, began to mount. In February 1994, as Serbs made gains in eastern Bosnia, the United Nations declared several regions there to be "safe areas" and threatened NATO air strikes to maintain them. But when NATO carried out its first air strikes on Serb forces near Goražde in April 1994, the Bosnian Serbs responded with their own attacks on the "safe areas." In 1995, the Serbs seized 270 UN peacekeepers and shackled them to potential bombing targets. French Gen. Bernard Janvier, whose troops made up more than one-half of the hostages, arranged for their release with Mladić, but the price was a halt of air attacks on the Serbs. The deal left the United Nations powerless, and the 40,000 Bosnian Muslims in Srebrenića—officially still under UN protection—were now defenseless. The result was genocide.[31]

As early as spring and early summer 1992, the U.S. government had evidence that the Serbs were conducting widespread massacres of Muslims. The government knew conclusively that in the northern town of Brčko, Serbs had herded 3,000 Muslim men into an abandoned warehouse and tortured and killed them. U.S. satellites had recorded a part of the slaughter. The United States had even intercepted telephone conversations in which Mladić made it clear that he also intended to cleanse Goražde and

Žepa.[32] The fall of Srebrenića in July 1995 was accompanied by yet another massacre, this one of between 6,000 and 8,000 Muslim men and boys. This time, Madeleine Albright, the U.S. ambassador to the United Nations, revealed photographs of fresh graves taken from U-2 spy planes. According to eyewitnesses, Mladić had been present at the killings at Srebrenića.

In May 1993, the UN Security Council established an "International Criminal Tribunal for the Former Yugoslavia," the first international war crimes proceedings since the Nuremberg and Tokyo war crimes trials after World War II. In May 1996, a young Croat, Drazen Erdemović, who had fought for the Serbs, became the first person to plead guilty of war crimes—confessing he had murdered scores of unarmed Muslim men at Srebrenića. His defense was that he had been ordered by the Serbs to participate in the killings; fearing for his life, he had only obeyed orders. At that time, the United Nations had a scant seven low-ranking individuals in custody out of a total of fifty-seven indicted suspects—among them forty-six Serbs, eight Croats, and three Muslims.[33] Mladić and Karadžić, still popular among the Serbs, remained at large—mainly because the United Nations, NATO, and the United States showed no inclination to go after them so as not to endanger the lives of their forces.

At the end of summer 1995, the tide turned against the Serbs when Croatian forces retook the Kraijina (a region in southeastern Croatia) from the Serbs, sending more than 170,000 Serbs fleeing in fear. After this Serb defeat, in October 1995 the three warring sides—by now thoroughly exhausted—agreed to a cease-fire and to hold talks in the United States.

Bosnian Muslims hoped a settlement of the conflict would not recognize the partition of Bosnia and the consequences of "ethnic cleansing." "Bosnia is the place to draw the line against ultranationalism on the march," a Bosnian journalist pleaded. "Appeasement of Serbian conquests and ethnic partition of Bosnia would encourage such forces."[34] But his plea was to no avail. The Dayton agreement of November 1995 divided Bosnia between a Serbian-controlled region and the Bosnian Federation (of Croats and Muslims) by a ratio of forty-nine to fifty-one, respectively. In essence, the split rewarded Serb aggression, although the agreement did not grant Karadžić's Serbian Republic official recognition. A small NATO force was left behind to monitor a precarious cease-fire.

Officially, Bosnia remained a single country but one divided into two republics. As of June 1996, 1,319,250 Bosnian refugees had made their way to European nations that did not want them. They were unable to return to their former domicile, however, which—as likely as not—had been "ethnically cleansed." Yet, if the refugees resettled in other regions, it would ratify the "cleansing" and mock the West's attempt to recreate a multiethnic state.[35]

There were still scores to be settled. Muslims in Bosnia remained bitter that the world had done little to protect them, and Serbs in the Kraijina, who had been put to flight, dreamed of retribution. An English reporter noted that Serb women, after running from a gauntlet of rocks hurled by a mob of Croats, had picked up some of the same rocks. When he asked the reason, one woman offered this vision of the future: "Lost things should be returned to their owners. I am going to send this back one day."[36]

RECOMMENDED READINGS

Ash, Timothy Garton. *The Magic Lantern: The Revolution of '89 Witnessed in Warsaw, Budapest, Berlin and Prague.* New York: Vintage, 1993.
An eyewitness account by a British journalist whose specialty is Eastern Europe.
Balcerowicz, Leszek. *Socialism, Capitalism, Transformation.* New York: Oxford University Press, 1996.
By the former Polish finance minister who introduced the changes from socialism to capitalism.
Behr, Edward. *Kiss the Hand You Cannot Bite: The Rise and Fall of the Ceauşescus.* New York: Villard Books, 1991.
Political biography that focuses on the deep social and cultural roots of the dictatorship. The final chapters point out that Ceauşescu's overthrow was the result of a palace coup rather than a popular revolution.
Clemens, Walter C., Jr. *Baltic Independence and Russian Empire.* New York: St. Martin's, 1991.
Djilas, Aleksa. *The Contested Country: Yugoslav Unity and Communist Revolution, 1919–1953.* Cambridge, Mass.: Harvard University Press, 1993.
An analysis of why Tito's concept of a unified Yugoslavia eventually failed.
Gati, Charles. *The Bloc That Failed: Soviet–East European Relations in Transition.* Bloomington: Indiana University Press, 1990.
Brief history of the Soviet bloc in Eastern Europe, with the emphasis on the impact of Gorbachev's reforms.
Goldman, Minton F. *Revolution and Change in Central and Eastern Europe: Political, Economic, and Social Changes.* Armonk, N.Y.: M. E. Sharpe, 1996.
Stokes, Gail. *From Stalinism to Pluralism: A Documentary History of Eastern Europe Since 1945.* New York: Oxford University Press, 1996.

NOTES

1. The Communist parties of Yugoslavia and Albania had come to power on their own in the wake of World War II; they were not Stalin's creation.

2. World Bank, *World Development Report, 1989* (Washington, D.C.: World Bank, 1989), p. 165.

3. "A Survey of Eastern Europe," *The Economist,* August 12, 1989, p. 10.

4. The Peasants' Party, with 76 seats, and Solidarity, with 161 seats, controlled over half of the 460 seats in the Sejm. Communists controlled 173 seats, the Christian parties 23, and the Democrats 27.

5. Craig Whitney, "East Europe Joins the Market and Gets a Preview of the Pain," *New York Times,* January 7, 1990, p. E3.

6. Stephen Engelberg, "Polish Economic About-Face Draws Criticism," *New York Times,* February 21, 1992, p. A8.

7. Radek Sikorski, "How We Lost Poland: Heroes Do Not Make Good Politicians," *Foreign Affairs,* September–October 1996, pp. 15–22.

8. Lawrence Wechsler, "A Reporter at Large: Deficit," *New Yorker,* May 11, 1992, pp. 70–73.

9. Previously in 1989, 77,000 East Germans had left for West Germany, three-quarters of them legally; "Goodbye to Berlin," *The Economist,* September 16, 1989, pp. 49–50.

10. Honecker apparently ordered the use of force against the 50,000–70,000 demonstrators, but it was never used. Who countermanded Honecker remains unclear. It may have been Egon Krenz, Honecker's protégé and the youngest member of the Politburo, or, as former West German Chancellor Willy Brandt believed, the Soviet military commanders; Jackson Diehl, "Leipzig's Leaders Prevent a Bloodbath," *Washington Post,* January 14, 1990, p. A36.

11. The Republican Party's chief, Franz Schönhuber, a former member of the Waffen-SS, declared in his autobiography that he was proud to have participated in Hitler's campaigns. His party's appeal rested on its opposition to foreigners in West Germany; moreover, the color of the Republican Party was brown, which dredged up the memory of Hitler's brownshirts.

12. "Kohl Stresses Need for 'Fair International Burden-Sharing' in Berkeley Speech," *The Week in Germany,* September 13, 1991, p. 2.

13. The Russian government also agreed to permit the Germans in Russia to reestablish their Volga Republic; see "German-Russian University Founded; Second Volga Republic to Be Established," *The Week in Germany,* July 24, 1992, p. 6; "Goethe-Institut schliessen 30 Bibliotheken," *Deutschland Nachrichten,* June 12, 1992, pp. 6–7; "Sprechen Sie Deutsch? More Employers Look for German Speakers," *The Week in Germany,* July 31, 1992, p. 6.

14. "Six Million Foreigners Make Their Home in Germany," *The Week in Germany,* July 17, 1992, p. 6.

15. Many of these foreigners were ethnic Germans who returned to Germany, at times after an absence of two centuries, from the east—from Romania, Poland, and the Soviet Union. The young, in particular, knew no German. The government granted them citizenship, but the public tended to view them as foreigners, as "Russians" or "Poles."

16. EMNID poll, "Divided Still," *The Economist,* November 9, 1996, p. 6.

17. In January 1989, Havel was arrested for participating in a ceremony in memory of Jan Palach, a young student who had set fire to himself in January 1969 to protest Brezhnev's invasion. One year later, in January 1990, Havel participated as the nation's chief of state in the ceremony honoring Palach.

18. For the statements, *New York Times,* December 5, 1989, p. A15.

19. Diana Jean Schemo, "Soviet Troops to Leave Czech Soil," *Baltimore Sun,* January 6, 1990, p. 2A.

20. Henry Kamm, "Language Bill Weighed as Slovak Separatists Rally," *New York Times,* October 25, 1990, p. A15.

21. Peter S. Green, "Slovaks Becoming Worried About Idea of an Independent State," *Baltimore Sun,* July 29, 1992, p. 6A.

22. Cited in William Pfaff, "Change in a Vulnerable Land," *Baltimore Sun,* December 22, 1989, p. 17A.

23. How many died remains unclear. The death toll in Timisoara probably ran into several hundreds, not the 4,500 initially reported. Mary Battiata, "State's Violence Sparked Rebellion," *Washington Post,* December 31, 1989, p. A1.

24. Edward Behr, *Kiss the Hand You Cannot Bite: The Rise and Fall of the Ceauşescus* (New York: Villard Books, 1991), chapter 13, pp. 251–268. Behr cites

a Romanian proverb: "A change of rulers is the joy of fools." Also, Antonia Rados, *Die Verschwörung der Securitate: Rumäniens verratene Revolution* (Hamburg: Hoffmann und Campe, 1990); Bartholomäus Grill, "Revolution der Funktionäre," *Die Zeit,* January 11, 1991, p. 30.

25. "Red" is the color of Communism; "brown" is that of German fascism, such as Hitler's "brownshirts." A similar "red-brown" bloc of Communists and racists challenged the Yeltsin government in Moscow; Leonid Vasilev, "Vlast vtorogo prizyva," *Novoe vremia,* no. 30 (1992), pp. 11–13.

26. William Pfaff, "Romania Moves Forward to the Past," *Baltimore Sun,* June 21, 1990, p. 11A; AP, "Iliescu Inaugurated with Pledge to Defend Democracy," *Baltimore Sun,* June 21, 1990, p. 4A.

27. Dusko Doder, "History Repeating Itself in Rebirth of Serbian Guerrillas, Nationalism," *Baltimore Sun,* July 15, 1991, p. 5A.

28. Helsinki Commission on Security and Cooperation in Europe, *The Referendum on Independence in Bosnia-Hercegovina,* February 29–March 1, 1992 (Washington, D.C.: U.S. Government Printing Office, 1992), p. 3.

29. Robert Block, "The Madness of General Mladic," *New York Review,* October 5, 1995, pp. 7–9.

30. Cited in Thomas L. Friedman, "Whose Balkan Menu?" *New York Times,* September 27, 1995, p. A23.

31. Newsday, "French General's Deal Ensured Massacre in Bosnia," *Baltimore Sun,* May 30, 1996, p. 18A.

32. Charles Lane and Thom Shanker, "Bosnia: What the CIA Didn't Tell Us," *New York Review,* May 9, 1996, pp. 10–15.

33. Commission on Security and Cooperation in Europe, "Prosecuting War Crimes in the Former Yugoslavia: An Update," *CSCE Digest,* May 1996, pp. 13, 21–27.

34. Kemal Kurspahić, former editor-in-chief of the Sarajevo daily, *Oslobodjenije,* " . . . And Don't Divide Bosnia," *Washington Post,* September 8, 1995, p. A25.

35. Provided by the United Nations High Commissioner for Refugees, "Doors Slam," *The Economist,* September 28, 1996, p. 64.

36. Cited in Patrick Bishop, *Daily Telegraph,* August 11, 1995, p. 10.

23

The Nuclear Arms Race

The Cold War of the 1950s and early 1960s produced an unchecked nuclear arms race. Throughout, the United States took the lead despite the campaign rhetoric of bomber and missile gaps favoring the Soviet Union. Presidential candidate John F. Kennedy's charge against the Eisenhower administration that it had been asleep at the helm and had permitted the Soviets to forge ahead in the missile race was laid to rest shortly after Kennedy's election when the Pentagon announced in 1961 a U.S. second-strike capability more powerful than a potential Soviet first-strike. This cold, cruel fact of the arms race, and the Soviet humiliation during the Cuban missile crisis the following year, put two items on the Kremlin's agenda: the closing of the gap favoring the United States and subsequent negotiations with Washington that acknowledged nuclear parity between the great powers.

The immediate consequence of the Cuban missile crisis, however, was a gradual improvement in East-West relations, for both sides had faced the moment of truth when they looked down the nuclear gun barrel. Détente of the 1960s and the early 1970s produced a number of agreements between the Soviet Union and the United States to limit the nuclear arms race. The first significant agreement between the nuclear powers was a direct consequence of the nuclear showdown. It produced the partial nuclear test ban treaty of 1963, one that prohibited nuclear testing in the atmosphere, in outer space, and on the high seas. The United States and the Soviet Union then took their nuclear weapons tests underground, thus limiting environmental contamination. More than a hundred nations signed the treaty. Notable exceptions were France (already a nuclear power) and Communist China (soon to become one when it exploded an atomic bomb in 1964).

Other agreements soon followed. They included the Outer Space Treaty (1967), which banned nuclear weapons in space and earth orbit; the Nuclear Non-Proliferation Treaty (1968), by which the Soviet Union, the United States, Great Britain, and eighty-three other nations pledged to prevent the spread of nuclear weapons and technology; the Seabed Pact (1971), which prohibited nuclear arms on the ocean floors beyond a nation's twelve-mile limit; and the Biological Warfare Treaty (1972), which outlawed the development, production, and stockpiling of biological weapons.

■ THE SALT TREATIES

Nonetheless, the superpowers continued to add to their nuclear arsenals by developing and testing new weapons and adding warheads. Toward the end of the decade, the governments of the United States and the Soviet Union, seeing the need for renewed efforts to control the open-ended arms race, initiated the Strategic Arms Limitation Talks (SALT). The purpose of these talks was to limit—and eventually abolish—a costly and potentially deadly nuclear arms race. When the talks began during the late 1960s, both sides had more than enough to destroy the other side many times over. Unrestrained stockpiling of nuclear weapons had become an obsession, and the SALT talks were meant to bring an element of control and rationality to the arms race.

President Richard Nixon and Communist Party chief Leonid Brezhnev signed the first SALT agreement in Moscow in May 1972. Its aim was a modest one, a limit on the deployment of "strategic weapons." Strategic weapons consist of nuclear warheads launched from one's territory and from submarines against the enemy's territory. They include the intercontinental bomber forces, intercontinental ballistic missiles (ICBMs), and submarine-launched ballistic missiles (SLBMs). SALT I, however, was a limited agreement that did not put a dent in anyone's nuclear arsenal. It merely put a ceiling on the destructive power each side possessed. But it marked a beginning of a process of mutual consultation on a pressing question. The negotiators expressed the hope that later treaties would address the more difficult problem of reducing nuclear arsenals.

SALT I froze the existing number of land-based missiles, the ICBMs, leaving the Soviet Union with an advantage in ICBMs: 1,398 to 1,052. The Nixon administration, to appease its domestic critics, argued that the agreement had prevented the buildup of the Soviet arsenal of SS-9s.[1] Moreover, the treaty offered the United States several advantages. It ignored the questions of intercontinental bombers (in which the United States always enjoyed a marked superiority), intermediate-range missiles in Europe (which became a major issue during the arms reduction talks of the early 1980s), and the French and British arsenals. In each instance, the United States and its NATO allies had a decided advantage. The Soviets also accepted, if only for the time being, a U.S. advantage in the number of strategic warheads, a category in which the United States led by a ratio of two to one.

But the treaty did not address the question of limiting MIRVed missiles, a U.S. invention, where the United States held a large, if only temporary, lead. MIRV is short for "multiple independently-targeted reentry vehicle," a missile capable of carrying several warheads, each with the ability of finding a different target. In other words, the missile—the expensive component—carries a number of warheads—the less expensive components. During the SALT I negotiations the United States had refused to discuss the Soviet proposal of banning MIRVed missiles, because the United States saw no reason to give away what at the time was the most sophisticated nuclear weapon either side possessed. U.S. negotiators soon had reasons to regret their decision, however.

SALT I was not expected to halt the arms race. For one, the treaty did not prevent the improvement in the quality of weapons, which continued to become increasingly more sophisticated. The emphasis on limiting launchers (bombers, missiles, submarines) was beginning to make less and less sense, since launchers, particularly missiles, were beginning to carry more and more warheads. And it is the warheads that do the damage. By the mid-1970s, the Soviet Union had begun to deploy its own MIRVed missiles. By then, MIRVed missile technology had begun to work to the Soviet Union's advantage because the Soviet missiles were larger and more powerful than the U.S. ICBMs and thus capable of carrying up to thirty warheads. The U.S. Minuteman III missile, in contrast, carried but three warheads. SALT II, which the negotiators hammered out by 1979, attempted, therefore, to limit not only launchers but also the number of warheads. This was done by placing a ceiling on missiles that could be MIRVed.

In June 1979, after years of difficult negotiations, Brezhnev and President Jimmy Carter met in Vienna to sign SALT II. The treaty placed a ceiling of 2,400 missile launchers for each side, of which only 1,320 could be fitted with MIRVs. The agreement also limited the number of warheads in an ICBM to ten. SALT II thus put a cap on the Soviet Union's strategic strength, its land-based ICBMs. But it also left the Soviet Union with a five-to-two advantage in ICBM-launched warheads. U.S. advocates of the treaty argued that the gap in this category would have been much wider had it not been for the treaty, which, after all, limited Moscow's arsenal. The treaty also left Washington with a decided advantage in other categories, particularly in SLBMs.

The signing ceremony proved to be the last act of détente. By that time a climate of mutual suspicion had already set in. U.S. critics of negotiations with the Soviet Union were becoming increasingly vocal. They pointed out that the Soviet Union could not have it both ways. It could not have peaceful relations with the West accompanied by increased trade with Western Europe and the United States and arms limitations agreements, and at the same time support revolutionary movements in Africa and Asia.

Détente, they insisted, must be tied to improved Soviet behavior, especially abroad. The international climate worsened when, in November 1979, the Iranian hostage crisis began, for which some even blamed the Soviet Union, followed in December by the Soviet intervention in Afghanistan. Soviet actions (and the U.S. political reactions) drove the last nail into the coffin of détente. And with the end of détente, arms negotiators could point to no progress during the first half of the 1980s.

Even more important than Soviet behavior abroad was the charge that détente and the SALT treaties had made it possible for the Soviet Union to pass the United States in the arms race. The most vocal critic of détente by 1980 was the Republican presidential hopeful, Ronald Reagan, who declared that the SALT treaties had opened a "window of vulnerability" and that only one side, the Soviet Union, was engaged in the arms race. The United States, he declared, had in effect disarmed unilaterally. As a political argument, Reagan got considerable mileage out of it. But, in fact, during the decade of the 1970s, the United States had doubled its strategic arsenal. By the time of the presidential election year of 1980, the Soviet Union had closed the wide gap, but the United States continued to lead in the arms race. It was never a race with one contestant.

Détente thus became a casualty of the renewed Cold War. Détente had already been in trouble, but the events of 1979 finished it off. The U.S. Senate never ratified SALT II, in part because critics such as Reagan had hammered home the point that it was advantageous to the Soviet Union. Once Reagan became president, however, he gave tacit recognition to the fact that the treaty had after all put a limit on the Soviet Union's strategic strength, a fact the Joint Chiefs of Staff had acknowledged when they urged the treaty's ratification, calling it "a modest but useful step."[2] President Reagan agreed, therefore, to abide by the unratified terms of SALT II for the next five years.

■ THE CORRELATION OF FORCES

A discussion of the number and types of nuclear weapons generally focused on numbers. But it became clear that one could not readily prove that one side or the other was "ahead" in the arms race merely by counting. What criteria did one use to determine who was ahead? What did one count? How did the weapons compare? What were the needs of the two sides? The geographic considerations? The nature of the threat each faced? The questions that may be raised are many.

The Soviet Union relied largely on powerful land-based ICBMs, equipped with up to ten warheads. U.S. missiles were smaller and contained smaller, but more accurate warheads. Which type is preferable? Which is more deadly? The Soviet Union, because its missiles were less

GLOSSARY

ABM Anti-Ballistic Missile; a defensive missile to destroy incoming enemy missiles

ASAT Anti-Satellite Missile; a missile to neutralize satellites in earth orbit; a central component of Star Wars

CSCE Conference on Security and Cooperation in Europe

ICBM Intercontinental Ballistic Missile

INF Intermediate-Range Nuclear Forces; see "theater weapons" below

IRBM Intermediate-Range Ballistic Missile (such as the Pershing II and the SS-20)

MIRV Multiple Independently-targeted Reentry Vehicle; a missile carrying several smaller missiles, each capable of reaching a different target

payload destructive power of a warhead; measured in *megatonnage* (1 megaton equals 1 million tons of TNT; a kiloton is the equivalent of 1,000 tons of TNT); a bomb with an explosive force of about 12 kilotons destroyed Hiroshima, where at least 70,000 died; in the 1970s, U.S. strategic warheads carried an average payload of more than 4 megatons, or more than 300 times the destructive power of the bomb dropped on Hiroshima; the warheads of the Soviet Union were even larger

SALT Strategic Arms Limitations Talks; the emphasis is on *strategic* and *limitations*

SDI Strategic Defense Initiative; the official name of Star Wars

SLBM Submarine-Launched Ballistic Missile

START Strategic Arms Reduction Talks; the emphasis is on *reduction* rather than *limitation*

strategic weapons weapons capable of delivering warheads over long distances (usually over 3,000 miles); they include intercontinental missiles, bombers, and submarine-launched missiles

tactical weapons short-range nuclear battlefield weapons (such as artillery shells)

theater weapons intermediate-range weapons for use in a specific global region, or theater (such as Europe or the Far East); also known as INF

warhead a nuclear bomb

accurate, relied on the larger missiles and thus enjoyed an advantage in the category known as "payload," also known as "megatonnage." (One megaton is equal to 1 million tons of TNT.) As missiles became increasingly more accurate, both sides reduced their megatonnage. The United States, because of its more precise missiles, did not need to build large warheads. Thus, if one focused on the payload category, then the Soviet Union was ahead in the arms race; but if one took into account missile accuracy, then the advantage went to the United States.

During the first half of the 1980s, there was no progress toward nuclear disarmament; instead, both sides produced more and more improved nuclear weapons at a furious pace. In December 1981, the Soviet Union walked out of arms reduction talks in Geneva when it failed to halt the deployment of U.S. intermediate-range missiles, the Pershing II and cruise missiles. The talks were not resumed until March 1985. During the intervening forty months, both sides added approximately a warhead a day to their strategic arsenals—and this did not take into account intermediate-range nuclear weapons, which both sides continued to deploy. In all, during the first half of the 1980s, each side added more than 2,000 strategic warheads to its already bloated arsenal.

The configuration of strategic forces, approximately equal in numbers, was not identical, however. The Soviet Union put most of its eggs into one basket: 65 percent of its nuclear warheads were in land-based missiles; 27 percent in submarines; and a scant 8 percent (an amount sufficient to destroy the United States, however) in intercontinental bombers.

In contrast, the United States had a more balanced strategic arsenal, a "triad" of three components. The strongest leg was the submarine-based nuclear deterrent, with 51 percent of its warheads in submarines; 27 percent in the air force's intercontinental bomber force; and only 19 percent in land-based missiles. As such, the United States had the more sensible balance. Should the Soviets have knocked out one of the triad's legs, U.S. retaliatory power still would have been more than enough to provide a credible second-strike deterrent. And unlike those of the Soviets, most U.S. warheads were not in stationary missiles on land, whose location was all too well known to the spy satellites in orbit, but were instead constantly in motion in the oceans of the world.[3]

All of this caused a problem in determining an equitable formula in the attempt to limit the arms race. The Soviet Union, with its massive land-based force, was not about to sit down to negotiate solely a reduction in its strength, its land-based missiles.[4] But this is also where the Soviet Union was most vulnerable. Its missiles in the ground were inviting targets. These missiles, powerful and deadly once launched, were nevertheless slow to fire, for they were propelled by a liquid fuel. U.S. missiles, in contrast, could be fired virtually at will, for they contained a solid-fuel propellant. For this reason, the Soviet Union moved toward the deployment of a smaller, mobile, solid-fuel intercontinental ballistic missile. Such a mobile ICBM promised to add new elements to the arms race—an increasing difficulty in verification and the ability to effect a quicker response.

By the end of 1985, the strategic balance of terror stood approximately as shown in Table 23.1.[5] Various studies over the previous three decades had concluded that between 200 and 300 warheads could destroy the Soviet Union. An equal number could mean the ruination of the United States. The strategic arsenal both sides had was thus of a fantastic dimension. "Overkill," the ability to destroy the enemy several times over, however, became institutionalized—and thus rationalized. And there was, of course, a cold logic behind it all if one sought security in sheer numbers—in which case, neither side could ever have enough. In the mid-1980s, the United States possessed the capability of destroying the Soviet Union fifty times with its strategic arsenal alone. It was little wonder that U.S. strategic planners ran out of targets. The surfeit of atomic warheads made possible the luxury of targeting grain elevators in Ukraine and open fields Soviet bombers could conceivably use on their return trips from the United States.[6] And the Soviet Union's ability to destroy the United States was no different. The pointlessness of continuously adding to one's nuclear arsenal led Henry Kissinger to ask in 1974: "What in the name of God is strategic superiority? . . . What do you do with it?"[7]

The Europeans, and the Soviets in particular, with their record of suffering and defeat, had a better understanding than most in the United States that history is all too often tragedy. The destruction wreaked by World War II, a conventional war fought with primitive weapons by

Table 23.1 U.S. and Soviet Strategic Arsenal, 1985

Weapon Carrier	Number of Warheads	Percentage of Strategic Arsenal
United States		
1,025 ICBMs	2,125	19
36 submarines with 640 missiles	5,728	51
263 B-52 bombers, 98 of which carry		
12 cruise missiles each	3,072	27
61 FB-111 bombers	366	3
Total	11,291	100
Soviet Union		
1,398 ICBMs	6,420	65
62 submarines with 924 missiles	2,688	27
173 bombers, 25 of which carry		
10 cruise missiles each	792	8
Total	9,900	100

Source: New York Times, October 4, 1985.

today's standards, was still a recent memory. Berlin, Stalingrad, and many other cities still contained the ruins, now displayed as memorials and museum pieces, of that war. The persistence of attempts to negotiate if only a limitation to the arms race was mute tribute to the uncomfortable fact that a nuclear war could not have winners. The ruins of the Soviet Union and Germany in 1945 did not reveal which country had won the war and which had lost.

■ INTERMEDIATE-RANGE WEAPONS

The late 1970s saw the end of détente and the beginning of what some have called Cold War II. The reasons for the deterioration of relations between the Soviet Union and the West were many and were the responsibility of both sides. One factor, however, was the lack of understanding by the Soviets of the U.S. definition of détente. Détente, in the U.S. mind, was always linked to a change in Soviet behavior. To the Soviets, however, it meant Western acceptance of the Soviet Union as a major power, an equal of the United States—and with it an acceptance of the global role that a great power traditionally plays. After all, they argued, the Soviet Union and the United States had normalized their relations at a time when the United States was engaged in pursuing its global interests in a war against "international Communism" in Vietnam. But from the U.S. viewpoint, Soviet good behavior, particularly in Afghanistan, was a precondition to maintaining détente. The Soviet Union countered by arguing that, for them, détente had been more important than Vietnam—but, for the United States, Afghanistan was more important than détente.[8] With détente at an end, the arms race began to take ominous twists and turns. The introduction of a new and increasingly more sophisticated generation of intermediate-range nuclear weapons added to the complexity of the debate on how to limit these weapons.

The strategic arsenal, originally the sole line of deterrent, was joined by shorter-range weapons whose purpose was to determine the outcome in a particular theater of war, such as the European or Pacific theater. From the early 1960s, both sides accumulated an extraordinarily destructive arsenal of these intermediate-range nuclear arms. Military strategists saw Europe as the most likely stage where such weapons might be employed. There, the Soviets put into place their most sophisticated medium-range missiles—the mobile SS-20s—capable of devastating all of Europe.

The SS-20 was a significant improvement over the older single-warhead, liquid-fuel SS-4s and SS-5s. It had a range of over 3,000 miles, was mobile, contained three independently targeted warheads, and was a solid-fuel missile that could be fired with a minimum of delay. This new addition to the Kremlin's military might produced a psychological shock among the West's military strategists. The SS-20 did not change the nuclear balance of terror, but it did give the appearance of a Soviet escalation of the arms race, a perception that was largely correct.

The United States responded, predictably, with its own enhanced intermediate-range weapons in Europe, the Tomahawk cruise missile and the Pershing II. The cruise missile hugged the ground on its approach and was therefore difficult to detect. It was a slow-moving projectile with a range of 2,000 miles and thus capable of reaching the Soviet Union from West European soil. The Pershing II was a fast-flying missile with a range of over 1,100 miles. Its mobility, range, accuracy, and speed made it one of the premier weapons in the U.S. arsenal. It was a potential first-strike weapon suitable for the elimination or "decapitation" of the Soviet command structures. The distinction between "strategic" and "theater" missiles became increasingly blurred. What was the difference between a Minuteman missile fired from Wyoming (thirty minutes flying time to a Soviet target) and a Pershing II missile fired from West Germany (six minutes flying time)?

For the Soviet Union this round in the arms race was filled with contradictions and irony, something all participants in this dangerous game experienced. The United States was first to witness this strange twist of logic. The atomic bomb had given the United States the "ultimate weapon," only to subject the country to the prospect of nuclear annihilation within ten short years. Similarly, the SS-20 briefly gave the Kremlin a decided advantage in case of a nuclear exchange in Europe—provided the contest could be limited to Europe, in itself a most unlikely prospect. Within a few years, however, the United States countered with the deployment of increasingly more dangerous weapons. The result was that the Soviet Union became less secure.

To be effective, U.S. intermediate-range missiles had to be stationed on European soil. Presidents Carter and Reagan had their work cut out in selling their deployment to their NATO allies. The Europeans understood all too well that both the Soviet and the U.S. arsenal threatened to turn Europe into a nuclear shooting gallery—particularly after President Reagan said, "I could see where you could have the exchange of tactical weapons in the field [in Europe] without it bringing either one of the major powers to pushing the button."[9] The upshot was a split in the NATO alliance. Still, the United States was able to convince its European allies to accept 464 cruise and 108 Pershing II missiles, for a total of 572.[10]

This round of escalation produced a series of ill-fated discussions at Geneva beginning in the spring of 1981. The negotiating postures of both sides were the essence of simplicity. Each sought to eliminate the other side's missiles and at the same time hold on to what it had. It was a prescription for a deadlock. Negotiators, instead seeking compromises, played to larger audiences, notably the people back home and the nervous Europeans. Propaganda and accusations of bad faith became the order of the day.

The two chief negotiators, Yuli Kvitsinsky for the Soviet Union and Paul Nitze for the United States, did manage at one point to agree on a compromise formula, their so-called "walk in the woods" proposal. It called for a rough balance between the Soviet Union's seventy-five SS-20s (each carrying three warheads) and the United States's seventy-five Tomahawk cruise launchers (each with four warheads). By this agreement, the Soviets would have had to curtail, but not scrap, the deployment of their SS-20s, while the United States would have had to forgo the deployment of its deadly Pershing IIs. Hard-liners in Moscow and Washington quickly denounced this attempt at a compromise. In December 1981, the Soviets left the conference table when the United States proceeded to deploy on schedule the first cruise and Pershing II missiles in Great Britain and West Germany, respectively. The deadlock lasted three and a half years, while missile deployment accelerated.

In April 1985, about one month after the Soviet and U.S. negotiators had resumed their talks in Geneva, the new Soviet leader, Mikhail Gorbachev, announced a freeze on further deployment of SS-20s until November 1985, provided the United States halted the deployment of its missiles. Yet, there was nothing in Gorbachev's proposal suggesting a reduction of the Soviet arsenal—whose deployment was largely completed. The Soviet gesture was too little and too late. Instead of facing seventy-five slow-moving cruise missiles, as proposed in the "walk in the woods," the Soviets now faced fifty-four of the deadly Pershing IIs and forty-eight cruise missiles, with the prospect of more to come. And Western Europe faced 250 of the Soviet Union's 414 SS-20s.

■ STAR WARS: THE STRATEGIC DEFENSE INITIATIVE

In March 1983, the arms race took another twist when President Reagan went public with a military research program long on the drawing board. It was a missile defense system officially called the Strategic Defense Initiative (SDI), but commonly known as Star Wars. Its purpose was to develop the means to offer U.S. land-based missiles a measure of protection in case of a nuclear war with the Soviet Union, particularly in the event that the Soviet Union struck first with its powerful and accurate land-based missiles, notably the SS-18s. With this pronouncement, Reagan officially committed the United States to the creation of a brand new, futuristic defense against Soviet ICBMs. The research program was now no longer a scientific quest for a hypothetical defensive weapon. Instead, the government of the United States fully committed its resources to finding a technological breakthrough to neutralize hostile projectiles.

Thus far, the prevention of nuclear war had been based on deterrence, a balance of terror, that is, on the assumption that neither side wanted to commit suicide. It was a strategy known as Mutually Assured Destruction, better known by its acronym, MAD. And in fact, this balance of terror kept the peace. The Soviet Union and the United States became hostages of the nuclear arsenals pointed at them.

In the late 1960s, the Soviets entertained the idea of a defensive shield of their own, which, however, was unacceptable to the United States. U.S. officials pointed out that such an action would only invite similar measures by the United States, as well as an increase in the number of U.S. warheads. The result would be an escalation of the arms race, one that promised no security for anyone. The United States prevailed upon the Soviet Union to abandon its missile defense program. The resultant accord, the Anti-Ballistic Missile (ABM) treaty between the United States and the Soviet Union (1972), permitted both sides to create two limited defensive systems each, which neither bothered to develop fully. The agreement put an end to the prospect of a new element in the nuclear arms race—the building of anti-missile defenses only to witness the adversary drastically increase its nuclear arsenal to overwhelm the defenses.

The ABM treaty became part and parcel of the SALT I agreement, without which SALT I would have been impossible. The U.S. military and political establishments were not about to sign an agreement with the Soviets by which the United States limited its missile strength and at the same time sat by idly as the Soviets took unilateral steps via a defensive shield to neutralize a portion of the U.S. strategic arsenal. Once the Soviets understood this, the door was opened for the ratification of SALT I and the limited ABM treaty. The simple, brutal deterrent of Mutually Assured Destruction remained intact.

In March 1983, eleven years after the superpowers had agreed to limit their nuclear firepower and their antinuclear defenses, President Reagan announced plans to build a highly complex system over the next twenty-five years to guard the United States against a nuclear attack. Reagan had never been comfortable with arms agreements accepting Soviet parity with the United States. That and his unlimited faith in U.S. ingenuity and technical skills led him to opt for a program that, he argued, would not cause an escalation of the arms race.

Reagan's proposal challenged the policy of Mutually Assured Destruction. It was immoral, he insisted, to rely on a military strategy predicated on the assured annihilation of the nation. He proposed instead the development of high-technology barriers to make nuclear war impossible. In fact, he went so far as to suggest that once U.S. scientists had solved the riddle of how to intercept incoming Soviet rockets, the U.S. government would hand over the secret to the Soviets. Nuclear war would then become impossible and peace would prevail. The ultimate goal, President Reagan said, was "to eliminate the weapons themselves."[11]

Star Wars played to mixed reviews. Its theoretical underpinnings could not be faulted readily. But there were several serious problems in implementing a defense of such staggering complexity. First, to be effective it would have to be nearly perfect. Since 2 percent of the Soviet Union's strategic arsenal could destroy the United States, a 90 percent efficiency in the Star Wars defense system—which according to some scientists was the best that could be gained—would not be nearly enough to protect the United States. Mutually Assured Destruction therefore would continue to prevail and the rubble would still bounce, for even 10 percent of a strategic arsenal of 10,000 warheads would destroy the United States several times over.

Star Wars, even if only 90 percent efficient, threatened, however, to bring about the unilateral U.S. neutralization of a sizable portion of the Kremlin's arsenal, something it was not likely to accept. Star Wars promised only to contribute to another spiral of the arms race, for the Soviets threatened to produce an ever increasing number of warheads. In short, the Soviets were being given the alternative of accepting U.S. nuclear superiority or of deploying enough weapons capable of overwhelming the Star Wars defense.

Second, there was the staggering cost. Reagan requested a budget of $30 billion ($3.7 billion for fiscal 1986) for research and development during the first five years. There was some doubt whether the U.S. government, already running a record deficit of over $200 billion a year, could afford the program.

Third, there was the very complexity of the system. Star Wars called for a new generation of sensors for the surveillance, tracking, and destruction of enemy missiles. The sensors would have to work almost flawlessly in the face of thousands of incoming warheads and decoys. The program also envisioned the deployment of energy weapons consisting primarily of powerful lasers based either on the ground (and deflected by huge mirrors in orbit) or in orbit. The most crucial part of the entire program, "systems concepts and battle management," called for an error-free computer system that instantaneously linked the system's diverse elements.[12]

Fourth, ways had to be found to protect the system from destruction by hostile elements. Mirrors and spy satellites in orbit would be inviting targets that could be neutralized easily. They would have to be defended somehow.

Last, the Soviet scientists were sure to work overtime to find ways over, under, around, and through any missile defense thought up by their U.S. counterparts.

In light of these obstacles, it was little wonder that Pentagon officials told Congress, which after all had to come up with the money to finance all of this, that this was a long-range program of at least twenty-five years duration. There was talk, however, of an "interim deployment" to protect land-based missiles, presumably the MX missile. This, of course, put first things first; civilians would have to wait. Former Defense Secretary Harold Brown admitted that "technology does not offer even a reasonable prospect of a population defense."[13]

Domestic critics of Star Wars feared that it would only militarize space, add little to anyone's security, and bankrupt the government. The deployment of a space-based defense promised to produce an open-ended contest in space. To the Soviets, it loomed as an attempt to disarm them. *Pravda* repeatedly announced that the Soviet Union would not idly accept Star Wars. It would join the race into space. Reagan's secretary of defense, Caspar Weinberger, when asked how he would view a unilateral deployment of a Soviet version of Star Wars, replied that such an act "would be one of the most frightening prospects I could imagine."[14]

■ GORBACHEV'S PEACE OFFENSIVE

In April 1985, one month after Mikhail Gorbachev came to power in Moscow, the Kremlin launched its most significant "peace offensive" of the Cold War. Gorbachev set out determined to bring about not only a domestic *perestroika* but one in foreign relations as well. "We will rob you of your enemy," he told the West. His proposal to freeze the deployment of Soviet SS-20 intermediate-range missiles was but his first move.

Soon the world witnessed a number of summit meetings between Gorbachev and Reagan, who had previously resolutely refused to sit down with his Soviet counterparts. Brezhnev, Andropov, and Chernenko were clearly dying men; moreover, Reagan felt there was nothing to talk about with the leaders of what he had called early in his presidency the "evil empire." The first meeting between Reagan and Gorbachev was a get-acquainted session in November 1985, in neutral Geneva. Several factors played a role in Reagan's turnabout. First, he had been criticized at home as being the first president since 1945 who had not met with Soviet leaders. Second, his foreign policy was in shambles and he sought the opportunity to put his mark on the course of history. Third, he realized he was dealing with a new type of Soviet leader. The Reagan-Gorbachev summits led to a series of negotiations that produced for the first time a reduction of nuclear armaments on both sides.

The first order of business was the recent escalation of the nuclear race in the heart of Europe: the deployment of intermediate-range nuclear forces (INF) such as the U.S. Pershing II and cruise missiles and the

Soviet SS-20. Gorbachev surprised the Reagan administration when he suddenly dusted off an old Western proposal, the zero-option: if the Soviet Union did not deploy its missiles, the United States would not counter with the deployment of its own rockets. Gorbachev would undo Brezhnev's error; he would take Soviet INF forces out of Europe if the United States were to do the same. Moscow called Washington's bluff; if Reagan rejected Gorbachev's proposal of eliminating all INFs, the U.S. position would be exposed as another example of Cold War propaganda.

Reagan responded positively. The consequence—after a year of difficult negotiation—was the INF treaty of May 1988, which eliminated an entire category of nuclear rockets, those with a range between 310 and 3,400 miles. The superpowers then proceeded to dismantle the costly weapons—1,752 Soviet and 867 U.S. rockets[15]—under the watchful eyes of on-site inspectors from the other side.

Reagan was then able to turn to one of his favorite programs, namely START, the Strategic Arms Reduction Talks. Early in his presidency, he had argued correctly that SALT had accomplished little. It had merely kept the nuclear arms race within certain parameters, making it possible, nevertheless, for both sides to increase their strategic arsenals. At the time of the signing of the INF treaty, the U.S. arsenal still contained 13,134 strategic warheads, the Soviet 10,664.[16] The time had come to reduce them. Reagan found a responsive partner in Gorbachev. Earlier, in October 1985, Gorbachev had already proposed a 50 percent reduction of strategic nuclear forces, which would lessen the Soviet threat against U.S. land-based missiles and narrow down what Reagan had called the U.S. "window of vulnerability." In October 1987, at their meeting in Reykjavik, Iceland, Gorbachev went so far as to offer Reagan the elimination of *all* strategic nuclear weapons. A surprised Reagan was on the verge of accepting before his advisers interfered. They feared that a world free of nuclear weapons would leave Western Europe at the mercy of the superior Soviet conventional forces.

Gorbachev was not finished with his surprises, however. On December 7, 1988, he launched another volley in his peace offensive. He announced—unilaterally and without precondition—the reduction in the Soviet armed forces of 10 percent (500,000 soldiers), 800 airplanes, 8,500 pieces of artillery, and 5,000 tanks within two years. Included in the offer was the promise to dissolve six of the fifteen divisions in East Germany, Hungary, and Czechoslovakia by 1991. But most important, Gorbachev included the withdrawal of assault troops and mobile bridges for crossing rivers. Gorbachev's speech marked a 180-degree turn in Soviet military doctrine as it had existed since the early 1960s. The East German party chief Erich Honecker recognized immediately what he called the "immense historical significance" of the Soviet troop withdrawal.[17] Gorbachev's speech also shocked many in the U.S. defense community; some

Soviet leader Mikhail Gorbachev and U.S. President Ronald Reagan in Geneva for their first summit meeting, Nov. 19, 1985. (*AP/Wide World Photos*)

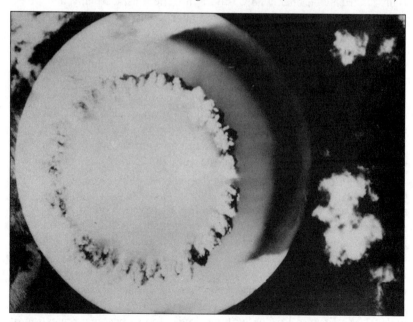

Radioactive substances released in the U.S. nuclear bomb test, boiling skyward—taken from a plane directly above the blast, July 12, 1948. (*National Archives*)

saw it as another Pearl Harbor, a propaganda offensive designed to disarm the West.

The Western critics of Gorbachev's speech of December 7, 1988, were in part correct. The first casualty of that speech was the U.S. program of "modernizing" the short-range Lance rocket, a tactical nuclear weapon. The Lance II, a new rocket with a range of just under the 310-mile limit as stipulated by the INF treaty, would not only be a deterrent but would also make possible the circumvention of the spirit, if not the letter, of the INF treaty. Lance II would give the United States a back door to an INF arsenal.

West German politics torpedoed the U.S. "modernization" program. Many in West Germany, especially the powerful Social Democratic Party in opposition, insisted that the shorter-range rockets, too, must go. "The shorter the rockets, the deader the Germans" became the West German watchword. Yet, Brent Scowcroft, U.S. President George Bush's national security adviser, reacted as if nothing had changed, as if the Cold War was still in full bloom, and pressed ahead to convince Bonn to accept the Lance II. In February 1989, Egon Bahr, the national security expert of the West German Social Democratic Party, explained to him that the United States had no chance to deploy the missiles. If the conservative government in Bonn capitulated to U.S. pressure and accepted them, his party would win the next election and take them out.[18] West German Foreign Minister Hans-Dietrich Genscher, who was born in Halle, East Germany, and whose relatives still lived there, declared: "I have sworn an oath to avert harm from the German people and that includes East Germany."[19]

East German scientists joined the debate. Even in case of conventional war, they argued, Europe would still be contaminated with nuclear fallout. The continent contained 220 civilian reactors that if damaged would turn into radioactive weapons. Because of the type of fuel they used, they would emit greater doses of radiation than atomic weapons. The large concentrations of chemical plants—such as along the Rhine River in Western Europe and in the region of Halle and Leipzig in East Germany—would spill their deadly poison on humans, plants, and animals. Even a conventional war would turn Europe into an "atomic, chemical and genetically contaminated desert." It would lead to the "destruction of what the aggressor would seek to conquer and what the victims of aggression have to defend."[20]

Gorbachev stood in stark contrast to the cautious Bush, who only late in 1989 began to accept the idea that he, too, could play a role in affecting the course of history. Gorbachev had been the engine of change, Bush a mere spectator. The demise of the Communist parties in Eastern Europe produced a situation in January 1990 whereby Czechoslovakia,[21] Hungary, and Poland insisted that the Soviet Army leave their territories by the end of 1991. An Eastern Europe without Soviet forces became a question of when, not if. It was at this point that Bush took the initiative and proposed the reduction of U.S. and Soviet forces to a level of 195,000 each in Central Europe. "New thinking" finally came to Washington. Previously, Bush had insisted on a U.S. troop ceiling of 275,000 in Central Europe, but budget considerations—the United States spent $150 billion a year for its troop deployment in Europe—gave the cautious Bush little choice but to accept a lower level. Moreover, as even the most hawkish officials in the Pentagon admitted, in the fourteen months since Gorbachev's speech of December 7, 1988, the Soviet Union had dismantled its capability to invade Western Europe. Bush's speech was welcomed news in Warsaw, Budapest, Prague, and Moscow because it facilitated the Soviet Army's withdrawal from its forward position in Eastern Europe. The military confrontation in the heart of Europe was coming to an end.

After the last Russian combat troops stationed in Poland pulled out in October 1992, President Lech Walesa declared: "Polish sovereignty has finally been confirmed." Problems of logistics and the lack of adequate housing at home for the Russian troops and their dependents produced a longer timetable for the withdrawal from the newly independent Baltic states and what had been East Germany. The departure from there was finally completed by 1993 and 1994, respectively.

■ THE START TREATIES

The START negotiations, begun in 1982, initially proceeded at a snail's pace for eight years, during which the intricacies of attaining balanced reductions in Soviet and U.S. arsenals were debated in twelve rounds of formal negotiations, thirteen foreign minister meetings, and six summit conferences. Finally, in May 1990, at a Bush-Gorbachev summit meeting in Washington, the two leaders announced the framework of a treaty they pledged to have ready for signing by year's end. As it turned out, it would take another fourteen months to complete the treaty.

There were other disarmament talks under way that had a bearing on the START talks. With the end of the Cold War in Europe, the Conference on Security and Cooperation in Europe (CSCE), composed of both NATO and Warsaw Pact nations, convened to take up the issue of reduction of conventional forces. In November 1990, a Conventional Forces in Europe (CFE) treaty was signed establishing greatly reduced limits on battle tanks, artillery, combat helicopters, and other weapons. Only after Moscow and Washington resolved their differences on this treaty were the two superpowers ready for the summit at which START was finally signed.[22]

Ironically, the signing of the treaty in Moscow in late July 1991 was attended with little fanfare—certainly not what had been expected for the signing of one of the most important nuclear disarmament treaties ever negotiated. After all, it reversed the forty-five-year-old strategic nuclear arms race. START seemed anticlimactic because it had been so long in coming and its main features had long since been known. Moreover, the deteriorating situation in the Soviet Union and the fading of the Soviet military threat made the treaty seem less significant. START, however, broke new ground by calling for a *reduction* rather than merely a limit on the growth of strategic weapons. The U.S. arsenal would be cut from 12,646 warheads to 8,556 and the Soviet Union's from 11,012 to 6,163 by 1999.[23] To the distinct advantage of the United States, START reduced the Soviets' heavy ICBMs by 50 percent, yet allowed the United States to retain a three-to-one advantage in sea-launched nuclear missiles. The treaty, however, did not place limitations on nuclear weapons modernization. Thus, it left the development of weapons systems such as the U.S. B-2 bomber and the Trident submarine, not to mention the SDI program, unhampered.

By the end of 1991, the Soviet Union had ceased to exist, and Washington now had to deal with Boris Yeltsin, the president of the new Russian Federation, and with the heads of the other fourteen successor states of the former Soviet Union. Yeltsin made clear immediately his commitment to stand by the START treaty and the disarmament pledges made by Gorbachev. In addition to Russia, however, three of the new sovereign republics—Belarus, Ukraine, and Kazakhstan—now had nuclear weapons. All three announced their intention of getting rid of them. Confident that Russian security was not threatened by the United States and greatly in need of slashing military costs and attaining Western economic assistance, Yeltsin declared his intentions of scrapping still more nuclear weapons.

At the first U.S.-Russian (as opposed to U.S.-Soviet) summit, in Washington in February 1992, Yeltsin joined Bush in signing a "Declaration of Friendship" and agreed to begin new negotiations for further nuclear disarmament. Four months of negotiations produced another startling agreement, one that promised far deeper cuts in strategic nuclear forces than the yet-to-be-ratified START treaty had called for. Yeltsin, given to grandstanding, came with offers Bush could hardly refuse, and the result was a spectacular agreement, the basis for a second treaty, START II, which called for the reduction of strategic nuclear weapons on each side to 3,000–3,500 by the year 2003. This was just over one-half of what START I allowed and amounted to a reduction of 73 percent of the existing strategic nuclear warheads. The most extraordinary feature of the Bush-Yeltsin agreement was its call for banning all MIRVed land-based missiles, leaving each side with only 500 single-warhead, land-based strategic weapons. This represented a Russian abandonment of its long-held advantage in heavy land-based missiles, which Washington had regarded as Moscow's first-strike capacity. In announcing this concession, Yeltsin stated that Russia now needed only a "minimum-security level" of nuclear forces and said that it was abandoning the concept of nuclear parity, which had caused Russia "to have half its population living below the poverty line."[24] In return for this concession, Bush agreed to a ceiling on submarine-launched missiles of 1,744, a 70 percent reduction.

But which delivery systems were to be destroyed? At the very end of 1992, a compromise was reached. Russia agreed to the conversion of U.S. strategic bombers (including the new B-2, or Stealth bomber) to conventional use, rather than destroying them. The United States, in its turn, agreed that Russia, as a cost-cutting measure, could keep 90 of its SS-18 silos for conversion to use by single-warhead SS-25 missiles as well as 105 of its 170 MIRVed (6 warheads) SS-19s, provided they were refitted with single warheads. Similarly, the United States would convert its Minuteman III missile to carry but a single warhead. The compromise became possible only after each side accepted unprecedented verification procedures. Bush and Yeltsin then signed START II in Moscow in January 1993. It pledged the two powers to return by 2003 to approximately where they had been in the early 1970s, before the MIRVing of their missiles. As such, it was a tacit admission of the mindlessness of the nuclear arms race.

The following chart provides comparative data on the size of the arms reductions called for in the START treaties.

1991 Strategic Warhead Levels

	Land-based (ICBMs)	Sea-based (SLBMs)	Air-launched (bombers)	Totals
U.S.	2,450	5,760	4,436	12,646
USSR	6,612	2,804	1,596	11,012
				23,658

START I, to be implemented by 1999; a reduction of 38% from the 1991 levels

	Land-based (ICBMs)	Sea-based (SLBMs)	Air-launched (bombers)	Totals
U.S.	1,400	3,456	3,700	8,556
USSR	3,153	1,744	1,266	6,163
				14,719

START II, to be implemented by 2003; a reduction of 73% from the 1991 levels

	Land-based (ICBMs)	Sea-based (SLBMs)	Air-launched (bombers)	Totals
U.S.	500	1,728	1,272	3,500
Russia	500	1,744	752	2,996
				6,496

Implementation of these agreements proved to be a difficult matter.[25] Ratification of START I was delayed mainly by complications caused by the breakup of the Soviet Union. Both Washington and Moscow wanted to be certain that all four former Soviet republics with strategic weapons abided by the treaty. In May 1992, the four successor states to the Soviet Union—Russia, Belarus, Ukraine, and Kazakhstan—signed a protocol making them parties to START I. They agreed to place their strategic weapons under Russian control, to remove them in accordance with the terms of START I, and then to sign the Non-Proliferation Treaty (NPT) as non-nuclear nations. Satisfied with these arrangements, the U.S. Senate finally ratified the START I treaty in October 1992, and one month later the Russian parliament did so as well.

But the START I treaty was not yet put into force. In ratifying START I, the Russian parliament stipulated that it would not exchange ratifications of the treaty with the United States until Belarus, Ukraine, and Kazakhstan each entered into binding agreements with Moscow unequivocally ceding its nuclear weapons to Russian jurisdiction. (Washington insisted on this as well.) Kazakhstan ratified START I in July 1992 and Belarus did so in February 1993. Ukraine, however, in contrast to its earlier professed intentions of becoming a nuclear-free nation, had second thoughts about giving up its nuclear weapons without something in return, namely substantial financial assistance for its struggling economy.[26] START I was being held up by Ukraine's blackmailing of the United States for economic assistance. This blocked not only START I but also START II, the far-reaching proposals of the Bush-Yeltsin agreement.

In November 1994, Ukrainian President Leonid Kuchma was finally able to convince his parliament to ratify the NPT. He argued that the nation could not afford nuclear arms and would gain nothing by holding on to them. He then called for a show of hands of legislators willing to accept nuclear test sites in their districts. Ukraine's ratification of the NPT opened the way for the formal signing ceremony of START I in Budapest in December 1994 at a meeting of the Conference on Security and Cooperation in Europe. The ratification of START II was now on the agenda.

The Ukrainian wish to be paid to disarm pointed to an additional, unforseen problem regarding the removal and destruction of the thousands of missiles: the high cost involved. Russia and the other three republics could ill afford the cost of dismantling so many missiles. In order to accelerate the process of disarming these weapons, Washington pledged some $800 million for this purpose. This was, in effect, payment for the security that disarmament offered, and compared to the enormous cost of the arms race itself, it was a bargain.

But it was only a down payment. The cost of nuclear disarmament figured to be much higher. Some experts estimated that the final cost of transporting, storing, and dismantling the Soviet nuclear weapons would run into many billions of dollars. Moreover, there was still the cost of the environmental cleanup. One estimate of the cost to clean up the nuclear weapons environmental mess in the United States alone was $300 billion.[27] Once these costs were factored in, nuclear weapons did not turn out after all to be the financial bargain its defenders had claimed. Eventually, the piper would also have to be paid in the former Soviet Union, where environmental pollution and safety hazards at many of its nuclear weapons sites had reached crisis proportions.

The U.S. Senate ratified START II in January 1996; in Russia, however, the treaty ran into opposition. President Boris Yeltsin sought ratification, but the volatile domestic political situation forced the treaty onto the back burner until after the presidential election in June 1996. Russian nationalists and Communists stressed that START II sold out national interests. The ultranationalist Vladimir Zhirinovsky, leader of the Liberal Democratic Party—the second-largest in the Duma (parliament)—glossed over the fact that the treaty called for parity between the United States and Russia and charged that the reduction of nuclear weapons "makes Russia a secondary state." His party would not ratify an agreement that would "humiliate, insult or limit Russia as a great nation."[28]

After the election, some Russian lawmakers wanted an extension of the disarmament timetable until 2008 because of financial difficulties. The cuts, after all, were extremely expensive to carry out. Other lawmakers linked their support for the treaty to their opposition to the expansion of NATO. The U.S. position was that these were separate issues, a view not readily shared by Russian officials.

☐ The Expansion of NATO

When Gorbachev agreed to withdraw Soviet troops from Eastern Europe, he made it clear that this region must remain a neutral buffer between the NATO powers and the Soviet Union. NATO was not to expand into a military vacuum once occupied by the Warsaw Pact. But then came the sudden end of the Soviet Union, after which Poland, Hungary, and the Czech Republic asked for membership in NATO as insurance against renewed Russian military ambitions. The United States then took the lead in preparing the eastward extension of NATO.

NATO tried to present the expansion as benign, meant largely to shore up democracy in Eastern Europe and somehow "strengthen European security." But the Russians well remembered the numerous invasions of their land from the west—through Germany and Poland—and repeatedly declared that NATO must not push toward Russia's borders. In June 1996, at a Berlin meeting of the foreign ministers of the sixteen NATO nations, Russian Foreign Minister Yevgeny Primakov warned that NATO expansion was "unacceptable." Primakov was only stating what a number of other

Russian politicians (including Yeltsin) had said for several years. Alexander Lebed, Yeltsin's national security adviser, had gone so far as to declare that a NATO push eastward would mean World War III.

Gorbachev joined the debate by pointing out that the agreement regulating the Soviet withdrawal from East Germany had demanded that East German troops must not be integrated into the unified German army. The "borders" of NATO must not expand, as doing so "does not strengthen, but weakens the security of Europe." Such a move could only have one meaning—namely, the isolation of Russia from Europe, resulting in "highly unpredictable consequences."[29]

The expansion of NATO raised the specter of Germany's renewed ambitions in the east, as well as the remilitarization of eastern Germany, this time under the aegis of a unified German state and the United States. Expansion also put on hold the ratification of START II by the Russian parliament and marked another humiliation of a Russia impotent in the face of expansion by its victorious Cold War adversary. NATO's ambitious move came at a time when much of Russia's military-industrial complex had been dismantled, its nuclear and conventional forces had been reduced, and its emphasis had shifted to defense.

NATO based its expansion on the questionable assumption that a military vacuum existed in Eastern Europe and that NATO had to fill it. The East European armed forces had been rebuilt and rearmed, however, and faced a weakened Russian military that had been unable to put down the secessionist movement in Chechnya, a province the size of Rhode Island. Moreover, NATO was hardly the means by which to shore up democracy; the European Union, with its insistence that its members be democracies (never a criterion for NATO membership), was a better vehicle to that end.[30]

■ NUCLEAR PROLIFERATION

As the superpowers rushed to eliminate thousands of nuclear weapons, other countries were working feverishly and surreptitiously to develop such weapons of their own. Suddenly, in the early 1990s nuclear proliferation began to replace superpower confrontation as the leading potential threat to international peace and security. Two developments in particular alerted the world to this danger: the discovery that Iraq had come much closer to building its own nuclear weapon than even its enemies had suspected and the breakup of the Soviet Union, which increased the availability of nuclear materials, arms, technicians, and scientists for other countries anxious to acquire them.

The 1968 Non-Proliferation Treaty required signatory nations *without* nuclear weapons not to produce or receive them and to open their nuclear power facilities to inspection by the International Atomic Energy Agency

(IAEA). Signatory nations *with* nuclear weapons were treaty-bound not to make such weapons available to non-nuclear nations and to negotiate in good faith toward nuclear disarmament. Only in 1992 did China and France sign the NPT, bringing all five declared nuclear powers under its regime. By that time, 149 nations of the world had signed the treaty. There were several holdouts however—notably India, Pakistan, Israel, Argentina, Brazil, and Algeria, all of which had nuclear weapons programs in various stages of development. These nations were thus beyond the pale of IAEA inspectors. Other nations that had signed the NPT, such as Iraq, North Korea, South Africa, Iran, and possibly Libya, had nonetheless managed to acquire nuclear materials and had begun nuclear weapons programs.

Several nations took steps to halt their nuclear weapons production and permit external inspection. South Africa, which had begun its nuclear weapons project in secret in the 1970s, closed its nuclear plants in 1990, signed the NPT, and opened its nuclear facilities to IAEA inspectors, thus becoming the first nation to abandon its nuclear weapons program voluntarily. In March 1993, South Africa admitted that by 1989 it had built six nuclear bombs, which, however, it had destroyed prior to the signing of the NPT. Brazil and Argentina both built large uranium enrichment facilities in the 1980s and thus developed the potential for making nuclear weapons. In December 1990, they too accepted inspection of their nuclear materials and facilities and permitted full IAEA monitoring.[31]

Other nations with secret nuclear weapons projects were not as forthcoming. Some were involved in regional nuclear arms races. India, which had tested a "nuclear device" as early as 1974, never admitted to having a nuclear arsenal, yet it refused to sign the NPT. It maintained its nuclear arms program as a deterrent to an attack by either China, or its hostile neighbor, Pakistan. It was likely that Pakistan, which also refused international inspection, finally succeeded in achieving, with some assistance from China, nuclear weapons capability in 1991 after many years of secret endeavor.[32] Its nuclear program was designed as a deterrent to India; but instead of providing security, the program threatened to provoke India into expanding its nuclear weapons arsenal and thus escalate a South Asian nuclear arms race.

Another regional nuclear arms race took place in the Middle East. It was mainly to counter Israel's nuclear bomb that Muslim nations such as Iraq, Iran, and Algeria sought to develop nuclear weapons. In 1981, Israeli fighter planes destroyed a nuclear reactor Iraq had purchased from France, and ever since then Iraq labored in secret to develop nuclear weapons, all the while profusely denying any such intention. After the Gulf War, UN inspectors armed with a Security Council resolution sought to remove and destroy all of Iraq's nuclear weapons materials and equipment. They were able to detect, despite continued Iraqi deception, a far larger and more fully developed nuclear weapons production program than suspected, including a calutron (a large atom-splitting facility) designed to produce uranium-235, and fissionable material needed for a nuclear bomb. The inspectors calculated that, if the Gulf War had not occurred, Iraq could have had a nuclear weapon within eighteen months. They also speculated that if Iraq had succeeded in concealing from them only a quarter of its critical nuclear facilities, Iraq would have been able to resurrect its nuclear weapons program.[33]

Before Iraq's nuclear ambitions were stymied, Iran and Algeria were already at work on nuclear projects. Both began secretly in the mid-1980s to build nuclear reactors with Chinese assistance, and after being detected and subjected to international pressures, both agreed to permit IAEA inspections. The initial probes in 1992 failed to detect conclusive evidence of weapons programs but did not erase the inspectors' suspicions that Iran and Algeria, like Iraq and North Korea, had mastered the skills of both nuclear engineering and nuclear deception.

Iraq's nuclear program was an eye-opener that pointed to the inadequacy of the NPT and to the necessity for improving the IAEA inspections system. Not only had Iraq succeeded in evading detection of its large nuclear weapons project with its many sites and thousands of workers, it had also been able to acquire a vast amount of material and highly technical equipment through a global procurement network it had developed. It proved that it was possible, even under NPT-ordered inspections, to obtain in secret the essential ingredients for building nuclear weapons—fissionable material (either plutonium or enriched uranium), nitric acid, nuclear graphite, and nuclear experts (engineers, chemists, and explosive specialists)—and to build and hide the necessary nuclear plants and facilities.[34]

The danger of nuclear proliferation suddenly increased in 1991 with the collapse of the Soviet Union and the prospect that its critical nuclear material, technology, and technicians might become available to the highest bidder. In 1991, the Soviet Union had over 40,000 nuclear weapons; about 700,000 people worked at its nuclear weapons plants, over 2,000 of whom had access to the key technical information; and since the 1940s it had produced some 100–150 tons of weapons-grade plutonium and 500–700 tons of enriched uranium, only a pound of which is needed for a Hiroshima-size bomb.[35] The problem was how to keep nuclear fuel and technology out of unauthorized hands or the hands of rulers with past records of, or propensity for, military aggression. The UN Security Council took a step toward this end in January 1992, when it declared that nuclear proliferation constituted a threat to international peace and security, thus making violators of the NPT subject to collective action by the UN. It was clear, however, that much more remained to be done to strengthen the NPT and the IAEA inspection system to stop nuclear proliferation.

☐ The Case of North Korea

The most severe challenge to the NPT system was North Korea's suspected development of nuclear weapons. It was well known that in the 1980s North Korea had built nuclear reactors and a plutonium processing plant capable of turning spent nuclear fuel from the reactors into weaponsgrade plutonium. What was not known outside of this tightly closed Communist society was whether such plutonium had already been produced and, if so, how much. All the while, Pyongyang remained tight-lipped, denying possession of a bomb or the intention of building one yet skillfully creating uncertainty and playing on the fears of others. There was indeed much to fear. A nuclear-armed North Korea would seriously threaten South Korea, which had forsworn nuclear weapons, and would likely cause Japan to reconsider its renunciation of nuclear weapons. Moreover, the prospect of North Korean bombs or nuclear technology exported to other nations would pose grave danger to the global nonproliferation effort and international security.

In 1994, the issue of the possible North Korean bomb became an international crisis. North Korea, which had signed the NPT in 1985, suddenly barred all further monitoring by IAEA inspectors in September 1993. But on the promise of future high-level talks with the United States on a range of issues, in January 1994, it agreed to allow the international inspectors to continue their work. Two months later when the inspectors arrived back in North Korea, they were prevented from entering the key plutonium processing plant and testing samples. Pyongyang was following a familiar pattern of making agreements, gaining concessions, then obstructing implementation of the agreements. Washington followed its own pattern of carrot-and-stick diplomacy; this time the stick was the dispatch of Patriot missiles to South Korea. Pyongyang again backed down in May 1994, allowing the inspectors to observe the planned replacement of fuel rods in one of its nuclear reactors, but it again hedged by not allowing them to conduct measurements of those rods—a procedure that would have provided the necessary evidence of whether fissionable fuel had already been diverted for weapons production.

At this point, tensions escalated rapidly. The Clinton administration sounded the call for UN sanctions and began talks with China and others to rally support for such a move. North Korea's response—that sanctions would be regarded as an act of war—in turn, provoked talk of war in Washington. A visit by former U.S. President Jimmy Carter to Pyongyang in mid-June 1994 served to cool things off. Carter secured from North Korean President Kim Il Sung a pledge not to expel IAEA inspectors as long as good-faith negotiations continued between the two countries. President Clinton then declared that talks would resume only if North Korea would "freeze" its nuclear weapons program and accept international safeguards.

Kim agreed in principle, and a new round of talks at a higher level was begun in Geneva. But these talks had barely opened when Kim Il Sung, the eighty-two-year-old Stalinist leader who had ruled North Korea since the 1940s, died. The negotiations were suspended while the North Korean government regrouped under its new ruler, Kim Jong Il, son of the long-lived dictator.

In August 1994, the negotiations in Geneva resumed. They soon produced an outline of an agreement whereby the United States pledged to help North Korea substitute its existing nuclear reactors with safer ones and North Korea would take steps to freeze its nuclear fuel production. More specifically, the United States would replace North Korea's graphite rod nuclear reactors with light water reactors, which have far less potential for producing weapons fuel. The new reactors were to be produced jointly by the United States, Japan, and South Korea at an estimated cost of $4 billion. Moreover, the same three nations would provide North Korea with fuel oil to meet its energy needs until the new reactors were in operation. This was the price North Korea was able to extract for agreeing not to go forward with its nuclear weapons program. It was the price the United States and its allies were willing to bear to remove the menace of a potential nuclear bomb in the hands of a nation with a track record of recklessness and to preserve the NPT system.

Other issues remained to be resolved before an agreement was ready for signing. The United States insisted that the 8,000 fuel rods North Korea had already removed from its nuclear reactors be delivered to a third country for inspection; when Pyongyang balked at that suggestion, it was ultimately agreed that the rods would remain in North Korea and would be sealed to protect against possible diversion for weapons production. The agreement, which rewarded North Korea handsomely for ceasing its violations of the NPT, was finally signed in October 1994.

☐   **The Search for a Comprehensive Nuclear Test Ban**

The partial nuclear test ban treaty of 1963 had done little to halt the spread of nuclear weapons. The treaty had committed the signatories to cease testing in the atmosphere, on the high seas, and in outer space; it thus simply drove nuclear testing underground. By the 1990s, three of the five declared nuclear powers—the United States, Britain, and Russia—were bound by the treaty. The other two—China and France—however, continued to test their weapons in the atmosphere. (Such tests are crucial in giving a nation its first reliable nuclear weapons or the ability to reconfigure them.) To curtail nuclear proliferation, a comprehensive international treaty was needed that would end all tests by both declared and undeclared nuclear powers. To that end, in 1996 the United Nations worked out a Comprehensive Test Ban Treaty at a thirty-seven-member UN Conference on Disarmament in

Geneva. India, however, one of the participating members at the conference, repeatedly resisted such an agreement. India presented two arguments against the treaty: it preserved the division between nuclear haves and have-nots, and it did not commit the haves to get rid of their weapons by a certain date.

When the vote came before the UN General Assembly in September 1996, India voted against the treaty (along with Libya and Bhutan, whose foreign policy India controlled). After 2,045 nuclear explosions since the first one in the New Mexico desert fifty-one years earlier, a permanent nuclear ban became a possibility. Still, for the treaty to become international law, the legislatures of all forty-four countries possessing nuclear reactors had to ratify it.[36] A provision in the treaty called for a review conference in 1999 to try to bring it into universal force. The vote of 158 to 3 did mean, however, that all future nuclear testing would fly in the face of world opinion.

Table 23.2 Known Nuclear Tests, 1945–1996

	U.S.	USSR	France	Britain	China	India
Atmospheric	215	219	50	21	23	0
Underground	815	496	159	24	22	1
Total	1,030	715	209	45	45	1

Sources: UN; Physicians for Social Responsibility; Barbara Crosette, "U.N. Endorses a Treaty to Halt All Nuclear Testing," *New York Times,* September 11, 1996, p. A3.

RECOMMENDED READINGS

Bottome, Edgar M. *The Balance of Terror: A Guide to the Arms Race.* 2d rev. ed. Boston: Beacon Press, 1986.

Broad, William J. *Teller's War: The Top-Secret Story Behind the Star Wars Deception.* New York: Simon and Schuster, 1992.
> How Edward Teller, the "father" of the U.S. hydrogen bomb, managed to sell SDI to the Reagan administration.

Bundy, McGeorge. *Danger and Survival: Choices About the Bomb in the First Fifty Years.* New York: Random House, 1988.
> John Kennedy's national security adviser describes how successive U.S. governments worked out a "tradition of non-use."

Cockburn, Andrew. *The Threat: Inside the Soviet Military Machine.* New York: Random House, 1983.
> A sober assessment of Soviet capabilities and weaknesses.

Cox, Arthur Macy. *Russian Roulette: The Superpower Game.* New York: Times Books, 1982.

Freedman, Lawrence. *The Evolution of Nuclear Strategy.* New York: St. Martin's, 1981.

Garthoff, Raymond L. *Deterrence and the Revolution in Soviet Military Doctrine.* Washington, D.C.: Brookings Institution, 1990.

Explains the Soviet emphasis on war prevention instead of deterrence.

Gervasi, Tom. *The Myth of Soviet Military Supremacy.* New York: Harper and Row, 1986.
Challenges the claims that the Soviet Union had overtaken the West in the arms race in the 1980s.

Holloway, David. *Stalin and the Bomb: The Soviet Union and Atomic Energy, 1936–1956.* New Haven, Conn.: Yale University Press, 1994.

McDougall, Walter A. *The Heavens and the Earth: A Political History of the Space Age.* New York: Basic Books, 1984.

Newhouse, John. *Cold Dawn: The Story of SALT.* New York: Holt, Rinehart and Winston, 1973.

Office of Technology Assessment. *SDI: Technology, Survivability and Software.* Princeton: Princeton University Press, 1988.
Reprint of a study conducted for the House Armed Services and Senate Foreign Relations committees that concluded that SDI would fail in case of war.

Rhodes, Richard. *Dark Sun: The Making of the Hydrogen Bomb.* New York: Simon and Schuster, 1995.
A definitive study of the first two decades of the nuclear arms race.

Schell, Jonathan. *The Fate of the Earth.* New York: Knopf, 1982.
The best seller on the potential consequences of nuclear war.

Smith, Gerard. *Doubletalk: The Story of SALT I.* Garden City, N.Y.: Doubleday, 1980.
By the chief U.S. arms negotiator at the talks.

Soviet Military Power. Washington, D.C.: U.S. Government Printing Office, six editions, 1981–1987.
The Pentagon's assessment of the Soviet threat.

Spector, Leonard S. *Nuclear Ambitions: The Spread of Nuclear Weapons, 1989–1990.* Boulder, Colo.: Westview Press, 1990.
The fifth in a series by this recognized expert provides a detailed country-by-country analysis.

Talbott, Strobe. *Endgame: The Inside Story of SALT II.* New York: Harper and Row, 1979.
This book and the following book by the same author, a former correspondent for *Time,* are among the most detailed and lucid accounts of recent arms negotiations.

Talbott, Strobe. *Deadly Gambits: The Reagan Administration and the Stalemate in Nuclear Arms Control.* New York: Knopf, 1984.

Union of Concerned Scientists. *The Fallacy of Star Wars.* 1983.

Zuckerman, Solly. *Nuclear Illusion and Reality.* New York: Random House, 1982.
A critical view of the nuclear arms race by a former scientific adviser to the British Ministry of Defense: neither side can gain nuclear advantage.

NOTES

1. SS (surface-to-surface) is the U.S. designation of Soviet missiles. As soon as a Soviet missile was tested, the Pentagon assigned it a number.

2. George McGovern, "SALT II: A Political Autopsy," *Politics Today,* March–April 1980, p. 64.

3. The Seabed Pact prohibited the stationing of weapons on the ocean floor beyond a nation's twelve-mile limit; it did not cover submarines that may approach the enemy's territorial waters.

4. This was the basis of Ronald Reagan's "window of vulnerability." It went something like this: the Soviet Union's land-based arsenal, which during the late 1970s had become increasingly more accurate, was capable of overwhelming the U.S. land-based missiles in their silos and thereby threatens the very existence of the United States. This argument always focused on only one facet of the arms race. It ignored the fact that either of the other two legs of the U.S. "triad," the submarines and the bomber force, was more than enough to keep the Soviets honest. Reagan promised that, if elected president, he would close this window. In 1984, he declared that he had closed the window—without, however, having done anything to protect U.S. land-based missiles.

5. Source for Tabhle 23.1 is *New York Times,* October 4, 1985. All figures are estimates of classified information. They were compiled from Pentagon publications, the International Institute for Strategic Studies, the Arms Control Association, and the Center for Defense Information.

6. Thomas Powers, "Nuclear Winter and Nuclear Strategy," *Atlantic Monthly,* November 1984, p. 60.

7. Lawrence Freedman, *The Evolution of Nuclear Strategy* (New York: St. Martin's, 1981), p. 363.

8. Georgy Arbatov, director of the Institute of U.S. and Canadian Studies of the Academy of Sciences of the Soviet Union, in Arthur Macy Cox (with a Soviet commentary by Georgy Arbatov), *Russian Roulette: The Superpower Game* (New York: Times Books, 1982), pp. 177–178, 182.

9. Leonid Brezhnev and Ronald Reagan, "Brezhnev and Reagan on Atom War," transcripts of statements, *New York Times,* October 21, 1981, p. 5.

10. Great Britain accepted 160 cruise missiles; West Germany, 108 Pershing II and 96 cruise missiles; Italy, 112 cruise missiles; Belgium and Holland, 48 cruise missiles each. Norway, Denmark, Greece, and Turkey rejected U.S. missiles. Turkey, by virtue of the agreement between the Soviet Union and the United States in the wake of the Cuban missile crisis of 1962, was prohibited from stationing U.S. missiles. The Greek government of Andreas Papandreou carved out a neutralist position between the United States and the Soviet Union despite the fact that Greece was a member of NATO. Papandreou considered Turkey, a fellow member of NATO, to be a greater threat to Greece than the Warsaw Pact to the north. In Norway and Denmark, pacifist sentiment prevented the acceptance of U.S. weapons.

11. Ronald Reagan, quoted in "President's Speech on Military Spending and a New Defense," *New York Times,* March 24, 1983, p. A20.

12. Star Wars "system concepts and battle management" was one of five components of Star Wars research; Wayne Biddle, "Request for Space Weapons Reflects Early Goals," *New York Times,* February 4, 1985, p. A10. With a computer-driven system the fate of the world would be in the hands (or the chips and software) of computers. "Perhaps we should run R2-D2 for president in the 1990s," declared Senator Paul Tsongas (D-Mass.) at a congressional hearing. "At least he'd be on line all the time. Has anyone told the President that he's out of the decision-making process?" George Keyworth, President Reagan's science adviser, replied, "I certainly haven't." George Keyworth, quoted in Philip M. Boffey, "'Star Wars' and Mankind: Consequences for Future," *New York Times,* March 8, 1985, p. A14. In January 1987, the Office of Technology Assessment, on behalf of the House Armed Services and Senate Foreign Relations committees, conducted workshops on potential Soviet responses to SDI and on the feasibility of producing SDI software, to determine whether the controversial program would in fact work. Its report concluded that the software would have to be written "without the benefit of

data or experience from battle use," that is, it could not be properly tested. It would have to rely on theoretical "peacetime testing," which, however, would offer "no guarantee that the system would not fail catastrophically . . . as a result of a software error . . . in the system's first battle." Office of Technology Assessment, *SDI: Technology, Survivability and Software* (Princeton: Princeton University Press, 1988), p. 249.

13. Harold Brown, December 1983, quoted in Boffey, "Star Wars," p. A14.

14. Caspar Weinberger quoted in ibid., p. A14.

15. The Soviet SS-20 rockets carried three warheads each, so the Soviet Union gave up more than three times as many warheads as the United States.

16. Arms Control Association, from data supplied by the U.S. Defense Department, the Joint Chiefs of Staff, and the Arms Control and Disarmament Agency, *New York Times,* May 26, 1988, p. A12.

17. "Wir werden euch des Feindes berauben," *Der Spiegel,* December 12, 1988, p. 22.

18. Christian Schmidt-Häuer, "Die Armee gerät unter Beschuss," *Die Zeit,* November 11, 1988, p. 8.

19. "Unsere Antwort wird Nein sein," *Der Spiegel,* May 1, 1989, p. 21.

20. "'Der Iwan kommt—und feste druff,'" *Der Spiegel,* May 1, 1989, pp. 23–27.

21. Wolfgang Schwarz of the Institute for International Politics and Economy in East Berlin, in a report to the East German Council of Ministers, "DDR-Wissenschaftler warnt vor Atomverseuchung Europas," *Frankfurter Rundschau,* June 21, 1989, p. 2.

22. At a meeting of the Warsaw Pact in December 1989, the five members—the Soviet Union, Poland, Hungary, East Germany, and Bulgaria—that had invaded Czechoslovakia in 1968 to crush the "Prague Spring" apologized for the invasion.

23. Gorbachev had taken the position that the reorganized armed forces of the Warsaw Pact, which at the time was being dissolved as a military alliance, should not come under the provisions of the CFE treaty, and the United States opposed that position. The Bush administration insisted it would not sign a START treaty until Moscow came on board the CFE treaty. Gorbachev conceded.

24. John F. Cushman Jr., "Senate Endorses Pact to Reduce Strategic Arms," *New York Times,* October 2, 1992, pp. A1, A6.

25. Jack Mendelsohn, "Big Deal at the Summit," *Baltimore Sun,* June 21, 1992, p. 3G. Yeltsin's offer was not cleared with nor necessarily supported by the government in Moscow. Some deputies in Moscow expressed shock at the extent of the cuts Yeltsin had proposed.

26. Although either government could begin voluntarily to implement all or part of the agreement signed by the presidents, neither was legally obliged to do so. An agreement does not become legally binding until it becomes a treaty ratified by each government.

27. Serge Schmemann, "Ukraine Asks Aid for Its Arms Curbs," *New York Times,* November 12, 1992, p. A10. Ukraine transferred all its tactical nuclear weapons to Russia, but still retained 176 ICBMs with more than 1,200 warheads with which it was determined not to part "for free."

28. George Petrovich, "Counting the Costs of the Arms Race," *Foreign Policy,* Winter 1991/92, p. 87.

29. Cited in David Hoffman, "Russian Says Arms Treaty Vote Should Follow Election," *Washington Post,* February 1, 1996, p. A17.

30. Mikhail Gorbachev, "'Geroi' razrusheniia Sovetskogo Soiuza izvestny . . . ," *Novoe vremia,* nos. 2–3 (1995), p. 27.

31. Thomas L. Friedman, "Bigger Isn't Better," *New York Times,* June 9, 1996, p. E15. In response to the argument that an expanded NATO would "strengthen European security," a Russian official replied that the West "must think we're blind and deaf"; Anatol Lieven, "A New Iron Curtain," *Atlantic Monthly,* January 1996, p. 20.

32. Leonard S. Spector, "Repentant Nuclear Proliferants," *Foreign Policy,* Fall 1992, pp. 26–27.

33. Tai Ming Cheung, "Nuke Begets Nuke," *Far Eastern Economic Review,* June 4, 1992, p. 22, states that India and Pakistan "have all the necessary components to assemble bombs within weeks. But they have held off production so far for fear of starting a subcontinental arms race."

34. Stephen J. Hedges and Peter Cary, "Desert Drama: Inside Saddam Hussein's Nuclear Nightmare," *U.S. News and World Report,* November 25, 1991, pp. 36–42.

35. For a succinct explanation of the necessary ingredients for building nuclear weapons, how would-be nuclear nations acquire or produce them, and the problems in halting proliferation, see John M. Deutch, "The New Nuclear Threat," *Foreign Affairs,* Summer 1992, pp. 119–134.

36. "A Nice Red Afterglow," *The Economist,* March 14, 1992, p. 43.

37. The 1969 Vienna Convention governing treaties stipulated, however, that between the signing and the ratification of a treaty, a state had a legal obligation not to act in a fashion that contradicted the agreement.

24

Epilogue:
The End of the Postwar Age

If historical processes are a combination of continuity and change, it was inevitable that half a century after World War II the world would be different from that the Big Three had faced in their moment of triumph in 1945. The new order the victors created in 1945 had considerable staying power but it was bound to end one day. Since the French Revolution of 1789, none of the international configurations of power survived much longer than a biblical generation of forty years.[1] Since 1945, the world has seen a number of major trends that, taken together, have put us at the beginning of a new, uncertain era. Among the major changes in the world since 1945 are the following.

☐ 1. The Fall of Communism

The most surprising and sudden development since 1945 took place in Eastern Europe, where all the Communist parties gave up their once seemingly immutable hold on power in the short span of two years, between 1989 and 1991. Soviet socialism's most visible accomplishment had been the creation of a powerful security apparatus designed to deal with threats from without and within. In short, East European Communist leaders neglected what Communist ideology always had considered significant, the substructure upon which the socialist house rested, namely the economic base. Gorbachev's *perestroika* eventually came to the conclusion that a new base was needed. Once that position was reached, Communism as an ideology, as defined by Lenin and particularly Stalin, became a thing of the past.

☐ 2. The End of the Cold War

Equally astonishing was the end of the Cold War and its most dangerous feature, the military confrontation, when the Soviet Army withdrew from

Eastern Europe. The demise of the Warsaw Pact then put into question the further need for NATO, the West's military alliance, particularly as the European Community began to contemplate the strengthening of its military and diplomatic component outside the U.S. umbrella. The nuclear arms reduction agreements ended a dangerous contest by the superpowers paralyzed into immobility. The agreements, however, came at a late hour as the genie of nuclear proliferation already had made its way out of the bottle. After the Soviet Union broke the U.S.-British monopoly in 1949, France, the People's Republic of China, India, and Israel joined the ranks of nuclear powers and a number of aspirants began to appear, among them North Korea, Iraq, Iran, and Pakistan.

☐ 3. The Triumph of Capitalism

The demise of Communism and the ideological message of U.S. President Ronald Reagan contributed to a return to a form of capitalism unchecked and deeply ideological in its content. *Perestroika,* designed to save Soviet socialism, opened instead the floodgate of criticism of Communism and produced a wild swing to a type of primitive capitalism the Western world had modified 100 years earlier because of its destructive and cruel nature. The primordial aspects of capitalism were making their way also into the arena of international trade, where pretense of open and mutually beneficial trade began to give way to fierce competition, a zero-sum contest, and the continuation of war by other means, in which there were invariably winners and losers. The unlimited right of one individual or nation to amass great wealth guaranteed the right of another individual to have little. By the early 1990s, the 1944 Bretton Woods ideals of free trade were severely tested by nationalist tendencies. This characteristic of international trade lay at the heart of the friction among the economic powers— the United States, the European Union, and Japan.

☐ 4. The Age of High Tech

After the 1970s, the world witnessed a new stage in the industrial revolution, a shift from "smokestack" industries. The production of steel, once the yardstick by which industrial progress had been measured, lost its importance to knowledge-intensive industries, such as computers and their offshoots—robots, digital communication, and the like. A fundamental flaw in the Soviet economy, for instance, had been the continued emphasis on the production of basic materials such as steel and oil in which it led the world in production. During the heyday of the "smokestack" industries, catching up with other industrialized nations was a difficult, yet relatively easy, process if one compared the hurdles underdeveloped countries faced at the end of the twentieth century. The gulf between the haves and the have-nots grew increasingly wider.

☐ 5. The Relative Decline of the United States

The decades following 1945 witnessed a gradual, yet steady erosion of U.S. economic power relative to other parts of the world—to East Asia (notably Japan) and Western Europe. The relative decline was the result of a number of factors. For one, the United States had spent vast sums of money on its national security state without taking the necessary steps to ensure the viability of its economic base. It continued to lead the world in technological breakthroughs, particularly as they applied to weapons research and development, but gave up its dominant position in the production of consumer goods. The "American century," to use the phrase of Henry Luce, the publisher of *Time,* scarcely lasted a generation.

☐ 6. The Reemergence of Germany

As the two superpowers declined, their old antagonists of World War II began to reassert themselves. Germany did so particularly after its unification in 1990. The Gulf War witnessed the stationing of German troops abroad for the first time (in Turkey), and during the Yugoslav crisis German warships began to make their appearance in the Adriatic Sea. In the 1950s, the first West German chancellor, Konrad Adenauer, devoted himself to the integration of his nation into the West European community. But in the early 1990s, Germany began to play once again its traditional role in Eastern Europe, taking the lead in the economic penetration of that region and in the recognition of breakaway republics of the Soviet Union and Yugoslavia.

☐ 7. The Reemergence of Japan

Japan's reassertion was more muted. After its disastrous defeat in World War II, it abandoned militarism in favor of pacifism and was content to remain under the U.S. defensive and diplomatic umbrella as long as possible while pursuing economic growth. But shortly after the end of the Allied Occupation in the 1950s, the United States already began to urge Japan to take a more active role as an ally in the Cold War. Once the Cold War ended, it was the United States that encouraged Japan to play a greater part in international affairs, particularly since Japan had the financial means to assist in underwriting U.S. and UN initiatives. Japan was cajoled into funding a portion of the Gulf War (after all, it was heavily dependent on oil from the region) and to participate in a peacekeeping force in Cambodia, where Japanese soldiers set foot on the Asian mainland for the first time since 1945. A reason for Japan's reluctance to play a role other than economic in East Asia was the resistance from nations it had controlled before and during World War II, notably Korea and China. German and Japanese military involvement abroad put to a severe test the clauses in their constitutions that permitted only acts of defense.

☐ 8. The Rise of East Asia

Beginning with Japan's "economic miracle" of the 1960s, East Asia emerged as an arena of dynamic economic growth and new prosperity. First, the "four tigers" (South Korea, Taiwan, Hong Kong, and Singapore) imitated Japan, registering in the early 1980s the world's highest economic growth rates. Then, by the early 1990s, this economic success was emulated by Southeast Asian countries (Thailand, Malaysia, and Indonesia) to attain honors as the world's fastest-growing economies. Their success, like that of Japan, represented a blend of a Western-derived capitalist system and elements of traditional Asian culture, an amalgam featuring state-directed economic modernization and capital formation, high rates of personal savings and capital investment, abundant and cheap labor consisting of disciplined workers, emphasis on new high-tech industries, and export-driven industrial growth. The People's Republic of China also exhibited significant new economic productivity resulting from its conversion to a market economy in the 1980s. The economic competitiveness of Asian nations posed a challenge to a smug industrialized West and to a struggling Third World.

☐ 9. The Fragmentation of the World

The bipolar camps had been the result of the Cold War, and once that confrontation had come to an end there was no further need to rally around one camp's flag or the other. Even at the height of the Cold War, a number of nations had refused to be drawn into it. De Gaulle of France, for example, feared too close an embrace on the part of the United States, and Nehru of India wanted no part of either bloc. Communist Yugoslavia's break with Stalin underscored the fact that "international Communist solidarity" existed primarily in theory only. Other Communist nations (China, Vietnam, Romania, Albania, and Cuba) tended to guard their independence against both Washington and Moscow. The fragmentation only increased after the end of the Cold War. The Soviet Union's East European bloc was no more, the EC witnessed an unprecedented degree of disunity, and the United States could no longer take its allies for granted.

☐ 10. Globalism vs. Nationalism

During the late 1980s, two conflicting currents came into collision. On the one hand, the "global village" was becoming smaller and many of its citizens began to see themselves as members of one large family facing common problems and a common future; on the other hand, the world was becoming increasingly fragmented and parochial as nationalities asserted their claims to independence and made war on one another. Rapid communication and economic change were among the forces behind the trend toward internationalization. This in turn gave rise to economic integration, to what some called the "borderless economy," to regional groupings and trade blocs such as the European Community and others formed in Asia and North America, and to regular summit meetings of the "Group of Seven," the heads of state of the leading market-economy nations.

Hitler and the horrors of World War II had discredited talk of blood that tied individuals to their collective tribe, but his defeat had only driven such talk underground waiting for its recrudescence. Eventually, ethnic consciousness gradually began to make a resounding comeback. This was evident in the Soviet Union, for example, after *glasnost* removed the restraints on its nationalities. With it came the call for separatism and "ethnic cleansing." Russians demanded the expulsion of Jews, and Estonians demanded the expulsion of Russians. Elsewhere, the Irish wanted Britain out of Northern Ireland; and Quebec wanted out of Canada, the Biafrans out of Nigeria, the Basques out of Spain, Tibet out of China, the Sikhs out of India, and the Kurds out of Turkey, Iran, and Iraq. Bulgaria expelled members of its Turkish minority; Arabs sought to drive Israelis into the sea, and Israelis demanded the expulsion of Palestinian Arabs; the nationalities of Yugoslavia decided they could not live in a Greater Serbia; and the misery in the Horn of Africa was in part the result of attempts to recreate a Greater Ethiopia and a Greater Somalia out of the same territory. Every East European nation had its "irredentists"[2] who claimed land at the expense of a neighbor. The Maastricht Treaty, the "deepening" of the EC, came at a time when much of the world was breaking up into ethnic fragments.

☐ 11. The End of Colonialism

The first significant development after World War II was the demand for the rapid dissolution of the European colonial control of much of the world. What Europe had accomplished between the time of the first Crusade in the late eleventh century and the turn of the twentieth century was largely undone in less than three decades. The colonial powers had been able to contain the anticolonial movements until the dam finally burst after World War II. At first blush, independence promised a happier future, free of foreign domination. In sub-Saharan Africa, in particular, the hope was that the continent now would develop its economic and human potential. Instead, the colonial power left behind artificially drawn borders and governments that clung to power at all cost by canceling elections and murdering their political opponents. Ethnic groups across the breadth of Africa repeatedly went to war against one another, leaving behind a devastated continent where the standard of living was lower in 1990 than it had been in 1960.

☐ 12. Superpower Competition in the Third World

In retrospect, it became clear that neither Cold War protagonist intended to begin a war in Europe. The contest then moved to another venue, into the Third World, generally the former colonies. There, the superpowers competed for the hearts and minds of tyrants, their ideological beliefs (or generally the lack thereof) notwithstanding. The Soviet Union supported Nasser of Egypt, Sukarno of Indonesia, and Hussein of Iraq (none of whom had qualms about jailing local Communists). It also supported India against Communist China and the Sandinistas against the Nicaraguan Communist Party. The United States propped up a host of military dictators in Latin America, Africa, and Southeast Asia as well as in southern Europe. It even supported Marxist insurgents and governments in Somalia, Yugoslavia, Angola, and China against Moscow, the ostensible center of international Marxism. In the process, the superpowers strengthened dictators around the globe, many of whom remained in power for decades. Gorbachev's "new thinking" led the Soviet Union to abandon its clients, and the United States no longer had the need to prop up its own associates. The Cold War ended, but its legacy remained—devastated countries and military factions armed to the teeth. In many nations (Afghanistan, Somalia, Angola, Cambodia) the bloodletting continued. The sale of weapons also continued, this time for commercial reasons, rather than those of state. Russia and the United States continued to do what they had done efficiently, namely produce weapons, and their economic woes dictated they sell them abroad. By the 1980s, they were joined in this by a new arms merchant—the People's Republic of China.

☐ 13. The Emergence of Militant Islam

The late 1970s saw the appearance of a third global ideology challenging those of the superpowers, that of militant Islam as embodied in the sermons of Iran's Ayatollah Khomeini. It was the first significant ideological movement on a global scale since 1945. Militant Islam was in part an appeal to the poverty-stricken masses of the Muslim world's 1 billion believers, most of whom lived in the Third World. It attacked the Western influence within Iranian society (as well as those of the Arab-speaking world, notably Lebanon, Kuwait, Iraq, Sudan, Saudi Arabia), which it denounced as a corruption of the Koran and the consequence of Western influence. Militant Islam also sought to restore the Muslim world to its former power and glory and to eliminate its dependency on outside forces that long had humiliated it.

☐ 14. A Fragile Ecological Balance

By the early 1970s, the world became aware that the blessings of the industrial revolution had a darker side—a record growth in population and
the ecological degradation of the globe. The world's population increased from approximately 2.4 billion in 1945 to nearly 6 billion in
1993 and was accompanied by an even more explosive growth in industry. U.S. factories had polluted Lake Erie (but not irreversibly); Soviet irrigation had ruined Lake Aral (perhaps irreversibly); German, French,
and Swiss industry had poisoned the Rhine River; and the air and water
in large cities (Mexico City, Cairo, Shanghai, Los Angeles, Moscow) had
become scarcely suited for human use. Toxic wastes from nuclear
weapons and power plants in many countries threatened serious ecological damage.

☐ 15. The Haves and the Have-Nots

The greatest challenges for the world's leaders on the eve of the twenty-
first century were not of a technological nature. Neil Armstrong already
had set foot on the moon, computers were able to conduct complex calcu-
lations in nanoseconds, and machines were able to perform what once had
been backbreaking work. The potentially explosive problems were of a
human nature. Many individuals faced a superfluous existence. They were
the members of a dispensable underclass of greater numbers, primarily in
the Third World. Mostly young and poverty-stricken, they witnessed a
world capable of producing great wealth denied to them. This situation had
the potential of producing great political turmoil. It was not something a
magical "free market" or a "new world order" could resolve.

Year Zero came for Japan and Western Europe in 1945 when they
began anew by putting the pieces back together again. For Eastern Europe,
Year Zero came only in 1989; for the states of the former Soviet Union it
did not come until 1991. China with its billion people started over after
Mao's death in 1976. Year Zero came in 1960 to the societies of sub-
Saharan Africa, who eventually had to realize that they had gone back in
time; they were still grasping for the takeoff point, another Year Zero that
would take them to a happier future. The Shiite Muslims regard the Iranian revolution of 1979 as Year Zero.

NOTES

1. The French revolutionary system ended with Napoleon's defeat in 1815,
and the "restored" conservative order lasted only until 1848. The wars for the
unification of Germany and Italy rearranged the map of Europe by 1871 only to

be destroyed by World War I (1914–1918). The international system that came out of World War I lasted until the outset of World War II (1939–1945).

2. From the Latin *terra irredenta*, "land unredeemed," the land of our forefathers that must be returned; first used by Italian nationalists during the nineteenth century, *Italia irredenta*.

■ Index

■ About the Book

The fourth edition of *The World Since 1945* moves beyond the demise of the Soviet Union into the uncertain post–Cold War age—the chaotic "new world order."

The text has been updated to discuss issues at the forefront of world politics today: the changing character of the European Union, events in Eastern Europe and the former Soviet Union, the movement toward resolution of the Israeli-Palestinian conflict, the new order in South Africa, the sharpening of the economic and political conflict between the United States and its trading partners in East Asia, and the unresolved disputes between North and South Korea and the two Chinas. There are also interpretive revisions based on new documents and studies of the Cold War, the Middle East conflicts, the nuclear arms race (including the Cuban missile crisis), and events in Afghanistan, El Salvador, and India.

Comprehensive, yet concise, this widely acclaimed study of the major political, economic, and ideological patterns in the global arena since World War II—written for introductory courses in international relations or world history—serves as a corrective to often one-sided, Western-centered approaches to the salient issues of recent decades.

Wayne C. McWilliams and **Harry Piotrowski** are professors in the Department of History at Towson University.